Essentials of Health Care Finance

Fourth Edition

William O. Cleverley, PhD
President
The Center for Healthcare Industry Performance Studies
Professor
Graduate Program in Health Services Management and Policy
The Ohio State University
Columbus, Ohio

AN ASPEN PUBLICATION®
Aspen Publishers, Inc.
Gaithersburg, Maryland
1997

Library of Congress Cataloging-in-Publication Data

Cleverley, William O.
Essentials of health care finance / William O. Cleverley.—4th ed.
p. cm.
Includes index.
ISBN 0-8342-0736-2 (hardcover : alk. paper)
1. Hospitals—Finance. 2. Hospitals—Accounting. 3. Health
facilities—Finance. 4. Health facilities—Accounting. I. Title.
[DNLM: 1. Costs and Cost Analysis. 2. Financial Management.
3. Health Services—economics. W 74 C635e 1997]
RA971.3.C528 1997
362.1'068'1—dc21
DNLM/DLC
for Library of Congress
96-29878
CIP

Orders: (800) 638-8437
Customer Service: (800) 234-1660

About Aspen Publishers • For more than 35 years, Aspen has been a leading professional publisher in a variety of disciplines. Aspen's vast information resources are available in both print and electronic formats. We are committed to providing the highest quality information available in the most appropriate format for our customers. Visit Aspen's Internet site for more information resources, directories, articles, and a searchable version of Aspen's full catalog, including the most recent publications: **http://www.aspenpub.com**
Aspen Publishers, Inc. • The hallmark of quality in publishing
Member of the worldwide Wolters Kluwer group.

Editorial Resources: Donald L. Delauter
Library of Congress Catalog Card Number: 96-29878
ISBN: 0-8342-0736-2

Printed in the United States of America

6   7   8   9

To my best friend and life-long companion,
my wife Linda.

Contents

Preface

This book represents the fourth edition of a book published originally in 1978, entitled *Essentials of Hospital Finance*. The text has evolved from a book containing seven chapters that dealt largely with understanding and interpreting hospital financial statements to a comprehensive financial text. The fourth edition has eighteen chapters that cover most of the major areas of financial decision making that health care executives deal with on a daily basis. The text continues to provide a large number of problems with related solutions at the end of each chapter.

Before discussing the coverage of this book, it is important to understand the objective, which has not changed in twenty years. This text is intended to provide a relevant and readable text for health care management students and executives. This is important to understand because *Essentials of Health Care Finance* is not a traditional finance text, nor is it a traditional management or financial accounting text. It attempts to blend the topics of both accounting and finance that have become part of the everyday life of most health care executives. This text does not provide as much coverage of cost of capital, capital structure, and capital budgeting topics that is present in most financial management texts. *Essentials of Health Care Finance* likewise does not provide major coverage of man-

agement control and budgeting systems that are present in most cost accounting and management accounting texts. This book has tried to cover those types of financial decisions that health care executives are most likely to be involved with, and to provide material that will help them understand the conceptual basis and mechanics of financial analysis and decision making as it pertains to the health care industry sector.

CONTENT OF THE BOOK

The general basis of financial decision making in any business is almost always built upon understanding three critical elements. First, most financial decisions are based upon the use of accounting information. It is difficult to make intelligent decisions without having at least a basic understanding of accounting information. The user does not need to be a CPA, but it is essential to have a little understanding of what accounting is and is not. Second, all business units operate within an industry. The health care industry is a huge, complex industry that is unlike other industries in many areas. Unless, the student has an appreciation for these critical differences, major mistakes can be made. Finally, both accounting and finance are, in many ways, subsets of economics. The principles of economics form the conceptual basis upon which many types of business decisions are made.

Chapter 1 provides some introductory linkages to the role of information in decision making. Chapters 2 and 3 provide detailed information about the economic environment of health care firms. Specific coverage of payment methods for all types of providers, from hospitals to physicians, is included. Extensive coverage of managed care, its definition, concepts, organizational structures, and its financial implications is included in Chapter 3 and woven in throughout the remainder of the text.

Chapters 4, 5, and 6 cover financial reporting for health care firms. Specific discussion of accounting jargon is included; but, perhaps more importantly, the accounting terms are related to health care issues such as self insurance of professional liability.

Chapters 7, 8, and 9 cover financial analysis and financial planning. Chapter 8 provides specific coverage of health care firms other than hospitals. Comparative financial and operating benchmark values are included for hospitals, HMOs, nursing homes, and medical groups that are used later to evaluate the financial position of a number of different kinds of health care firms.

Chapters 10 through 13 cover cost finding, pricing, break-even analysis, budgeting, and other managerial cost accounting topics. Special integration of managed care examples and concepts has been included in this edition.

Chapters 14 through 16 include coverage of capital budgeting and capital formation topics as they pertain to health care firms. Special attention is given to capital formation in both taxable and voluntary nonprofit situations. Chapters 17 and 18 cover the topics of working capital management and cash budgeting.

ACKNOWLEDGMENTS

I have received the support and assistance of many people in the preparation of this fourth edition. I have been extremely fortunate to have taught health care finance for more than twenty years to a large number of very bright and very positive students both at Ohio State University and in countless adult education seminars around the country. Much of the material that is presented in this book is a direct result of my teaching experiences.

Larry Goldberg of Deloitte and Touche deserves special thanks for contributing to Chapter 2. He provided details of current reimbursement provisions for major payers, especially Medicare.

Aspen Publishers conducted a very useful survey of university faculty who have adopted *Essentials of Health Care Finance*. The results of that survey provided many suggestions for improvement, which are contained in this fourth edition. I also want to thank Molly Bessey and Shelley Hamilton who spent much time creating and proofing the final document.

Finally, I want to thank my wife and three children for their understanding, love, and support. They have been a constant reminder to say things as simply as possible. I hope that this text is clearly spoken.

I have tried my best to create a text that is relevant and readable for health care students. However, this book will evolve as the health care industry evolves.

1

Financial Information and the Decision-Making Process

This book is intended to improve decision makers' understanding and use of financial information in the health care industry. It is not an advanced treatise in accounting or finance but an elementary discussion of how general and health care industry financial information is interpreted and used. It is written for people who are not experienced health care financial executives. Its aim is to make the language of health care finance understandable and relevant for decision makers in the health care industry.

Three interdependent factors have created the need for this book. They are the following:

1. rapid expansion and evolution of the health care industry,
2. health care decision makers' general lack of business and financial background, and
3. the increasing importance of financial and cost criteria in decisions relating to health care.

The health care industry's expansion is a trend visible even to people not involved in the health care system. The hospital industry, the major component of the health care industry, consumes about 4.5 percent of the gross national product; other types of health care systems, although

smaller than those in the hospital industry, are expanding at even faster rates. Table 1–1 lists the types of major health care institutions and indexes their relative size.

The rapid growth of health care facilities providing direct medical services has substantially increased the numbers of decision makers who need to be familiar with financial information. Effective decision making in their jobs depends on an accurate interpretation of financial information. Many health care decision makers involved directly in health care delivery—doctors, nurses, dietitians, pharmacists, radiation technologists, physical therapists, respiratory care practitioners—are medically or scientifically trained but often lack education and experience in business and finance. Their specialized education, in most cases, did not include such courses as accounting. However, advancement and promotion within health care organizations increasingly entail assumption of administrative duties, requiring almost instant, knowledgeable reading of financial information. Communication with the organization's financial executives is not always helpful. As a result, nonfinancial executives often ignore financial information.

Governing boards, significant users of financial information, are expanding in size in many health care facilities—in some cases, to accom-

Table 1–1 Health Care Expenditures 1990–1994 (Billions)

	1994	1990	Annual Growth Rate (%)
Total health expenditures	949.4	697.5	8.0
Percentage of gross national product	13.7	12.1	3.1
Health services and supplies	919.2	672.9	8.1
Personal health care	831.7	614.7	7.9
Hospital care	338.5	256.4	7.2
Physicians' services	189.4	146.3	6.7
Dentists' services	42.2	31.6	7.5
Home health	26.2	13.1	18.9
Other professional services	49.6	34.7	9.3
Drugs and medical supplies	78.6	59.9	7.0
Vision products and other durables	13.1	10.5	5.7
Nursing home care	72.3	50.9	9.2
Other health services	21.8	11.2	18.1
Expenses for prepayment and administration	58.7	38.6	11.1
Government public health	28.8	19.6	10.1
Research and construction	30.2	24.5	5.4

Source: Reprinted from Health Care Financing Administration, Office of Financial and Actuarial Analysis, Division of National Cost Estimates.

modate demands for more consumer representation. This trend can be healthy for both the community and the facilities. However, many board members, even those with backgrounds in business, are being overwhelmed by financial reports and statements. There are important distinctions between the financial reports and statements of business organizations (with which some board members are familiar) and those of health care facilities, which governing board members must recognize if they are to carry out their governing missions satisfactorily.

Decision makers involved in regulation have also multiplied. These decision makers work primarily with quantitative information provided by the facilities they regulate; much of these important and influential decision makers have some background in accounting and finance, but it may not be sufficient for their assigned tasks. In most situations, the agency staff serves only as a source of input for decisions that are made

by a governing board. Members of these boards usually represent a public constituency and may have little or no understanding of or experience with financial data. It is important for these members to have some minimum level of financial awareness if effective regulatory decisions are to be made.

The increasing importance of financial and cost criteria in health care decision making is the third factor creating a need for more knowledge of financial information. For many years, accountants and others involved with financial matters have been caricatured as individuals with narrow vision, incapable of seeing the forest from the trees. In many respects, this may have been an accurate portrayal. However, few people in the health care industry today would deny the importance of financial concerns, especially cost. Careful attention to these concerns requires a variety of decision makers to knowledgeably consume financial information. It is not an overstatement to state that inattention to financial criteria can lead to excessive costs and eventually to insolvency.

INFORMATION AND DECISION MAKING

The major function of information in general and financial information in particular is to "oil" the decision-making process. Decision making is basically the selection of a course of action from a defined list of possible or feasible actions. In many cases, the actual course of action followed may be essentially no action; decision makers may decide to make no change from their present policies. It should be recognized, however, that both action and inaction represent policy decisions.

Figure 1–1 shows how information is related to the decision-making process and gives an example to illustrate the sequence. Generating information is the key to decision making. The quality and effectiveness of decision making depend on accurate, timely, and relevant information. The difference between data and information is more than semantic: data become information only when they are useful and appropriate to the decision. Many financial data never become information because they are not viewed as relevant or are unavailable in an intelligible form.

For the illustrative purposes of the ambulatory surgery center (ASC) example in Figure 1–1, only two possible courses of action are assumed: to build or not to build an ASC. In most situations, there may be a continuum of alternative courses of action. For example, an ASC might vary by size or facilities included in the unit. In this case, prior decision making seems to have reduced the feasible set of alternatives to a more manageable and limited number of analyses.

Once a course of action has been selected during the decision-making phase, it must be accomplished. Implementing a decision may be extremely complex. In the ASC example, carrying out the decision to build the unit would require enormous management effort to ensure that the projected results are actually obtained. Periodic measurement of results in a feedback loop, as depicted in Figure 1–1, is a method commonly used to make sure that decisions are actually implemented according to plan.

As previously stated, results that are forecast are not always guaranteed. Controllable factors, such as failure to adhere to prescribed plans, and uncontrollable circumstances, such as a change in reimbursement, may obstruct planned results.

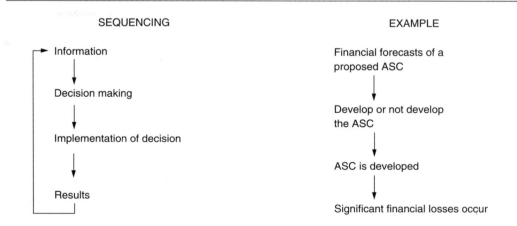

Figure 1–1 Information in the Decision-Making Process

Decision making is usually surrounded by uncertainty. No anticipated result of a decision is guaranteed. Events may occur that have been analyzed but not anticipated. A results matrix concisely portrays the possible results of various courses of action, given the occurrence of possible events. Table 1–2 provides a results matrix for the sample ASC; it shows that approximately 50 percent utilization will enable this unit to operate "in the black" and not drain resources from other areas. If forecasting shows that utilization below 50 percent is unlikely, decision makers may very well elect to build.

A good information system should enable decision makers to choose those courses of action that have the highest expectation of favorable results. Based on the results matrix of Table 1–2, a good information system should specifically do the following:

- list possible courses of action,
- list events that might affect the expected results,
- indicate the probability that those events will occur, and
- estimate the results accurately, given an action/event combination (for example, profit in Table 1–2).

One thing an information system does not do is evaluate the desirability of results. Decision makers must evaluate results in terms of their organizations' or their own preferences. For example, construction of an ASC may be expected to lose $200,000 a year, but it could provide a needed community service. Weighing these results, or criteria, is purely a decision maker's responsibility—not an easy task, but one that can be improved with accurate and relevant information.

USES AND USERS OF FINANCIAL INFORMATION

As a subset of general information, financial information is important in the decision-making process. In some areas of decision making, financial information is especially relevant. For our purposes, we identify five uses of financial information that may be important in decision making. They are as follows:

1. evaluating the financial condition of an entity,
2. evaluating stewardship within an entity,
3. assessing the efficiency of operations,
4. assessing the effectiveness of operations, and
5. determining the compliance of operations with directives.

Financial Condition

Evaluation of an entity's financial condition is probably the most common use of financial information. Usually, an organization's financial condition is equated with its viability or capacity to continue pursuing its stated goals at a consistent level of activity. Viability is a much more restrictive term than solvency; some health care organizations may be solvent but not viable. For

Table 1–2 Results Matrix for the ASC

| Alternative Actions | Event | | |
	25% Utilization	50% Utilization	75% Utilization
Build unit	$400,000 Loss	$10,000 Profit	$200,000 Profit
Do not build unit	0	0	0

example, a hospital may have its level of funds restricted so that it must reduce its scope of activity but still remain solvent. A reduction in approved rates by a designated regulatory or rate-setting agency may be the vehicle for this change in viability.

Assessment of the financial condition of business enterprises is essential to our economy's smooth and efficient operation. Most business decisions in our economy are directly or indirectly based on perceptions of financial condition. This includes the largely nonprofit health care industry. Although attention directed at organizations usually treats these organizations as whole units, assessment of the financial condition of organizational divisions is equally important. In the ASC example, information on the future financial condition of the unit is valuable. If continued losses from this operation are projected, impairment of the financial condition of other divisions in the organization could be in the offing.

Assessment of financial condition also includes consideration of short-run versus long-run effects. The relevant time frame may change, depending on the decision being considered. For example, suppliers typically are interested only in an organization's short-run financial condition because that is the period during which they must expect payment. However, investment bankers, as long-term creditors, are interested in the organization's financial condition over a much longer period.

Stewardship

Historically, evaluation of stewardship was the most important use of accounting and financial information systems. These systems were originally designed to prevent the loss of assets or resources through employees' malfeasance. This use is still very important. In fact, the relatively infrequent occurrence of employee fraud and embezzlement may be due in part to the well-designed accounting systems.

Efficiency

Efficiency in health care operations is becoming an increasingly important objective for many decision makers. Efficiency is simply the ratio of outputs to inputs, not the quality of outputs (good or not good), but the lowest possible cost of production. Adequate assessment of efficiency implies the availability of standards against which actual costs may be compared. In many health care organizations, these standards may be formally introduced into the budgetary process. Thus, a given nursing unit may have an efficiency standard of 4.3 nursing hours per patient day of care delivered. This standard then may be used as a benchmark by which to evaluate the relative efficiency of the unit. For example, actual employment of 6.0 nursing hours per patient day may cause management to assess staffing patterns.

Effectiveness

Assessment of the effectiveness of operations concerns the attainment of objectives through production of outputs, not the relationship of outputs to cost. Measuring effectiveness is much more difficult than measuring efficiency because most organizations' objectives or goals are typically not stated quantitatively. Because measurement of effectiveness is difficult, there is a tendency to place less emphasis on effectiveness and more on efficiency. This may result in the delivery of services that are not needed at an efficient cost. For example, development of outpatient surgical centers may reduce costs per surgical procedure and thus create an efficient means of delivery. However, the necessity of those surgical procedures may still be questionable.

Compliance

Finally, financial information may be used to determine whether compliance with directives has occurred. The best example of an organization's internal directives is its budget, an agreement between two management levels regarding use of resources for a defined period. External parties also may impose directives, many of them financial in nature, for the organization's adherence. For example, rate-setting or regulatory agencies may set limits on rates determined within an organization. Financial reporting by the organization is required to ensure compliance.

Table 1–3 presents a matrix of users and uses of financial information in the health care industry. It identifies areas or uses that may interest particular decision-making groups. It does not consider relative importance.

Not every use of financial information is important in every decision. For example, while approving a health care organization's rates, a governing board may be interested in only two uses of financial information: (1) evaluation of financial condition, and (2) assessment of operational efficiency. Other uses may be irrelevant. The board wants to ensure that services are being provided efficiently and that the rates being established are sufficient to guarantee a stable or improved financial condition. As Table 1–3 illustrates, most health care decision-making groups use financial information to assess financial condition and efficiency.

FINANCIAL ORGANIZATION

It is important to understand the management organizational structure of businesses in general and health care organizations in particular. Figure 1–2 outlines the financial management structure of a typical hospital.

The Financial Executives Institute has categorized financial management functions as either controllership or treasurership. Although few health care organizations have specifically identified treasurers and controllers at this time, the separation of duties is important to the understanding of financial management. The following describes functions in the two categories designated by the Financial Executives Institute:

1. Controllership
   a. planning for control
   b. reporting and interpreting

Table 1–3 Users and Uses of Financial Information

	Uses				
Users	Financial Condition	Stewardship	Efficiency	Effectiveness	Compliance
External					
Health care coalitions	X		X	X	
Unions	X		X		
Rate-setting organizations	X		X	X	X
Creditors	X		X	X	
Third-party payers			X		X
Suppliers	X				
Public	X		X	X	
Internal					
Governing board	X	X	X	X	X
Top management	X	X	X	X	X
Departmental management			X		X

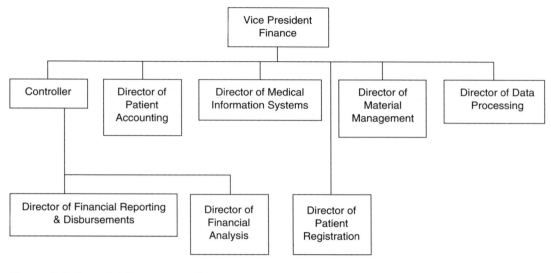

Figure 1–2 Financial Organization Chart

c. evaluating and consulting
d. administrating taxes
e. reporting to government
f. protecting assets
g. appraising economic health
2. Treasurership
a. providing capital
b. maintaining investor relations
c. providing short-term financing
d. providing banking and custody
e. overseeing credits and collections
f. choosing investments
g. providing insurance

The effectiveness of financial management in any business is the product of many factors, such as environmental conditions, personnel capabilities, and information quality. A major portion of the total financial management task is the provision of accurate, timely, and relevant information. Much of this activity is carried out through the accounting process. An adequate understanding of the accounting process and the data generated by it are thus critical to successful decision making.

SUMMARY

The health care sector of our economy is growing rapidly in both size and complexity. Understanding the financial and economic implications of decision making has become critical to health care decision makers. Successful decision making can lead to a viable operation capable of providing needed health care services. Unsuccessful decision making can and often does lead to financial failure. The role of financial information in the decision-making process cannot be overstated. It is incumbent on all health care decision makers to become accounting-literate in our financially changing health care environment.

ASSIGNMENTS

1. Only in recent years have hospitals begun to develop meaningful systems of cost accounting. Why did they not begin such development sooner?
2. Your hospital has been approached by a major employer in your market area to negotiate a preferred provider arrangement. The employer is seeking a 25 percent discount from your current charges. Describe a structure that you might use to summarize the financial implications of this decision. Describe the factors that would be critical in this decision.
3. What type of financial information should be routinely provided to board members?

SOLUTIONS AND ANSWERS

1. Before 1983, most hospitals were paid actual costs for delivering hospital services. With the introduction of Medicare's prospective payment system in 1983, hospitals now receive prices based on diagnosis-related groupings that are fixed in advance. Cost control and, therefore, cost accounting are critical in a fixed-price environment. The expansion of managed care has further restricted revenue and fostered greater interest in costing.

2. This problem could be set up in a results matrix (see Table 1–2). The two actions to be charted are to accept or to reject the preferred provider arrangement opportunity. Possible events would center on the magnitude of volume changes, for example, to lose 1,000 patient days or to gain 500 patient days. A key concern while estimating the financial impact would be the hospital's incremental revenue and incremental cost positions. In short, how large would the revenue reduction and cost reduction be if significant volume was lost? Actual gains or losses of business would be functions of the hospital's market position.

3. Board members do not need to see detailed financial information that relates to their established plans to ensure that the plans are being met. If significant deviations have occurred, more details may be necessary to take corrective action or to modify established plans.

2

Financial Environment
of Health Care Organizations

Almost any measure of size would indicate that the health care industry is big business. Its proportion of the gross national product (GNP) has been steadily increasing for several decades and now represents 14 percent of the GNP and one trillion dollars in expenditures. Paralleling this growth, the pressures for cost control within the system have increased tremendously, especially at the federal and state levels for control of Medicare and Medicaid. Health care organizations (HCOs) that are not able to deal effectively with these pressures face an uncertain future. In short, as the expected demand for health services continues to increase during the next several decades as our population ages, successful HCOs must become increasingly cost-efficient.

FINANCIAL VIABILITY

An HCO is a basic provider of health services but is also a business. The environment of an HCO viewed from a financial perspective could be schematically represented as depicted in Figure 2–1.

The author thanks Lawrence Goldberg of Deloitte and Touche LLP for updating reimbursement provisions in this chapter.

In the long run, the HCO must receive dollar payments from the community in an amount at least equal to the dollar payments it makes to its suppliers. In very simple terms, this is the essence of financial viability.

The community in Figure 2–1 is the provider of funds to the HCO. The flow of funds is either directly or indirectly related to the delivery of services by the HCO. For our purposes, the community may be categorized as follows:

- Patients
  1. Self-payer
  2. Third-party payer
     –Blue Cross and Blue Shield
     –Commercial insurance, including managed care
     –Medicaid
     –Medicare
     –Self-insured employer
     –Other
- Nonpatients
  1. Grants
  2. Contributions
  3. Tax support
  4. Miscellaneous

In most HCOs, the greater proportion of funds is derived from patients who receive services directly. The largest percentage of these payments

Figure 2–1 Financial Environment of Health Care Organizations

usually comes from third-party sources such as Blue Cross, Medicare, Medicaid, and managed care organizations. In addition, some nonpatient funds are derived from government sources in the form of grants for research purposes or direct payments to subsidized HCOs, such as county facilities. Some HCOs also receive significant sums of money from individuals, foundations, or corporations in the form of contributions. Although these sums may be small relative to the total amounts of money received from patient services, their importance in overall viability should not be understated. In many HCOs, these contributed dollars mean the difference between net income and loss.

The suppliers in Figure 2–1 provide the HCO with resources that are necessary in the delivery of quality health care. The major categories of suppliers are the following:

- employees,
- equipment suppliers,
- service contractors,
- vendors of consumable supplies, and
- lenders.

Payments for employees usually represent the largest single category of expenditures. For example, in many hospitals, payments for employees represent about 60 percent of total expenditures. Table 2–1 is an example of an income

Table 2–1 Statement of Operations for Memorial Hospital, Year Ended 1999 (000s Omitted)

	1999	%
Net patient service revenue	$48,306	96.99
Other revenue	1,499	3.01
Total revenue	49,805	100.0
Operating expenses	24,189	48.57
Salaries and wages	4,174	8.38
Employee benefits	1,628	3.27
Professional fees	15,307	30.73
Depreciation and amortization	3,586	7.20
Interest	819	1.64
Total expenses	$49,703	99.79
Operating income	102	0.21
Investment income	474	0.95
Excess of revenues over expenses	$ 576	1.16

statement that shows percentages of revenues and expenses for a hospital. Payments for physicians' services also represent important financial requirements. In addition, lenders such as commercial banks or investment bankers supply dollars in the form of loans and receive from the HCO a promise to repay the loans with interest according to a defined repayment schedule. This financial requirement has grown steadily as HCOs have become more dependent on debt financing.

SOURCES OF OPERATING REVENUE

Table 2–2 provides a historical breakdown of the relative size of the health care industry and its individual industrial segments. The largest segment is the hospital industry, which absorbs about 36 percent of all health care expenditure dollars. This percentage has been declining over the last few years and is expected to decline further as other industry segments grow more quickly. The physician segment absorbs approximately 20 percent of total health care expenditures; this represents a modest increase over the last decade when expressed as a percentage of total health care expenditures. Nursing homes represent the third largest health care segment, constituting about 8 percent of all health care expenditures. Many people believe that this segment will grow the fastest as the population ages.

Table 2–3 depicts the sources of operating funds for the three largest health care segments: hospitals, physicians, and nursing homes. Dra-

Table 2–2 National Health Care Expenditures

	1985	1994	Annual Growth Rate (%)
National health care expenditures (billions)	$ 428	$ 949	9.3
Population (millions)	247	271	1.0
Per capita expenditures			
Personal health care			
Hospital care	$ 682	$1,251	7.0
Physicians' services	339	700	8.4
Dentist's services	88	156	6.6
Other professional services	67	183	11.8
Home health care	23	97	17.3
Drugs and other medical nondurables	150	291	7.6
Vision aids and other medical nondurables	27	48	6.6
Nursing home care	124	267	8.9
Other personal health care	25	81	14.0
Total personal health care	$1,525	$3,074	8.1
Program administration and insurance costs	96	217	9.5
Government public health	47	106	9.5
Research and construction	66	112	6.1
Total national health care expenditures	$1,734	$3,509	8.2

Source: Reprinted from Health Care Financing Administration, Office of Financial and Actuarial Analysis, Division of National Cost Estimates.

Table 2–3 Sources of Health Services Funding, 1994

Source	Hospitals	Physicians	Nursing Homes
Private payments (%)			
Out of pocket	3	15	33
Private insurance	34	49	2
Other private	4	2	2
Total private payments	41	66	37
Government payments (%)			
Medicare	30	20	9
Medicaid	15	7	52
Other	14	7	2
Total government payments	59	34	63
Total payments (%)	100.0	100.0	100.0

Source: Reprinted from Health Care Financing Administration, Office of Financial and Actuarial Analysis, Division of National Cost Estimates.

matic differences in financing among these three segments can be seen easily.

The hospital industry derives more than 50 percent of its total funding from public sources, largely from Medicare and Medicaid. Of the two, Medicare is by far the larger, representing about 30 percent of all hospital revenue. This gives the federal government enormous control over hospitals and their financial positions. Few hospitals can choose to ignore the Medicare program because of its sheer size. Another 34 percent of total hospital funding results from private insurance, largely from Blue Cross, commercial insurance carriers, managed care organizations, and self-insured employers. Direct payments by patients to hospitals represent approximately 3 percent of total revenue. The implication of this distribution for hospitals is the creation of an oligopsonistic marketplace. The buying power for hospital services is concentrated in relatively few third-party purchasers, namely the federal government, the state government, Blue Cross, a few commercial insurance carriers, and some large self-insured employers.

The physician marketplace is somewhat different from the marketplace for hospital services. A much larger percentage of physician funding is derived from direct payments by patients (approximately 15 percent). And compared with hospital funding, a slightly larger percentage of physician funding results from private insurance sources, largely from Blue Cross and commercial insurance carriers. Physicians derive approximately 49 percent of their total funds from this source; the hospital segment derives 34 percent of total funds from this source. Public programs, although still significant, are the smallest source of physician funding, representing 34 percent of total funds. This situation results because more physician services, such as routine physical examinations and many deductible and copayment services, are excluded from Medicare payment.

The nursing home segment receives almost no funding from private insurance sources. The major public program for nursing homes is Medicaid, not Medicare. However, the federal government pays more than 50 percent of all Medicaid expenditures. Medicare payments to nursing homes are largely restricted to skilled nursing care, whereas the majority of Medicaid payments to nursing homes are for intermediate-level (custodial) care.

HOSPITAL PAYMENT SYSTEMS

One of the most important financial differences between hospitals and other businesses is the way in which their customers or patients make payment for services received. Most businesses have only one basic type of payment: billed charges. Each customer is presented with a bill that represents the product of the quantity of goods or services received and their appropriate prices. The price may be discounted to move inventory during slack periods or to encourage large volume orders. The basic payment system, however, remains the same: a fixed price per unit of service that is set by the business, not the customer.

In contrast, the typical hospital will have several different payment systems in effect at any given time. Each of these payment systems has a different effect on the hospital's financial position and might lead to different conclusions regarding business strategy. Thus, it is extremely important to understand the financial implications of the various payment systems hospitals use. This book discusses the following four major payment systems:

1. historical cost reimbursement,
2. specific services (charge payment),
3. negotiated bids and capitated rates, and
4. diagnosis-related groups.

Historical Cost Reimbursement

Until recently, cost reimbursement was the predominant form of payment for most hospitals. In addition to Medicare, most state Medicaid plans and a large number of Blue Cross plans paid hospitals on the basis of "reasonable" historical costs. Today, the major payers have abandoned historical cost reimbursement and have replaced it with other payment systems.

Two key elements in historical cost reimbursement are reasonable cost and apportionment. Reasonable cost is simply a qualification introduced by the payer to limit total payment by excluding certain categories of cost or placing limits on costs that the payer deems reasonable. Examples of costs often defined as unreasonable, and therefore not reimbursable, are costs for charity care, patient telephones, and nursing education. Apportionment refers to the manner in which costs are assigned or allocated to a specific payer such as Medicaid. For example, assume that a hospital has total reasonable costs of $10 million, which represent the costs of servicing all patients. If Medicaid is a historical cost reimbursement payer, an allocation or apportionment of that $10 million is necessary to determine Medicaid's share of the total cost. Often, the apportionment is related to the hospital's billed charges. For example, if charges for services to Medicaid patients were $3 million and total charges to all patients were $15 million, then 20 percent of the $10 million cost would be apportioned to Medicaid.

Several important financial principles of cost reimbursement should be emphasized. First, cost reimbursement can somewhat insulate those in management from the results of poor financial planning. New clinical programs that do not achieve targeted volume or exceed projected costs may still be viable because of extensive cost reimbursement. This assumes that the payer does not regard the costs as unreasonable. Second, cost reimbursement often can be increased through careful planning, just as taxes often can be reduced through tax planning. The key objective is to maximize the amount of cost apportioned to cost payers subject to any tests for reasonableness.

Specific Services

Usually, some hospital patients make payment based on charges for the specific services provided, such as nursing, surgery, pharmacy, or laboratory services. These charges may be regulated by external parties, such as state rate-setting commissions, or they may be completely unregulated and left to the discretion of hospital management. Commercial insurance carriers, self-insured employers, and self-pay patients are usually the largest sources of payment for specific services.

Payment for specific services has several important implications for financial management. First, revenue from specific services may represent the major source of profit to the hospital. In this case, pricing or rate setting becomes an important hospital policy (rate setting is addressed later in this chapter). Second, the hospital's rate structure should be based on projected volume and cost factors. Any unexpected deviation from the hospital's plan merits prompt attention.

Negotiated Bids and Capitated Rates

Negotiated bids and capitated rates represent a new type of payment for many hospitals. This type of payment results from a specific contractual arrangement between the hospital and a payer. A special contract with a health maintenance organization or a local employer is a common example of a negotiated bid or capitated arrangement. In some states, Medicaid also might be considered a source of negotiated bid revenue. For example, in 1983, California hospitals bid for Medicaid contracts on the basis of a rate per patient day. Hospitals that submitted low bids (for example, a low rate per patient day) often would receive contracts to provide hospital services to Medicaid patients in a given area.

In a negotiated bid or capitated payment environment, financial planning and control are critical—even more critical than in a specific services payment situation. The fee arrangement is usually contractually fixed for a period of one year. Unexpected increases in costs usually will not be a basis for contract renegotiation. Cost accounting and analysis are also important. It is imperative that management knows what it costs to provide a unit of service required in the contract. For example, if the negotiated rate is to

provide all hospital services to subscribers of a health maintenance organization for a fixed fee per subscriber (or capitation), the hospital must know both the volume and the cost of the required services. Ideally, the cost accounting system should define in a given contract the incremental costs likely to be incurred so that they can be compared to the incremental revenue likely to result from the contract. In addition, actuarial services also are essential to project utilization on a per-member basis.

Diagnosis-Related Groups

Payment by diagnosis-related groups (DRGs) became prevalent for hospitals in 1983 when Medicare initiated payment on this basis. Because of the sheer size of the Medicare program in most hospitals, hospital management was quickly forced to become familiar with the DRG payment system. In the Medicare DRG payment system, specific prices are established for 495 specific diagnostic categories. These prices are updated each year by Medicare to reflect inflationary changes as well as changes in treatment protocols.

From the hospital's perspective, the prices established by Medicare are fixed and not appealable. The hospital may decide not to continue providing a given DRG service because it loses money when providing this service; however, it cannot get Medicare to change prices in specific DRGs. The financial implications of DRG payment are fairly clear. First, cost control becomes critical to long-term financial viability. Hospitals must produce a given DRG at a reasonable cost. There are four primary ways in which costs for a DRG can be reduced. They are the following:

1. Reduce the prices paid for resources.
2. Reduce the length of stay.
3. Reduce the intensity of service provided.
4. Improve production efficiency.

Note that two of the four methods for DRG cost reduction involve medical staff decision making, namely reducing length of stay and reducing service intensity. Thus, it is necessary that hospital management focus more intensely on product lines. Ultimately, hospitals need to analyze the relative profitability of given DRGs comprising particular clinical services, such as psychiatry or surgery. Clearly, cost accounting by DRG is essential to any intelligent analysis of relative DRG profitability. Hospital cost accounting systems are usually structured around departments, such as dietary, laboratory, and physical therapy departments. However, DRGs require services from a number of departments, and therefore costs must be assigned from these departments to individual DRGs. This is not a small problem, and accurate cost information is essential.

RATE/PRICE SETTING

Stages in the Rate-Setting Process

Rate setting is an extremely complex and important management activity. The success or failure of the organization ultimately may depend on the quality of management decision making in this area. Assuming that reasonably accurate projections of both output and expense are available, there are at least three stages in the rate-setting process. They are the following:

1. determining required net income,
2. determining patient payment composition, and
3. determining bad debt and charity deductions.

In most situations, net income is essential to the viability of the organization. The real issue is how much net income is acceptable. In this short discussion, it is not possible to answer this question in detail. However, in general, the rates must be established at levels that will meet budgeted financial requirements, that is:

Budgeted financial requirements =
Total revenue

where:

Total operating revenue =
Gross patient service revenue −
Allowances and uncollectable +
Other revenue

The required amount of income now can be defined as:

Required net income =
Budgeted financial requirements −
Budgeted expenses

The previous calculations ignore the existence of nonoperating revenue. If sizable and stable sums of nonoperating revenue are available, they may be used to subsidize operations. This is clearly an important policy determination and should be made by the board after careful consideration of projected financial plans.

Budgeted financial requirements are cash requirements or expenditures that an entity must meet during the budget period. These requirements usually comprise the following four elements:

1. budgeted expenses, excluding depreciation,
2. debt principal payments,
3. increases in working capital, and
4. capital expenditures.

Budgeted expenses at the departmental level should include both direct and indirect or allocated expenses. Depreciation charges are excluded because depreciation is an expense, not an expenditure; it does not require an actual cash outlay.

Debt principal payments include only the principal portion of debt service due. In some cases, additional reserve requirements may be established, and these may require additional funding. Interest expense is already included in budgeted expenses and should not be included in this category.

Working capital requirements include such things as necessary increases in inventory, accounts receivable, and precautionary cash balances. Planned financing of increases in working capital is a legitimate financial requirement.

Capital expenditure requirements may be of two types. First, actual capital expenditures may be made for approved projects. Those projects not financed with indebtedness require a cash investment and represent a financial requirement. Second, prudent fiscal management requires that funds be set aside and invested to meet reasonable requirements for future capital expenditures. This amount should be related to the replacement cost depreciation of existing fixed assets. An HCO should fund some proportion of its replacement cost depreciation, especially a not-for-profit HCO that cannot obtain new equity from selling stock.

Determination of the patient payment composition is the next important stage in effective rate setting. It must be remembered that not all patients actually will pay the rates established. Many third-party payers—especially Blue Cross, Medicare, managed care organizations, and Medicaid—do not pay billed charges. Therefore, the rate structure should incorporate the effect of these contractual allowances in the establishment of rates.

Finally, estimates of the expected write-off of charges for bad debts and charity care must be made. It is important to emphasize that these elements will be treated as deductions from gross patient service revenue, and not expenses. Although the correct financial reporting of bad-debt expense is to treat it as an expense, we will treat bad debt as a deduction from revenue. Some hospitals may have especially large bad debt and charity care loads if they serve a high percentage of medically indigent patients.

A Rate-Setting Model

It is possible to develop a simple but realistic rate-setting model based on the previous discussion. In algebraic form, revenue should be determined as follows:

Revenue =

$$\frac{\text{Budgeted expenses} + \text{Desired net income} - \text{Noncharge-paying patient payments}}{\text{Proportion of charge-paying patients}}$$

The following example may help illustrate this formula. Let us assume that a hospital has 25 patients in the following payment categories:

Managed care	5
DRG patients	10
Cost-paying patients	4
Charity care patients	1
Charge-paying patients	5
Total	25

Furthermore, assume that the hospital has budgeted operating expenses of $27,500, or $1,100 per patient, the DRG payment rate is $1,000 per patient, and the managed care rate is $1,050 per patient. If the hospital needs to earn a $3,000 net income, it must set its rates as follows:

Revenue =

$$\frac{27,500 + 3,000 - 10,000 - 4,400 - 5,250}{5/25}$$

= 54,250 or $2,170 per patient

The following income statement would result if the previous expectations were realized:

Gross patient revenue

Managed care (5 × $2,170)	$10,850
DRG patients (10 × $2,170)	21,700
Cost patients (4 × $2,170)	8,680
Charity patients (1 × $2,170)	2,170
Charge patients (5 × $2,170)	10,850
Total	$54,250

Allowances and uncollectables

Managed care	
[5 × ($2,170 − $1,050)]	$ 5,600
DRG patients	
[10 × ($2,170 − $1,000)]	11,700
Cost patients	
[4 × ($2,170 − $1,100)]	4,280
Charity patients	
[1 × ($2,170 − 0)]	2,170
Charge patients	
[5 × ($2,170 − $2,170)]	0
Total	$23,750

Net patient revenue	30,500
Operating expenses	27,500
Net operating income	$ 3,000

A number of conclusions can be drawn from this example. First, rates often may be significantly above actual expenses. The hospital in this example had a rate structure that was almost 100 percent above its expenses, but it realized just $3,000 or 5.5 percent of its gross patient revenue as income. Health care executives and board members should not be surprised by this occurrence. Second, payer subsidies clearly exist. In this example, charge-paying patients paid almost twice the rate of cost paying patients ($1,100) and 2.2 times the rate of DRG patients ($1,000). Third, the impact of charity care is directly related to the marginal cost of providing that care. In our example, removing the one charity care patient with no resulting reduction in expense would change required rates only marginally:

$$\text{Revenue} = \frac{\$27,500 + 3,000 - 10,000 - 4,583 - 5,250}{5/24}$$

$$= \$51,201 \text{ or } \$2,133 \text{ per patient}$$

However, removing $1,100 of cost (the average cost of treating one patient) would lead to a sizable reduction in rates:

$$\text{Revenue} = \frac{\$26,400 + 3,000 - 10,000 - 4,400 - 5,250}{5/24}$$

$$= \$46,800 \text{ or } \$1,950 \text{ per patient}$$

Finally, reductions in operating expenses can lead to sizable reductions in required rates if the percentage of cost-paying patients is relatively low. In our example, a 10 percent reduction in operating expense ($2,750) would yield a 21 percent reduction in rate per patient:

$$\text{Revenue} = \frac{\$24,750 + 3,000 - 10,000 - 3,960 - 5,250}{5/25}$$

$$= \$42,700 \text{ or } \$1,708 \text{ per patient}$$

Cost reduction has, in fact, become a primary objective for many hospitals as their percentage of cost payment business declines.

MEDICARE PROSPECTIVE PAYMENT SYSTEM FOR HOSPITALS

It is somewhat risky to describe in detail the mechanics of Medicare's prospective payment system (PPS), given the fact that the system is complex. However, the enormous impact that this payment system has on the entire health care system dictates that some attempt be made here to examine its operation and implications. Still, readers are cautioned that the information provided here may not be accurate at the time of reading.

PPS was officially launched by Medicare on October 1, 1983. All hospitals participating in the Medicare program are required to participate in PPS, except those excluded by statute. These include the following:

- psychiatric hospitals,
- rehabilitation hospitals,
- children's hospitals,

- long-term care hospitals,
- distinct psychiatric and rehabilitation units,
- hospitals outside the fifty states, and
- hospitals in states with an approved waiver.

PPS provides payment for all hospital nonphysician services provided to hospital inpatients. This payment also covers services provided by outside suppliers, such as laboratory or radiology units. Medicare makes one comprehensive, all-inclusive payment to the hospital, which is then responsible for paying outside suppliers or nonphysician services.

The basis of PPS payment is the DRG system developed by Yale University. The DRG system takes all possible diagnoses from the *International Classification of Diseases, 9th Revision, Clinical Modification* (ICD9–CM) system and classifies them into twenty-five major diagnostic categories based on organ systems. These twenty-five categories are further broken down into 495 distinct medically meaningful group-

ings or DRGs (Appendix 2–A contains a list of the 495 DRGs). Medicare contends that the resources required to treat a given DRG entity should be similar for all patients within a DRG category.

Total payments to a hospital under Medicare can be split into the following elements (Figure 2–2):

- Prospective payments
  1. DRG operating payment
  2. DRG capital payment
- Reasonable cost payments

The DRG operating payment results from the multiplication of the hospital dollar rate and the specific case weight of the DRG. Appendix 2–A provides the most recent case weight for the 495 DRGs. The case weight for DRG #1, craniotomy, age older than 17 years, except for trauma, is 3.0932. This measure indicates that in terms of expected cost, DRG #1 would cost

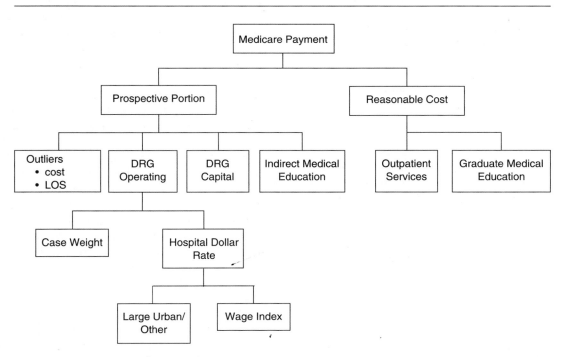

Figure 2–2 Breakdown of Medicare Payments to a Hospital

about 3.0932 times more than the average case. A specific value is assigned to each of the 495 DRGs.

The dollar rate depends on the hospital's designated status as large urban or "other." Large urban areas are metropolitan areas with more than 1 million people. Rates for each of these categories are defined once a year by Medicare. Table 2–4 presents hypothetical rates as might be defined by Medicare.

Every hospital in the United States has a wage index value assigned to it. That wage index is multiplied by the labor component of the Medicare standardized payment to yield the DRG operating payment. If we assume that a large urban hospital has a wage index of 1.2509, its DRG operating payment for DRG #1 would be calculated as follows:

$$\$ = \text{DRG weight} \times [(\text{Labor amount} \times \text{wage index}) + \text{Nonlabor amount}]$$

$$\$ = 3.0932 \ [(\$2,741 \times 1.2509) + \$1,098] = \$14,002$$

This dollar payment may be further increased by additional payments to cover the following areas:

- indirect medical education,
- disproportionate share, and
- outlier payments.

An add-on to a teaching hospital is given and referred to as an indirect medical education adjustment. This allowance is related to the number of interns and residents at the hospital and the number of beds in a hospital. The allowance is over and above salaries paid to interns and residents, which are already covered as a reasonable cost included in graduate medical education. The additional payment is meant to cover the additional costs that the teaching hospital incurs in the treatment of patients by medical residents.

A separate payment is also provided to a hospital that treats a large percentage of Medicare and Medicaid patients. This payment is referred to as a disproportionate share payment.

Outlier payments are additional payments for patients who use an unusually large amount of resources. There are two categories of outlier payments: (1) cost and (2) day. Cost outliers must exceed the DRG payment by $15,150. Day outliers represent cases in which the actual length of stay (LOS) is three standard deviations from the geometric mean LOS, or 23 days from the geometric mean LOS. Appendix 2–A provides the day outlier threshold in the last column. For DRG #1, a patient would need to have a LOS in excess of 32 days before any additional payment would be granted. After the thirty-second day, a per diem equal to 45 percent of the average cost would be paid.

The multiplication by 45 percent reflects the fact that only a portion of the hospital's cost is variable. Medicare assumes that the variable costs of outlier patients are 45 percent; alternatively, it assumes that the fixed costs are 55 percent.

Calculations for cost outliers are complex and beyond the scope of this book. As in the case of LOS outliers, only the cost beyond the cutoff point is reimbursed, and then only at 80 percent. For example, a cost outlier with an $84,000 total cost and a cutoff cost value of $44,000 would generate only $32,000 additional reimbursement (.80 × $40,000). Medicare uses a variable cost percentage of 80 percent for cost outliers as contrasted with 45 percent for day outliers.

There is still a portion of the total Medicare payment that is related to reasonable cost (Figure 2–2). Costs that are still paid for on this basis include the following:

Table 2–4 Hypothetical Medicare Rates According to Hospital Status

Hospital Status	Rate	
	Labor	Nonlabor
Large urban	$2,741	$1,098
Other areas	$2,698	$1,081

- direct medical education costs,
- kidney acquisition costs,
- bad debts for copayments and deductibles,
- outpatient operating costs, and
- outpatient capital costs.

Effective October 1, 1992, Medicare began to pay for inpatient capital costs on a prospective basis also. Before this date, capital costs had been paid for on a reasonable cost basis. There is a ten-year phase-in for capital cost payment that is complicated and is not covered here. There is also a floor on capital cost payment that is currently set at 70 percent of inpatient capital costs. This means that the lowest payment for inpatient capital costs will at least equal 70 percent of the hospital's allocated inpatient capital costs. Capital costs include interest, depreciation, and lease rental costs. Taxes and insurance are also considered capital costs if they are related to capital assets.

There is a national standardized federal payment rate for capital costs that is similar to the national rates for labor and nonlabor costs discussed earlier. In 1996, the federal rate for capital costs was $461.96. This rate would be adjusted for the following factors:

- case mix, using the DRG relative weight,
- indirect medical education,
- outlier adjustments (the adjustment is much lower than before, to recognize the presumed fixed-cost nature of capital costs),
- disproportionate share adjustment,
- geographic adjustment using the wage index to impute higher costs to higher wage areas, and
- large urban adjustment of three percent, to reflect higher costs.

As an illustration, assume that we wish to calculate capital payment for DRG #1 when the federal payment rate was $461.96. We also will assume that our hospital is in a large urban area with a wage index of 1.2509. No other adjustments are applicable. The amount of payment would be

Capital payment =
$461.96 \times 3.0932 \times 1.03 \times 1.2509 = \$1,841.08$

MEDICARE PAYMENT FOR PHYSICIANS

Beginning in January 1992, Medicare began paying for physician services using a resource-based relative value scale (RBRVS). This payment system replaced the old reasonable charge method that had been the basis for physician payment since the inception of the Medicare program in the 1960s. Medicare pays the lesser of the actual billed charge or the fee schedule amount.

From Medicare's perspective, physicians are categorized as participating or nonparticipating physicians. A participating physician is a physician who agrees to accept Medicare's payment for a service as payment in full and will bill the patient for the copayment portion only. The copayment portion is usually 20 percent of the Medicare allowable charge. As an example, assume that a patient received a service from a physician that had an approved fee schedule of $100. The participating physician would receive $80 directly from Medicare and would bill the patient for $20, which would represent the copayment portion of the bill. If the physician's bill for the service was only $80, Medicare would pay 80 percent, or $64, and the patient would be billed 20 percent, or $16. A participating physician agrees to accept assignment on each and every Medicare patient that he or she treats.

A nonparticipating physician can choose to accept assignment on a case-by-case basis. Although this arrangement initially might seem advantageous, there are several major drawbacks. First, a nonparticipating physician has a lower fee schedule. The amount that could be billed would be equal to 95 percent of the approved fee schedule. If the physician in the illustration just discussed was nonparticipating, the amount of the Medicare payment would be $95, not $100. This difference may not seem all that important if the physician can recover any of the difference from the patient. However, Medicare has placed some limits on the amount that a nonparticipating physician can recover from the patient. Medicare sets a maximum fee for a nonparticipating physician equal to 115 percent of the approved fee for a nonparticipating physician, which is already only 95 percent of the approved fee schedule for a participating physician.

A simple illustration may help to better explain this narrative. Assume that a nonparticipating physician provides services to a patient who has charges of $200, but Medicare's approved schedule for a participating physician is only $100. How much can the physician collect? The answer depends on whether the physician accepts or rejects Medicare assignment. First, assume that the physician rejects assignment. The maximum amount that can be collected from this service is

$$\$109.25 = [.95 \times \$100] \times 1.15$$

The entire amount will come directly from the patient. No check will be sent to the physician from Medicare. The final total payment could be allocated as follows:

Medicare payment to patient	
(.8 × $95.00)	$76.00
Patient's copayment	
(.2 × $95.00)	19.00
Additional patient payment	14.25
Total payment to physician	$109.25

The nonparticipating physician also can choose to accept assignment on a case-by-case basis. The advantage realized with assignment is that Medicare now will pay the physician directly for its portion of the bill. The disadvantage is that the physician must accept the fee schedule for nonparticipating physicians, which will be only 95 percent of the fee approved for participating physicians. In the previous example, the nonparticipating physician who agreed to accept assignment regarding this patient would receive the following payments:

Medicare payment to physician	
(.8 × $95.00)	$76.00
Patient's copayment	
(.2 × $95.00)	19.00
Total payment to physician	$95.00

The participating physician would be able to receive $100 for this service because of the higher approved fee schedule. Of the total $100 in payment, $80 would come directly from Medicare and $20 from the patient as the copayment portion.

Presently, there are Medicare payment rates for almost all of the 7,000 current procedural terminology (CPT) codes. There are specific values for those codes that vary by region; presently, there are distinct values for each of the approximately 200 Medicare carrier localities. These payment rates result from the multiplication of three relative values and geographical cost indexes. For every procedure there are three relative value units (RVUs) that together reflect the cost of a particular procedure. They are the following:

1. Work (RVUw)—This factor represents not only physician time involved, but also skill levels, stress, and other factors.
2. Practice expense (RVUpe)—This factor represents nonphysician costs, excluding malpractice costs.
3. Malpractice (RVUm)—This factor represents the cost of malpractice insurance.

Each of the individual relative values is then multiplied by a region-specific set of price indexes. To illustrate this adjustment, the weighted value for coronary artery bypass for Los Angeles, California, is presented in Table 2–5. To determine the payment rate for this procedure in Los Angeles, the index-adjusted relative value would be multiplied by a conversion factor. If we assume that the conversion factor is 40.7986, the approved charge for coronary artery bypass in Los Angeles would be $2,613 (64.04 × 40.7986).

Table 2–5 Components of Price Adjustment for Coronary Artery Bypass in Los Angeles

	RVU	Geographical Cost Index for Los Angeles	Product
Work	23.16	1.056	24.46
Practice			
expense	29.55	1.207	35.67
Malpractice	5.20	0.752	3.91

Medicare Payment for SNF, HHA, and ASC Procedures

As you can tell from Medicare payments for inpatient and physician services, Medicare payment involves a complex set of rules. Medicare pays skilled nursing facilities (SNFs) on a reasonable cost basis, subject to a "schedule of limits." Similarly, Medicare pays for home health agency (HHA) services on a reasonable cost basis subject to a schedule of limits. Table 2–6 contains Medicare's latest proposed limits for HHAs (as of June 1996). These amounts are adjusted further to account for regional labor differences using the hospital area wage index amounts.

Regarding free-standing ambulatory surgical center (ASC) services—those surgical procedures that can be safely performed outside a hospital—Medicare pays for the "facility" portion of the procedure by classifying all such procedures into one of eight category groupings. Each grouping has a price. They are the following:

Group 1 $304
Group 2 $408
Group 3 $467
Group 4 $576
Group 5 $657
Group 6 ` $619 + $150 = $769
Group 7 $911
Group 8 $753 + $150 = $903

ASC facility fees, rates, or prices, however you term these amounts, are subject to the usual copayment amount from the patient. If an intraocular lens is inserted as part of a cataract procedure, the payment includes $150 as payment in full for the cost of the lens. Payment for physician services is recognized and paid separately

Table 2–6 Proposed Medicare Limits for HHAs

Location	Labor Portion	Nonlabor Portion
MSA		
Skilled nursing care	$76.57	$21.62
Physical therapy	83.84	23.59
Speech pathology	84.11	23.88
Occupational therapy	83.41	23.84
Medical social services	110.59	31.46
Home health aide	37.14	10.56
Non-MSA		
Skilled nursing care	$89.53	$20.09
Physical therapy	97.61	22.04
Speech pathology	106.31	24.30
Occupational therapy	105.06	24.24
Medical social services	149.82	43.21
Home health aide	38.87	8.73

using the Medicare physician RBRVS fee schedule.

SUMMARY

Compared with most businesses, health care organizations are financially complex. Not only do they provide a large number of specific services, but their individual services often have different effective price structures. One customer may choose to pay on the basis of cost, whereas another may pay full charges. This variation in payment patterns creates problems in the establishment of prices for products and services. Indeed, the revenue function of a typical health care entity is usually much more complex than that of a comparably sized non–health care business.

Health care entities also depend heavily on a very limited number of key clients for most of their operating funding. Their largest client is often the federal government or the state government. Doing business with the government involves a significant amount of reporting to ensure compliance and adherence to government regulations. Moreover, because the federal government is such a large purchaser of services, a thorough understanding of the nature and implications of the Medicare payment system's rules and regulations is a must for effective management of a health care organization. Yet, although health care organizations may be complex from a financial perspective, they are still businesses. Their financial viability requires the receipt of funds in amounts sufficient to meet their financial requirements.

ASSIGNMENTS

1. From the following data, determine the amount of revenue that needs to be generated to meet hospital financial requirements.

   Volume

Medicare cases	1,000
Cost-paying cases	400
Charity care and bad-debt cases	100
Charge-paying cases	500
Total cases	2,000

   Financial data

Budgeted expenses	$6,000,000
Debt principal payment	200,000
Working capital increase	250,000
Capital expenditures	400,000

   Present payment structure
   - Medicare pays only $2,800 per case, or a total of $2,800,000.
   - All other cost payers pay their share of existing expenses.

2. Why is the accumulation of funded reserves for capital replacement more critical for nonprofit health care entities than for investor-owned health care facilities?
3. Hospitals not located in large urban areas receive less payment for specific DRGs than do large urban hospitals. What might be the rationale to justify these differences?
4. Depreciation expense is recognized as a reimbursable cost by a number of payers who pay prospective rates for operating costs. Would you prefer accelerated depreciation (sum of the year's digits) or price-level depreciation for a five-year life asset with a $150,000 cost? Assume that inflation is projected to be six percent per year.
5. Nonprofit organizations should not make profits; instead, either their rates should be reduced or their services expanded. Evaluate the choices.
6. Using the data from Problem 1 (first item on this list), calculate the impact of a 10 percent reduction in operating expenses, that is, down to $5,400,000, on the required revenue and rate structure. Discuss the implications of your findings.
7. Assume that the wage index is 1.2509 for your geographical area. Using the limits defined in the text for home health agency visits, compute the maximum payment for a physical therapy visit.
8. Calculate the RBRVS rate for CPT 33426, repair of mitral valve for a physician in Chicago, Illinois. Assume the conversion factor is 40.7986. The following table provides relevant values to complete this calculation:

Repair of Mitral Valve
(33426)

	RVU	Chicago Index	Product
Work	26.07	1.028	26.80
Practice expense	31.96	1.080	34.52
Malpractice	5.80	1.382	8.02
			69.34

SOLUTIONS AND ANSWERS

1. The relevant calculation is as follows:

Revenue =

$$\frac{\text{Budgeted expense} + \text{Desired net income} - \text{Noncharge-paying patient payments}}{\text{Proportion of charge-paying patients}}$$

Revenue =

$$\frac{\$6,000,000 + \$850,000 - \$4,000,000}{.25} = \$11,400,000 \text{ or } \$5,700 \text{ per case}$$

Desired net income = $850,000 = $200,000 + $250,000 + $400,000

Noncharge-paying patient payments = Medicare payments + Cost-paying patient payments

$$= \$2,800,000 + (\frac{400}{2,000} \times \$6,000,000)$$

= $4,000,000

$$\text{Proportion of charge-paying patients} = \frac{500}{2,000} = .25$$

2. A nonprofit entity does not have the same opportunities for capital formation that an investor-owned organization does. Specifically, the nonprofit entity cannot sell new shares or ownership interests. Its sources of capital are limited to its accumulated funded reserves, and to new debt. In some special situations, nonprofit organizations may receive contributions, but these amounts are usually not significant.
3. The major rationale for urban and rural hospital payment differences relates to severity-of-illness difference. Many people believe that urban hospitals are more likely to treat more severely ill patients. Rural hospitals contend that much of the variation is due to differences in the efficiency and effectiveness of care. At this time, it is not clear precisely what the causes of urban and rural hospital cost differences are, but such differences do exist.
4. The relevant comparative data would be as follows:

	Price Level Depreciation*	Sum-of-the-Years Digits Depreciation**
Year 1	$ 31,800	$ 50,000
Year 2	33,708	40,000
Year 3	35,730	30,000
Year 4	37,874	20,000
Year 5	40,147	10,000
	$179,259	$150,000

* Depreciation in year $t = 150,000/5\ (1.06)^t$. This term reflects compounding of straight-line depreciation at 6 percent per year.

** Depreciation in year t of an N year life asset is equal to the historical cost times $2(N + 1 - t)/ N(N + 1)$.

In year 1, the depreciation would be: $\$150,000 \times 10/30$, or $\$50,000$.

In most cases, price-level-adjusted depreciation would be better. However, for short-lived assets, accelerated depreciation may provide greater levels of reimbursement in earlier years to offset lower returns in later years. The lower the rate of asset inflation, the more desirable accelerated depreciation becomes.

5. Profit is essential to most business organizations because accounting expenses do not equal cash requirements. Additional funds or profits must be available to meet the financial requirements of debt principal payments, increases in working capital, and capital expenditures.

6. The relevant calculation would be as follows:

$$\text{Revenue} = \frac{\$5,400,000 + \$850,000 - \$3,880,000}{.25}$$

= $\$9,480,000$ or $\$4,740$ per case

A 10 percent reduction in operating expenses permitted a 17 percent reduction in rates ($\$5,700$ to $\$4,740$ per case). Cost control is critical in health care entities, especially in those with relatively low levels of cost payers. A reduction in rates is especially important when competing for major contracts in which price is a predominant determinant.

7. The maximum allowed rate would be:

$\$128.47 = (1.2509 \times \$83.84) + \$23.59$

8. The RBRVS rate for this procedure would be:

$\$2,829 = \$40.7986 \times 69.34$

Appendix 2–A

List of Diagnosis-Related Groups (DRGs), Relative Weights, Geometric Mean Length of Stay (LOS), and LOS Outlier Cutoff Points

Source: Reprinted from Health Care Financing Administration.

DRG	MDC	Type	Description	Weight	Geometric Mean LOS	Outlier
001	01	SURG	CRANIOTOMY AGE >17 YEARS EXCEPT FOR TRAUMA	3.0932	8.7	32
002	01	SURG	CRANIOTOMY FOR TRAUMA AGE >17 YEARS	3.0095	9	32
003	01	SURG	CRANIOTOMY AGE 0–17 YEARS	1.8848	12.7	36
004	01	SURG	SPINAL PROCEDURES	2.3296	6.5	29
005	01	SURG	EXTRACRANIAL VASCULAR PROCEDURES	1.5798	4	27
006	01	SURG	CARPAL TUNNEL RELEASE	0.8124	2.4	25
007	01	SURG	PERIPH & CRANIAL NERVE & OTHER NERV SYST PROC W CC	2.6017	9.3	32
008	01	SURG	PERIPH & CRANIAL NERVE & OTHER NERV SYST PROC W/O CC	1.1794	3.1	26
009	01	MED	SPINAL DISORDERS & INJURIES	1.3047	5.7	29
010	01	MED	NERVOUS SYSTEM NEOPLASMS W CC	1.2299	6.2	29
011	01	MED	NERVOUS SYSTEM NEOPLASMS W/O CC	0.8	3.8	27
012	01	MED	DEGENERATIVE NERVOUS SYSTEM DISORDERS	0.9891	6	29
013	01	MED	MULTIPLE SCLEROSIS & CEREBELLAR ATAXIA	0.7858	5.4	28
014	01	MED	SPECIFIC CEREBROVASCULAR DISORDERS EXCEPT TIA	1.2065	6	29
015	01	MED	TRANSIENT ISCHEMIC ATTACK & PRECEREBRAL OCCLUSIONS	0.7227	3.8	27
016	01	MED	NONSPECIFIC CEREBROVASCULAR DISORDERS W CC	1.0639	5.4	28
017	01	MED	NONSPECIFIC CEREBROVASCULAR DISORDERS W/O CC	0.6026	3.2	26
018	01	MED	CRANIAL & PERIPHERAL NERVE DISORDERS W CC	0.9242	5.1	28
019	01	MED	CRANIAL & PERIPHERAL NERVE DISORDERS W/O CC	0.599	3.6	27
020	01	MED	NERVOUS SYSTEM INFECTION EXCEPT VIRAL MENINGITIS	2.1157	8.3	31
021	01	MED	VIRAL MENINGITIS	1.535	6.5	30
022	01	MED	HYPERTENSIVE ENCEPHALOPATHY	0.8127	4	27
023	01	MED	NONTRAUMATIC STUPOR & COMA	0.809	3.9	27
024	01	MED	SEIZURE & HEADACHE AGE >17 YEARS W CC	0.9908	4.6	28
025	01	MED	SEIZURE & HEADACHE AGE >17 YEARS W/O CC	0.5681	3.1	26
026	01	MED	SEIZURE & HEADACHE AGE 0–17 YEARS	0.8993	3.1	26
027	01	MED	TRAUMATIC STUPOR & COMA, COMA >1 HR	1.3476	3.9	27
028	01	MED	TRAUMATIC STUPOR & COMA, COMA <1 HR AGE >17 YEARS W CC	1.2001	5.2	28
029	01	MED	TRAUMATIC STUPOR & COMA, COMA <1 HR AGE >17 YEARS W/O CC	0.6217	3.1	26
030	01	MED	TRAUMATIC STUPOR & COMA, COMA <1 HR AGE 0–17 YEARS	0.3187	2	17

DRG	MDC	Type	Description	Weight	Geometric Mean LOS	Outlier
031	01	MED	CONCUSSION AGE >17 YEARS W CC	0.7934	3.8	27
032	01	MED	CONCUSSION AGE >17 YEARS W/O CC	0.4819	2.4	22
033	01	MED	CONCUSSION AGE 0–17 YEARS	0.2003	1.6	9
034	01	MED	OTHER DISORDERS OF NERVOUS SYSTEM W CC	1.0569	4.9	28
035	01	MED	OTHER DISORDERS OF NERVOUS SYSTEM W/O CC	0.5914	3.4	26
036	02	SURG	RETINAL PROCEDURES	0.593	1.4	7
037	02	SURG	ORBITAL PROCEDURES	0.8821	2.6	26
038	02	SURG	PRIMARY IRIS PROCEDURES	0.4243	2	17
039	02	SURG	LENS PROCEDURES WITH OR WITHOUT VITRECTOMY	0.5036	1.5	9
040	02	SURG	EXTRAOCULAR PROCEDURES EXCEPT ORBIT AGE >17 YEARS	0.7	2.3	25
041	02	SURG	EXTRAOCULAR PROCEDURES EXCEPT ORBIT AGE 0–17 YEARS	0.3244	1.6	7
042	02	SURG	INTRAOCULAR PROCEDURES EXCEPT RETINA, IRIS, & LENS	0.5615	1.6	12
043	02	MED	HYPHEMA	0.3665	3	25
044	02	MED	ACUTE MAJOR EYE INFECTIONS	0.615	4.8	28
045	02	MED	NEUROLOGIC EYE DISORDERS	0.646	3.4	25
046	02	MED	OTHER DISORDERS OF THE EYE AGE >17 YEARS W CC	0.7593	4.2	27
047	02	MED	OTHER DISORDERS OF THE EYE AGE >17 YEARS W/O CC	0.4539	3	26
048	02	MED	OTHER DISORDERS OF THE EYE AGE 0–17 YEARS	0.2859	2.9	26
049	03	SURG	MAJOR HEAD & NECK PROCEDURES	1.7701	4.7	28
050	03	SURG	SIALOADENECTOMY	0.7522	1.8	12
051	03	SURG	SALIVARY GLAND PROCEDURES EXCEPT SIALOADENECTOMY	0.7325	2	23
052	03	SURG	CLEFT LIP & PALATE REPAIR	0.8492	2.4	25
053	03	SURG	SINUS & MASTOID PROCEDURES AGE >17 YEARS	0.9392	2.3	25
054	03	SURG	SINUS & MASTOID PROCEDURES AGE 0–17 YEARS	0.4634	3.2	22
055	03	SURG	MISCELLANEOUS EAR, NOSE, MOUTH, & THROAT PROCEDURES	0.7238	1.9	22
056	03	SURG	RHINOPLASTY	0.8195	2.1	21
057	03	SURG	T&A PROC, EXCEPT TONSILLECTOMY &/OR ADENOIDECTOMY ONLY, AGE >17 YEARS	1.045	3.2	26
058	03	SURG	T&A PROC, EXCEPT TONSILLECTOMY &/OR ADENOIDECTOMY ONLY, AGE 0–17 YEARS	0.2631	1.5	4

DRG	MDC	Type	Description	Weight	Geometric Mean LOS	Outlier
059	03	SURG	TONSILLECTOMY &/OR ADENOIDECTOMY ONLY, AGE >17 YEARS	0.5963	2.1	19
060	03	SURG	TONSILLECTOMY &/OR ADENOIDECTOMY ONLY, AGE 0–17 YEARS	0.2004	1.5	4
061	03	SURG	MYRINGOTOMY W TUBE INSERTION AGE >17 YEARS	1.2221	3.1	26
062	03	SURG	MYRINGOTOMY W TUBE INSERTION AGE 0–17 YEARS	0.2837	1.3	5
063	03	SURG	OTHER EAR, NOSE, MOUTH, & THROAT O.R. PROCEDURES	1.1462	3.3	26
064	03	MED	EAR, NOSE, MOUTH, & THROAT MALIGNANCY	1.1887	5.1	28
065	03	MED	DYSEQUILIBRIUM	0.5162	2.9	22
066	03	MED	EPISTAXIS	0.5306	3	24
067	03	MED	EPIGLOTTITIS	0.806	3.4	25
068	03	MED	OTITIS MEDIA & URI AGE >17 YEARS W CC	0.7094	4.2	27
069	03	MED	OTITIS MEDIA & URI AGE >17 YEARS W/O CC	0.527	3.4	21
070	03	MED	OTITIS MEDIA & URI AGE 0–17 YEARS	0.3129	2.4	17
071	03	MED	LARYNGOTRACHEITIS	0.7206	3.6	25
072	03	MED	NASAL TRAUMA & DEFORMITY	0.6419	3	26
073	03	MED	OTHER EAR, NOSE, MOUTH, & THROAT DIAGNOSES AGE >17 YEARS	0.773	4	27
074	03	MED	OTHER EAR, NOSE, MOUTH, & THROAT DIAGNOSES AGE 0–17 YEARS	0.3223	2.1	20
075	04	SURG	MAJOR CHEST PROCEDURES	3.1034	9.3	32
076	04	SURG	OTHER RESP SYSTEM O.R. PROCEDURES W CC	2.5601	9.6	33
077	04	SURG	OTHER RESP SYSTEM O.R. PROCEDURES W/O CC	1.1219	3.9	27
078	04	MED	PULMONARY EMBOLISM	1.4136	7.4	30
079	04	MED	RESPIRATORY INFECTIONS & INFLAMMATIONS AGE >17 YEARS W CC	1.6625	7.8	31
080	04	MED	RESPIRATORY INFECTIONS & INFLAMMATIONS AGE >17 YEARS W/O CC	0.9508	5.7	29
081	04	MED	RESPIRATORY INFECTIONS & INFLAMMATIONS AGE 0–17 YEARS	0.9558	4.7	28
082	04	MED	RESPIRATORY NEOPLASMS	1.3166	6	29
083	04	MED	MAJOR CHEST TRAUMA W CC	0.9557	5.2	28
084	04	MED	MAJOR CHEST TRAUMA W/O CC	0.5002	3	25
085	04	MED	PLEURAL EFFUSION W CC	1.1917	5.9	29
086	04	MED	PLEURAL EFFUSION W/O CC	0.6848	3.6	27

DRG	MDC	Type	Description	Weight	Geometric Mean LOS	Outlier
087	04	MED	PULMONARY EDEMA & RESPIRATORY FAILURE	1.3589	5.3	28
088	04	MED	CHRONIC OBSTRUCTIVE PULMONARY DISEASE	1.0018	5.3	28
089	04	MED	SIMPLE PNEUMONIA & PLEURISY AGE >17 YEARS W CC	1.1211	6.2	29
090	04	MED	SIMPLE PNEUMONIA & PLEURISY AGE >17 YEARS W/O CC	0.6996	4.7	26
091	04	MED	SIMPLE PNEUMONIA & PLEURISY AGE 0–17 YEARS	0.8366	4.4	27
092	04	MED	INTERSTITIAL LUNG DISEASE W CC	1.2	6	29
093	04	MED	INTERSTITIAL LUNG DISEASE W/O CC	0.755	4.2	27
094	04	MED	PNEUMOTHORAX W CC	1.2378	6.2	29
095	04	MED	PNEUMOTHORAX W/O CC	0.6242	3.8	26
096	04	MED	BRONCHITIS & ASTHMA AGE >17 YEARS W CC	0.839	4.9	28
097	04	MED	BRONCHITIS & ASTHMA AGE >17 YEARS W/O CC	0.6089	3.8	23
098	04	MED	BRONCHITIS & ASTHMA AGE 0–17 YEARS	0.6696	4.2	27
099	04	MED	RESPIRATORY SIGNS & SYMPTOMS W CC	0.6959	2.9	26
100	04	MED	RESPIRATORY SIGNS & SYMPTOMS W/O CC	0.5034	2.1	14
101	04	MED	OTHER RESPIRATORY SYSTEM DIAGNOSES W CC	0.912	4.5	27
102	04	MED	OTHER RESPIRATORY SYSTEM DIAGNOSES W/O CC	0.5595	2.9	26
103	05	SURG	HEART TRANSPLANT	13.8273	27.4	50
104	05	SURG	CARDIAC VALVE PROCEDURES W CARDIAC CATH	7.3143	13.3	36
105	05	SURG	CARDIAC VALVE PROCEDURES W/O CARDIAC CATH	5.631	10	33
106	05	SURG	CORONARY BYPASS W CARDIAC CATH	5.6187	11.2	34
107	05	SURG	CORONARY BYPASS W/O CARDIAC CATH	4.1803	8.6	32
108	05	SURG	OTHER CARDIOTHORACIC PROCEDURES	5.9455	10.5	33
109	05		NO LONGER VALID	0	0	0
110	05	SURG	MAJOR CARDIOVASCULAR PROCEDURES W CC	4.1308	8.7	32
111	05	SURG	MAJOR CARDIOVASCULAR PROCEDURES W/O CC	2.2584	6.3	29
112	05	SURG	PERCUTANEOUS CARDIOVASCULAR PROCEDURES	1.9922	3.6	27
113	05	SURG	AMPUTATION FOR CIRC SYSTEM DISORDERS EXCEPT UPPER LIMB & TOE	2.7536	11.6	35
114	05	SURG	UPPER LIMB & TOE AMPUTATION FOR CIRC SYSTEM DISORDERS	1.5383	7.4	30

DRG	MDC	Type	Description	Weight	Geometric Mean LOS	Outlier
115	05	SURG	PERM CARDIAC PACEMAKER IMPLANT W AMI, HEART FAILURE, OR SHOCK	3.5513	9.5	33
116	05	SURG	OTH PERM CARDIAC PACEMAKER IMPLANT OR AICD LEAD OR GENERATOR PROC	2.3949	4.2	27
117	05	SURG	CARDIAC PACEMAKER REVISION EXCEPT DEVICE REPLACEMENT	1.1454	3	26
118	05	SURG	CARDIAC PACEMAKER DEVICE REPLACEMENT	1.526	2.2	25
119	05	SURG	VEIN LIGATION & STRIPPING	1.1247	3.4	26
120	05	SURG	OTHER CIRCULATORY SYSTEM O.R. PROCEDURES	1.9531	5.8	29
121	05	MED	CIRCULATORY DISORDERS W AMI & C.V. COMP DISCH ALIVE	1.6459	7	30
122	05	MED	CIRCULATORY DISORDERS W AMI W/O C.V. COMP DISCH ALIVE	1.1614	4.9	28
123	05	MED	CIRCULATORY DISORDERS W AMI, EXPIRED	1.437	2.8	26124
124	05	MED	CIRCULATORY DISORDERS EXCEPT AMI, W CARD CATH & COMPLEX DIAG	1.2933	4	27
125	05	MED	CIRCULATORY DISORDERS EXCEPT AMI, W CARD CATH W/O COMPLEX DIAG	0.8767	2.4	22
126	05	MED	ACUTE & SUBACUTE ENDOCARDITIS	2.6049	12.3	35
127	05	MED	HEART FAILURE & SHOCK	1.0302	5.2	28
128	05	MED	DEEP VEIN THROMBOPHLEBITIS	0.7929	6.3	29
129	05	MED	CARDIAC ARREST, UNEXPLAINED	1.1376	2.1	25
130	05	MED	PERIPHERAL VASCULAR DISORDERS W CC	0.9384	5.6	29
131	05	MED	PERIPHERAL VASCULAR DISORDERS W/O CC	0.6002	4.5	27
132	05	MED	ATHEROSCLEROSIS W CC	0.6861	3.1	23
133	05	MED	ATHEROSCLEROSIS W/O CC	0.5347	2.5	18
134	05	MED	HYPERTENSION	0.58	3.3	25
135	05	MED	CARDIAC CONGENITAL & VALVULAR DISORDERS AGE >17 YEARS W CC	0.8988	4.1	27
136	05	MED	CARDIAC CONGENITAL & VALVULAR DISORDERS AGE >17 YEARS W/O CC	0.5789	2.8	22
137	05	MED	CARDIAC CONGENITAL & VALVULAR DISORDERS AGE 0–17 YEARS	0.7866	3.3	26
138	05	MED	CARDIAC ARRHYTHMIA & CONDUCTION DISORDERS W CC	0.8049	3.7	27

DRG	MDC	Type	Description	Weight	Geometric Mean LOS	Outlier
139	05	MED	CARDIAC ARRHYTHMIA & CONDUCTION DISORDERS W/O CC	0.4945	2.5	18
140	05	MED	ANGINA PECTORIS	0.6312	3.1	22
141	05	MED	SYNCOPE & COLLAPSE W CC	0.7149	3.7	27
142	05	MED	SYNCOPE & COLLAPSE W/O CC	0.5216	2.7	20
143	05	MED	CHEST PAIN	0.5159	2.3	15
144	05	MED	OTHER CIRCULATORY SYSTEM DIAGNOSES W CC	1.0689	4.3	27,145
145	05	MED	OTHER CIRCULATORY SYSTEM DIAGNOSES W/O CC	0.6204	2.7	22
146	06	SURG	RECTAL RESECTION W CC	2.5898	10.2	33
147	06	SURG	RECTAL RESECTION W/O CC	1.5368	7.2	29
148	06	SURG	MAJOR SMALL & LARGE BOWEL PROCEDURES W CC	3.3264	11.7	35
149	06	SURG	MAJOR SMALL & LARGE BOWEL PROCEDURES W/O CC	1.5654	7.4	26
150	06	SURG	PERITONEAL ADHESIOLYSIS W CC	2.6561	10.1	33
151	06	SURG	PERITONEAL ADHESIOLYSIS W/O CC	1.2606	5.5	29
152	06	SURG	MINOR SMALL & LARGE BOWEL PROCEDURES W CC	1.886	8	31
153	06	SURG	MINOR SMALL & LARGE BOWEL PROCEDURES W/O CC	1.1257	5.7	26
154	06	SURG	STOMACH, ESOPHAGEAL & DUODENAL PROCEDURES AGE >17 YEARS W CC	4.2102	12.6	36
155	06	SURG	STOMACH, ESOPHAGEAL & DUODENAL PROCEDURES AGE >17 YEARS W/O CC	1.3885	5.4	28
156	06	SURG	STOMACH, ESOPHAGEAL & DUODENAL PROCEDURES AGE 0-17 YEARS	0.8101	6	29
157	06	SURG	ANAL & STOMAL PROCEDURES W CC	1.1048	4.3	27
158	06	SURG	ANAL & STOMAL PROCEDURES W/O CC	0.5789	2.3	18
159	06	SURG	HERNIA PROCEDURES EXCEPT INGUINAL & FEMORAL AGE >17 YEARS W CC	1.1707	4.1	27
160	06	SURG	HERNIA PROCEDURES EXCEPT INGUINAL & FEMORAL AGE >17 YEARS W/O CC	0.6746	2.5	17
161	06	SURG	INGUINAL & FEMORAL HERNIA PROCEDURES AGE >17 YEARS W CC	0.9554	3.1	26

DRG	MDC	Type	Description	Weight	Geometric Mean LOS	Outlier
162	06	SURG	INGUINAL & FEMORAL HERNIA PROCEDURES AGE >17 YEARS W/O CC	0.5365	1.8	11
163	06	SURG	HERNIA PROCEDURES AGE 0–17 YEARS	0.7578	3.5	27
164	06	SURG	APPENDECTOMY W COMPLICATED PRINCIPAL DIAG W CC	2.2374	8.5	31
165	06	SURG	APPENDECTOMY W COMPLICATED PRINCIPAL DIAG W/O CC	1.2365	5.3	25
166	06	SURG	APPENDECTOMY W/O COMPLICATED PRINCIPAL DIAG W CC	1.3695	4.9	28
167	06	SURG	APPENDECTOMY W/O COMPLICATED PRINCIPAL DIAG W/O CC	0.7892	3	16
168	03	SURG	MOUTH PROCEDURES W CC	1.1761	3.6	27
169	03	SURG	MOUTH PROCEDURES W/O CC	0.6434	2	17
170	06	SURG	OTHER DIGESTIVE SYSTEM O.R. PROCEDURES W CC	2.7116	9.1	32
171	06	SURG	OTHER DIGESTIVE SYSTEM O.R. PROCEDURES W/O CC	1.1628	4.4	27
172	06	MED	DIGESTIVE MALIGNANCY W CC	1.2898	6.1	29
173	06	MED	DIGESTIVE MALIGNANCY W/O CC	0.6569	3.2	26
174	06	MED	G.I. HEMORRHAGE W CC	0.988	4.7	28
175	06	MED	G.I. HEMORRHAGE W/O CC	0.5457	3.1	19
176	06	MED	COMPLICATED PEPTIC ULCER	1.0563	5	28
177	06	MED	UNCOMPLICATED PEPTIC ULCER W CC	0.827	4.4	27
178	06	MED	UNCOMPLICATED PEPTIC ULCER W/O CC	0.599	3.2	21
179	06	MED	INFLAMMATORY BOWEL DISEASE	1.0993	6	29
180	06	MED	G.I. OBSTRUCTION W CC	0.924	5	28
181	06	MED	G.I. OBSTRUCTION W/O CC	0.5231	3.4	23
182	06	MED	ESOPHAGITIS, GASTROENT & MISC DIGEST DISORDERS AGE >17 YEARS W CC	0.7794	4.1	27
183	06	MED	ESOPHAGITIS, GASTROENT & MISC DIGEST DISORDERS AGE >17 YEARS W/O CC	0.548	3	22
184	06	MED	ESOPHAGITIS, GASTROENT & MISC DIGEST DISORDERS AGE 0–17 YEARS	0.391	2.5	18
185	03	MED	DENTAL & ORAL DIS EXCEPT EXTRACTIONS & RESTORATIONS, AGE >17 YEARS	0.8892	4.1	27

36   ESSENTIALS OF HEALTH CARE FINANCE

DRG	MDC	Type	Description	Weight	Geometric Mean LOS	Outlier
186	03	MED	DENTAL & ORAL DIS EXCEPT EXTRACTIONS & RESTORATIONS, AGE 0–17 YEARS	0.3088	2.9	23
187	03	MED	DENTAL EXTRACTIONS & RESTORATIONS	0.6473	2.8	26
188	06	MED	OTHER DIGESTIVE SYSTEM DIAGNOSES AGE >17 YEARS W CC	1.0458	4.7	28
189	06	MED	OTHER DIGESTIVE SYSTEM DIAGNOSES AGE >17 YEARS W/O CC	0.5438	2.8	26
190	06	MED	OTHER DIGESTIVE SYSTEM DIAGNOSES AGE 0–17 YEARS	1.2379	4.6	28
191	07	SURG	PANCREAS, LIVER, & SHUNT PROCEDURES W CC	4.4495	12.9	36
192	07	SURG	PANCREAS, LIVER, & SHUNT PROCEDURES W/O CC	1.7103	6.4	29
193	07	SURG	BILIARY TRACT PROC EXCEPT ONLY CHOLECYST W OR W/O C.D.E. W CC	3.2131	12.3	35
194	07	SURG	BILIARY TRACT PROC EXCEPT ONLY CHOLECYST W OR W/O C.D.E. W/O CC	1.6937	6.9	30
195	07	SURG	CHOLECYSTECTOMY W COMMON DUCT EXPLORATION W CC	2.6147	9.4	32
196	07	SURG	CHOLECYSTECTOMY W COMMON DUCT EXPLORATION W/O CC	1.5695	6.2	29
197	07	SURG	CHOLECYSTECTOMY EXCEPT BY LAPAROSCOPE W/O C.D.E. W CC	2.2034	7.9	31
198	07	SURG	CHOLECYSTECTOMY EXCEPT BY LAPAROSCOPE W/O C.D.E. W/O CC	1.1355	4.6	24
199	07	SURG	HEPATOBILIARY DIAGNOSTIC PROCEDURE FOR MALIGNANCY	2.3309	9.2	32
200	07	SURG	HEPATOBILIARY DIAGNOSTIC PROCEDURE FOR NON-MALIGNANCY	3.0158	7.9	31
201	07	SURG	OTHER HEPATOBILIARY OR PANCREAS O.R. PROCEDURES	3.2951	11.7	35
202	07	MED	CIRRHOSIS & ALCOHOLIC HEPATITIS	1.3177	6.1	29
203	07	MED	MALIGNANCY OF HEPATOBILIARY SYSTEM OR PANCREAS	1.2187	5.9	29
204	07	MED	DISORDERS OF PANCREAS EXCEPT MALIGNANCY	1.202	5.5	28
205	07	MED	DISORDERS OF LIVER EXCEPT MALIG, CIRR, ALCOHOLIC HEPATITIS W CC	1.2276	5.8	29
206	07	MED	DISORDERS OF LIVER EXCEPT MALIG, CIRR, ALCOHOLIC HEPATITIS W/O CC	0.6801	3.6	27
207	07	MED	DISORDERS OF THE BILIARY TRACT W CC	1.0287	4.7	28
208	07	MED	DISORDERS OF THE BILIARY TRACT W/O CC	0.5943	2.8	23
209	08	SURG	MAJOR JOINT & LIMB REATTACHMENT PROCEDURES OF LOWER EXTREMITY	2.2707	6.8	27

DRG	MDC	Type	Description	Weight	Geometric Mean LOS	Outlier
210	08	SURG	HIP & FEMUR PROCEDURES EXCEPT MAJOR JOINT AGE >17 YEARS W CC	1.8616	8.2	31
211	08	SURG	HIP & FEMUR PROCEDURES EXCEPT MAJOR JOINT AGE >17 YEARS W/O CC	1.2893	6.3	28
212	08	SURG	HIP & FEMUR PROCEDURES EXCEPT MAJOR JOINT AGE 0–17 YEARS	1.1296	4.3	27
213	08	SURG	AMPUTATION FOR MUSCULOSKELETAL SYSTEM & CONNECTIVE TISSUE DISORDERS	1.7196	7.6	31
214	08	SURG	BACK & NECK PROCEDURES W CC	1.9184	5.7	29
215	08	SURG	BACK & NECK PROCEDURES W/O CC	1.0924	3.5	22
216	08	SURG	BIOPSIES OF MUSCULOSKELETAL SYSTEM & CONNECTIVE TISSUE	2.1075	8.6	32
217	08	SURG	WOUND DEBRID & SKIN GRFT EXCEPT HAND, FOR MUSCSKELET & CONNECTIVE TISSUE DISORDERS	2.8975	11.1	34
218	08	SURG	LOWER EXTREM & HUMER PROC EXCEPT HIP, FOOT, FEMUR AGE >17 YEARS W CC	1.4231	5.3	28
219	08	SURG	LOWER EXTREM & HUMER PROC EXCEPT HIP, FOOT, FEMUR AGE >17 YEARS W/O CC	0.9179	3.4	22
220	08	SURG	LOWER EXTREM & HUMER PROC EXCEPT HIP, FOOT, FEMUR AGE 0–17 YEARS	0.5611	5.3	28
221	08	SURG	KNEE PROCEDURES W CC	1.8463	6.3	29
222	08	SURG	KNEE PROCEDURES W/O CC	0.9747	3.3	26
223	08	SURG	MAJOR SHOULDER/ELBOW PROC, OR OTHER UPPER EXTREMITY PROC W CC	0.8364	2.3	17
224	08	SURG	SHOULDER, ELBOW OR FOREARM PROC, EXCEPT MAJOR JOINT PROC, W/O CC	0.6983	2	11
225	08	SURG	FOOT PROCEDURES	0.9504	3.3	26
226	08	SURG	SOFT TISSUE PROCEDURES W CC	1.3656	4.7	28
227	08	SURG	SOFT TISSUE PROCEDURES W/O CC	0.7273	2.4	20
228	08	SURG	MAJOR THUMB OR JOINT PROC, OR OTH HAND OR WRIST PROC W CC	0.9315	2.4	25
229	08	SURG	HAND OR WRIST PROC, EXCEPT MAJOR JOINT PROC, W/O CC	0.5965	1.8	14

DRG	MDC	Type	Description	Weight	Geometric Mean LOS	Outlier
230	08	SURG	LOCAL EXCISION & REMOVAL OF INT FIX DEVICES OF HIP & FEMUR	1.0399	3.5	27
231	08	SURG	LOCAL EXCISION & REMOVAL OF INT FIX DEVICES EXCEPT HIP & FEMUR	1.2131	3.5	26
232	08	SURG	ARTHROSCOPY	1.0578	2.6	26
233	08	SURG	OTHER MUSCULOSKELET SYS & CONN TISS O.R. PROC W CC	1.9275	6.8	30
234	08	SURG	OTHER MUSCULOSKELET SYS & CONN TISS O.R. PROC W/O CC	1.0039	3.3	26
235	08	MED	FRACTURES OF FEMUR	0.8501	5.2	28
236	08	MED	FRACTURES OF HIP & PELVIS	0.7818	5.2	28
237	08	MED	SPRAINS, STRAINS, & DISLOCATIONS OF HIP, PELVIS, & THIGH	0.5711	3.7	27
238	08	MED	OSTEOMYELITIS	1.4356	8.4	31
239	08	MED	PATHOLOGICAL FRACTURES & MUSCULOSKELETAL & CONNECTIVE TISSUE MALIGNANCY	1.0219	6.3	29
240	08	MED	CONNECTIVE TISSUE DISORDERS W CC	1.19	5.9	29
241	08	MED	CONNECTIVE TISSUE DISORDERS W/O CC	0.5986	3.8	27
242	08	MED	SEPTIC ARTHRITIS	1.1295	6.7	30
243	08	MED	MEDICAL BACK PROBLEMS	0.7248	4.7	28
244	08	MED	BONE DISEASES & SPECIFIC ARTHROPATHIES W CC	0.7446	4.6	28
245	08	MED	BONE DISEASES & SPECIFIC ARTHROPATHIES W/O CC	0.505	3.4	26
246	08	MED	NON-SPECIFIC ARTHROPATHIES	0.5646	3.7	27
247	08	MED	SIGNS & SYMPTOMS OF MUSCULOSKELETAL SYSTEM & CONNECTIVE TISSUE	0.5534	3.1	26
248	08	MED	TENDONITIS, MYOSITIS, & BURSITIS	0.7275	4.1	27
249	08	MED	AFTERCARE, MUSCULOSKELETAL SYSTEM & CONNECTIVE TISSUE	0.6558	3.1	26
250	08	MED	FRACTURE, SPRN, STRN & DISL OF FOREARM, HAND, FOOT AGE >17 YEARS W CC	0.7193	3.9	27
251	08	MED	FRACTURE, SPRN, STRN & DISL OF FOREARM, HAND, FOOT AGE >17 YEARS W/O CC	0.4423	2.4	21
252	08	MED	FRACTURE, SPRN, STRN & DISL OF FOREARM, HAND, FOOT AGE 0–17 YEARS	0.2438	1.8	15

DRG	MDC	Type	Description	Weight	Geometric Mean LOS	Outlier
253	08	MED	FRACTURE, SPRN, STRN & DISL OF UPARM, LOWLEG EXCEPT FOOT AGE >17 YEARS W CC	0.7637	4.7	28
254	08	MED	FRACTURE, SPRN, STRN & DISL OF UPARM, LOWLEG EXCEPT FOOT AGE >17 YEARS W/O CC	0.4365	3	26
255	08	MED	FRACTURE, SPRN, STRN & DISL OF UPARM, LOWLEG EXCEPT FOOT AGE 0–17 YEARS	0.2838	2.9	26
256	08	MED	OTHER MUSCULOSKELETAL SYSTEM & CONNECTIVE TISSUE DIAGNOSES	0.6419	3.2	26
257	09	SURG	TOTAL MASTECTOMY FOR MALIGNANCY W CC	0.8997	3.1	20
258	09	SURG	TOTAL MASTECTOMY FOR MALIGNANCY W/O CC	0.6965	2.4	11
259	09	SURG	SUBTOTAL MASTECTOMY FOR MALIGNANCY W CC	0.8765	2.6	26
260	09	SURG	SUBTOTAL MASTECTOMY FOR MALIGNANCY W/O CC	0.5749	1.7	8
261	09	SURG	BREAST PROC FOR NONMALIGNANCY EXCEPT BIOPSY & LOCAL EXCISION	0.808	1.9	13
262	09	SURG	BREAST BIOPSY & LOCAL EXCISION FOR NONMALIGNANCY	0.7115	2.6	26
263	09	SURG	SKIN GRAFT &/OR DEBRID FOR SKIN ULCER OR CELLULITIS W CC	2.2344	11.2	34
264	09	SURG	SKIN GRAFT &/OR DEBRID FOR SKIN ULCER OR CELLULITIS W/O CC	1.1633	6.7	30
265	09	SURG	SKIN GRAFT &/OR DEBRID EXCEPT FOR SKIN ULCER OR CELLULITIS W CC	1.4131	4.9	28
266	09	SURG	SKIN GRAFT &/OR DEBRID EXCEPT FOR SKIN ULCER OR CELLULITIS W/O CC	0.7451	2.8	26
267	09	SURG	PERIANAL & PILONIDAL PROCEDURES	0.8022	2.8	26
268	09	SURG	SKIN, SUBCUTANEOUS TISSUE & BREAST PLASTIC PROCEDURES	0.9068	2.7	26
269	09	SURG	OTHER SKIN, SUBCUTANEOUS TISSUE & BREAST PROC W CC	1.6495	6.7	30
270	09	SURG	OTHER SKIN, SUBCUTANEOUS TISSUE & BREAST PROC W/O CC	0.6796	2.4	25
271	09	MED	SKIN ULCERS	1.1157	7.2	30
272	09	MED	MAJOR SKIN DISORDERS W CC	1.0208	6.1	29
273	09	MED	MAJOR SKIN DISORDERS W/O CC	0.6403	4.5	27
274	09	MED	MALIGNANT BREAST DISORDERS W CC	1.0741	5.5	28
275	09	MED	MALIGNANT BREAST DISORDERS W/O CC	0.4845	2.4	25

DRG	MDC	Type	Description	Weight	Geometric Mean LOS	Outlier
276	09	MED	NONMALIGNANT BREAST DISORDERS	0.6418	4.2	27
277	09	MED	CELLULITIS AGE >17 YEARS W CC	0.8703	5.9	29
278	09	MED	CELLULITIS AGE >17 YEARS W/O CC	0.5822	4.6	27
279	09	MED	CELLULITIS AGE 0–17 YEARS	0.707	4.2	27
280	09	MED	TRAUMA TO THE SKIN, SUBCUTANEOUS TISSUE & BREAST AGE >17 YEARS W CC	0.6847	4	27
281	09	MED	TRAUMA TO THE SKIN, SUBCUTANEOUS TISSUE & BREAST AGE >17 YEARS W/O CC	0.4523	2.8	26
282	09	MED	TRAUMA TO THE SKIN, SUBCUTANEOUS TISSUE & BREAST AGE 0–17 YEARS	0.2467	2.2	19
283	09	MED	MINOR SKIN DISORDERS W CC	0.7171	4.4	27
284	09	MED	MINOR SKIN DISORDERS W/O CC	0.4307	3.1	26
285	10	SURG	AMPUTATION OF LOWER LIMB FOR ENDOCRINE, NUTRIT, & METABOLIC DISORDERS	2.388	11	34
286	10	SURG	ADRENAL & PITUITARY PROCEDURES	2.3163	6.9	30
287	10	SURG	SKIN GRAFTS & WOUND DEBRID FOR ENDOCRINE, NUTRIT, & METABOLIC DISORDERS	2.1126	10.7	34
288	10	SURG	O.R. PROCEDURES FOR OBESITY	2.0397	5.9	29
289	10	SURG	PARATHYROID PROCEDURES	1.0385	3	26
290	10	SURG	THYROID PROCEDURES	0.8537	2.3	16
291	10	SURG	THYROGLOSSAL PROCEDURES	0.4657	1.4	6
292	10	SURG	OTHER ENDOCRINE, NUTRIT, & METABOLIC O.R. PROC W CC	2.6301	9.2	32
293	10	SURG	OTHER ENDOCRINE, NUTRIT, & METABOLIC O.R. PROC W/O CC	1.1866	4.6	28
294	10	MED	DIABETES AGE >35 YEARS	0.7579	4.7	28
295	10	MED	DIABETES AGE 0–35 YEARS	0.7634	3.7	27
296	10	MED	NUTRITIONAL & MISC METABOLIC DISORDERS AGE >17 YEARS W CC	0.9166	5.1	28
297	10	MED	NUTRITIONAL & MISC METABOLIC DISORDERS AGE >17 YEARS W/O CC	0.5353	3.5	27
298	10	MED	NUTRITIONAL & MISC METABOLIC DISORDERS AGE 0–17 YEARS	0.4756	2.8	26

DRG	MDC	Type	Description	Weight	Geometric Mean LOS	Outlier
299	10	MED	INBORN ERRORS OF METABOLISM	0.979	4.2	27
300	10	MED	ENDOCRINE DISORDERS W CC	1.0919	5.8	29
301	10	MED	ENDOCRINE DISORDERS W/O CC	0.6181	3.6	27
302	11	SURG	KIDNEY TRANSPLANT	4.137	11.9	35
303	11	SURG	KIDNEY, URETER, & MAJOR BLADDER PROC FOR NEOPLASMS	2.6171	9.1	32
304	11	SURG	KIDNEY, URETER, & MAJOR BLADDER PROC FOR NEOPLASMS W CC	2.3715	8.1	31
305	11	SURG	KIDNEY, URETER, & MAJOR BLADDER PROC FOR NEOPLASMS W/O CC	1.16	4.2	27
306	11	SURG	PROSTATECTOMY W CC	1.2441	4.9	28
307	11	SURG	PROSTATECTOMY W/O CC	0.6639	2.7	17
308	11	SURG	MINOR BLADDER PROCEDURES W CC	1.4848	5	28
309	11	SURG	MINOR BLADDER PROCEDURES W/O CC	0.8061	2.5	21
310	11	SURG	TRANSURETHRAL PROCEDURES W CC	0.9694	3.3	26
311	11	SURG	TRANSURETHRAL PROCEDURES W/O CC	0.5486	1.9	12
312	11	SURG	URETHRAL PROCEDURES, AGE >17 YEARS W CC	0.8891	3.3	26
313	11	SURG	URETHRAL PROCEDURES, AGE >17 YEARS W/O CC	0.5008	1.9	15
314	11	SURG	URETHRAL PROCEDURES, AGE 0–17 YEARS	0.4756	2.3	25
315	11	SURG	OTHER KIDNEY & URINARY TRACT O.R. PROCEDURES	2.0612	5.7	29
316	11	MED	RENAL FAILURE	1.2996	5.7	29
317	11	MED	ADMIT FOR RENAL DIALYSIS	0.6556	2.7	26
318	11	MED	KIDNEY & URINARY TRACT NEOPLASMS W CC	1.1007	5.2	28
319	11	MED	KIDNEY & URINARY TRACT NEOPLASMS W/O CC	0.5432	2.2	25
320	11	MED	KIDNEY & URINARY TRACT INFECTIONS AGE >17 YEARS W CC	0.932	5.6	29
321	11	MED	KIDNEY & URINARY TRACT INFECTIONS AGE >17 YEARS W/O CC	0.6104	4.2	25
322	11	MED	KIDNEY & URINARY TRACT INFECTIONS AGE 0–17 YEARS	0.6651	3.9	27
323	11	MED	URINARY STONES W CC, &/OR ESW LITHOTRIPSY	0.7281	2.8	26
324	11	MED	URINARY STONES W/O CC	0.3992	1.8	11
325	11	MED	KIDNEY & URINARY TRACT SIGNS & SYMPTOMS AGE >17 YEARS W CC	0.6436	3.7	27
326	11	MED	KIDNEY & URINARY TRACT SIGNS & SYMPTOMS AGE >17 YEARS W/O CC	0.4233	2.6	21

DRG	MDC	Type	Description	Weight	Geometric Mean LOS	Outlier
327	11	MED	KIDNEY & URINARY TRACT SIGNS & SYMPTOMS AGE 0–17 YEARS	0.2302	3.1	26
328	11	MED	URETHRAL STRICTURE AGE >17 YEARS W CC	0.6672	3.2	26
329	11	MED	URETHRAL STRICTURE AGE >17 YEARS W/O CC	0.4233	1.9	13
330	11	MED	URETHRAL STRICTURE AGE 0–17 YEARS	0.3063	1.6	9
331	11	MED	OTHER KIDNEY & URINARY TRACT DIAGNOSES AGE >17 YEARS W CC	1.0122	4.9	28
332	11	MED	OTHER KIDNEY & URINARY TRACT DIAGNOSES AGE >17 YEARS W/O CC	0.6176	3.1	26
333	11	MED	OTHER KIDNEY & URINARY TRACT DIAGNOSES AGE 0–17 YEARS	0.8701	4.2	27
334	12	SURG	MAJOR MALE PELVIC PROCEDURES W CC	1.6948	6.1	25
335	12	SURG	MAJOR MALE PELVIC PROCEDURES W/O CC	1.3044	4.8	20
336	12	SURG	TRANSURETHRAL PROSTATECTOMY W CC	0.8802	3.6	25
337	12	SURG	TRANSURETHRAL PROSTATECTOMY W/O CC	0.6128	2.6	12
338	12	SURG	TESTES PROCEDURES, FOR MALIGNANCY	1.026	3.7	27
339	12	SURG	TESTES PROCEDURES, NONMALIGNANCY AGE >17 YEARS	0.933	3.1	26
340	12	SURG	TESTES PROCEDURES, NONMALIGNANCY AGE 0–17 YEARS	0.2723	2.4	13
341	12	SURG	PENIS PROCEDURES	1.0699	2.6	25
342	12	SURG	CIRCUMCISION AGE >17 YEARS	0.736	2.8	26
343	12	SURG	CIRCUMCISION AGE 0–17 YEARS	0.1479	1.7	6
344	12	SURG	OTHER MALE REPRODUCTIVE SYSTEM O.R. PROCEDURES FOR MALIGNANCY	1.0209	2.4	25
345	12	SURG	OTHER MALE REPRODUCTIVE SYSTEM O.R. PROC EXCEPT FOR MALIGNANCY	0.8435	3	26
346	12	MED	MALIGNANCY, MALE REPRODUCTIVE SYSTEM, W CC	0.9626	5.1	28
347	12	MED	MALIGNANCY, MALE REPRODUCTIVE SYSTEM, W/O CC	0.4853	2.5	25
348	12	MED	BENIGN PROSTATIC HYPERTROPHY W CC	0.7106	3.8	27
349	12	MED	BENIGN PROSTATIC HYPERTROPHY W/O CC	0.4241	2.3	22
350	12	MED	INFLAMMATION OF THE MALE REPRODUCTIVE SYSTEM	0.681	4.3	27
351	12	MED	STERILIZATION, MALE	0.2271	1.3	5
352	12	MED	OTHER MALE REPRODUCTIVE SYSTEM DIAGNOSES	0.5932	3.1	26

DRG	MDC	Type	Description	Weight	Geometric Mean LOS	Outlier
353	13	SURG	PELVIC EVISCERATION, RADICAL HYSTERECTOMY, & RADICAL VULVECTOMY	1.9483	7.5	30
354	13	SURG	UTERINE, ADNEXAL PROC FOR NON-OVARIAN/ADNEXAL MALIG W CC	1.4609	5.6	29
355	13	SURG	UTERINE, ADNEXAL PROC FOR NON-OVARIAN/ADNEXAL MALIG W/O CC	0.8881	3.8	12
356	13	SURG	FEMALE REPRODUCTIVE SYSTEM RECONSTRUCTIVE PROCEDURES	0.7323	2.9	13
357	13	SURG	UTERINE & ADNEXAL PROC FOR OVARIAN OR ADNEXAL MALIGNANCY	2.3679	8.5	31
358	13	SURG	UTERINE & ADNEXAL PROC FOR NONMALIGNANCY W CC	1.1458	4.3	20
359	13	SURG	UTERINE & ADNEXAL PROC FOR NONMALIGNANCY W/O CC	0.8072	3.2	10
360	13	SURG	VAGINA, CERVIX, & VULVA PROCEDURES	0.8739	3.3	23
361	13	SURG	LAPAROSCOPY & INCISIONAL TUBAL INTERRUPTION	1.1984	3.2	26
362	13	SURG	ENDOSCOPIC TUBAL INTERRUPTION	0.2902	1.4	5
363	13	SURG	D&C, CONIZATION & RADIOIMPLANT, FOR MALIGNANCY	0.6881	2.7	22
364	13	SURG	D&C, CONIZATION EXCEPT FOR MALIGNANCY	0.6667	2.6	26
365	13	SURG	OTHER FEMALE REPRODUCTIVE SYSTEM O.R. PROCEDURES	1.7739	6	29
366	13	MED	MALIGNANCY, FEMALE REPRODUCTIVE SYSTEM W CC	1.1405	5.5	29
367	13	MED	MALIGNANCY, FEMALE REPRODUCTIVE SYSTEM W/O CC	0.5179	2.5	25
368	13	MED	INFECTIONS, FEMALE REPRODUCTIVE SYSTEM	0.9841	5.5	29
369	13	MED	MENSTRUAL & OTHER FEMALE REPRODUCTIVE SYSTEM DISORDERS	0.513	2.7	26
370	14	SURG	CESAREAN SECTION W CC	0.9573	4.5	26
371	14	SURG	CESAREAN SECTION W/O CC	0.6531	3.4	11,372
372	14	MED	VAGINAL DELIVERY W COMPLICATING DIAGNOSES	0.5558	2.6	20
373	14	MED	VAGINAL DELIVERY W/O COMPLICATING DIAGNOSES	0.3446	1.8	8
374	14	SURG	VAGINAL DELIVERY W STERILIZATION &/OR D&C	0.6721	2.3	13
375	14	SURG	VAGINAL DELIVERY W O.R. PROC EXCEPT STERIL &/OR D&C	0.6587	4.4	27
376	14	MED	POSTPARTUM & POST ABORTION DIAGNOSES W/O O.R. PROCEDURE	0.4418	2.5	26
377	14	SURG	POSTPARTUM & POST ABORTION DIAGNOSES W O.R. PROCEDURE	0.8181	2.8	26

DRG	MDC	Type	Description	Weight	Geometric Mean LOS	Outlier
378	14	MED	ECTOPIC PREGNANCY	0.7409	2.4	14
379	14	MED	THREATENED ABORTION	0.3962	2.2	25
380	14	MED	ABORTION W/O D&C	0.3742	1.6	9
381	14	SURG	ABORTION W D&C, ASPIRATION CURETTAGE OR HYSTEROTOMY	0.4673	1.5	11
382	14	MED	FALSE LABOR	0.1922	1.2	7
383	14	MED	OTHER ANTEPARTUM DIAGNOSES W MEDICAL COMPLICATIONS	0.4587	3.1	26
384	14	MED	OTHER ANTEPARTUM DIAGNOSES W/O MEDICAL COMPLICATIONS	0.2818	1.6	10
385	15		NEONATES, DIED OR TRANSFERRED TO ANOTHER ACUTE CARE FACILITY	1.3219	1.8	25
386	15		EXTREME IMMATURITY OR RESPIRATORY DISTRESS SYNDROME, NEONATE	4.3591	17.9	41
387	15		PREMATURITY W MAJOR PROBLEMS	2.9772	13.3	36
388	15		PREMATURITY W/O MAJOR PROBLEMS	1.7964	8.6	32
389	15		FULL-TERM NEONATE W MAJOR PROBLEMS	2.3785	7.8	31
390	15		NEONATE W OTHER SIGNIFICANT PROBLEMS	0.6218	2.7	26
391	15		NORMAL NEWBORN	0.1465	3.1	11
392	16	SURG	SPLENECTOMY AGE >17 YEARS	3.1908	9.3	32
393	16	SURG	SPLENECTOMY AGE 0–17 YEARS	1.2949	9.1	32
394	16	SURG	OTHER O.R. PROCEDURES OF THE BLOOD AND BLOOD FORMING ORGANS	1.6252	4.9	28
395	16	MED	RED BLOOD CELL DISORDERS AGE >17 YEARS	0.8359	4.1	27
396	16	MED	RED BLOOD CELL DISORDERS AGE 0–17 YEARS	0.598	2.8	26
397	16	MED	COAGULATION DISORDERS	1.2825	4.8	28
398	16	MED	RETICULOENDOTHELIAL & IMMUNITY DISORDERS W CC	1.236	5.6	29
399	16	MED	RETICULOENDOTHELIAL & IMMUNITY DISORDERS W/O CC	0.6934	3.8	27
400	17	SURG	LYMPHOMA & LEUKEMIA W MAJOR O.R. PROCEDURE	2.6034	7.2	30
401	17	SURG	LYMPHOMA & NON-ACUTE LEUKEMIA W OTHER O.R. PROC W CC	2.4533	9	32
402	17	SURG	LYMPHOMA & NON-ACUTE LEUKEMIA W OTHER O.R. PROC W/O CC	0.9428	3.1	26
403	17	MED	LYMPHOMA & NON-ACUTE LEUKEMIA W CC	1.6823	6.9	30
404	17	MED	LYMPHOMA & NON-ACUTE LEUKEMIA W/O CC	0.814	3.8	27

DRG	MDC	Type	Description	Weight	Geometric Mean LOS	Outlier
405	17		ACUTE LEUKEMIA W/O MAJOR O.R. PROCEDURE AGE 0–17 YEARS	1.8358	4.9	28
406	17	SURG	MYELOPROLIFERATIVE DISORD OR POORLY DIFFERENTIATED NEOPLASMS W MAJ O.R. PROC W CC	2.6558	8.6	32
407	17	SURG	MYELOPROLIFERATIVE DISORD OR POORLY DIFFERENTIATED NEOPLASMS W MAJ O.R. PROC W/O CC	1.1626	4	27
408	17	SURG	MYELOPROLIFERATIVE DISORD OR POORLY DIFFERENTIATED NEOPLASMS W OTHER O.R. PROC	1.684	5.2	28
409	17	MED	RADIOTHERAPY	0.9475	4.9	28
410	17	MED	CHEMOTHERAPY W/O ACUTE LEUKEMIA AS SECONDARY DIAGNOSIS	0.7172	2.6	20
411	17	MED	HISTORY OF MALIGNANCY W/O ENDOSCOPY	0.5015	2.5	25
412	17	MED	HISTORY OF MALIGNANCY W ENDOSCOPY	0.453	2.1	24
413	17	MED	OTHER MYELOPROLIFERATIVE DISORD OR POORLY DIFFERENTIATED NEOPLASMS DIAG W CC	1.3422	6.4	29
414	17	MED	OTHER MYELOPROLIFERATIVE DISORD OR POORLY DIFFERENTIATED NEOPLASMS DIAG W/O CC	0.7285	3.9	27
415	18	SURG	O.R. PROCEDURE FOR INFECTIOUS & PARASITIC DISEASES	3.4769	12.4	35
416	18	MED	SEPTICEMIA AGE >17 YEARS	1.477	6.5	30
417	18	MED	SEPTICEMIA AGE 0–17 YEARS	0.8764	4.8	28
418	18	MED	POSTOPERATIVE & POST-TRAUMATIC INFECTIONS	0.9777	5.7	29
419	18	MED	FEVER OF UNKNOWN ORIGIN AGE >17 YEARS W CC	0.9223	4.8	28
420	18	MED	FEVER OF UNKNOWN ORIGIN AGE >17 YEARS W/O CC	0.6258	3.8	25
421	18	MED	VIRAL ILLNESS AGE >17 YEARS	0.6982	3.8	27
422	18	MED	VIRAL ILLNESS & FEVER OF UNKNOWN ORIGIN AGE 0–17 YEARS	0.5446	3.3	26
423	18	MED	OTHER INFECTIOUS & PARASITIC DISEASES DIAGNOSES	1.5828	6.8	30
424	19	SURG	O.R. PROCEDURE W PRINCIPAL DIAGNOSES OF MENTAL ILLNESS	2.4543	12.1	35
425	19	MED	ACUTE ADJUSTMENT REACT & DISTURBANCES OF PSYCHOSOCIAL DYSFUNCTION	0.7129	3.9	27
426	19	MED	DEPRESSIVE NEUROSES	0.5949	4.5	27
427	19	MED	NEUROSES EXCEPT DEPRESSIVE	0.5794	4.1	27

DRG	MDC	Type	Description	Weight	Geometric Mean LOS	Outlier
428	19	MED	DISORDERS OF PERSONALITY & IMPULSE CONTROL	0.6847	5.2	28
429	19	MED	ORGANIC DISTURBANCES & MENTAL RETARDATION	0.9537	6.6	30
430	19	MED	PSYCHOSES	0.867	7.5	30
431	19	MED	CHILDHOOD MENTAL DISORDERS	0.6362	5.3	28
432	19	MED	OTHER MENTAL DISORDER DIAGNOSES	0.7018	4.2	27
433	20	MED	ALCOHOL/DRUG ABUSE OR DEPENDENCE, LEFT AMA	0.308	2.6	26
434	20		ALC/DRUG ABUSE OR DEPEND, DETOX OR OTHER SYMPTOMATIC TREAT W CC	0.7373	4.7	28
435	20		ALC/DRUG ABUSE OR DEPEND, DETOX OR OTHER SYMPTOMATIC TREAT W/O CC	0.4249	3.9	27,436
436	20		ALC/DRUG DEPENDENCE W REHABILITATION THERAPY	0.8384	12.6	36
437	20		ALC/DRUG DEPENDENCE, COMBINED REHAB & DETOX THERAPY	0.7972	9.9	33
438			NO LONGER VALID	0	0	0
439	21	SURG	SKIN GRAFTS FOR INJURIES	1.6599	5.6	29
440	21	SURG	WOUND DEBRIDEMENTS FOR INJURIES	1.7792	7	30
441	21	SURG	HAND PROCEDURES FOR INJURIES	0.8785	2.3	25
442	21	SURG	OTHER O.R. PROCEDURES FOR INJURIES W CC	2.0836	5.7	29
443	21	SURG	OTHER O.R. PROCEDURES FOR INJURIES W/O CC	0.813	2.4	25
444	21	MED	TRAUMATIC INJURY AGE >17 YEARS W CC	0.729	4.4	27
445	21	MED	TRAUMATIC INJURY AGE >17 YEARS W/O CC	0.4664	2.9	26
446	21	MED	TRAUMATIC INJURY AGE 0–17 YEARS	0.2846	2.4	22
447	21	MED	ALLERGIC REACTIONS AGE >17 YEARS	0.4976	2.3	20
448	21	MED	ALLERGIC REACTIONS AGE 0–17 YEARS	0.0896	1	1
449	21	MED	POISONING & TOXIC EFFECTS OF DRUGS AGE >17 YEARS W CC	0.7886	3.3	26
450	21	MED	POISONING & TOXIC EFFECTS OF DRUGS AGE >17 YEARS W/O CC	0.4329	1.9	15
451	21	MED	POISONING & TOXIC EFFECTS OF DRUGS AGE 0–17 YEARS	0.2527	2.1	17
452	21	MED	COMPLICATIONS OF TREATMENT W CC	0.9127	3.9	27
453	21	MED	COMPLICATIONS OF TREATMENT W/O CC	0.4752	2.6	24
454	21	MED	OTHER INJURY, POISONING & TOXIC EFFECT DIAG W CC	0.8906	3.8	27

DRG	MDC	Type	Description	Weight	Geometric Mean LOS	Outlier
455	21	MED	OTHER INJURY, POISONING & TOXIC EFFECT DIAG W/O CC	0.4689	2.3	25,456
456	22	MED	BURNS, TRANSFERRED TO ANOTHER ACUTE CARE FACILITY	1.941	4.2	27
457	22	MED	EXTENSIVE BURNS W/O O.R. PROCEDURE	1.5849	2.5	26
458	22	SURG	NONEXTENSIVE BURNS W SKIN GRAFT	3.4645	12.8	36
459	22	SURG	NONEXTENSIVE BURNS W WOUND DEBRIDEMENT OR OTHER O.R. PROC	1.9398	8.2	31
460	22	MED	NONEXTENSIVE BURNS W/O O.R. PROCEDURE	0.9369	5.1	28
461	23	SURG	O.R. PROC W DIAGNOSES OF OTHER CONTACT W HEALTH SERVICES	1.0104	2.6	26
462	23	MED	REHABILITATION	1.4731	11.8	35
463	23	MED	SIGNS & SYMPTOMS W CC	0.7416	4.2	27
464	23	MED	SIGNS & SYMPTOMS W/O CC	0.4972	3	26
465	23	MED	AFTERCARE W HISTORY OF MALIGNANCY AS SECONDARY DIAGNOSIS	0.4362	1.9	20
466	23	MED	AFTERCARE W/O HISTORY OF MALIGNANCY AS SECONDARY DIAGNOSIS	0.5601	2.5	26
467	23	MED	OTHER FACTORS INFLUENCING HEALTH STATUS	0.4291	2.6	26
468			EXTENSIVE O.R. PROCEDURE UNRELATED TO PRINCIPAL DIAGNOSIS	3.5391	11.4	34
469			PRINCIPAL DIAGNOSIS INVALID AS DISCHARGE DIAGNOSIS	0	0	0
470			UNGROUPABLE	0	0	0
471	08	SURG	BILATERAL OR MULTIPLE MAJOR JOINT PROCEDURES OF LOWER EXTREMITY	3.6458	8	31
472	22	SURG	EXTENSIVE BURNS W O.R. PROCEDURE	10.6993	14.3	37
473	17	SURG	ACUTE LEUKEMIA W/O MAJOR O.R. PROCEDURE AGE >17 YEARS	3.4797	8.9	32
474			NO LONGER VALID	0	0	0
475	04	MED	RESPIRATORY SYSTEM DIAGNOSIS WITH VENTILATOR SUPPORT	3.7015	9.1	32
476		SURG	PROSTATIC O.R. PROCEDURE UNRELATED TO PRINCIPAL DIAGNOSIS	2.2703	11.5	35,477
477		SURG	NONEXTENSIVE O.R. PROCEDURE UNRELATED TO PRINCIPAL DIAGNOSIS	1.5682	5.8	29
478	05	SURG	OTHER VASCULAR PROCEDURES W CC	2.2709	6	29
479	05	SURG	OTHER VASCULAR PROCEDURES W/O CC	1.3864	3.7	27

DRG	MDC	Type	Description	Weight	Geometric Mean LOS	Outlier
480		SURG	LIVER TRANSPLANT	16.3066	24.4	47
481		SURG	BONE MARROW TRANSPLANT	11.6796	27.2	50
482		SURG	TRACHEOSTOMY FOR FACE, MOUTH, & NECK DIAGNOSES	3.662	12.4	35
483		SURG	TRACHEOSTOMY EXCEPT FOR FACE, MOUTH, & NECK DIAGNOSES	16.109	38.2	61
484	24	SURG	CRANIOTOMY FOR MULTIPLE SIGNIFICANT TRAUMA	5.4488	10.9	34,485
485	24	SURG	LIMB REATTACHMENT, HIP AND FEMUR PROC FOR MULTIPLE SIGNIFICANT TRAUMA	3.261	10.5	33
486	24	SURG	OTHER O.R. PROCEDURES FOR MULTIPLE SIGNIFICANT TRAUMA	4.8763	9.6	33
487	24	MED	OTHER MULTIPLE SIGNIFICANT TRAUMA	1.9932	6.8	30
488	25	SURG	HIV W EXTENSIVE O.R. PROCEDURE	4.2177	13.9	37
489	25	MED	HIV W MAJOR RELATED CONDITION	1.7856	7.8	31
490	25	MED	HIV W OR W/O OTHER RELATED CONDITION	1.0476	4.7	28
491	08	SURG	MAJOR JOINT & LIMB REATTACHMENT PROCEDURES OF UPPER EXTREMITY	1.6088	4	22
492	17	MED	CHEMOTHERAPY W ACUTE LEUKEMIA AS SECONDARY DIAGNOSIS	4.1529	11.8	35,493
493	07	SURG	LAPAROSCOPIC CHOLECYSTECTOMY W/O COMMON DUCT EXPLORATION. W CC	1.6501	4.3	27
494	07	SURG	LAPAROSCOPIC CHOLECYSTECTOMY W/O COMMON DUCT EXPLORATION W/O CC	0.8769	1.8	15
495		SURG	LUNG TRANSPLANT	9.5678	18.2	41

3

Managed Care

Managed care, health maintenance organizations (HMOs), preferred provider organizations (PPOs), physician organizations (POs), physician hospital organizations (PHOs), capitation, medical service organizations (MSOs), and integrated delivery systems are all terms and acronyms that are used freely in today's health care arena. These terms often represent different things to different people and often change in meaning over time. One common thread runs through all of these terms and it is the issue of change and market reform that is sweeping the health care industry. Our focus in this chapter will be primarily on the development of HMOs and their increasing reliance on capitation as a method of payment.

HMO AND MANAGED CARE DEVELOPMENT

Before describing the development of HMOs in the health care market, it is important to define what we mean by an HMO. HMOs are organizations that receive premium dollars from subscribers in exchange for a promise to provide all health care required by that subscriber for a defined period. They assume the risk of delivering both physician and hospital services to their enrolled populations for a fixed sum of money pro-

vided on a prepaid basis. HMOs are a type of health plan or health insurance company. In this regard, they are no different than any other type of health insurer.

Figure 3–1 presents a view of the money flows from subscribers to health plans to providers of health care services.

Health plans receive premium dollars from buyers who may be employers, groups, or individuals on a prepaid basis in return for a promise to provide payment for covered health care services when needed. Payments for those services can be paid to the subscriber or to the health care provider. Indemnity plans would make payments to the subscriber, or indemnify the subscriber, for covered health care services; but, in most cases, payments are made directly to the provider.

Health plans must make a profit to remain in business and it is easy to understand the principles of profitability in the health insurance marketplace. To earn positive profits, health plans must receive payments from subscribers greater than payments to health care providers. They must also cover their own internal administrative costs. Health plans also generate some additional revenue from the investment of prepaid health premiums. The amounts of investment income earned by health insurers are relatively small compared to life insurance com-

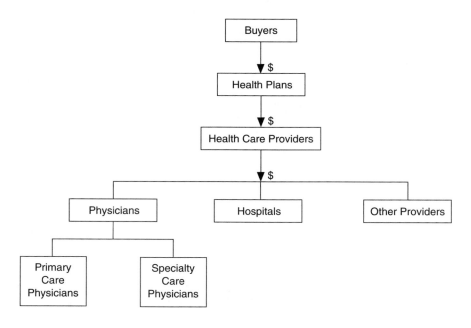

Figure 3–1 Health Care Insurance Market

panies where the premium dollars are received far in advance of payment.

What functions do health plans perform to justify their position in the health care marketplace? There are four primary activities, and they are described in the following text.

Underwriting

Health plans accept risk much in the same way that any insurance company accepts risk. They agree to provide payment for services that at the time of contract are not certain. Greater than expected utilization can easily destroy profits and cause payments to exceed receipts. Underwriting of risk is an important business function. Few of us would be willing to live in homes without homeowner's insurance because the occurrence of a fire could destroy us financially. Even though we may pay the insurance company much more in premiums over our lifetimes than we receive in payments, we are not willing to assume the risk of a fire. Health insurance is the

same situation. Payment for open heart procedures, kidney transplants, and other sophisticated medical procedures are very expensive, and we all hope that we never need them; but, if we do, it is comforting to know that we have a source of payment for these procedures. Our country is different than most other industrial countries regarding the percentage of private versus public financing. The United States relies on private financing of medical care to a much greater extent than most other countries. This places a much greater emphasis on health insurance in our country and less on public financing programs such as Medicare and Medicaid.

Marketing

Insurance companies in general and health insurers in particular must communicate the availability of their products to prospective buyers and convince buyers of the value of their product. Various media are used to accomplish this task, from individual salespersons to television and other media advertising. There are substantial costs associated with these efforts.

Utilization Review

Increasingly, health plans have sought to control escalating costs through a variety of utilization review techniques. Health plans employ doctors and nurses to review and approve the delivery of nonemergent medical care for necessity and appropriateness. Medical personnel at health plans also work with health providers to plan discharges from hospitals to less intense subacute settings as soon as possible. Case management of chronic conditions such as mental illness also is used by health plans to control costs. Much of the "managed" in managed care deals with health-plan review and approval of treatment protocols.

Claims Administration

Payments to health care providers for the provision of services to subscribers is a necessary administrative process. The health plan must verify that coverage for the services exists and that the services were in fact performed. In most cases, the health plan also must determine the amount of payment for the services, which is often different than the charges listed on a patient's bill or claim form. Verification of primary coverage also must be determined in cases when the individual has more than one insurer. The process of assigning payment responsibility when multiple insurers exist is called coordination of benefits.

HMOs are a subset of health plans and share all of the functions identified previously; but they are different in several areas, most notably regarding the pattern of relationships with their health care providers. First, most HMOs do not permit HMO subscribers to select providers who are out of the network. For example, an HMO subscriber who wished to use an orthopaedic surgeon not in the HMO's network may not be covered for charges incurred by that surgeon. A hybrid form of an HMO package called point of service (POS) has a provision that permits subscribers to go out of network for services, but subscribers must pay a greater percentage of the cost. We will review POS options later in the text. Secondly, most HMOs rely on a primary care gatekeeper concept. The HMO uses the primary care physician as a central triage point for the referral and approval of services. Before a subscriber can see a specialist, the referral must be first approved by the primary care physician. The use of the primary care physician as a gatekeeper is a central concept underlying HMO success and has been adopted by other health plans that might not be characterized as HMOs.

HMOs are often categorized by the pattern of provider relationships they maintain, especially physician provider relationships. HMOs are usually categorized into the following four types.

Staff Model HMO

In a staff model HMO, the physicians are either employees of the HMO or they provide most of their services to HMO members through a contractual relationship. The latter alternative is used in states where HMOs cannot employ physicians because of restrictions on employment of physicians by nonphysician-owned companies. Not all physicians may be employees, nor may they be under direct contract; but the critical segment is the primary care physicians. The HMO must control the primary care physician network to be a true staff model HMO. A staff model also may own other related health care providers such as hospitals, but ownership is not necessary.

Group Model HMO

In a group model HMO, the HMO contracts with one or more medical groups to provide all necessary services to HMO members. Usually, the groups are not exclusively bound to any one HMO and may provide services to several HMOs. The groups also may be primary care, specialty based, or multiple specialty based. The physicians in the groups, however, must come together and transfer all or most of their medical practice assets and liabilities to the group entity.

Independent Practice Association (IPA) Model HMO

An IPA model HMO is a much looser affiliation of independent physicians who have not come together and integrated their practices in any substantive way. The IPA contracts with the HMO for needed medical services, but the individual physicians maintain their own independent practices and use the IPA only to sign contracts with HMOs and other health plans. County medical societies often create an IPA for their physician members.

Network Model HMO

Network model HMOs are really a hybrid of the previous three forms. A network model HMO may contract with both medical groups and IPAs, as well as employ individual physicians. The key to their success is the ability to access a pool of cost-effective physicians who can manage care.

Alternative Health Insurance Plans

Table 3–1 provides a historical perspective on market share of alternative health insurance products in the private health care insurance market. The data show a dramatic reduction in indemnity style health plans, with a corresponding increase in both PPOs and HMOs. Table 3–2 summarizes some key characteristics for indemnity plans, PPOs, and HMOs.

Indemnity plans provide their members with the greatest access to health care providers, both

doctors and hospitals. Members are not restricted in terms of who they can see for treatment of any medical disorders. In short, freedom of choice is the highest in indemnity plans. HMOs are usually the most restrictive in terms of choice and often limit access to hospitals and physicians that are part of the network. PPOs may be as restrictive as HMOs, but usually have larger panels of both doctors and hospitals. They attempt to select providers who have a good track record on both quality and cost effectiveness.

HMOs usually provide the broadest range of medical benefits, whereas indemnity plans are often the most restrictive. HMO members often have access to liberal outpatient and drug benefits that other health plans do not offer. The cost for increased benefits is most often limited access. HMO members cannot go to any doctor or hospital they wish to visit, but are limited to the panel listed in the benefits directory. Without a POS provision, HMO members are precluded from going out of the network for services. PPOs often will provide provisions for out-of-network services, but require members to pay a portion of the cost for these benefits in the form of higher copayments and deductibles. A copayment is a provision that specifies a percentage of the approved charge that must be paid by the member. For example, a 20 percent copay would require a PPO member to pay 20 percent of the approved charge. The approved charge may be different from the charge made to the member for the service. A doctor may charge $2,000 for a procedure that the PPO says is approved at $1,200. The member would be required to pay the doctor 20 percent of the approved charge of $1,200, or $240, plus the difference between the approved charge and the actual charge, or $800, for a total payment of $1,040.

Indemnity plans usually pay providers, both hospitals and doctors, on the basis of charges. In some cases, there may be a fee schedule in effect that limits payment liability. PPOs usually negotiate some discount with the providers as a condition for participation in the network of providers. HMOs work in much the same way as PPOs

Table 3–1 Private Health Insurance Market

Health Insurance Type	Market Share %	
	1988	1993
Indemnity	72.6	33.3
HMO	17.2	22.4
PPO	10.0	43.0
POS Plan	0.2	1.3
Total	100.0	100.0

Source: Reprinted from National Center for Health Statistics.

Table 3–2 Health Care Insurance Alternatives

Parties	Alternative Plans		
	HMOs	*PPOs*	*Indemnity*
Subscribers	Restricted choice	Choice from panel	Free choice
	Generous benefits	Copays	Deductible and 80/20 copays
		Out of network with reduced benefits and higher cost	Major medical benefits
			Limited outpatient coverage
		Broader benefits	
Physicians	Limited access	Access by contracting	All participate
	Discounted reimbursement or capitation	Discounted charges or fee-schedule	Paid charges
	Utilization review (UR) requirements	UR—mostly hospital-based	
Hospitals	Limited access	Limited access	All participate
	Discounted charges, per diems, case rates, or capitation	Discounted charges or per diem	Paid charges
	UR	UR	
Employers	Reduced cost	Reduced cost	Expensive but most freedom for employees

and require a discount for participation in the network of providers. There is also a possibility of capitated payment to providers in an HMO arrangement. Capitation simply means the provider is not paid on the basis of services performed, but rather on the basis of HMO members assigned to their organization. This means the provider may be paid on a per-member-per-month (PMPM) basis. Finally, HMOs use stringent utilization review (UR) procedures at both the hospital and physician levels to eliminate unnecessary services and to provide cost-effective treatment plans. PPOs use UR procedures, but at the present time most of their efforts are directed at hospitals. Indemnity plans are also beginning to use UR procedures to curtail unnecessary utilization.

Costs of health care coverage to the employer are usually lowest in an HMO plan and highest in an indemnity plan. The reason for this observation is not hard to understand. HMOs try to reduce unnecessary utilization for both doctors and hospitals and they also try to curtail the amount paid for services to health care providers. PPOs have tried to reduce costs primarily through reduced prices to providers by selective provider contracting, but utilization reductions have not been substantial relative to those achieved in an HMO setting. The big advantage that PPOs have regarding their remarkable growth rate can be attributed to the ease of organization. It takes much less planning and effort, as well as capital, to create a PPO than it does to create an HMO. Most policy experts believe, however, that the evolutionary cycle eventually will change many of these PPOs to HMOs as continued cost pressure from major purchasers of health care—employers and the government—force health plans to further decrease costs. Most of the future reductions in health care costs will not likely flow from lower prices per unit of service, but rather from reduced utilization of expensive procedures, especially hospital inpatient procedures.

HMOs are not a new development and have been in existence for many years. Two of the earliest HMOs were Kaiser Permanente and Group Health of Puget Sound. Both of these HMOs could be described as staff model HMOs. Physicians and hospitals that participated in these HMOs derived most, if not all, of their business from the HMO. In the early 1970s, Dr. Paul Elwood of Interstudy, a consulting firm in Minneapolis, coined the term "health maintenance organization" to describe the kind of health plan represented by Kaiser and Group Health. The development of HMOs, although rapid, was not very impressive until the mid 1980s, when HMOs started to develop and grow. Most of the growth occurred in nonstaff model HMOs. Newly formed HMOs simply could not put together the ownership structures necessary to employ physicians directly and relied on contractual relationships with groups and IPAs. Physicians also were reluctant to give up their independent status for employee positions. Staff

model enrollment today represents approximately 10 percent of all HMO enrollment.

INTEGRATED DELIVERY SYSTEMS

With the growth of HMOs and PPOs, buying power was concentrated in fewer purchasing groups, and hospitals and physicians sought some way to reduce the trend to greater and greater discounts granted for participation in managed care contracts. To offset this concentration of purchasing power, hospitals and physicians began to develop integrated delivery system (IDS) structures to better position themselves and place themselves closer to the premium dollar. In some cases, these IDS organizations even approached employers directly to sell health insurance coverage. This eliminated the health plan, which they regarded as a middleman in the marketplace.

In the early 1990s, IDSs, which consisted of at least a hospital and physician component, began to develop. An IDS was thought of as a strategic alliance among doctors, hospitals, and other ancillary providers to deliver care to a defined population. There are few fully integrated delivery systems presently, and most consist of only hospital and doctor elements. IDS organizations initially sought to develop managed care contracts on behalf of both the hospitals and the physicians and served primarily as a contracting vehicle. There are a number of economic factors, however, that created the stimulus for the formation of IDSs. These factors are discussed in the following text.

Negotiation for Health Plan Contracts

One of the key driving forces behind hospital-physician integration has been the present need, or perceived future need, to provide health insurers with a single contract for health services. This will be easier to negotiate if the doctors and hospitals are within the same organizational system. Much of the consolidation now occurring in the health care delivery system is related to this factor.

Growing Importance of Payer Referrals

Physicians receive about 20 percent of each health care dollar in the United States, yet they control most of the expenditures. Hospitals and other institutional providers depend upon physician referrals to keep utilization in their facilities at reasonable levels. Although physician referrals are still the primary source of business for most health care providers, there has been a subtle but growing increase in payer referrals. Physicians and hospitals suddenly have found that they are no longer acceptable providers for some health plans and that they have been dropped. Most of the reasons for their exclusion relate to the high cost of their practice patterns with only minimal, if any, attention presently paid to quality of care. Fear of being excluded has caused many hospitals and doctors to create larger corporate structures. It is believed the sheer size of these hospital-physician combinations will strengthen their negotiating position with health plans.

Increasing Importance of Capitation

Under a capitated payment system, providers are paid a fixed amount for each person living in their covered service area. This is very different from the current practice of most payers (including most HMOs, who pay on the basis of services provided). The speed and extent to which the current system, which is largely dominated by retrospective payment for services, will be replaced with prospective captitation is debatable. It is clear, however, that capitation will increase and that this will cause a striking reversal of service incentives; instead of being paid for providing services to sick patients, hospitals and physicians will be paid a fixed amount for a population, regardless of what services are provided. Supporters believe that this will encourage preventive care and reduce unnecessary uti-

lization of services; others worry that it will create incentives for skimping on service or reducing quality. Whichever position is true, it is clear that in the future, more Americans will be covered under capitated payment schemes. At the present time, approximately forty million Americans are enrolled in HMO plans, which is up sharply from eleven million in 1982.

Shift of Hospital Services to Outpatient

In 1988, about 88 percent of all hospital revenue was derived from traditional inpatient services. By 1992, that figure had fallen to 64 percent, and it is expected that by the year 2000, 50 percent of all hospital revenue will come from outpatient sources. This shift is related to tremendous cost pressures to perform procedures on an outpatient basis when possible, technology that has made outpatient procedures more feasible, and a strong desire by patients to be treated on an outpatient basis. The cost pressures have forced hospitals to become more active in outpatient services that were traditionally the domain of the physician office, while the new technology has enabled doctors to provide services in their offices that were historically performed in hospitals. The outpatient market can either be an area where hospitals and physicians can productively collaborate, or it can degenerate into a fierce competitive battleground between the two. For an integrated delivery system to succeed, it is imperative that collaboration, not competition, occur. Only then can an appropriate continuum of care be assured for every patient.

Integrated Data Systems

Technology has made it possible to share vast quantities of information among various potential users. Shared clinical data among physicians, hospitals, and other providers can enhance both the quality and effectiveness of medical care. Data that are shared also permit some economies in business functions such as billing. Although shared data is an objective sought by many parties, it is much easier to accomplish in organizations that are formally related either through common ownership or business-related affiliations. Unfortunately, the health care industry is notoriously behind in using the power of modern computer systems to solve business and clinical problems. This is true partly because the hospital environment is complex, and partly because the system is fragmented. For instance, a person who can get cash instantly from an ATM machine while traveling in the Philippines still cannot access his or her medical records if admitted to a hospital one county away from his or her home. A person can call a travel agent to schedule a complex trip itinerary involving multiple airlines, yet cannot schedule a day's worth of diagnostic and treatment steps in a hospital without serious risk of delays or cancellations. The most important factor in the future success of the integrated delivery system likely will be its ability to use information as a competitive resource.

Vertical and Horizontal Integration Trends

There has been a concerted effort during the last few years to develop new entities that can dominate markets in selected areas. Major hospital chains have announced on a weekly basis some new merger that was designed to enhance their market position. Columbia–HCA, through its mergers, quickly has become the nation's largest hospital provider, with special strength in certain regions. This is an example of horizontal integration and can be a successful market strategy. Many other regional systems have chosen vertical integration as a means to market dominance. For example, Sentara Health System in Norfolk, Virginia, includes 4 hospitals, 1,859 physicians, 6 nursing homes, 3 assisted living centers, and its own HMO. The important lesson that most health care providers have realized is that it is dangerous to be small and unaffiliated in today's competitive markets. There is a major "shake-out" coming in the health care industry, and it will involve hospitals, physicians, and

payers. Those who are incorporated into larger systems are the most likely to have greater access to consumer and capital markets, and thus be better positioned for long-term survival.

Productivity

Many economists believe that improvements in productivity are the primary means for realizing increases in the standard of living within a nation. The same is true in an economic enterprise. Over the long term, a hospital, medical group, or insurance company cannot increase its financial performance without continually enhancing productivity. One of the key potential benefits of creating integrated delivery systems is the opportunity to reengineer processes across what were formerly impregnable barriers to communication, thereby reducing redundancy and cost.

Figure 3–2 presents a diagram of an IDS and shows its insertion between the health plan, the providers of medical services, and products that were shown in Figure 3–1. One of the developments discussed earlier that has led to the development of IDS organizations is the increasing importance of capitation as a form of payment to health care providers. As of 1994, it is estimated that 70 percent of the HMOs use capitation for paying primary care physicians, 50 percent use capitation for paying specialty care physicians, and 25 percent use capitation for hospital payment. These percentages are expected to increase dramatically in the future. It should be noted that these percentages do not reflect the actual percentages of payment made on a capitated basis, only the percentage of HMOs using capitation as a method of payment. For example, the average amount of capitated revenue in a typical hospital is still very small, approximately 5 percent or less. An HMO may use a capitated contract for several of its providers, but the majority of its provider contracts still may be on a fee-for-service basis of some kind.

HMOs have a strong financial incentive to capitate providers whenever possible because this guarantees their profit and locks in a fixed

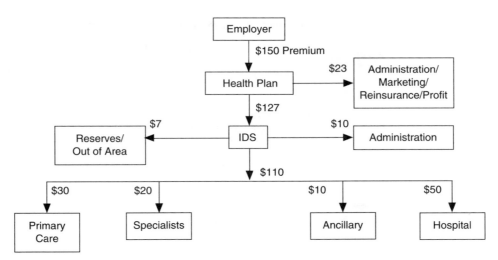

Figure 3–2 Integrated Delivery System Structure Funds Flow in an IDS

return. For example, the illustration in Figure 3–2 depicts a situation where the HMO could guarantee itself a $23 return PMPM if it could negotiate a fixed PMPM payment of $127 to an IDS for all health care services. Although HMOs have begun to push capitation on health care providers, the health care providers have asked themselves whether it is to their advantage to accept capitation and directly market an insurance product to major employers, thus eliminating the middle man health plan from the revenue stream. The providers assume that they can perform appropriate utilization review, administer claims, and market their product to employers. The only piece that they may be uncomfortable with is the assumption of risk or underwriting. If HMOs push capitation downward to them, this is no longer an issue. They are already capitated and must assume the medical underwriting risk anyway.

It is difficult to answer the question of who controls the IDS. In general, there are three alternatives. Hospitals can seek to control the IDS and protect their position in the health care marketplace as inpatient acute care utilization falls. Physicians may think that they are in better position to control the IDS because the emphasis is

increasingly on managing care, and this is a role that physicians are uniquely qualified to assume. Finally, organizers of health plans may believe that they are in the best position to control the IDS because of their closeness to the premium dollar and their historical interest in cost control. Health plans also presently have the cash reserves to finance much of the organizational development necessary to make this happen.

The primary vehicle for hospital control has been a PHO. The PHO may serve as the IDS in Figure 3–2 and contract on behalf of physicians and hospitals. The development of PHOs is relatively new and most were not started until 1993 or later. PHOs are, in theory, a partnership between hospitals and physicians. However, many have been tightly controlled by the hospital and do not always represent a true partnership. Figure 3–3 presents two possible PHO organizational structures. PHOs formed between a hospital and a formal physician organization often are better suited to tackle the issues of managed care because they have a structure in place to begin physician dialogue about cost-effective care. PHOs formed without a physician organization simply may represent shareholder interests of individual physicians or groups. This greatly di-

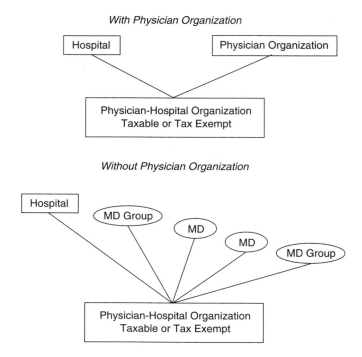

Figure 3–3 Physician Hospital Organizational Structure

minishes physician control in the PHO. Significant physician involvement is needed to create an effective integrated delivery system. A loosely organized physician body may give effective control to the hospital, but not really accomplish the physician–hospital integration essential to success.

PHOs may be formed on either a taxable or tax exempt basis. There are pros and cons for either alternative, but if the objective is the eventual acquisition or employment of physicians, a taxable basis appears to have fewer problems. The creation of a tax exempt nonprofit PHO may raise the issue of inurement, which will be discussed later.

A PHO is not usually a fully integrated delivery system. The major difficulty with many PHOs is determining how to divide the payments from the health plan or HMO among the hospital and its contracting physicians. Each party most likely wants to protect their level of income, and without common ownership or control, this revenue allocation may doom many PHOs in the long term. Hospital-dominated PHOs often are considered by physicians as an attempt to protect the hospital's declining market share and to perpetuate hospital domination of the health care market.

MSOs are an alternative organizational structure to a PHO that also may serve as an IDS and contract for medical services with a health plan. MSOs are often formed to provide management services to medical groups and may or may not have any hospital ownership or control. If an MSO is formed without hospital interest, the MSO may have to contract with a hospital if the MSO wishes to contract for both hospital and physician services.

POs are a relatively recent development. Most POs were developed in large part because of dissatisfaction with hospital-sponsored PHOs. They represented an attempt by physicians to take back control in the new managed care world. The primary problem many physicians encountered when creating a PO was a lack of capital and organizational management skills. Investors have begun to pour capital dollars into the development of POs because they recognize the gigantic opportunities for cost savings in health care and the pivotal role that physicians play in the realization of those cost savings. National corporations, as well as the American Medical Association, have been aggressively organizing and funding POs to put them in a position where they can begin forming their own managed care organizations and directly contract for health care services on a capitated basis.

Health insurers and HMOs are also actively entering the IDS arena and beginning to directly provide medical services, especially outpatient services. Acquisition of clinics and the employment of physicians have been undertaken by a number of insurers, and more are considering these types of ventures. Even large employers are beginning to ask the question, "Why should we buy health insurance when we believe that we can make our own delivery system and produce care cheaper than we buy it?" This is most often seen in the development of clinics for employees of a firm.

PAYING PROVIDERS IN A MANAGED CARE ENVIRONMENT

One of the most difficult problems in a less than fully integrated delivery system is splitting the revenue between individual health care providers. Let's assume that the IDS represented in Figure 3–2 does not own the individual health care providers to which it is distributing premium dollars. How does it determine that primary care physicians get $30 PMPM and specialty care physicians get $20 PMPM? Or at an

even more basic level, how does the IDS decide if it will pay physicians on a capitated PMPM basis or use a fee schedule?

The decisions referred to previously are related to pricing and are ultimately related to costs. No business wishes to produce products that are priced at levels lower than costs. If a business continued to do this, it would ultimately be forced to close its doors. Health care providers and insurers are not an exception. The health plan or HMO in Figure 3–2 knows that in its marketplace it can sell health care insurance for $150 on a PMPM basis. Of that $150, $23 is needed to cover internal administrative costs and marketing costs. Additional costs are allocated for reinsurance and profit for the health plan's investors. Reinsurance represents the additional costs paid to other insurers for assumption of unusual risks. For example, the health plan may have to pay the IDS additional payments for treating high-risk patients, such as patients with AIDS.

The health plan then pays the IDS $127 PMPM to provide all health care benefits or some subset of benefits. The IDS needs $10 PMPM to cover its costs of administration and another $10 to create a reserve position to meet out-of-service area costs. Reserves are needed because the IDS is obligating itself to pay for all health care costs that will be provided during the benefit period. The actual level of utilization is not certain. A reserve position will help them cover costs in situations when actual utilization exceeds estimates. Reserve requirements might also reflect a state requirement that the IDS entity be treated as an insurance company and, therefore, statutory reserve levels may be required. Out-of-area costs simply represent those payments that will be made to health care providers out of the service area. A subscriber may be traveling in another state and require emergency medical attention that could not be provided by a network provider.

The IDS now has $110 to pay the providers of health care services that are part of its regional network. Each of those providers will develop a budget of what expected costs are likely to be incurred for the insured population. For example, assume that the primary care physicians have developed the following schedule to estimate their costs:

Unit of service: Office visits

Annual frequency per 1,000 members: 4,000

Unit cost: $75

Net PMPM cost: $25

The primary care physicians have estimated that approximately 4,000 visits per 1,000 members will be required per year. At this rate of utilization, approximately four office visits per year will be required per member with an estimated cost of $75 per office visit. Therefore, the average cost per member per year is 4 × $75 or $300 per year. Dividing by twelve, the number of months in a year, yields a PMPM basis of $25. The primary care physicians would be willing to accept any amount greater than $25 PMPM to provide office visits for this insured population if they had confidence in their estimates, especially the estimated rate of utilization of four visits per year.

Estimating costs under a capitated contract basis is easy to understand from a conceptual basis. Cost can be expressed simply as follows:

PMPM cost =

$$\frac{\text{Expected encounters per year} \times \text{Cost per encounter}}{12}$$

With this framework, the IDS (or the health plan if there is no intermediate IDS entity) has three primary forms of payment. These forms are discussed in the following text.

Salary or Budget

If the providers are owned by the IDS or health plan, or are employees of the organiza-

tion, there is no real revenue-sharing arrangement in effect. The IDS is merely trying to determine what costs it will incur when it treats the insured population for the budget period. A Kaiser-owned hospital receives a budget based upon expected utilization during the coming year. Salaried physicians are not paid on a volume basis but are paid a salary with perhaps some incentives for above-average performance. The key relationship in this arrangement is determining the required physician and hospital staffing necessary to meet expected utilization.

Fee for Service

Doctors and hospitals in this payment mode are paid on a volume-related basis. For doctors, there are two primary alternatives: charges or fee schedule. In a charge-based payment system, the doctor usually would be paid on the basis of total charges, most often some negotiated percentage of total charges such as 80 percent. In a fee schedule arrangement, the doctor would be paid based upon some contractually specified fee structure. The Resource Based Relative Value Scale (RBRVS) described in Chapter 2 would be an example. Hospitals usually are paid on one of three bases: charges, per diems, or per case. As with physicians, a hospital being paid on a charge basis most likely would not receive 100 percent of charges, but rather some lower percentage. Per diem payment is common among many HMOs and simply guarantees the hospital so much per patient day, for example $900 for every medical surgical patient day. Different rates may be in effect for maternity and intensive care days. Case payment may be similar to Medicare's diagnosis-related groups (DRGs) and could relate payment to specific DRGs. Case payment could be some aggregation of case categories such as medical cases, obstetrical cases, and surgical cases. Hospital outpatient services most often are based upon discounted charges, but ambulatory visit groups (AVGs) and other classification methods are becoming more popular and could be used to devise a fee schedule.

Capitation

Presently, capitation arrangements are much more common for physicians, especially primary care physicians, than they are for hospitals. Physicians are in a much better position to control and manage costs than hospitals, who largely provide services ordered and administered by physicians. In a flat rate capitation arrangement, the provider would receive a flat amount, $30 PMPM, to provide all contracted services. A percentage arrangement pays the provider some fixed percentage, for example 25 percent of the PMPM premium payment. Floors or adjustments are sometimes included in capitated arrangements to protect the provider. For example, utilization is usually a function of age, gender, prior health status, and other variables. If an HMO contracted with a primary care group for $30 PMPM, that rate might be sufficient for insured individuals between twenty-five and fifty-five years old, but grossly inadequate for the population older than sixty-five years. The primary care group may therefore adjust its PMPM payment based upon age.

Withholds and Risk Pools

The last element of provider payment that needs to be addressed is the presence of withholds and risk pools. Withholds are most common in fee-for-service arrangements and provide a mechanism for reducing the risk to the IDS or health plan. Table 3–3 presents an example that we will use to illustrate the concept of withholds and risk pools. There are three categories of providers: primary care physicians who are paid $30 PMPM, specialty care physicians who are paid on a fee schedule basis, and the hospital that is paid $850 per patient day. There are 10,000 people who are insured by the HMO, and budgets are projected for each category.

The hospital budget is projected to be $3,400,000 and is derived as follows assuming 400 patient days per 1,000 members with 10,000 members:

$$= 4{,}000 \text{ Patient days} \times \$850$$
$$= \$3{,}400{,}000$$

The hospital also is subject to a 10 percent withhold, which means they will be paid $765 per diem (90 percent of $850). Now assume that actual days were 450 days per 1,000. Payments would be calculated as follows:

Initial hospital payment		
(4,500 Days × $765)	=	$3,442,500
Risk pool (Budget – Paid)		
($3,400,000 – $3,442,500)	=	–$42,500
Additional payments		
to hospital	=	0

Table 3–3 HMO Payment Example

	Primary Care Physicians (PCP)	Specialty Care Physicians (SCP)	Hospital
Payment	$30 PMPM	Fee schedule	$850 per diem
Annual budget for 10,000 covered lives	$3,600,000	$2,400,000	$3,400,000
Risk pool	0	$240,000	$340,000
Parties splitting risk pool	None	PCP, SCP, HMO	PCP, hospital, HMO
Withhold	None	None	10%

If actual days were 350 instead of 450, the following payments would result:

Initial hospital payment
(3,500 × $765)   = $2,677,500
Risk pool (Budget − Paid)
($3,400,000 − $2,677,500) = $722,500
Additional payments
to hospital (one third
of risk pool)   = $240,833

In the first example of excessive utilization, the risk pool is a negative value at the end of the year and the hospital would receive no additional moneys. An interesting question is whether the negative risk pool balance would be divided among the primary care physician, the hospital, and the HMO. We will assume that in this example, only the HMO is assuming the negative variance. In the second example, there is a surplus in the risk pool. The balance in the risk pool would be split equally among the three parties: the HMO, the hospital, and the primary care physicians. The critical factor in each situation is utilization. Some may wonder why the primary care physicians would be able to participate in the hospital risk pool, but it is this group of decision makers that makes the referral and admission decisions that ultimately impact hospital utilization. Sharing in the risk pool gives them an incentive to keep utilization in check. The primary care physicians also share in the specialty care risk pool for the same reason. It is their referral decisions that will determine actual utilization; therefore, they determine the total payments given a fixed fee schedule for payment to specialty care physicians.

The use of withholds and risk pools can be confusing to even the most experienced financial analyst. It is important to work out several examples to make certain that the contract language is understood by all parties. The examples also may be part of the contract to help clarify actual interpretation.

SETTING PRICES IN CAPITATED CONTRACTS

Pricing in any market is a function of a variety of factors, but it ultimately rests on the relationship between costs and expected prices. In most markets, prices already are established within some narrow band. An HMO cannot decide to price a policy at $300 PMPM when its closest competitor is pricing a similar product at $200 PMPM. It would have few buyers, if any, and would be forced out of that market. The HMO must therefore decide if it can provide coverage for approximately $200 PMPM to remain competitive in the marketplace.

Table 3–4 presents recent data from the 1995–1996 edition of *HMO Industry Profile*, published by the American Association of Health Plans (AAHP), which shows average PMPM expenses. The table is useful to help identify the major categories of expense and their relative importance in the cost structures of HMOs.

Revenues for HMOs consist of three categories: premiums, copayments, and coordination of benefits. The largest element is premiums received from HMO subscribers. In addition to those premiums, HMOs also may receive additional revenues from copayments for selected services. For example, the HMO may have a $5 copayment for physician office visits, which is usually collected at the time of the visit. This copayment generates some additional revenue, and it also provides an incentive for subscribers not to overuse physician services. Coordination of benefits relates to the recovery of payments from other insurers when two or more insurance policies are involved. For example, an HMO may have made payments to health care providers on behalf of a member for services rendered, but discovered later that the member also had coverage under a spouse's policy. The two insurance companies would work together to determine the amount that each insurance company is liable to pay and the HMO might receive some payment from the other insurance company for services that it has already paid.

Table 3–4 PMPM Revenue and Expense Averages

Revenue (including copayments and coordination of benefits)	$136.00
Expenses	
Inpatient	$ 39.08
Physician	46.31
Other professional	9.22
Outside referral	7.38
Emergency room and out of area	4.36
Other expenses	21.34
Administration	13.49
Total expenses	$ 128.42*

* Individual expenses do not add to total

Source: Reprinted with permission from AAHP HMO & PPO Industry Profile, 1995–1996 Edition, © American Association of Health Plans.

The two largest categories of expense for HMOs are inpatient expenses and physician payments. Inpatient expenses are mostly payments to hospitals for covered admissions, whereas physician payments reference amounts paid to both primary care and specialty care physicians. As discussed earlier, these payments could be fee for services or capitation. Other professional services relate to payments for diagnostic lab and radiology, home health, and other professional services. Outside referral payments are payments to physicians and others for services not contracted with existing providers. Emergency room payments are payments to hospitals for emergency room visits, and out-of-area payments relate to payments for services to members who become ill and need medical attention while traveling outside the plan's service area. Other expenses represent a "catch all" category designed to include expenses not previously included in the other categories. Lastly, administrative expenses refer to the marketing and administrative costs of plan management. Also included here are premium taxes charged against health insurance sales.

An HMO or an intermediate IDS that is attempting to either set a price or assess the profitability of an existing price will have to determine its expected costs of servicing the defined population. To do this, the following cost relationship would be used:

$$PMPM = \frac{\text{Expected encounters per year} \times \text{Cost per encounter}}{12}$$

Cost is a simple function of expected utilization and cost per type of encounter. We will now discuss each of these factors in detail and use the pricing example of Table 3–5. Table 3–5 presents four categories of provider expenses: hospital inpatient, hospital outpatient, physician, and other. Each cost category in the table converts to a budgeted cost on a PMPM basis. To understand this more clearly, let's go through the first item, medical surgical benefits. It is currently expected that 350 days per 1,000 lives will

Table 3–5 Development of PMPM Rate

Category	Annual Frequency per 1,000	Unit Cost	PMPM	Copay Frequency per 1,000	Copay Amount	Copay PMPM	Net PMPM
Hospital inpatient							
Medical surgical	350	$ 900	$ 26.25	300	$ 100	$ 2.50	$ 23.75
Maternity	20	900	1.50	20	100	.17	1.33
Mental health	30	300	.75	—	—	—	.75
Subtotal			$ 28.50			$ 2.67	$ 25.83
Hospital outpatient							
Surgery	70	$1,200	$ 7.00	—	—	—	$ 7.00
X-ray & lab	400	250	8.33	—	—	—	8.33
Emergency room	120	250	2.50	80	50	.33	2.17
Subtotal			$ 17.83			$ .33	$ 17.50
Physician							
Inpatient visits	200	$ 100	$ 1.67	—	—	—	$ 1.67
Inpatient surgery	70	1,500	8.75	—	—	—	8.75
Outpatient surgery	400	200	6.67	—	—	—	6.67
Maternity	15	2,000	2.50	15	100	.13	2.37
Office visits	4,000	75	25.00	3,000	10	2.50	22.50
Emergency room	120	100	1.00	—	—	—	1.00
Mental health	350	125	3.65	350	10	.29	3.36
Subtotal			$ 49.24			$ 2.92	$ 46.32
Other							
Home Health	50	$ 200	$ .83	—	—	—	$ .83
Diagnostic X-ray & lab	700	125	7.29	—	—	—	7.29
Durable med. equip.	30	300	.75	—	—	—	.75
Ambulance	35	400	1.17	35	50	.15	$ 1.02
Subtotal			$ 10.04			$ .15	$ 9.89
Total			$105.61			$ 6.07	$ 99.54
Coordination of benefits (2%)							(1.99)
							97.55
Net health care cost retention (15%)							14.63
PMPM requirement							$112.18

be used and that the HMO will pay the hospital(s) an average rate of $900 per day. To convert this to PMPM basis, the following calculation would be performed:

$$\$26.25 = \frac{.350 \times \$900}{12}$$

There is also a copayment provision in this insurance package that requires a $100 copayment, but it is not expected that all 350 days will be subject to the copayment provision. Most likely, the copayment is in the form of a deductible payment that is paid upon admission. The expected copayment to be received for medical surgical patients is .300 times $100, or

$30, which is then converted to a PMPM basis of $2.50. The net PMPM cost of medical surgical benefits is then $23.75 ($26.25 − $2.50). The copayment is subtracted from the expected payments to providers because this payment from the subscriber offsets provider payments. The health plan will pay $26.25 per member per month to providers, but it will recover $2.50 in direct payments from the subscriber to the health plan. Similar methodology would be applied to the other cost categories.

The total cost of health care benefits expected to be paid using Table 3–5 is $99.54. This amount is net of copayments, but does not reflect any coordination of benefit (COB) recoveries. COB recoveries are expected to be 2 percent of the total and reduce the health care cost of this insurance package to $97.55. The HMO needs to mark up this amount by 15 percent to cover administrative costs and reserves, and to build in a profit requirement. The required PMPM price is then $112.18.

The process of pricing is relatively easy as the example shows. The most difficult part is forecasting, and the most difficult area is expected utilization. For example, how certain are we that 350 days of medical-surgical care will be delivered as the forecast states? If 400 days of medical-surgical care were required rather than the budgeted 350, the additional cost would be $3.75 PMPM. This may seem like a small variance, but it should be remembered that margins in most HMOs are not large. Small variations in utilization can have disastrous effects on the financial performance of an HMO.

Tables 3–6 and 3–7 provide some utilization averages from the AAHP. The tables clearly show that major differences exist among gender, age, and region. Females in child-bearing years are more likely to use medical services than males of the same age. The pacific region of the United States has lower utilization than other regions, perhaps attributed to higher managed care penetration rates or to differences in practice patterns of physicians. The type of benefit package also can have a dramatic influence on utili-

Table 3–6 Inpatient Utilization Rates

Region	Acute Inpatient Days per 1,000	
	0–64 Years	Over 65 Years
New England	237	937
South Atlantic	317	1,237
East North Central	242	1,174
Pacific	192	1,172

Source: Reprinted with permission from AAHP HMO & PPO Industry Profile, 1995–1996 Edition, © American Association of Health Plans.

zation. A policy with liberal benefits for mental health probably will have much greater mental health utilization than one with more stringent benefits. Perhaps the best source of information on expected utilization is prior utilization for the covered population. What were inpatient usage rates last year? How many office visits were made? What kinds of chronic conditions exist in the population? Have physician practice patterns changed or are they likely to change as a result of different financial incentives? The HMO should have data that answer these questions as well as others and should be willing to release that data in the contracting phase.

Table 3–7 Ambulatory Utilization

Region	Ambulatory Encounters per Year	
	0–64 years	Over 65 years
New England	5.1	6.2
South Atlantic	5.0	NA
East North Central	3.7	6.6
Pacific	4.3	4.1

Source: Reprinted with permission from AAHP HMO & PPO Industry Profile, 1995–1996 Edition, © American Association of Health Plans.

One of the first major effects of managed care programs is a dramatic reduction in inpatient usage. The biggest area of cost is in inpatient usage, and plans that provide financial incentives for reducing inpatient days almost always experience significant declines in inpatient days per 1,000. The use of withholds and risk pools described earlier provide strong financial incentives for physicians to decrease usage rates. Some analysts are predicting that inpatient days per 1,000 could drop as low as 100 for the population younger than 65 years in mature managed care markets.

The cost per unit is not a terribly difficult item to forecast and usually is established in the contract. The HMO knows, for example, they will pay $900 per medical–surgical inpatient day, subject only to a withhold and/or risk pool. The only real issue confronted here is one of negotiation. The HMO wants to get the lowest possible price from the provider, and the provider wants to get the highest possible price from the HMO. If the provider is reasonably certain that dramatic reductions in utilization can occur, it might make sense to negotiate a capitation arrangement. For example, the hospital in Table 3–5 may decide that rather than receive $900 per day for medical-surgical care, it would rather have $23.75 PMPM, subject to its collection of the copayment. If it can keep usage rates down, the hospital stands to make much more money. However, if usage rates increase above 350 days per 1,000, it will lose money. This is a fundamental principle behind risk return tradeoffs. The entity assuming the risk gets the return or loss.

A provider or the provider's appointed IDS agent, however, needs to make an important decision during negotiation. Namely, the provider must decide whether to provide the services internally or buy contractually required services. For example, the hospital is scheduled to receive $300 a day for inpatient mental health services. Should it provide this service internally, assuming it has the delivery capability, or should it contract this out to a specialized mental health provider? The hospital may decide that it is bet-ter off to contract out inpatient mental health benefits for $300 a day and divert its resources to areas where it has a significant competitive advantage, such as cardiology or orthopedics. In some cases, there is no choice because the provider may not have the capability. For example, a primary care medical group that did not have any specialists would be required to negotiate contracts with specialty physicians to provide services if the primary care group contracted for all physician services.

Before we conclude this section on pricing, there are several issues that are of paramount importance to providers or their IDS agents who are negotiating capitated rates with an HMO or directly with an employer.

Delineation of the Set of Covered Services

A provider and health plan should carefully define the set of services covered under their agreement. For example, are transplants and AIDS patients included under the plan? A useful way to summarize this discussion is through a responsibility matrix. The responsibility matrix would list services in the rows and parties responsible in the columns. This matrix could be a part of the formal contract. Included in this category is the specific listing of carve-outs or services that are not included as part of the provider's responsibility, such as mental health.

Determination of Break-Even Service Volumes

Providers that accept a capitation rate have a different break-even structure as Figure 3–4 shows. In a capitation environment, revenue is fixed and costs vary with volume. For a fixed number of covered people, the provider wishes to minimize services or encounters. The provider accepting a capitation rate must carefully determine the maximum amount of service that could be provided before costs would exceed revenues.

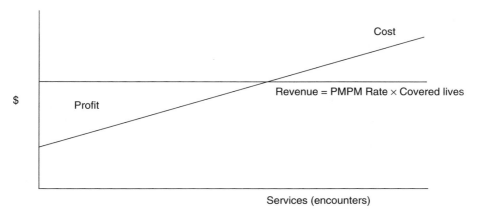

Figure 3–4 Break-Even Analysis in a Capitated Environment

Cost and Use of Stop Loss Coverage

Providers may have the option of buying stop loss coverage from the HMO or another insurer to cover costs of patients with catastrophic illnesses. For example, a hospital may negotiate a $75,000 stop loss on inpatient care. Whenever a patient incurred charges greater than $75,000, the stop loss insurer would pay the hospital for all costs above the threshold. In a like manner, physicians may negotiate lower stop loss limits of $7,500 per patient for physician charges.

Adverse Selection Provisions

Some reference should be made to adverse selection of HMO members. If a significant number of chronically ill patients, such as patients with AIDS, are attracted to the HMO, both the HMO and the providers may lose. However, if the HMO has subcapitated all its providers with no adverse selection provisions, it might be encouraged to market its policies to anyone at lower-than-required rates because the HMO has a guaranteed cost because it has capitated its providers.

Reporting Requirements

In capitated contracts, providers must closely monitor utilization rates frequently. Small changes in usage rates can destroy profitability quickly. Data systems must be in place to collect and report this information frequently. Providers also must be aware of the potential for an unrecorded liability referred to as incurred but not reported (IBNR). This covers situations when services have been delivered but no claim has been received to date. Providers under capitation may be obligated to pay for services not performed in their network and should be aware of this potential liability. For example, a hospital that contracted out mental health services may not know at any point in time the total outstanding liability. These amounts, although small in relationship to total cost, can produce severe distortions of estimated profitability on contracts unless information about these changes is reported promptly and reasonable estimates of expected costs are made.

MEDICARE AND MEDICAID RISK CONTRACTS

Perhaps the last frontier for major managed care expansion is the Medicare and Medicaid markets. Figure 3–5 presents a graph showing the recent growth in managed care programs. Both Medicare and Medicaid have experienced dramatic growth in managed care and it is ex-

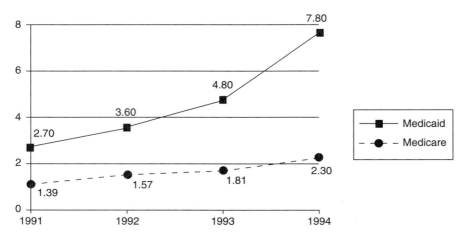

Figure 3–5 Medicare and Medicaid Managed Care Population (Millions)

pected that this growth will accelerate even more in the future. The reason for the growth of managed care in Medicare and Medicaid is the potential for cost reduction, especially in inpatient areas. Medicare inpatient days per 1,000 average approximately 2,700 to 2,800 in the traditional fee-for-service plans but decrease to 1,200 in Medicare risk contracts. Medicaid inpatient days per 1,000 average 1,100 in traditional programs but decrease to 600 in managed care programs. The potential for cost reduction is enormous and government fiscal pressure is forcing the movement to managed care.

Because Medicaid is a state-run health care program, there is no uniform program. Each state has defined its own program and will be different from programs in other states. As of 1994, there were twelve states that had received Section 1115 waivers that permit states to engage in Medicaid demonstration projects. These waivers are largely used to expand Medicaid enrollment in HMOs. In many of these contracts, long-term care is eliminated or carved out because nursing home expenditures are such a large percentage of the total Medicaid budget, and prediction of utilization can be speculative.

Medicare is encouraging beneficiaries to drop fee-for-service arrangements and switch to an HMO or a competitive medical plan (CMP). A CMP is similar to an HMO but does not have to meet all the requirements to become federally qualified. The Medicare HMO/CMP plan is at risk for all services provided by Medicare. Medicare reimburses health plans 95 percent of the estimated fee-for-service payment. The base rate is known as the adjusted average per capita cost (AAPCC) and is computed for each county in the United States. The AAPCC is the government's estimate of what fee-for-service costs would have been in the next fiscal year. Individual county rates are published in the Health Care Financing Administration AAPCC rate book. Categories include demographic cost factors for Medicare Part A and Part B. These county rates are further adjusted for gender, age, and institutionalized status. Rates can vary enormously by region of the country. In one recent year, the range was $680 PMPM in New York City to $180 PMPM in South Dakota. Potential contractors must review their projected costs using a format similar to the one presented in Table 3–5 and compare those with the allowed Medicare AAPCC.

LEGAL AND REGULATORY ISSUES

There are a number of legal and regulatory issues that affect the formation and operation of provider-based managed care organizations, especially integrated delivery systems. Among them are the following:

Antitrust

One concern with loose affiliations of physicians, such as an IPA, is the potential for price fixing. If the physicians do not share risk and have not commingled their assets and liabilities, the government may view an IPA arrangement that forms to negotiate prices with insurers as an attempt to fix prices. Similar arguments would apply to loose affiliations of hospitals or other providers who are not financially integrated, but who merely created an association to negotiate prices.

Inurement

If a nonprofit entity is involved in the creation of an IDS with physicians, it must be careful to ensure that it is not giving away more than it is receiving in value. This covers situations of physician practice acquisition, rental of space, or the provision of other services to physicians or other groups. The nonprofit entity must not have its resources used to the benefit of any individual. A "commercially reasonable" test is often used to assess the potential of inurement. Did the nonprofit entity pay more for something that was commercially reasonable or provide services at a price less than commercially reasonable? In the areas of physician practice acquisition, did the nonprofit entity pay more than fair market value for the practice?

Licensure As an Insurer

It is not clear at this stage whether a provider or provider group, such as an IDS, is required to be licensed as an HMO if it accepts payment on a capitated basis for services that it does not provide. For example, if a primary care group contracted with an HMO for all physician services, not just primary care, would it be required to be licensed by the state as an HMO? Increasingly, many IDS organizations are being required to become licensed as HMOs if they contract out some of the medical services to organizations that are not part of its corporate system.

Incentive Payments to Physicians To Reduce Services

Payments to physicians that provide incentives for fewer services may not be legal if they provide incentives to provide services less than medically necessary. Practically all present HMO arrangements currently have financial rewards for reduced services and the pivotal point may be the term "medically necessary."

Intentional Torts

If physicians or other health care providers commit an act of malpractice because they wish to make more money, this may be construed as an intentional tort and their malpractice insurance may not be obligated to pay if wrongdoing was found to occur. Physicians may be potentially liable under existing payment arrangements if their malpractice insurer could argue medical services were denied to make more money. For example, a doctor who failed to authorize a mammogram for a woman with a history of family breast cancer may be liable for an intentional tort if the physician was capitated and routinely scheduled mammograms for non-HMO patients with similar histories.

Corporate Practice of Medicine

In some states, physicians are precluded from being employed in corporations that are not owned by physicians. This may limit the kind of organizational structure that can be used to acquire physician practices.

There are many other legal and regulatory issues that may affect business practices in managed care relationships. Outside legal advice should be sought to investigate possible problems and solutions for those areas cited previously, as well as others.

SUMMARY

This chapter has dealt with the topic of managed care and the evolving issues that affect financial management in managed care situations. Managed care is not a new development in many respects. Health plans always have been in the business of accepting prepaid dollars in return for the promise to pay for any contractual medical benefits provided to the plan member. The new twist in managed care is really on the payment side. Health plans have historically paid providers, doctors, and hospitals on a fee-for-service basis. The health plan then assumed all the risk for utilization variances, whereas the provider assumed the risk of production, being able to provide services at costs less than negotiated prices. HMOs and other managed care organizations are also trying to shift utilization risk to providers by capitating payment to them.

Capitation payment systems require providers to know much more about the populations they are obligated to provide health care services to, and to do a much better job of forecasting. Pricing under a capitation payment system is easy to conceptualize but difficult to implement because most providers have little experience with utilization variation in a covered population. Historical use rates may be available, but managed care has created sizable shifts in utilization rates and forecasting the magnitude of those changes is difficult.

IDSs have formed to try to place providers closer to the premium dollar flowing from the employer. Many of these IDS organizations are presently hospital-dominated, but physicians are increasingly asking why they should not take charge in the managed care world because they have the most experience and the greatest ability to actually manage care and achieve cost savings. It is not clear whether the capital and organizational ability of the hospital or the patient management ability of the physician will win, or whether true partnerships will evolve.

ASSIGNMENTS

1. HMOs are a subset of alternative health insurance options. How does an HMO differ from a traditional indemnity health insurance plan?
2. You have been hired as a consultant to a major health insurance company to help identify ways to reduce payments for health care benefits. Please identify some possible methods that may be useful in cutting costs.
3. You represent a medical group that is considering joining a PHO whose sole objective is to negotiate with HMOs and employers for the provision of hospital and physician services on a capitated basis. If your state regards this PHO as a health insurance company and requires licensure, what possible effects might this have?
4. Your multispecialty group has been approached by an HMO that wishes you to contract with them for the provision of all physician services for a fixed capitated rate on a PMPM basis. How would you decide what to do in this situation?
5. You represent an integrated delivery system that is in negotiations with an HMO for a capitated rate to cover all hospital and physician services for a defined population. The following utilization data have been given to you, which details last year's usage rates. You have included in this table your expected costs for selected services. Using the data presented in Exhibit 3–1, calculate a required break-even rate for this contract, assuming that you need a 15 percent retention factor to cover administrative costs.

Exhibit 3–1

Category	Annual Frequency per 1,000	Unit Cost	PMPM	Copay Frequency per 1,000	Copay Amount	Copay PMPM	Net PMPM
Hospital inpatient							
Medical-surgical	400	$1,000		0	0		
Maternity	15	$1,000		0	0		
Mental health	50	$ 400		0	0		
Subtotal							
Hospital outpatient							
Surgery	100	$1,500		0	0		
X-ray & lab	500	$ 300		0	0		
Emergency room	150	$ 300		150	$50		
Subtotal							
Physician							
Inpatient surgery	100	$2,000		0	0		
Outpatient surgery	500	$ 300		0	0		
Office visits	5,000	$ 100		5,000	$10		
Inpatient visits	250	$ 150		0	0		
Mental health	400	$ 150		400	$20		
Subtotal							
Total							

6. Memorial Hospital is trying to calculate their expected payments from a proposed fee structure with a local HMO. The HMO projects its hospital budget at 465 patient days per 1,000 members, with a payment rate of $1,000 per patient day. The covered population is 25,000 members, which produces a hospital budget of $11,625,000 (465 × 25 × $1,000). The HMO proposes that a 10 percent withhold be put into effect, which translates to an actual per diem payment of $900. The risk pool would be shared equally by the doctors (one half) and the hospital (one half). Any negative balance in the risk pool would be assumed by the HMO. Calculate the amount of payment to Memorial Hospital under two assumptions: 550 patient days per 1,000 and 430 patient days per 1,000.

SOLUTIONS

1. HMOs differ from traditional indemnity plans in several ways. First, HMOs usually provide a wider range of benefits, especially in the area of outpatient benefits. To offset the cost of wider benefits, most HMOs restrict the panel of providers, hospitals, and doctors that can be seen. HMO members wishing to see a doctor or hospital not in the network would be required to pay for those benefits themselves. Sometimes an HMO may offer a POS option that does permit members to seek care from providers not in the HMO's network, but the member must pay a portion, sometimes a substantial portion, of the cost. HMOs may also pay their health care providers on a capitated basis. This is in contrast to indemnity plans, which usually pay providers on a fee-for-service basis.

2. Health care benefit cost can be expressed as the product of utilization and price. Possible methods for reducing prices paid to providers would include selective contracting with the providers on a discounted basis, use of copayment provisions and deductibles to shift some of the cost to the insured health plan member, and development of a fee schedule for all providers that limit payments. Utilization options for reducing costs would include methods that either reduced the frequency of procedures or used less expensive procedures. For example, better utilization review and prior authorization for medical procedures could be implemented. Case management of chronic conditions might also cut utilization by reducing the use of expensive inpatient procedures. Incentive structures for physicians such as capitation payments or risk pools might also be useful in decreasing utilization.

3. Aside from the legal filing requirements and increased government supervision of the PHO, it is also likely that certain reserve requirements must be maintained. These reserves may range from several hundred thousand dollars to several million dollars. This will create additional capital requirements for the PHO creation.

4. The critical issue to be resolved is the maximum amount of service that could be provided under the PMPM rate and still break even. In a fixed PMPM payment system, revenue is fixed, while costs vary with volume. The group needs to carefully consider the expected costs per unit. If total expected cost on a PMPM basis is less than the PMPM premium, it might make sense to accept the capitated rate.

5. Exhibit 3–2 (see page 74) calculates a required net PMPM rate of $138.50. When that rate is increased 15 percent to cover retention, the required PMPM rate would be $159.28.

6. Exhibit 3–3 (see page 74) provides the calculations for hospital payment under the two assumptions.

Exhibit 3–2

Category	Annual Frequency per 1,000	Unit Cost	PMPM	Copay Frequency per 1,000	Copay Amount	Copay PMPM	Net PMPM
Hospital inpatient							
Medical-surgical	400	$1,000	$33.33	0	0	$0.00	$33.33
Maternity	15	$1,000	1.25	0	0	0.00	1.25
Mental health	50	$ 400	1.67	0	0	0.00	1.67
Subtotal			$36.25			0.00	$36.25
Hospital outpatient							
Surgery	100	$1,500	12.50	0	0	0.00	12.50
X-ray & lab	500	$ 300	12.50	0	0	0.00	12.50
Emergency room	150	$ 300	3.75	150	$50	0.63	3.12
Subtotal			$28.75			$0.63	28.12
Physician							
Inpatient surgery	100	$2,000	16.67	0	0	0.00	16.67
Outpatient surgery	500	$ 300	12.50	0	0	0.00	12.50
Office visits	5,000	$ 100	41.67	5,000	$10	4.17	37.50
Inpatient visits	250	$ 150	3.13	0	0	0.00	3.13
Mental health	400	$ 150	5.00	400	$20	0.67	4.33
Subtotal			$78.97			$4.84	$74.13
Total			$143.97			$5.47	$138.50

Exhibit 3–3

Patient Day Level	Hospital Payment @ $900 per Day	Risk Pool (Budget - Paid)	Hospital Share of Risk Pool	Total Hospital Payment
550 PD per 1,000	$12,375,000	$(750,000)	Negative /0 Share	$12,375,000
430 PD per 1,000	$ 9,675,000	$1,950,000	$975,000	$10,650,000

4

General Principles of Accounting

Information does not happen by itself; it must be generated by an individual or a formally designed system. Financial information is no exception. The accounting system generates most financial information to provide quantitative data, primarily financial in nature, that are useful in making economic decisions about economic entities.

FINANCIAL VERSUS MANAGERIAL ACCOUNTING

Financial accounting is the branch of accounting that provides general-purpose financial statements or reports to aid many decision-making groups, internal and external to the organization, in making a variety of decisions. The primary outputs of financial accounting are four financial statements that are discussed in Chapter 5 (see Tables 5–1, 5–2, 5–3, and 5–4 and Exhibit 5–1). They are the following:

1. balance sheet,
2. statement of revenues and expenses,
3. statement of cash flows, and
4. statement of changes in fund balances.

The field of financial accounting is restricted in many ways regarding how certain events or business transactions may be accounted for. The term "generally accepted accounting principles" is often used to describe the body of rules and requirements that shape the preparation of the four primary financial statements. For example, an organization's financial statements that have been audited by an independent certified public accountant (CPA) would bear the following language in an unqualified opinion:

We have audited the accompanying balance sheets of the XYZ Hospital (the Hospital) as of December 31, 19X9 and 19X8, and the related statements of operations, changes in net assets, and cash flows for the years then ended. These financial statements are the responsibility of the Hospital's management. Our responsibility is to express an opinion on these financial statements based on our audits.

We conducted our audits in accordance with generally accepted auditing standards. Those standards require that we plan and perform the audit to obtain reasonable assurance about whether the financial statements are free of material misstatement. An audit includes examining, on a test basis, evidence supporting the amounts and disclosures in the financial statements.

An audit also includes assessing the accounting principles used and significant estimates made by management, as well as evaluating the overall financial statement presentation. We believe that our audits provide a reasonable basis for our opinion.

In our opinion, such financial statements present fairly, in all material respects, the financial position of the Hospital at December 31, 19X9 and 19X8, and the results of its operations and its operations and its cash flows for the years then ended in conformity with generally accepted accounting principles.

Financial accounting is not limited to preparation of the four statements. An increasing number of additional financial reports are being required, especially for external users for specific decision-making purposes. This is particularly important in the health care industry. For example, hospitals submit cost reports to a number of third-party payers, such as Blue Cross, Medicare, and Medicaid. They also submit financial reports to a large number of regulatory agencies, such as planning agencies, rate review agencies, service associations, and many others. In addition, CPAs often prepare financial projections that are used by investors in capital financing. These statements, although not usually audited by independent CPAs, are, for the most part, prepared in accordance with the same generally accepted accounting principles that govern the preparation of the four basic financial statements.

Managerial accounting is primarily concerned with the preparation of financial information for specific purposes, usually for internal users. Because this information is used within the organization, there is less need for a body of principles restricting its preparation. Presumably, the user and the preparer can meet to discuss questions of interpretation. Uniformity and comparability of information, which are desired goals for financial accountants, are clearly less important to management accountants.

PRINCIPLES OF ACCOUNTING

In addressing the principles of accounting, we are concerned with both sets of accounting information, financial and managerial. Although managerial accounting has no formally adopted set of principles, it relies strongly on financial accounting principles. Understanding the principles and basics of financial accounting is therefore critical to understanding both financial and managerial accounting information.

The case example in our discussion of the principles of financial accounting is a newly formed, nonprofit health care organization, which we refer to as "Alpha HCO."

Accounting Entity

Obviously, in any accounting there must be an entity for which the financial statements are being prepared. Specifying the entity on which the accounting will focus defines the information that is pertinent. Drawing these boundaries is the underlying concept behind the accounting entity principle.

Alpha HCO is the entity for which we will account and prepare financial statements. We are not interested in the individuals who may have incorporated Alpha HCO or other health care organizations in the community, but solely in Alpha HCO's financial transactions.

Defining the entity is not as clear-cut as one might expect. Significant problems arise, especially when the legal entity is different from the accounting entity. For example, if one physician owns a clinic through a sole proprietorship arrangement, the accounting entity may be the clinic operation, whereas the legal entity includes the physician and the physician's personal resources as well. A hospital may be part of a university or government agency, or it might be owned by a large corporation organized on a profit or nonprofit basis. Indeed, many hospitals now have become subsidiaries of a holding company as a result of corporate restructuring. Careful attention must be paid to the definition of the accounting entity in these situations. If the entity is not properly defined, evaluation of its financial information may be useless at best and misleading at worst.

The common practice of municipalities directly paying the fringe benefits of municipal employees employed in the hospital illustrates this situation. Such expenses may never show up in the hospital's accounts, resulting in an understatement of the expenses associated with running the hospital. In many cases, this may produce a bias in the rate-setting process.

Money Measurement

Accounting in general, and financial accounting in particular, are concerned with measuring economic resources and obligations and their changing levels for the accounting entity under consideration. The accountant's yardstick for measuring is not metered to size, color, weight, or other attributes; it is limited exclusively to money. However, there are significant problems in money measurement, which will be discussed in the following text.

Economic resources are defined as scarce means, limited in supply but essential to economic activity. They include supplies, buildings, equipment, money, claims to receive money,

and ownership interests in other enterprises. The terms economic resources and assets may be interchanged for most practical purposes. Economic obligations are responsibilities to transfer economic resources or provide services to other entities in the future, usually in return for economic resources received from other entities in the past through the purchase of assets, the receipt of services, or the acceptance of loans. For most practical purposes, the terms "economic obligations" and "liabilities" may be used interchangeably.

In most normal situations, assets exceed liabilities in money-measured value. Liabilities represent the claim of one entity on another's assets; any excess or remaining residual interest may be claimed by the owner. In fact, for entities with ownership interest, this residual interest is called "owner's equity."

In most nonprofit entities, including health care organizations, there is no residual ownership claim. Any assets remaining in a liquidated not-for-profit entity, after all liabilities have been dissolved, legally become the property of the state. Residual interest is referred to as "fund balance" or "net assets" for most nonprofit health care organizations.

In the Alpha HCO example, assume that the community donated $1,000,000 in cash to the health care organization at its formation, hypothetically assumed to be December 31, 19X6. At that time, a listing of its assets, liabilities, and fund balance would be prepared in a balance sheet and read as presented in Exhibit 4–1.

Exhibit 4–1

Alpha HCO Balance Sheet
December 31, 19X6

Assets	*Liabilities and Net Assets*
Cash $1,000,000	Net assets $1,000,000

Duality

One of the fundamental premises of accounting is a simple arithmetic requirement: the value of assets must always equal the combined value of liabilities and residual interest, which we have called fund balance. This basic accounting equation, the duality principle, may be stated as follows:

Assets = Liabilities + Net assets

This requirement means that a balance sheet will always balance: the value of the assets will always equal the value of claims, whether liabilities or fund balance, on those assets.

Changes are always occurring in organizations that affect the value of assets, liabilities, and fund balance. These changes are called transactions and represent the items that interest accountants. Examples of transactions are borrowing money, purchasing supplies, and constructing buildings. The important thing to remember is that each transaction must be carefully analyzed under the duality principle to keep the basic accounting equation in balance.

To better understand how important this principle is, let us analyze several transactions in our Alpha HCO example:

- Transaction 1. On January 2, 19X7, Alpha HCO buys a piece of equipment for $100,000. The purchase is financed with a $100,000 note from the bank.
- Transaction 2. On January 3, 19X7, Alpha HCO buys a building for $2,000,000, using $500,000 cash and issuing $1,500,000 worth of 20-year bonds.
- Transaction 3. On January 4, 19X7, Alpha HCO purchases $200,000 worth of supplies from a supply firm on a credit basis.

If balance sheets were prepared after each of these three transactions, they would appear as presented in Exhibit 4–2.

In each of these three transactions, the change in asset value is matched by an identical change in liability value. Thus, the basic accounting equation remains in balance.

It should be noted that, as the number of transactions increases, the number of individual asset and liability items also increases. In most organizations, there is a large number of these individual items, which are referred to as accounts. The listing of these accounts is often called a chart of accounts; it is a useful device for categorizing transactions related to a given health care organization. There is already significant uniformity among hospitals and other health care facilities in the chart of accounts used; however, there is also pressure, especially from external users of financial information, to move toward even more uniformity.

Cost Valuation

Many readers of financial statements make the mistake of assuming that reported balance sheet values represent the real worth of individual assets or liabilities. Asset and liability values reported in a balance sheet are based on their historical or acquisition cost. In most situations, asset values do not equal the amount of money that could be realized if the assets were sold. However, in many cases, the reported value of a liability in a balance sheet is a good approximation of the amount of money that would be required to extinguish the indebtedness.

Examining the alternatives to historical cost valuation helps clarify why the cost basis of valuation is used. The two primary alternatives to historical cost valuation of assets and liabilities are market value and replacement cost valuation.

Valuation of individual assets at their market value sounds simple enough and appeals to many users of financial statements. Creditors especially are often interested in what values assets would bring if liquidated. Current market

Exhibit 4–2

• *Transaction 1*

Alpha HCO Balance Sheet
January 2, 19X7

Assets		Liabilities and Net Assets	
Cash	$1,000,000	Notes payable	$ 100,000
Equipment	100,000	Net assets	1,000,000
Total	$1,100,000	Total	$1,100,000

Assets: Increase $100,000 (equipment increases by $100,000)
Liabilities: Increase $100,000 (notes payable increase by $100,000)

• *Transaction 2*

Alpha HCO Balance Sheet
January 3, 19X7

Assets		Liabilities and Net Assets	
Cash	$ 500,000	Notes payable	$ 100,000
Equipment	100,000	Bonds payable	1,500,000
Building	2,000,000	Net assets	1,000,000
Total	$2,600,000	Total	$2,600,000

Assets: Increase $1,500,000 (cash decreases by $500,000 and building increases by $2,000,000)
Liabilities: Increase $1,500,000 (bonds payable increase by $1,500,000)

• *Transaction 3*

Alpha HCO Balance Sheet
January 4, 19X7

Assets		Liabilities and Net Assets	
Cash	$ 500,000	Accounts payable	$ 200,000
Supplies	200,000	Notes payable	100,000
Equipment	100,000	Bonds payable	1,500,000
Building	2,000,000	Net assets	1,000,000
Total	$2,800,000	Total	$2,800,000

Assets: Increase $200,000 (supplies increase by $200,000)
Liabilities: Increase $200,000 (accounts payable increase by $200,000)

values give decision makers an approximation of liquidation values.

The market value method's lack of objectivity, however, is a serious problem. In most normal situations, established markets dealing in second-hand merchandise do not exist. Decision makers must rely on individual appraisals. Given the current state of the art of appraisal, two appraisers are likely to produce different estimates of market value for identical assets. Accountants' insistence on objectivity in measurement thus eliminates market valuation of assets as a viable alternative.

Replacement cost valuation of assets measures assets by the money value required to replace them. This concept of valuation is extremely useful for many decision-making purposes. For example, management decisions to continue delivery of certain services should be affected by the replacement cost of resources, not their historical or acquisition cost—which is considered to be a sunk cost, irrelevant to future decisions. Planning agencies or other regulatory agencies also should consider estimates of replacement cost to avoid bias. Considering only historical cost may improperly make old facilities appear more efficient than new or proposed facilities and projects.

Replacement cost may be a useful concept of valuation; however, it too suffers from lack of objectivity in measurement. Replacement cost valuation depends on how an item is replaced. For example, given the rate of technologic change in the general economy, especially in the health care industry, few assets today would be replaced with like assets. Instead, more refined or capable assets probably would replace them. What is the replacement cost in this situation? Is it the cost of the new, improved asset or the present cost of an identical asset that most likely would not be purchased? Compound this question by the large number of manufacturers selling roughly equivalent items and you have some idea of the inherent difficulty and subjectivity in replacement cost valuation.

Historical cost valuation, with all its faults, is thus the basis that the accounting profession has

chosen to value assets and liabilities in most circumstances. Accountants use it rather than replacement cost largely because it is more objective. There is currently some fairly strong pressure from inside and outside the accounting profession to switch to replacement cost valuation, but it is still uncertain whether this pressure will be successful.

One final, important point should be noted: At the time of initial asset valuation, the values assigned by historical cost valuation and replacement cost valuation are identical. The historical cost value is most often criticized for assets that have long, useful lives, such as building and equipment. Over a period of many years, the historical cost and replacement cost values tend to diverge dramatically, in part because general inflation in our economy erodes the dollar's purchasing power. A dollar of today is simply not as valuable as a dollar of ten years ago. This problem could be remedied, without sacrificing the objectivity of historical cost measurement, by selecting a unit of purchasing power as the unit of measure: Transactions then would not be accounted in dollars but in dollars of purchasing power at a given point in time, usually the year for which the financial statements are being prepared. This issue is addressed later in this chapter, under Stable Monetary Unit.

Required Return on Investment and Valuation Alternatives

Business firms, both voluntary nonprofit and investor-owned, must produce returns on their investment greater than the cost of capital used to finance their investment. For example, a business could not borrow money at 10 percent and invest the proceeds in projects earning only 5 percent and expect to stay in business. Valuation of the investment at cost, market value, or replacement cost can have a significant effect on basic business decisions such as expansion or closure. To illustrate this point, consider James Nursing Home, a fictitious voluntary nonprofit clinic, with the following financial data:

James Nursing Home
Financial Data
19X9

Cash Flow	$ 10,000
Cost of Capital	12%
Investment Cost	$ 80,000
Investment–Replacement Cost	$150,000
Investment–Market Value	$ 60,000

Return on investment (ROI) for James Nursing Home is 12.5 percent under a cost valuation ($10,000/$80,000), 6.7 percent under replacement-cost valuation ($10,000/$150,000), and 16.7 percent under a market-value valuation ($10,000/60,000). What should the management and board of James Nursing Home do?

First, the ROI calculated under cost valuation is meaningless for future decisions. An ROI based upon historical cost tells you how well the investment has done, not how well it will do in the future. ROI calculated under replacement-cost valuation will tell the decision maker the return using current replacement-cost values. In our example, the James Nursing Home is not profitable given current replacement cost values

and is not viable in the future. Unless expectations about future cash flows change, the nursing home should not receive significant new investment. ROI calculated under market values shows the James Nursing Home to be viable in the short run. It is generating an ROI of 16.7 percent, which exceeds its cost of capital, 12 percent.

Figure 4–1 illustrates the decision framework.

Accrual Accounting

Accrual accounting is a fundamental premise of accounting. It means that transactions of a business enterprise are recognized during the period to which they relate, not necessarily during the periods in which cash is received or paid.

It is common to hear people talk about an accrual versus a cash basis of accounting. Most of us think in cash-basis terms. We measure our personal financial success during the year by the amount of cash we realized. Seldom do we consider such things as wear and tear on our cars and other personal items or the differences between earned and uncollected income. Perhaps if we

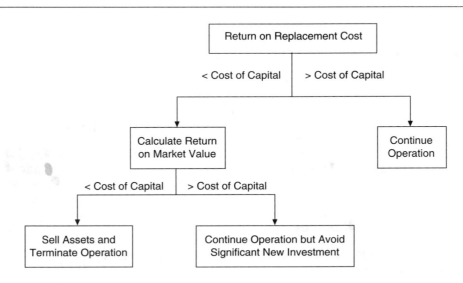

Figure 4–1 Return on Investment Relationships

accrued expenses for items such as depreciation on heating systems, air conditioning systems, automobiles, and furniture, we might see a different picture of our financial well-being.

The accrual basis of accounting significantly affects the preparation of financial statements in general; however, its major impact is on the preparation of the statement of revenues and expenses. The following additional transactions for Alpha Hospital illustrate the importance of the accrual principle:

- Transaction 4. Alpha HCO bills patients $100,000 on January 16, 19X7, for services provided to them.
- Transaction 5. Alpha HCO pays employees $60,000 for their wages and salaries on January 18, 19X7.
- Transaction 6. Alpha HCO receives $80,000 in cash from patients who were billed earlier in Transaction 4 on January 23, 19X7.
- Transaction 7. Alpha HCO pays the $200,000 of accounts payable on January 27, 19X7, for the purchase of supplies that took place on January 4, 19X7.

Balance sheets prepared after each of these transactions would appear as presented in Exhibit 4–3.

In Transactions 4 and 5, there is an effect on Alpha HCO's residual interest or its fund balance. In Transaction 4, an increase in fund balance occurred because patients were billed for services previously rendered. Increases in fund balance or owner's equity resulting from the sale of goods or delivery of services are called revenues. It should be noted that this increase occurred even though no cash was actually collected until January 23, 19X7, illustrating the accrual principle of accounting. Recognition of revenue occurs when the revenue is earned, not necessarily when it is collected.

In Transaction 5, a reduction in fund balance occurs. Costs incurred by a business enterprise to provide goods or services that reduce fund balance or owners equity are called expenses. Under the accrual principle, expenses are recognized when assets are used up or liabilities are incurred in the production and delivery of goods or services, not necessarily when cash is paid.

The difference between revenue and expense is often referred to as net income. In the hospital

---

Exhibit 4–3

- *Transaction 4*

Alpha HCO Balance Sheet
January 16, 19X7

Assets		Liabilities and Net Assets	
Cash	$ 500,000	Accounts payable	$ 200,000
Accounts receivable	100,000	Notes payable	100,000
Supplies	200,000	Bonds payable	1,500,000
Equipment	100,000	Net assets	1,100,000
Building	2,000,000		
Total	$2,900,000	Total	$2,900,000

Assets: Increase $100,000 (accounts receivable increase by $100,000)
Net assets: Increases $100,000

continues

Exhibit 4–3 continued

• *Transaction 5*

Alpha HCO Balance Sheet
January 18, 19X7

Assets		Liabilities and Net Assets	
Cash	$ 440,000	Accounts payable	$ 200,000
Accounts receivable	100,000	Notes payable	100,000
Supplies	200,000	Bonds payable	1,500,000
Equipment	100,000	Net assets	1,040,000
Building	2,000,000		
Total	$2,840,000	Total	$2,840,000

Assets: Decrease by $60,000 (cash decreases by $60,000)
Net assets: Decreases by $60,000

• *Transaction 6*

Alpha HCO Balance Sheet
January 23, 19X7

Assets		Liabilities and Net Assets	
Cash	$ 520,000	Accounts payable	$ 200,000
Accounts receivable	20,000	Notes payable	100,000
Supplies	200,000	Bonds payable	1,500,000
Equipment	100,000	Net assets	1,040,000
Building	2,000,000		
Total	$2,840,000	Total	$2,840,000

Assets: No change (cash increases by $80,000; accounts receivable decrease by $80,000)

• *Transaction 7*

Alpha HCO Balance Sheet
January 27, 19X7

Assets		Liabilities and Net Assets	
Cash	$ 320,000	Accounts payable	$ 0
Accounts receivable	20,000	Notes payable	100,000
Supplies	200,000	Bonds payable	1,500,000
Equipment	100,000	Net assets	1,040,000
Building	2,000,000		
Total	$2,640,000	Total	$2,640,000

Assets: Decrease by $200,000 (cash decreases by $200,000)
Liabilities: Decrease by $200,000 (accounts payable decrease by $200,000)

and health care industry, this term may be used interchangeably with the term excess of revenues over expenses or revenues and gains in excess of expenses.

The income statement or statement of operations summarizes the revenues and expenses of a business enterprise over a defined period. If an income statement is prepared for the total life of an entity, that is, from inception to dissolution, the value for net income would be the same under both an accrual and a cash basis of accounting.

In most situations, frequent measurements of revenue and expense are demanded, creating some important measurement problems. Ideally, under the accrual accounting principle, expenses should be matched to the revenue that they helped create. For example, wage, salary, and supply costs usually can be easily associated with revenues of a given period. However, in certain circumstances, the association between revenue and expense is impossible to discover, necessitating the accountant's use of a systematic, rational method of allocating costs to a benefiting period. In the best example of this procedure, costs such as those associated with building and equipment are spread over the estimated useful life of the assets through the recording of depreciation.

To complete the Alpha HCO example, assume that the financial statements must be prepared at the end of January. Before they are prepared, certain adjustments must be made to the accounts to adhere fully to the accrual principle of accounting. The following adjustments might be recorded:

- Adjustment 1. There are currently $100,000 of patient charges that have been incurred but not yet billed.
- Adjustment 2. There are currently $50,000 worth of unpaid wages and salaries for which employees have performed services.
- Adjustment 3. A physical inventory count indicates that $50,000 worth of initial supplies have been used.

- Adjustment 4. The equipment of Alpha Hospital has an estimated useful life of ten years, and the cost is being allocated over this period. On a monthly basis, this amounts to an allocation of $833 per month.
- Adjustment 5. The building has an estimated useful life of forty years, and the cost of the building is being allocated equally over its estimated life. On a monthly basis, this amounts to $4,167.
- Adjustment 6. Although no payment has been made on either notes payable or bonds payable, there is an interest expense associated with using money for this one-month period. This interest expense will be paid later. Assume that the note payable carries an interest rate of 8 percent and the bond payable carries an interest rate of 6 percent. The actual amount of interest expense incurred for the month of January would be $8,167 ($667 on the note and $7,500 on the bond payable).

The effects of these adjustments on the balance sheet of Alpha Hospital and on the ending balance sheet that would be prepared after all the adjustments were made, are presented in Exhibit 4–4.

It is also possible to prepare the statement of revenues and expenses presented in Exhibit 4–5.

Note that the difference between revenue and expense during the month of January was $26,833, the exact amount by which the net assets of Alpha Hospital changed during the month. Alpha Hospital began the month with $1,000,000 in its net asset account and ended with $1,026,833. This illustrates an important point to remember when reading financial statements: the individual financial statements are fundamentally related to one another.

Stable Monetary Unit

The money measurement principle of accounting discussed earlier restricted accounting

Exhibit 4–4

Adjustment	Change	Account(s) Increased	Account(s) Decreased
1	$100,000	Net assets Accounts receivable	None None
2	$50,000	Wages and salaries payable	Net assets
3	$50,000	None	Net assets Supplies
4	$833	None *Accumulated depriciay*	Net assets Equipment
5	$4,167	None	Net assets Building
6	$8,167	Interest payable	Net assets

Alpha HCO Balance Sheet
January 31, 19X7

Assets		Liabilities and Net Assets	
Cash	$ 320,000	Wages and salaries payable	$ 50,000
Accounts receivable	120,000	Interest payable	8,167
Supplies	150,000	Notes payable	100,000
Equipment	99,167	Bonds payable	1,500,000
Building	1,995,833	Net assets	1,026,833
Total	$2,685,000	Total	$2,685,000

measures to money. In accounting in the United States, the unit of measure is the dollar. At the present time, no adjustment to changes in the general purchasing power of that unit is required in financial reports; a 1990 dollar is assumed to be equal in value to a 1998 dollar. This permits arithmetic operations, such as addition and subtraction. If this assumption was not made, addition of the unadjusted historical cost values of assets acquired during different periods would be inappropriate, like adding apples and oranges. Current, generally accepted accounting principles incorporate the stable monetary unit principle.

The stable monetary unit principle may not seem to pose any great problems. However, even modest rates of inflation at around 4 percent per year can quickly compound to produce major financial distortions. For example, a dollar paid in the year 2000 would be equivalent to 67 cents

Exhibit 4–5

Alpha HCO
Statement of Revenues and Expenses
For month ended January 31, 19X7

Revenues	$200,000
Less expenses	
Wages and salaries	$110,000
Supplies	50,000
Depreciation	5,000
Interest	8,167
Total	$173,167
Excess of revenues over expenses	$ 26,833

paid in 1990 with a 4 percent annual inflation rate. Imagine that the inflation rate in the economy is currently 100 percent, compounded monthly. Consider a neighborhood health care center that has all its expenses, except payroll, covered by grants from governmental agencies. Its employees have a contract that automatically adjusts their wages to changes in the general price level. (With a monthly inflation rate of 100 percent, it is no wonder.) Assume that revenues from patients are collected on the first day of the month after the one in which they were billed,

but that the employees are paid at the beginning of each month. Rates to patients are set so that the excess of revenues over expenses will be zero. With the first month's wages set equal to $100,000, the income and cash flow positions presented in Exhibit 4–6 result for the first six months of the year.

Note the tremendous difference between income and cash flow. Although the income statement would indicate a break-even operation, the cash balance at the end of June would be a negative $3,150,000. Obviously, the health care

Exhibit 4–6

	Income Flows			Cash Flows		
	Expense	Revenue	Net Income	Inflow	Outflow	Difference
January	$ 100,000	$ 100,000	0	$ 50,000	$ 100,000	($ 50,000)
February	200,000	200,000	0	100,000	200,000	(100,000)
March	400,000	400,000	0	200,000	400,000	(200,000)
April	800,000	800,000	0	400,000	800,000	(400,000)
May	1,600,000	1,600,000	0	800,000	1,600,000	(800,000)
June	3,200,000	3,200,000	0	1,600,000	3,200,000	(1,600,000)
	$6,300,000	$6,300,000	0	$3,150,000	$6,300,000	($3,150,000)

*$50,000 is equal to the revenue billed in December.

center's operations cannot continue indefinitely in light of the extreme cash hardship position imposed.

Fortunately, the rate of inflation in our economy is not 100 percent. However, smaller rates of inflation compounded over long periods could create similar problems. For example, setting rates equal to historical cost depreciation of fixed assets leaves the entity with a significant cash deficit when it is time to replace the asset. Many health care boards and management organizations of nonprofit firms do not adequately reflect increasing replacement costs in their pricing.

Fund Accounting

Fund accounting is a system in which an entity's assets and liabilities are segregated in the accounting records. Each fund may be considered an independent entity with its own self-balancing set of accounts. The basic accounting equation discussed under "Duality" must be satisfied for each fund: assets must equal liabilities plus fund balance for the particular fund in question. This is, in fact, how the term fund balance developed; a fund balance originally represented the residual interest for a particular fund.

The Financial Accounting Statement Board (FASB) pronouncement #117 changed the nature of fund accounting for voluntary nonprofit health care organizations. It stipulated that only three classifications of net assets or fund balance be used. They are the following:

• unrestricted net assets,
• temporarily restricted net assets, and
• permanently restricted net assets.

The last two categories of net assets, temporarily and permanently restricted net assets, are related to the existence of a donor-imposed restriction. The difference between the two is based upon the nature of the donor's restriction. Temporarily restricted assets are funds that can be used for a specific purpose only, or funds that

may be released for a specific purpose only, funds that may be released for general purposes after a passage of time. Permanently restricted net assets are often of an endowment nature. Only the income of the fund can be used, and the principal cannot be used to fund any purpose. Generally, donor-restricted net assets can consist of the following three common types:

1. specific-purpose funds,
2. plant replacement and expansion funds, and
3. endowment funds.

Specific-purpose funds are donated by individuals or organizations and restricted for purposes other than plant replacement and expansion or endowment. Monies received from government agencies to perform specific research or other work are examples of specific-purpose funds.

Plant-replacement and expansion funds are restricted for use in plant replacement and expansion. Assets purchased with these monies are not recorded in the fund. When the monies are used for plant purposes, the amounts are transferred to the unrestricted net assets. For example, if $200,000 in cash from the plant-replacement fund were used to acquire a piece of equipment, equipment and unrestricted net assets would be increased.

Endowment funds are contributed to be held intact for generating income. The income may or may not be restricted for specific purposes. Some endowments are classified as "term" endowments. That is, after the expiration of some period, the restriction on use of the principal is lifted. The balance is then transferred to the general fund.

CONVENTIONS OF ACCOUNTING

The accounting principles discussed up to this point are important in the preparation of financial statements. However, several widely accepted conventions modify the application of these principles in certain circumstances. Three of the more important conventions are discussed in the following text:

1. conservatism,
2. materiality, and
3. consistency.

Conservatism affects the valuation of some assets. Specifically, accountants use a "lower of cost" or "market rule" for valuing inventories and marketable securities. The lower of cost or market rule means that the value of a stock of inventory or marketable securities would be the actual cost or market value, whichever is less. For these resources, there is a deviation from cost valuation to market valuation whenever market value is lower.

Materiality permits certain transactions to be treated out of accordance with generally accepted accounting principles. This might be permitted because the transaction does not materially affect the presentation of financial position. For example, theoretically, paper clips may have an estimated useful life greater than one year. However, the cost of capitalizing this item and systematically and rationally allocating it over its useful life is not justifiable; the difference in financial position that would be created by not using generally accepted accounting principles would be immaterial.

Consistency limits the accounting alternatives that can be used. In any given transaction, there is usually a variety of available, generally acceptable, accounting treatments. For example, generally accepted accounting principles permit the use of double-declining balance, sum-of-

the-year digits, or straight-line methods for allocating the costs of depreciable assets over their estimated useful life; but the consistency convention limits an entity's ability to change from one acceptable method to another.

SUMMARY

In this chapter, we discussed the importance of generally accepted accounting principles in deriving financial information. Although these principles are formally required only in the preparation of audited financial statements, they influence the derivation of most financial information. An understanding of some of the basic principles is critical to an understanding of financial information in general.

The following six specific principles of accounting were discussed in some detail:

1. accounting entity,
2. money measurement,
3. duality,
4. cost valuation,
5. accrual accounting, and
6. stable monetary unit.

In addition to these, the general importance of fund accounting as it relates to the hospital and health care industry was discussed. The chapter concluded with a discussion of three conventions that may modify the application of generally accepted accounting principles in specific situations.

ASSIGNMENTS

1. ABC Medical Center has undergone a recent corporate reorganization. The structure presented in Exhibit 4–7 resulted. What difficulties might be experienced in preparing financial statements for the ABC Hospital?
2. Does the value of total assets represent the economic value of the entity?
3. What is the difference between stockholders' equity and fund balance or unrestricted net assets?
4. A home health care firm has purchased five automobiles. Each automobile costs $12,000 and has an estimated useful life of three years. Each year, the replacement cost of the automobiles is expected to increase 10 percent. At the end of the third year, replacement cost would be $15,972. The firm anticipates that each automobile will be used to make 1,500 patient visits per year. If the firm prices each visit to recover just the historical cost of the automobiles, it will include a capital cost of $2.67 per visit ($12,000 divided by 4,500 total visits). Assuming the revenue generated from this capital charge is invested at 10 percent, will the firm have enough funds available to meet its replacement cost? How would this situation change if price level depreciation were used to establish the capital charge?
5. A health maintenance organization (HMO) has just been formed. During its first year of operations, the organization reported an accounting loss of $500,000. Cash flow during the same period was a positive $500,000. How might this situation exist, and which measure better describes financial performance?
6. What is the difference between restricted and unrestricted net assets?
7. Why is consistency in financial reporting critical to fairness in financial representation?

Exhibit 4–7

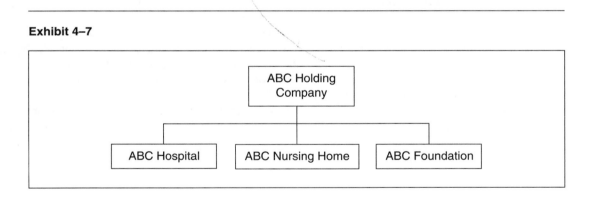

SOLUTIONS AND ANSWERS

1. It may be difficult to associate specific assets and liabilities for the ABC Hospital. For example, debt may have been issued by the holding company to finance projects for both the hospital and the nursing home. In addition, commonly used assets may be involved, such as a dietary department providing meals for both hospital and nursing home patients. Some expenses also may be difficult to trace to either the hospital or the nursing home. For example, how should expenses that are common to the hospital, the nursing home, and the foundation (such as administrative expenses of the holding company) be allocated? Thus, many problems of jointness may make preparation of the financial statements for the hospital difficult, but such statements are still likely to be a necessity for adequate planning and control.

2. Only coincidentally would the value of total assets equal the economic value of the entity. Total assets, as reported in the balance sheet, represent the undepreciated historical cost of assets acquired by the entity. Economic value of an entity is related to the discounted value of future earnings or the market value of the entity if sold.

3. Both stockholders' equity and fund balance or net assets represent the difference between total assets and total liabilities. Stockholders' equity is used in investor-owned corporations to designate the residual owners' claims. Net assets are used in not-for-profit corporations in which there is no residual ownership interest.

4. Exhibit 4–8 presents data relevant to the pricing decision of the home health care firm regarding the five automobiles. Funds available are shown with historical cost depreciation per automobile. Exhibit 4–9 presents funds available with price level depreciation per automobile. Thus, the prices should be set equal to expected replacement cost. Clearly, pricing services to recover capital costs is critical to long-term financial survival.

5. The HMO could have received large payments in advance for providing health services to major employers. This would mean that a liability to provide future services exists. Both accounting loss and cash flow are important in assessing financial performance. The accounting loss is symbolic of a critical operational problem regarding revenue and expense relationships. The positive cash flow may be temporary unless revenue exceeds expenses in future periods.

6. A restricted fund has a third-party donor restriction placed on the utilization of the funds. An unrestricted fund has no such restriction.

7. Changes in financial reporting can impair the comparability of financial results between years for a given firm.

Exhibit 4–8

	Depreciation	Years Invested (10%)	Value, End of Third Year
Year 1	$ 4,000	2	$ 4,840
Year 2	4,000	1	4,400
Year 3	4,000	0	4,000
	$12,000		$13,240

Shortage = $15,972 – $13,240 = $2,732 per automobile

Exhibit 4–9

	Depreciation*	Years Invested (10%)	Value, End of Third Year
Year 1	$ 4,400	2	$ 5,324
Year 2	4,840	1	5,324
Year 3	5,324	0	5,324
	$14,564		$15,972

*Price level depreciation in year $t = \dfrac{\$12,000\ (1.10)^t}{3}$

Shortage = $15,972 – $15,972 = 0

5

Financial Statements

Understanding the principles of accounting is a critical first step in understanding financial statements. However, the average reader may not be able to understand the format and language of financial statements. In this chapter, we discuss in some detail the following four major general purpose financial statements:

1. balance sheet,
2. statement of revenues and expenses or statement of operations,
3. statement of cash flows, and
4. statement of changes in fund balances or net assets.

In addition, we examine the footnotes to the financial statements.

The balance sheet and statement of revenues and expenses are more widely published and used than the other two statements. Understanding them enables a reader to use the other two financial statements and financial information in general. Therefore, in the following discussion, we pay major attention to the balance sheet and statement of revenues and expenses. Omega Health Foundation (OHF) is the entity in our example.

ORGANIZATIONAL STRUCTURE

When reviewing the financial position of any firm, a useful first step is to clearly define the scope of the business being reviewed. Exhibit 5–1 provides an organizational chart for OHF. The basis for this chart is contained in Item 1 in Exhibit 5–2.

OHF is a complex business with two hospitals, Omega and Able Memorial, plus a number of related medical-service providers. All of the related entities are nonprofit with the exception of Omega Medical Management Inc. (OMMI). OMMI is a wholly owned taxable subsidiary that is involved in a variety of business ventures, among them the operation of family medicine centers where physicians are directly employed. To create incentive programs for employed doctors, many nonprofit health care firms have created taxable subsidiaries such as OMMI, which permits them more latitude in structuring compensation programs that are not subject to the same issues of inurement examined by the Internal Revenue Service in nonprofit firms.

BALANCE SHEET

Current Assets

Assets that are expected to be exchanged for cash or consumed during the operating cycle of the entity (or one year, whichever is longer) are classified as current assets on the balance sheet. The operating cycle is the length of time between acquisition of materials and services and

Due 3/15/0? (handwritten note in left margin)

Exhibit 5–1 Omega Health Foundation Organizational Structure

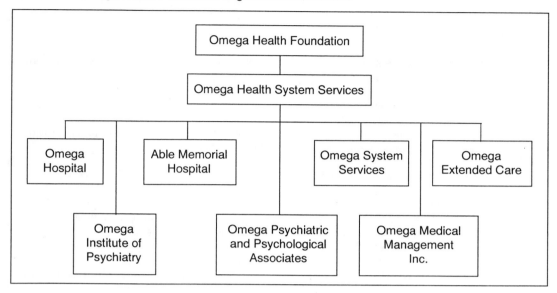

collection of revenue generated by them. Because the operating cycle for most health care organizations is significantly less than one year (perhaps three months or less), current assets are predominantly those that may be expected to be converted into cash or used to reduce expenditures of cash within one year.

Cash and Cash Equivalents

Cash consists of coin, currency, and available deposited funds at banks. Negotiable instruments such as money orders, certified checks, cashier's checks, personal checks, or bank drafts are also viewed as cash. Cash equivalents include savings accounts, certificates of deposit, and other temporary marketable securities. Categorization as a cash equivalent requires that two criteria be met. First, management must intend to convert the investment into cash within one year or during the operating cycle, whichever is longer. Second, the investment must be readily marketable and capable of being transformed into cash easily.

In Table 5–1, OHF has $7,929,000 in cash and cash equivalents plus $1,763,000 in short-term investments for a total of $9,692,000 at the end

of 1999. These monies are readily available to meet normal daily demands for cash such as wages and salaries, federal and state withholding, and supplier invoices. OHF also has $990,000 held by a trustee for payment of the current portion of long-term debt as Item 6 in Exhibit 5–2 suggests. OHF also has an additional $2,264,000 held in a self-insurance trust fund. Item 9 explains the current insurance arrangements of OHF, which self insures for both workers' compensation and professional liability. OHF is estimating that actual claims paid the next year, 2000, will amount to $2,264,000.

Accounts Receivable

Accounts receivable represent legally enforceable claims on customers for prior services or goods. OHF has net accounts receivable of $24,324,000 at the end of 1999. This value represents the amount of money that OHF expects to collect in the next year (2000) from services provided to patients and other customers in 1999 that as yet have not been paid. There are several other accounts in the current asset and current liability section of the balance sheet that need to be considered when calculating the amount of

Exhibit 5–2 Notes to Combined Financial Statements for Omega Health Foundation

1. Basis of Presentation

The combined financial statements of Omega Health Foundation (OHF) and its controlled entity, Omega Health System Services (OHSS), include the accounts of the following:

- Omega Health Foundation (Foundation), a tax-exempt, nonprofit corporation, engaged in investment and fund-raising activities for the benefit of its controlled entities
- Omega Health System Services (OHSS) a tax-exempt, nonprofit entity engaged in providing management services to its controlled entities and subsidiary

The following are the controlled entities and subsidiary of OHSS:

- Omega Hospital (Hospital), a tax-exempt, nonprofit acute-care hospital
- Able Memorial Hospital (Able), a tax-exempt entity whose principal operations include an acute-care and long-term care hospital and a home health care agency
- Omega System Services (OSS), a tax-exempt, nonprofit entity engaged in providing physician and management services to the Hospital and OMMI
- Omega Institute of Psychiatry (OIP), a tax-exempt, nonprofit entity organized to provide outpatient mental health services
- Omega Psychiatric and Psychological Associates (OPPA), a tax-exempt, nonprofit entity, organized to provide mental health services to the public, other organizations, and institutions serving the public
- Omega Extended Care (OEC), a tax-exempt, nonprofit entity, whose principal operations include providing health and wellness services to the public and other organizations and operating an assisted-living personal residence community for the elderly
- Omega Medical Management, Inc., and subsidiaries (OMMI), a wholly owned, taxable subsidiary of OHSS, whose principal operations include rental of durable medical equipment, operation of family medicine center, and various joint venture operations.

2. Summary of Significant Accounting Policies

The significant accounting policies OHF follows in the accompanying combined financial statement are as follows:

Principles of Combination
The combined financial statements include the accounts of OHF. All significant intercompany accounts and transactions have been eliminated in combination.

Net Patient Service Revenue
Net patient service revenue is reported at the estimated net realizable amounts from patients, third-party payers, and others for services rendered, including estimated retroactive adjustments under reimbursement agreements with third-party payers. Retroactive adjustments are accrued on an estimated basis during the period the related services are rendered and will be adjusted in future periods for tentative and final settlements.

continues

Exhibit 5–2 continued

Charity Care
OHF provides care to patients who meet certain criteria under its charity care policy without charge or at amounts less than its established rates. Because OHF does not pursue collection of amounts qualifying as charity care, they are not reported as revenue.

Statements of Revenues and Expenses of General Funds
For purposes of display, transactions deemed by management to be ongoing, major, or central to the provision of health care services are reported as revenue and expenses. Transactions management deem incidental to operations are reported as nonoperating gains and losses.

Cash and Cash Equivalents
Cash and cash equivalents include cash management funds and repurchase agreements, excluding amounts that have limited use, designated by the Board of Directors.
OHF typically maintains cash and cash equivalents in local banks.

Short-Term Investments
Short-term investments, which consist of combined investment trust funds, are carried at the lower of cost or market value. Realized gains and losses on sales of investments are based on cost.

Investments
Investments in cash management funds, real estate, U.S. government obligations, and other interest-bearing accounts are carried at cost. Investments in the combined investment trust, mutual funds, bonds, and common stock funds are carried at the lower of cost or market value. Realized gains and losses on sales of investments are based on cost (specific identification method). The combined investment trust includes a variety of financial instruments such as preferred and common stocks, U.S. government obligations, and mutual funds.

Inventories
Inventories of pharmaceutical and medical supplies are stated at lower of cost (first-in, first-out method) or market. Inventories of durable medical equipment, owned for lease to others, are valued at the lower of cost, net of depreciation, or net realizable sales value.

Assets That Have Limited Use
Assets that have limited use include self-insurance trust funds, board-designated funds, funded depreciation, and the portion of funds held by a trustee that has not been reflected as a current asset to meet the current portion of long-term debt. Self-insurance trust funds represent monies designated to fund current and future liabilities for payment of professional liability, workers' compensation, and employee health care benefit claims. Board-designated funds and funded depreciation represent amounts designated by the board of directors of the Hospital for capital acquisition and debt retirement.
OHF has a Workers' Compensation Security Trust (Security Trust). The Security Trust was established under agreement with the state of New York to meet the state's statutory requirements for self-insured workers' compensation arrangements.

continues

Exhibit 5–2 continued

Property, Plant, and Equipment

Property, plant, and equipment are stated as cost. Depreciation is computed using the straight-line method over the estimated useful lives of the assets. Gains and losses resulting from the sale of property, plant, and equipment are included in nonoperating gains, net.

Investments in Partnerships and Advances to Partnerships

OHSS, through its controlled entities and subsidiary, maintains an ownership interest in several partnerships that provide various clinical and nonclinical services. Under the terms of the partnership agreements, OHSS may be required to occasionally make additional cash contributions and provide working capital advances to the partnerships. The investments in partnerships are accounted for by the equity method.

Deferred Financing Costs

Deferred financing costs represent the costs incurred in connection with the issuance of the 1994 hospital revenue refunding bonds and the series of 1992 revenue bonds. These costs are being amortized over the life of the bonds based on the interest method.

Deferred Third-Party Reimbursement

Deferred third-party reimbursement consists of the reimbursement effect arising from the timing differences in recognizing the loss on the advanced refunding of the 1990 hospital revenue refunding bonds, the funding of self-insurance trust funds, and the funding of pension and other postretirement benefits for financial accounting and third-party purposes. The Hospital accounts for deferred reimbursement based on existing definitive legislation, management's estimate of future utilization, and management's estimate of future recoverability.

Accrued Insurance Costs

Accrued insurance costs consist of reserves for incurred but not reported claims related to medical malpractice incidents and workers' compensation incidents.

Retirement Programs

OHF has a noncontributory defined benefit pension plan covering most of its employees. OHF has a supplemental noncontributory defined benefit pension plan covering certain executives of OHF.

There is a defined contribution tax-sheltered annuity thrift plan covering most OHF employees except those employed by OMMI. OMMI sponsors a 401(k) tax-deferred savings plan covering most of its employees. Both plans allow participating employees to contribute up to 20 percent of their annual salaries. Employee contributions are matched at a rate of fifty cents per dollar up to the first 6 percent of the employee's annual earnings.

Taxes (Income Taxes)

All entities, except OMMI, are exempt from federal income tax under section 501(c)(3) of the Internal Revenue code. On such basis, these entities will not incur any liability for federal income taxes, except for possible unrelated business income. As of June 30, 1999, OMMI had net operating loss carryforwards of approximately $4,775,000 expiring in various years through 2014.

Fair Value of Financial Instruments

Statement of Financial Accounting Standards No. 107, "Disclosures about Fair Value of Financial Instruments" (SFAS No. 107), requires that OHF disclose the estimated fair values for certain

continues

Exhibit 5–2 continued

of its financial instruments. Financial instruments include cash and cash equivalents, accounts receivable, accounts payable, and long-term debt. The carrying amounts reported in the balance sheets for accounts receivable and accounts payable approximate their fair values as of June 30, 1999, and 1998.

3. Third-Party Agreements

Payments to Omega Hospital and Able Hospital from the Medicare and New York Medical Assistance programs for inpatient hospital services were made on a prospective basis. Under these programs, specific, predetermined payments are made for each discharge based on the patient's diagnosis. Blue Cross reimburses the Hospital for inpatient services on a reasonable cost basis. Medicaid pays the Hospital and Able for capital costs on a prospective basis. Medicare makes additional payments for the cost of approved graduate medical education programs and for cases that involve an extremely long hospital stay or unusually high costs compared to national or statewide averages.

Medicare reimburses the Hospital for outpatient services on a reasonable cost basis, except for clinical lab services, of which reimbursement is based upon a fee schedule, and ambulatory surgery and diagnostic radiology services, of which reimbursement is based upon the lower of cost or blended rate.

Revenue received under agreements with third-party payers is subject to audit and retroactive adjustment. Included in net patient service revenue for 1999 and 1998 are favorable (unfavorable) expense adjustments related to the settlements of prior year cost reports of approximately $334,000 and $43,000, respectively. Adjustments related to final settlements with third-party payers are included in the determination of revenue and gains in excess of expenses and losses during the year in which such adjustments become known.

Capital Cost Payment by Medicare

The Health Care Financing Administration (HCFA) promulgated regulations changing the method by which the Medicare program reimburses hospitals for inpatient capital costs effective beginning fiscal year 1991.

For fully prospective hospitals, these regulations set forth a prospective payment based on rates using a blend of the June 30, 1990, hospital-specific, base-period capital cost per Medicare discharge and the national average Medicare cost per discharge. Annually, the proportion of the hospital-specific rate and the national rate (10 percent for the hospital-specific rate and 90 percent for the national rate as of June 30, 1991) will be adjusted 10 percent over a ten-year implementation period until the prospective payments based on 100 percent of the national rate are made.

4. Charity Care, Community Expense, and Bad Debt

OHF provides services to patients who meet the criteria of its charity care policy without charge or at amounts less than the established rates. Criteria for charity care consider family income levels, household size, and ability to pay. Federal poverty guidelines are used as a means to determine the patient's ability to pay. Individuals who qualify for charity care do not have insurance or other coverage.

Charges foregone for providing charity care to individuals as determined in accordance with the AICPA Audit guide will be approximately $1,843,000 and $2,033,000 in 1999 and 1998, respectively. Such amounts have been excluded from net patient service revenue.

continues

Exhibit 5–2 continued

5. Property, Plant, and Equipment and Accumulated Depreciation and Amortization

Property, plant, and equipment as of June 30, 1999, and 1998 consist of:

	1999	*1998*
Land	$ 3,845,050	$ 3,599,917
Land improvements	1,315,653	860,188
Building and building improvements	84,015,323	79,866,619
Equipment, including capitalized leases of $260,007	57,532,494	52,768,949
	146,708,520	137,095,673
Accumulated depreciation, including amortization on capital leases	(70,803,892)	(63,252,010)
	75,904,628	73,843,663
Construction-in-progress	55,478	965,386
	$75,960,106	$74,809,049

6. Long-Term Debt

Long-term debt as of June 30, 1999, and 1998 consists of:

	1999	*1998*
Omega Hospital revenue refunding bonds, series 1994	$48,480	$49,405
Variable rate Hospital revenue bonds	6,143	6,286
Term loan payable in monthly installments of $16,600 including interest, collateralized by certain equipment of OPPA (7.25 percent and 6 percent at June 30, 1999, and 1998, respectively)	852	998
Various mortgages, loans, and capitalized leases, at various interest rates	707	806
	56,182	57,495
Less current portion:		
Long-term debt and capitalized leases	411	581
Revenue bonds (included in payable from funds held by trustee)	990	925
	$54,781	$55,989

continues

Exhibit 5–2 continued

Maturity requirements on long-term debt, including capitalized leases, during the next five years and thereafter are as follows:

2000	$ 1,401
2001	1,488
2002	1,566
2003	1,806
2004	1,715
Thereafter	48,204
	$ 56,180

7. Funds Held by Trustee

Funds held by trustee as of June 30, 1999, and 1998 consist of (data in thousands):

	1999	*1998*
Able Mastersite project fund		$ 386
Debt service and revenue funds	$1,011	947
Debt service reserve fund	317	317
	1,328	1,650
Less current portion	990	925
	$ 338	$ 725

8. Retirement Programs

OHF sponsors a noncontributory defined benefit pension plan (Plan) covering most employees. Plan benefits are generally based on the employee's highest average rate of earnings for any five consecutive years during the last ten years of employment. OHF's policy is to annually fund at least the minimum amount required by the Employee Retirement Income Security Act of 1974.

The Plan's aggregate funded status and amounts recognized in the combined balance sheets as of June 30, 1999, and 1998 follow.

continues

Exhibit 5–2 continued

	1999	1998
Accumulated present value of benefit obligation:		
Vested	$ 33,387,862	$ 29,117,999
Nonvested	642,769	745,054
	$ 34,030,631	$ 29,863,053
Projected benefit obligation	(49,675,796)	(43,584,435)
Plan assets at fair value	42,726,273	40,718,368
Plan assets in excess of (less than) projected		
benefit obligation	(6,949,523)	(2,866,067)
Unrecognized net assets	(1,055,892)	(1,187,878)
Unrecognized prior service cost	109,195	130,356
Unrecognized net loss	5,957,690	3,650,026
Contributions during fourth quarter	699,999	500,001
(Accrued) prepaid pension cost	$ (1,238,531)	$ 226,438

Plan assets consist principally of listed stocks and U.S. government obligations.

Aggregate pension costs were $3,864,969 and $2,571,502 for the years ending June 30, 1999, and 1998, respectively. In addition, OHF offered early retirement to certain individuals in 1999, resulting in special termination benefits of $951,303.

Net periodic pension costs for 1999 and 1998 consisted of the following components:

	1999	1998
Service cost benefits earned during the period	$ 2,623,847	$ 2,242,670
Interest cost on projected benefit obligation	3,219,007	2,835,990
Actual return on plan assets	(973,906)	(3,809,141)
Net amortization and deferral	(1,955,282)	1,301,983
Special termination benefits	951,303	
Net periodic pension costs charged to operations	$ 3,864,969	$ 2,571,502

Assumptions used in determining the actuarial value of the projected benefit obligation for 1999 and 1998 were:

	1999	1998
Discount rate	7.25%	7.25%
Rate of increase in compensation levels	6.00%	6.00%
Expected long-term rate of return on assets	7.00%	7.00%

9.   Insurance Coverage

OHF maintains self-insurance trust funds for workers' compensation and excess professional liability claims. OHF's contributions to its professional liability self-insurance trust fund are based on actuarial assumptions from independent actuaries; OHF's contributions to its workers' compensation trust fund are based on estimated claims and statutory funding limits.

continues

Exhibit 5–2 continued

Directors' and officers' liability coverage is underwritten through Aetna. Coverages are provided under a guaranteed cost agreement on a claims-made policy.

OHF is insured under a comprehensive liability policy provided by ABC insurance company. Coverages are provided under a retrospectively rated agreement on a claims-made policy. Before April 1998, coverages were provided under a guaranteed cost agreement on a claims-made policy. Coverages included in this contract are general liability, institutional professional liability, and physician professional liability.

As of June 30, 1999, OHF's professional liability limits were $200,000 for each occurrence and $1,000,000 in the aggregate, and physicians' liability limits were $200,000 for each occurrence and $600,000 in the aggregate. Additionally, OHF participates in a catastrophic loss fund with limits of $1,000,000 for each occurrence and $3,000,000 in the aggregate. An excess liability policy covers individual and aggregate claim liability between $1,200,000 and $11,200,000. OHF maintains excess general liability coverage under an umbrella policy with a limit of $10,000,000. OHF purchases directors' and officers' liability coverage with limits of $5,000,000 and excess workers' compensation insurance with statutory limits over a self-insured retention of $400,000 per occurrence.

10. Restructuring Costs

During fiscal 1999, OHF underwent a comprehensive restructuring process to optimize work flow and contain operating costs, which resulted in a charge to expenses for restructuring costs of approximately $5,110,000 for severance and termination benefits and consulting fees. The remaining liability as of June 30, 1999, is approximately $2,100,000.

---

outstanding receivables. The following schedule recasts accounts receivable as of 1999:

	1999 Value
Accounts receivable	$24,324,000
Add: Due from third-party payers	280,000
Subtract: Due to third-party payers	11,571,000
Net accounts receivable due at 6/30/99	$13,033,000

OHF has a substantial "due to third-party payers," a current liability account, in both 1999 and 1998. The values for both due to and from third-party payers usually reflect differences between interim payments for medical services in the preceding year and estimated final payments. For example, a large payer such as Medicare may agree to make biweekly payments of $1,000,000 for services to its beneficiaries. At year end, a final accounting will be made to determine the actual amounts that should have been paid based on actual utilization and cost. In the case of OHF, a large balance is due to the payers, which may be offset against future payments from the payer. OHF has reduced its investment in accounts receivable substantially by getting its payers to pay for medical services before these services are rendered, enabling OHF to benefit from an interest-free loan.

OHF also has an "advance from third-party payers" listed in its current liability section of $1,205,000 in 1999. This amount is usually associated with a working capital advance by a third-party payer. These advances are usually made to provide funding for medical providers to recognize that the providers must incur costs before payments for those services are made. Few third-party payers have such an arrangement in today's economic climate.

Table 5–1 Balance Sheet for Omega Health Foundation (Data in Thousands) as of June 30, 1999 and 1998

Assets

	1999	1998
Current		
Cash and cash equivalents	$ 7,929	$ 7,827
Short-term investments	1,763	1,629
Accounts receivable, less uncollectable accounts of $8,532 in 1999 and $8,372 in 1998	24,324	25,597
Due from third-party payers		56
Due from donor-restricted funds	280	179
Inventories	1,763	2,251
Prepaid expenses and other assets	1,135	1,520
Current portion of funds held by trustee	990	925
Current portion of self-insurance trust funds	2,264	2,284
Total current assets	40,448	42,268
Assets that have limited use		
Self-insurance trust funds, net of current portion *current portion need to be funded*	9,321	9,013
Board-designated funds	4,959	4,609
Funded depreciation	50,835	37,717
Funds held by trustee, net of current portion	338	726
	65,453	52,065
Property, plant, and equipment, net	75,990	74,829
Investments in and advances to partnerships	2,497	2,226
Deferred financing costs, net	1,139	1,306
Deferred third-party reimbursement		674
Other assets	1,067	654
Total	$ 186,594	$ 174,022

Liabilities

	1999	1998
Current		
Current portion of long-term debt	$ 411	$ 581
Notes payable		250
Accounts payable and accrued expenses	11,087	7,215
Accrued salaries, wages, and fees	4,342	4,238
Accrued restructuring costs	2,078	
Accrued vacation	3,288	3,331
Accrued insurance costs	2,234	2,284
Advance from third-party payer	1,205	1,142
Due to third-party payers	11,571	10,688
Total current liabilities	36,216	29,729

continues

Table 5–1 continued

Accrued retirement costs	8,846	1,736
Accrued insurance costs, net of current portion	4,636	3,450
Deferred third-party reimbursement	3,489	3,488
Long-term debt, net of current portion	54,781	55,989
Other liabilities	1,228	927
Total liabilities	109,196	95,319
Unrestricted net assets	77,398	78,703
Total	$ 186,594	$ 174,022

A characteristic of hospitals and other health care organizations that makes their accounts receivable different from those of most other organizations is that the charges actually billed to patients are often settled for substantially less amounts. The differences also are known as allowances. The following four major categories of allowances are used to restate accounts receivable to expected, realizable value:

1. charity allowances,
2. courtesy allowances,
3. doubtful account allowances, and
4. contractual allowances.

A charity allowance is the difference between established service rates and amounts actually charged to indigent patients. Many health care facilities, especially clinics and other ambulatory care settings, have a policy of scaling the normal charge by some factor based on income. A courtesy allowance is the difference between established rates for services and rates billed to special patients, such as employees, physicians, and clergy. A doubtful account allowance is the difference between rates billed and amounts expected to be recovered. For example, a medically indigent patient might actually receive services that have an established rate of $100, but be billed only $50. If it is anticipated that the patient will not pay even the $50, then that $50 will show up as a doubtful account allowance.

In most situations, contractual allowances represent the largest deduction from accounts receivable. A contractual allowance is the difference between rates billed to a third-party payer, such as Medicare, and the amount that actually will be paid by that third-party payer. For example, a Medicare patient may receive hospital services priced at $4,000 but actually pay the hospital only $3,000 for those services, based on the patient's diagnosis-related group classification. If this account is unpaid at the fiscal year end, the financial statements would include the net amount of cash expected to be received, not the gross prices charged. Accounts receivable represent the amount of cash expected to be received, not the gross prices charged. Because most major payers, such as Medicare, Medicaid, and Blue Cross, have a contractual relationship that permits payment on a basis other than charges, contractual allowances can be, and usually are, very large.

The allowances are estimates and will, in all probability, differ from the actual value of accounts receivable that eventually will be written off. For example, OHF shows an expected value of accounts receivable to be collected as $24,324,000 in 1999, but it actually has $32,856,000 of outstanding accounts receivable.

Net accounts receivable	$24,324,000
Allowances	8,532,000
Accounts receivable gross	$32,856,000

Because estimation of allowances is so critical to the reported value of accounts receivable, the methodology should be scrutinized. Just how was the estimate developed? Has the estimating method been used in the past with any degree of reliability? An external audit performed by an independent certified public accountant can usually provide the required degree of reliability and assurance.

Inventories/Supplies

Inventories in a health care facility represent items that are to be used in the delivery of health care services. They may range from normal business office supplies to highly specialized chemicals used in a laboratory.

Prepaid Expenses

Prepaid expenses represent expenditures already made for future service. In OHF, they may represent prepayment of insurance premiums for the year, rents on leased equipment, or other similar items. For example, an insurance premium for a professional liability insurance policy may be $600,000 per year, due one year in advance. If this amount was paid on January 1, then on June 30, $300,000 (one-half of the total) would be shown as a prepaid expense.

Property and Equipment

Property and equipment are sometimes called fixed assets or shown more descriptively as plant property and equipment. Items in this category represent investment in tangible, permanent assets; they are sometimes referred to as the capital assets of the organization. These items are shown at the historical cost or acquisition cost, reduced by allowances for depreciation.

Land and Improvements

Land and improvements represent the historical cost of land owned by the health care facility and the historical cost of any improvements erected on it. Such improvements might include water and sewer systems, roadways, fences, sidewalks, shrubbery, and parking lots. Although land may not be depreciated, land improvements may be depreciated. Land held for

investment purposes is not shown in this category but appears as an investment in the other assets section.

Buildings and Equipment

Buildings and equipment represent all buildings and equipment owned by the entity and used during the normal course of its operations. These items are also stated at historical cost. Buildings and equipment not used in the normal course of operations should be reported separately. For example, real estate investments would not be shown in the fixed asset or plant property and equipment section but in the other assets section. Equipment in many situations is classified into three categories: (1) fixed equipment—affixed to the building in which it is located, including items such as elevators, boilers, and generators, (2) major movable equipment—usually stationary but capable of being moved, including reasonably expensive items such as automobiles, laboratory equipment, and X-ray apparatuses, and (3) minor equipment—usually low in cost with short estimated useful lives, including such items as wastebaskets, glassware, and sheets.

Construction in Progress

Construction in progress represents the amount of money that has been expended on projects that are still not complete when the financial statement is published. In OHF, there is currently $55,478 of construction in progress (Item 5 in Exhibit 5–2). When these projects are completed, the values will be charged to property and equipment.

Allowance for Depreciation

Allowance for depreciation represents the accumulated depreciation taken on the asset to the date of the financial statement. The concept of depreciation is important and useful regarding a wide variety of decisions. The following example illustrates the depreciation concept: A $500 desk is purchased and depreciated over a five-year life. The balance sheet values are presented in the following:

	Year				
	1	*2*	*3*	*4*	*5*
Historical equipment cost	$500	$500	$500	$500	$500
Allowance for depreciation	100	200	300	400	500
Net	$400	$300	$200	$100	$ 0

In the case of OHF, there is $70,803,892 of accumulated depreciation as of June 30, 1999. The historical cost base for this amount is $146,708,520 (Item 5 in Exhibit 5–2), the historical cost value of buildings and equipment. This means that 48.3 percent of the historical cost of present facilities has been depreciated in prior years. As the ratio of allowance for depreciation to building and equipment increases, it usually signifies that a physical plant will need to be replaced in the near future. OHF appears to be in such a situation, which may partially explain the current construction.

Assets That Have Limited Use

Most organizations will have some amounts listed under assets that have limited use. In Table 5–1 OHF has $65,453,000 at the end of 1999. The nature of the asset limitation usually derives from one of two ways. First, the board may restrict certain funds to be used in only designated ways. For example, the board has restricted $9,321,000 for paying insurance costs and $50,835,000 for funded depreciation. These monies have been set aside and restricted by the board for these designated purposes. They could not be spent for any other purpose without the formal approval of the board.

Aside from a board restriction, funds also may be restricted by a third party. These restrictions are not from a third-party donor. If they were, there would be a balance shown as either temporarily or permanently restricted net assets. OHF has only unrestricted net assets presently. A common third-party nondonor restriction is an indenture agreement. OHF has $338,000 of funds restricted under bond indenture. These are funds held by the bond trustee, usually for one or more purposes. Item 7 to OHF's financial statements (Exhibit 5–2) describes the nature of the restrictions under bond indenture.

Other Assets

Other assets are assets that are neither current nor involve property and equipment. Typically, they are either investments or intangible assets. OHF has several categories of investments. It has some investment in partnership through its Ohio Medical Management subsidiary. OHA also has some deferred financing costs. Deferred financing costs are costs incurred initially by a borrower to issue bonds. Such costs include legal fees, accounting fees, and underwriter's costs. The costs are amortized over the life of the bonds, much like depreciation.

Two other intangible asset items that may be included in some health care facility balance sheets are goodwill and organization costs. Goodwill represents the difference between the price paid to acquire another entity and the fair market value of the acquired entity's assets, less any related obligations or liabilities. Goodwill is included mainly in balance sheets of proprietary facilities, although increasingly, it is also being seen in balance sheets of voluntary not-for-profit organizations as they acquire other health care entities, especially physician practices. Organization costs are expended for legal and accounting fees and other items incurred at the formation of the entity. The cost of these items is usually amortized over some allowable life.

Current Liabilities

Current liabilities are obligations that are expected to require payment in cash during the coming year or operating cycle, whichever is longer. Like current assets, they are generally expected to be paid in one year.

Accounts Payable

Accounts payable may be thought of as the counterpart of accounts receivable. They represent the entity's promise to pay money for goods or services it has received.

Accrued Liabilities

Accrued liabilities are obligations that result from prior operations. They are thus a legal obligation to make future payment. The expense of accruing interest, discussed in Chapter 4, is an example. Other examples of accrued expenses are payroll, vacation pay, tax deductions, rent, and insurance. In some cases, especially payroll, accrued liabilities are desegregated to show material categories. OHF classifies accrued liabilities into the following four categories: (1) salaries and wages, (2) vacation, (3) insurance, and (4) restructuring. Accrued restructuring costs represent costs incurred in a "reengineering" program that is explained in Item 10.

Current Portion of Long-Term Debt

Current portion of long-term debt represents the amount of principal that will be repaid on the indebtedness within the coming year. It does not equal the total amount of the payments that will be made during that year. Total payments include both interest and principal; current portion of long-term debt includes just the principal portion. For example, if at the June 30 fiscal year close, a total of $360,000 ($30,000 per month) will be paid on long-term indebtedness during the coming year and of this amount, only $120,000 is principal payment, then $120,000 would be shown as a current portion of the long-term debt.

Noncurrent Liabilities

Noncurrent liabilities include obligations that will not require payment in cash for at least one year or more. Omega Health Foundation shows five types of noncurrent liabilities, accrued retirement costs, accrued insurance costs, deferred third-party reimbursement, long-term debt, and other liabilities.

Accrued Insurance Costs

OHF has recorded $4,636,000 of estimated noncurrent insurance costs at the close of 1999.

In Exhibit 5–2, item 9 describes this account and its derivation in more detail. The amount reported for estimated insurance costs represents the present value of expected or "estimated" claims that the organization will be responsible for paying. In the case of OHF, there are $4,636,000 of estimated claims that OHF will be responsible for paying that are not covered by their insurer. OHF has sufficient reserves to cover the expected present value of professional liability and workers' compensation claims at the present time. The asset side of the balance sheet shows $9,321,000 of long-term reserves, far in excess of the current estimated future costs.

Long-Term Debt

Long-term debt represents the amount of long-term indebtedness that is not due in the next year. OHF reported $54,781,000 in 1999. When the current portion of long-term debt ($411,000) is added to the long-term portion, the total amount of debt is determined. The footnotes to financial statements (Item 6, Exhibit 5–2, for OHF) usually provides additional information on maturities, interest rates, and types of outstanding debt.

Unrestricted Net Assets

Unrestricted net assets, as discussed earlier, represent the difference between assets and the claim to those assets by third parties or liabilities. Increases in this account balance usually arise from one of two sources: (1) contributions or (2) earnings.

In the nonprofit health care industry, there is usually no separation in the fund balance account to recognize these two sources. Thus, there is no indication of how much of OHF's unrestricted net assets of $77,398,000 was earned and how much was contributed. Financial statements prepared for proprietary entities do show this breakdown. Earnings of prior years, reduced by dividend payments to stockholders, are shown in an account labeled "retained earnings."

In any given year, however, it is possible to determine the sources of change in unrestricted net assets by examining the statement of changes in fund balance. Table 5–2 shows that OHF's increase in its unrestricted net assets did not result totally from the excess of revenues over expenses in either 1998 or 1999.

The value of the unrestricted net assets account at any point is often confused with the cash position of the entity. However, cash and unrestricted net assets rarely will be equal. In most situations, the cash balance will be much less than the fund balance. For example, in Table 5–1, OHF has $77,398,000 in unrestricted net assets as of December 31, 1999, but only $7,929,000 in cash (Table 5–1) at the same date. Thus, the assumption that the $77,398,000 reported as unrestricted net assets can be converted into cash is false.

STATEMENT OF REVENUES AND EXPENSES

The statement of revenues and expenses (Table 5–3) has become increasingly important in both the proprietary and nonproprietary sectors. It represents operations in a given period better than a balance sheet does. A balance sheet summarizes the wealth position of an entity at a given point by delineating its assets, liabilities, and unrestricted net assets. An income statement provides information concerning how that wealth position was changed through operations.

An entity's ability to earn an excess of revenue over expenses is an important variable in many external and internal decisions. A series of income statements indicates this ability well. Creditors use income statements to determine the entity's ability to pay future and present debts; management and rate-regulating agencies use them to assess whether current and proposed rate structures are adequate.

The entity principle is an important factor in analyzing and interpreting the statement of revenue and expense. Income, the excess of revenue over expenses, comes from a large number of individual operations within a health care entity and is aggregated in the statement of revenues and expenses. For example, OHF has aggregated the revenues and expenses from its subsidiaries to create a consolidated statement of revenues and expenses. Individuals interested in details about any of the individual entities that constitute OHF would need to see income statements for those organizations. Information about revenues and expenses by product line also are often needed when making managerial decisions. Here, however, our focus is on the general-purpose statement of revenues and expenses, which is an aggregate of individual product lines.

Revenue

Generally speaking, revenue in a health care facility comes from three sources:

1. patient services revenue,
2. other revenue, and
3. nonoperating gains (losses).

Table 5–2 Statements of Changes in Unrestricted Net Assets for Omega Health Foundation

	1999	1998
Balance, beginning of year	$78,703	$71,003
Excess of revenues over expenses	(904)	5,706
Change in net unrealized gains and losses on other than trading securities	(498)	1,963
Decrease in unrecognized net periodic pension cost	97	31
Balance, end of year	$77,398	$78,703

Table 5–3 Statements of Revenues and Expenses for Omega Health Foundation

	1999	1998
Revenues:		
Net patient service revenue	$160,574	$162,323
Equity in net income from partnership	732	1,135
Gifts and bequests	258	435
Other	8,760	8,742
Total revenues	170,324	172,635
Expenses:		
Salaries and wages	81,032	81,476
Fringe benefits	18,627	19,876
Professional fees	8,980	12,743
Supplies and other	39,607	38,539
Interest	4,364	4,369
Bad-debt expense	4,551	6,419
Depreciation and amortization	8,545	7,861
Restructuring costs	5,110	
Total expenses	170,816	171,283
Income (loss) from operations	(492)	1,352
Nonoperating gains (losses):		
Income on investments, including net realized gains on sale of investments of approximately $1,150,000 in 1994 and $1,367,000 in 1993	4,717	4,658
Gifts and bequests	41	297
Loss on disposal of assets	(84)	(601)
Nonoperating gains, net	4,674	4,354
Excess of revenues over expenses before cumulative effect of change in accounting principle	4,182	5,706
Cumulative effect of change in accounting principle	(5,086)	
Excess of revenues over expenses	$ (904)	$ 5,706

Patient Services Revenue

Patient services revenue represents the amount of revenue that results from the provision of health care services to patients. It is often shown on a net basis in the statement of revenues and expenses with additional detail in the foot-notes. OHF reported net patient services revenue of $160,574,000 in fiscal year 1999. This value is the amount that OHF expects to collect from the patient services it has provided. Actual changes for these services would have been much higher but are reduced for contractual allowances and charity care.

Charity care represents services provided for which payment was never expected. Most health care organizations have some stated policy regarding charity care. There is no charge generated for a charity patient because payment is not pursued, but it is sometimes useful to identify the amount of charges or costs incurred to provide charity care. Item 4 in Exhibit 5–2 shows that OHF provided $1,843,000 in charges to charity patients.

It should be emphasized that bad debts are different from charity care. Bad debts are incurred on patients for whom services were provided and payment was expected, but no payment was forthcoming. Bad debts are not reported as a deduction from gross patient services revenue. Instead, bad debts are reported as an expense. As shown in Table 5–3, OHF had $4,551,000 of bad debt expense in 1999. This value represents the amount of charges to patients who are not expected to pay.

The value that is reported for net patient services revenue is part fact and part estimate. At the close of the fiscal year, someone must estimate what amounts actually will be paid by third-party payers under existing contracts. This is not an easy task in most situations, and there is likely to be some error. This is important to recognize when revenue figures are examined for periods shorter than one year (for example, monthly) and when those statements are not audited by an independent auditor. This does not mean that the data are not valid, only that some caution should be exercised in using them.

Usually, it is important to get some information about major third-party payers, such as how they pay and what their relative volume is. Oftentimes, the footnotes can be helpful in this regard. Item 3 in Exhibit 5–2 also explains how Medicare, Blue Cross, and Medicaid make payments to the hospitals.

Other Revenue

Other revenue is generated from normal day-to-day operations not directly related to patient care. In Table 5–3, Omega Hospital reports $8,760,000 of other revenue for 1999. There is no indication regarding the source of this revenue in the financial statements, but the usual sources include revenue from the following:

- educational programs,
- research and grants,
- rentals of space or equipment,
- sales of medical and pharmacy items to nonpatients,
- cafeteria sales,
- gift shop sales,
- parking lot sales,
- investment income on borrowed funds held by a trustee, and
- investment income on malpractice trust funds.

It is not entirely clear in all cases whether an item should be categorized as other revenue or as nonoperating gain or loss. The general rule is that items are categorized as nonoperating gains or losses when they are peripheral or incidental to the activities of the health care provider. For example, donations could be classified as a gain to some organizations and as other revenue to other organizations.

Nonoperating Gains (Losses)

Gains and losses result from peripheral or incidental transactions. The definitions of peripheral and incidental transactions are not exactly clear, and the terms could be treated inconsistently. For example, OHF reports $4,717,000 of investment income in 1999 (Table 5–3). Most likely, these earnings resulted from funds restricted by the board for funded depreciation. Is the investment of funded depreciation or capital replacement reserves incidental to OHF? OHF must believe that it is, but another organization with exactly the same situation might choose to categorize it differently.

In general, the following items are often categorized as nonoperating gains or losses:

- contributions or donations that are unrestricted income from endowments,
- income from the investment of unrestricted funds,

- gains or losses on sale of property, and
- net rentals of facilities not used in the operation of the facility.

Operating Expenses

In these days of increasing concern regarding health care costs, decision makers are paying more attention to health care facilities' operating expenses. Generally speaking, there are two ways that expenses may be categorized: (1) by cost or responsibility center or (2) by object or type of expenditure.

In most general-purpose financial statements, costs are reported by cost object. OHF breaks down expenses into the following categories:

1. salaries and wages,
2. fringe benefits,
3. professional fees,
4. supplies,
5. interest,
6. bad debt expense,
7. depreciation and amortization, and
8. restructuring costs.

Fringe-benefit costs represent amounts for employee benefits and tax payments. Among items included are social security, unemployment tax, workers' compensation, retirement costs, health insurance, and other fringe-benefit programs.

Bad-debt provisions recognize the amount of gross charges that will not be collected from patients from whom payment was expected. For example, if a patient had commercial insurance coverage that paid 80 percent of the patient's bill of $10,000, the hospital would bill the patient for $2,000. If the patient refused to pay the $2,000 and no payment was expected, the $2,000 charge would be written off as a bad debt. OHF had $4,551,000 of bad-debt expense in 1999.

Depreciation and interest are two special accounts that have great importance in financial analysis and are discussed in Chapter 7.

It should be noted that expense and expenditure (or payment of cash) may not be equivalent

in any given period. For example, a health care facility may incur an expenditure of $1,000,000 to buy a piece of equipment but may charge only $200,000 as depreciation expense in a given year. In general, expenditure reflects the payment of cash, whereas expense recognizes prior expenditure that has produced revenue. The following three major categories of expenditures usually are not treated as expenses:

1. retirement or repayment of debt,
2. investment in new fixed assets, and
3. increases in working capital or current assets.

One major category of expense—depreciation of fixed assets—does not involve a cash expenditure. In addition, other normal accruals, such as vacation and sick leave benefits, may be recognized as expense but involve no immediate cash outlay.

STATEMENT OF CASH FLOWS

The statement of cash flows is designed to give additional information on the flow of funds within an entity. As we have noted, the concept of expense does not necessarily give decision makers information on funds flow. The statement of cash flows is designed to give information on the flow of funds within an entity, and to summarize the sources that make funds available and the uses for those funds during a given period.

OHF reports its statement of cash flows in Table 5–4. In general, there are three activities that generate or use cash flows for an organization: (1) operating activities, (2) investing activities, and (3) financing activities. OHF derived $23,883,000 of cash flow from operating activities during 1999. It then spent $22,307,000 on investments, primarily property, equipment, and funded depreciation. It also spent $1,473,000 for financing activities during 1999. The difference is the net increase in cash and cash equivalents during the year, or $102,000. A statement of cash flows can be thought of simply as a state-

Table 5–4 Statements of Cash Flows of General Funds for Omega Health Foundation

	1999	1998
Cash flows from operating activities and gains and losses		
Revenue and gains in excess of (less than)		
expenses and losses	$ (904)	$ 5,706
Adjustments to reconcile revenue and gains in excess		
of expenses and losses to net cash provided by		
operating activities and gains and losses:		
Gain on investments	(1,150)	(1,367)
Provision for bad debts	4,551	6,419
Depreciation and amortization	8,545	7,861
Loss on disposal of assets	84	346
Equity in earnings of partnerships	(732)	(1,135)
Amortization of deferred financing costs	167	87
Change in assets and liabilities:		
Increase in patient accounts receivable	(3,278)	(8,482)
Increase in due from donor-restricted funds, net	(100)	(132)
Decrease in inventories	487	1,610
Decrease (increase) in prepaid expenses and other assets	181	(836)
Increase in accounts payable and accrued expenses	3,871	256
Increase in accrued salaries and vacation	61	601
Increase in accrued insurance	1,135	693
Decrease in amounts due from third-party payers	730	
Increase in accrued restructuring costs	2,078	
Increase in advance from third parties	63	200
Increase in amounts due to third-party payers	883	1,859
Increase in accrued retirement costs	7,206	160
Net cash provided by operating activities	23,878	13,846
Cash flows from investing activities		
Purchase of property, plant, and equipment	(9,791)	(14,843)
Cash invested in self-insurance trust funds	(258)	1,581
Cash invested in and advances to partnerships	(358)	(209)
Distributions and payments received from partnerships	519	832
Cash acquired in acquisitions		66
Cash paid for acquisitions		(596)
Change in minority interest	(3)	(4)
Cash invested in short-term investments	(133)	(164)
Cash invested in board-designated funds, funds		
held by trustee and funded depreciation	(12,281)	(3,128)
Net cash used by investing activities	(22,305)	(16,465)
Cash flows from financing activities		
Repayments of long-term debt	(1,312)	(1,411)
Issuance (repayments) of notes payable	(249)	21
Issuance of equity in OMMI	88	1,957
Net cash provided by (used by) financing activities	(1,473)	567

continues

Table 5–4 continued

Net (decrease) increase in cash and cash equivalents	102	(2,049)
Cash and cash equivalents at beginning of year	$7,827	$9,876
Cash and cash equivalents at end of year	$7,929	$7,827

ment that explains the sources for changes in the cash accounts during the year.

The amount of cash flow generated from operating activities can be thought of as the amount of excess of revenues over expenses subject to several adjustments: The first adjustment is for expenses that did not involve an actual outlay of cash. The biggest items here are depreciation and provision for bad debts. Provision for bad debts is added back because the expense did not involve an outlay of cash, merely a write-off of a receivable.

Another major use of cash flow involves working capital items, the difference between current assets and current liabilities. OHF experienced an increase of $3,278,000 in its patient accounts receivable. In general, the following equation will define the amount of cash flow used to increase patient accounts receivable:

[Ending accounts receivable –
Beginning accounts receivable +
Provision for bad debts] = Cash
change in accounts receivable

[$24,324 – $25,597 + $4,551] = $3,278

Other working capital items such as a decrease in accounts payable can use cash and reduce cash flow.

STATEMENT OF CHANGES IN UNRESTRICTED NET ASSETS

The statement of changes in unrestricted net assets merely accounts for the changes in unrestricted net assets during the year. Table 5–2 shows that the majority of the change in unre-

stricted net assets is attributed to excess of revenues over expenses, or net income. OHF does, however, show sizable values for changes in net unrealized gains and losses on other than trading securities. In 1999, OHF experienced a $498,000 reduction compared to an increase of $1,963,000 in 1998. These changes represent valuation adjustments for nontrading securities, usually equity investments, with objective market values, such as publicly traded values. For example, in 1999, OHF's market value of its stock investments may have decreased $498,000 from their beginning market value. When the securities are finally sold, the difference between the sales price and acquisition cost will be recognized as a realizable gain.

SUMMARY

In this chapter, we have discussed the contents of the following four general-purpose financial statements:

1. balance sheet,
2. statement of revenues and expenses,
3. statement of cash flows, and
4. statement of changes in unrestricted net assets.

Primary attention was directed at the first two, balance sheet and statement of revenues and expenses, which provide a basis for most financial information.

This chapter focused on understanding the basic information available in these four financial statements. Later chapters describe how that information can be interpreted and used in actual decision making.

ASSIGNMENTS

1. Determine the amount of net operating income that would result for a hospital whose payer mix and expected volume (100 cases) is as follows:

30 Medicare cases	pay $2,000 per case
30 BCBS cases	pay average cost
20 commercial cases	pay 100 percent of charges
10 Medicaid cases	pay average cost
8 self-pay cases	pay 100 percent of charges
2 charity cases	pay nothing

   Average cost per case is expected to be $2,200, and the average charge per case is $2,500.

2. How could you determine the amount of debt principal that will be retired during the next year through an examination of the financial statements?

3. What are the titles of the four financial statements that are usually included in an audited financial report?

4. Shady Rest nursing home has just acquired a home health firm for $850,000 in cash. The balance sheet of the home health firm looked as follows just before the acquisition:

Current assets	$200,000
Net fixed assets	100,000
Total	$300,000
Current liabilities	$100,000
Shareholder's equity	200,000
Total	$300,000

   Assume that the fair market value of the net fixed assets is $300,000 and fair market value of current assets is $200,000. Describe how this acquisition might be reflected on the balance sheet of Shady Rest.

5. Describe several items that are treated as expenses in the income statement but do not require any expenditure of cash in the present period.

6. A major medical supplier has donated $45,000 worth of medical supply items to your firm. These items are then used in the treatment of patients. Explain how this transaction would be recorded in your firm's financial statements.

7. Your HMO is experiencing a critical shortage of funds. Using the statement of cash flows as a framework for discussion, explain how you might attempt to reduce the need for additional funds.

8. Your hospital has experienced negative levels of net income for the last five years. The total amount of accumulated deficits is $5 million, but you have noticed that unrestricted net assets has increased $2 million during the same period. How might this situation be explained?

9. You have been reading the footnotes to your hospital's financial statements and were surprised to see that the actuarial present value of accumulated pension plan benefits is $4,500,000. A footnote cites a fund of $8,500,000 that has been established to pay these benefits. However, you can find no mention of either the liability or the fund in the balance sheet. What might explain this situation?

SOLUTIONS AND ANSWERS

1. The calculations to determine the hospital's net operating income would be as follows:

Gross patient revenue	
Medicare (30 × $2,500)	$ 75,000
BCBS (30 × $2,500)	75,000
Commercial (20 × $2,500)	50,000
Medicaid (10 × $2,500)	25,000
Self-pay (8 × $2,500)	20,000
Charity (2 × $2,500)	5,000
Total	$ 250,000
Deductions from gross patient revenue	
Medicare [30 × ($2,500 − $2,000)]	$ 15,000
BCBS [30 × ($2,500 − $2,200)]	9,000
Commercial [20 × ($2,500 − $2,500)]	0
Medicaid [10 × ($2,500 − $2,200)]	3,000
Self-pay [8 × ($2,500 − $2,500)]	0
Charity [2 × ($2,500 − 0)]	5,000
Total deductions	$ 32,000
Net patient revenue	$ 218,000
Total expenses (100 × $2,200)	$ 220,000
Excess of revenues over expenses	$ (2,000)

2. The value reported for current maturities of long-term debt in the balance sheet should represent the value of debt principal that will be retired during the next fiscal year.

3. The four financial statements are the following:

   1. balance sheet,
   2. statement of revenues and expenses or statements of operations,
   3. statement of cash flows, and
   4. statement of changes in unrestricted net assets.

4. First, fair market value of the assets acquired by Shady Rest would be determined. In this example, we will assume that the current asset value would not change, but that the fixed assets would be restated to $300,000 at fair market value. Shady Rest is thus acquiring total assets worth $500,000 and assuming liabilities of $100,000 for a net book value of $400,000. Because Shady Rest is paying $850,000 for these assets, there would be a goodwill account of $450,000 created for the residual. The following account changes would occur:

   • cash—decrease of $850,000
   • current assets—increase of $200,000
   • net fixed assets—increase of $300,000
   • goodwill—increase of $450,000
   • current liabilities—increase of $100,000

The goodwill value would be charged to expense in future periods.

5. Pension expense would not require an actual expenditure of cash at the present time, although a payment may be made to a trustee for investment. Other accruals—such as vacation benefits, sick-leave benefits, and FICA (Federal Insurance Contributions Act) accruals—may not require immediate cash expenditures.
6. The fair market value of the items donated would be treated as other revenue. In this case, if $45,000 is the fair market value, that amount would be shown as other revenue.
7. Major categories of fund usage in the statement of cash flows are the following:

   • repayment of debt,
   • purchase of fixed assets, and
   • increase in working-capital items such as accounts receivable.

   Conservation of funds could occur in any one of these three areas. For example, the HMO could postpone or delay new fixed-asset acquisitions. It also could try to restructure its debt, especially in situations when a large proportion of the debt is short-term. Finally, it could attempt to reduce the amount of funds necessary for working-capital increases. This could be accomplished through a reduction in the HMO's receivable cycle or through an increase in its payable cycle.
8. In this example, the hospital has increased its total equity by $7 million through sources other than income. The most likely sources of these funds are transfers from restricted net assets, such as from plant replacement, or from direct equity transfers from related parties, such as a holding company. It is important to note that the funds were not derived from unrestricted contributions. Unrestricted contributions would have been shown as revenue and thus included in the computation of excess of revenues over expenses. It is also possible that unrealized gains on other than trading securities could have taken place.
9. Pension funds in a defined benefit plan are often held by a trustee and are not shown on the firm's financial statements. This is most likely the situation here. It is important to examine periodically the relationship between the pension fund and the actuarial present value of the pension fund liability. Changes in actuarial assumptions—for example, in mortality, investment yield, or inflation rates—can have a dramatic influence over the size of the liability. The relevant information can be found in the footnotes to the financial statements.

6

Accounting for Inflation

To adjust for the effects of changing price levels, the Financial Accounting Standards Board (FASB) has issued a number of pronouncements over the last thirty years. In September 1979, the FASB issued Statement 33, which required large public enterprises to provide supplemental information on the effects of changing price levels in their annual financial reports. This was a major step for the FASB and represented for the first time that firms were required to report price-level effects in their financial reports.

In 1986, the FASB substantially modified its initial position set forth in Statement 33 with the publication of Statement 9. This pronouncement left much of Statement 33 intact, except that it designated the reporting as voluntary. Business enterprises were encouraged but not required to report supplementary information on the effects of changing prices in the following areas for the most recent five years:

- net sales and operating revenues, using constant purchasing power,
- income from continuing operations on a current cost basis,
- purchasing power gains or losses from holding monetary items,
- increases in specific prices of net plant, property, and equipment net of inflation,
- foreign currency translation adjustments on a current cost basis,

- net assets (assets less liabilities) on a current cost basis,
- income per common share from continuing operations on a current cost basis,
- cash dividends per common share, and
- market price per common share at year end.

The rationale for these changes in financial reporting stems from the inaccuracy and inability of present, unadjusted, and historical cost reports to measure financial position accurately in an inflation-riddled economy. Unless inflationary pressures in the economy are removed, it seems logical to assume that alternative financial reporting systems that can account for the effects of changing price levels will be adopted. It also seems logical to expect that the accounting profession eventually will extend alternative reporting requirements to all business organizations. Hospitals and other health care organizations will, in all probability, be included.

Presently, the effect of these financial-reporting changes has not been clearly demonstrated. Thus, many individuals have formed beliefs and expectations about financial-reporting changes that may not be accurate.

The major purpose of this chapter is to discuss and describe the major alternatives for reflecting the effects of inflation in financial statements. Specific methods are described and the adjustments that need to be made to convert historical cost statements are illustrated. This discussion should provide a basis for understanding and using financial statements that have been adjusted for inflation.

REPORTING ALTERNATIVES

Methods of financial reporting can be categorized using two dimensions: (1) the method of asset valuation and (2) the unit of measurement. Two major methods of asset valuation are (1) acquisition (or historical) cost and (2) current (or replacement) value.

Asset valuation at acquisition cost means that the value of the asset is not changed over time to reflect changing market values. Amortization of the value may take place, but the basis is the acquisition cost. Depreciation is recorded, using the acquisition (historical) cost of the asset. Use of an acquisition cost valuation method postpones the recognition of gains or losses from holding assets until the point of sale or retirement. Current valuation of assets revalues the assets in each reporting period. The assets are stated at their current value rather than their acquisition cost. Likewise, depreciation expense is based on the current value, not the historical cost. Current valuation recognizes gains or losses from holding assets before sale or retirement.

There are also two major alternative units of measurement in financial reporting: (1) nominal (unadjusted) dollars and (2) constant dollars measured in units of general purchasing power. Use of a nominal dollar unit of measurement simply means that the attribute being measured is the number of dollars. From an accounting perspective, a dollar of one year is no different from a dollar of another year. No recognition is given to changes in the purchasing power of the dollar because the attribute is not measured. The major outcome associated with the use of this measure unit is that gains or losses, regardless of when they are recognized, are not adjusted for changes in purchasing power. For example, if a piece of land that was acquired for $1 million in 1979 were sold for $5 million in 1999, it would

have generated a $4 million gain, regardless of changes in the purchasing power of the dollar during the twenty-year period.

A constant dollar measuring unit reports the effects of all financial transactions in terms of constant purchasing power. The unit that is usually used is the purchasing power of the dollar at the end of the reporting period or the average during the fiscal year. The measurement is made by multiplying the unadjusted, or nominal, dollars by a price index to convert to a measure of constant purchasing power. During periods of inflation, when using a constant dollar measuring unit, gains from holding assets are reduced, whereas losses are increased. Thus, in the previous land sale example, the initial acquisition cost would be restated to 1999 dollars to reduce the gain in Exhibit 6–1.

Constant dollar measurement has a further significant effect on financial reporting: The gains or losses created by holding monetary liabilities or assets during periods of purchasing power changes are recognized in the financial reporting. For example, an entity that owed $25 million during a year when the purchasing power of the dollar decreased by 10 percent would report a $2.5 million (0.10 × $25 million) purchasing power gain. All gains or losses would be recognized, regardless of the valuation basis used.

Monetary assets and liabilities are defined as those items that reflect cash or claims to cash that are fixed in terms of the number of dollars, regardless of changes in prices. Almost all liabilities are monetary items, whereas monetary assets consist primarily of cash, marketable securities, and receivables. Purchasing power

Exhibit 6–1

Sale price of land (1999 dollars)	$5,000,000
Less acquisition cost restated (1999 dollars)	2,038,504
Gain on sale	$2,961,496

gains or losses are recognized on monetary items because there is an assumption that the gains or losses are already realized, because repayments or receipts are fixed.

The interfacing of the valuation basis and the unit of measurement basis produces four alternative financial reporting methods (Table 6–1). Each of the four methods is a possible basis for financial reporting. The unadjusted historical cost (HC) method represents the present method used by accountants; the other three methods are alternatives that would provide some degree of inflationary adjustment not present in the HC method. The HC–general price level adjusted (HC–GPL) method is referred to as historical cost/constant dollar accounting, whereas the current value–general price level adjusted (CV–GPL) method is referred to as current cost accounting.

Table 6–2 summarizes the effects the four reporting methods would have on the following three major income statement items: (1) depreciation expense, (2) purchasing power gains or losses, and (3) unrealized gains in replacement values. However, the net effect of the changes in these items on net income for an individual institution cannot be predicted; the composition and age of the assets, as well as the prior patterns of financing, will determine whether the net effect will be positive or negative and to what degree.

USES OF FINANCIAL REPORT INFORMATION

The measurement of financial position is an important function, and its results are useful to a

great variety of decision makers, both internal and external to the organization. Changes in financial reporting methods unquestionably will alter the resulting measures of financial position reported in financial statements. These changes are likely to produce changes in the decisions that are based on the financial reports (Figure 6–1).

Lenders represent an important category of financial statement users who may change their decisions on the basis of a new financial reporting method. The lender's major concern is the relative financial position of both the individual firm and the industry. A decrease in the relative financial position of the industry could seriously affect both the availability and the cost of credit. If, for a variety of reasons, new measurements of financial position make the health care industry appear weaker than other industries, financing terms could change. Particularly for the health care industry, which is increasingly dependent on debt financing, the importance of changes in financial reporting methods cannot be overstated. Research on the results of changing to an HC–GPL method has shown that the relative financial positions of individual firms and industries are also likely to change.

Changes in financial reporting methods also could have an effect on decisions reached by regulatory and rate-setting organizations. As a result of such changes, comparisons of costs across institutions may be more meaningful than they were previously. For example, depreciation in firms that operate in relatively new physical plants cannot be compared with the unadjusted historical depreciation costs of older facilities.

Table 6–1 Alternative Financial Reporting Bases

Unit of Measurement	Asset Valuation Method	
	Acquisition Cost	Current Value
Nominal dollars	Unadjusted historical cost (HC)	Current value (CV)
Constant dollars	Historical cost–general price level adjusted (HC–GPL) Constant dollar accounting	Current value–general price level adjusted (CV–GPL) Current cost accounting

Table 6–2 Major Effect of Alternative Reporting Methods on Net Income Measurement

| | | *Impact Variables* | |
	Depreciation Expense	*Purchasing Power Gains/Losses*	*Unrealized Gains in Replacement Value*
Reporting Methods			
HC	No change	No change/not recognized	No change/not recognized
HC–GPL	Increase/GPL depreciation is recognized	Gain or loss/ depends on the net monetary asset position	No change/not recognized
CV	Increase/will recognize replacement cost	No change/not recognized	Gain/will recognize increase in replacement cost
CV–GPL	Increase/will recognize current replacement cost	Gain or loss/ depends on the net monetary asset position	Gain/will recognize increase in replacement cost but will reduce amount by changes in the GPL

Without financial reporting adjustments, new facilities may appear to have higher costs and thus be less efficient, whereas, in fact, the opposite may be true.

The actions of interested community leaders who have access to, and make decisions based on, financial statements also might be affected by reporting method changes. For example, suppose that individual, corporate, and public agency giving is in part affected by reported income. Many, in fact, regard reported income as a basic index of need, and the relationship between income and giving seems logical. Thus, because each of the alternative financial reporting methods we have discussed will produce a different measure of income, total giving in each case could be affected.

Internal management decisions also might change with a new financial reporting method. Perhaps the most obvious example of such a change would be rate-setting. Organizations that have control over pricing decisions and are not

reacting to market-determined prices should set prices at levels at least high enough to recover their costs. The use of any of the three alternative methods of reporting will increase reported cost levels and therefore increase rates.

CASE EXAMPLE: WILLIAMS CONVALESCENT CENTER

In the remainder of this chapter, we show how adjustments are made in the income statement and balance sheet of Williams Convalescent Center, a 120-bed skilled and intermediate care facility, to take into account the effects of inflation. The center's two financial statements are shown in Tables 6–3 and 6–4. You will note that values are reported for each of the following three reporting methods: (1) HC, (2) HC–GPL, and (3) CV–GPL. In this discussion, we do not describe or apply the CV method. This method is not being seriously considered by the accounting profession presently, and it is not likely to be

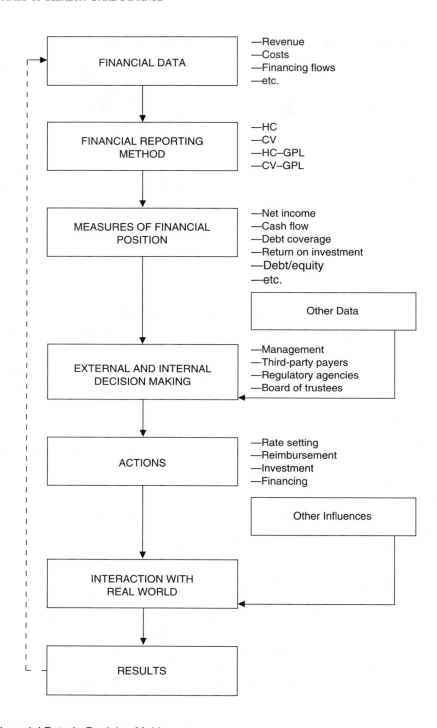

Figure 6–1 Financial Data in Decision Making

Table 6–3 Statement of Income for Williams Convalescent Center (000s Omitted)

	HC 19Y4	Constant Dollar (HC–GPL) 19Y4	Current Cost (CV–GPL) 19Y4
Operating revenue	$3,556	$3,625	$3,625
Operating expenses	3,253	3,316	3,316
Depreciation	74	177	185
Interest	102	104	104
Net income	$ 127	$ 28	$ 20
Purchasing power gain from holding net monetary liabilities during the year	—	$ 43	$ 43
Increase in specific prices of property, plant, and equipment during the year	—	—	$ 136
Less effect of increase in general price level	—	—	$ 144
Increase in specific prices over (under) increase in the general price level	—	—	$ (8)
Change in equity due to income transactions	$ 127	$ 71	$ 55

considered in the future. The CV method suffers from a serious flaw: it does not recognize the effects of changing price levels on equity. In short, the CV method would treat increases in the replacement cost of assets as a gain and not restate them for changes in purchasing power.

Table 6–5 presents values for the consumer price index (CPI). The CPI is the price index that is presently used by the accounting profession to adjust financial statements for the effects of inflation.

Price Index Conversion

Both of the two methods we have selected to adjust the financial statements of the Williams Convalescent Center (CV–GPL and HC–GPL) use a constant dollar as the unit of measurement. This means that purchasing power, not the dollar, is the unit of measurement.

That is, all reported values in the financial statements are expressed in dollars of a specified purchasing power. Usually, the purchasing power used is the period end value. In our case example, Williams Convalescent Center uses purchasing power as of December 31, 19Y4, as its unit of measurement.

Restatement of nominal or unadjusted dollars to constant dollars is a relatively simple process, at least conceptually. All that is required are the following three pieces of information:

1. the unadjusted value of the account in historical or nominal dollars,
2. a price index that reflects the purchasing power in which the unadjusted value is currently expressed, and
3. a price index that reflects the purchasing power at the date the account is to be restated.

Table 6–4 Balance Sheet for Williams Convalescent Center (000s Omitted)

	HC 19Y3	HC 19Y4	Constant Dollar (HC–GPL) 19Y4	Current Cost (CV–GPL) 19Y4
Current assets				
Cash	$ 98	$ 21	$ 21	$ 21
Accounts receivable	217	249	249	249
Supplies	22	27	27	27
Prepaid expenses	36	36	36	36
Total current assets	$ 373	$ 333	$ 333	$ 333
Property and equipment				
Land	200	200	530	525
Building and equipment	2,102	2,228	5,333	5,570
	2,302	2,428	5,863	6,095
Less accumulated depreciation	783	844	2,020	2,186
Investments	161	596	596	596
Total assets	$2,053	$2,513	$4,772	$4,838
Current liabilities	412	493	493	493
Long-term debt	1,203	1,478	1,478	1,478
Partners' equity	438	542	2,801	2,867
	$2,053	$2,513	$4,772	$4,838

For example, Williams Convalescent Center's long-term debt at December 31, 19Y3, is $1,203 (see Table 6–4). To express that amount in constant dollars as of December 31, 19Y4, the following adjustment would be made:

Unadjusted amount ×

$$\frac{\text{Price index converting to}}{\text{Price index converting from}} =$$

Constant dollar value

or

$$\$1,203 \times \frac{315.5}{303.5} = \$1,251$$

The value of the beginning long-term debt for the center would be $1,251, expressed in purchasing power as of December 31, 19Y4. The previously described adjusted method is the same for all other accounts. The price index to which the conversion is made is usually the price index at the ending balance sheet date (December 31, 19Y4, in our example). The price index from which the conversion is made represents the purchasing power in which the account is currently expressed. This value will vary depending on the classification of the account as either monetary or nonmonetary.

Monetary versus Nonmonetary Accounts

When restating financial statements from one based on an HC method to one based on a con-

Table 6–5 Consumer Price Index, Year-End Values

Year	CPI
19X0	119.1
19X1	123.1
19X2	127.3
19X3	138.5
19X4	155.4
19X5	166.3
19X6	174.3
19X7	186.1
19X8	202.9
19X9	229.9
19Y0	258.4
19Y1	283.4
19Y2	292.4
19Y3	303.5
19Y4	315.5

Source: Reprinted from United States Department of Labor, Bureau of Labor Statistics.

stant dollar method, it is critical to distinguish between monetary accounts and nonmonetary accounts. Monetary accounts are automatically stated in current dollars and therefore require no price level adjustments. Monetary items, discussed earlier in this chapter, consist of cash, claims to cash, or promises to pay cash that are fixed in terms of dollars, regardless of price-level changes. Nonmonetary accounts require price-level adjustments to be stated in current dollars.

Because of the fixed nature of monetary items, holding them during a period of changing price levels creates a gain or loss. This can be seen in Table 6–6, which includes data from the Williams Convalescent Center (000s omitted).

The data in Table 6–6 assume that a repayment and new issue occurred at the midpoint of the year, June 30, 19Y4. The price index at that point would have been approximately 309.5. This resulted from taking the average of the beginning and ending values (303.5 + 315.5)/2. In constant dollars, the Williams Convalescent Center would have reported $1,531 of long-term debt as of December 31, 19Y4. However, the actual value of the long-term debt at that date was $1,478. The difference of $53 represents a purchasing power gain to the center during the year. Because the price level increased during 19Y4, the value of the long-term debt actually owed by the center declined when measured in constant purchasing power.

Nonmonetary asset accounts always must be restated to purchasing power as of the current date. The price index at the time of acquisition represents the price index from which the conversion is made. The price index at the current date represents the index to which the conversion is made. To illustrate the adjustment, assume that the building and equipment account of the Williams Convalescent Center has the age distribution presented in Table 6–7.

Table 6–6 Computation Purchasing Power Gains and Losses

	Unadjusted	Conversion Factor	Constant Dollars
Beginning long-term debt (12/31/Y3)	$1,203	315.5/303.5	$1,251
−Repayment (6/30/Y4)	152	315.5/309.5	155
+ New debt (6/30/Y4)	427	315.5/309.5	435
Ending long-term debt (12/31/Y4)	$1,478		$1,531
−Actual ending long-term debt (12/31/Y4)			$1,478
Purchasing power gain			$ 53

Table 6–7 Restatement of Nonmonetary Assets

Year Acquired	Cost	Conversion Factor	Constant Dollar Cost (12/31/Y4)
19X0	$1,500	315.5/119.1	$3,974
19X8	401	315.5/202.9	624
19Y1	201	315.5/283.4	224
19Y4	126	315.5/315.5	126
	$2,228		$4,948

The data in Table 6–7 show that assets with a historical cost of $2,228 represent $4,948 of cost when stated in dollars as of December 31, 19Y4. The latter value is much more meaningful than the former as a measure of actual asset cost in 19Y4. It provides the center with a measure of cost that is expressed in dollars as of the current date and thus better represents its actual investment. Depreciation expense also should be restated in 19Y4 dollars to accurately portray the center's actual cost of using its building and equipment in the generation of current revenues. (Please note that the value reported for building and equipment cost in Table 6–4 does not match the $4,948 calculated because a different method was used to estimate cost.)

Adjusting the Income Statement

Operating Revenues

If one assumes that revenues are realized equally throughout the year, the restatement is significantly simplified. If the assumption is valid—and in most cases it is—it means that the revenues can be considered realized at the midpoint of the year, in our case, June 30, 19Y4. As already noted, the price index at June 30, 19Y4 can be assumed to be the average of the beginning and ending price index, or 309.5. The restated operating revenue would be calculated as follows:

$$\$3,556 \times 315.5/309.5 = \$3,625$$

Operating Expenses

Based on the same assumption that we used with operating revenues, the adjustment for operating expenses would be as follows:

$$\$3,253 \times 315.5/309.5 = \$3,316$$

Operating expenses do not include depreciation or interest. Separate adjustments for these two items may be required.

Depreciation

The depreciation expense adjustment is different from the earlier adjustments in two ways. First, depreciation expense represents an amortization of assets purchased over a long period, usually many years. This means that the midpoint conversion method used for operating revenues and operating expenses is clearly not appropriate. Second, the adjustment methods for the constant dollar and current cost methods diverge. Depreciation expense may vary considerably because the current cost of the assets may differ dramatically from the constant dollar cost. Remember, a price index represents price changes for a large number of goods and services; specific price changes of individual assets may vary significantly from that index.

Constant Dollar Adjustment. Two methods can be used to adjust depreciation expense to a constant dollar amount. The most accurate method is to perform an adjustment for each asset. This can be a time-consuming process, however, and may not be worth the effort. Alternatively, the average acquisition date can be estimated by first determining the average age of the assets as follows:

$$\text{Average age} =$$

$$\frac{\text{Accumulated depreciation}}{\text{Depreciation expense}} =$$

$$\frac{\$844}{\$74} = 11.4 \text{ years}$$

Straight-line depreciation, which estimates average age, is reasonably reliable. For Williams Convalescent Center, an average of 11.4 years would imply that the assets were purchased sometime in 19X3. Interpolation would yield a price index of 131.8. Thus, depreciation expense in 19Y4, expressed in constant dollars, would be the following:

$$\$74 \times 315.5/131.8 = \$177$$

Current Cost Adjustment. The identification of the current cost of existing physical assets is a subjective and complex process. To many individuals, the current cost method provides little additional value compared with the constant dollar method. Whether it will be eventually eliminated and replaced by the constant dollar method is not clear at this time.

The first issue to address in the adjustment is the definition of current cost. By and large, current cost can be equated to the replacement cost of the assets. In short, we must determine what the cost of replacing assets in today's dollars would be. This could be estimated through a variety of techniques using, for example, insurance appraisals or specific price indexes. In the case of Williams Convalescent Center, we will assume that a recent insurance appraisal indicated a replacement cost of $5,570 for buildings and equipment. With this estimate, depreciation expense could be adjusted as follows:

$$\frac{\text{Appraisal cost}}{\text{Historical cost}} \times \text{Depreciation expense} =$$

Restated depreciation expense

or

$$\frac{\$5,570}{\$2,228} \times \$74 = \$185$$

Interest Expense

We will again assume that interest expense is paid equally throughout the year. This assumption would produce the following interest expense adjustment:

$$\$102 \times 315.5/309.5 = \$104$$

Purchasing Power Gains or Losses

A purchasing power gain results if one is a net debtor during a period of increasing prices, whereas a purchasing power loss results if one is a net creditor during such a period. In most health care firms, purchasing power gains result because liabilities exceed monetary assets. A firm is thus paying its debts with dollars that are of less value than the ones it received.

To calculate purchasing power gains or losses, net monetary asset positions must first be calculated. The net monetary position for Williams Convalescent Center is presented in Table 6–8.

The actual calculation of the purchasing power gain for Williams Convalescent Center is presented in Table 6–9.

Because the center was in a net monetary liability position during the year, it experienced a purchasing power gain of $43. This value is not an element of net income; it is, rather, shown below the net income line in Table 6–3. It thus affects the change in equity.

Table 6–8 Net Monetary Asset Schedule

	Beginning (12/31/Y3)	Ending (12/31/Y4)
Monetary assets		
Cash	$ 98	$ 21
Accounts receivable	217	249
Prepaid expenses	36	36
Investments	161	596
Total monetary	$ 512	$ 902
Monetary liabilities		
Current liabilities	$ 412	$ 493
Long-term	1,203	1,478
Total monetary liabilities	$ 1,615	$ 1,971
Net monetary assets	$(1,103)	$(1,069)

Increase in Specific Prices Over General Prices

The adjustment to consider—an increase in specific prices over general prices—is made only in the current cost method. The constant dollar method does not recognize any increases (or reductions) in prices that are different from the general price level. In short, no gains or losses from holding assets are permitted in the constant dollar method.

The calculations involved in this adjustment can be complex. In our Williams Convalescent Center example, we will make some assumptions to simplify the arithmetic without impairing the reader's conceptual understanding of the adjustment. We will assume the following data:

Insurance appraisal of buildings and equipment, 12/31/Y3	$5,015
Insurance appraisal of buildings and equipment, 12/31/Y4	$5,570
Appraised value of land, 12/31/Y3	$ 500
Appraised value of land, 12/31/Y4	$ 525
New equipment bought on 12/31/Y4	$ 126

Table 6–10 shows the increase in specific prices over general prices.

These data show that, during 19Y4, the value of physical assets held by Williams Convales-

Table 6–9 Purchasing Power Gain (Loss) Schedule

	Actual Dollars	Conversion Factor	Constant Dollars
Beginning net monetary liabilities	$1,103	315.5/303.5	$1,147
–Decrease	34	315.5/309.5	35
Ending net monetary liabilities	$1,069		$1,112
–Actual			$1,069
Purchasing power gain			$ 43

Table 6–10 Increase in Specific over General Prices Schedule

	Building and Equipment	Land	Total
Ending appraised value			
less acquisitions	$5,444	$525	$5,969
−Accumulated depreciation			
on appraised value	2,186	0	2,186
Ending net appraised value	$3,258	$525	$3,783
Beginning appraised value	$5,015	$500	$5,515
−Accumulated depreciation			
on appraised value	1,868	—	1,868
Beginning net appraised value	$3,147	$500	$3,647
Increase in specific prices			
during the year			$ 136
Effect of increase in general price level	$3,647 × [(315.5/303.5) − 1.0]		$ 144
Increase in specific prices over			
general price level			$ (8)

cent Center did not increase more than the general price level. This may be a positive sign for the center if it is not contemplating a sale. The replacement cost for its assets is increasing less than the general price level. Therefore, revenues could increase less than the general price level and replacement could still be ensured.

Adjusting the Balance Sheet

Monetary Items

None of the monetary items—cash, accounts receivable, prepaid expenses, investments, current liabilities, or long-term debt—requires adjustment. The values of these items already reflect current dollars.

Land

In our discussion of the increase in specific prices over the general price level in the Will-

iams Convalescent Center's income statement, we assumed an appraisal value for land of $525. That value will be used here with the current cost method. With the constant dollar method, we will assume that the land was acquired in 19X0 for $200. To restate that amount to purchasing power as of December 31, 19Y4, the following calculation would be made:

$$\$200 \times 315.5/119.1 = \$530$$

Buildings and Equipment

Values for the center's buildings and equipment and the related accumulated depreciation already have been cited for the current cost method. We will assume those same values here. This produces a value for buildings and equipment of $5,570 (000s omitted) based on an appraisal. The value for accumulated depreciation was derived as follows:

Adjusted accumulated depreciation =

Unadjusted accumulated depreciation ×

$$\frac{\text{Appraised value} - \text{Current year acquisitions}}{\text{Historical cost} - \text{Current year acquisitions}}$$

or

$$\$2,186 = \$844 \times \frac{(\$5,570 - \$126)}{(\$2,228 - \$126)}$$

The constant dollar method values can be derived by using the estimated average age of the plant. In earlier discussions relating to depreciation expense, we computed the average age to be 11.4 years and the related price index at acquisition to be 131.8. With this information, the following values result:

Buildings and equipment =
$2,228 × 315.5/131.8 = $5,333

Accumulated depreciation =
$844 × 315.5/131.8 = $2,020

Equity

Equity calculations are not discussed in any detail here. It is enough for our purposes to recognize that equity is a derived figure. Equity must equal total assets less liabilities. In our Williams Convalescent Center example, this generates values of $2,801 for the constant dollar method and $2,867 for the current cost method.

SUMMARY

Financial reporting suffers from its current reliance on the HC valuation concept. Inflation has made many of the reported values in current financial reports meaningless to decision makers. The example used in this chapter illustrates this point. The total asset investment of Williams Convalescent Center is approximately 100 percent larger when adjusted for inflation under the current cost or constant dollar method. Net income, however, decreased. The result is a dramatic deterioration in return on investment—the single most important test of business success.

Table 6–11 summarizes return on assets and return on equity for Williams Convalescent Center.

These reductions are so drastic that they would prompt an investor to seriously question the continuation of the present investment, let alone replacement. More profitable avenues of investment very likely may be available.

To the extent that our Williams Convalescent Center example is representative of many health care firms—and it probably is—decisions re-

---

Table 6–11 Effect of Alternative Reporting Methods on Financial Measures

	Historical Cost	Constant Dollar	Current Cost
Return on assets (ROA)			
Net income/Total assets	5.1%	0.6%	0.4%
Revised ROA			
Change in equity due to			
Income transaction/Total assets	5.1	1.5	1.1
Return on equity (ROE)			
Net income equity	23.4	1.0	0.7
Revised ROE			
Change in equity due to			
income transactions/Equity	23.4	2.5	1.9

garding health care business continuation must be evaluated seriously. It is imperative that health care companies, like all other businesses, adjust their financial reports to reflect inflation.

Whether the method used is current cost or constant dollar is not the issue. The important point is that ignoring the effects of inflation is unwise at best.

ASSIGNMENTS

Use the data and information presented in Exhibit 6–2 to answer the following questions:

1. What index was used to restate to constant dollars?
2. What method was used to determine current cost values?
3. Is the American Medical Firm (AMF) a net debtor or a net creditor?
4. In 1996, AMF showed a minus $24 million value for the increase in specific prices over general prices. What does this mean?
5. Why are AMF's net operating revenues in 1999 identical for the HC, constant dollar, and current cost methods of reporting?
6. Why is depreciation expense greater in the current cost method than in the constant dollar method?

Exhibit 6–2 Supplementary Financial Information for American Medical Firm (AMF)

Effects of Changing Prices	The company's financial statements have been prepared in accordance with generally accepted accounting principles and reflect historical cost. The goal of the supplemental information that follows is to reflect the decline in the purchasing power of the dollar resulting from inflation. This information should be viewed only as an indication, however, and not as a specific measure of the inflationary impact.
	The constant dollars were calculated by adjusting historical cost amounts by the CPI. Current costs, however, reflect the changes in specific prices of land, buildings, and equipment from the date acquired to the present; they differ from constant dollar amounts to the extent that prices in general have increased more or less rapidly than specific prices. The current cost of buildings and equipment was determined by applying published indices to the historical cost.
	Net income has been adjusted only for the change in depreciation expense. Other operating expenses, which are the result of current transactions, are, in effect, recorded in amounts approximating purchasing power on the primary financial statements. Depreciation expense was determined by applying primary financial statement depreciation rates to restated building and equipment amounts. Because only historical costs are deductible for income tax purposes, the income tax expense in the primary financial statements was not adjusted.
	During a period of inflation, the holding of monetary assets (cash, receivables, etc.) results in a purchasing power loss, whereas owing monetary liabilities (current liabilities, long-term debt, deferred credits, etc.) results in a gain. Net monetary gains or losses are not included in the adjusted net income amounts reported.

continues

Exhibit 6–2 continued

Consolidated Statement of Income Adjusted for Changing Prices	(dollar amounts are expressed in millions)	For the Year Ended December 31, 1999		
		As Reported in Primary Statements (Historical Cost)	Adjusted for General Inflation (Constant $)	Adjusted for Changes in Specific Prices (Current Costs)
	Net operating revenue	$2,065	$2,065	$2,065
	Operating and administrative expenses	$1,698	$1,698	$1,698
	Depreciation and amortization	84	98	111
	Interest	91	91	91
	Total cost and expenses	$1,873	$1,887	$1,900
	Income from operations	$ 192	$ 178	$ 165
	Investment earnings	$ 24	$ 24	$ 24
	Income before taxes on income	$ 216	$ 202	$ 189
	Taxes on income	95	95	95
	Net income	$ 121	$ 107	$ 94
	Effective income tax rate	44%	47%	50%

Changing price gains not included in adjusted income:
Increase in specific prices (current cost) of property,
plant, and equipment held during the year* $ 139
Less effect of increase in general price level   68

Excess of increase in specific prices over increase in the
general price level $ 71

*As of December 31, 1999, current cost of property, plant, and equipment, net of accumulated depreciation, was $1,915 (historical cost $1,349). "Property, plant, and equipment" in both the previous and following data includes land held for expansion.

continues

Exhibit 6–2 continued

Selected Supplementary Financial Data Adjusted for Effects of Changing Prices	(dollar amounts, except pre-share amounts, are expressed in millions) For the Years Ended Dec. 31				
		1999	1998	1997	1996	1995
Net operating revenues Adjusted for general inflation	$2,065	$1,852	$1,271	$1,070	$832
Net Income Adjusted for general inflation	107	85	73	54	36
Adjusted for changes in specific prices	94	73	64	46	27
Earnings per share Adjusted for general inflation	1.54	1.29	1.18	.95	.82
Adjusted for changes in specific prices	1.35	1.12	1.04	.82	.61
Purchasing power gain from holding net monetary liabilities during the year	28	15	16	22	32
Increase in specific prices of property, plant, and equipment over (under) increases in the general price level	71	85	16	(24)	77
Net assets at year end (total assets less total liabilities) Adjusted for general inflation	1,095	972	756	657	413
Adjusted for changes in specific prices	1,332	1,162	894	809	470
Cash dividends declared per common share Adjusted for general inflation	$ 0.43	$ 0.39	$ 0.34	$ 0.28	$0.21
Market price per common share at year end: adjusted for general inflation	$20.24	$29.41	$12.39	$24.30	$11.66
Average CPI–all urban consumers	303.9	293.4	280.3	257.5	230.0

SOLUTIONS AND ANSWERS

1. AMF used the CPI, which is required by Financial Accounting Standards Board Statement 33 to restate historical costs to constant dollars.
2. AMF used specific price indexes to restate historical costs to current costs. This method contrasts with the use of appraisals discussed in the chapter example.
3. AMF is a net debtor. It has experienced a purchasing power gain in each year from 1995 to 1999. Because prices were increasing during that period, AMF must have had a net monetary liability position in each year.
4. In 1996, the specific prices of AMF's fixed assets must have increased less than the general price level as determined by using the CPI.
5. AMF does not restate revenues or expenses to the fiscal year end, December 31. Instead, they restate to the midpoint of the fiscal year, June 30. Because it is usually assumed that revenues are received equally throughout the year, the midpoint (June 30) would represent the index from which the conversion is made. Because AMF is converting to the midpoint index, the adjustment is 1.0.
6. Depreciation expense under the current cost method exceeds depreciation expense under the constant dollar method because the current cost value of depreciable assets exceeds the constant dollar value of depreciable assets.

7

Analyzing Financial Statements

The major purpose of this chapter is to introduce some analytical tools for evaluating the financial condition of health care entities. Think for a moment how confusing and difficult it would be, without a key, to reach any conclusions about financial position from any of the financial statements presented in Chapter 5. Unless your training is in business or finance, the statements may look like a mass of endless numbers with little meaning. In short, there may be too much information in most financial statements to be digested easily by a general-purpose user.

An exhaustive list of people who might use general-purpose financial information would be difficult to prepare. The following are some of the potential users and their reasons for measuring financial condition.

- boards of trustees, to evaluate the solvency of their facilities and establish a framework for various decisions, such as those relating to investment, financing, and pricing
- creditors, to determine the amounts and terms of credit to be granted to health care facilities and to evaluate the security of presently outstanding credit obligations

- employee unions, to evaluate the financial condition of a health care facility and its ability to meet increasing demands for higher wages; also, to assess the capability of the facility to meet existing contractual relationships for deferred compensation programs, such as pension plans
- departmental managers, to better understand how operations and activities under their direct control contribute to the entity's overall financial position
- rate-regulating agencies, to assess the adequacy of existing and proposed rates of a health care facility that is subject to rate review
- grant-giving agencies (public and private), to determine a grantee's ability to continue to provide services supported by a grant and to assess the need for additional funding
- public, to determine a community health care facility's financial condition and assess its need for rate increases and its use of prior funds to enhance and improve the delivery of health care services; also, as a basis for assessing the need for money in a fund drive

ASSESSING FINANCIAL PERFORMANCE: SUSTAINABLE GROWTH

Understanding financial performance in any business requires some global or summary measure of financial success. For many health care organization executives, this measure is often the operating margin (operating income divided by revenues). We believe that this measure is wrong and can be misleading in many situations. For example, low operating margins may not always be "bad" and high operating margins may not always be "good."

What should be the primary criterion for financial success in health care organizations? We believe that a financially successful organization is capable of generating the resources needed to meet its mission. This creates two immediate questions. First, what are resources? Second, what level of resources are needed to fulfill the mission? Economic resources that are owned or controlled by a business firm are referred to as assets and would include such items as supplies, equipment, buildings, and other factors of production that must be present to produce health services. Human resources are not usually shown as assets because the firm does not own an individual, but human resources also are required in the production of products or services. Resources or assets owned by a health care organization are shown in its balance sheet, which provides a listing of its assets and the pattern of financing used to acquire those assets. The level of resources required by a health care organization depends largely on the range and quantity of health services envisioned in the mission statement. In situations when there is no scientific standard for resource requirements, benchmarking against other health care organizations may be used to partially address the issue of resource need. A hospital or health care firm can find itself in a situation when it may have too little investment in assets to meet the production needs for services, or it may have excessive investment in assets of a certain category.

Resources can be financed with either debt or equity funds as any balance sheet clearly shows. A financially successful organization must therefore be capable of generating the amount of funds through debt and/or equity that is needed to finance the required level of resources. Figure 7–1 depicts a simple balance sheet that illustrates these concepts. In this example, our health care organization needs to increase its investment in assets, or resources, by $100 million over the next seven years to fulfill its mission. This level of future investment should be a by-product of the hospital's strategic plan. A strategic plan should provide some information about projected service levels, which in turn should drive expected investment. Strategic financial planning will be the topic of a later chapter. The rate of annual compounded asset growth for the example in Figure 7–1 is approximately 10 percent per year. This rate equals the average rate of asset growth in voluntary nonprofit hospitals during the last five years. Although this growth rate may seem high, remember that this rate incorporates replacement of assets at higher prices, new technology, entry into new product lines requiring new investment, and increases in working capital such as accounts receivable. The health care organization depicted in Figure 7–1 has chosen a financing mix of 50 percent equity and 50 percent debt. This means that seven years later, the target financing mix will be $100 million of debt and $100 million of equity to finance the $200 million investment in assets.

The principle of sustainable growth states that no business entity can generate a growth rate in assets (10 percent in our example) that is greater than its growth rate in equity (also 10 percent in our example) for a prolonged period. It may be possible to generate new asset growth, of 15 percent for several years when equity growth is only 5 percent by changing the percentages of equity and debt financing. There is no mystery in the principle of sustainable growth, and it is not some esoteric finance concept that bears no relationship to reality. Any business will have its asset growth rates limited by its ability to generate

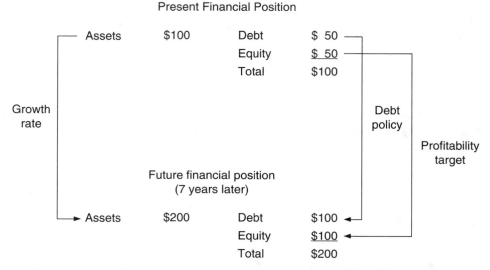

Figure 7–1 Sustainable Growth

new equity growth. To not believe in the validity of this concept would imply that a firm could always increase its percentage of debt financing to any level. There are no exceptions to this theorem. It is not something that represents a nice target; it is a fundamental principle of business from which no one is exempt. Some governmental health care organizations may argue that they always generate growth rates in equity less than their asset growth because they get capital funds directly from their governmental sponsors. Those transfers represent a transfer of equity and are a part of equity growth.

There is no other financial objective that is more important than equity growth for measuring long-term financial success in any business entity. Health care organizations that expect low rates of equity growth in the future most likely will not be able to provide the level of resources sufficient to meet their mission. If your health care organization anticipates growth rates in equity of only 5 percent over the next decade, it is almost certain that your asset growth potential will be no greater than 5 percent. Although the objective is not to add assets or investments for the sake of growth, health care organizations

that remain viable must add new investments. Health care organizations with low rates of growth in equity most likely will experience most of their asset growth in working capital areas such as accounts receivable and supplies. These firms will invest very little in renovation and replacement of existing equipment and plant, and very little in new capital required for entry into new markets. If they are surrounded by firms that are not experiencing low equity growth rates, their market share will decrease as their relative delivery capability deteriorates.

Growth rate in equity (GRIE) can be expressed as follows:

$$\frac{\text{Change in equity}}{\text{Equity}} =$$

$$\frac{\text{Net income}}{\text{Equity}} \times \frac{\text{Change in equity}}{\text{Net income}} =$$

$$\frac{\text{Return on equity}}{\text{Reported income index}}$$

Where reported income index =
net income/change in equity

Most voluntary nonprofit health care organizations do not have a source of equity other than net income. This means that no transfers of funds from government or large restricted endowments exist to increase the hospital's change in equity from the level of reported net income. In these situations, the reported income index equals one, and therefore, GRIE can be defined as net income divided by equity, or return on equity (ROE). ROE is therefore the primary financial criterion that should be used to evaluate and target financial performance for voluntary nonprofit health care organizations when transfers of new equity are not likely. ROE is also the primary financial criterion that should be used to evaluate and target financial performance for taxable for-profit firms.

ROE can be factored into a number of components that help executives analyze and improve their ROE values. The following equation defines ROE:

$$\frac{(\text{Operating income} + \text{Nonoperating income})}{\text{Revenue}} \times$$

$$\frac{\text{Revenue}}{\text{Assets}} \times \frac{\text{Assets}}{\text{Equity}}$$

The previous relationship tells us that there are a variety of ways that an organization can improve its ROE. First, it can improve its operating margins (operating income divided by revenue). Second, it can increase its nonoperating gain ratio (nonoperating income divided by revenue). Third, it can increase its total asset turnover (revenue divided by assets). Fourth, it can reduce its equity financing ratio (equity divided by assets). Operating margin improvement is an important strategy for improving ROE, but it is not the only way that ROE can be increased and sustainable growth achieved. Figure 7–2, which depicts a strategic management model, breaks down the ROE relationship further and identifies specific relationships that can have a direct bearing on ROE for hospitals.

RATIO ANALYSIS

The technique used to assess financial condition is financial ratio analysis, the examination of the relation of two pieces of financial information to obtain additional information. In this process, the new information is both easier to understand and usually more relevant than the unrelated, free-standing information found in general-purpose financial statements. For example, the values of fund balance and total assets may have little meaning when stated independently in a balance sheet. When the ratio of the two is taken, however, it is possible to indicate the proportion of assets that has been financed with sources other than debt.

Financial ratios are not another attempt by financial specialists to confuse and confound decision makers. Financial ratios have been empirically tested to determine their value in predicting business failure. The results to date have been impressive: financial ratios can, in fact, discern potential problems in financial condition even five years before their emergence.

Unfortunately, much financial information is never subjected to financial ratio analysis; the mass of figures just seems too voluminous ever to be synthesized. Decision makers tend to assume that if the entity is "breathing" at the end of the year and is capable of publishing a financial statement, all must be well. If something goes wrong later, the accountant is blamed for not warning the decision makers. Sometimes the accountant is at fault. However, the decision makers are often responsible because they did not analyze and interpret the financial information given to them in published financial statements.

Meaningful ratio analysis relies heavily on the existence of relevant, comparable data. Absolute values of ratios usually are more valuable than the underlying financial information; but they are even more valuable when they can be com-

Level 1

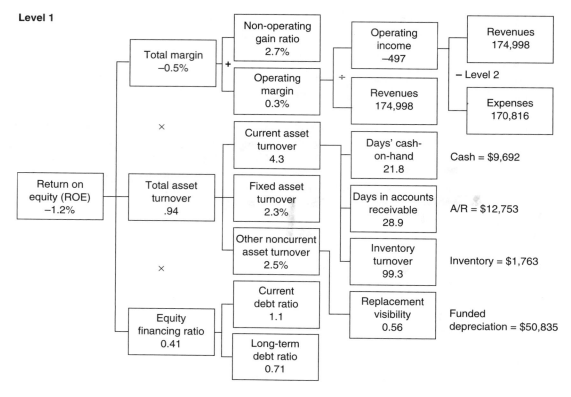

Level 2

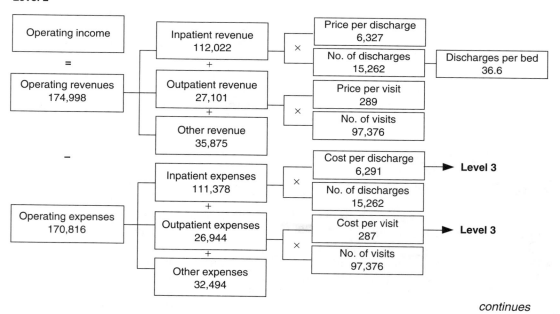

continues

Figure 7–2 Strategic Management Model

Figure 7–2 continued

Level 3

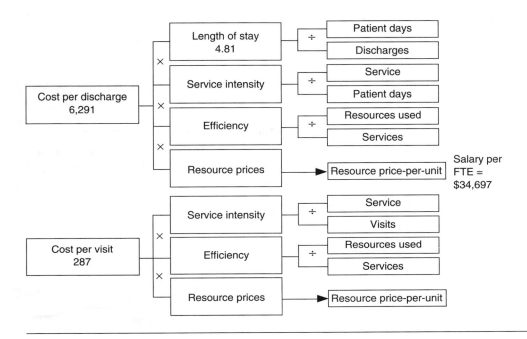

pared with existing standards. For example, the statement that a hospital earned 3 percent on its revenues in the previous year is useful, but a statement of the relationship of this 3 percent to some standard would be much more valuable.

Usually, the analysis of financial ratios involves two types of comparisons. Temporal comparison of ratios, the comparison of year-end ratios to prior-year values, gives the analyst some idea of both trend and desirability. A projected financial ratio similarly may be compared with prior actual values to test the validity of the projection and the desirability of the proposed plan of operation.

A second method of comparison uses industry averages as the relevant standards for comparison. The Center for Healthcare Industry Performance Studies (CHIPS) produces a large number of financial, operating, and clinical

benchmarks for the hospital industry. Financial standards for other industry segments are supplied by other firms and will be discussed in the next chapter.

Financial ratios can be classified into the following five major categories for the purposes of this chapter:

1. liquidity ratios,
2. capital structure ratios,
3. activity ratios,
4. profitability ratios, and
5. other ratios.

In the following discussion, individual ratios within each of these categories are defined regarding their assessment of financial condition. The specific indicators described are a subset of the ratios used by CHIPS. Additional information about CHIPS data sets can be obtained by contacting CHIPS at 1-800-859-2447. The financial statement of Omega Health Foundation (OHF), shown in Tables 5–1 and 5–3, illustrates the discussion.

It may seem to some that undue emphasis is being placed on financial reporting and financial analysis in the hospital sector. Regarding coverage in this chapter, this is true. However, ratios are general in nature and are just as relevant in other health care settings. For example, use of a current ratio that measures an entity's liquidity is valid and helpful not only for hospitals but also for nursing homes, health maintenance organizations (HMOs), outpatient clinics, and surgicenters. Furthermore, understanding the application of financial ratios in the relatively more complex hospital environment makes their application in other settings easier. The next chapter will include discussion of financial standards for other industry segments.

Liquidity Ratios

Liquidity is a term frequently used by people in the business and financial world. It refers to the ability of a firm to meet its short-term maturing obligations. The more liquid a firm, the better it is able to meet its short-term obligations or current liabilities. Liquidity is an important dimension in the assessment of financial condition. Most firms that experience financial problems do so because of a liquidity crisis; they are unable to pay current obligations as they become due. Measuring an entity's liquidity position is central to determining its financial condition. Other long-term factors, such as a poor accounts receivable collection policy, may explain a poor liquidity position; but the worsening of a liquidity position is usually the first clue that something more basic is wrong.

Current Ratio

One of the most widely used measures of liquidity is the current ratio:

$$\frac{\text{Current assets}}{\text{Current liabilities}}$$

For OHF, the current ratio values for 1999 and 1998 are as follows:

1999	1998
$\dfrac{40,448,000}{36,216,000} = 1.12$	$\dfrac{42,268,000}{29,729,000} = 1.42$

The higher the ratio value, the better the firm's ability to meet its current liabilities. A value commonly used in industry as a standard is 2.00; this means that $2 of current assets (assets expected to be realized in cash during the year) are available for each dollar of current liabilities (obligations expected to require cash within the year). The CHIPS national median was 1.96. On both a trend basis and a standard comparison basis, OHF is in an unfavorable position (Table 7–1).

The current ratio is a basic measure that is widely used. However, if used alone, it does not tell the whole story. Some types of assets—cash and marketable securities, for example—are more liquid than accounts receivable or inventory. The current ratio does not account for these differences.

Days in Patient Accounts Receivable Ratio

The current ratio is a useful measure of a firm's liquidity, but it does not differentiate between categories of current assets. For example, cash is much more liquid than inventory or accounts receivable. In many situations, high current ratios result from excessive investment in accounts receivable. Days in patient accounts receivable is a liquidity ratio that further refines liquidity measurements and may pinpoint an area for correction. It is defined as all net patient accounts receivable divided by average daily net patient revenue:

$$\frac{\begin{array}{c}\text{Net patient accounts receivable +}\\ \text{Due from third parties –}\\ \text{Due to third parties}\end{array}}{\text{Net patient revenue/365}}$$

Table 7–1 Financial Ratio Analysis of Omega Health Foundation (OHF)

Ratio	1999	1998	CHIPS National Median	Evaluation Trend	Standard
Liquidity					
Current	1.12	1.42	1.96	Unfavorable	Unfavorable
Days in patient accounts receivable	28.9	33.7	56.7	Favorable	Favorable
Average payment period	81.5	66.4	57.0	Unfavorable	Unfavorable
Days' cash-on-hand	21.6	21.1	26.8	Favorable	Unfavorable
Capital structure					
Equity financing	0.41	0.45	0.52	Unfavorable	Unfavorable
Long-term debt to equity	0.71	0.71	0.55	Stable	Unfavorable
Times interest earned	0.79	2.31	3.17	Unfavorable	Unfavorable
Debt service coverage	2.12	3.10	3.32	Unfavorable	Unfavorable
Cash flow to debt	0.08	0.16	0.21	Unfavorable	Unfavorable
Activity					
Total asset turnover	0.94	1.02	1.01	Unfavorable	Unfavorable
Fixed asset turnover	2.30	2.37	2.20	Unfavorable	Favorable
Current asset turnover	4.33	4.19	3.57	Favorable	Favorable
Other asset turnover	2.49	3.11	5.11	Unfavorable	Unfavorable
Average age of plant	8.30	8.00	8.53	Unfavorable	Favorable
Profitability					
Total margin %	−0.5	3.3	3.8	Unfavorable	Unfavorable
Operating margin %	−0.3	0.8	2.7	Unfavorable	Unfavorable
Operating margin, price-level-adjusted %	−1.6	−0.3	0.8	Unfavorable	Unfavorable
Nonoperating gain %	2.7	2.5	1.0	Favorable	Favorable
Return on equity %	−1.2	7.3	7.4	Unfavorable	Unfavorable
Other					
Replacement viability	0.56	0.48	0.17	Favorable	Favorable

For OHF, days in accounts receivable for 1999 and 1998 are the following:

1999

$$\frac{24,324,000 + 0 - 11,571,000}{(160,574,000/365)} = 28.9$$

1998

$$\frac{25,597,000 + 56,000 - 10,688,000}{(162,323,000/365)} = 33.7$$

Values for this ratio indicate the number of days in the average collection period. For example, OHF in 1999 had 28.9 days outstanding in accounts receivable at year end. This implies that it took OHF 28.9 days on average to turn its accounts receivable into cash. High values for this ratio could indicate problems in collection time that may be due to faulty collection policies and billing systems of the entity. However, a high value might also indicate that the underlying quality of the accounts receivable is poor, that is, their collectability may be in doubt. This might imply that the write-off policy of the entity should be re-examined. A good way to evaluate the collectability of accounts receivable is to perform an aging of accounts receivable by payer.

OHF is in a favorable position regarding accounts receivable when compared to the CHIPS median of collecting on accounts receivable of 56.7 days. OHF has a collection cycle that is 27.8 days (56.7 − 28.9) shorter than the average U.S. hospital. This is a sizable difference and should translate into larger cash reserves. The potential increase in cash resulting from a short collection cycle for OHF in 1999 can be calculated as follows:

$$\frac{\text{Net patient revenue}}{365} \times \text{Reduced days} =$$

$$\frac{\$160,574,000}{365} \times 27.8 = \$12,230,000$$

There is also a potential risk for OHF, however. OHF's present low days in accounts receivable is partly attributable to a large "due to third-party payer" of $11,571,000. If this balance drops, OHF's receivables will increase sharply and create a major short-term financing need.

Care must be exercised when using any of the liquidity ratios if seasonality is a factor. For example, if the dates for financial statement presentation occur during a slack period of the year, certain values of current assets may be understated and others overstated. In particular, the values of accounts receivable and inventory might be at their lowest point of the year, and the corresponding values of cash and marketable securities at their highest, or vice versa, giving a biased view of the liquidity position of the firm. In addition, standards may vary by type of health care facility and region of the country. Clinics and HMOs can be expected to spend significantly fewer days focusing on accounts receivable than most hospitals. The collection period

also depends heavily on the composition of payers and their payment practices. Medicaid may pay on a prompt and timely basis in one state and yet be delinquent in another. The same holds true for Blue Cross and other major third-party payers.

Average Payment Period Ratio

Another index that provides information about causes of a worsening liquidity position is the average payment period ratio. It is as follows:

$$\frac{\text{Current liabilities}}{(\text{Total operating expenses} - \text{Depreciation})/365}$$

For OHF, the values of this ratio for 1999 and 1998 are the following:

1999

$$\frac{36,216,000}{(170,816,000 - 8,545,000)/365} = 81.5$$

1998

$$\frac{29,729,000}{(171,283,000 - 7,861,000)/365} = 66.4$$

From a financial condition standpoint, low values of this ratio are better than higher values. Creditors often use the following, which is a slight adaptation of this ratio:

$$\frac{\text{Accounts payable}}{\text{Purchases}/365}$$

If the data are available, both of the previous ratios should be calculated. However, in the OHF example, a separate listing of purchases for the year is not available.

The average payment period ratio indicates the length of time an entity takes to pay its obligations. The denominator, which is total expenses less depreciation divided by 365, provides an index of average daily cash expenses. (Remember, depreciation is a noncash expense.) The numerator (current liabilities) represents obligations for expenditures during the coming year. Most normal supply items are expensed within the year in which they are purchased. The same is true of payroll expenses, which usually constitute the largest single element of accrued liabilities and expenses. A standard value for this ratio derived from CHIPS is 57.0. On this basis, OHF has an unfavorable trend and an unfavorable standard comparison.

Days' Cash-on-Hand Ratio

A final measure of liquidity is days' cash on hand:

$$\frac{\text{Cash + Marketable securities}}{(\text{Total operating expenses} - \text{Depreciation})/365}$$

For OHF, the values of this ratio for 1999 and 1998 are:

1999

$$\frac{7,929,000 + 1,763,000}{(170,816,000 - 8,545,000)/365} = 21.6$$

1998

$$\frac{7,827,000 + 1,629,000}{(171,283,000 - 7,861,000)/365} = 21.1$$

Higher values of this ratio imply a more liquid position, other factors remaining constant. The ratio measures the number of days an entity could meet its average daily expenditures (as measured by the denominator) with existing liquid assets, namely cash and marketable securities. It attempts to define a maximum period of safety, assuming the worst of all conditions—for example, no conversion of accounts receivable into cash.

OHF has cash balances in short-term accounts that are slightly below national CHIPS averages. The differences do not cause any alarm, however, because OHF has cash reserves held for replacement that are above CHIPS averages (see replacement viability ratio discussion).

Capital Structure Ratios

Capital structure ratios are useful when assessing the long-term solvency or liquidity of a firm. Although the liquidity ratios just discussed are useful when detecting immediate solvency problems, the capital structure ratios are especially useful when assessing long-term financial condition. They are also valuable when detecting some short-term problems. Capital structure ratios are evaluated carefully by long-term creditors and bond-rating agencies to determine an entity's ability to increase its amounts of debt financing. In the last twenty years, the hospital and health care industries have increased their percentages of debt financing. This trend makes capital structure ratios vitally important to many individuals. Evaluation of these ratios may well determine the amount of credit available to the industry and thus directly affect its rate of growth.

Equity Financing Ratio

A basic capital structure ratio is the equity financing ratio. It is as follows:

$$\frac{\text{Net assets}}{\text{Total assets}}$$

For OHF, the values for this ratio in 1999 and 1998 are the following:

1999	1998
$\frac{77,398,000}{186,594,000} = .41$	$\frac{78,703,000}{174,022,000} = .45$

Higher values for this ratio are regarded as positive indicators of a sound financial condition, all other things being equal. After all, if an entity had zero debt or a net assets to total assets ratio of 1.0, there would not be any possible claimants on the entity's assets and thus no fear of bankruptcy or insolvency. The ratio indicates the percentage of total assets that have been financed with sources other than debt. In segments of the health care industry in which there is a greater stability in earnings, lower equity financing ratios may be permitted because there is less business risk.

OHF has a capital structure that contains more debt than the CHIPS averages. The addition of more debt in an organization's capital structure can improve the organization's ROE if the organization can realize returns on its borrowed funds greater than the interest rate on these funds. OHF's decline in its equity financing ratio from 1998 to 1999 is not due to the addition of more long-term debt as the balance sheet in Chapter 5 shows. The primary cause for the decline is related to a sizable increase in accrued retirement costs that resulted from an accounting change in the recognition of post-retirement benefits.

Long-Term Debt to Equity Ratio

Another capital structure ratio used by many analysts is the long-term debt to equity ratio. This is as follows:

$$\frac{\text{Long-term debt}}{\text{Net assets}}$$

For OHF, the values for this ratio in 1999 and 1998 are as follows:

1999	1998
$\frac{54,781,000}{77,398,000} = .71$	$\frac{55,989,000}{78,703,000} = .71$

One deficiency of the equity financing ratio is that it includes short-term sources of debt financing, such as current liabilities as well as noncurrent liabilities that are not debt instru-

ments, such as accrued insurance costs. When assessing solvency and the ability to increase long-term financing, it is sometimes desirable to focus on "permanent capital." Permanent capital consists of sources of financing that are not temporary, including long-term debt and net assets. Low values for the long-term debt to equity ratio may indicate to creditors an entity's ability to carry additional long-term debt.

The average value for this ratio in the *Standard & Poor's 400 Industrials* was 42 percent. In the health care industry, this value may be higher, especially for hospitals. A maximum value used by some investment bankers is 2.0. In other words, they are willing to allow $2 of long-term debt for every $1 of equity for some hospitals. In part, this reflects the stability of the industry. It also reflects the relative difficulty in acquiring equity capital in a largely nonprofit industry because nonprofit firms do not sell new equity shares.

OHF has high long-term debt to equity ratios when compared to CHIPS national averages. Often, higher long-term debt to equity ratios are present in organizations that have just undergone major renovation or expansion, and this results in a younger average age of plant. OHF, however, has an average age of plant that is similar to U.S. averages, which makes its more leveraged capital structure more of a problem. Maintaining excellent profitability will help OHF service its existing debt and maintain access to capital markets for future financing. As we will discuss shortly, profitability is a critical concern for OHF.

Times Interest Earned Ratio

A traditional capital structure ratio that attempts to measure the ability of an entity to meet its interest payment is the times interest earned ratio. It is as follows:

$$\frac{\text{Excess of revenues over expenses} + \text{Interest expense}}{\text{Interest expense}}$$

For OHF, the values for this ratio in 1999 and 1998 are the following:

1999	1998

$$\frac{-904 + 4,364}{4,364} = .79 \qquad \frac{5,706 + 4,369}{4,369} = 2.31$$

Even though a firm has a very low percentage of debt financing, it may not be able to carry additional debt because its profitability cannot meet the increased interest payment. Repayment of interest expense is an important consideration in long-term financing. Failure to meet interest payment requirements on a timely basis could result in the entire principal value of the loan becoming due. Meeting the fixed annual interest expense obligations is thus highly critical to solvency. The times interest earned ratio measures the extent to which earning could slip and still not impair the entity's ability to repay its interest obligations. High values for this ratio are obviously preferable. An absolute minimum standard in general industry is 1.5. The CHIPS national median for the times interest earned ratio was 3.17.

OHF has a poor trend and an unfavorable national comparison in both years. As discussed previously, OHF is a leveraged organization, but the poor national comparison is linked directly to poor profitability. Much of the decline in 1999 is attributable to a one-time charge to income, reflecting severance and termination benefits from a restructuring program in 1999. This should make OHF more viable in future years and increase profitability; but it did adversely affect 1999 performance.

Debt Service Coverage Ratio

A commonly used capital structure ratio that measures the ability to pay both components of long-term indebtedness—interest and principal—is the debt service coverage ratio. It is as follows:

$$\frac{\text{Excess of revenues over expense + Depreciation + Interest}}{\text{Principal payment + Interest expense}}$$

Values for OHF's debt principal repayments in 1999 and 1998 can be identified in Table 5–4 (statement of cash flows). By using these values, debt service coverage ratios for OHF in 1999 and 1998 are the following:

1999

$$\frac{-904 + 8,545 + 4,364}{1,312 + 4,364} = 2.12$$

1998

$$\frac{5,706 + 7,861 + 4,369}{1,411 + 4,369} = 3.10$$

The debt service coverage ratio is a broader measure of debt repayment ability than the times interest earned ratio because it includes the second component of a debt obligation—the repayment of debt principal. The numerator of the debt service coverage ratio defines the funds available to meet debt service requirements of principal and interest. The ratio indicates the number of times that the debt service requirements can be met from existing funds. Higher ratios indicate that an entity is better able to meet its financing commitments.

A standard minimum debt service coverage ratio value used by investment bankers in the hospital industry is 1.5. The CHIPS national median for the debt service coverage ratio was 3.32. With this value as a standard, OHF has both an unfavorable trend and an unfavorable standard comparison evaluation.

Values for OHF's debt service coverage ratio corroborate our earlier findings for the times interest earned ratio. The hospital is not in a good position to assume additional long-term debt. Ultimately, further improvement in these ratios must be linked directly to improvements in profitability.

Cash Flow to Debt Ratio

One of the best predictors of financial failure is the cash flow to debt ratio. It is as follows:

$$\frac{\text{Excess of revenues over expenses + Depreciation}}{\text{Current liabilities + Long-term debt}}$$

For OHF, the values of the cash flow to debt ratio in 1999 and 1998 are as follows:

1999

$$\frac{-904 + 8,545}{37,206 + 54,781} = .083$$

1998

$$\frac{5,706 + 7,861}{30,654 + 55,989} = .157$$

The cash flow to debt ratio has been found to be an excellent predictor of financial failure, even as much as five years before such failure. The numerator (cash flow) can be thought of as the firm's source of total funds, excluding financing. The denominator (total debt) provides a measure of a major need for future funds, namely, debt retirement. A low value for this ratio often indicates a potential problem in meeting future debt payment requirements.

OHF's values for cash flow to total debt exhibit a pattern similar to the times interest earned and debt service coverage ratio. Values in 1998 were low but dropped sharply in 1999 because of the large loss that resulted from restructuring. OHF needs a significant improvement in profitability if it is to survive and be in a position to service its debt.

Activity Ratios

Activity, or turnover, ratios measure the relationship between revenue and assets. The numerator is always revenue; it may be thought of as a surrogate measure of output. The denominator is investment in some category of assets; it may be thought of as a measure of input. These ratios are also referred to as efficiency ratios, because efficiency ratios measure output to input. As noted in a later context, activity ratios also have an important relationship to measures of profitability.

Total Asset Turnover Ratio

The most widely used activity ratio is the total asset turnover ratio. It is as follows:

$$\frac{\text{Total revenue}}{\text{Total assets}}$$

where:

Total revenue = Total revenue + Net nonoperating gains

For OHF, the values of the total asset turnover ratio in 1999 and 1998 are as follows:

1999

$$\frac{170,324 + 4,674}{186,594} = .94$$

1998

$$\frac{172,635 + 4,354}{174,022} = 1.02$$

A high value for this ratio implies that the entity's total investment is being used efficiently; that is, many services are being provided to the community from a limited resource base. However, the ratio can be deceptive. For example, a facility that is relatively old, with most of its plant assets fully depreciated, is likely to show a high total asset turnover ratio; yet, it may not be nearly as efficient as a newer facility that has plant and equipment assets that are largely undepreciated.

A measure that may be used to partially evaluate the existence of this problem by detecting the age of a given physical plant is the following:

$$\frac{\text{Allowance for depreciation}}{\text{Depreciation expense}} =$$

Average age of plant

By using this measure for OHF, the values for 1999 and 1998 are the following:

1999	1998
$\frac{70,804}{8,545} = 8.3$	$\frac{63,252}{7,861} = 8.0$

The CHIPS national median for the average age of plant ratio was 8.5. OHF is, therefore, slightly younger than the U.S. norm. All other factors being equal, this should suggest that the total asset turnover and fixed asset turnover ratios should be lower. OHF's total asset turnover ratio is slightly lower than the national median of 1.0, but its fixed asset turnover ratio is higher. OHF's favorable fixed asset turnover and favorable current asset turnover are, however, offset by a low other asset turnover ratio. Because much of the unfavorable difference in the other asset turnover ratio results from high levels of replacement reserves, the overall impression is that OHF is being efficient regarding its present investment in assets. This will be explained in more detail as we review the individual categories of investment.

Fixed Asset Turnover Ratio

Another common turnover ratio is the fixed asset turnover ratio. It is as follows:

$$\frac{\text{Total revenue}}{\text{Net fixed assets}}$$

For OHF, the values of the fixed asset turnover ratio in 1999 and 1998 are the following:

1999

$$\frac{170,324 + 4,674}{75,990} = 2.30$$

1998

$$\frac{172,635 + 4,354}{74,829} = 2.37$$

The fixed asset turnover ratio is identical to the total asset turnover ratio, except that fixed assets, a specific subset of total assets, are substituted in the denominator. This substitution is an attempt to assess the relative efficiency of an individual category of assets. In fact, all the turnover ratios discussed subsequently are further segregations of various categories of assets.

Fixed assets represent the number one investment in most health care entities. The fixed asset turnover ratio can thus be of major importance in assessing the relative efficiency of plant investments. The CHIPS national median for the fixed asset turnover ratio was 2.20. Because OHF's average age of plant is younger than the U.S. norm, OHF has a favorable position regarding fixed asset investment, as evidenced by its fixed asset turnover ratio. Organizations with low fixed asset turnover ratios can track the problem to one of the following three areas:

1. excessive investment in fixed assets,
2. inadequate volume for existing capacity, and
3. low prices for services.

Current Asset Turnover Ratio

The complement of the fixed asset turnover ratio is the current asset turnover ratio. It is as follows:

$$\frac{\text{Total revenue}}{\text{Current assets}}$$

For OHF, the values of this ratio in 1999 and 1998 are the following:

1999

$$\frac{170,324 + 4,674}{40,448} = 4.33$$

1998

$$\frac{172,635 + 4,354}{42,268} = 4.19$$

The current asset turnover ratio focuses on the relative efficiency of the investment in current assets regarding the generation of revenue. The valuation of current assets is not subject to the same difficulties encountered in the measurement of fixed assets. The ratio is thus more comparable across facilities. OHF has a very favorable comparison with the CHIPS national median of 3.58. The primary reason for this favorable comparison is the relatively smaller investment in patient accounts receivable and cash. OHF had 28.9 days in patient accounts receivable in 1999 and 21.8 days' cash-on-hand. Both values are well below the national median.

Other Asset Turnover Ratio

The last activity ratio to be discussed is the other asset turnover ratio. It is as follows:

$$\frac{\text{Total revenue}}{\text{Other assets}}$$

Other assets are defined as the following:

Total assets – Current assets – Fixed assets

For OHF, the values of this ratio in 1999 and 1998 are the following:

1999

$$\frac{170,324 + 4,674}{186,594 - 40,448 - 75,990} = 2.49$$

1998

$$\frac{172,635 + 4,354}{174,022 - 42,268 - 74,829} = 3.11$$

In most situations, a high other asset turnover ratio is desirable because it signals an ability to provide services with minimal investment. If the cause of a high other asset turnover ratio is the lack or absence of replacement funds, the high other asset turnover ratio may not be desirable. OHF has relatively low other asset turnover ratios and their values are declining. Should OHF be worried about this situation? Probably not, because the primary cause for the relatively poor showing is high investment levels in funded depreciation reserves. OHF had $50,835,000 in funded depreciation reserves in 1999, which was up sharply from $37,717,000 in 1998. Assuming reasonable yields on these reserves, this investment should be a source of strength, not weakness, for OHF.

Profitability Ratios

To talk of profit in a largely nonprofit industry may appear to many to be a contradiction in terms. Yet few, if any, health care facilities could remain liquid and solvent if profits were held to zero. In such a situation, cash flow would not be sufficient to meet normal nonexpense cash flow requirements, such as repayment of debt principal and investment in additional fixed and current assets.

However, recognizing the basic need for profit is not the same thing as determining how much is needed. It is not healthy either for the public or for the health care entity if the entity's profitability is either too great or too small. Discussion of the need for profitability thus centers on a definition of financial requirements. Here, we are concerned only with the interpretation of several commonly used financial ratios of profitability.

Total Margin Ratio

A common profitability ratio is the following total margin ratio:

$$\frac{\text{Excess of revenues over expenses}}{\text{Total revenue}}$$

For OHF, total margin ratios in 1999 and 1998 are the following:

1999	1998
$\frac{-904}{174,998} = -0.5\%$	$\frac{5,706}{176,989} = 3.2\%$

The total margin ratio defines the percentage of total revenue plus net nonoperating gains that have been realized in the form of net income, or revenues and gains in excess of expenses and losses. It is used by many analysts as a primary measure of total profitability. Although this measure is extremely useful, we believe that income should be related to some measure of investment to be meaningful. An alternative measure of profitability, discussed later, that does provide a measure of investment in the denominator is the return on equity ratio.

It is possible to improve the total margin ratio by either improving operating margin performance or increasing nonoperating gains. For most health care firms, short-term improvements will result primarily from increases in operating margins. The total margin ratio will, in most situations, be equal to the following:

Operating margin ratio +
Nonoperating gain ratio

There may be some limited circumstances when an item affects excess of revenues over expenses but does not appear in either net nonoperating gains or income from operations. OHF's performance in 1999 is a good illustration of this exception, as the following schedule shows:

	1999	1998
Income from operations	(492)	1,352
Nonoperating gains	4,674	4,354
Change in accounting principle	(5,086)	0
Revenues and gains in excess of expenses	(904)	5,706

OHF had a sizable reduction in net income in 1999 that would not be reflected in either its operating margin or nonoperating gain ratios. For 1999, total margin will not equal operating margin plus nonoperating gain ratio as Table 7–1 shows.

OHF experienced a sharp decrease in its total margin during 1999, which is directly traced to two areas. First, operating margins decreased because OHF experienced a loss of $492,000 from operations. Secondly, OHF wrote off $5,086,000 in costs associated with a change in accounting principle. Item 10 of Exhibit 5–2 explains this one-time charge incurred for restructuring. In short, OHF laid off large numbers of employees in 1999 and had many others take early retirement. These actions will make OHF more cost competitive in the future, but these actions did raise costs significantly in 1999.

Operating Margin Ratio

The most commonly cited measure of profitability is the following operating margin ratio:

$$\frac{\text{Net operating income}}{\text{Total revenue}}$$

For OHF, the values of this ratio in 1999 and 1998 are the following:

1999   1998

$$\frac{-492}{174,998} = -0.3\% \quad \frac{1,352}{176,989} = 0.8\%$$

To realize an increase in operating margins, one of the following two options exists: (1) raise net prices or (2) reduce cost per unit. An increase in volume is sometimes cited as a third option, but an increase in volume reduces cost per unit when fixed costs exist. For many health care firms, the primary way to enhance profitability is through cost reduction, because prices may be fixed by external payers such as Medicare.

OHF has relatively low operating margins in both years. The primary cause for their poor position can be traced to high operating costs. OHF must get its cost structure in line with that of its competitors if it wishes to survive in an increasingly price-sensitive market. The issue of costs at OHF will be addressed later.

Operating Margin, Price-Level-Adjusted Ratio

It is often useful to adjust the operating margin ratio to reflect replacement cost depreciation. The operating margin, price-level-adjusted ratio is as follows:

$$\frac{(\text{Operating income} + \text{Depreciation}) - \text{Price level depreciation}}{\text{Total revenue}}$$

For OHF, the values for this ratio in 1999 and 1998 are the following:

1999

$$\frac{(-492 + 8,545) - (8,545 \times 1.275)}{174,998} = -1.6\%$$

1998

$$\frac{(1,352 + 7,861) - (7,861 \times 1.247)}{176,989} = -0.3\%$$

The operating margin, price-level-adjusted ratio is identical to the operating margin ratio except that it substitutes price level depreciation for depreciation expense reported on an unadjusted historical cost basis. The ratio defines the proportion of operating revenue net of deductions that is retained as income after deducting price-level-adjusted depreciation. Although not totally accurate, this measure of operating profitability attempts to reflect the replacement costs of operating fixed assets in the calculation of the operating margin.

Values of this ratio that are less than zero imply that the organization is not currently earning enough operating income to provide funds for the eventual replacement of its fixed assets. Future replacement needs may have to be met from an increased reliance on debt (if available) or from other equity sources, such as grants and contributions (if available). Values for this ratio that exceed zero are not to be interpreted as a guarantee of future fund availability for replacement. To the extent that increased working capital needs are financed with equity, an erosion of the replacement potential of the hospital will occur. Also, it should be remembered that the index used for price-level restatement is the consumer price index for urban wage earners, which may understate the real replacement cost of the hospital.

OHF's operating margins adjusted for price-level effects match the same trend observed for unadjusted operating margins. OHF simply is not generating enough income from operations to replace its present depreciable assets, let alone to provide for any expansion into new markets.

Nonoperating Gain Ratio

A profitability ratio that provides a means of analyzing the source of profit is the nonoperating gain ratio. It is as follows:

$$\frac{\text{Net nonoperating gains}}{\text{Total revenue}}$$

For OHF, the values for this ratio in 1999 and 1998 are the following:

1999	1998

$$\frac{4,674}{174,998} = 2.7\% \qquad \frac{4,354}{176,989} = 2.5\%$$

The nonoperating gain ratio defines the proportion of total revenue plus net nonoperating gains that was derived from net nonoperating gains. The major sources of nonoperating gains most likely will be donations, income on nonborrowed funds, and other gains and losses. Some firms may report negative values for this ratio if they experience large losses in a given year.

To some extent, nonoperating gains can be used to subsidize poor operating margins, if net nonoperating gains are expected to be present year after year. For many health care firms, development activity has become increasingly important as a source of income to supplant eroding operating profits. Improvements in the nonoperating gain ratio will have a positive impact on most profitability ratios.

OHF has a favorable nonoperating gain position relative to CHIPS national averages. The primary cause for this position is large amounts of investment income realized on funded depreciation reserves, $4,717,000 in 1999 and $4,658,000 in 1998. OHF has relied heavily on its nonoperating income to subsidize poor operating profitability. A critical question to raise is whether OHF can continue this level of nonoperating income generation in the future.

Return on Equity Ratio

One of the primary tests of profitability for both voluntary and investor-owned health care firms is the return on equity ratio. It is as follows:

$$\frac{\text{Excess of revenues over expenses}}{\text{Net Assets}}$$

For OHF, the values for this ratio in 1999 and 1998 are the following:

1999	1998

$$\frac{-904}{77,398} = -1.2\% \qquad \frac{5,706}{78,703} = 7.3\%$$

The return on equity ratio defines the amount of net income or excess of revenues over expenses earned per dollar of equity investment. This ratio has been discussed by decision makers in some hospitals, especially investor-owned hospitals, as an alternative way to establish rates. Many financial analysts consider the return on equity ratio the primary test of profitability. Failure to maintain a satisfactory value for this ratio may prevent the hospital from obtaining equity capital in the future.

The return on equity ratio can be expressed as a product involving the following four ratios:

(Operating margin ratio +

Nonoperating gain ratio) ×

$$\frac{\text{Total asset turnover ratio}}{\text{Equity financing ratio}}$$

For health care firms without access to donor-restricted funds, government tax support, or other sources of new equity, asset growth will be limited to return on equity. This principle is referred to as "sustainable growth." The principle simply says that a firm cannot generate a growth rate in assets greater than its growth rate in equity for a prolonged period. If a firm can generate a return on equity of only 5 percent per year, its new growth in asset investment will be limited to 5 percent per year.

Figure 7–2 displays the relationships between ROE and other financial and operating measures for OHF. This chart can be used to "drill down" to the specific problems that are causing a poor ROE performance. This "drill down" approach will be used to summarize our discussion of OHF financial performance. At this point, we simply will note that ROE at OHF is very low and dramatic improvement is required.

Other Ratios

Replacement Reserve Adequacy

The issue of replacement fund adequacy is especially important for voluntary nonprofit health care organizations. Unlike for-profit organizations, most nonprofit firms cannot raise new equity funds in any manner other than through profit. A for-profit firm could issue new stock to finance new or replacement capital, but a nonprofit firm is limited to retained profits invested in funded depreciation reserves.

Replacement Viability Ratio

To assess the feasibility of future plant replacement, the replacement viability ratio is frequently used. It is as follows:

$$\frac{\text{Funded depreciation}}{\text{Price-level-adjusted accumulated depreciation}}$$

For OHF, the values for replacement viability in 1999 and 1998 are the following:

1999

$$\frac{50,835}{70,804 \times 1.275} = .56$$

1998

$$\frac{37,717}{63,252 \times 1.247} = .48$$

The replacement viability ratio is used to measure the adequacy of current investments to meet replacement needs. The numerator is a measure of current funds available to meet potential replacement needs. The denominator is a measure of the present need. Price-level-adjusted accumulated depreciation is a measure of the current cost of fixed assets that has been written off as depreciation. It is not a perfect measure of a hospital's replacement need, but it gives a much better estimate than that produced by simply using unadjusted historical cost accumulated depreciation.

A value of .50 would imply that 50 percent of the firm's replacement cost need is currently funded. This also would imply a projected debt to equity mix of 50 percent debt to 50 percent equity. OHF's 1999 replacement viability ratio value of .56 implies that OHF could use a 56 percent equity and 44 percent debt mix to replace its depreciable assets. High values for the replacement viability ratio imply not only a potential reduction in future debt financing but also provide investment income that can be used to subsidize poor operating profitability. OHF's strong replacement reserve position has helped it offset low or negative operating margins with investment income.

Table 7–2 presents a framework for assessing total cash adequacy. We will assume targets of 20 days for short-term cash and a .50 replacement viability ratio for OHF.

OHF presently has surplus cash and reserves of $6,497,956 ($804,436 + $5,693,520), based upon targets of 20 days worth of cash-on-hand for short-term uses and a replacement viability ratio of .50. Changes in the target values for OHF would have an impact on these calculations.

SOME CAVEATS

In this chapter, we have demonstrated, through an examination of twenty separate financial ratios, the use of financial ratio analysis in the assessment of the financial condition of health care facilities. At this point, it is appropriate to add some general limitations that should

Table 7–2 Assessment of Cash Position for Omega Health Foundation, 1999

	Short-Term Cash	Replacement Reserves
Present balance	$9,692,000	$50,835,000
Target ratio value	20 Days' cash-on-hand	.50 Replacement viability
Actual ratio value	21.8	.563
Target/actual	.917	.888
Desired cash/investment	$8,887,564	$45,141,480
Surplus (deficit)	$ 804,436	$ 5,693,520

be recognized when evaluating financial condition through financial ratio analysis.

Validity of Standards

The standards used in this chapter should be helpful in many health care settings. They are, however, of special importance for hospital medical centers because that is where they were derived. These ratios will vary by region of the country and period. This implies that standards should be updated frequently. It also implies the importance of using adequate trend data.

Financial ratios should be calculated over a minimum of five years, if meaningful trends are to be discovered. The two-year comparisons developed in this chapter were used only to discuss basic methodology and are clearly inadequate. In this connection, participation in a financial service, such as CHIPS, is strongly encouraged.

Cost Valuation

The values reported in a balance sheet are usually stated in unadjusted historical cost. Although this valuation does have some advantages in terms of objectivity of reporting, it limits the utility of comparisons across facilities when inflation is a predominant factor. The need

for adjustment of ratios that use balance sheet values, especially fixed-asset values, cannot be overstated.

Projections

Financial ratio analysis uses historical data. It provides a "picture" of where the entity has been; it does not necessarily indicate where it is going. Budgetary data are required for this purpose. The value of financial ratio analysis as a predictor relies on the assumption that past behavior validly indicates future behavior.

Accounting Alternatives

It should be recognized that a number of acceptable accounting alternatives for measuring the financial effects of various transactions are available. The use of different accounting methods can create significantly different values for financial ratios, even when the underlying financial events are identical. There even may be situations when differences in accounting methods impair the comparability of financial ratios across health care facilities or over time. Consistent use of a given set of accounting methods can help a health care facility avoid such comparability problems and should be encouraged.

OPERATING INDICATORS

Before this discussion of measuring financial position is concluded, attention should be focused on cost control. In most health care firms, the most likely cause of either good or bad financial performance is traceable to operating income. As results from operations improve, so does overall financial performance. Operating income can be defined simply as the following:

Revenue – Costs

Revenue is always the product of volume multiplied by the price, but the unit of volume sold may vary from a covered individual under a capitation arrangement, to a discharge in a case payment system, or to a procedure in fee-for-service payment systems. Presently, there are two primary categories of patient encounters for hospitals, an inpatient admission and an outpatient visit. Revenue could be expressed as follows:

Capitation

Revenue = Covered lives × Premium
            per covered life

Fee-for-service

Revenue = Encounters × Price per
            encounter
        = [Inpatient discharges ×
            Net price per discharge] +
            [Outpatient visits × Net
            price per outpatient visit]

In a similar manner, cost also can be broken down as follows:

Capitation:

Cost = Covered lives x Cost per
            covered life

Cost per covered life =

$$\frac{\text{Encounters}}{\text{Covered lives}} \times \frac{\text{Services}}{\text{Encounters}} \times$$

$$\frac{\text{Resources}}{\text{Services}} \times \text{Price or wages of resources}$$

Fee-for-service:

Cost = Encounters × Cost per encounter

Cost per discharge =

$$\frac{\text{Patient days}}{\text{Discharges}} \times \frac{\text{Services}}{\text{Patient days}} \times$$

$$\frac{\text{Resources}}{\text{Services}} \times \text{Price or wages of resources}$$

Cost per visit =

$$\frac{\text{Services}}{\text{Visits}} \times \frac{\text{Resources}}{\text{Services}} \times$$

Price or wages of resources

The relationships defined previously provide a structure for breaking down revenue and cost into components that can suggest possible problems. Figure 7–2 expresses these relationships in the Level 2 and Level 3 segments of the strategic management model.

To illustrate these concepts, let us focus on the inpatient sector in Levels 2 and 3 of the strategic management model in Figure 7–2, especially cost per discharge. Cost per discharge is affected by the following factors:

1. Length of stay (patient days/discharges).
2. Service intensity (services/patient days)—Services are departmental outputs and would consist of lab tests per patient day, radiology procedures per patient day, or pharmacy doses per patient day.
3. Efficiency (resources/services)—This reflects departmental efficiency such as staff hours per lab test or staff hours per pharmacy dose.
4. Resource prices or wages—This reflects salary costs and prices paid for drugs and other supplies.

Ideally, management will monitor actual performance in all of these areas through a comparison of actual indicator values to budgeted values. When significant deviations occur, some management action should be taken to correct the situation. In our discussion, thirteen macroindicators are defined and suggested for monitoring. These values should be compared with those of the budget fairly frequently, at least quarterly and, ideally, monthly.

It is also useful to compare these indicators with industry averages when they are available. We will again use comparative national medians for the thirteen indicators, which were taken

from the CHIPS strategic operating indicator data set. Data used to define the indicator values for Omega Hospital are presented in Table 7–3. Data from Omega Hospital for only one year is used in this analysis. Omega Hospital, which is a subsidiary of Omega Health Foundation, becomes the focal point for analysis now for two reasons. First, these operating indicators are hospital-specific and, therefore, the consolidated entity, OHF, cannot be evaluated. Second, Omega Hospital represents 80 percent of the entire revenue of OHF and, therefore, represents the ideal focal point for analysis. The indicators, the definitions of the indicators, Omega-calcu-

Table 7–3 1999 Operating Indicator Data for Omega Hospital (dollar amounts in thousands)

	Inpatient	Outpatient	Total
Gross patient revenue	$221,610	$53,612	$275,222
Less contractual allowances	109,588	26,511	136,099
Net patient revenue	$112,022	$27,101	139,123
Other revenue			2,993
Total revenue			$142,116
Operating expenses			
Salaries and wages	$ 44,012	$10,647	$ 54,659
Fringe benefits	10,211	2,470	12,681
Interest	3,248	786	4,034
Depreciation	5,552	1,343	6,895
Bad debt	2,855	691	3,546
Professional liability	1,378	333	1,711
Direct medical education	2,267	549	2,816
Other operating expenses	41,855	10,125	51,980
Total expenses	$111,378	$26,944	$138,322
Medicare discharges			5,520
Total discharge			15,262
Outpatient visits			97,376
Licensed beds			417
Staff beds			396
Patient days			88,473
Case-mix index			1.2048
FTEs	1,317	319	1,636
Wage index			0.9628

lated values for 1999, and the CHIPS national medians are presented in Table 7–4.

Occupancy

Occupancy can be either a measure of volume or a measure of productivity, depending on one's view. If actual occupancy levels are below budgeted levels, an adverse impact on average costs may result. This occurs because a significant percentage of total cost is usually fixed in the short run: costs will not decline proportionally with a change in volume. Usually, significant and permanent declines in occupancy signal a need for management to alter the cost structure of the hospital. In addition, some adjustment in the rate structure may be necessary to maintain desired levels of profitability.

Omega has a 1999 occupancy percentage of 58.1. This value is above the CHIPS median. Although Omega clearly has some additional capacity to service more inpatients, its values do not suggest a major problem with utilization.

Length of Stay, Case-Mix Adjusted

This measure is identical to the traditional length-of-stay measure, except that it is adjusted for case-mix differences. This enhances the comparability across hospitals with different case mixes.

Increasing values for length-of-stay, case-mix adjusted data almost always will have a negative impact on profitability because most hospitals receive a fixed fee per case. Medical staff involvement in evaluating length of stay and treatment protocols is no longer only desirable, it is an absolute necessity.

Omega has a 1999 length-of-stay, case-mix adjusted value of 4.81, which is above the median of 4.76. Although this value is not significantly above the median, it does suggest a closer examination of individual case types. A reduction in this value could lower Omega's costs.

Net Price per Discharge, Case-Mix and Wage Index Adjusted

This indicator provides management and the board with a measure of the average amount of revenue realized per discharge. This measure is case-mix adjusted, so that differences due to kinds of cases seen should be eliminated. The data also are adjusted for cost-of-living differences through division by the hospital's wage index. Hospitals with heavy Medicare and Medicaid patient loads may find it more difficult to generate more revenue per case because Medicare and Medicaid pay a fixed price per diagnosis-related group that is not negotiable.

Omega Hospital has a price structure that is well above the CHIPS national median by $1,180 per discharge on a case-mix and wage-index adjusted basis. Because operating profits at Omega are relatively low, the problem can be immediately traced to high costs, which we will discuss shortly. Improvements in future profitability must be linked to cost reductions that were begun in 1999 through restructuring.

Cost per Discharge, Case-Mix and Wage Index Adjusted

Hospitals that fail to control their costs are often more likely to fail. With increasing percentages of hospital revenue coming from payers who pay fixed prices, it is important to monitor and compare costs. Hospitals with high costs per discharge must realize higher prices per discharge. If price competition exists in the market area, or if the vast majority of patients pay fixed non-negotiable prices, higher costs certainly will lead to much lower profit per discharge. The case-mix adjustment will remove much of the interhospital variation that stems from case-mix differences; however, severity still may be a problem.

Omega Hospital's cost per discharge is high when compared to the CHIPS national medians. The strategic management model flow in Figure 7–2 shows that the problem of high costs is related to poor productivity, high salaries, and

Table 7–4 1999 Cost Control Indicators for Omega Hospital

Indicator	Definition	CHIPS National Medians	1999 Omega Value
1. Occupancy %	$\dfrac{\text{Patient days}}{365 \times \text{Licensed beds}} \times 100$	47.6	58.1
2. Length of stay, case-mix adjusted	$\dfrac{\text{Patient days}}{\text{Case-mix index} \times \text{Discharges}}$	4.76	4.81
3. Net price per discharge, case-mix and wage index adjusted	$\dfrac{\text{Net inpatient revenue}}{\text{Total discharges} \times \text{Case-mix index} \times \text{Wage index}}$	$5,147	$6,327
4. Cost per discharge, case-mix and wage index adjusted	$\dfrac{\text{Inpatient operating expenses}}{\text{Total discharges} \times \text{Case-mix index} \times \text{Wage index}}$	$5,107	$6,291
5. Inpatient staff hours per discharge, case-mix adjusted	$\dfrac{\text{Inpatient FTEs} \times 2,080}{\text{Total discharges} \times \text{Case-mix index}}$	136.5	149.0
6. Other costs per discharge, case-mix and wage index adjusted	$\dfrac{\text{Inpatient other costs}}{\text{Total discharges} \times \text{Case-mix index} \times \text{Wage index}}$	$1,714	$2,364
7. Salary per FTE, wage index adjusted	$\dfrac{\text{Salaries}}{\text{FTEs} \times \text{Wage index}}$	$32,564	$34,697
8. Capital costs per discharge, case-mix and wage index adjusted	$\dfrac{\text{Inpatient capital costs}}{\text{Total discharges} \times \text{Case mix} \times \text{Wage index}}$	$398	$497
9. Net price per visit, wage index adjusted	$\dfrac{\text{Net outpatient revenue}}{\text{Total visits} \times \text{Wage index}}$	$226	$289
10. Cost per visit, wage index adjusted	$\dfrac{\text{Total outpatient costs}}{\text{Total visits} \times \text{Wage index}}$	$227	$287
11. Outpatient staff hours per visit	$\dfrac{\text{Outpatient FTEs} \times 2,080}{\text{Total visits}}$	6.08	6.81
12. Outpatient revenue %	$\dfrac{\text{Net outpatient revenue} \times 100}{\text{Total revenue}}$	32.5	19.1

*FTEs = Full-Time Employees

Source: Center for Healthcare Industry Performance Studies, SOI National Values for 1995.

high capital costs. Omega needs to address these issues quickly if it is to remain competitive in a marketplace that is increasingly focused on price. At this point, we simply will identify the gap in cost per discharge between Omega and the CHIPS national median at $1,184 ($6,291 – $5,107).

Inpatient Man-Hours per Discharge, Case-Mix Adjusted

The inpatient man-hours per discharge, case-mix-adjusted indicator, provides an overall measure of inpatient labor productivity. Because of the labor intensity of hospital services, control over labor costs and staffing is critical to efficient and financially viable operations.

This measure assumes that the measure of activity or volume is a case-mix-adjusted discharge. This adjustment should make comparisons across hospitals reasonably valid. Hospitals with high values for inpatient man-hours per discharge adjusted for case mix may want to examine several areas. First, is the hospital using more staffing but lower cost staffing? For example, a hospital that employs more lower cost employees, such as aides, might have more hours worked per adjusted discharge but still have lower costs. This situation could be examined through a review of the salary per full-time equivalent (FTE) indicator. Second, high staffing could result from excessive length of stay. In this regard, length of stay adjusted for case mix should be reviewed. Third, staffing may vary depending on the extent of contract services. Hospitals with low staffing ratios may have larger amounts of contract labor. This should be reflected in higher values for other costs per discharge adjusted for case mix.

Omega Hospital used 12.5 more man-hours per case-mix-adjusted discharge than the CHIPS national median. What does this lower productivity cost Omega? Assume an average salary cost per hour of $16.68 ($34,697/2,080) and inflate this by 23 percent to reflect fringe benefits, which is Omega's present average. This yields an average total compensation cost of $20.52 per

hour. This implies that the poor productivity at Omega creates additional costs of $256.50 per discharge (12.5 hours × $20.52).

Other Costs per Discharge, Case-Mix and Wage Index Adjusted

This measure is adjusted for both case mix and wage index, or cost-of-living differences. What exactly is included in "other costs"? Other costs include all costs that are not categorized as either salary, fringe benefits, professional liability, or capital costs. Much of this cost category includes costs for drugs, medical supplies, and other supply costs, as well as costs for purchased services, education, travel, and other items.

Omega Hospital has other costs that far exceed the CHIPS national median, $650 ($2,364 – $1,714). This difference explains about 50 percent of the total cost difference (Table 7–5). Some of this excess cost may be due to restructuring costs incurred in 1999.

Salary per FTE, Wage Index Adjusted

The salary per FTE indicator provides a basic measure for the per-unit cost of the largest resource item used in producing hospital services. Control over wage rates is an important element in overall cost control.

It is important to recognize that many factors may influence salary per FTE. First, wage rates may vary significantly by geographical region. Hospitals in New York City clearly will have higher salaries than hospitals in less expensive cost-of-living areas. It is, therefore, critical to ensure that a relevant peer group is matched with your hospital for comparison purposes. The wage index adjustment methodology should remove regional wage differences. Second, labor mix also may impact the values for salary per FTE. Hospitals that employ staffs of only registered nurses (RNs) may have higher salary per FTE values but should experience lower staffing, as measured by inpatient man-hours per discharge adjusted for case mix. Finally, the extent of contract labor services also may affect re-

Table 7–5 Explanation of Omega Cost Difference from National Median

Cause	Dollar Amount	Percentage
Productivity	$256	21.6
Other costs	650	54.9
Salary	153	12.9
Capital	99	8.4
Unexplained	26	2.2
Total	$1,184	100.0

ported values of salaries per FTE. Hospitals that contract out relatively low-paid areas, such as housekeeping, may experience higher salary per FTE values.

Hospitals with high salary per FTE values should consider all of the comparability factors cited previously, but they also should evaluate their present wage and salary structure. In today's competitive environment, it is difficult to survive paying employees $25 per hour when your competitors are paying an average wage rate of $20 per hour, if there are no differences in productivity.

Omega Hospital has a salary structure that is well above CHIPS national medians by $2,133 per FTE, or $1.03 more per hour. Omega has a labor pool that is expensive and also less productive. This combination is disastrous for Omega if they wish to control their costs. The excessive salary per hour costs Omega $153 more per discharge ($1.03 × 149 hours per discharge).

Capital Costs per Discharge, Case-Mix and Wage Index Adjusted

The capital costs per discharge indicator measures the total amount of interest and depreciation expense per discharge. High values for capital costs per discharge may be the result of several factors. First, low volume may be a factor in high capital costs per discharge. Because capital costs are largely fixed costs, low volume would mean that the fixed capital costs of inter-

est and depreciation would be spread over fewer units. Second, age of the plant also may be an issue. Hospitals with relatively new plants often will have both higher depreciation and interest costs. Third, the percentage of debt financing and the relative cost of that debt often will affect measures of capital costs per discharge. Hospitals with heavy percentages of debt financing or expensive costs of debt (or both) frequently will have higher capital costs per discharge. Finally, the use of operating leases also will have an impact. If the hospital leases assets on an operating basis, its depreciation and interest may be lower, resulting in lower capital costs per discharge.

Omega has relatively high capital costs, almost $100 greater per discharge than the CHIPS national median. This is to be expected, given our earlier discussion of Omega's higher financial leverage and greater debt financing. The added burden of more debt has raised interest costs and increased Omega's capital costs per discharge.

Net Price per Visit, Wage Index Adjusted

Net price per visit defines the amount of revenue collected per outpatient visit. A key to the comparability of this indicator across hospitals is a uniform definition of an outpatient visit. The definition used by CHIPS is related to an "encounter" concept and is defined as follows: "Each outpatient visit to each clinic or service is counted as one. For example, a patient who visits the emergency room, cardiology clinic, and ophthalmology clinic on the same or subsequent day(s) would be counted as three visits."

It is usually important to monitor prices in the outpatient area. Often, there is a greater price sensitivity in outpatient services compared with inpatient services because patients frequently pay all or a greater portion of the bill directly because of lower insurance coverage.

Omega Hospital has high net prices per outpatient visit, which is consistent with the earlier conclusion of high inpatient prices. This high price structure may not be sustainable in the future.

Cost per Visit, Wage Index Adjusted

The cost per visit measure is an analogue to the cost per discharge measure. It provides an overall measure of the cost of production in the outpatient area. The basic unit of production in the outpatient area is the visit. Unfortunately, a visit is not always identified in the same manner across hospitals. Care must be exercised when making comparisons with group medians. It is possible that the definitions of an outpatient visit are not uniform within the group. Over time, we expect the definition of an outpatient visit to be increasingly standardized.

There is also no adjustment for case mix in the outpatient area. A hospital seeing a high percentage of emergency patients may have a much higher cost per visit. Hospitals with extensive nonemergency patients may have significantly lower costs per visit.

Omega Hospital has relatively high outpatient visit costs. This finding is again consistent with our earlier conclusion of high inpatient costs.

Outpatient Staff Hours per Visit

The outpatient staff hours per visit measure provides an overall measure of labor productivity for outpatient services. A high value would tend to imply excessive staffing and should be investigated. There are, however, several possible causes for high values that may not be related to poor labor productivity. First, it is possible that a visit in one hospital may not be comparable to a visit in other hospitals. This problem already has been discussed for other indicators measured on a per-visit basis. Great care should be exercised to ensure that visits are at least defined consistently over time and, ideally, consistently across hospitals.

Second, the complexity of a visit may vary. There is no case-mix adjustment for an outpatient visit as there is for inpatient discharges. Third, if outpatient expenses, including labor costs, are allocated according to outpatient revenue percentages, there may be some bias.

Omega has poor productivity, as seen in the outpatient man hours per visit. In 1999, Omega used 6.81 hours per visit, compared with the norm of 6.08.

Outpatient Revenue Percentage

The outpatient revenue percentage provides a measure of the hospital's reliance on outpatient revenue. A high value is not necessarily good or bad. The indicator merely provides a measure of the hospital's current reliance on outpatient revenue.

In general, the hospital industry has been increasing its overall reliance on outpatient revenue sources in the past. Many of the new growth areas are concentrated in the outpatient areas as the location of many health care services shifts from inpatient to outpatient settings.

A hospital experiencing an increase in outpatient revenue percentages needs to determine the cause. An increase that results totally from a decline in inpatient business is, of course, not a favorable indication. An increase resulting from substantial relative growth in outpatient care may be highly favorable if the inpatient care side of the equation is stable to increasing. The key to assessment is profitability. Expanding any business line, inpatient or outpatient, is beneficial if reasonable returns are being generated.

Omega Hospital is well below CHIPS national norms regarding outpatient revenue. Omega should seriously explore opportunities for future growth in this area given current and projected market conditions.

SUMMARY

Assessing the financial condition of a firm is a joint management and board responsibility. It is essential that periodic evaluations be performed to enable better long-term strategic decisions and midcourse corrections to avert financial problems. Many of the indicators described in this chapter should be helpful in the measurement of financial position. Comparative data, such as those provided by CHIPS, also should be sought to provide some relevant benchmarks for assessing performance.

ASSIGNMENTS

1. Operating margins in your hospital have been consistently below national norms for the past three years. Discuss the factors that might have created this situation and the ways in which you might determine specific causes.
2. Your firm reported net income of $5,000,000, but the change in equity was only $3,000,000. What could account for this difference?
3. How could a firm have a negative times interest earned ratio and a positive debt service coverage ratio?
4. Your firm's current liquidity ratio is 1.2. Is your liquidity position poor? What other factors would you check?
5. Your total asset turnover ratio has been declining over the past few years. How might you determine the cause for this decline?
6. Your firm has a replacement viability ratio of .20. If you were to replace your fixed assets today, what percentage of debt financing would you use?
7. Howard Ruhl has just been selected as the new chief executive officer (CEO) of Suburban Hospital, a well-known, 600-bed teaching hospital located in the suburb of a stable western city of approximately 1.5 million population. Howard is concerned about the future of the hospital. He fears that, over the years, it has relied too much on its good location and excellent medical staff. Although all the operating indicators point to a good future—for example, outpatient and inpatient volumes are up—Howard is especially concerned about the financial welfare of the hospital.

   The man whom Howard is replacing is well respected and was unquestionably a good manager. He personally brought the hospital through a significant growth period and is probably the major cause of its current success. He was, however, not well versed in finance and did not recruit competent fiscal help. The present chief fiscal officer is an old friend of the outgoing CEO and has no financial background; he received a master's in health administration (MHA) more than 20 years ago from the same school as the outgoing CEO.

   Suburban Hospital has borrowed very little in the past. Most of its present plant was financed with county general-obligation bonds—that financing vehicle is no longer available.

   At the present time, Suburban has a fairly active outpatient clinic operation. It does not have an attached medical office building. Howard believes that major growth in a number of areas is essential if Suburban is to remain strong. However, he is not certain which areas of growth to suggest to his fiscally conservative board, or how to suggest them. As a first step, Howard has asked for and received the two most recent financial statements. His present fiscal officer has calculated some key financial ratios for him to consider in his review. These statements and ratios are shown in Table 7–6.

   (a) Define key areas of concern for Suburban Hospital and state the rationales for your concern.

   (b) Propose a set of possible actions that may correct the problems in these key areas.

Table 7–6 Financial Statements and Ratios for Suburban Hospital (dollar amounts in thousands)

	1999	1998
Income statement		
Operating revenues		
Routine services	$28,453	$22,914
Ancillary services	33,376	27,133
Total patient revenues	$61,829	$50,047
Deductions from revenue		
Charity	$ 2,160	$ 1,549
Contractual adjustments	3,263	2,388
Other	229	63
Total deduction from revenue	(5,652)	(4,000)
Net patient revenue	56,177	46,047
Other operating revenues	2,547	48
Total operating revenues	$58,724	$46,095
Operating Expenses		
Salaries	$30,620	$24,670
Supplies and other	27,026	20,723
Total operating expenses	57,646	45,393
Net operating gain	1,078	702
Nonoperating revenues – net excess	1,363	497
of revenues over expense before	2,441	1,199
changes in method of accounting	671	—
Excess of revenues over expenses	$ 3,112	$ 1,199
Balance sheet		
Assets		
Current assets		
Cash and cash equivalents	$ 974	$ 2,606
Accounts receivable	8,734	6,398
Other current assets	988	1,829
Current assets	10,696	10, 833

continues

Table 7–6 continued

Other assets		
Replacement funds	4,668	7,215
Other funds	2,256	1,182
Other assets	6,924	8,397
Property, plant, and equipment	36,579	31,508
Total assets	$54,199	$50,738
Liabilities and current liabilities		
Accounts payable	$ 1,948	$ 2,644
Accrued expenses	3,005	2,174
Current maturities of long-term debt	1,031	837
Other	85	792
Current liabilities	6,069	6,447
Long-term debt	13,658	13,213
State equity	1,408	1,372
Net assets	33,064	29,706
Total liabilities and fund balance	$54,199	$50,738

Financial ratios

Liquidity		
Current	1.760	1.680
Days in patient accounts receivables	56.700	50.700
Average payment period	40.100	54.200
Days' cash-on-hand	6.400	21.900
Capital structure		
Equity financing	.610	.590
Long-term debt to equity	.420	.450
Times interest earned	4.430	4.350
Debt service coverage	3.660	2.880
Cash flow to total debt	.260	.150
Activity		
Total asset turnover	1.080	.910
Fixed asset turnover	1.610	1.460
Current asset turnover	5.490	4.260
Profitability		
Operating margin	.018	.015
Nonoperating revenue	.440	.410

continues

Table 7–6 continued

Reported income index	.970	.270
Return on total assets	.057	.024
Return on equity	.094	.040
Other		
Average age of plant	8.500	9.090
Operating margin, price-level adjusted	−.029	−.029
Replacement viability	.42	.78

SOLUTIONS AND ANSWERS

1. Low operating margins are the result of either low prices or high costs. Low prices may be difficult to change in either competitive markets or situations involving high fixed-price payers such as Medicare. High costs may result from excessive length of stay, poor productivity, or high salaries.

2. A transfer of funds out of the entity may have taken place. This is often the case in investor-owned companies, because of the payment of dividends. It also may occur in a voluntary entity because of a corporate restructuring.

3. The firm may have an extensive amount of depreciation and very low debt principal payments. This is often the case in the early years immediately after a major construction program.

4. A low current ratio is not always an indication of a poor liquidity position. If significant cash reserves are available, as measured by a high days' cash-on-hand ratio or a high replacement viability ratio, a liquidity problem may not exist. Alternatively, a high current ratio that results from a high days in patient accounts receivable position may not indicate good liquidity.

5. A declining total asset turnover usually can be traced to a declining fixed asset turnover ratio or a declining current asset turnover ratio. A declining fixed asset turnover ratio often results from declining utilization or from new plant investment, which should be associated with a declining average age of plant ratio. A declining current asset turnover ratio can be traced to an increasing days in patient accounts receivable, an increasing days' cash-on-hand, or a declining inventory turnover ratio.

6. The required percentage of debt financing for the firm would be 80 percent or, alternatively, 20 percent equity financing. The following formula can be used:

$$\text{Required debt financing \%} = [1.0 - \text{Replacement viability ratio}] \times 100.0\%$$
$$= [1.0 - .20] \times 100.0\%$$
$$= 80.0\%$$

7. (a) The major areas of concern for Suburban Hospital are the following:
   - relatively low operating profitability
   - relatively old physical plant
   - dramatic decline in liquid assets, as evidenced by days' cash-on-hand

   (b) Possible courses of action to be considered are the following:
   - Increase rates or curtail operating expenses.
   - Investigate the reasons for the buildup of accounts receivable. The increase appears to have required Suburban to expend more of its cash reserves to meet operating expenses.
   - Consider additional debt financing to meet physical asset replacement and expansion needs. Suburban appears to have additional debt capacity at the present time. However, a successful financing package is highly contingent on an improvement in operating profitability.

8

Financial Analysis of Alternative
Health Care Firms

In the last chapter, we discussed the measures and concepts of financial analysis in some detail, but most of the examples and industry standards were from the hospital sector. The hospital industry is by far the largest sector in the health care industry, but it is not the only sector, and its rate of growth in recent years has been slower than in other areas. This chapter will provide some additional information for alternative health care firms. Specifically, we will discuss the financial characteristics of the following three alternative sectors:

1. nursing homes,
2. medical groups, and
3. health plans.

It is impossible to describe all of the specific operating characteristics for these three sectors in one chapter, but we will try to highlight the important differences that affect financial measures. It is important to remember that the financial measures and concepts discussed in the previous chapter are still applicable. For example, the concept and measurement of liquidity is the same for a hospital as it would be for a health plan. However, operating differences between health plans and hospitals will produce different values and standards. Health plans have much lower days in receivables than hospitals, and are required to carry much higher cash balances

to meet transaction needs, namely claims payment.

It is not just the higher relative growth rates of nonhospital sectors that cause us to separately examine the topic of financial analysis for alternative health care firms. Many of the alternative health care firms have been consolidating through both horizontal and vertical mergers and have now become major corporations in our nation's economy. For example, Med Partners, Aetna, and Beverly Enterprises are among the largest corporations in the country, employing large numbers of people and absorbing large amounts of capital to finance their continued growth. Much financial analysis and discussion are now devoted to these firms because of the firms' almost continuous financing needs. Major brokerage houses now have analysts who devote their time to narrow sectors of the health care industry, such as home health firms or medical groups.

Table 8–1 presents financial ratio standards for the three sectors along with comparative values for the investor-owned hospital industry sector. These values were derived from information taken from financial statements filed with the Securities and Exchange Commission (SEC). The financial averages for these four sectors are therefore representative of large for-profit firms. There are no not-for-profit firms represented in these industry ratio medians.

Table 8–1 Financial Ratio Medians

Financial Ratio	Skilled and Intermediate Care Facilities (SIC Code 805x)	Physician Offices (SIC Code 8011)	Hospital and Medical Service Plans (SIC Code 6324)	Hospital (SIC Code 806x)
Liquidity				
Current	1.64	2.17	1.32	1.55
Days in receivables	60.0	155.2	22.5	56.1
Days' cash-on-hand	17.6	14.5	89.9	7.4
Capital structure				
Equity financing percent	38.6	51.4	48.9	36.4
Long-term debt to equity percent	51.4	32.6	13.0	50.0
Cash flow to total debt percent	11.4	19.6	15.0	17.5
Times interest earned	1.79	3.53	13.1	2.55
Activity				
Total asset turnover	.95	.76	1.55	.92
Fixed asset turnover	1.86	4.50	16.8	1.80
Current asset turnover	3.71	1.88	2.88	4.06
Profitability				
Total margin percent	2.5	4.2	3.6	4.4
Return on equity percent	6.1	6.3	11.6	11.1

SIC = standard industry code assigned by the Department of Commerce.

Source: Center for Healthcare Industry Performance Studies.

LONG-TERM-CARE FACILITIES AND NURSING HOMES

It is not always clear what types of firms individuals are referring to when they talk about the long-term-care industry. For our purposes, we will be primarily referring to nursing homes, both skilled and intermediate care facilities. The nursing-home industry has experienced significant growth during the last decade, and expectations about the aging of America have led many analysts to project even more rapid growth in the future. Growth in the nursing-home industry is inextricably linked to government payment and regulatory policy.

As of 1993, there were approximately 16,000 nursing homes in the United States, and of those, approximately 70 percent were investor-owned. Investor-owned presence in the nursing-home industry is much larger than it is in the hospital industry where only 15 percent of hospital capacity is investor-owned. Many of the investor-owned nursing homes are part of large national chains, such as Beverly Enterprises and Manor Care. However, there still are many investors that may own as few as one or two nursing homes to as many as twenty. Most of the large investor-owned chains became involved in the industry when the government started to finance a sizable percentage of nursing-home care through the Medicaid program. Heavy government financing provided a stable source of payment that was not present before Medicaid.

Financing of nursing-home care is a critical driver of nursing-home supply, as it is for most other health care sectors. Table 8–2 summarizes sources of financing for nursing homes as of 1994.

The data in Table 8–2 show a dramatic increase in the percentage of nursing-home financing that is derived from public sources, and a corresponding reduction in private financing. The percentage of Medicare financing has increased sharply as hospitals have discharged more patients into nursing-home settings to cut their costs per case and maximize their profit per Medicare case. Much of this shift is probably related to the financial incentives created by the Medicare program when Medicare shifted to a per-case payment system in 1983.

Table 8–2 Financing Percentages for Nursing-Home Expenditures

	1985	1990	1994
Private financing	49	46	37
Insurance	2	3	2
Out-of-pocket	44	41	33
All other	3	2	2
Public financing	51	54	63
Medicare	2	4	9
Medicaid—federal	26	27	30
Medicaid—state	21	21	22
All other	2	2	2

Source: Reprinted from Health Care Financing Administration.

Although the federal government pays more than 50 percent of Medicaid nursing-home costs, actual nursing-home payments for Medicaid patients are set by the states. There is wide variation among the states between retrospective and prospective systems. In many states, there may be a mix of both systems. For example, capital costs may be paid on a retrospective basis whereas all other costs may be paid on a prospective basis. Many states also use a case-mix-adjustment methodology to provide higher payments for nursing homes treating more severely ill patients.

Medicaid payments from states are usually the second largest state expenditure and, as a result, are subject to dramatic changes based upon the economic condition in the state. When economic times are bad and states have a difficult time meeting their budgets, one of the areas usually affected is nursing-home payments.

The level of nursing-home beds by state varies dramatically. Many states have used the supply of nursing-home beds as a means to control state expenditures for nursing-home care. The number of nursing-home beds per 1,000 people older than 75 years ranges from 66.4 in Florida to 189.9 in Louisiana. Licensure laws and Certificate of Need have been the primary means for controlling nursing-home beds in most states. Rates of payment for Medicaid patients also serve as an indirect method of controlling nursing-home capacity. As rates are held down, less capital becomes available for expansion and renovation. Major national nursing-home chains have been known to sell all their nursing homes in certain states where they believed that reasonable profits would be difficult to obtain because of restrictive state payment policies.

It is expected that demand for nursing-home care will increase dramatically in the next thirty years as the population ages and baby boomers reach the age of 75 plus, which is the age when nursing-home demand peaks. Nursing homes are also diversifying and expanding their product lines. For example, many nursing homes are becoming continuing care retirement centers (CCRCs). In a CCRC, there is a continuum of care that runs the gamut from independent living, to assisted living, to skilled care.

CCRCs also have discovered that their resident populations are desirable targets for HMOs that are seeking to expand their Medicare risk contracts. The CCRC is in a strong position to market itself to a managed care group because of the economies of scale provided from its continuum of care and its personal relationship to a Medicare population. At the same time, hospitals are looking for ways to expand their revenue base and have begun to develop skilled care units and other subacute units that can expand their business along the continuum of care and compete with existing nursing homes. In many respects, some of the historical distinctions among health care industry segments are becoming blurred as vertical integration accelerates.

The financial statements in Tables 8–3 and 8–4 reflect the operations of Friendly Village, a church-owned CCRC. A review of these financial statements will give the reader some idea of the nature of business operations in this type of health care organization. A CCRC usually provides three levels of care: nursing-home care, assisted living, and independent living. Often, residents progress through these three levels of care. An elderly person may enter the CCRC in an independent-living status and occupy one of the independent-living apartments. These apartments often are similar to apartments in other settings except that the residents are all retired and there is usually a variety of social activities to keep the residents active and united. As the health of a resident erodes, that resident may move to an assisted-living environment. In an assisted-living environment, there will be some health care services provided to enable the resident to maintain daily activities. For example, medication or medical monitoring or some help with daily-living functions such as bathing, toileting, and cooking may be required. Many residents are prolonging admission into an assisted-living center, and assisted-living residents are becoming similar to the nursing-home residents of ten years ago. The last level of care is nursing-home services, either intermediate or skilled. Many CCRCs also may have specialized units to treat patients with Alzheimer's disease or who have experienced a stroke.

The income statement of Table 8–4 depicts revenues from a variety of sources. The largest share is from the nursing home and is referred to as routine health care center services ($6,033,751 in 1999). The second largest source of revenue is from fees generated from care and services provided to residents of the assisted-living center or the independent-living apartments ($3,922,230 in 1999). Some other revenue is generated from entrance fees and consists of $1,049,160 from an amortization of entrance fees and $2,111,079 from investment income earned on the entrance fee fund. Some residents pay entrance fees upon entrance into the independent-living or assisted-living center. These deposits guarantee that a nursing-home bed will be available if needed and that the rate for that nursing-home bed will be less than the nursing home's current rates. For example, the CCRC may guarantee that the resident would have to pay only 50 percent of the posted rate for a nursing-home bed if needed.

The amount of the entrance fee may be based upon age at entrance. The fund is then amortized or recognized as income as the patient ages or dies. There is also income earned on the deposits that is recognized as income each year. The entrance-fee fund is listed several times in the balance sheet depicted in Table 8–3. On the asset side, there is a receivable from the church, which holds the entrance fees, in both the current asset and assets that have limited use sections. On the liability side, there are accounts in both the current and noncurrent sections that represent deferred entrance fees. We will discuss shortly what these accounts represent because they are one of the most confusing accounting aspects of CCRCs.

The expense structure of a CCRC or nursing home is similar to other health care providers and is labor-intensive. At Friendly Village, salaries and wages plus benefits constitute slightly more than 50 percent of total expenses. Also, notice that depreciation is not shown in the ex-

Table 8–3 Friendly Village and Subsidiary Consolidated Balance Sheets

	June	
	1999	1998
Assets		
General Funds		
Current assets:		
Cash and cash equivalents	$ 222,032	$ 168,091
Investments (at cost—approximate market value of $293,000 in 1999 and $530,000 in 1998)	193,991	397,469
Cash and investments that have limited use	616,425	301,582
Receivable—Friendly Church entrance-fee fund (Note 3)	2,089,315	2,106,442
Resident and patient accounts receivable, less allowance for doubtful accounts (1999—$195,000; 1998—$115,000)	780,227	432,321
Mortgage escrow deposits	29,991	79,574
Inventories, prepaid expenses and other assets	115,112	139,896
Total current assets	$ 4,047,093	$ 3,625,375
Assets that have limited use:		
Cash and investments (at cost, which approximates market value):		
Under bond indenture agreement—held by trustee (Note 4)	$ 4,954,756	$ 642,929
Repair and replacement—held by trustee	274,931	345,041
Resident deposits	284,235	276,455
	$ 5,513,922	$ 1,264,425
Less cash and investments required for current liabilities	(616,425)	(301,582)
	$ 4,897,497	$ 962,843
Receivable—Friendly Church entrance-fee fund, less portion classified as current assets (Notes 3 and 5)	5,691,916	4,992,891
	$10,589,413	$ 5,955,734
Property and equipment, less allowances for depreciation (Notes 4 and 6)	$12,925,048	$10,433,986
Unamortized debt financing costs	535,631	219,515
Total general funds	$28,097,185	$20,234,610
Donor-restricted funds		
Cash and investments (at cost—approximate market value of $1,121,000 in 1999 and $1,210,000 in 1998)	$ 1,171,460	$ 1,043,801
Recievable—Friendly Foundation	192,635	184,085
Due from general funds	190,868	183,104
Due from nurse scholarship recipients	13,939	5,887
Due from employee hardship recipients	3,171	—
Total donor-restricted funds	$ 1,572,073	$ 1,416,877

continues

Table 8–3 continued

Liabilities and fund balances
General funds
  Current liabilities:

Accounts payable	$ 862,611	$ 674,165
Interest payable	330,544	169,475
Salaries, wages, and related liabilities	737,374	676,173
Funds held for others	29,672	29,201
Due to donor-restricted funds	190,868	183,104
Estimated third-party settlement (Note 2)	44,507	428
Current portion of deferred entrance fees	800,000	958,496
Current portion of note payable to Friendly		
Church entrance-fee fund (Note 5)	27,467	39,698
Current portion of long-term liabilities (Note 5)	413,750	363,750
Total current liabilities	$ 3,436,793	$ 3,094,490
Deferred entrance fees, less current portion (Notes 1 and 5)	2,888,683	4,159,368
Deposits—residents	279,650	266,581
Note payable to the entrance-fee fund, less current portion (Note 5)	617,258	647,135
Long-term liabilities, less current portion (Note 4)	15,507,312	8,025,153
Refundable entrance fees	27,291	29,036
Obligation to provide future services and use of facilities	185,000	185,000
General fund balance	5,155,198	3,827,847
Total general funds	$28,097,185	$20,234,610

Donor-restricted funds
  Fund balances:

Sustaining fund	$ 729,814	$ 672,155
Foundation fund	192,634	184,085
Medical-memorial fund	334,618	326,378
Specific-purpose fund	190,869	183,104
Nurse-scholarship fund	46,069	44,295
Employee-hardship fund	11,871	6,860
Pooled-income fund	66,198	—
Total donor-restricted funds	$ 1,572,073	$ 1,416,877

pense section but is separately shown as other expense. This is not uncommon for not-for-profit CCRCs that oftentimes regard capital as a gift and do not regard replacement of the existing assets as an operating expense.

Perhaps the most unusual feature of a CCRC's financial statement relates to the entrance-fee fund and the deferred revenue that results from the receipt of those moneys upon admission to the retirement community. To understand the

Table 8–4 Friendly Village and Subsidiary Consolidated Statements of Revenues and Expenses of General Funds

	Year ended June 30	
	1999	1998
Revenues		
Routine health care center services—net	$ 6,033,751	$ 5,692,688
Care and service fees—net	3,922,230	3,685,316
Amortization of entrance fees	1,049,160	958,497
Other medical services	670,479	656,520
Applicant fees	6,200	5,900
Investment income on restricted funds	278,894	94,432
Other	276,467	203,349
Total revenues	$12,237,181	$11,296,702
Expenses		
Salaries and wages	$ 5,731,524	$ 5,418,725
Employee benefits	1,022,276	935,969
Purchased services	994,078	948,193
Other medical services	757,452	741,082
Supplies	1,044,831	925,812
Repairs and maintenance	133,882	105,871
Utilities	582,935	519,091
Equipment rental	7,531	4,739
Interest and amortization	1,274,492	770,507
Provision for doubtful accounts	63,804	24,675
Taxes	376,858	359,522
Insurance—property, liability, and general	76,534	91,050
Other	81,649	85,066
Total expenses	$12,147,846	$10,930,302
Gain from operations before depreciation and other operating revenues	$ 89,335	$ 366,400
Other operating revenues and expenses		
Unrestricted contributions	19,230	65,538
Investment income on entrance-fee fund—net(1)	2,111,079	752,331
Gain from operations before depreciation	$ 2,219,644	$ 1,184,269
Provision for depreciation	(895,632)	(801,185)
Gain from operations	$ 1,324,012	$ 383,084
Nonoperating loss		
Loss on disposal of property and equipment	(49,594)	(9,802)
Excess of revenues over expenses and nonoperating loss	$ 1,274,418	$ 373,282

concepts of entrance fees and their amortization and deferred revenue recognition, we will use a simple example and then relate those concepts to the data for Friendly Village. Let's assume that a resident enters the CCRC at the beginning of the year and contributes $35,000 to the entrance-fee fund. This amount will be amortized over the expected life of the resident, which we will assume to be seven years. During the year, the resident spends twenty days in the skilled nursing facility and is required to pay only 60 percent of the $150 per-day charge, or $90 per day. This means that a payment of $60 per day for twenty days, or $1,200, will be paid to the skilled nursing facility for 40 percent of the residents' charges by the entrance-fee fund. Finally, assume that the $35,000 entrance-fee fund earned investment income during the year in the amount of $2,000. The following entries would be made:

Entry No. 1. Record receipt of the $35,000 entrance fee.
Increase entrance-fee fund by $35,000.
Increase deferred revenue by $35,000.

Entry No. 2. Record transfer of money to skilled nursing facility.
Increase unrestricted cash by $1,200.
Decrease entrance-fee fund by $1,200.

Entry No. 3. Record annual amortization of entrance-fee fund.
Increase revenue account—
amortization of entrance fees by $5,000.
Decrease deferred revenue by $5,000.

Entry No. 4. Record the investment income earned during the year.
Increase entrance-fee fund by $2,000.
Increase investment income on entrance-fee fund by $2,000.

These are the accounting entries that would be made to reflect activities related to the entrance-fee fund and the deferred revenue account relating to the entrance-fee fund. The entrance-fee fund is an asset account that represents the funds available to meet contractual commitments to provide future health care services to residents. The deferred revenue account is a liability account that represents the estimated present value of future contractual obligations to provide health care services to residents. With this simple illustration of accounting entries, we will now discuss the entrance-fee fund and the deferred-entrance-fees account. Exhibit 8–1 shows

Exhibit 8–1 Change in entrance-fee related accounts

Change in entrance-fee fund

Current portion of entrance-fee fund June 30, 1998	$2,106,442
Long-term portion of entrance-fee fund June 30, 1998	$4,992,891
Beginning entrance-fee fund	$7,099,333
Add: Investment income on entrance-fee fund	$2,111,079
New fees paid by residents	$445,319
Deduct: Payments made for nursing services	$1,874,500
Current portion of entrance-fee fund June 30, 1999	$2,089,315
Long-term portion of entrance-fee fund June 30, 1999	$5,691,916
Ending entrance-fee fund	$7,781,231

Change in deferred entrance fees

Current portion of deferred entrance fees June 30, 1998	$958,496
Long-term portion of deferred entrance fees June 30, 1998	$4,159,368
Beginning entrance-fee fund	$5,117,864
Add: New fees paid by residents	$445,319
Deduct: Amortization of entrance fees	$1,874,500
Current portion of deferred entrance fees June 30, 1999	$800,000
Long-term portion of deferred entrance fees June 30, 1999	$2,888,683
Ending entrance-fee fund	$3,688,683

the beginning and ending values, and the transactions creating the changes for Friendly Village.

MEDICAL GROUPS

Expenditures for physician services amount to approximately $200 billion and are second only to hospital expenditures. Physician expenditures have been increasing more rapidly than expenditures of most other sectors of the health care industry, which has increased the relative importance of physicians. However, it is not just the absolute level of expenditures made to physicians that make doctors an important element in our health care industry. It is widely believed that doctors directly or indirectly control up to 85 percent of all health care expenditures. Doctors admit and discharge patients to hospitals; they prescribe drugs, order expensive diagnostic imaging services, and schedule rehabilitative services. The stroke of a doctor's pen directs a massive amount of health care resources to or away from an individual patient. Managed care plans realized the demand-influencing behavior of physicians early and have attempted to incorporate incentives for cost control in physician payment plans.

Although few would debate the importance of physicians in controlling health care costs, physicians have yet to realize their importance in the medical marketplace because of their lack of organization. Of the 700,000 physicians in the United States, two thirds operate in one- or two-person practices. It is difficult for physicians to realize their central role in cost and quality decision making in health care negotiations when most of them are part of delivery organizations that are too small to exert much, if any, bargaining leverage in health care negotiations. Physicians are slowly realizing this weakness and are now becoming part of larger organizations that are being developed by hospitals, health plans, large practice-management companies, and large physician-controlled medical groups.

Table 8–5 presents some data on sources of financing for the physician sector of the health care industry. Perhaps the most significant trend is the dramatic reduction in the percentage of physician expenditures financed by out-of-pocket payments from patients. In the period from 1985 to 1994, the percentage dropped from 25 to 15. It is not exactly clear what has caused this decrease, but the decline of indemnity coverage and the corresponding increase in HMO and PPO plans may be possible causes. Many HMO plans require a low copayment or no copayment for routine office visits, whereas most traditional indemnity programs have a co-insurance and deductible provision. For ex-

Table 8–5 Financing Percentages for Physician Expenditures

	1985	1990	1994
Private financing	71	68	66
Insurance	44	48	49
Out-of-pocket	25	18	15
All other	2	2	2
Public financing	29	32	34
Medicare	20	21	20
Medicaid—federal	2	3	4
Medicaid—state	2	2	3
All other	5	6	7

Source: Reprinted from Health Care Financing Administration.

ample, indemnity programs may require a subscriber to make all routine physician payments until some deductible is met, for example $500.

Physicians do receive a much larger percentage of their total revenue from the private sector than most other major health care sectors. In 1994, physicians received 66 percent of their total revenues from the private sector, whereas hospitals received only 44 percent. Medicare covers nearly 100 percent of hospital service charges for the elderly, but is subject to a 20 percent coinsurance for most physician services. Most Medicare beneficiaries will finance this payment with supplemental insurance, which creates a shift from public to private financing.

Physician expenditures are increasing because there is increasing usage of physician services. Table 8–6 documents the increasing number of physician contacts per person, especially in the older age groups. As the population ages, demand for physician services is expected to increase sharply. The substitution of ambulatory care for inpatient care also will further accelerate demand for physicians.

As we discussed earlier, physicians are beginning to align themselves with larger groups and are moving quickly from one- or two-person practices to large groups. Some of this movement is a reflection of personal tastes. Physicians who practice in larger groups can make arrangements for weekend or evening coverage. Large group practices often provide their doctors with better consultative services and also reduce administrative burden, permitting greater

patient-contact time. Lifestyle considerations may be an important cause of physicians joining larger groups, but the primary cause is related to economics. Physicians have seen hospitals and health plans merge and become more and more dominant in the local health care marketplace. Prior to increasing physician organization to counterbalance these large bargaining entities, physicians perceived themselves as being at a disadvantage.

Physicians can choose whether to align with other physicians or to remain independent. If they choose to align with other physicians, there are four primary organizational alternatives for them to consider. They are the following:

- alignment with other medical groups,
- alignment with hospitals,
- alignment with health plans, and
- alignment with physician practice management firms.

Alignment with physicians is, in some respects, most appealing to physicians because their control is maximized in this type of organizational setting. Oftentimes, the critical limitation is capital. To achieve large-scale integration and development of new information systems and administrative structures, massive amounts of both financial and human capital are required. Only recently have outside investors come forward to provide this external capital. For integration with other physicians to be successful, a physician activist is needed who will not only ar-

Table 8–6 Physician Contacts per Person per Year

Age Group	1987	1990	1993
Younger than 15 years	4.5	4.5	4.9
15 to 44	4.6	4.8	5.0
45 to 64	6.4	6.4	7.1
65 to 74	8.4	8.5	9.9
Older than 74 years	9.7	10.1	12.3

Source: Reprinted from National Center for Health Statistics.

range the financing of capital needs, but also will provide the administrative leadership.

Hospitals have the financial capital to create large groups; but in some cases, their administrative experiences with physician practice management is limited. This limitation coupled with differing incentives can lead to organizational conflict. In a managed care environment, the objective is to empty hospital beds, not fill them, and this oftentimes leads to conflict between hospitals and doctors. Hospitals also have been dominated by specialists, but primary care physicians are the key in managed care markets. Primary care physicians often believe that hospitals do not understand them or their needs.

Health plans also have the capital to put together large medical groups, but a conflict may arise between the incentives of health plans and its employee doctors. The health plan has a strong incentive to reduce fees or salaries of its doctors and also to control utilization. Physicians do not react favorably to lower income and also object to mandates or controls over their practice patterns.

Physician practice management firms are a relatively recent development that has evolved to meet the needs of both the physicians and the marketplace. Many of these firms are publicly traded and have tremendous capital and management pools to draw on to develop large integrated organizations. Physician practice management firms usually offer physicians some type of profit sharing and also provide for an equity stake in the firm. This equity participation can make the attraction of merger or acquisition by a physician practice management firm hard to resist. In short, physician practice management firms often can afford to pay large sums of money to acquire physician practices and they also promise physicians a strong degree of autonomy.

The financial statements in Tables 8–7 and 8–8 provide financial information for Waverly Health Care (WHC), a hospital-owned network of eight primary care clinics with twenty-four full-time physicians and 110 nonphysician employees who recorded 101,542 patient encoun-

ters during the past year. WHC is a separately incorporated for-profit subsidiary of the hospital, and all of its physicians are salaried with profit and productivity incentives.

The financial statements of WHC provide some interesting information about physician practices, especially those owned by hospitals. We can see that the practice lost $1,697,568 in the current year. It is not unusual for hospital-owned physician practices to lose money. Revenues from the practice are oftentimes less than expenses. Many hospital executives argue that although the direct revenues and expenses of the practice may show a loss, there are substantial benefits realized from operating the practice that result from admitting and referral patterns of the acquired physician practices, which raise volume at the hospital. Greater integration with the physicians themselves also may result in better cost control, which is important for managed care contracts. Although all of this may be true, in many cases, it is simply poor management that creates the financial loss. Most of these acquired practices were profitable before hospital acquisition, yet once they become hospital-owned and operated, they suddenly become unprofitable. A review of the financial information for WHC can help shed some light on the most common reasons for lack of profitability. Table 8–9 shows values for WHC expressed on a per-physician full-time equivalent (FTE) basis, compared to national values for primary care medical group practices derived from a study by the Center for Healthcare Industry Performance Studies (CHIPS) in 1996.

WHC has much more operating expenses than a typical medical group. Some of this is due to staffing. WHC has 4.58 support staff persons per FTE physician, whereas the national norm is close to 4.0. The bottom line is that WHC spends more than $100,000 per physician FTE above what a typical medical group would spend for operating expenses. WHC also generates less revenue per physician FTE than the national norm, about $24,000 less. Some of this problem is directly related to lower physician productivity. WHC physicians saw fewer patients than

Table 8–7 Balance Sheet, Waverly Health Clinic, December 31, 1999

Assets

Current assets

Cash	$ 364,631
Net accounts receivable	1,411,013
Prepaid expenses	143,481
Other current assets	731,550
Total current assets	$2,650,675

Net property, plant, and equipment	1,855,869
Intangible assets	188,941

Total assets	**$4,695,485**

Liabilities and Equity

Current liabilities

Accounts payable	$ 168,131
Withheld taxes	84,694
Employee benefits withheld	3,281
Accrued salaries and wages	335,513
Other current liabilities	98,482
Total current liabilities	$ 690,101

Equity

Contributed capital	$8,234,890
Retained earnings	(4,229,506)
Total equity	4,005,384

Total liabilities and equity	**$4,695,485**

---

expected when compared to national averages—4,231 encounters compared to 6,500.

WHC is losing money because its physicians see fewer patients and have significantly larger overhead associated with their practice. It is doubtful that these same physicians practiced in this manner when they were in private practice. The critical factor for the long-term success of owning physician practices is directly related to the incentive structures used for physicians. Ide-

ally, incentives should promote and not destroy physician entrepreneurial spirit.

HEALTH PLANS

Most individuals in the United States are covered by either public or private health insurance. In some cases, both public and private coverage may be combined. For example, many Medicare beneficiaries have obtained private health insur-

Table 8–8 Income Statement, Waverly Health Clinic, Year Ending December 31, 1999

Revenue

Gross physician charges	$10,147,800
Other revenue	2,186,088
Adjustments and write-offs	−2,350,116
Net revenue	$ 9,983,772

Operating Expenses

Personnel expense	$ 4,545,228
Supplies expense	404,412
Occupancy expense	1,861,248
Purchased services	202,632
General and administrative expense	868,296
Total operating expense	$ 7,881,816
Physician expense	3,799,524
Total expense	$11,681,340
NET PROFIT	$ (1,697,568)

ance to pay for health expenses not covered by Medicare. At the end of 1993, approximately 29 million Medicare beneficiaries (almost all Medicare beneficiaries) had obtained Medicare supplemental insurance from private insurance companies. Although the vast majority of Americans have health insurance of some type, many Americans do not have either public or private health insurance. In 1994, the Bureau of the Census estimated that approximately 40 million Americans were uninsured. This large pool of noncovered Americans creates costs of treatment that must be paid by someone. To date, it is not clear who will be responsible for paying for

Table 8–9 Comparative Operating Norms for Waverly Health Clinic

Indicator	WHC Value	CHIPS Median
Operating expense per physician FTE	$328,409	$236,000
Revenue per physician FTE	$415,991	$440,000
Physician compensation per physician FTE	$158,313	$145,000
Support staff per physician FTE	4.58	4.03
Operating expense to net revenue percent	79%	53%
Patient encounters per physician FTE	4,231	6,500

this group of people. Will it be the government, the health plans, or the providers?

The cost of private health insurance has been rapidly increasing during the last 20 years, as Table 8–10 shows.

Health insurance companies always have been big business, but the amount of money spent in selling, administration, reserve retention, and profit has increased greatly. In 1994, $46.5 billion was spent by private health insurance firms for either administrative costs, reserve retention, or profit. Actual claims paid to providers amounted to $266.8 billion in 1994. Adding the cost of private health insurance, $46.5 billion, to actual claims paid, $266.8 billion, would produce total premiums paid to private health insurance firms of $313.3 billion. Table 8–10 shows that the cost of private health insurance in relation to claims paid has been increasing sharply. It is this administrative cost that has caused much discussion among policy analysts. They have argued that most of these moneys spent for administration and profit are not necessary and add to the cost of health care in the United States. It seems unreasonable to pay 17.4 cents per dollar of claims paid.

The costs of private health insurance may not, however, be wasteful. The nature of risk and regulation in the industry may require these levels of expenditures. Insurance companies agree to provide a benefit package of services for some specified sum of money. If costs of services exceed this amount, the insurance company loses money. This is often referred to as underwriting risk. In addition, insurance companies are regulated and are required to maintain certain reserve balances to protect policyholders in the event of a financial catastrophe. The only alternative to private health insurance would be some type of government-financed and managed program. Government costs might be just as high or higher.

Health care insurance companies come in many different forms. The Health Insurance Association of America (HIAA) categorizes health care insurance firms as commercial, Blue Cross Blue Shield, and health maintenance organizations (HMOs). The trend toward managed care has blurred some of these distinctions. Commercial insurance companies often provide an HMO option as do most Blue Cross Blue Shield plans. HMOs have broadened their coverage plans to include more traditional indemnity programs, and most provide some point-of-service (POS) option whereby enrollees can go outside the HMO network for care if they are willing to pay higher copayments or deductibles.

HIAA, in their 1995 *Source Book of Health Insurance Data,* has defined managed care as a system that integrates the financing and delivery of appropriate health care services to covered individuals. The most common examples of managed care organizations are HMOs and PPOs (preferred provider organizations). A PPO typically offers more flexibility than an HMO by allowing more provider choice, but it attempts to direct patients to providers with whom it has negotiated special contracts.

Table 8–10 Private Health Insurance Trends

Year	All Personal Health Care Expenditures (Billions)	Private Insurance Payments (Billions)	Cost of Private Health Insurance (Billions)	Cost of Private Health Insurance to Private Health Insurance Payments
1994	$831.7	$266.8	$46.5	17.4%
1990	$614.7	$201.8	$30.6	15.2%
1980	$217.0	$ 62.0	$ 7.7	12.4%

Usually, there are five types of HMOs that are defined in the literature. They are the following:

1. Staff model. Physicians practice as employees of the HMO and are usually paid a salary.
2. Group model. The HMO pays the physician group a per capita rate, which the physi-

cian group then distributes among its members.
3. Network model. The HMO contracts with two or more groups and pays them on a per capita rate, which the groups then distribute to individual physicians.
4. Independent practice association (IPA) model. The HMO contracts with individual

Table 8–11 Hospital HMO Balance Sheet

	1999	1998
Assets		
Current assets		
Cash and cash equivalents	$1,324,206	$1,669,372
Short-term investments	1,659,278	1,451,923
Premiums receivable	789,735	1,198,034
Investment income receivables	28,208	44,018
Amounts due from affiliates	7,502	2,513
Total current assets	$3,808,929	$4,365,860
Other assets		
Restricted cash and other assets	$ 172,783	$ 135,009
Long-term investments	688,292	929,423
Total other assets	$ 861,075	$1,064,432
Property and equipment		
Total property and equipment	386,254	239,851
Total assets	$5,056,258	$5,670,143
Liabilities and Net Worth		
Current liabilities		
Accounts payable	$ 394,333	$ 523,907
Claims payable (reported and unreported)	1,032,715	1,174,091
Unearned premiums	98,113	156,619
Aggregate write-ins for current liabilities	10,000	13,000
Total current liabilities	1,535,161	1,867,617
Other liabilities		
Amounts due to affiliates (Schedule J)	1,628,923	2,217,411
Total liabilities	3,164,084	4,085,028
Net worth		
Total net worth	1,892,174	1,585,115
Total liabilities and net worth	$5,056,258	$5,670,143

Table 8–12 Hospital HMO Statement of Revenue, Expenses, and Net Worth

	1999	*1998*
Member months	174,967	191,465
Revenues		
Premium	$20,882,715	$21,367,747
Fee-for-service	0	0
Title XVIII-Medicare	0	0
Investment	59,014	26,623
Aggregate write-ins for other revenues	45,668	74,308
Total revenues	$20,987,397	$21,468,678
Expenses		
Medical and hospital		
Physician services	$ 1,535,928	$ 1,640,367
Other professional services	1,781,773	1,736,742
Outside referrals	4,175,302	4,217,545
Emergency room and out-of-area	935,322	1,384,142
Inpatient	7,635,927	7,245,575
Aggregate write-ins for other medical and hospital expenses	2,729,462	2,713,019
Subtotal	$18,793,714	$18,937,390
Reinsurance expenses net of recoveries	365,574	359,954
Total medical and hospital	$19,159,288	$19,297,344
Administration		
Compensation	$ 876,327	$ 758,889
Occupancy, depreciation, and amortization	81,368	102,907
Aggregate write-ins for other administration expenses	668,015	524,879
Total administration	$ 1,625,710	$ 1,386,685
Total expenses	20,784,998	20,684,029
Net income (loss)	$ 202,399	$ 784,649

physicians or with associations of independent physicians and pays them a per capita rate, or a negotiated fee-for-service rate.

5. Mixed model. This model combines two or more of the previous options.

The information in Tables 8–11 and 8–12 present financial statements for a small hospital-owned HMO. It is important to point out that financial and operating information on any HMO is usually available publicly by contacting the Department of Insurance in the state where the HMO operates. In fact, this is the source of the financial information used in our example.

The data in Tables 8–11 and 8–12 reveal a lot about the structure of HMOs. First, you will note that a small percentage of the total assets of the HMO is invested in property, plant, and equipment—less than 8 percent. HMOs are not fixed-asset intensive; the bulk of their investment is in cash and investments. Our HMO has $1,892,174

Table 8–13 PMPM Profitability

	1999	1998
Premiums	$119.35	$111.66
Expenses:		
Physicians services	$ 8.78	$ 8.57
Other professional services	10.18	9.07
Outside referrals	23.86	22.02
ER and out-of-area	5.35	7.23
Inpatient	43.64	37.84
Other medical and hospital	15.60	14.17
Reinsurance net of recoveries	2.09	1.88
Total medical and hospital	$109.50	$100.78
Administration	9.29	7.24
Total expenses	$118.79	$108.02
Net income	$ 1.16	$ 4.10

in equity at the end of 1999, which represented about 37 percent of the total assets. This gives the appearance of a debt-laden organization relative to the financial standards listed in Table 8–1, but it should be noted that a loan due to an affiliate in the amount of $1,628,923 also exists. The sponsoring hospital granted this loan and, in some ways, reflects equity. A large portion of this loan was paid off during 1999, which can be seen from the decline in the loan balance from $2,217,411 in 1998 to $1,628,923 at the end of 1999.

The income statement in Table 8–12 depicts a large decrease in net income, from $784,649 in 1998 to $202,399 in 1999. One of the reasons for this decline is the drop in member months, from 191,465 in 1998 to 174,967 in 1999. Table 8–13

analyzes the expenses on a per-member-per-month (PMPM) basis.

The decline in net income for our HMO example is the direct result of premiums on a PMPM basis increasing less than expenses. Although not the largest increase, administration expenses increased sharply on both an absolute basis and a PMPM basis. Much of the cost in this area is fixed and cannot be reduced when volume declines. Inpatient expenses also sharply increased. It is not clear from this information whether the cause is higher rates per hospital visit or higher utilization. Additional information in the insurance filing show that inpatient days in 1999 were 4,187, or 287 days per 1,000 members. In 1998, inpatient days per 1,000 members were 278, or 4,447 total days. The av-

Table 8–14 Inpatient HMO Use Rates

Utilization Measure	Use Rate per 1,000 Members
Acute inpatient discharges	68.7
Acute inpatient days	258.8
Ambulatory encounters	4.3

Source: HMO Industry Profile 1995–1996 Edition, American Association of Health Plans.

erage price per inpatient day paid in 1999 was $1,824 compared to $1,629 in 1998. Therefore, both increased use and higher per diems paid to the hospitals contributed to the inpatient expense increase.

The Group Health Association of America publishes the *HMO Industry Profile,* which provides numerous financial, operating, and utilization statistics. For example, the 1994 edition of this book provides utilization information for enrollers under 65 years of age (Table 8–14).

SUMMARY

This chapter briefly examined the financial and operating characteristics of alternative health care firms. Although the concepts of financial analysis are the same across all firms, there are some industry specifics that will alter the interpretation of financial results. It is important to become familiar with the industry sector being analyzed before reaching general conclusions regarding the performance of any given firm.

ASSIGNMENTS

1. Using the information presented in Table 8–15 for United Healthcare, a major HMO, discuss some of the primary observations that you would conclude regarding the financial performance of the firm. Relate your discussion to the values presented in Table 8–1.

Table 8–15 United Healthcare Corp Balance Sheet (Data in Thousands)

Fiscal Year Ending	12/31/95	12/31/94	12/31/93
Assets			
Cash	$ 940,110	$1,519,049	$ 228,260
Marketable securities	863,815	135,287	172,610
Receivables	550,313	167,369	169,075
Other current assets	512,883	86,510	44,023
Total current assets	$2,867,121	$1,908,215	$ 613,968
Prop, Plant, Equipment	$ 417,166	$ 273,431	$ 215,628
Less Accumulated Depreciation	149,514	110,834	88,886
Net Prop and Equipment	$ 267,652	$ 162,597	$ 126,742
Investment in Subsidiaries	$1,274,470	$1,115,054	$ 768,563
Intangibles	1,751,743	303,613	278,081
Total assets	$6,160,986	$3,489,479	$1,787,354
Liabilities			
Accounts payable	$1,236,217	$ 470,591	$ 535,863
Accrued expenses	566,770	122,993	52,027
Other current liabilities	631,009	70,718	70,844
Total current liabilities	$2,433,996	$ 664,302	$ 658,734
Noncurrent capital leases	38,970	29,721	39,099
Total liabilities	$2,472,966	$ 694,023	$ 697,833
Preferred stock	500,000	NA	NA
Common stock net	1,752	1,728	1,691
Capital surplus	822,429	752,472	659,359
Retained earnings	2,358,640	2,085,056	424,468
Other equities	5,199	–43,800	–108
Shareholder equity	$3,688,020	$2,795,456	$1,085,410
Total liability and net worth	$6,160,986	$3,489,479	$1,783,243

continues

Table 8–15 continued

Annual Income (000$)

Fiscal Year Ending	12/31/95	12/31/94	12/31/93
Net sales	$5,670,878	$3,768,882	$3,115,202
Cost of goods	3,930,933	2,643,107	2,236,588
Gross profit	$1,739,945	$1,125,775	$ 878,614
Selling, general, and administration	1,030,906	555,649	491,635
Income before depreciation and amortization	$ 709,039	$ 570,126	$ 386,979
Depreciation and amortization	94,458	64,079	50,628
Non-operating income	−153,796	−35,940	122
Interest expense	771	2,163	3,046
Income before tax	460,014	467,944	333,427
Provision for income tax	170,205	177,822	119,379
Minority interest	3,845	1,983	1,970
Net income before extraordinaries	285,964	288,139	212,078
Extraordinary items and discontinued operations	NA	1,377,075	NA
Net income	$ 285,964	$1,665,214	$ 212,078

2. Using the information presented in Table 8–16 for Manor Care, a major nursing-home firm, discuss some of the primary observations that you would conclude regarding the financial performance of the firm. Relate your discussion to the values presented in Table 8–1.

Table 8–16 Manor Care Inc., Balance Sheet (Data in Thousands)

Fiscal Year Ending	05/31/95	05/31/94	05/31/93
Assets			
Cash	$ 75,060	$ 60,487	$ 80,844
Receivables	96,149	84,766	82,820
Inventories	17,138	12,954	13,489
Other current assets	42,028	25,145	17,106
Total current assets	230,375	183,352	194,259
Net prop & equip	993,791	824,350	753,746
Intangibles	61,565	64,454	67,343
Deposit & other assets	130,576	114,369	91,158
Total assets	$1,416,307	$1,186,525	$1,106,506

continues

Table 8–16 continued

Fiscal Year Ending	05/31/95	05/31/94	05/31/93
Liabilities			
Accounts payable	$ 94,281	$ 50,231	$ 44,504
Current long-term debt	5,468	5,869	45,338
Accrued expenses	101,732	97,597	85,377
Income taxes	NA	12,681	5,254
Total current liabilities	$ 201,481	$ 166,378	$ 180,473
Mortgages	209,630	119,333	124,838
Deferred charges/inc	222,652	209,397	183,601
Long-term debt	157,671	157,602	255,600
Total liabilities	$ 791,434	$ 652,710	$ 744,512
Common stock, net	$ 6,553	$ 6,545	$ 6,047
Capital surplus	168,699	167,316	68,471
Retained earnings	491,520	402,520	329,532
Treasury stock	42,608	42,535	42,408
Other equities	709	−31	352
Shareholder equity	624,873	533,815	361,994
Total liabilities & net worth	$1,416,307	$1,186,525	$1,106,506
Annual Income			
Net sales	$1,321,993	$1,163,072	$1,009,675
Cost of goods	983,261	871,599	756,721
Gross profit	$ 338,732	$ 291,473	$ 252,954
Sell gen & admin exp	78,569	67,445	57,891
Inc bef dep & amort	$ 260,163	$ 224,028	$ 195,063
Depreciation & amort	76,215	66,540	60,999
Non-operating inc	2,953	10,655	3,889
Interest expense	27,115	31,281	37,070
Income before tax	$ 159,786	$ 136,862	$ 100,883
Prov for inc taxes	65,300	58,500	38,500
Net inc bef ex items	$ 94,486	$ 78,362	$ 62,383
Ex items & disc ops	NA	NA	−3,019
Net income	$ 94,486	$ 78,362	$ 59,364

3. Using the information presented in Table 8–17 for Phy Cor, a major physician-practice management firm, discuss some of the primary observations that you would conclude regarding the financial performance of the firm. Relate your discussion to the values presented in Table 8–1.

Table 8–17 Phy Cor Inc. Balance Sheet (Data in Thousands)

Fiscal Year Ending	12/31/95	12/31/94	12/31/93
Assets			
Cash	$ 18,827	$ 6,460	$ 3,200
Receivables	167,028	118,175	61,600
Inventories	8,939	5,840	3,994
Other current assets	22,727	14,407	8,658
Total current assets	$217,521	$144,882	$ 77,452
Net prop & equip	108,813	58,761	26,757
Other non-cur assets	NA	712	712
Intangibles	308,963	137,635	63,688
Deposits and oth asset	8,289	9,395	2,565
Total assets	$643,586	$351,385	$171,174
Liabilities			
Accounts payable	$ 20,020	$ 10,269	$ 5,931
Current long-term debt	587	148	65
Cur port cap leases	1,799	1,533	1,826
Accrued expenses	32,064	24,822	13,952
Income taxes	2,714	NA	NA
Other current liabilities	48,917	27,577	8,751
Total current liabilities	$106,101	$ 64,349	$ 30,525
Deferred charges/inc	8,030	8,258	1,630
Convertible debt	59,369	51,487	61,190
Long-term debt	65,905	32,150	2,597
Non-cur cap leases	1,637	1,261	3,050
Other long-term liabilities	13,722	9,755	2,177
Total liabilities	$254,764	$167,260	$101,169
Common stock, net	363,211	180,388	77,943
Retained earnings	25,611	3,737	−7,938
Shareholder equity	388,822	184,125	70,005
Total liability & net worth	$643,586	$351,385	$171,174

continues

Table 8–17 continued

Fiscal Year Ending	12/31/95	12/31/94	12/31/93
Annual Income			
Net sales	$441,596	$242,485	$167,381
Cost of goods	233,627	125,579	97,153
Gross profit	$207,969	$116,906	$ 70,228
Sell gen & admin exp	140,380	85,547	50,033
Inc bef dep & amort	$ 67,589	$ 31,359	$ 20,195
Depreciation & amort	$ 21,445	$ 12,229	$ 8,394
Non-operating inc	−5,117	1,334	309
Interest expense	5,230	3,963	3,878
Income before tax	$ 35,797	$ 16,501	$ 8,232
Prof for inc taxes	13,923	4,826	1,092
Net income	$ 21,874	$ 11,675	$ 7,140

SOLUTIONS

1. Table 8–18 provides financial ratio values for United Healthcare for the last three years.

Table 8–18 United Healthcare Financial Ratios

	Health Plan Median 1995	1995	1994	1993
Liquidity				
Current	1.32	1.18	2.87	0.93
Days in receivables	22.5	35.4	16.2	19.8
Days' cash-on-hand	89.9	128.3	178.7	51.3
Capital structure				
Equity financing %	48.9	59.9	80.1	60.7
Long-term debt to equity %	13.0	1.0	1.1	3.6
Cash flow to total debt %	15.0	15.6	260.3	37.6
Times interest earned	13.1	372.0	771.0	70.6
Activity				
Total asset turnover	1.55	0.90	1.07	1.74
Fixed asset turnover	16.8	20.6	23.0	24.6
Current asset turnover	2.88	1.93	1.96	5.08
Profitability				
Total margin %	3.6	5.2	44.6 (7.6)	6.8
Return on equity %	11.6	7.8	61.2 (10.3)	19.5

United Healthcare is and has been a very profitable health plan. Profitability was especially high in 1994, but much of this increase was the result of a large, extraordinary gain on the sale of a subsidiary. Total margin and return on equity would have been 7.6 and 10.3 percent, respectively, in 1994 without the gain. Although profitability in 1995 was above the industry median, there was a substantial decrease that should be watched closely. Revenues are increasing at rates less than costs, which may be a result of more competition in United Healthcare's markets.

United Healthcare has a very good liquidity position. The firm is carrying a lot of cash, much of it generated from the sale of the subsidiary in 1994, and is well above industry medians. There is a potential for reducing accounts receivable. United Healthcare appears to have almost 50 percent more days in accounts receivable than the industry median.

United Healthcare has very little long-term debt that is consistent with industry norms. Most of its debt is current and most likely represents significant claims payable amounts.

United Healthcare does have lower asset efficiency ratios. Much of the difference is a result of its very heavy investment in cash and marketable securities. This is not a bad situation if United Healthcare has a purpose for the cash. United Healthcare also has excess receivables and also may have more plant, property, and equipment than the norm.

Overall, United Healthcare appears to be a very strong HMO and has experienced significant growth during the last three years.

2. Table 8–19 provides financial ratios for Manor Care for the last three years.

Table 8–19 Manor Care Financial Ratios

	Nursing Home Median 1995	1995	1994	1993
Liquidity				
Current	1.64	1.14	1.10	1.08
Days in receivables	60.0	26.5	26.6	29.9
Days' cash-on-hand	17.6	23.7	21.5	33.1
Capital structure				
Equity financing %	38.6	44.1	45.0	32.7
Long-term debt to equity %	51.4	126.6	122.3	205.5
Cash flow to total debt	11.4	30.0	32.7	21.5
Times interest earned	1.79	4.5	3.5	2.6
Activity				
Total asset turnover	0.95	0.94	0.99	0.92
Fixed asset turnover	1.86	1.33	1.42	1.35
Current asset turnover	3.71	5.75	6.40	5.22
Profitability				
Total margin %	2.5	7.1	6.7	5.9
Return on equity %	6.1	15.1	14.7	16.4

Manor Care has experienced a period of increasing margins and is well above industry standards regarding profitability. High return on equity values are a result of both margins as well as relatively high use of debt or financial leverage.

Manor Care has a relatively low current ratio, which may be partly due to very low values of days in accounts receivable. Present days in receivable are less than 50 percent of the industry norm.

Manor Care has relied much more heavily on debt financing than other nursing-home chains. This can be seen in its long-term debt to equity ratio, which is decreasing, but is still better than twice the industry average. Coverage of this debt does not appear to be a problem, however, because of Manor Care's present high margins. The extensive use of long-term debt also has helped to improve its return on equity.

Manor Care does appear to have a lot of fixed assets relative to the amount of revenue being generated from those assets, as can be determined from Manor Care's low fixed asset turnover ratios. This may be a result of a newer physical plant than that of average nursing homes.

Overall, Manor Care appears to be a very profitable nursing home chain relative to industry norms. Manor Care's return on equity has been double its industry average.

3. Table 8–20 provides financial ratio values for Phy Cor for the last three years.

Table 8–20 Phy Cor Financial Ratios

| | Medical Group Median | | | |
	1995	1995	1994	1993
Current	2.17	2.05	2.25	2.53
Days in receivables	155.2	138.1	177.9	134.3
Days' cash-on-hand	14.5	19.5	11.8	8.3
Capital structure				
Equity financing %	51.4	60.4	52.4	40.9
Long-term debt to equity %	32.6	32.6	45.6	39.2
Cash flow to total debt %	19.6	17.6	15.0	15.6
Times interest earned	3.53	5.18	3.95	2.84
Activity				
Total asset turnover	0.76	0.69	0.69	0.98
Fixed asset turnover	4.50	4.05	4.13	6.3
Current asset turnover	1.88	2.03	1.68	2.15
Profitability				
Total margin %	4.2	5.0	4.8	4.3
Return on equity %	6.3	5.6	6.3	10.2

Phy Cor has experienced phenomenal growth during the last three years in both sales and assets. To a large extent, Phy Cor's growth has been financed with new equity and not debt. New debt increased approximately $150 million, whereas equity increased approximately $318 million. Much of this equity represented an issuance of new equity shares.

Phy Cor's growth will be linked to its ability to maintain and increase profitability. At the present time, its margins are slightly above industry averages, and have been improving. This is typical of a firm that is growing, in which margins improve as new businesses are integrated into the corporate structure. Return on equity is lower than industry averages because Phy Cor has relied less on debt financing than the industry average and has lower total asset turnover ratios. Again, much of this may change as Phy Cor consolidates growth and improves its asset efficiency and margins.

Phy Cor has a large balance in accounts receivable, but this balance is not out of line with industry norms. Liquidity in general appears similar to other firms in this rapidly evolving sector.

Phy Cor has lower total asset turnover ratios than industry averages. Much of the total asset investment of Phy Cor is listed as intangible assets—$308,963,000 in 1995. Much of this investment represents goodwill and other intangible assets that are a part of the value of physicians' practices acquired by Phy Cor. This investment will be amortized against earnings in future years and could have a depressing effect upon earnings. Phy Cor needs to be careful that it does not overpay for its acquisitions.

The overall assessment of Phy Cor is that it is a relatively strong firm within the practice-management sector of the health care industry. There is, however, much risk, and future growth seems contingent upon corresponding growth in earnings.

Phy Cor is in a growth sector of the industry, but one that has significant elements of risk.

9

Strategic Financial Planning

Is there a need to define corporate financial policy in a health care firm? If so, who should be responsible—the board of trustees, the chief executive officer, the chief financial officer, or some combination of these? How should the definition of financial policy be accomplished? What are the steps required?

These kinds of questions are only now beginning to surface in the health care industry. Finance and financial management have long been areas of concern, but their orientation has recently shifted. Reimbursement and payment system management have given way to financial planning. Survival tomorrow is no longer guaranteed. Health care firms must establish realistic and achievable financial plans that are consistent with their strategic plans. The primary purpose of this chapter is to help provide a basis for the crucial task of forming financial policies in health care firms.

THE STRATEGIC PLANNING PROCESS

Most observers probably would agree that financial policy and financial planning should be closely integrated within the strategic planning process. Thus, understanding the strategic planning process is a first step in defining and developing financial policy and financial planning. It would be ideal if there was agreement among leading experts regarding the definition of strategic planning, but this is not the case. The literature on strategic-planning is fairly recent; most of it has appeared since 1965. And the application of strategic planning principles to the health care industry is even more recent; the bulk of the literature on such applications has been published since 1980.

One trend in health care strategic planning does appear clear, however: there is a definite movement away from "facilities planning" to a more market-oriented approach. Health care firms can no longer decide which services they want to deliver without assessing the economics of demand. This requirement appears consistent with the concept of strategic planning as it is used in general industry. Indeed, as the business environments of the health care industry and general industry become more alike, strategic planning in the two areas should become increasingly similar.

Much of the literature that deals with the strategic-planning process in business organizations appears to be concerned with two basic decision outcomes: first, a statement of mission or goals (or both) is required to provide guidance to the organization. Second, a set of programs or activities to which the organization will commit resources during the planning period is defined.

Figure 9–1 shows the integration of the financial-planning process with the strategic-planning process. Financial planning is fashioned by

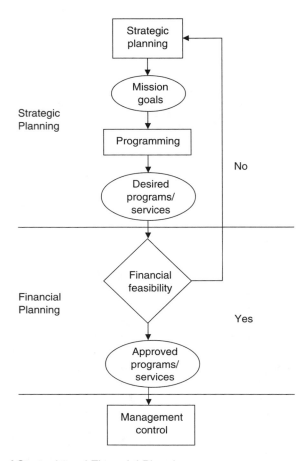

Figure 9–1 Integration of Strategic and Financial Planning

the definition of programs and services and then assesses the financial feasibility of those programs and services. In many cases, a desired set of programs and services may not be financially feasible. This may cause a redefinition of the organization's mission and its desired programs and services. For example, a hospital may decide to change from a full-scale hospital to a specialty hospital, or it may decide to eliminate specific clinical programs, such as pediatrics or obstetrics.

Three points concerning the integration of strategic and financial planning should be emphasized. First, both strategic planning and fi-

nancial planning are the primary responsibility of the board of trustees. This does not exclude top management from the process, because they should be active and participating members of the board. Second, strategic planning should precede financial planning. In some situations, the board may make strategic decisions based on the availability of funding. Although this may be fiscally conservative, it often can inhibit creative thinking. Third, the board should play an active, not a passive, role in the financial-planning process. The board should not await word concerning the financial feasibility of its desired programs and services; it should actively provide guidelines for management or its consultants (or both) to use in developing the financial plan. Specifically, the board should establish key financial policy targets in the following three major areas:

1. growth rate in assets,
2. debt policy, and
3. profitability objective (return on equity).

Financial-Policy Targets

The term financial feasibility is often associated with an expensive study performed by a consulting firm in conjunction with the issue of debt. In such cases, the financial projections are so incredibly complex that few people profess to understand them, and even fewer actually do. In many people's minds, financial planning consists of a large number of mathematical relationships that can simulate future financial results, given certain key inputs. The validity of the projections is dependent on the reliability of the mathematical relationships, or model, and on the accuracy of the assumptions. Most financial feasibility studies developed in this way are never reviewed and never updated.

But conditions are changing and changing rapidly. A large number of health care firms are now beginning to develop formal strategic plans. They are beginning to redefine, or at least reconsider, their basic mission and to identify future market areas. It is increasingly clear that their financial plans and financial strategies must be integral parts of their overall strategic plan.

Granted that health care board members and health care executives have an urgent need to understand financial policy and financial planning, can the requisite body of knowledge be conveyed in a manner that is capable of being understood? Must board members and executives remain passive observers in financial planning, or can they be given the means to establish key policy directives?

Figure 9–2 identifies the critical financial-planning relationships, and also the sequencing of the financial-planning process. The premise on which the financial plan is built rests on some projection of services or levels of activity. The strategic plan usually provides this information by indicating which product lines the firm expects to provide during the next five years, and at what level of expected activity. The first line in Figure 9–2 is from the income statement and shows present and projected revenues. The projection of revenues can be directly related to the strategic plan. After all, revenue is merely the product of price multiplied by quantity. If the strategic plan specifies volume of services, then multiplying those volumes by expected price yields revenues.

Projected revenue serves as the basis for projecting the required level of investment or assets, which is the second step in the financial-planning process set forth in Figure 9–2. In any business firm, there are usually some specific relationships between investment required and production. For example, a health care firm with no existing clinic capacity that expected to provide 50,000 clinic visits per year five years from now would be required to invest heavily in physician practices to acquire this capacity. In the simple illustration of Figure 9–2, there appears to be a one-to-one relationship between revenue and investment: one dollar of investment in assets is required for every dollar of revenue.

The third step is for the board to establish a debt policy for the organization. Stated simply, what percentage of the firm's investment will the board permit to be financed with debt? In Figure 9–2, the debt policy appears to be set at 50 percent. Fifty percent of the $2,000 investment in year 5 is financed with debt, which leaves the remaining 50 percent to be financed with equity.

The fourth and final step would appear to be the easiest stage in the planning process. If balance sheets balance, and they always do, the firm illustrated in Figure 9–2 will need to have $1,000 in equity at the end of year 5. A $1,000 equity balance when combined with the board-approved debt target of $1,000 will exactly finance the $2,000 required investment in assets.

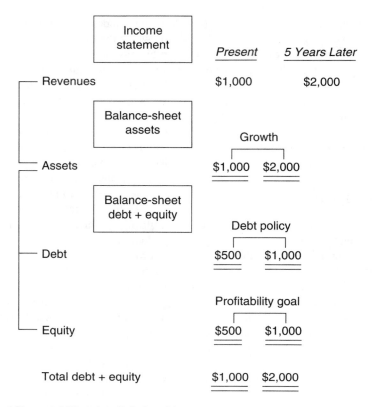

Figure 9–2 Critical Financial Planning Relationships

The critical question, however, is can the firm generate $500 in new equity during the next five years? Because most, if not all, of this equity must be generated from profits of the firm, the feasibility of this increase in equity relates directly to the reasonableness of forecasted profitability targets or goals. If the firm is not able to generate $500 in new equity, what will happen? First, a balance sheet must always balance, so the firm is faced with one of two decisions. It must either reduce its level of investment, which of course translates into fewer services. Or it must increase its risk exposure through the addition of higher debt limits. This process is most likely iterative and can be related to Figure 9–1. When the financial plan is feasible, an approved set of programs and services is in place and resources are allocated to accomplish the firm's

goals. The financial plan then serves as the basis for management control.

Requirements for Effective Policy Making

The preceding discussion of the elements of financial planning and the three major target areas of financial policy suggest certain requirements for effective financial planning and policy making. The following ten requirements are of special importance.

1. The accounting system should be capable of providing data on cost, revenue, and investment along program lines.

Programs, or "strategic business units," are the basic building blocks of any strategic plan. The financial plan must be developed on a basis consistent with the strategic plan. Unfortunately, present accounting systems are geared to provide data along responsibility center or departmental lines. For example, psychiatry may represent a program in the strategic plan, but the financial data on costs, investments, and revenues for the program may be intertwined with those of many departments, such as dietary, housekeeping, occupational therapy, and pharmacy. Still, this problem is not unique to health care firms. Many organizations have programs that cut across departmental lines. In such cases, the financial data can be accumulated along programmatic lines, but some adjustments in cost and revenue assignments are necessary.

With the advent of the diagnosis-related group (DRG) payment system, the hospital industry has been making major advancements in the accumulation of financial data in terms of DRG categories. It is now possible to define major programs or product lines in a hospital as consisting of a specific set of DRGs. For example, if obstetrics was a program, it might be defined as DRG #370 (Cesarean section with CC) to DRG #391 (normal newborns).

It is important to note that although problems exist in obtaining financial data along program lines, they are not insurmountable. The health care industry is, of course, different from the automotive industry, but the differences do not necessarily imply greater difficulties in costing.

2. No growth does not imply a zero-growth rate in assets.

The fact that no growth does not necessarily imply zero growth in assets is so obvious that it is often overlooked by many planning committees. Inflation will create investment needs that exceed present levels, even though the organization's strategic plan may call for program stabilization or an actual retrenchment. An annual rate of inflation equal to 7 percent means a doubling of investment values every ten years. For example, a nursing home with assets of $25 million today should plan on being a $50-million-asset firm ten years from now. Just because the investment involved may not represent an in-

crease in productive capacity does not negate the need for a financial plan that will generate $25 million in new equity and debt financing over the next ten years.

Over time, of course, expectations about future rates of inflation may change. The financial plan should reflect the best current thinking in this area. This may necessitate periodic changes in the financial plan (Requirement 9). It is also important to recognize that there may be differences in investment inflation rates across programs. In some programs, such as oncology, in which dramatic technologic changes are likely to occur, a greater relative inflation rate may have to be assigned.

3. Working capital is a major element in computing total future asset needs.

In computing future investment needs, it is not uncommon to omit the working capital category. Most investment in any strategic plan is usually in bricks, mortar, and equipment. However, working capital can still be a rather sizable component, accounting for 20 to 30 percent of total investment in many health care firms.

The term "net working capital" is often used to describe the amount of permanent financing required to finance working capital or current assets. Net working capital is defined as current assets less current liabilities. It is important to remember this, because some current liability financing is automatic or unnegotiated. Just as inflation increases the dollar value of outstanding accounts receivable, it also increases wages or salaries payable and accounts payable. It is the net amount of working capital that must be financed.

Working capital requirements vary by program. New programs usually have significant working capital requirements, whereas existing programs may experience only modest increases resulting from inflation. One of the primary causes for failure in new business ventures is often an inadequate amount of available working capital. New programs also may have significantly different working-capital requirements. For example, a home-health program may require little fixed investment in plant and equipment, but significant amounts of working capital may be required to finance a long collection cycle and initial development costs. Many firms that rushed into the development of home-health agency programs have become acutely aware of this problem.

If inadequate amounts of working capital are projected in the financial plan, the entire plan may be jeopardized. For example, an unanticipated $2 million increase in receivables requires an immediate source of funding, such as the liquidation of investments. If those investments are essential to provide needed equity in a larger financing program, certain key investments may be delayed or canceled in the future. A number of firms have had to reduce the scope of their strategic plans because of unanticipated demands for working capital.

4. There should be some accumulation of funds for future investments critical to long-term solvency.

Saving for a rainy day has not been a policy practiced by many health care firms to any significant degree. As of 1995, the average hospital had approximately 17.5 percent of its replacement needs available in investments. This implies that the average hospital would need to borrow 82.5 percent of its replacement needs. This level of debt financing may no longer be feasible in the hospital industry as lenders reassess the relative degree of risk involved.

It is critical that health care boards and management establish formal policies for retention of funds for future investment. Health care firms can no longer expect to finance all of their investment needs with debt. They must set aside funds for investment to meet future needs in the same manner that pension plans are funded. An actuarially determined pension funding requirement is analogous to a board policy of replacement reserve funding. Yet, few health care firms set aside sufficient replacement funds for future investment needs, which partially explains the dramatic growth in debt in the hospital industry.

5. A formally defined debt capacity ceiling should be established.

Few health care firms have formally defined their debt capacity or debt policy. This is in sharp contrast to most other industries. Without such a formally established debt policy, one of two unfavorable outcomes may result. First, debt may be viewed as the balancing variable in the financial plan. If a firm expects a $25 million increase in its investment and a $5 million increase in equity, $20 million of debt is required to make the strategic plan financially feasible. The firm will then try to arrange for $20 million of new debt financing. This is the situation in which many hospitals have found themselves. In the past, additional debt usually could be obtained and adequate debt service coverage could be demonstrated to lenders. Cost reimbursement had its advantages in that it could be used to provide payment for debt-service costs. The strategic plan could remain unchanged, but a potential problem was that the debt to equity ratio might increase significantly.

Second, the balancing variable in the financial plan may shift to the investment side, but on an ex post facto basis. An approved financial plan may be unrealistic because the level of indebtedness required to finance the strategic plan exposes the hospital to excessive risks. Management may not realize this until the actual financing is needed. At that point, it may be required to scale down the programs specified in the strategic plan. If a realistic debt-capacity ceiling had been established earlier, existing funded programs might have been canceled or cut back to make funds available for more desirable programs.

Debt capacity can be defined in a number of ways. It can be expressed as a ratio, such as a long-term debt to equity ratio, or it can be defined in terms of demonstrated debt-service coverage. Whatever the method used, some limit on debt financing should be established. That limit should represent a balance between the organization's desire to avoid financial risk exposure and the investment needs of its strategic plan. Debt policy should be clearly and concisely established before the fact; it should not be an ad hoc result.

6. Return on investment (ROI) by program area should be an important criterion in program selection.

The principle that ROI by program area should govern program selection is related to the need for accounting data along product lines, as discussed previously. To calculate ROI along program lines, financial data on revenues, expenses, and investment must be available along program lines. ROI should be used as part of an overall system of program evaluation and selection.

Portfolio analysis is a buzzword that has been used lately to categorize programs in terms of market share and growth rate. Health care writers have applied the concept to the literature on health care planning and marketing. However, one difficulty with the application of portfolio analysis in the health care industry is the selection of the dimensions for developing the portfolio matrix. In most portfolio matrices, the dimensions used are market share and growth. Market share and growth are assumed to have an explicit relationship to cash flow. High market share is associated with high profitability and, thus, with good cash flow. High market growth is assumed to require cash flow for investment. For example, a program with a high market share and low growth is regarded as a "cash cow." It produces high cash flow but requires little cash flow for reinvestment because of its low-growth needs.

Here we will use a slight modification of the portfolio analysis paradigm, incorporating the dimension of profitability. Figure 9–3 illustrates the revised portfolio analysis matrix. Its two dimensions are (1) ROI and (2) community need. ROI is used as the measure of profitability because it is most directly related to strategic and financial planning. Profit is merely new equity that can be used to finance new investment. Absolute levels of profit or cash flow mean little unless they are related to the underlying investment. For example, if program A has a profit of $100,000 and an investment of $2,000,000, whereas program B has a profit of $50,000 and an investment of $100,000, which program is a better cash cow if both programs have low community need? In this example, B is clearly the better cash cow because it generates a much better return on its investment.

In our revised portfolio analysis matrix, community need replaces the traditional marketing dimensions of growth and market share. Community need may be difficult to measure quantitatively, but the concept appears closely aligned to the missions of most voluntary health care firms—firms that usually were formed to provide health care services to some reasonably well-defined market.

Figure 9–3 categorizes programs as "dogs," "cash cows," "stars," and "Samaritans." With the exception of Samaritans, these terms are identical to those used in the existing literature.

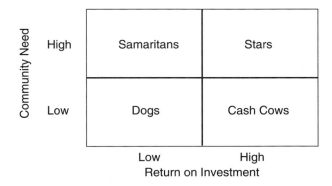

Figure 9–3 Revised Portfolio Analysis Matrix

An example of a Samaritan program is one with a small or negative ROI but a high community need. For example, a hospital may provide a drug-abuse program that loses money but meets a community need not met by any other health care provider. The program can continue if—and only if—the hospital has some stars or cash cows to subsidize the program's poor profitability. Dogs, that is, programs with low community need and low profit, should be considered in light of the resources they draw from potential Samaritans. The new payment environment makes this kind of analysis mandatory.

7. Nonoperating sources of equity should be included in the financial plan.

In the preceding discussion of ROI, we were concerned primarily with operating profitability. However, in many voluntary health care firms, nonoperating income also can be extremely important. In fact, in 1995, nonoperating revenue accounted for 32 percent of total reported net income in the hospital industry. If nonoperating income can be improved, a significant new source of funding will be available to help finance the strategic plan. This could mean either that a greater percentage of desired programs can be undertaken or that reduced levels of indebtedness are possible. The primary source of nonoperating income for most health care firms is investment income and gains.

The investment portfolio of many health care firms is large. Funds are available for retirement plans, professional liability self-insurance plans, funded depreciation, bond funds, endowments, and other purposes. Thus, small increases in investment yields can create sizable increases in income. For example, a 1-percent improvement in the yield on invested pension funds may reduce annual pension expense by as much as 10 percent. Clearly, management should formally establish and incorporate target investment yields in its financial plans.

New equity also can come from sources other than operating and nonoperating income. Corporate restructuring arrangements can create proprietary subsidiaries that can issue stock. Joint-venture relationships with medical staff and others can be used to finance plant assets. It is important that both board members and executives have a clear understanding of the possible alternatives available for raising new equity to finance the strategic plan. Raising new equity through stock or partnerships is no longer the exclusive domain of investor-owned firms.

8. The financial plan must be integrated with the management control system.

The integration of the financial plan with the management-control system is an obvious requirement, but it is often overlooked. Frequently, a large fee is paid to a consultant or enormous amounts of internal staff time are used to develop a financial plan that is never used.

Ideally, the financial plan should be the basis for the annual budget. The key link between the budget and the financial plan should be the ROI targets specified in the financial plan. These ROI targets are critical to the long-run fulfillment of the strategic plan. Failure to achieve the targeted levels of profit will require revisions in the strategic plan.

Health care board members would not have to be involved in pricing debates if approved financial plans were available. In such situations, the profitability targets by program already would have been approved in the plans. The primary issues in the budgeting process should be the translation of profit targets by program lines to departmental lines via pricing allocations and the assessment of departmental operating efficiencies. Long, involved discussions about whether budgeted profit is too much or not enough should not be necessary.

9. The financial plan should be updated at least annually.

Management should have the most recent financial "road map" available at all times. Few people would plan a drive to San Francisco from Boston with a five-year-old road map, yet many organizations operate either with no long-range financial plan or with an outdated one. This can be especially dangerous for health care firms at the present time, as the business environment continues to change rapidly. Today, financial plans based on yesterday's financial environment may be useless, or even misleading. In all financial plans, a careful reassessment of relative program profitability is periodically required, possibly prompting major revisions of the strategic plan. Knowing both where you are going and how you expect to get there is critical to survival in a competitive environment.

10. The financial plan is a board document and should be formally approved by the board.

In many firms, the financial plan, if it exists, is regarded as a management document. The board may be only mildly interested in reviewing it and not interested at all in relating it to the strategic plan. This is rather strange behavior. Most boards would never dream of letting management operate without a board-approved annual budget for fear of failing to fulfill their board responsibilities. Yet planning for periods longer than one year is not regarded as important.

A recent hospital board meeting that followed a two-day strategic planning retreat illustrates this traditional perspective. During the retreat, strategic discussions about the future were held. The board and management agreed on a plan for the future that called for significant expansion into new market areas, such as long-term care. At the subsequent board meeting, the chief executive officer and the chief finance officer presented the strategic plan and the related financial plan. The board members regarded approval of the financial plan as a waste of time. They did approve it, but in body only, not in spirit. Their rationale for apathy was clear. They could not foresee any problem with the financing. Most of them had been board members for a long time. Whenever money was needed in the past, they raised rates or borrowed, and they could not see any reason to change this policy in the future. This type of behavior in today's market is not only unwise, it is suicidal.

Fortunately, this kind of reaction is becoming less common. Board members today are beginning to realize that the financial plan and the strategic plan are integrally related. It is impos-sible to develop one without the other, and both are ultimately the responsibility of the board.

DEVELOPING THE FINANCIAL PLAN

In this section, we describe in some detail the steps involved in preparing a financial plan, using an actual case example. For our purposes, a financial plan may be defined as the bridge between two balance sheets. It is the income statement that provides the major connection between two balance sheets, and so we will describe both balance sheet and income statement projection.

The Developmental Process

Four steps are involved in the development of a financial plan:

1. Assess financial position and prior growth patterns.
2. Define growth needs in total assets for the planning period.
3. Define acceptable level of debt for both current and long-term categories.
4. Assess reasonableness of required growth rate in equity.

Assessment of Present Financial Position

The first step in the development of a financial plan is the assessment of present financial position. It is extremely important to determine the present financial health and position of the firm. Without such information, projections about future growth can be dangerous at best. In most situations, past performance is usually a good basis for projecting future performance. For example, a financial plan may call for a future growth rate in equity of 15 percent per year. If, however, the prior five-year period showed an average annual growth rate in equity of only 5 percent, there may be some doubt about the validity of the assumption of 15 percent and thus the reasonableness of the financial plan.

The following two categories of financial information need to be assembled to assess present financial position:

1. financial statements for the past three to five years, and
2. financial evaluation of the firm, using ratio analysis.

To illustrate the application of this information in financial planning, the balance sheets presented in Table 9–1 are used. These balance sheets provide historical information for Omega Health Foundation (OHF) for the years 1997 through 1999.

Tables 9–1, 9–2, and 9–3 present some useful historical data that will be helpful in assessing the present financial position and projecting asset growth rates. After a review of the three tables, the following summary may help to organize our thinking about OHF's 1999 financial position.

A complete review of OHF's financial position can be found in Chapter 7 where the individual financial ratios of OHF were calculated and discussed. This brief summary will cover only the highlights of OHF's present financial position.

- OHF has good levels of investment reserves. Its present replacement viability ratio is 0.56, which is better than three times the CHIPS national average of 0.17. The present funded depreciation account has $55,794,000 in it and also has created a sizable amount of investment income.
- Present operating profitability at OHF is not good and an operating loss of $492,000 was experienced in 1999. The primary cause for this poor operating position is an excessive cost structure. OHF took a restructuring charge of $5,086,000 in 1999, which reflects its commitment to further cost reduction.

- Age of plant at OHF is close to the national average and might suggest higher levels of capital expenditures in the future. The board has, however, approved capital expenditures of $10,000,000 per year during the next five years.
- OHF has a capital structure that reflects slightly more debt than national norms, but it has not issued any new debt in the last three years. The board's policy for future financing calls for no new long-term debt. Repayment of existing debt will continue using the existing debt principal schedule.
- Present days in accounts receivable are very low, primarily because of the netting of due-to-third-party-payer amounts shown in the current liability section. It is expected that this present situation will continue.

Defining Growth Rate in Assets

Table 9–4 defines the assumptions that will be used to develop the five-year financial plan for OHF. As discussed earlier, it is impossible to forecast asset investment without first forecasting revenues and also expenses. Revenue forecasts are an integral part of asset forecasts because the level of service drives the underlying required investment. For example, growth in property, plant, and equipment is directly related to the range and level of services expected to be provided in the planning period. Even items as mundane as accounts receivable are directly related to revenue forecasts. Projecting revenues leads to a forecast of expenses. When a firm defines its expected production levels, requirements for staffing, supplies, and other expense items are often directly tied to these forecasts. In addition, certain areas of asset investment are often directly related to expense levels. For example, short-term cash is often directly related to expense levels, and inventory investment is often tied to expected annual supplies expense.

In the remainder of this section, we will discuss some of the more significant assumptions used in the financial plan developed for OHF. The projected balance sheet, income statement,

Table 9–1 Balance Sheet for Omega Health Foundation as of June 30, 1999, 1998, and 1997 (Data in Thousands)

GENERAL FUNDS

Assets

	1999	1998	1997
Current			
Cash and short-term investments	$ 9,692	$ 9,456	$ 11,388
Accounts receivable	24,324	25,597	23,381
Due from third-party payers	0	56	185
Due from donor-restricted funds	280	179	47
Inventories	1,763	2,251	2,252
Prepaid expenses and other assets	1,135	1,520	1,963
Current portion of funds held by trustee	990	925	1,580
Current portion of self-insurance trust funds	2,264	2,284	2,917
Total current assets	$ 40,448	$ 42,268	$ 43,713
Assets that have limited use:			
Self-insurance trust funds, net of current portion	$9,321	$9,013	$9,962
Board-designated funds and fund depreciation	55,794	42,326	37,520
Funds held by trustee, net of current portion	338	726	1,037
	$ 65,453	$ 52,065	$ 48,519
Property, plant, and equipment, net	$ 75,990	$ 74,829	$ 66,317
Investments in and advances to partnerships	2,497	2,226	1,759
Deferred financing costs, net	1,139	1,306	1,394
Deferred third-party reimbursement	—	674	983
Other assets	1,067	654	575
Total	$186,594	$174,022	$163,260

Liabilities

	1999	1998	1997
Current			
Current portion of long-term debt	$ 1, 401	$ 1, 506	$ 1,784
Notes payable	—	250	—
Accounts payable and accrued expenses	11,087	7,215	6,791
Accrued salaries, wages, and fees	4,342	4,238	3,724
Accrued restructuring costs	2,078	—	—
Accrued vacation	3,288	3,331	3,223
Accrued insurance costs	2,234	2,284	2,917
Advance from third-party payer	1,205	1,142	941
Due to third-party payers	11,571	10,688	9,150
Total current liabilities	$37,206	$30,654	$28,530

continues

Table 9–1 continued

Accrued retirement costs	$8,846	$1,736	$1,576
Accrued insurance costs, net of current portion	4,636	3,450	2,124
Deferred third-party reimbursement	3,489	3,488	3,604
Long-term debt, net of current portion	54,781	55,989	56,369
Other liabilities	238	2	—
Total liabilities	$109,196	$ 95,319	$ 92,203
Unrestricted net assets	77,398	78,703	71,057
Total	$186,594	$174,022	$163,260

Table 9–2 Statements of Revenues and Expenses of General Funds for Omega Health Foundation (Data in Thousands)

	1999	1998	1997
Revenues			
Net patient service revenue	$160,574	$162,323	$147,596
Equity in net income from partnership	732	1,135	1,216
Gifts and bequests	258	435	296
Other	8,760	8,742	7,655
Total revenues	$170,324	$172,635	$156,763
Expenses			
Salaries and wages	$ 81,032	$ 81,476	$ 75,942
Fringe benefits	18,627	19,876	16,391
Professional fees	8,980	12,743	13,541
Supplies and other	39,607	38,539	30,658
Interest	4,364	4,369	4,421
Bad-debt expense	4,551	6,419	8,026
Depreciation and amortization	8,545	7,861	7,167
Restructuring costs	5,110✓	—	—
Total expenses	$170,816	$171,283	$156,146
Income (loss) from operations	$ (492)	$ 1,352	$ 617
Nonoperating gains (losses)			
Income on investments	$4,717	$4,658	$3,837
Gifts and bequests	41	297	—
Loss on disposal of assets	(84)	(601)	(150)
Nonoperating gains, net	$ 4,674	$ 4,354	$ 3,687
Excess of revenues over expenses before cumulative effect of change in accounting principle	$ 4,182	$ 5,706	$ 4,304
Cumulative effect of change in accounting principle	(5,086) ✓	—	—
Excess of revenues over expenses	$ (904)	$ 5,706	$ 4,304

Table 9–3 Historical Financial Ratios for Omega Health Foundation

	1997	1998	1999	National Median*
Profitability				
Total margin percent	2.7	3.2	−0.5	3.8
Operating margin percent	0.4	0.8	−0.3	2.7
Nonoperating gain percent	2.3	2.5	2.7	1.0
Return on equity percent	6.1	7.3	−1.2	7.4
Liquidity				
Current	1.53	1.38	1.09	1.96
Days in accounts receivable	35.7	33.7	28.9	56.7
Average payment period	69.9	68.5	83.2	57.0
Days' cash-on-hand	27.8	21.2	21.8	26.8
Capital structure				
Equity financing percent	43.5	45.2	41.5	52.0
Long–term debt to equity percent	79.4	71.1	70.8	55.0
Cash flow to debt percent	13.5	15.7	8.3	21.0
Times interest earned	1.97	2.31	0.79	3.17
Activity				
Total asset turnover	0.98	1.02	0.94	1.01
Fixed asset turnover	2.42	2.37	2.30	2.20
Other asset turnover	3.01	3.10	2.49	5.11
Current asset turnover	3.67	4.18	4.32	3.57
Other ratios				
Average age of plant	7.5	8.0	8.3	8.5
Replacement viability	0.44	0.48	0.56	0.17

*Median source: The 1995 Almanac of Hospital Financial and Operating Indicators, CHIPS.

and financial ratios are presented in Tables 9–5, 9–6, and 9–7.

- Net patient revenues. Net patient revenues were projected at an annual 2-percent growth rate. Net patient revenue actually decreased slightly in 1999, but increased 9.4 percent in 1998. What should we forecast? Clearly, revenues should be set equal to volumes of services expected multiplied by expected net prices. At first, 2 percent might seem like a relatively small growth rate, but remember that OHF presently has a very high price structure, which it may not

be able to maintain. A 2-percent growth rate is predicated on zero growth in net prices, but a 2-percent growth in volume of services. A 2-percent growth in services seems reasonable given previous growth in outpatient and clinic services. The assumptions made about revenue growth (volume and price) are the most important variables in terms of impact upon the financial plan. Small changes in these assumptions can have a sizable influence on projected financial results.

- Salaries and wages. In the labor-intensive health care industry, the second most im-

Table 9–4 Financial Planning Assumptions for Omega Health Foundation Years 2000 to 2004

Account	Assumptions
Revenues	
Net patient revenue	2 percent growth per year
Equity in partnerships	5 percent growth per year
Gifts and bequests	5 percent growth per year
Other	5 percent growth per year
Expenses	
Interest expense	7.5 percent of prior year long-term debt + current maturities of long-term debt
Salaries and wages	1 percent growth per year
Fringe benefits	23 percent of salaries and wages
Professional fees	5 percent growth per year
Supplies	5 percent growth per year
Restructuring costs	$2,078,000 in 2000, zero thereafter
Depreciation expense	5.8 percent of gross property and equipment
Bad-debt expense	2.8 percent of net patient revenue
Nonoperating gains	
Investment Income	8.3 percent of average balance in board-designated and funded depreciation
Gifts and bequests	$50,000 per year
Loss on disposals	$100,000 per year
Assets	
Cash and short-term investments	20 days' cash-on-hand
Accounts receivable	15 percent of net patient revenue
Due from donor-restricted funds	$300,000 per year
Current portion held by trustee	Schedule $1,055,000 in 2000, increasing by $65,000 per year
Current portion self-insurance	5 percent growth per year
Total current assets	Subtotal of previous items
Gross property and equipment	Net new capital expenditures of $10,000,000 per year
Accumulated depreciation expense	Beginning balance plus depreciation expense
Self-insurance trust	5 percent growth per year
Board-designated and funded depreciation	Balancing account, all surplus cash flow will be invested here
Funds held by trustee	$338,000 per year
Investments in partnerships	5 percent growth per year
Deferred financing costs	Schedule/$972,000 in 2000, decreasing by $167,000 per year
Other assets	10 percent growth per year
Liabilities	
Current maturities of long-term debt	Schedule based upon debt principal due
Accounts payable	5 percent growth per year
Accrued salaries and wages	5.3 percent of salaries and wages expense

continues

Table 9–4 continued

Accrued restructuring costs	Value goes to zero in 2000 and remains at zero
Accrued vacation	Stable at $3,288,000
Accrued insurance costs	5 percent growth per year
Advances from third-party payers	0.75 percent of net patient revenue
Due to third-party payers	7.2 percent of net patient revenue
Total current liabilities	Subtotal of previous items
Long-term debt	Schedule based upon payment of debt principal
Accrued retirement costs	5 percent growth per year
Accrued insurance costs	5 percent growth per year
Deferred third-party reimbursement	Stable at $3,489,000
Other liabilities	5 percent growth per year
Unrestricted net assets	Addition of net income to prior balance

portant assumption in any financial forecast is salaries and wages. Salary and wage cost are the product of three factors:

Salary and wage costs =
Volume of services × Staffing ratios ×
Wage rates

OHF has poor productivity, as discussed in Chapter 7. It has undergone massive restructuring to try to reduce given staff levels and become more efficient. These staff reductions showed up as one-time restructuring costs in 1999, and finally will be written off in 2000. It is expected that future labor force reductions will be accomplished through attrition. It is, therefore, expected that salary and wages will increase only 1 percent per year over the next five years. Wage rates are expected to increase anywhere between 3 to 5 percent per year, but the reduction in staffing ratios resulting from attrition will keep the total increase to 1 percent. Any change in this assumption also will have a dramatic effect upon projected financial results.

- Fringe benefits. Fringe benefits on average have constituted between 20 to 24 percent of salaries and wages. It is expected that future fringe benefit costs will constitute ap-

proximately 23 percent of salary and wage costs.
- Interest expense. Projected average interest on existing long-term debt is expected to be 7.5 percent. This interest rate is applied to the beginning total of long-term debt plus current maturities of long-term debt.
- Restructuring costs. Restructuring costs were $5,086,000 in 1999, due in large part to costs associated with early retirement and layoffs. There are $2,078,000 of these costs still remaining as a current liability at the end of 1999. These costs will be expensed in 2000, and will be zero thereafter.
- Depreciation expense. Depreciation expense was 5.8 percent of gross property, plant, and equipment in 1999. This value is consistent with national averages and was used to forecast future depreciation.
- Bad-debt expense. Bad-debt expense has been declining in recent years. In 1999, bad-debt expense was 2.8 percent of net patient revenue. It is expected that future declines will be difficult to achieve and that present relationships will stabilize.
- Cash and short-term investments. Cash balances in this account are needed to meet normal transaction needs for cash such as salary, wages, and accounts payable. A

Table 9–5 Forecasted Balance Sheet for Omega Health Foundation as of June 30, 2000, 2001, 2002, 2003, and 2004 (Data in Thousands)

GENERAL FUNDS

Assets

	2000	2001	2002	2003	2004
Current					
Cash and cash equivalents	$ 8,907	$ 8,988	$ 9,190	$ 9,400	$ 9,616
Accounts receivable	24,568	25,059	25,560	26,072	26,593
Due from third-party payers	0	0	0	0	0
Due from donor-restricted funds	300	300	300	300	300
Inventories	1,830	1,921	2,017	2,118	2,224
Prepaid expenses and other assets	1,192	1,251	1,314	1,380	1,449
Current portion of funds held by trustee	1,055	1,120	1,185	1,250	1,315
Current portion of self-insurance trust funds	2,377	2,496	2,621	2,752	2,890
Total current assets	$ 40,229	$ 41,135	$ 42,187	$ 43,272	$ 44,387
Other assets					
Gross property, plant, and equipment	$156,794	$166,794	$176,794	$186,794	$196,794
Less total accumulated depreciation	79,898	89,572	99,826	110,660	122,074
Net property, plant, and equipment	$ 76,896	$ 77,222	$ 76,968	$ 76,134	$ 74,720
Self-insurance trust funds, net of current portion	$ 9,787	$ 10,276	$ 10,790	$ 11,330	$ 11,896
Board-designated funds	59,896	67,757	76,476	85,499	95,429
Funds held by trustee, net of current portion	338	338	338	338	338
Investments in and advances to partnerships	2,622	2,753	2,891	3,035	3,187
Deferred financing costs, net	972	805	638	471	304
Deferred third-party reimbursement	0	0	0	0	0
Other assets	1,174	1,292	1,420	1,562	1,718
Total other assets	$ 74,789	$ 83,221	$ 92,553	$102,235	$112,872
Total assets	$191,914	$201,578	$211,708	$221,641	$231,979

continues

Table 9–5 continued

Liabilities					

Current

Current portion of long-term debt	$ 1, 488	$ 1, 566	$ 1,806	$ 1,715	$ 1,525
Accounts payable and accrued expenses	11,641	12,223	12,835	13,476	14,150
Accrued salaries, wages, and fees	4,338	4,381	4,425	4,469	4,514
Accrued restructuring costs	0	0	0	0	0
Accrued vacation	3,288	3,288	3,288	3,288	3,288
Accrued insurance costs	2,346	2,463	2,586	2,715	2,851
Advance from third-party payer	1,228	1,253	1,278	1,304	1,330
Due to third-party payers	11,793	12,028	12,269	12,514	12,765
Total current liabilities	$ 36,122	$ 37,202	$ 38,487	$ 39,481	$ 40,423
Accrued retirement costs	$ 9,288	$ 9,753	$ 10,240	$ 10,752	$ 11,290
Accrued insurance costs, net of current portion	4,868	5,111	5,367	5,635	5,917
Deferred third-party reimbursement	3,489	3,489	3,489	3,489	3,489
Long-term debt, net of current portion	53,380	51,892	50,326	48,520	46,805
Other liabilities	250	262	276	289	304
Total liabilities	$107,397	$107,709	$108,185	$108,166	$108,228
Unrestricted net assets	$ 84,518	$ 93,869	$103,524	$113,473	$123,752
Total liabilities and unrestricted net assets	$191,915	$201,578	$211,709	$221,639	$231,980

typical transaction balance is approximately twenty days.

- Accounts receivable. Accounts receivable have been approximately 15 percent of net patient revenue, or 55 days. Please note that this value is much higher than the reported value of days in receivables because OHF has been experiencing significant overpayments by third-party payers, which can be seen in due-to-third-party-payer balances shown in the current liability section of the balance sheet. It is expected that the present pattern of receivables will remain stable over the next five years.
- Gross property and equipment. Gross property and equipment will increase each year by the amount of capital expenditures less

any assets that are sold or disposed. Table 9–8 shows the board-approved capital expenditure plan.

Definition of Debt Policy

Having defined the desired levels of investment for OHF, the next step to be undertaken is the definition of debt policy during the five-year forecast period. Debt should not be viewed as the balancing variable in the financial plan. That is, the financial plan should not project assets and equity and then balance the equation with debt. Sound financial policy requires that the board and management define in advance what their position is regarding the assumption of debt. Table 9–9 presents OHF's management and board policy on debt for the next five years.

Table 9–6 Forecasted Income Statement for Omega Health Foundation (Data in Thousands)

	2000	2001	2002	2003	2004
Revenues					
Net patient service revenue	$163,785	$167,061	$170,402	$173,810	$177,287
Equity in net income from partnership	769	807	847	890	934
Gifts and bequests	271	284	299	314	329
Other	9,198	9,658	10,141	10,648	11,180
Total revenues	$174,023	$177,810	$181,689	$185,662	$189,730
Expenses					
Salaries and wages	81,842	82,661	83,487	84,322	85,165
Fringe benefits	18,824	19,012	19,202	19,394	19,588
Professional fees	9,429	9,900	10,395	10,915	11,461
Supplies and other	41,587	43,667	45,850	48,143	50,550
Interest	4,214	4,115	4,009	3,910	3,768
Bad-debt expense	4,586	4,678	4,771	4,867	4,964
Depreciation and amortization	9,094	9,674	10,254	10,834	11,414
Restructuring costs	2,078	0	0	0	0
Total expenses	$171,654	$173,707	$177,968	$182,385	$186,910
Income from operations	$ 2,369	$ 4,103	$ 3,721	$ 3,277	$ 2,820
Nonoperating gains (losses)					
Income on investments	$ 4,801	$ 5,298	$ 5,986	$ 6,722	$ 7,509
Gifts and bequests	50	50	50	50	50
Loss on disposal of assets	(100)	(100)	(100)	(100)	(100)
Nonoperating gains, net	$ 4,751	$ 5,248	$ 5,936	$ 6,672	$7,459
Excess of revenues over expenses	$ 7,120	$ 9,351	$ 9,657	$ 9,949	$ 10,279

• Long-term debt. Board members at OHF have determined that they do not wish to borrow any additional moneys on a long-term basis over the next five years. They believe that their present capital structure has too much long-term debt as evidenced by a high long-term debt to equity ratio. The present debt will, therefore, be repaid in accordance with existing debt amortization schedules. Table 9–9 summarizes OHF's long-term debt position over the next five years.

• Accrued salaries and wages. Although it may not be thought of as a form of debt, all current liabilities represent a form of fi-nancing. Accrued salaries and wages represent a form of financing from the firm's employees. The employees have contributed their labor before receiving their wages. Accrued salaries and wages, on average, have constituted about 5 percent of salaries and wages and constituted 5.3 percent in 1999. This value is used in the forecast.

• Due to third-party payers. This current liability account represents overpayment by third-party payers during the course of the year and is a sizable account for OHF. In 1999, the account balance was $11,571,000. OHF has consistently report-

Table 9–7 Forecasted Financial Ratios for Omega Health Foundation

	2000	2001	2002	2003	2004
Profitability					
Total margin percent	4.0	5.1	5.1	5.2	5.2
Operating margin percent	1.3	2.2	2.0	1.7	1.4
Nonoperating gain percent	2.7	2.9	3.2	3.5	3.8
Return on equity percent	8.4	10.0	9.3	8.8	8.3
Liquidity					
Current	1.11	1.10	1.09	1.09	1.09
Days in accounts receivable	28.5	28.5	28.5	28.5	28.5
Average payment period	81.1	82.7	83.7	84.0	84.0
Days' cash-on-hand	20.0	20.0	20.0	20.0	20.0
Capital structure					
Equity financing percent	44.0	46.6	48.9	51.2	53.3
Long-term debt to equity percent	63.2	55.3	48.6	42.8	37.8
Cash flow to debt percent	18.1	21.4	22.4	23.6	24.9
Times interest earned	2.69	3.27	3.40	3.54	3.72
Activity					
Total asset turnover	0.93	.90	.88	.86	.85
Fixed asset turnover	2.32	2.37	2.43	2.52	2.63
Other asset turnover	2.39	2.20	2.02	1.88	1.74
Current asset turnover	4.44	4.45	4.44	4.44	4.44
Other ratios					
Average age of plant	8.7	9.2	9.7	10.2	10.6
Replacement viability	49.0	50.1	51.1	51.4	51.0

Table 9–8 Forecasted Property and Equipment for Omega Health Foundation

	2000	2001	2002	2003	2004
Beginning gross property and equipment	$146,794	$156,794	$166,794	$176,794	$186,794
+ Net capital expenditures	10,000	10,000	10,000	10,000	10,000
Ending gross property and equipment	$156,794	$166,794	$176,794	$186,794	$196,794

Table 9–9 Forecasted Long-Term Debt for Omega Health Foundation

	2000	2001	2002	2003	2004
Beginning long-term debt (LTD)	$54,781	$53,380	$51,892	$50,326	$48,520
− Beginning current maturities of LTD	1,401	1,488	1,566	1,806	1,715
Ending long-term debt	$53,380	$51,892	$50,326	$48,520	$46,805

ed sizable values for this account and this overpayment situation is expected to continue into the future. It is expected that the present relationship between net patient revenue and due to third-party payers will stabilize at approximately 7.2 percent. This is a critical relationship and represents interest-free financing that is currently being provided by OHF's third-party payers. Any change in this relationship would have a significant influence on OHF's financial projections.

Assessing the Reasonableness of Required Equity Growth

At this stage in the development of the financial plan, we have projected balance sheets (Table 9–5), income statements (Table 9–6), and financial ratios (Table 9–7). The following two questions must be answered before our financial plan can be accepted:

1. Can we actually achieve the results currently projected, or are our assumptions realistic?
2. Are the financial results projected acceptable, or are we satisfied with the current projected financial performance?

Regarding the first question about the realistic nature of our assumptions, we already have discussed these assumptions and the basis for them. This does not mean that they are attainable and we should review again the critical assumptions on which the forecast is based. Especially important are the assumptions regarding revenue and expense growth.

One useful way to review the validity of a financial plan is to compare the projected financial ratios with historical values. Comparing the financial ratio values found in Table 9–3 and 9–7 seems to indicate that the plan may be reasonable. The only major significant change appears in the area of profitability, especially margins. Operating income is projected to increase sharply from 1999 levels. The basis for this increase is directly related to a modest 1-percent

growth in salaries and wages. If we remain convinced that this goal is achievable because of scheduled productivity improvements, our initial forecast appears to be attainable.

Regarding the second question of acceptability, a comparison of historical and projected financial ratios will prove useful. In the initial forecast, there was no target set for board-designated and funded depreciation reserves. Surplus cash generated in the forecast was added to this balance, and any cash deficits would be subtracted from beginning balances. During the five-year forecast, OHF has added almost $40 million in new board-designated and funded depreciation reserves. The ending balance in 2004 is projected to be $95,429,000. On the surface, this seems like a healthy increase. But how does this compare to our replacement cost needs? A review of the projected replacement viability ratios in Table 9–7 suggests stability over the five-year period. Even though OHF has added nearly $40 million in new reserves, it still has a replacement viability ratio of approximately 50 percent. This value is almost identical to OHF's initial starting value and suggests equilibrium. From this perspective, the financial plan appears acceptable.

A further review of the financial ratios suggests only one area that may need some revision. The net plant and equipment actually declines during the five-year financial-planning period. Furthermore, OHF's average age of plant increases from 8.3 to 10.6 years. This may signal an under-investment in plant and equipment. For the present time, however, we will assume that the projected level of capital expenditures is adequate, given the current surplus investment in inpatient facilities that will not require replacement. Most of the new capital will be deployed to fast-growing outpatient and clinic operations.

INTEGRATION OF THE FINANCIAL PLAN WITH MANAGEMENT CONTROL

The development of a financial plan is a useless exercise unless that plan is integrated into the management-control process. Management needs to know whether the plan is being realized and, if it is not, what corrective action can be taken. In some cases, there may be little that management can do. For example, assume that the entity has experienced an unusually large reduction in its operating margins as a result of declining prices due to increased competition. In this case, perhaps the only course of action open to management is to revise its plan to reflect more accurately the current situation or to cut expenses if possible. Indeed, it is important for management to assess the accuracy of its financial plan annually and to make appropriate changes as needed.

To integrate the financial plan with the management-control process, some structure is needed. Financial ratios provide that structure. The chart in Figure 9–4 depicts detailed targets for OHF, reflecting its financial plan. In the chart, specific ratio values are delineated. The primary targets involve the four major ratios that together determine the hospital's return on equity. The secondary targets are concerned with additional data that can be used to monitor actual performance and detect possible problems.

To understand how the chart in Figure 9–4 might be used in management control, let us assume that the year 2000 has just ended and the financial data essential to the calculation of the

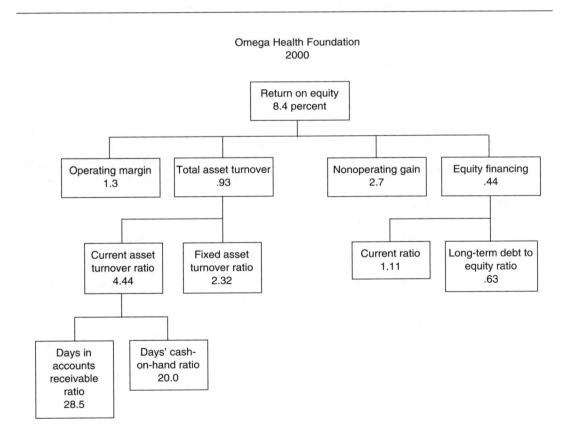

Figure 9–4 Financial Ratio Targets for Omega Health Foundation

ratios are now available. OHF's actual return on equity for 2000 is assumed to be 7.6 percent, which represents an unfavorable variance from the required value of 8.4 percent.

Actual values for the primary indicators are the following:

	2000 Values
Operating margin ratio percent	1.0
Total asset turnover ratio	.93
Equity financing ratio percent	44.0
Nonoperating gain percent	2.6

The major cause of the unfavorable variance in return on equity deviates from the expected operating margin of 1.3 percent to 1.0 percent. In addition, the nonoperating gain ratio also was below expectations, with an actual value of 2.6 percent compared with an expected value of 2.7 percent. All other ratio targets that determine equity growth were met. This would narrow any corrective actions to the two areas of operating margins and nonoperating gains.

It is extremely important to remember the concept of "sustainable growth" introduced in Chapter 7: sustainable growth simply means that no organization can generate a growth rate in assets that exceeds its growth rate in equity for a prolonged period. Ultimately, an organization is limited by the rate at which it can generate new equity.

Return on equity can be defined as follows:

$$\text{Return on equity} = \frac{[OM + NOR] \times TAT}{EF}$$

where:

OM = operating margin ratio
NOR = nonoperating gain ratio
TAT = total asset turnover ratio
EF = equity financing ratio

If top management and board members concentrate on this simple formula and the key relationships represented by it, financial focus and direction will improve dramatically.

SUMMARY

In the process of identifying the requirements for effective financial-policy formulation in health care firms, it is especially important to relate the strategic plan to the financial plan. The financial plan should not be developed in isolation from strategic planning, nor should the strategic plan be developed in isolation from the financial plan. Both plans need to be developed together, reflecting in that context their individual requirements and assumptions. A strategic plan is not valid if it is not financially feasible, and a financial plan is of little value if it does not reflect the strategic decisions reached by management and the board.

A financial plan should be updated at least annually, projecting a forecast period of three to five years. Financial plans that are not updated stand a good chance of becoming invalid. The environment of health care delivery is changing, and a health care entity's financial plan must reflect the changes. In fact, a failure to update its financial plan can have disastrous consequences for an entity, leading perhaps to market share retrenchment or even financial failure.

Finally, financial plans should be integrated into the management-control process. Financial ratios can be useful in this regard. In particular, specific ratios can be usefully related to the key financial planning target of growth rate in equity.

ASSIGNMENTS

1. A financial plan may be thought of as a bridge between two balance sheets. What are the major categories of assumptions that must be specified to project a future balance sheet, given a current balance sheet?
2. What problems result from the present responsibility center or departmental orientation of most accounting systems in providing data for financial planning?
3. Your director of marketing is urging you to develop a new drug-abuse program. She has argued that there is no capital investment involved in the development of the new service. Do you believe this is an accurate statement?
4. Your hospital has a current replacement viability ratio of .20. What are the implications of this indicator for your hospital's financial planning?
5. Your controller has just provided you with ROI figures for your firm's major product lines. You have noticed that obstetrics has a very low ROI. What factors should be considered before you eliminate this service?
6. You are in the process of developing your firm's financial plan for the next five years. As an initial step, you are analyzing financial ratios for the last five years. You notice that, over the five-year period, the average age of plant ratio has increased from 8.5 years to 12.2 years. What are the implications of this for your financial plan?
7. If current assets are expected to increase by $4 million over the next five years and you wish to increase your current ratio from 1.5 to 2.0, what additional amount of new equity must be generated to finance the increase in the current ratio on the incremental $4.0?
8. Beginning equity is $50 million and equity in five years is projected to be $100 million. What is the annual rate of growth implied by these values?
9. You are assessing the financial plan developed for you by a prestigious "Big 6" accounting firm. You are especially interested in the attainability of the projected growth rate in equity. You know that if that growth rate is not realistic, the financial plan is not valid and you may have to scale back your projected increase in assets. Table 9–10 summarizes your findings. Does the accounting firm's plan appear to be reasonable?
10. Using the data presented for Omega Health Foundation in this chapter, revise the existing financial plan. Assume that salaries and wages will increase 2 percent per year, not the original 1 percent used in the forecast. Prepare a revised forecasted balance sheet, income statement, and ratios for OHF.

Table 9–10 Financial Plan Summary Values

	Historical Average	*Five-Year Projections*
Reported income index ratio	1.000	.900
Operating margin ratio	.025	.027
Total asset turnover ratio	1.100	1.200
Nonoperating gain ratio	.011	.011
Equity financing ratio	.500	.500
Equity growth rate	7.86 percent	10.29 percent

SOLUTIONS AND ANSWERS

1. Projection of a future balance sheet requires assumptions in the following three categories:
   a. rates of growth for individual asset accounts
   b. debt-financing policy for both current and long-term debt
   c. realizable rate of growth in equity that is factored into five ratio areas:
      —operating margins
      —nonoperating revenue
      —equity financing
      —total asset turnover
      —reported income index (defined as net income divided by the change in equity)
2. Strategic financial planning is usually done along program or product lines, not responsibility centers or departments. This requires the financial planner to transfer revenue, cost, and investment assignments from responsibility centers to product lines. This can be a difficult process.
3. Although some new investment in fixed assets may be required to start a drug-abuse program, the investment in working capital may be sizable. Some projection of the investment should be made to assess the potential return on investment that is likely to result.
4. A replacement viability ratio of .20 implies that your hospital will need to borrow 80 percent of its replacement needs in the future. The percentage of debt financing is derived by the following formula:

   Debt financing = 100 percent – Replacement viability ratio

   This directly affects the debt-policy assumptions that will be used in the financial plan. It also will have an impact on the firm's operating margins because of the potentially large increase in debt and the resulting increase in interest expense.
5. Eliminating a product line solely on the basis of an inadequate ROI may not be consistent with the firm's goals and objectives. Specifically, obstetrics may meet a community need and may be essential to the firm's mission; it may, in fact, be classified as a Samaritan (see Figure 9–3). Alternatively, a low ROI can sometimes be deceiving. The product line may have important externalities. For example, obstetrics may lose money, but gynecology may be very profitable. Eliminating obstetrics may mean that the firm's gynecology line, and its profits, would be reduced.
6. The current average age of plant ratio implies that the firm has a very old plant relative to industry norms. This almost will certainly mean that significant new investment will be required in the planning period.
7. Use of a current ratio of 2.0 implies that the incremental investment of $4 million in current assets would be financed with $2 million of current liabilities. Use of a current ratio of 1.5 would imply current liability financing of $2.67 million. Therefore, the change in the current ratio implies that an additional equity requirement of $670,000 would be required.
8. The implied annual rate of growth is 14.86 percent.
9. The accounting firm's plan specifies a 30-percent increase in the annual growth rate in equity, compared with the historical five-year average (7.86 percent versus 10.29 percent). The major changes are in the reported income index and total asset turnover ratios. In the past five years, the firm has had no unreported income because the value for the reported income index is 1.0. It is important to determine the expected source of the new equity. The increase in total asset turnover, although not large, does play an important role in the higher projected growth rate in equity. Reasons for this increase should be verified.

10. Tables 9–11 through 9–13 list the revised forecasts for Omega Health Foundation. Note the dramatic reduction in profit from such a small change in one item. Also, OHF now will have $77,156,000 in board-designated funded depreciation in 2004, not the original amount of $95,429,000.

Table 9–11 Revised Forecasted Balance Sheet for Omega Health Foundation as of June 30, 2000, 2001, 2002, 2003, and 2004 (Data in Thousands)

GENERAL FUNDS

Assets

	2000	2001	2002	2003	2004
Current					
Cash and cash equivalents	$ 8,962	$ 9,099	$ 9,359	$ 9,628	$ 9,906
Accounts receivable	24,568	25,059	25,560	26,072	26,593
Due from third-party payers	0	0	0	0	0
Due from donor-restricted funds	300	300	300	300	300
Inventories	1,830	1,921	2,017	2,118	2,224
Prepaid expenses and other assets	1,192	1,251	1,314	1,380	1,449
Current portion of funds held by trustee	1,055	1,120	1,185	1,250	1,315
Current portion of self-insurance trust funds	2,377	2,496	2,621	2,752	2,890
Total current assets	$40,284	$41,246	$42,356	$43,500	$44,677
Other assets					
Property, plant, and equipment, gross	$156,794	$166,794	$176,794	$186,794	$196,794
Less total accumulated depreciation	79,898	89,572	99,826	110,660	122,074
Property, plant, and equipment, net	$76,896	$77,222	$76,968	$76,134	$ 74,720
Self-insurance trust funds, net of current portion	$9,787	$10,276	$10,790	$11,330	$11,896
Board-designated funds	58,844	64,491	69,700	73,773	77,156
Funds held by trustee, net of current portion	338	338	338	338	338
Investments in and advances to partnerships	2,622	2,753	2,891	3,035	3,187
Deferred financing costs, net	972	805	638	471	304
Deferred third-party reimbursement	0	0	0	0	0
Other assets	1,174	1,291	1,420	1,562	1,718
Total other assets	$73,737	$79,954	$85,777	$90,509	$94,599
Total assets	$190,917	$198,422	$205,101	$210,143	$213,996

continues

Table 9–11 continued

	Liabilities				
	2000	*2001*	*2002*	*2003*	*2004*
Current					
Current portion of long-term debt	$1, 488	$1, 566	$1,806	$1,715	$1,525
Accounts payable and					
accrued expenses	11,641	12,223	12,835	13,476	14,150
Accrued salaries, wages, and fees	4,381	4,468	4,557	4,650	4,741
Accrued restructuring costs	0	0	0	0	0
Accrued vacation	3,288	3,288	3,288	3,288	3,288
Accrued insurance costs	2,346	2,463	2,586	2,715	2,851
Advance from third-party payer	1,228	1,253	1,278	1,304	1,330
Due to third-party payers	11,793	12,028	12,269	12,514	12,765
Total current liabilities	$ 36,165	$37,289	$38,619	$39,662	$40,650
Accrued retirement costs	$ 9,288	$ 9,753	$ 10,240	$ 10,752	$ 11,290
Accrued insurance costs,					
net of current portion	4,868	5,111	5,367	5,635	5,917
Deferred third-party reimbursement	3,489	3,489	3,489	3,489	3,489
Long-term debt,					
net of current portion	53,380	51,892	50,326	48,520	46,805
Other liabilities	250	262	276	289	304
Total liabilities	$107,440	$107,796	$108,317	$108,347	$108,455
Unrestricted net assets	83,447	90,626	96,784	101,796	105,541
Total liabilities and unrestricted net assets	$191,887	$198,422	$205,101	$210,143	$213,996

Table 9–12 Revised Forecasted Income Statement for Omega Health Foundation (Data in Thousands)

	2000	2001	2002	2003	2004
Net patient service revenue	$163,785	$167,061	$170,402	$173,810	$177,287
Equity in net income from partnership	769	807	847	890	934
Gifts and bequests	271	284	299	314	329
Other	9,198	9,658	10,141	10,648	11,180
Total revenues	$174,023	$177,810	$181,689	$185,662	$189,730
Expenses					
Salaries and wages	$ 82,653	$ 84,306	$ 85,992	$ 87,712	$ 89,466
Fringe benefits	19,010	19,390	19,778	20,174	20,577
Professional fees	9,429	9,900	10,395	10,915	11,461
Supplies and other	41,587	43,667	45,850	48,143	50,550
Interest	4,214	4,115	4,009	3,910	3,768
Bad-debt expense	4,586	4,678	4,771	4,867	4,964
Depreciation and amortization	9,094	9,674	10,254	10,834	11,414
Restructuring costs	2,078	0	0	0	0
Total expenses	$172,651	$175,730	$181,049	$186,555	$192,200
Income from operations	$ 1,372	$ 2,081	$ 639	$ (892)	$ (2,469)
Nonoperating gains (losses)					
Income on investments	$ 4,757	$ 5,118	$ 5,569	$ 5,954	$ 6,264
Gifts and bequests	50	50	50	50	50
Loss on disposal of assets	(100)	(100)	(100)	(100)	(100)
Nonoperating gains, net	$ 4,707	$ 5,068	$ 5,519	$ 5,904	$ 6,214
Revenues before taxes	$ 6,079	$ 7,149	$ 6,158	$ 5,012	$ 3,745
Revenues after taxes	$ 6,079	$ 7,149	$ 6,158	$ 5,012	$ 3,745

Table 9–13 Revised Forecasted Financial Ratios for Omega Health Foundation

	2000	2001	2002	2003	2004
Profitability					
Total margin percent	3.4	3.9	3.3	2.6	1.9
Operating margin percent	.8	1.1	.3	−.5	−1.3
Nonoperating gain percent	2.6	2.8	2.9	3.1	3.2
Return on equity percent	7.3	7.9	6.4	4.9	3.5
Liquidity					
Current	1.11	1.10	1.09	1.09	1.09
Days in accounts receivable	28.5	28.5	28.5	28.5	28.5
Average payment period	80.7	81.9	82.5	82.3	82.0
Days' cash-on-hand	20.0	20.0	20.0	20.0	20.0
Capital structure					
Equity financing percent	43.7	45.7	47.2	48.4	49.3
Long-term debt to equity percent	63.9	57.3	52.0	47.7	44.3
Cash flow to debt percent	16.9	18.9	18.5	18.0	17.3
Times interest earned	2.44	2.73	2.53	2.28	1.99
Activity					
Total asset turnover	.93	.92	.91	.91	.91
Fixed asset turnover	2.32	2.36	2.43	2.51	2.62
Other asset turnover	2.42	2.28	2.18	2.11	2.07
Current asset turnover	4.43	4.43	4.42	4.40	4.38
Other ratios					
Average age of plant	8.7	9.2	9.7	10.2	10.6
Replacement viability	48.1	47.7	46.6	44.3	41.2

10

Cost Concepts and Decision Making

In the last five chapters, we have focused on understanding and interpreting the financial information prepared through the financial accounting system and presented in general-purpose financial statements. This chapter focuses more on the use of cost information in decision making. Cost information is produced through an entity's cost accounting system. In most situations, cost information is shaped by the financial accounting system and the generally accepted principles of financial accounting on which financial accounting is based. However, cost information must be flexible because it usually provides information for identifiable and specific decision-making groups, such as budgetary cost variance reports to department managers, cost reports to third-party payers, and forecasted project cost reports to planning agencies.

Cost is a noun that never really stands alone. In most situations, two additional pieces of information are added that enhance the meaning and relevance of the cost statistic. First, the object being costed is defined. For example, we might state that the cost of a clinic visit is $85. Objects of costing are usually of two types: (1) products (outputs or services) and (2) responsibility centers (departments or larger units). Often, we oversimplify this classification system and refer to cost information about products as planning information and cost information about responsibility centers as control information.

Second, usually an adjective is added to modify cost. For example, we might state that the direct cost of routine nursing care in a hospital is $400 per day. A number of major categories of modifiers refine the concept of cost; they are all used to improve the decision-making process by precisely defining cost to make it more relevant to decisions.

This chapter discusses some of the basic concepts of cost used in cost analysis. It is important to explain this jargon if decision makers are to use cost information correctly. Different concepts of cost are required for different decision purposes. In most situations, these concepts require specific, unique methodologies of cost measurement.

CONCEPTS OF COST

Cost may be categorized in a variety of ways to meet decision makers' specific needs. However, in most situations, the total value of cost is the same. Using one cost concept in place of another simply slices the total cost pie differently. For example, in Table 10–1, the total cost of a laboratory for June 1999 is $21,360. Of that amount, $20,000 could be classified as direct cost and $1,360 as indirect cost. However, clas-

Table 10–1 Cost Report, Laboratory, June 1999

	Amount
Direct costs	
Salaries	$10,000
Supplies	5,000
Other	5,000
Total direct costs	$20,000
Allocated costs	
Employee benefits	$ 150
Administration	500
Maintenance	250
Housekeeping	200
Laundry	100
Depreciation	160
Total indirect costs	$ 1,360
Total costs	$21,360
Relative value units (RVUs)	10,000

sifying costs by controllability might determine that $15,000 of the laboratory cost was controllable and $6,360 was not controllable. The total cost, however, is the same in both cases.

This brings us to another important point. Because, in most cases, different concepts of cost simply slice total cost in different ways, there may be underlying relationships among the various concepts of costs. For example, direct costs and controllable costs may be related. In many situations, there are standard "rules of thumb" that may be used to relate cost measures.

The difference between cost and expense is another crucial definitional point. Accountants have traditionally defined cost in a way that leads one to think of cost as an expenditure. However, most people who are not accountants use the term "cost" to refer to expense. For example, in Table 10–1, depreciation is listed as a cost. However, depreciation is not an actual expenditure of cash but an amortization of prior cost. In the present context, unless otherwise indicated, when we are discussing cost statistics,

the terms "costs" and "expenses" may be used interchangeably.

For purposes of discussion, we examine the following four major categories of costs:

1. traceability to the object being costed,
2. behavior of cost to output or activity,
3. management responsibility for control, and
4. future costs versus historical costs.

Traceability

Of all cost classifications, traceability is the most basic. Two major categories of costs classified by traceability are (1) direct costs and (2) indirect costs. A direct cost is specifically traceable to a given cost objective. For example, the salaries, supplies, and other costs in Table 10–1 are classified as direct costs of the laboratory. Indirect costs cannot be traced to a given cost objective without resorting to some arbitrary method of assignment. In Table 10–1, depreciation, employee benefits, and costs of other departments would be classified as indirect costs.

Not all costs classified as indirect actually may be indirect, however. In some situations, they could be redefined as direct costs. For example, it might be possible to calculate employee benefits for specific employees; these costs then could be charged to the departments in which the employees work and thus become direct costs. However, the actual costs of performing these calculations might be prohibitive.

The classification of a cost as either direct or indirect depends on the given cost objective. This is a simple observation, but one that is forgotten by many users of cost information. For example, the $20,000 of direct cost identified in Table 10–1 is a direct cost only regarding the laboratory department. If another cost objective is specified, the cost may no longer be direct. For example, dividing the $20,000 of direct costs by the number of relative value units (RVUs) yields a direct cost per RVU of $2, but this is not a true figure. The direct cost of any given RVU may be higher or lower than the $2 calculated, which is the average value for all RVUs and not necessarily the cost for any specific unit.

Incorrect classification is a common problem in cost accounting. Costs are accumulated on a department or responsibility-center basis and may be direct or indirect regarding that department. However, it can be misleading to state that the same set of direct costs is also direct regarding the outputs of that department.

The major direct cost categories of most departments would include the following:

- salaries,
- supplies, and
- other (usually fees and purchased services such as dues, travel, and rent).

Indirect cost categories usually include the following:

- depreciation,
- employee benefits, and
- allocated costs of other departments.

The concept of direct versus indirect cost may not seem to have much specific relevance to decision makers. To some extent, this is true; however, the concept of direct versus indirect costs is pervasive. It influences both the definition and measurement of other alternative cost concepts that do have specific relevance.

Cost Behavior

Cost is also classified by the degree of variability in relation to output. The actual measurement of cost behavior is influenced by a department's classification of cost, which provides the basis for categorizing costs as direct or indirect.

For our purposes, we can identify four major categories of costs that are classified according to their relationship to output:

1. variable,
2. fixed,
3. semifixed, and
4. semivariable.

Variable costs change as output or volume changes in a constant, proportional manner. That is, if output increases by 10 percent, costs also should increase by 10 percent; that is, there is some constant cost increment per unit of output. Figure 10–1 illustrates, graphically and mathematically, the concept of variable cost for the laboratory example of Table 10–1. It is assumed that all supply costs in this case are variable. For each unit increase in RVUs, supply costs will increase by $.50.

Fixed costs do not change in response to changes in volume. They are a function of the passage of time, not output. Figure 10–2 illustrates fixed cost behavior patterns for the depreciation costs of the laboratory example. Each month, irrespective of output levels, depreciation cost will be $160.

Semifixed (step) costs do change regarding changes in output, but they are not proportional. A semifixed cost might be considered variable or fixed, depending on the size of the steps rela-

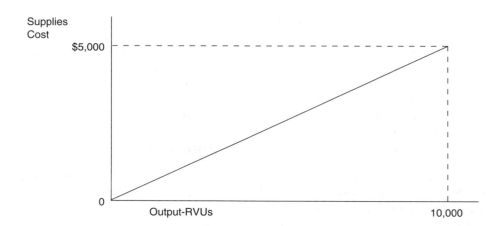

Note: Supplies cost = $.50 × number of RVUs.

Figure 10–1 Cost Behavior of Supplies Cost, Variable

tive to the range of volume under consideration. For example, in Figure 10–3, it is assumed that the salary cost of the laboratory is semifixed. If the volume of output under consideration was between 6,000 and 8,000 RVUs, salary costs could be considered fixed at $9,000. Some semifixed costs may be considered variable for cost analysis purposes. For example, if people could be employed other than as full-time equivalents (FTEs), such as by using overtime or part-time pools, the size of the steps might be significantly smaller than the 2,000 RVUs in our laboratory example. Presently, it is assumed that one additional FTE must be employed for every increment of 2,000 RVUs. Treating salary costs as variable in this situation might not be bad practice (Figure 10–3).

Semivariable costs include elements of both fixed and variable costs. Utility costs are good examples. There may be some basic, fixed re-

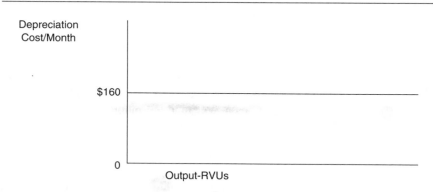

Note: Depreciation cost = $160 per month.

Figure 10–2 Cost Behavior of Depreciation, Fixed

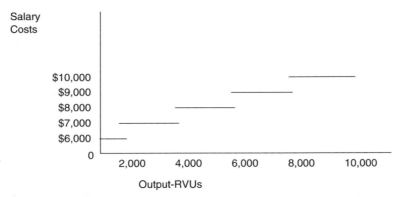

Note: Salary costs = $6,000 if RVUs are less than 2,000; $7,000 if RVUs are between 2,001 and 4,000; $8,000 if RVUs are between 4,001 and 6,000; $9,000 if RVUs are between 6,001 and 8,000; and $10,000 if RVUs are between 8,001 and 10,000.

Figure 10–3 Cost Behavior of Salary Costs, Semifixed

quirement per unit of time (month, year), regardless of volume—such as normal heating and lighting requirements. But there is also likely to be a direct, proportional relationship between volume and the amount of the utility cost. As volume increases, costs go up. Figure 10–4 illustrates semivariable costs in our laboratory example.

In many situations, we do not focus on specific cost elements but aggregate several cost categories of interest. It is interesting to see what type of cost behavior pattern emerges when we do this. Figure 10–5 aggregates the four cost categories discussed earlier: variable, fixed, semifixed, and semivariable. A semivariable cost behavior pattern closely approximates the actual aggregated cost behavior pattern; this is true for many types of operations. In the next section, we discuss some simple but useful methods for approximating this cost function.

Controllability

One of the primary purposes of gathering cost information is to aid the management control process. To facilitate evaluation of the manage-ment control process, costs must be assigned to individual responsibility centers, usually departments, where a designated manager is responsible for cost control. A natural question that arises is, for what proportion of the total costs charged to a department is the manager responsible? The answer to this question requires costs to be separated into two categories: controllable and noncontrollable costs.

Controllable costs can be influenced by a designated responsibility center or departmental manager within a defined control period. It has been stated that all costs are controllable by someone at some time. For example, the chief executive officer of a health care facility, through the authority granted by the governing board, is ultimately responsible for all costs.

The matrix of costs shown in Figure 10–6 categorizes the laboratory cost report data of Table 10–1. All costs must fall into one of the six cells of the matrix; however, it may be possible to categorize a cost that falls into several different categories into more than one cell of the matrix. In the laboratory example, other cost was viewed as semivariable, implying that part of the cost would be described as a direct variable cost ($4,000) and part as a direct fixed cost ($1,000).

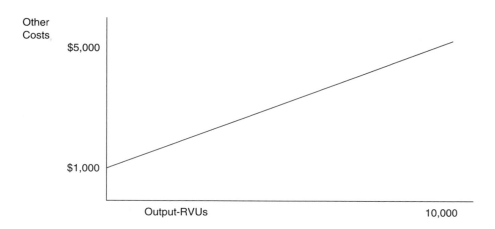

Note: Other costs = $1,000 per month + $.40 × RVUs.

Figure 10–4 Cost Behavior of Other Costs, Semivariable

There is a tendency in developing management control programs, especially in the health care industry, to use one of three approaches in designating controllable costs. First, controllable costs may be defined as the total costs charged to the department; the department manager would view all costs in the previous six categories as controllable. In our example, all $21,360 of cost would be viewed as controllable by the laboratory manager. In most normal situations, however, this grossly overstates the amount of cost actually controllable by a given department manager. The result of this overstatement has been negative in many situations.

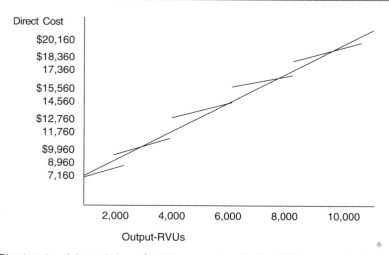

Note: Direct cost and depreciation = $7,160 per month + $1.30 × RVUs (approximation).

Figure 10–5 Cost Behavior of Aggregated Costs, Direct Cost, and Depreciation

Traceability	Variable		Fixed		Semifixed		Total
	Other	$4,000	Other	$1,000	Salaries	$10,000	
	Supplies	5,000					
Direct		$9,000		$1,000		$10,000	$20,000
	Employee		Depreciation	$160	Maintenance	$250	
	Benefits	$150	Administration	$500	Laundry	$100	
Indirect	Housekeeping	100	Housekeeping	$100			
		$250		$760		$350	$1,360
Totals		$9,250		$1,760		$10,350	$21,360

Figure 10–6 Laboratory Cost Behavior Categorization

Department managers have rightfully viewed this basis of control as highly inequitable.

Second, controllable costs may be limited to those costs classified as direct. This system is also not without fault: specifically, there may be fixed costs attributed directly to the department that should not be considered controllable. Rent for pieces of equipment, for example, may not be under the department manager's control. There also may be indirect costs, especially costs that are variable, that the department manager can control. For example, employee benefits may legitimately be the department manager's responsibility.

Third, in some situations, controllable costs may be defined as only those costs that are direct or variable. This limits costs that are controllable by the department manager to their lowest level. However, it excludes what could be a relatively large amount of cost influenced by the department manager. Failure to include the latter cost in the manager's control sphere may weaken management control.

Future Costs

Decision making involves selection among alternatives; it is a forward-looking process. Actual historical cost may be useful as a basis for projecting future costs, but it should not be used without adjustment unless it can be assumed that future conditions will be identical to past conditions.

A variety of concepts and definitions has been used in current discussion of costs for decision-making purposes. The following four types of costs seem to be basic to the process of selecting among alternative decisions:

1. avoidable costs,
2. sunk costs,
3. incremental costs, and
4. opportunity costs.

Avoidable Costs

Avoidable costs will be affected by the decision under consideration. Specifically, they are costs that can be eliminated or saved if an activity is discontinued; they will remain only if the activity continues. For example, if a hospital was considering curtailing its volume by 50 percent in response to cost-containment pressures, what would it save? The answer is those costs that are avoidable. In most situations, multiplication of current average cost per unit of output (patient days or admissions) by the projected change in output would overstate avoidable costs because much of the cost might not be able to be reduced, at least in the short run. For example, depreciation and interest expenses might not change. Variable costs are almost always a subset of avoidable costs, but avoidable costs might include some fixed costs. For example, administrative staffing might be drastically reduced in a nursing home if 50 percent of the beds were taken out of service. Most likely, administrative staffing costs would have been classified as fixed, given earlier expectations regarding volume. Most variable costs are avoidable, but some fixed costs also may be avoidable when large changes in volume are under consideration.

Sunk Costs

Sunk costs are unaffected by the decision under consideration. In the previous example, large portions of cost—depreciation, administrative salaries, insurance, and others—are sunk or not avoidable in the proposed 50-percent reduction in volume in the nursing home.

The distinction between fixed and variable costs, on the one hand, and sunk and avoidable costs, on the other, is not perfect. Many costs classified as fixed also may be thought of as sunk, but some are not. For example, malpractice insurance premiums generally may be considered fixed cost, given an expected normal level of activity. However, if the institution is considering a drastic reduction in volume, malpractice premiums may not be entirely fixed. In summary, sunk costs are almost always a subset of fixed costs, but not all fixed costs need be sunk. In the evaluation of a decision to close a hospital, most of the hospital's costs (both fixed and variable) probably would be eliminated and therefore would be categorized as avoidable and not sunk regarding the closure decision.

Incremental Costs

Incremental costs represent the change in cost that results from a specific management action. For example, someone might want to know the incremental cost of signing a managed-care contract that would generate 200 new admissions a year. There is a strong relationship between incremental and avoidable costs. They can be thought of as different sides of the same coin. We use the term incremental costs to reference the change in costs that results from a management action that increases volume. The term avoidable costs defines the change in cost that results from a management action that reduces volume. For decisions involving only modest changes in output, incremental costs and variable costs may be used interchangeably. In most situations, however, incremental costs are more comprehensive. A decision to construct a surgicenter adjacent to a hospital would involve fixed and variable costs. Depreciation of the facility would be a fixed cost, but it would be incremental to the decision if a new surgicenter is constructed.

Opportunity Costs

Opportunity costs are values foregone by using a resource in a particular way instead of in its next best alternative way. Assume that a nursing home is considering expanding its facility and would use land acquired twenty years ago. If the land had a historical cost of $1 million but a present market value of $10 million, what is the opportunity cost of the land? Practically everyone would agree that if sale of the land constituted the next best alternative, the opportunity cost would be $10 million, not $1 million. Alternatively, a hospital might consider converting part of its acute care facility into a skilled nursing facility because of a reduction in demand or obsolescence in the facility. The question arises, what is the value, or what would be the cost of the facility, to the skilled nursing facility operation? If there is no way that the facility can be renovated or if the facility is not needed for the provision of acute care, its opportunity cost may be zero. This could contrast sharply to the recorded historical cost of the facility.

COST MEASUREMENT

In this section, we examine the methods of cost measurement for two cost categories: (1)

direct and indirect cost and (2) variable and fixed cost. Both of these cost categories are useful in financial decisions, but the cost accounting system does not directly provide estimates for them.

Direct and Indirect Cost

In most cost accounting systems, costs are classified by department or responsibility center and by type of expenditure. Costs are charged to the departments to which they are traceable. Costs are also classified by object of expenditure; they may be identified as supplies, salaries, rent, insurance, or some other category.

Departments in a health care facility can be classified generally as direct or indirect departments, depending on whether they provide services directly to the patient. Sometimes the terms revenue and nonrevenue are substituted for direct and indirect. In the hospital industry, the following breakdown is used in general-purpose financial statements:

Operating Expense Area	Type of Department
Nursing services area	Direct/revenue
Other professional services	Direct/revenue
General services	Indirect/nonrevenue
Fiscal services	Indirect/nonrevenue
Administrative services	Indirect/nonrevenue

Whatever the nomenclature used to describe the classification of departments, cost allocation is usually required. The costs of the indirect, nonrevenue departments need to be allocated to the direct revenue departments for many decision-making purposes. For example, some payers reimburse on the basis of the full costs of direct departments and are interested in the costs of indirect departments only insofar as they affect the calculation of the direct departments' full costs (both direct and indirect). Pricing decisions need to be based on full costs, not just direct costs, if the costs of the indirect departments are to be covered equitably. It is also critical to include indirect costs when evaluating the financial return of specific programs or product lines. For example, some indirect costs would need to be assigned to an ambulatory surgery program to evaluate properly whether the program was financially viable.

Equity is a key concept in allocating indirect department costs to direct departments. Ideally, the allocation should reflect, as nearly as possible, the actual cost incurred by the indirect department to provide services for a direct department. Department managers who receive cost reports showing indirect allocations are vitally interested in this equity principle, and for good reason. Even if indirect costs are not regarded as controllable by the department manager, the allocation of costs to a given direct department can have an important effect on a variety of management decisions. Pricing, expansion, or contraction of a department; the purchase of new equipment; and the salaries of department managers are all affected by the allocation of indirect costs. An outpatient surgery program that has unreasonable amounts of hospital overhead allocated to it may find itself noncompetitive.

Costs of indirect departments are in most cases not directly traceable to direct departments. If they were, they could be reassigned. In such cases, they must be allocated to the direct departments in some systematic and rational manner. In general, the following two allocation decisions must be made: (1) selection of the allocation basis and (2) selection of the method of cost apportionment.

Table 10–2 provides sample data for a cost allocation. In this example, there are four departments: two are indirect (laundry/linen and housekeeping), and two are direct (radiology and nursing). How much the laundry weighs is the only allocation basis under consideration for the laundry and linen department. The housekeeping department can use one of two allocation bases, either square feet of area served or hours of service actually worked.

In general, there are only three acceptable methods of cost allocation:

Table 10–2 Cost Allocation Example

Department	Direct Cost	Pounds of Laundry Used	Hours of Housekeeping	Square Feet
Laundry/linen	$15,000	—	150	50,000
Housekeeping	$30,000	5,000	—	—
Radiology	$135,000	5,000	900	10,000
Nursing	$270,000	90,000	1,950	140,000
Total	$450,000	100,000	3,000	200,000

1. step-down method,
2. double-distribution method, and
3. simultaneous-equations method.

Most health care facilities still use the step-down method of cost allocation. In this method, the indirect department that receives the least amount of service from other indirect departments and provides the most service to other departments allocates its cost first. A similar analysis follows to determine the order of cost allocation for each of the remaining indirect departments. This determination can be subjective to allow some flexibility, as we shall observe shortly.

In the step-down allocation process illustrated in Table 10–3, the laundry and linen department allocates its cost first. Then, housekeeping allocates its direct cost, plus the allocated cost of laundry and linen, to the direct departments of radiology and nursing, based on the ratio of services provided to those departments. The num-

bers in parentheses represent the proportion of cost charged to that department.

The order of departmental allocation can be an important variable in a step-down method of cost allocation. Table 10–4 depicts an alternative step-down cost allocation in which housekeeping allocates its cost first, preceding the laundry and linen department.

The double-distribution method of cost allocation is just a refinement of the step-down method. Instead of closing the individual department after allocating its costs, it is kept open and receives the costs of other indirect departments. After one complete allocation sequence, the former departments are then closed, using the normal step-down method.

The simultaneous-equations method of cost allocation is used in an attempt to calculate the exact cost allocation amounts. A system of equations is established, and mathematically correct allocations are computed. In the previous example, if simultaneous equations had been used,

Table 10–3 Step-Down Allocation Method—Alternative 1

	Direct Cost	Laundry/Linen	Housekeeping (Hours)	Total
Laundry/linen	$ 15,000	$15,000		
Housekeeping	30,000	750 (.05)	$30,750	
Radiology	135,000	750 (.05)	9,711 (.3158)	$145,461
Nursing	270,000	13,500 (.90)	21,039 (.6842)	304,539
Total	$450,000	$15,000	$30,750	$450,000

Table 10–4 Step-Down Allocation Method—Alternative 2

	Direct Cost	Housekeeping (Hours)	Laundry/Linen	Total
Housekeeping	$ 30,000	$30,000		
Laundry/linen	15,000	1,500 (.05)	$16,500	
Radiology	135,000	9,000 (.30)	868 (.0526)	$144,868
Nursing	270,000	19,500 (.30)	15,632 (.9474)	305,132
Total	$450,000	$30,000	$16,500	$450,000

the cost of radiology would be $145,075 and the cost of nursing would be $304,925, using the following system of equations:

Laundry cost (LC) =
$15,000 + .05 HC

Housekeeping cost (HC) =
$30,000 + .05 LC

Radiology cost (RC) =
$135,000 + .05LC + .30HC

Nursing cost (NC) =
$270,000 + .90LC + .65 HC

Finally, it should be noted that using a different allocation base can create differences in cost allocation. For example, the use of square footage for housekeeping, instead of hours served, produces the pattern of cost allocation shown in Table 10–5 when housekeeping allocates its cost first, using the step-down method.

The important point in this discussion is that full cost is not as objective and as exact of a figure as one might normally think. Indirect costs can be allocated in a variety of ways that can create significant differences in full costs for given departments. This flexibility should be remembered when examining and interpreting full-cost data.

Variable and Fixed Cost

An important and widely used cost concept is variability regarding output. It is involved in determining a number of other costs such as avoidable, sunk, incremental, and controllable costs. However, accounting records do not directly yield this type of cost information. Instead, the costs are classified by department and by object of expenditure. Thus, to develop estimates of variable and fixed costs, the relevant data must be analyzed in some way.

Table 10–5 Step-Down Allocation Method—Alternative 3

	Direct Cost	Housekeeping (Square Feet)	Laundry/Linen	Total
Housekeeping	$ 30,000	$30,000		
Laundry/linen	15,000	7,500 (.25)	$22,500	
Radiology	135,000	1,500 (.05)	1,125 (.05)	$137,625
Nursing	270,000	21,000 (.70)	21,375 (.95)	312,375
Total	$450,000	$30,000	$22,500	$450,000

Our discussion of cost concepts classified by variability regarding output indicated that a semivariable cost pattern may be a good representation of many types of costs. A semivariable cost function has both a fixed and variable element. A semivariable cost function often results when various types of costs are aggregated together.

Estimating Methods

Estimation of a semivariable cost function requires separation of the cost into variable and fixed components. A variety of methods, varying in complexity and accuracy, may be used. Four of the simplest methods are (1) visual-fit, (2) high-low, (3) semi-averages, and (4) regression.

To illustrate each of these methods, assume that we are trying to determine the labor cost function for the radiology department and we have the six biweekly payroll data points presented in Table 10–6.

In the visual-fit method of cost estimation, the previous individual data points are plotted on graph paper. A straight line is then drawn through the points to provide the best fit. Visual fitting of data is a good first step in any method of cost estimation. Figure 10–7 shows a visual fitting of the previous radiology data.

The high-low method is a simple technique that can be used to estimate the variable and fixed-cost coefficients of a semivariable cost function. The variable cost parameter is solved first. It equals the change in cost from the highest to the lowest data point, divided by the change in output. In the previous radiology example, the variable hours worked would be calculated as follows:

$$\text{Variable labor hours/film} = \frac{320 - 110}{600 - 180} =$$

$$\frac{210}{420} = .50$$

The fixed-cost parameter then may be solved by subtracting the estimated variable cost (deter-

Table 10–6

Pay Period	No. of Films (x)	Hours Worked (y)	
1	300	180	(low)
2	240	140	(low)
3	400	230	(high)
4	340	190	(high)
5	180	110	(lowest)
6	600	320	(highest)
Total	2,060	1,170	

mined by multiplying the variable cost parameter estimate by output at the high level) from total cost. In our radiology example, fixed labor hours would equal the following:

Fixed labor hours per pay period =
$320 - (.50 \times 600) = 320 - 300 = 20$

Alternatively, it is possible to plot the high and low points and then draw a straight line through them.

The semi-averages method is similar to the high-low method regarding its mathematical solution. To derive the estimate of variable cost, the difference between the mean of the high-cost points and the mean of the low-cost points is divided by the change in output from the mean of the high-cost points to the mean of the low-cost points. In the radiology example, variable cost would be calculated as follows:

Variable labor hours/film =

$$\frac{\dfrac{320 + 230 + 190}{3} - \dfrac{180 + 140 + 110}{3}}{\dfrac{600 + 400 + 340}{3} - \dfrac{300 + 240 + 180}{3}}$$

$$= \frac{246.67 - 143.33}{446.67 - 240.00} = .50$$

Fixed cost is solved in a manner identical to that used in the high-low method. In the radiol-

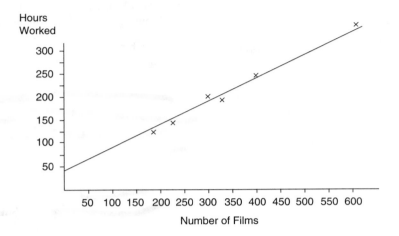

Figure 10–7 Visual Fitting of Radiology Data

ogy example, fixed labor hours would equal the following:

Fixed labor hours per pay period =
246.67 − (.50 × 446.67) = 23.34

The simple regression method will produce estimates of variable cost (V) and fixed cost (F) that will minimize the variance between predicted and actual observations. The formulas for estimation are presented in the following where Q refers to output, C refers to cost, and N refers to the number of observations:

1. $V = \dfrac{\Sigma QC - N\overline{Q}\,\overline{C}}{\Sigma Q^2 - N\overline{Q}^2}$

2. $F = \overline{C} - V\overline{Q}$

Applying the previous formulas to the radiology data produces the following estimates:

1. $V = \dfrac{456{,}000 - 401{,}696}{815{,}600 - 707{,}253} = .5012$

2. $F = 195 - (.5012 \times 343.33) = 22.92$

These four methods of estimating variable and fixed costs are highly simplistic. They are useful in only limited ways to provide a basis for further discussion and analysis of what the true cost behavioral pattern might be. However, in most situations, a limited attempt, based on simplistic methods, to discover the underlying fixed and variable cost patterns is better than no attempt.

Data Checks

When any of the previous methods are used, several data checks should be performed. First, the cost data being used to estimate the cost behavior pattern should be stated in a common dollar. If the wages paid for employees have changed dramatically from one year to the next, the use of unadjusted wage and salary data from the two years can create measurement problems. In our radiology example, we used a physical quantity measure of cost, namely, hours worked. A physical measure of cost should be used whenever possible.

Second, cost and output data should be matched; the figures for reported cost should relate to the activity of the period. In most situations, accounting records provide this type of relationship based on the accrual principle of accounting. However, in some situations, this may not happen; supply costs may be charged to a department when the items are purchased, not when they are used.

Third, the period during which a cost function is being estimated should include stable technology and a case mix. If the technology under consideration has changed dramatically during that period, there will be measurement problems. Estimating a cost function based upon two different production technologies will produce a cost function that reflects neither.

BREAK-EVEN ANALYSIS

Certain techniques can be applied when analyzing the relationships among cost, volume, and profit. These techniques rely on categorizing costs as fixed and variable. They can serve as powerful management-decision aids and may be valuable in a wide range of decisions. An understanding of these techniques is crucial for decision makers whose choices affect the financial results of health care facilities.

Profit in a health care facility is influenced by various factors, including the following:

- rates or prices,
- volume,
- variable cost,
- fixed cost,
- payer mix, and
- bad debts.

The primary value of break-even analysis, or, as it is sometimes called, cost-volume-profit analysis, is its ability to quantify the relationships among the previous factors and profit.

Traditional Applications

Break-even analysis has been used in industry for decades with a high degree of satisfaction. Its name comes from the solution to an equation that sets profit equal to zero and revenue equal to

costs. To illustrate, assume that a hospital has the following financial information:

Variable cost per case	$1,000
Fixed cost per period	$100,000
Price per case	$2,400

The break-even volume can be solved by dividing fixed costs by the contribution margin, which is the difference between price and variable cost.

Break-even volume in units =

$$\frac{\text{Fixed cost}}{\text{Price} - \text{Variable cost}} = \text{Contribution Margin}$$

Thus, in our hospital example, break-even volume would be the following:

Break-even volume in units =

$$\frac{\$100,000}{\$2,400 - \$1,000} = 71.4 \text{ Cases}$$

If volume exceeds seventy-two cases, the hospital will make a profit; but if volume goes below seventy-one cases it will incur a loss. Sometimes, a revenue and cost relationship is put into graphic form to illustrate profit at various levels. Such a presentation is referred to as a break-even chart. For our hospital example, a break-even chart is shown in Figure 10–8.

In many cases, some targeted level of net income or profit is desired. The break-even model is easily adapted to this purpose; the new break-even point would become the following:

Break-even volume in units =

$$\frac{\text{Fixed cost} + \text{Targeted net income}}{\text{Price} - \text{Variable cost}}$$

In our example, assuming that a profit of $6,000 was required, the new break-even point would be the following:

Break-even volume in units =

$$\frac{\$100,000 + \$6,000}{\$1,400} = 75.7 \text{ Cases}$$

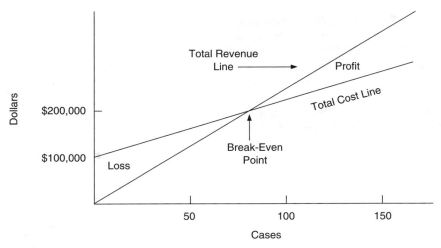

Figure 10–8 Break-Even Chart

Multiple-Payer Model

Although break-even analysis is a powerful management tool, it cannot be used in the health care industry without adaptation. The major revision required relates to the revenue function. The preceding discussion of break-even analysis assumed that there was only one payer or purchaser of services. That payer was assumed to pay a fixed price per unit of product. However, this situation does not exist in the health care industry, where there may be three or more major categories of payers. For our purposes, we will assume that there are three categories of payers:

1. cost payers (paying average cost of services provided);
2. fixed-price payers [paying an established fee per unit of service, for example, a fixed price per diagnosis-related group (DRG)]; and
3. charge payers (paying on the basis of internally set prices, but maybe discounted).

The break-even formula in these three payer situations can be generalized as follows:

Break-even volume in units =

$$\frac{(1 - CO)F + NI}{(CH \times P_I) + (FP \times P_E) - (1 - CO)V}$$

This formula may look complex at first glance, but it is actually similar to the previous one-payer break-even formula. In fact, the previous equation can be used in the one-payer situation and provides an identical result. To aid in our understanding of the formula, we should first define the individual variables:

V = Variable cost per unit of output
F = Fixed cost per period
NI = Targeted net income
P_I = Internally set price that is paid by charge payers
P_E = Externally set price paid by fixed-price payers
CO = Proportion of cost payers
CH = Proportion of charge payers
FP = Proportion of fixed-price payers

Let us now examine each term in the equation:

• $(1 - CO)F$—This term represents the proportion of fixed costs (F) that is not paid by cost payers. Cost payers are assumed to pay their proportionate share of fixed costs. This leaves the residual portion $(1 - CO)$ unpaid; it is included in the numerator as a financial requirement that must be covered before break even occurs. If there were no cost payers, $(1 - CO)$ would be 1, and all of the fixed costs would be included. This is the case in traditional break-even analysis.

- NI—This term, targeted net income, is included as a financial requirement as in the traditional break-even formula. NI is not reduced by the cost payer portion because it is assumed that cost payers are not contributing toward meeting the net income requirement. Cost payers pay cost—nothing less and nothing more.

- $CH \times P_I$—This term represents the weighted price paid by charge payers. When added to the next term $(FP \times P_E)$, we have a measure of the price paid by the two price-paying categories of customers—charge payers and fixed-price payers. It should be emphasized that P_I represents the price received, not the charge made. For example, if 10 percent of the patients paid established charges of $2,400 per case and 20 percent paid 90 percent of established charges of $2,400 per case, the following values would result:

$$CH = .10 + .20 = .30$$

$$P_I = (1.0 \times \$2,400) \times 1/3 + (.90 \times \$2,400) \times 2/3 = \$2,240$$

- $FP \times P_E$—This term represents the weighted price paid by fixed-price payers. The addition of this term to $CH \times P_I$ yields a measure of the price received for price-paying patients. The summation of the two terms can be compared with the price term used in the traditional break-even formula. Again, there may be circumstances when subweighting may be necessary. For example,

assume that Medicare pays $2,000 per case and that 40 percent of the cases are Medicare. Also assume that 10 percent of the cases are from a health maintenance organization (HMO) that pays $2,200 per case. The following values would result:

$$FP = .40 + .10 = .50$$

$$P_E = [(.40/.50) \times \$2,000] + [(.10/.50) \times \$2,200] = \$2,040$$

- $(1 - CO)V$—This term represents the net variable cost that remains after reflecting the proportion paid by cost payers. Cost payers pay their share of both fixed and variable costs. If there were no cost payers, the entire value of the variable cost per unit would be subtracted to yield the contribution margin per unit.

To determine that the traditional break-even formula is actually derived from our more general three-payer model, let us compute the break-even point using the data from the case example developed in our discussion of traditional break-even analysis:

$$\text{Break-even volume in units} = \frac{(1 - 0) \times \$100,000 + \$6,000}{(1.0 \times \$2,400) + (0 \times \$0) - (1 - 0) \times \$1,000}$$

$$= 75.7 \text{ cases}$$

Now, having tested the accuracy of the three-payer break-even formula in a one-payer situation, let us expand our initial case example to a more realistic multiple-payer situation. The data in Table 10–7 are assumed.

Also assume that the variable cost is $1,000 per case and fixed costs are $100,000 per period. In addition, the firm needs a profit of $6,000 to meet other financial requirements. The use of these data in our break-even model would produce the following result:

Table 10–7 Multiple Payer Case Example

Payer Proportion	Payment Method
.20	Pay average cost
.40	Pay $2,000 per case (fixed-price payer)
.10	Pay $2,200 per case (fixed-price payer)
.10	Pay 100 percent of charges, $2,400 per case
.20	Pay 90 percent of charges, $2,160 per case

Break-even volume in cases =

$$\frac{(.8 \times \$100,000) + \$6,000}{(.3 \times \$2,240) + (.5 \times \$2,040) - (.8 \times 1,000)}$$

$$= \frac{\$86,000}{\$892} = 96.413$$

To demonstrate the accuracy of the break-even formula, we can derive the following income statement for our case example, assuming 96.4 cases as the break-even volume:

Patient revenue		
.20 × 96.4 × $2,037.34*	$39,279.92	
.40 × 96.4 × $2,000.00	77,120.00	
.10 × 96.4 × $2,200.00	21,208.00	
.10 × 96.4 × $2,400.00	23,136.00	
.20 × 96.4 × $2,160.00	41,644.80	
Net patient revenue	$202,388.72	
Less fixed cost	100,000.00	
Less variable cost		
(96.4 × $1,000)	96,400.00	
Net income	$ 5,988.72	

*Average cost = ($100,000 + 96,400)/96.4
= $2,037.34

This income statement demonstrates that, at a volume of 96.4 patients, the firm's net income would be $5,988.72. This value does not exactly match the targeted net income level of $6,000 because of a small rounding error; the actual break-even volume was 96.413, not 96.4.

Before concluding this discussion of break-even analysis, it is useful to mention output de-termination. For the break-even model to be ap-plicable, there must be one measure of output. It makes no difference whether the measure of ac-tivity is macro, such as a case, a patient day, or a covered life, or whether the measure of activity is micro, such as a procedure or a laboratory test. The following two conditions, however, are nec-essary:

1. It must be possible to define an average price paid for that unit for both fixed-price payers and charge payers. For ex-ample, both Medicare and Medicaid may pay a fixed rate per case, but all charge payers may pay some percentage of the billed charges. This would require some-one to aggregate average charge-payer amounts for individual billed services to an expected price per case. This might also require an assignment of a per-case amount paid by Medicare to an estimated amount for a specific service such as a physical therapy treatment if the focus of analysis was at the treatment level. In a situation of capitation, some transfer price must be established on a case, per diem, or procedure basis to apply break-even analysis if an output unit other than members or covered lives is used.

2. A variable cost per unit of the defined output measure also must be established. This may mean aggregating across de-partments to create a variable cost value for an aggregated output measure such as

a case or a patient day. Disaggregation is not nearly as great a problem in variable cost measurement because costing systems usually provide reasonably good detail at the departmental level.

Special Applications

The break-even formula has many applications other than that of computing break-even points. Two specific applications are (1) the computation of marginal profit of volume changes and (2) rate-setting analysis.

Computation of Marginal Profit of Volume Changes

In most business situations, executives are concerned about the impact of volume changes on operating profitability. At the beginning of a budget period, management may not be sure what its actual volumes will be, but it still needs to know how sensitive profit will be to possible swings in volume. If the payer mix is expected to remain constant, the following simple formula can be used to calculate the marginal changes in profit associated with volume swings:

Change in profit = Change in units × Profitability index

where:

Profitability index = $CH(P_I - V)$ + $FP(P_E - V)$

The profitability index remains constant and is simply multiplied by projected volume change to determine the profit change. Using our earlier case example, the profitability index would be

Profitability index = .3($2,240 – $1,000) + .5($2,040 – $1000) = $892

The value for the profitability index is actually the weighted contribution margin per unit of output. This fact is easily observed by comparing the value calculated previously with that from our three-payer break-even example. The

values are the same, $892 in each case. This means that for every one unit change in output the profit will increase on average by $892. An increase of one unit will increase profit by $892, and a decrease of one unit will decrease profit by $892. A useful question to ask at this point is, how large a reduction in volume can the firm experience before its profit decreases to $2,000? Using the preceding formula, the answer would be the following:

Change in profit = Volume change × Profitability index

($6,000 – $2,000) = Volume change × $892

Volume change = 4.48 cases

If volume decreases by 4.48 cases, the firm's profit will decrease to $2,000. Further analysis could be used to portray other scenarios or to answer other "what-if" type questions. In each case, the resulting data could be displayed in a table or graph.

Rate-Setting Analysis

Rate setting is an extremely important activity for most health care organizations. Usually, the objective is not profit maximization, but rather covering financial requirements. In general, pricing services can be stated in the following conceptual terms:

Price = Average cost + Profit requirement + Loss on fixed-price patients

If Q represents total budgeted volume in units, we can use our earlier break-even model to develop the following pricing formula:

$$P_I = AC + \frac{NI}{CH \times Q} + \frac{(AC - P_E) \times (FP \times Q)}{CH \times Q}$$

where:

$$AC = \text{Average cost per unit} = \frac{F}{Q} + V$$

Again, it is useful to examine the individual terms to understand their conceptual relationship.

- AC—This term represents the average cost per unit. Average cost is the basis on which the firm marks up to establish a price that can meet its financial requirements.
- $NI/(CH \times Q)$—This term divides the target net income (NI) by the number of charge-paying units $(CH \times Q)$. This payment source generates the firm's profit. Internally set prices will not affect the amount of payment received from cost payers or fixed-price payers.
- $(AC - P_E) \times (FP \times Q)/(CH \times Q)$—This term is complex but has a simple interpretation. The difference between average cost (AC) and the fixed price (P_E) represents an additional requirement that must be covered by the firm's charge-paying units. This difference per unit is then multiplied by total fixed-price payer units $(FP \times Q)$ to generate the total loss resulting from selling services to fixed-price payers. Dividing by the number of charge payers $(CH \times Q)$ translates this loss into an additional pricing increment that must be recovered from the charge payers. It is important to note that if the fixed price paid by fixed-price payers (P_E) exceeds average cost (AC), this term will be negative. Prices to the charge payers then could be reduced because the fixed-price payers would be making a positive contribution to the firm's profit requirement.

To test the validity of the pricing formula, let us apply it to the data in our earlier three-payer break-even example. Assume that the volume is 96.4 cases.

$$P_I = \$2,037.34 + \frac{\$6,000}{.3 \times 96.4} +$$

$$\frac{(\$2,037.34 - 2,040) \times .5 \times 96.4}{.3 \times 96.4} =$$

$$\$2,037.34 + \$207.47 - 4.43 = \$2,240.38$$

The required price as determined previously, \$2,240.38, is approximately equal to the price established for charge payers, \$2,240. Again, a small discrepancy exists because of rounding errors.

It should be noted that \$2,240 is not the actual charge or price set per case. The actual posted charge is \$2,400. P_I represents the net amount actually received. Because the firm had one category of charge payers who paid 90 percent of charges, the effective price realized was only \$2,240. When using this pricing formula to define hospital charges, the defined price must be increased to reflect write-off due to discounts, bad debts, or charity care. The following general formula represents the mark-up requirement:

$$\text{Price} = P_I /(1 - \text{Write-off proportion})$$

The write-off proportion is not based on total revenue; it is based only on the revenue from charge payers. For example, in our case example, the charge payers represented 30 percent of total cases. Of that 30 percent, 10 percent paid 100 percent of charges and 20 percent paid 90 percent of charges. The write-off percentage is thus the following:

$$(1/3) \times 0 + (2/3) \times .10 = .0667$$

Using this value to mark up the required net price of \$2,240 would yield \$2,400.

$$\$2,400 = \frac{\$2,240}{1 - .0667}$$

An important issue for many health care organizations concerns the maximization of profit per dollar of rate increase. In a number of states and regions, rate regulations impose restraints on a firm's ability to increase its rates. In addition, boards may wish to minimize rate increases in any given budgetary cycle.

The percentage of any price increase that will be realized as profit can be expressed as follows:

Percent price increase realized as
profit =
(Percent charge payers)
× (1 − Write-off proportion)
− Physician fee percent

Let us assume that a nursing home is interested in learning what effect a $5 increase in its per diem would have on its profitability. Its present payer mix and write-off proportions are presented in Table 10–8.

Thus, a $5 per diem increase would generate $2.25 per day in additional profit.

50 percent × (1 − .10) = 45 percent

Evaluating Incremental Profit of New Business

One of the most common examples of the use of marginal analysis methods is evaluating the profitability of new business. Many health care providers are being approached on an almost daily basis with a proposal for a new block of patients. For example, a preferred provider organization (PPO) may present a hospital with the opportunity to be in the PPO's network if the hospital is willing to accept a discount from its present price structure. It is easy to define a conceptual model to organize the financial evaluation of this proposal or a similar one.

Change in profit =
Change in volume
(Price per unit − Incremental cost per unit) − Change in existing price ×
Volume affected

The terms are defined as follows:

- Change in volume—In many cases, there will be a reasonably good measure of what the new volume will be. For example, the PPO may be able to deliver twenty new cases per year. It is important to structure a contract that has a volume trigger related to the range of discounts. If high volumes are realized, then the full discount will be granted. However, if volumes are significantly lower than expected, the discount will get smaller. This provides an incentive for the contractor to send as much volume as possible to the provider firm.
- Price per unit—This variable is almost always known with some degree of precision. In many instances, it actually may be a given figure. Prices for services are established in the contract itself.
- Incremental cost per unit—This variable is often difficult to calculate, but not impossible. If the expected change in volume is relatively small, variable cost per unit would be a good approximation.
- Change in existing price—Once a contract is signed and new business is serviced, there may be a negative effect on existing prices. If the organization has granted a discount to attract the client, it may find that its existing clients will demand similar discounts. In many areas of the country, Blue Cross has a most-favored nation clause that guarantees it the lowest price charged by a hospital. Any hospital that lowers prices to another payer below the Blue Cross pay-

Table 10–8 Nursing Home Pricing Data

Payer Percentage	Payer Mode	Write-off Proportion
10 percent	Medicare—pays cost	NA
50 percent	Private payer—pays charges	.10
40 percent	Medicaid—pays fixed charge per diem	NA

ment rate may find itself facing an immediate reduction in price to Blue Cross and a possible lawsuit. The presence of cost payers also will create an automatic reduction in price. As more volume is delivered, the cost per unit will decrease as fixed costs are spread over more units. This means that cost payers will automatically benefit from increases in volume. Many hospitals, nursing homes, and other health care providers have some sizable blocks of cost payers. For example, there is still a substantial block of Medicare outpatient business that is cost-reimbursed in most hospitals.

SUMMARY

Cost accounting systems can be designed to provide different measures of cost for different decision-making purposes. This is a desirable characteristic, not an exercise in playing with numbers. To understand what measure of cost is needed for a specific purpose, the decision maker must have some knowledge of the variety of alternative concepts of cost. The terms covered in this chapter should be useful in helping decision makers define their needs more precisely.

Break-even analysis presents management with a set of simple analytical tools to provide information about the effects of costs, volume, and prices on profitability. In this chapter, we examined the application of several break-even models for health care providers with three categories of payers. These models should help analysts understand the conceptual framework for improving profitability in their health care organization.

ASSIGNMENTS

1. What are the two major categories of decisions that use cost information?
2. What does it mean to state that a cost is direct?
3. Define the terms variable costs and fixed costs. Give some examples of each.
4. Is it true that indirect costs should never be included in the determination of controllable costs?
5. A hospital is considering using a vacant wing to set up a skilled nursing facility. What is the cost of the space?
6. A free-standing ambulatory care center averages $60 in charges per patient. Variable costs are approximately $10 per patient, and fixed costs are about $1.2 million per year. Using these data, how many patients must be seen each day, assuming a 365-day operation, to reach the break-even point?
7. You are attempting to develop a break-even for a capitation contract with a major HMO. Your hospital has agreed to provide all inpatient hospital services for 10,000 covered lives. You will receive $38 per member per month (PMPM) to cover all inpatient services. It is anticipated that ninety-three admissions per 1,000 covered lives will be provided with an average length of stay equal to 5.0, or 465 days per 1,000.

   You anticipate that your hospital will incur fixed costs, or readiness to serve costs, of $1,860,000 for these 10,000 covered lives. Variable costs per patient day are expected to be $600.

   Calculate the break-even point in patient days under this contract.
8. Your hospital's board of trustees has just determined that the maximum revenue increase it will permit next year is 5 percent. It also has specified maximum and minimum rate increases by department. Data for the hospital's five departments are depicted in Table 10–9.

   Given the previous information, develop a rate change plan that will maximize the hospital's net income yet still adhere to the board's guidelines.
9. Develop an estimate of fixed and variable costs for labor expenses, based on the data presented in Table 10–10. Develop your estimates by using the high-low and semi-averages methods, and simple regression.

Table 10–9 Rate Optimization Data

			Payer Composition Percentage					Rate Change Percentage	
	Current Charges	*Budgeted Cost*	*Cost*	*Fixed Price*	*Charge*	*Bad Debt*	*Physician Fee*	*Min.*	*Max.*
Nursing	$2,000	$2,200	30	30	40	10	0	5	20
Emergency Room	200	190	70	10	20	10	0	0	10
Operating Room	300	330	35	40	25	20	0	10	25
Laboratory	1,000	750	50	30	20	15	10	–10	20
Anesthesiology	360	300	40	30	30	10	30	0	10
	$3,860	$3,770							

Table 10–10 Data for Variable/Fixed Cost Example

Period	Output in Units	Hours Worked
1	16,156	3,525
2	19,160	4,151
3	17,846	3,829
4	20,238	4,454
5	21,198	4,657
6	14,640	3,406

10. An interdepartmental service structure and its direct costs are depicted in Table 10–11.

Table 10–11 Data for Cost Allocation Example

Department	Direct Costs	Percentage of Service Consumed By					
		S1	S2	S3	R1	R2	R3
Service center 1	$10,000	–	10	10	40	20	20
Service center 2	12,000	10	–	10	20	40	20
Service center 3	10,000	10	10	–	20	20	40
Revenue center 1	30,000						
Revenue center 2	25,000						
Revenue center 3	50,000						

Compute the total costs, direct and allocated, for each of the three revenue centers using the direct and step-down methods of cost apportionment.

11. Your hospital was denied a contract with an HMO last year. Legal counsel believes that there was a breach of contract and wishes to bring suit against the HMO for damages. The chief executive officer has asked you to work with the controller to develop a defensible measure of the damages experienced during the last year. Explain how you would organize your work to estimate the amount of damages.

SOLUTIONS AND ANSWERS

1. The two major categories of decisions that use cost data are planning and control. Planning decisions usually require costs that are accumulated by program or product line, whereas control decisions usually require costs that are accumulated by responsibility centers or departments.

2. A direct cost can be traced or associated with a specific cost objective, usually related to a department or responsibility center.

3. A variable cost changes proportionately with volume. Common examples are materials and supplies. A fixed cost does not change with volume but remains constant. Common examples are rent, depreciation, and interest. Fixed costs are usually constant only for some "relevant range" of volume. For example, depreciation probably will increase if a facility experiences volume increases that exceed existing capacity.

4. It is not invariably true that indirect costs should never be included in the determination of controllable costs. There are some costs that may be classified as indirect but could be controlled by a manager. For example, housekeeping costs may be classified as an indirect cost to the physical therapy department. However, the actual amount of housekeeping services required by the physical therapy department may be affected by the actions of the physical therapy department manager.

5. The opportunity cost of the space—that is, its value in the next best alternative use—should be measured. Possible alternative uses might be as physician offices or as sleeping accommodations for patient families.

6. The number of patients that must be seen is 65.75 per day, based on the following calculation:

$$\text{Annual break-even volume} = \frac{1{,}200{,}000}{\$50} = 24{,}000 \text{ patients per year}$$

$$\text{Daily break-even volume} = \frac{24{,}000}{365} = 65.75$$

7. Fixed annual revenue = $10{,}000 \times \$38 \times 12 = \$4{,}560{,}000$
   Fixed costs = $\$1{,}860{,}000$
   Variable cost per patient day = $\$600$

$$\text{Break-even point} = \frac{\$4{,}560{,}000 - \$1{,}860{,}000}{\$600} = 4{,}500 \text{ Patient days}$$

If utilization is above 4,500 patient days, the hospital will lose money. See the following graph to illustrate this concept.

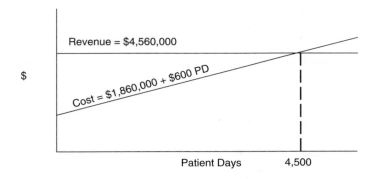

8. The rate change plan could be developed in the manner depicted in Table 10–12. Results of loading as much of the rate increase as possible into nursing are depicted in Table 10–13.

Table 10–12 Departmental Price Change Coefficients

Department	Percentage of Price Realized As Profit
Nursing	40.0% × .9 = 36.0%
Emergency room	20.0% × .9 = 18.0%
Operating room	25.0% × .8 = 20.0%
Laboratory	(20.0% × .85) − 10.0% = 7.0%
Anesthesiology	(30.0% × .9) − 30.0% = −3.0%

Table 10–13 Optimal Departmental Charges

Department	Current Charges	Required Minimum	Additional Charges	Final Charges
Nursing	$2,000	$100	$163	$2,263
Emergency room	200	0	0	200
Operating room	300	30	0	330
Laboratory	1,000	−100	0	900
Anesthesiology	360	0	0	360
	$3,860	$ 30	$163	$4,053

9. Table 10–14 depicts estimates of fixed and variable costs for labor expenses that could be developed.
10. The total costs for the three revenue centers would be as depicted in Table 10–15.
11. A reasonable framework for the estimation of damages would be the equation introduced earlier in this chapter:

> Change in profit = Change in volume [Price per unit – Incremental cost per unit]
> – Change in existing price × Volume affected

The change in volume would be an estimate of the lost volume resulting from the breach of contract. Price per unit could be obtained from a price schedule used by the HMO to pay the hospital or other similar hospitals. Incremental cost per unit could be approximated by variable cost. Finally, if the hospital has cost payers, some recognition must be given to the higher levels of payment made by cost payers because of the lower volumes, which would have raised average cost per unit because of the presence of fixed costs. In short, the hospital would have experienced an increase in its existing price from its cost payers.

Table 10–14 Variable and Fixed Cost Estimates

	Variable Hours/Unit	Fixed Hours
High-low method	.1908	613
Semi-averages method	.2093	193
Simple regression	.1990	375

Table 10–15 Solution for Cost Allocation Example

	Cost Apportionment Method	
	Direct	Step-Down
Revenue center 1	$ 40,500	$ 40,000
Revenue center 2	36,000	35,889
Revenue center 3	60,500	61,111
	$137,000	$137,000

11

Product Costing

Practically every health care provider expresses a strong and urgent interest in developing better cost accounting systems. The basis for this interest is easy to understand and relates to the nature of payment systems for health care providers. Before 1983, hospitals and many other health care providers were paid on the basis of actual cost. Hospitals, for example, were paid on a cost basis by Medicare, many Blue Cross plans, and most Medicaid programs. In this type of payment environment, costing was important, but allocation of costs to heavily cost reimbursed areas was emphasized, rather than accurate costing. Reimbursement maximization, not accurate costing, was the primary objective. With the advent of prospective payment systems in the early 1980s and the growing importance of managed care in the late 1980s, hospitals and other health care providers became concerned with the actual cost of service delivery. Providers wanted to know what the actual costs of producing a medical or surgical procedure were so they could compare these costs with the revenue received and make more intelligent decisions about products and product lines.

Interest in costing is not confined to the health care industry. Industry in general has expressed a renewed interest in accurate costing that is related to heightened global competition. Perhaps the most often used buzzword for improved

costing systems in the '90s has been activity-based costing or ABC. ABC is a relatively new term that describes a system of costing that assigns costs to products or customers based on the resources they consume. The assignment of cost to products or customers on the basis of resources consumed is not a new objective. All costing systems try to relate resource consumption to cost objects. The new feature of ABC relates to the identification of activities that are essential to the production of a product or service. It is these activities that are costed and then related to the completed product.

The approach to costing in this chapter builds on the principles of ABC, but we shall refer to activity-based costing concepts more generally as product costing. The critical objective is to determine the cost of resources for either a product or a customer.

RELATIONSHIP TO PLANNING, BUDGETING, AND CONTROL

Cost information is of value only as it aids in the management decision-making process. Figure 11–1 presents a schematic that summarizes the planning-budgeting-control process in a business. Of special interest is the decision output of the planning process. The planning process should detail the products or product lines

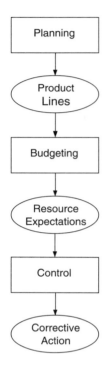

Figure 11-1 The Planning-Budgeting-Control Process

that the business will produce during the planning horizon, typically three to five years.

Products and Product Line

The terms "product" and "product line" seem simple and easy to understand regarding most businesses. For example, a finished car is the product of an automobile company; individual types of cars then may be grouped to form product lines, such as the Chevrolet product line of General Motors.

Can this definition of a product be transposed to the health care sector? Many people think that products cannot be defined so easily in health care firms. The major dilemma seems to arise in the area of patients versus products. In short, is the product the patient or is it the individual services provided, such as laboratory tests, nursing

care, and meals? In most situations, we believe that the patient is the basic product of a health care firm. This means that the wide range of services provided to patients—such as nursing, prescriptions, and tests—are to be viewed as intermediate products, not final products. There is, in fact, little difference between this interpretation and that applied in most manufacturing settings. For example, automobile fenders are, on one hand, a final product; on the other, they are only an intermediate product in preparation of the final product, the completed automobile. Ultimately, it is the automobile that is sold to the public, not the fenders. In the same vein, it is the treated patient who generates revenue, not the individual service provided in isolation. Indeed, a hospital that provided only laboratory tests would not be a hospital but rather a laboratory. In short, patients must exist for an individual or an entity to be a health care provider.

Product lines represent an amalgamation of patients in a way that makes business sense. Sometimes people use the term "strategic business units" to refer to areas of activity that may stand alone. For our purpose, a product line is a unit of business activity that requires a go or no-go decision. For example, eliminating one diagnosis related group (DRG) is probably not possible because that DRG may be linked to other DRGs within a clinical specialty area; it may be impossible to stop producing DRG 36 (retinal procedures) without also eliminating other DRGs, such as DRG 39 (lens procedure). Thus, in many cases, it is the clinical specialty, for example, ophthalmology, that defines the product line.

Budgeting and Resource Expectations

The budgeting phase of operations involves a translation of the product-line decisions made earlier into a set of resource expectations. The primary purpose of this is twofold. First, management must assure itself that there will be a sufficient funds flow to maintain financial solvency. Just as you and I must live within our financial means, so must any health care business entity. Second, the resulting budget serves as a basis for management control. If budget expectations are not realized, management must discover why not and take corrective actions. A budget or set of resource expectations can be thought of as a standard costing system. The budget represents management's expectations of how costs should behave, given a certain set of volume assumptions. It is important to remember that it is the forecasted or budgeted costs of a product that are of the greatest interest to management. Historical costs are useful, but only insofar as those costs indicate future costs.

The key aspect of budgeting is the translation of product-line decisions into precise and specific sets of resource expectations. This involves five basic steps:

1. Define the volumes of patients by case type to be treated in the budget period.
2. Define the standard treatment protocol by case type.
3. Define the required departmental or activity center volumes.
4. Define the standard cost profiles for departmental or activity center outputs.
5. Define the prices to be paid for resources.

The primary output of the budgeting process is a series of departmental or activity center budgets that explicates what costs should be during the coming budget period. Two separate sets of standards are involved in the development of these budgets (these standards are described later in the chapter).

We now will use a simple, hypothetical nursing-home example to illustrate how these five steps would be integrated into the budgeting process. We will assume that our nursing home is a 100-bed facility with a simple organizational structure. It only has three departments: a dietary department, a nursing department, and an administration department.

Define Volumes of Patients (Step 1)

The first step in any budgetary process is to estimate the critical volume statistics. These sta-

tistics, when defined, will enable managers to determine levels of activity in each of the departments. In our nursing-home example, we will assume that the facility will average 95 percent occupancy, or 34,675 patients, during the next year. For most nursing homes, patient days would be the critical measure of patient volume. In a hospital, it might be discharges, patient days, and outpatient visits. Ideally, these macro measures then would be broken down further into more specific case types. For example, in a nursing home we might categorize patients by their acuity, whereas a hospital might use DRG categories, and a medical group might use procedure codes.

Define Standard Treatment Protocol (Step 2)

The second step in the budgetary process is to define the relationship between patient volumes and departmental volumes. If 34,675 patients are seen in our nursing home next year, what does that mean in terms of individual departmental activity for the dietary, nursing, and administration departments?

The major connection here is the determination of a "standard treatment protocol." What departmental service is required to provide a patient day of care? In our nursing-home example, we will assume that there are only two real products required to treat a nursing home patient: (1) three patient meals per patient day and (2) two hours of nursing time.

Define Required Departmental Volumes (Step 3)

Given the standard treatment protocol defined in Step 2, it is relatively easy to determine departmental volumes. To treat 34,675 patients, our nursing home will need to provide the following service:

3 Meals × 34,675 = 104,025 Meals in dietary

2 Nursing hours × 34,675 = 69,350 Nursing hours

Define Standard Cost Profiles (Step 4)

Given the level of activity required in the departments, it is now time to define the "standard cost profiles." This set of standards simply relates departmental volume to expected resource levels. In short, what resources are required to provide a patient day of care? We will assume that the departmental managers have developed the following standard cost profiles. Dietary will be purchasing individual food packages from an outside vendor for every meal.

Dietary
   1 purchased food package
   10 minutes of dietary labor
Nursing
   1 hour of RN labor
   1 hour of aide labor
Administration
   5 full-time equivalents (FTEs) to provide 34,675 patient days of care

You will notice that the administration department has a requirement for resources, but it did not specify any service required in Step 2, standard treatment protocol specification. There will be a number of areas, such as administration, in which there is no clear connection between service and patient volume. It is possible only on a macro basis to determine staffing or resource profiles for a specified range of activity, for example, 34,675 patient days.

One of the major advantages of ABC cited by proponents is better costing of overhead areas like administration. This better costing results from detailed analysis of the activities performed in the overhead areas. For example, administration may be broken into several patient-related activities such as billing and purchasing. The costs for these activities then may be traced or assigned directly to the product—a patient day in our nursing-home example. At some point, however, most overhead areas cannot be further divided into activity centers with product-traceable outputs, and the remaining costs must be assigned to the products in some reasonable manner.

Define Resource Prices (Step 5)

The last step in completing the budget is to determine the expected resource prices to be in effect during the budget period. Those prices are determined below:

Purchased food package	$2/meal
Dietary labor	$6/hour
RN labor	$15/hour
Aide labor	$8/hour
Administrative labor	$28,000/FTE

Table 11–1 summarizes the completed budget for the nursing-home example, assuming that 34,675 patient days of care are provided next year.

Control and Corrective Action

The control phase of business operations monitors actual cost experience and compares it with budgetary expectations. If there are deviations from expectations, management analyzes the causes of the deviation. If the deviation is favorable, management may seek to make whatever created the variance a permanent part of operations. If the variance is unfavorable, action will be taken in an attempt to prevent a recurrence. Much of the control phase centers around the topic of variance analysis, which is explored in depth in Chapter 13.

THE COSTING PROCESS

Most firms, whether they are hospitals, nursing homes, or steel manufacturers, have similar costing systems. In fact, in most cases, the similarities outweigh the differences. Figure 11–2 presents a schematic of the cost-measurement process that exists in most businesses.

Valuation

Valuation always has been a thorny issue for accountants—one that has not been satisfactorily resolved even today. We need only to con-

Table 11–1 Nursing Home Budget

Dietary	
Purchased food packages ($2.00 × 3 × 34,675)	$ 208,050
Dietary labor ($6.00 × (1/6) × 3 × 34,675)	104,025
Total dietary	$ 312,075
Nursing	
RN labor ($15.00 × 34,675)	$520,125
Aide labor ($8.00 × 34,675)	277,400
Total nursing	$ 797,525
Administration	
Salaries (5 × $28,000)	$140,000
Total cost	$1,249,600

sider the current controversy over replacement costs versus historical costs to realize the full problem. Here, for discussion purposes, we have chosen to split the valuation process into two areas: (1) basis and (2) assignment over time. These two areas are not mutually exclusive; to some degree, they overlap. However, both areas determine the total value of a resource that is used to cost a final product.

The valuation basis is the process by which a value is assigned to each and every resource transaction occurring between the entity being accounted for and another entity. In most situations, this value is historical cost.

Having established a basis value for the resource transaction, there are two major types of situations when that value will have to be assigned over time: First, the value may be expended before the actual reporting of expense; the best example of this is depreciation. Second, the expense may be recognized before an actual expenditure. Normal accruals such as wages and salaries are examples of this situation. As the period being costed increases, the problems caused by assignment over time become less severe. For example, if the period being costed is one year, normal accruals for wages and salaries represent a very small percentage of total wage

and salary costs. It may be perfectly acceptable to simply use the actual dollar amount paid for wages and salaries. But, if the period being costed is one week, estimates of costs or accruals must be made because no actual wages may have been paid during the one-week period.

Allocation

The end result of the cost-allocation process is the assignment of all costs or values determined during the valuation phase of costing to direct departments. A direct department provides a service or product directly traceable to a patient. Two phases of activity are involved in this assignment: First, all resource values to be recorded as expenses during a given period are assigned or allocated to the direct and indirect departments as direct expenses. Second, once the initial cost assignment to individual departments has been made, a further allocation is required. In this phase, the expenses of the indirect departments are assigned to the direct departments.

By using this framework for analysis, costing issues may be subcategorized. In the initial cost-assignment phase, the following two major decisions appear to be involved in the costing pro-

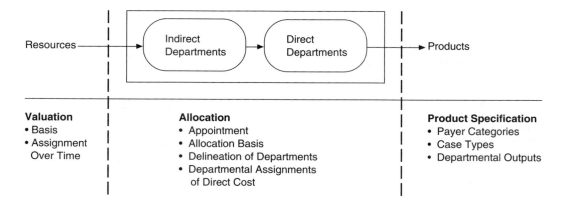

Figure 11–2 The Cost Measurement Process

cess: (1) assigning the cost to departments and (2) defining the indirect and direct departments.

In the first category, a situation may arise in which the departmental structure currently specified is not questioned, but some of the initial value assignments are. For example, premiums paid for malpractice insurance might be charged to administration, or they may be charged directly to the nursing and professional departments that are involved. In the second category, a situation may arise in which the existing departmental structure has to be revised. For example, the administration department may be divided into several new departments, such as nonpatient telephone, data processing, purchasing, admitting, business office, and other. Splitting an existing department into a number of activity centers may greatly improve the costing process and is a significant part of so-called ABC systems. The analysis focuses on the discovery of activities that are related to the products being produced. For example, admitting activities may be a significant activity within the administration department that is clearly traceable to an individual patient. Dividing administration into admitting and other activity centers may greatly improve the accuracy of individual costing and permit management to better mea-

sure the actual costs of producing a product. There are numerous examples of overhead departments that could be split into component activities that then may be traced to the patient or procedure being produced.

During the second phase of cost allocation—the reassignment from indirect departments to direct departments—the following two primary decisions are involved: (1) selection of the cost-apportionment method and (2) selection of the appropriate allocation basis. Regarding the first category, cost-apportionment methods—such as step-down, double distribution, and simultaneous equations methods, are simply mathematical algorithms that redistribute cost from existing indirect departments to direct departments, given defined allocation bases. An example of the second type of decision is the selection of square feet or hours worked for housekeeping as an appropriate allocation basis for an indirect department. Sometimes the term "cost driver" is used to describe the selection of an appropriate allocation base. Ideally, the allocation basis selected should be that variable that has the most direct or causal relationship to cost. For example, square feet would not appear to be as accurate an allocation basis or cost driver for housekeeping as hours worked.

Product Specification

In most health care firms, there are two phases in the production (or treatment) process. The schematic in Figure 11–3 illustrates this process and also introduces a few new terms.

In Stage 1 of the production process, resources are acquired and consumed within departments or activity centers to produce a product, defined as a service unit (SU). Here, two points need to be emphasized. First, all departments have SUs, but not all departments have the same number of SUs. For example, the nursing department may provide the following four levels of care: acuity levels 1, 2, 3, and 4. A laboratory, in contrast, may have 100 or more separate SUs that relate to the provision of specific tests. Second, not all SUs can be directly associated with the delivery of patient care; some of the SUs may be only indirectly associated with patient treatment. For example, housekeeping cleans laboratory areas, but there is no direct association between this function and patient treatment. However, the cleaning of a patient's room could be regarded as a service that is directly associated with a patient.

Stage 2 of the production process relates to the actual consumption of specific SUs during the treatment of a patient. Much of the production process is managed by the physician. This is true regardless of the setting (hospital, nursing home, home health care firm, or clinic). The physician prescribes the specific SUs that will be required to treat a given patient effectively.

The lack of management authority in this area complicates management's efforts to budget and control its costs. This is not meant to be a negative criticism of current health care delivery systems; all of us would prefer to have a qualified physician rather than a lay health care executive direct our care. Yet, this is perhaps the area of greatest difference between health care firms and other business entities. Management at General Motors can decide which automobiles will have factory-installed air-conditioning and tinted glass and which will not. In contrast, a health care executive will have great difficulty in attempting to direct a physician to either prescribe or not prescribe a given procedure in the treatment of a patient.

Health care products to be costed may vary depending on the specific decision being considered. At one level, management may be interested in the cost of a specific SU or departmental output. Prices for some SUs (for example, radiograph procedures) may have to be established, and to do that, management must know their costs. In other situations, knowing the cost for one treated patient or for a group of treated patients may be desired. For example, management may wish to bid on a contract to provide home health services to a health maintenance organization (HMO). In this case, it is important for management to understand what the costs of treating HMO patients are likely to be. If the contract is signed, management then needs to determine the actual costs of treating the patients from the HMO to measure the overall profitability from that segment of the business. Alternatively, it may be necessary to group patients by specialty. A hospital may wish to know whether it is losing money from treating a particular DRG entity or some grouping of DRGs, such as obstetrics. This kind of cost information is especially critical to management decision making involving the expansion or contraction of specific clinical service areas and the recruitment of new medical staff.

STANDARD DEVELOPMENT

The key to successful product costing is management's ability to develop and maintain the following two systems: (1) a system of standard cost profiles and (2) a system of standard treatment protocols. The relationship between these two systems is shown in Figure 11–3. The "linchpin" between them is the SU concept. Specifically, management must know what it costs to produce an SU, and it must know what particular SUs are needed to treat a given patient.

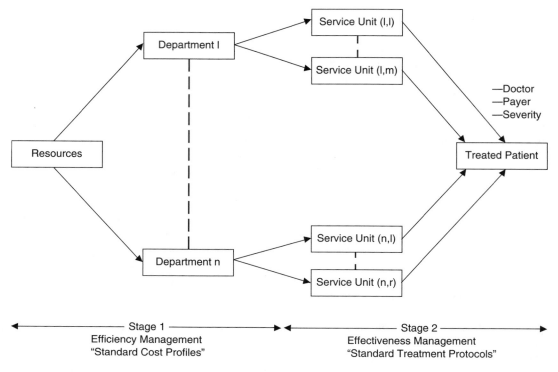

Stage 1 ──────────────▶ ◀────────────── Stage 2

Efficiency Management   Effectiveness Management
"Standard Cost Profiles"   "Standard Treatment Protocols"

Figure 11–3 The Production Process for Health Care Firms

Standard Cost Profiles

The standard cost profile (SCP) is not a new concept; it has been used in manufacturing cost accounting systems for many years. For our purposes, there are two key elements in an SCP: (1) the definition of the SU being costed and (2) the profile of resources required to produce the SU.

As noted earlier, the number of SUs in a given department may vary; some departments may have one, whereas others may have 100 or more. If the number of SUs is very large, however, there may be an unacceptable level of costing detail involved to make the system feasible. In these situations, it may be useful to aggregate some of the SUs. For example, the laboratory may perform 1,000 or more tests. In this situation, it may make sense to develop cost profiles for only the most commonly performed tests and

to use some arbitrary assignment method for the remaining noncommon tests.

The SU does not have to be a product or service that is directly provided or performed for a patient. Many indirect departments do not provide services or products to the patient; instead, their products or services are consumed by other departments, both direct and indirect. However, many indirect departments have SUs that are provided directly to the patient. For example, the dietary department, often regarded as an indirect department, may not have revenue billed for its product to the patient. However, a meal that the dietary department furnishes to a patient is an SU that is just as direct as a laboratory test or a chest radiograph. In a similar vein, housekeeping may provide cleaning for a patient's room that is, in effect, a direct service consumed by the patient.

Thus, SUs may be categorized as either direct or indirect. A direct SU is associated with a given patient. An indirect SU is provided to another department of the hospital, as opposed to a patient. The differentiation between direct and indirect SUs is important, not only in the development of standard cost profiles but also in the development of standard treatment protocols. Direct SUs must be identified when standard treatment protocols are defined, whereas indirect SUs need not be specifically identified, although some estimate of allocated cost is often required.

In the development of an SCP for a given SU, the following resource expense categories are listed: (1) direct expenses (labor, materials, and departmental overhead) and (2) allocated overhead. Ideally, the expense also should be categorized as variable or fixed. This distinction is particularly important in certain areas of management decision making, as noted in Chapter 10. Specifically, the differentiation between variable and fixed cost is critical to many incremental pricing and volume decisions. It is also important in flexible budgeting systems and management control. These topics are explored in greater depth in Chapters 12 and 13.

Table 11–2 presents an SCP for a regular patient meal in a dietary department. The total cost of providing one regular patient meal, or SU 181, is $2.70. The variable cost per meal is

$1.40, and the average fixed cost per meal is $1.30.

In most situations, direct labor is the largest single expense category. In our dietary meal example, this is not true because the direct material cost, mostly raw food, is larger. It is possible, and in many cases desirable, to define direct labor costs by labor category. Thus, in our dietary meal example, we might provide separate listings for cooks, dietary aides, and dishwashers.

An important point here is the division of cost into fixed and variable quantities. Table 11–2 indicates that .05 units of variable labor time is required per meal, and .05 units of fixed labor is required per meal. (In Chapter 10, we discussed several methods for splitting costs into fixed and variable elements.) The fixed-cost assignment is an average based on some expected level of volume. This is an important point to remember when developing SCPs; a decline in volume below expected levels will increase the average cost of production because the fixed cost is spread over fewer units of ouput.

The third column of Table 11–2 presents unit cost. This represents management's best guess as to the cost or price of the resources to be used in the production process. Our dietary meal SCP indicates a price of $8 per unit of direct labor. This value reflects the expected wage per hour to be paid for direct labor in the dietary department. Again, it might be possible and desirable to di-

Table 11–2 Standard Cost Profile for a Dietary/Regular Patient Meal SU 181

Cost Category	Quantity Variable	Required Fixed	Unit Cost	Variable Cost	Average Fixed Cost	Average Total Cost
Direct labor	.05	.05	$8.00	$ .40	$ .40	$ .80
Direct materials	1.00	.00	1.00	1.00	.00	1.00
Department overhead	.00	1.00	.50	.00	.50	.50
Allocated costs						
Housekeeping	.00	.10	1.00	.00	.10	.10
Plant operation	.00	1.00	.10	.00	.10	.10
Administration	.00	.02	10.00	.00	.20	.20
Total				$1.40	$1.30	$2.70

vide direct labor further into specific job classifications. This usually permits better costing, but it also requires more effort.

Any fringe benefit cost associated with labor should be included in the unit cost. For example, the average direct hourly wage in our dietary meal example might be $6.40 per hour, but fringe benefits may average 25 percent. In this case, the effective wage would be $8 per hour.

Departmental overhead consists of expenses that are charged directly to a department and do not represent either labor or materials. Common examples are equipment costs, travel allowances, expenses for outside-purchased services, and cost of publications. Usually, these items do not vary with level of activity or volume but remain fixed for the budgetary period. If this is the case, assignment to an SCP can be based on a simple average. For example, assume that our dietary department expects to provide 200,000 regular patient meals next year. Assume further that the department has been authorized to spend $100,000 in discretionary areas that constitute departmental overhead. The average cost per meal for these discretionary costs would be $.50 and would be fixed.

Allocated costs are probably the most difficult to assign in most situations. In our dietary example, we include only three allocated cost areas. This is probably a low figure; a number of other departments most likely would provide service to the dietary department and should be properly included in the SCP.

There are two major alternatives to using estimates of allocated costs in an SCP. First, individual costing studies could be performed, and services from one department to another could be recorded. This process may be expensive, however, and not worth the effort. For example, if separate meters were installed, utility costs could be associated with each user department. However, the installation of such meters is probably not an effective expenditure of funds; costing accuracy would not be improved enough to justify the extra expenditure.

The second alternative would be a simple averaging method. All overhead costs might be aggregated and apportioned to other departments on the basis of direct expenses, FTEs, or some other criterion. This method is relatively simple, but its accuracy would be suspect if significant variation in departmental utilization exists.

We believe that the best approach to costing is to identify all possible direct SUs. These SUs, which can be directly associated with a patient, are much more numerous than one would suspect. For example, a meal provided to a patient is a direct SU but is currently treated as an indirect product in most costing systems. Laundry and linen departments have certain SUs that are directly associated with a patient, such as clean sheets and gowns. Housekeeping provides direct services to patients when its personnel cleans rooms. The administration and medical records departments also provide specific direct services to patients in the form of processed paper work and insurance forms. If such costs, currently regarded as indirect, were reclassified as direct, there would be a substantially lower level of indirect costs that would require allocation. This would improve the costing of patients—the health care product—and make the allocation of indirect costs less critical. Currently, indirect costs in many health care settings are in excess of 50 percent of total cost. With better identification of services or SUs, we believe that level could be reduced to 25 percent or lower. This identification of services or activities is the "heart" of ABC costing systems.

Standard Treatment Protocols

There is an analogy between a standard treatment protocol (STP) and a job-order cost sheet used in industrial cost accounting. In a job-order cost system, a separate cost sheet is completed for each specific job. This is necessary because each job is different from jobs performed in the past and jobs to be performed in the future. Automobile repairs are an excellent example of a job-order cost system. A separate cost sheet is prepared for each job. That cost sheet then serves as the bill or invoice to the customer.

Health care firms also operate in a job-cost setting. Patient treatment may vary significantly across patients. The patient's bill may be thought of as a job-order cost sheet in that it reflects the actual services provided during the course of the patient's treatment. Of course, not all of the services provided are shown in the patient's bill. For example, meals provided are rarely charged for as a separate item.

In a typical job-order cost setting, standards may not always be applied. When you leave your car at the dealership for servicing, the dealer does not prepare a standard job-order cost sheet. Dealers have no incentive to do this because they expect that customers will pay the actual costs of the service when they pick up their cars. If they do not, the dealer may take possession of the car as collateral.

In the past, a similar situation existed among health care firms; the client or patient would pay for the actual cost of services provided. Today, this is no longer true for the majority of health care products. Today, most health care firms are paid a fixed fee or price regardless of the range of services provided. Medicare's DRG payment system is an example of this type of payment philosophy. Health care providers who have accepted capitation have an additional dilemma because cost is now a function of both utilization and cost per episode. The provider must estimate the number of episodes of care as well as the cost per episode. It is similar to an automobile manufacturer providing a warranty. The manufacturer must determine both the frequency of claims and the average cost per claim.

Little revenue realized by a health care provider is derived from cost payers in today's marketplace and the majority of revenue is fixed price on either a case, per diem, procedure, or capitated basis. Because the revenue is fixed, understanding the cost of a treatment protocol is essential to effective management. Table 11–3

shows a hypothetical STP for DRG 208 (disorder of biliary tract). (This STP is for illustrative purposes only; it should not be regarded as a realistic STP for DRG 208.)

In the STP depicted in Table 11–3, costs are split into fixed and variable components. Thus, the STP requires twenty-five patient meals at a variable cost of $1.40 per meal and a fixed cost of $1.30 per meal. The basis for these data is the SCP (see Table 11–2). As noted earlier, this division between fixed and variable costs is extremely valuable for management when it makes its planning and control decisions. For example, if Medicare paid the hospital $1,400 for every DRG 208 patient treated, we would conclude that, at least in the short run, the hospital would be financially better off if it continued to treat DRG 208 cases, because the payment of $1,400 exceeds the variable cost of $1,017 and the hospital is therefore making a contribution to fixed costs.

Table 11–3 depicts two areas in which no actual quantity is specified: pharmacy prescriptions and other laboratory tests. In these instances, the total cost of the services is instead divided between fixed and variable costs. Because of the large number of products provided in each of these two areas, it would be impossible to develop an SCP for each product item. However, some of the heavier volume laboratory tests or pharmacy prescriptions may be separately identified and costed; for example, laboratory complete blood count is listed as a separate SU.

Some of the items shown in Table 11–3 may not be reflected in a patient's bill. For example, patient meals, linen changes, room preparation, and admission processing usually would not be listed in the bill. Also, separation of nursing care by acuity level may not be identified in the bill; many hospitals do not distinguish between levels of nursing care in their pricing structures.

A final point to emphasize is that not all SUs will show up in an STP. Only those SUs that are classified as direct are listed. A direct SU can be

Table 11–3 Standard Treatment Protocol for DRG 208/Disorder of Biliary Tract

Service Unit No.	Service Unit Name	Quantity	Variable Cost/ Unit	Fixed Cost/ Unit	Total Cost/ Unit	Total Variable Cost	Total Fixed Cost	Total Cost
1	Admission process	1	$48.00	$52.00	$100.00	$48.00	$52.00	$100.00
7	Nursing care level 1	1	80.00	40.00	120.00	80.00	40.00	120.00
8	Nursing care level 2	7	85.00	45.00	130.00	595.00	315.00	910.00
9	Nursing care level 3	1	110.00	45.00	155.00	110.00	45.00	155.00
29	Pharmacy prescriptions		38.00	19.00	57.00	38.00	19.00	57.00
38	Chest radiograph	1	12.00	8.00	20.00	12.00	8.00	20.00
46	Laboratory complete blood count	1	4.00	3.50	7.50	4.00	3.50	7.50
49	Other laboratory tests		85.00	55.00	140.00	85.00	55.00	140.00
57	Patient meals	25	1.40	1.30	2.70	35.00	32.50	67.50
65	Linen changes	5	.60	.50	1.10	3.00	2.50	5.50
93	Room preparation	1	7.00	3.00	10.00	7.00	3.00	10.00
	Totals					$1,017.00	$575.50	$1,592.50

directly traced or associated with patient care. The costs associated with the provision of indirect SUs are allocated to the direct SUs. At the same time, the objective should be to create as many direct SUs as possible. The creation of traceable SUs is one of the objectives of ABC systems.

VARIANCE ANALYSIS

In general, given the systems of standards discussed previously (SCPs and STPs),the following four types of variances may be identified in the variance analysis phase of control:

1. price (rate),
2. efficiency,
3. volume, and
4. intensity.

The first three types of variances are a direct result of the development of the SCPs; they are the product of departmental activity. A rate or price variance is the difference between the price

actually paid and the standard price multiplied by the actual quantity used. The equation is as follows:

Price variance = (Actual price – Standard price) × Actual quantity

For example, assume that our dietary department of Table 11–2 produced 1,500 patient meals for the period in question when budgeted volume was 1,600 meals. To produce these meals, it used 180 hours of labor and paid $8.25 per hour. In this case, the price or rate variance would be the following:

($8.25 – $8.00) × 180 hours = $45.00

This variance would be unfavorable because the department paid $8.25 per hour when the expected rate was $8.00.

An efficiency variance reflects productivity in the production process. It is derived by multiplying the difference between actual quantity used and standard quantity by the standard price:

Efficiency variance = (Actual quantity –
Standard quantity) × Standard price

In our dietary example, the efficiency variance would be

(180 hours – 155 hours) × $8 = $200

Standard labor is derived by multiplying the variable labor requirement of .05 by the number of meals produced, or 1,500. The budgeted fixed-labor requirement of 80 hours is added to this sum (.05 × 1,600 meals). In our example, the department used twenty-five more hours of labor than had been expected. As a result, it incurred an unfavorable efficiency variance of $200.

The volume variance reflects differences between expected output and actual output. It is a factor to be considered in situations involving fixed costs. If no fixed costs existed, the resources required per unit would be constant. This would mean that the cost per unit of production should be constant. For most situations, this is not a reasonable expectation; normally, fixed costs are present.

The volume variance is derived by multiplying the expected average fixed cost per unit by the difference between budgeted volume and actual volume. The equation is as follows:

Volume variance = (Budgeted volume –
Actual volume) × Average fixed cost per
unit

In the case of direct labor in our dietary example, the volume variance would be an unfavorable $40:

(1,600 – 1,500) × $.40

Notice that in our example, the total of these variances equals the difference between actual costs incurred for direct labor and the standard cost of direct labor assigned to the SU, a patient meal:

Actual direct labor	
($8.25 × 180 hours)	$1,485
Less standard cost	
($.80 × 1,500 meals)	1,200
Total variance	$285
Price variance	$45.00
Efficiency variance	200.00
Volume variance	40.00
Total variance	$285.00

The intensity variance is the difference between the quantity of SUs actually required when treating a patient and the quantity necessary in the STP. For example, if twenty meals were provided to a patient categorized in DRG 208, there would be a favorable variance of five meals, given the STP data of Table 11–3.

Intensity variances are generically defined as follows:

Intensity variance =
(Actual SUs – Standard SUs) ×
Standard cost per SU

Thus, in our example, the intensity variance for the DRG 208 patient regarding meals would be a favorable $13.50 ([20 meals – 25 meals] × $2.70).

It may be useful to divide intensity variances into fixed and variable elements. In our example, it is probably not fair to state that $13.50 was saved because five fewer meals were delivered. Five times $1.40, the variable cost, may be a better reflection of short-term realized savings.

One final statement about variance analysis: It is important to specify the party responsible for variances. This is, after all, part of the rationale for standard costing—to be able to take corrective action through individuals to correct unfavorable variances. In our example, three variances—price, efficiency, and volume—are distinguished in the departmental accounts. However, the department manager may not be responsible for all of this variation, especially in the volume area. Usually, department managers have little control over volume; they merely re-

Table 11–4 Relative Value Weights

CPT #	Number of Procedures	Physician Work Weight	Total Work Units	Practice Weight	Total Practice Units	Malpractice Weight	Total Malpractice Units
67800	1,000	1.5	1,500	1.0	1,000	.05	50
66985	500	8.5	4,250	14.0	7,000	.75	375
Total	1,500		5,750		8,000		425

act to the volume of services requested from their departments.

The intensity variance can be largely associated with a given physician. Most of the SUs are of a medical nature, resulting from physician decisions regarding testing or length of stay. It may be helpful, therefore, to accumulate intensity variances by physicians. Periodic discussions regarding these variations can be most useful to both the health care executive and the physician. Ideally, physicians should participate actively in the development of STPs.

Relative Value Unit Costing

In a number of settings, the costing of individual products is difficult to accomplish and may not be worth the time and effort required. For example, medical groups often produce a large number of different medical procedures. Ancillary providers such as laboratories or imaging centers may produce hundreds of different procedures. Costing of any specific procedure is virtually impossible. Imagine for a moment the effort involved in costing a routine visit to a physician's office. Once you identified the individual activities involved in the delivery of service and the indirect support costs associated with service delivery, it would be an accounting "nightmare" to assign those costs to 100 or more procedures routinely performed in the doctor's office.

One solution that is used in many settings is relative value unit (RVU) costing. In RVU costing, some relative weights are assigned for each of the commonly produced outputs. For medical groups, the most commonly accepted classification of outputs is current procedural terminology (CPT) codes. Medicare uses CPT codes in its resource-based relative value system discussed in Chapter 2. These assigned weights can be used to cost individual procedures. For example, consider an ophthalmology practice that performs only two procedures (Table 11–4).

If we assume that the total expenses of the practice are presented as in Table 11–5, we then could develop a cost per procedure using the RVU concept.

The cost for each of the two procedures would then be calculated as shown in Table 11–6.

Table 11–5 Cost per Weighted Procedure

	Total Expenses	Total Weighted Units	Cost Per Weighted Unit
Physician compensation	$200,000	5,750	$34.78
Practice expenses	450,000	8,000	56.25
Malpractice expense	7,500	425	17.65

Table 11–6 Cost per Procedure

	CPT 67800	*CPT 66985*
Physician work units	1.5	8.5
× cost per unit	$34.78	$34.78
Physician cost per procedure	$52.17	$295.63
Practice work units	1.0	14.0
× cost per unit	$56.25	$56.25
Practice cost per procedure	$56.25	$787.50
Malpractice work units	.05	.75
× cost per unit	$17.65	$17.65
Malpractice cost per procedure	$0.88	$13.24
Total cost per procedure	$109.30	$1,096.37

SUMMARY

Product costing has become much more critical to health care executives today than it was before 1983. The emphasis on prospective prices and competitive discounting creates a real need to define costs. For health care purposes, the product is a treated patient. Various aggregations of patients also may be useful. For example, we may want to develop cost data by DRG, by clinical specialty, or by payer category.

To develop a standard cost system in a health care firm, two sets of standards must be defined. First, a series of SCPs must be developed for all SUs (intermediate departmental products) pro-

duced by the firm. This part of standard costing is analogous to that of most manufacturing systems. Second, a set of STPs must be defined for major patient-treatment categories. These STPs must identify all the service units to be provided in the patient treatment. Physician involvement is critical in this area.

The purpose of standard costing is to make planning decisions, such as those involved in pricing and product mix, more precise and meaningful. Standard costing is also useful when making control decisions. Variance analysis is based on the existence of standard cost and the periodic accumulation of actual cost data. Timely analysis of variances can help management achieve desired results.

ASSIGNMENTS

1. An HMO has asked your hospital to provide all of its obstetric services. It has offered to pay your hospital $2,000 for a normal vaginal delivery, without complications (DRG 373). You have looked at the STP for this DRG and discovered that your hospital's cost is $2,400. What should you do?

2. Dr. Jones is scheduled to meet with you this afternoon. She has been an active admitter, but you would like to see her practice increase. After reviewing Dr. Jones' financial report, shown in Table 11–7, what recommendations would you make?

3. Using the data presented in Table 11–8, explain why some DRGs have negative values for deductions.

4. In Table 11–8, DRG 14 has the largest revenue of all the case types listed, yet it lost money. Why?

5. The data in Table 11–9 represent a cost accountant's effort to define the variable cost for DRG 104 (cardiac valve procedures with cardiac catheter). Evaluate this method.

Table 11-7 Dr. Jones' Financial Report

DRG Number	Type Description	No. of Discharges	ALOS*	Comp LOS*	LOS Var	Total Charges	Deductions	Net Revenue	Variable Cost	Gross Margin	Fixed Cost	Net Income
0316	Renal Failure	7	11.7	6.7	5.0	$ 19,371	$ 4,484	$ 14,887	$ 7,372	$ 7,515	$ 6,926	$ 589
0315	Other Kidney Uri	5	42.4	12.7	29.7	28,945	6,270	22,675	12,375	10,300	8,866	1,434
0468	Unrelated OR Procedures	5	32.2	11.3	20.9	87,309	12,739	71,570	33,421	38,149	30,955	7,194
0130	Vascular	3	6.0	8.8	-2.8	8,166	1,834	6,332	3,055	3,277	3,297	-20
0138	Cardiac Arrhythm	3	4.3	7.4	-3.1	3,524	1,027	2,497	1,351	1,146	985	161
0182	Esophagitis GI + D	3	7.3	6.7	.6	14,171	3,427	10,744	5,308	5,436	5,503	-67
0331	Other Kid + Urina	3	8.7	7.6	1.1	10,983	2,539	8,444	3,900	4,544	4,390	154
0024	Seizure + Headache	2	16.0	6.8	9.2	4,625	1,156	3,469	1,651	1,818	1,459	359
0127	Heart Failure +	2	4.0	10.4	-6.4	1,827	592	1,235	606	629	348	281
0140	Angina Pectoris	2	7.0	6.6	.4	5,290	1,179	4,111	2,079	2,032	1,765	267
0188	Other Digest/sys	2	9.5	6.5	3.0	4,733	1,148	3,585	1,551	2,034	1,926	108
0296	Nutri + Misc Met	2	8.0	8.9	-.9	2,840	625	2,215	1,103	1,112	995	117
0321	Kid + Urinary Tra	2	23.0	4.6	18.4	12,377	248	12,129	4,103	8,026	4,505	3,521
0442	Other OR Proc In	2	6.5	11.6	-5.1	11,415	2,629	8,786	4,533	4,253	4,082	171
0443	Other OR Proc In	2	8.5	5.6	2.9	8,974	2,227	6,747	3,392	3,355	3,225	130
0452	Complications Tr	2	44.5	6.0	38.5	1,827	482	1,345	562	783	693	90
0467	Other Factors In	2	1.5	3.1	-1.6	1,461	396	1,065	452	613	518	95
0010	Nervous Syst Neo	1	35.0	13.5	21.5	267	99	168	62	106	35	71
0016	Nonspec Cerebrov	1	8.0	11.0	-3.0	4,984	1,093	3,891	2,064	1,827	2,034	-207
0066	Epistaxis	1	7.0	4.6	2.4	302	112	190	86	104	68	36
0085	Pleural Effusion	1	19.0	12.1	6.9	675	251	424	393	31	220	-189
0088	Chronic Obstruct	1	3.0	9.1	-6.1	2,634	694	1,940	1,087	853	946	-93
0112	Vasc Proc No Maj	1	9.0	26.2	-17.2	6,357	1,380	4,977	2,445	2,532	2,482	50
0120	Other OR Procedu	1	71.0	16.4	54.6	10,448	3,461	6,987	2,862	4,125	2,178	1,947
0143	Chest Pain	1	6.0	4.2	1.8	5,659	1,179	4,480	2,333	2,147	2,070	77
0144	Other Circ Diagn	1	2.0	9.3	-7.3	2,085	439	1,646	858	788	713	75
0152	Minor Small + Lar	1	93.0	13.7	79.3	1,084	403	681	241	440	149	291
0171	Other Digest/sys	1	35.0	6.9	28.1	2,136	793	1,343	555	788	358	430
0175	G. I. Hemmorhage A	1	6.0	5.8	.2	3,734	883	2,851	1,676	1,175	1,027	148
0224	Up Extr Proc No	1	23.0	4.3	18.7	10,977	5,544	5,433	3,672	1,761	4,165	-2,404
OP 30 Case types		62	17.9	8.6	9.3	$279,180	$59,333	$216,847	$105,148	$111,699	$96,883	$14,816

* ALOS = average length of stay. LOS = length of stay.
See Appendix 2–A for key to abbreviations.

Table 11–8 Financial Statement by DRG Category

DRG Number	Description	Total Charges	Total Deductions	Net Revenue	Variable Cost	Gross Margin	Total Margin Percent	Fixed Cost	Net Income	Income Percentage
0001	Craniotomy Age 17 No Trau	$14,115	$3,317	$10,798	$4,709	$6,089	43.1	$4,192	$1,897	13.4
0002	Craniotomy Age 17 W/Trau	1,170	435	735	302	433	37.0	220	213	18.2
0004	Spinal Procedures	5,553	–251	5,804	2,278	3,526	63.4	1,596	1,930	34.7
0005	Extracranial Vasc Procedu	14,814	2,310	12,504	5,641	6,863	46.3	4,898	1,965	13.2
0006	Carpal Tunnel Release	12,488	1,991	10,497	4,441	6,056	48.4	4,649	1,407	11.2
0007	Periph + Cranial Nerv/Syst	2,586	–1,900	4,486	586	3,900	150.8	424	3,476	134.4
0008	Periph + Cranial Nerv/Syst	6,742	605	6,137	2,577	3,560	52.8	2,806	754	11.1
0010	Nervous Syst Neoplasms Ag	36,194	5,602	30,592	13,594	16,998	46.9	13,625	3,373	9.3
0011	Nervous Syst Neoplasms Ag	9,075	2,869	6,206	3,058	3,148	34.6	2,885	263	2.8
0012	Degenerative Nerv/Syst Di	49,084	11,628	37,456	18,392	19,064	38.8	18,500	564	1.1
0013	Multiple Sclerosis and Cere	4,249	532	3,717	1,448	2,269	53.4	1,417	852	20.0
0014	Spec Cerebrovascular Dis	129,884	37,434	92,450	48,146	44,304	34.1	45,014	–710	–.5
0015	Transient Ischemic Attack	39,989	10,813	29,176	13,768	15,408	38.5	14,098	1,310	3.2
0016	Nonspec Cerebrovascular D	7,272	1,713	5,559	2,855	2,704	37.1	2,496	208	2.8
0017	Nonspec Cerebrovascular D	544	11	533	147	386	70.9	223	163	29.9
0018	Cranial plus Periph Nerve Diso	12,807	895	11,912	4,305	7,607	59.3	4,680	2,927	22.8
0019	Cranial plus Periph Nerve Diso	4,083	–160	4,243	1,311	2,932	71.8	1,535	1,397	34.2
0020	Nerv/Syst Infect No Viral	8,246	619	7,627	2,405	5,222	63.3	2,519	2,703	32.7
0021	Viral Meningitis	3,443	1,334	2,109	1,180	929	26.9	971	–42	–1.2
0022	Hyperten Encephalopathi	589	147	442	194	248	42.1	135	113	19.1

See Appendix 2–A for key to abbreviations.

Table 11–9 Format for Defining Variable Cost for DRG 104 (Cardiac Valve Procedures with Cardiac Catheter)

Department	Average Charges	Ratio of Direct Costs to Charges	Estimated Costs	Estimated Variable Costs (As Percent of Total Estimated Costs)	Estimated Variable Costs
General nursing	$1,240	.71	$ 880	70	$ 616
Special care unit	1,810	.68	1,231	70	862
Central supply	180	.28	50	75	38
Laboratory	270	.47	127	10	13
EKG	50	.37	19	20	4
EEG	60	.38	23	20	5
Nuclear medicine	190	.37	70	30	21
Diagnostic radiology	95	.38	36	25	9
Operating room	650	.47	306	65	199
Emergency department	105	.49	51	40	21
Transfusion	405	.63	255	70	179
Pharmacy	320	.28	90	75	67
Anesthesiology	180	.44	79	30	24
Respiratory therapy	295	.35	103	25	26
Physical therapy	85	.61	52	25	13
Clinic	110	.53	58	30	17
Totals	$6,045		$3,430		$2,114

SOLUTIONS AND ANSWERS

1. Hopefully, the STP for DRG 373 separates the costs into variable and fixed elements. If the variable cost is less than $2,000, your hospital may earn some marginal profit from the additional business. However, the HMO physicians should closely examine the STP. There may be some patient-management differences, especially regarding length of stay, that could result in more or less cost. An agreement on the STP with the HMO physicians should be negotiated.

2. Most of the income generated by Dr. Jones is in areas where the LOS is significantly above the normal level. For example, DRGs 468, 321, and 120 accounted for 85 percent of the total income that she generated for the hospital. In each of these three DRG categories, her LOS was well above normal. Because these cases were profitable, they must not have been billed to Medicare. If it is likely that some of your major payers may shift to a prospective case payment basis, you may not want to encourage Dr. Jones to increase her practice. The data in her financial report indicate a relatively high LOS in almost all areas.

3. DRG 7 has a minus $1,900 deduction. This means that payment received for treating this DRG category exceeded charges by $1,900. This probably reflects payment by Medicare in excess of charges. This situation may change if other hospitals have a similar experience because Medicare may change its payment. Presently, however, DRG 7 is a profitable product for the hospital (134.4 percent).

4. The deductible provision provides one reason why DRG 14 lost money. Approximately 29 percent of the DRG charges were written off. You may want to pay special attention to the firm's STP for this case type. Perhaps the firm's LOS or ancillary services are excessive.

5. The first potential weakness in the cost accountant's method is the use of a cost-to-charge ratio. There is no guarantee that charges for departmental services always will be related to costs. The method also may miss a large block of indirect departmental costs that may be variable. Finally, the method simply does not relate well to the two-stage definition of standard costs involving SCPs and STPs, as discussed in this chapter. In fairness, it must be noted that the cost accountant's method would cost significantly less than other methods. And it is not clear whether the improved accuracy that might result from some other, more sophisticated, system would be worth the extra cost.

12

The Management Control Process

Twenty years ago, the word "budgeting" could not have been found in the vocabularies of many health care executives. Today, this is no longer true. Most hospitals and other health care firms now develop and use budgets as an integral part of their overall management control process.

To a large extent, the attention health care providers pay to budgeting is attributable to changes in the environment. In ten years, the health care industry has experienced a dramatic shift in its revenue function from cost-related to fixed prices on either a procedure, case, or covered-life basis. Firms that sell products or services in markets where prices are fixed must control their costs. Budgeting is, of course, a logical way for any business organization to control its costs.

External market forces thus certainly have stimulated the development of budgets in the health care industry; but most likely, such budgets would have been developed in any case. Hospitals and health care firms have grown larger and more complex, in both organization and finances. And budgeting is imperative in organizations in which management authority is delegated to many individuals.

ESSENTIAL ELEMENTS

For our purposes, a budget is defined as a quantitative expression of a plan of action. It is an integral part of the overall management control process of an organization.

Anthony and Young (*Management Control in Nonprofit Organizations* [Meowed, Ill.: Richard D. Irwin, 1988], 16–33) discuss management control in great detail. They define it as a process by which managers ensure that resources are obtained and used effectively and efficiently while accomplishing an organization's objectives (p. 16).

Efficiency and Effectiveness

In the previous definition, special emphasis is placed on attaining efficiency and effectiveness. In short, they determine the success or failure of management control.

These two terms have precise meanings. Often, people talk about the relative efficiency and effectiveness of their operations as if efficiency and effectiveness were identical, or at least highly correlated. They are not identical, nor are they necessarily correlated. An operation may be effective without being efficient, and vice versa. A well-managed operation ideally should be both effective and efficient. Efficiency is easier to measure and its meaning is fairly well understood; efficiency is simply a relationship between outputs and inputs. For example, a cost per patient day of $1,100 is a measure of efficiency; it tells how many resources, or inputs, were used to provide one day of care, the measure of output.

Managers and other persons wishing to assess performance in the health care industry are increasing their use of efficiency measures. In most situations, efficiency is measured by comparison with some standard. Several basic considerations should be understood if efficiency measures are to be used intelligently. First, output measures may not always be comparable. For example, comparing the costs per patient day of care in a fifty-bed rural hospital with those in a 1,000-bed teaching hospital is not likely to be meaningful. A day of care in a teaching hospital typically entails more service. Second, cost measures may not be comparable or useful for the specific decision being considered. For example, two operations may be identical, but one may be in a newer facility and thus would have a higher depreciation charge; or the two operations may account for costs differently. One hospital may use an accelerated depreciation method, such as the sum of the year's digits, whereas the other may use straight-line depreciation. Third, the cost concepts used may not be relevant to the decision being considered. For example, a certificate-of-need review to decide which of two hospitals should be permitted to develop a cardiac catheterization lab obviously will consider cost. However, comparing the full costs of a procedure in each institution and selecting the least expensive one could produce bad results: for this specific decision, the full-cost concept is wrong. Incremental or variable cost is the relevant cost concept in this case. The focus of interest is on what the future additional cost would be, not what the historical average cost was.

Effectiveness is concerned with the relationship between an organization's outputs and its objectives or goals. A health care firm's typical goals might include solvency, high quality of care, low cost of patient care, institutional harmony, and growth. Measuring effectiveness is more difficult than measuring efficiency for at least two reasons. First, defining the relationship between outputs and some goals may be difficult because many firms' goals or objectives are not likely to be quantified. For example, exactly how does an alcoholism program contribute to quality of care? Still, objectives and goals usually can be stated more precisely in quantitative terms. In fact, they should be quantified to the greatest extent possible. In the alcoholism program example, quality scales, such as frequency of repeat visits or new patients treated, might be developed. Second, the output usually must be related to more than one organization goal or objective. For example, both solvency and reasonable cost are legitimate objectives for a hospital. Yet, continuing a home health operation might affect solvency negatively and simultaneously reduce patient-treatment costs. How should decision makers weigh these two criteria to determine an overall measure of effectiveness?

Control Unit

In most health care facilities, management controls various responsibility centers. These centers are generally referred to as departments. Figure 12–1 presents an organizational chart of a hospital and its departments.

Usually, the departments perform special functions that contribute to overall organization goals, directly or indirectly. They receive resources or inputs and produce services or outputs. Figure 12–2 illustrates this relationship.

Responsibility centers are the focus of management control efforts. Emphasis is placed on the effectiveness of their operations. Measurement problems occur when the responsibility structure is not identical to the program structure. Decision makers are frequently interested in a program's total cost. Yet, in the case of a burn-care program, for example, it is unlikely that all the resources used in the program will be

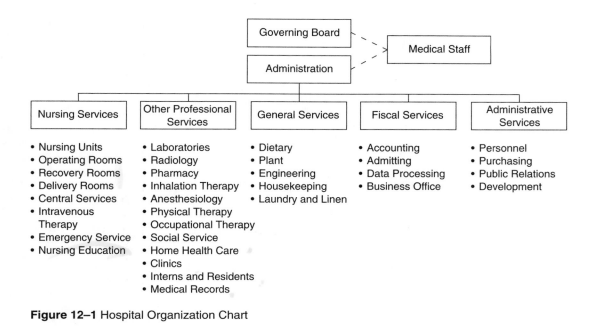

Figure 12–1 Hospital Organization Chart

assigned to it directly; the costs of medical support services (such as physical therapy, laboratory, and radiology services, as well as other general and administrative services) will not likely be contained in the burn-care unit. Program lines typically run across responsibility center or departmental lines. This necessitates cost allocations for decisions that require program cost information. It should be remembered that when cost allocations are involved, the accuracy of the information as well as its comparability may be suspect. For example, one may be interested in the specific costs of a burn-care program, but then find that those costs must be allocated from various departments or responsibility centers, such as laboratory, radiology, and housekeeping departments.

Responsibility centers vary greatly, depending on the controlling organization. For a regulatory agency, the responsibility center might be an entire health care firm; for a health care firm manager, it may be an individual department; for a department manager, it may be a unit within the department. The only requirement is that a designated person be in charge of the identified responsibility center.

Phases of Management Control

Figure 12–3 illustrates the relationship of various phases of the management control process to each other and to the planning process. Management control relies on the existence of goals and objectives; without them, the structure and evaluation of the management control process is incomplete. Poor or no planning usually limits the value of management control. Effectiveness becomes impossible to assess without

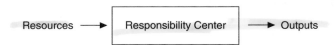

Figure 12–2 Responsibility Center Production Relationship

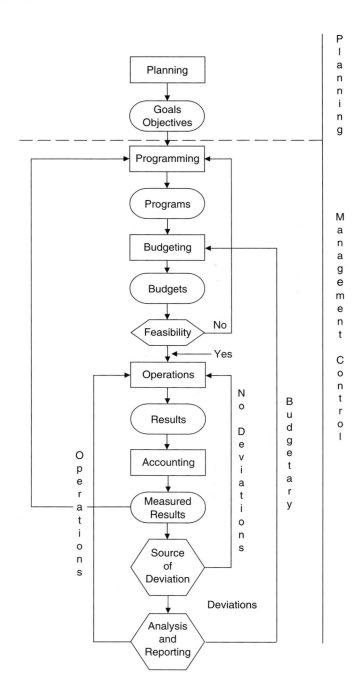

Figure 12–3 The Management Control Process

stated goals and objectives; in such cases, one can focus only on measuring and attaining efficiency. The organization can assess only whether it has produced outputs efficiently; it cannot evaluate the desirability of those outputs.

For the purposes of this discussion, we shall be concerned with the four phases of management control that Anthony and Young have identified in their work on management control (see previous citation):

1. programming,
2. budgeting,
3. accounting, and
4. analysis and reporting.

Programming

Programming is the phase of management control that determines the nature and size of programs an organization will provide to accomplish its stated goals and objectives. It is the first phase of the management control process and interrelates with planning. In some cases, the boundary dividing the two activities may in fact be difficult to establish. Programming usually lasts three to five years—longer than budgeting, but shorter than planning.

Programming decisions deal with new and existing programs. The methodology for programming is different in these two areas. Programming decisions for new programs involve capital investment or capital budget decision making (this process is examined more extensively in Chapter 15). The method for making programming decisions for existing programs is often referred to as zero-base review, or zero-base budgeting (this method is discussed later in this chapter).

To illustrate the programming process, assume that a stated objective of a hospital organization is to develop and implement an ambulatory care program in the community. The decision makers in the programming phase of management control would take this stated objective and evaluate alternative programs to accomplish it, such as a surgicenter, an outpatient clinic, or a mobile health-screening unit. After this analysis, a decision might be made to construct a ten-room surgicenter on a lot adjacent to the hospital. This would be a program decision.

Budgeting

Budgeting is the management control phase of primary interest. It was defined earlier as a quantitative expression of a plan of action. Budgets are usually stated in monetary terms and cover a period of one year.

The budgetary phase of management control follows the determination of programs in the programming phase. In many cases, no real review of existing programs is undertaken; the budgeting phase then may be based on a prior year's budget or on the actual results of existing programs. Proponents of zero-base budgeting have identified this practice as a major shortcoming.

The budgeting phase primarily translates program decisions into terms that are meaningful for responsibility centers. The decision to construct a ten-room surgicenter will affect the revenues and costs of other responsibility centers, such as the laboratory, radiology, and anesthesiology departments and the business office. The effects of program decisions thus must be carefully and accurately reflected in the budgets of each of the relevant responsibility centers.

Budgeting also may change programs. A more careful and accurate estimation of revenues and costs may prompt one to re-evaluate prior programming decisions as financially unfeasible. For example, the proposed ten-room surgicenter may be shown, through budget analysis, to produce a significant operating loss. If the hospital cannot or will not subsidize this loss from other sources, the programming decision must be changed. The size of the surgicenter may be reduced from ten rooms to five to make the operation "break even."

Accounting

Accounting is the third phase of the management control process. Once the decision about which programs to implement has been made and budgets have been developed for them along responsibility center lines, the operations phase begins. The accounting department accumulates and records information on both outputs and inputs during the operating phase.

It is important to note that cost information is provided along both program and responsibility center lines. Responsibility center cost information is used in the reporting and analysis phase to determine the degree of compliance with budget projections. Programmatic cost information is used to assess the desirability of continuing a given program at its present size and scope in the programming phase of management control.

Analysis and Reporting

The last phase of management control is analysis and reporting. In this phase, differences between actual costs and budgeted costs are analyzed to determine the probable cause of the deviations and are then reported to the individuals who can take corrective action. The method used in this phase is often referred to as variance analysis, which is discussed in greater detail in Chapter 13. Those doing the analysis and reporting rely heavily on the information provided from the accounting phase to break down the reported deviations into categories that suggest causes.

In general, there are three primary causes for differences between budgeted and actual costs:

1. Prices paid for inputs were different from budgeted prices.
2. Output level was higher or lower than budgeted.
3. Actual quantities of inputs used were different from budgeted levels.

Within each of these causal areas, the problem may arise from either budgeting or operations. A budgetary problem is usually not controllable; no operating action can be taken to correct the situation. For example, the surgicenter may have budgeted for ten registered nurses (RNs) at $2,500 each per month. However, if there was no way to employ ten RNs at an average wage

less than $2,600 per month, the budget would have to be adjusted to reflect the change in expectations. Alternatively, the problem may arise from operations and be controllable. Perhaps the nurses of the surgicenter are more experienced and better trained than expected. If this is true, and the mix of RNs originally budgeted is still regarded as appropriate, some action should be taken to change the actual mix over time.

THE BUDGETING PROCESS

Elements and Participants

Budgeting is regarded by many as the primary tool that health-care managers can use to control costs in their organizations. The objectives of budgetary programs, as defined by the American Hospital Association, are fourfold:

1. to provide a written expression, in quantitative terms, of the policies and plans of the hospital;
2. to provide a basis for the evaluation of financial performance in accordance with the plans;
3. to provide a useful tool for the control of costs; and
4. to create cost awareness throughout the organization.

The budgetary process encompasses a number of interrelated but separate budgets. Figure 12–4 provides a schematic representation of the budgetary process and the relationships between specific types of budgets.

The individuals and roles involved in the budgetary process may vary. In general, the following individuals or parties may be involved:

- governing board,
- chief executive officer (CEO),
- controller,
- responsibility center managers, and
- budgetary committee.

The governing board's involvement in the budgetary process is usually indirect. The board

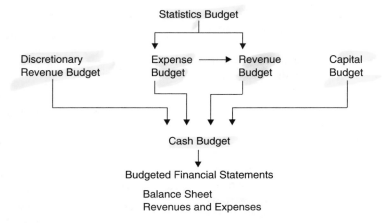

Figure 12–4 Integration of the Budgetary Process

provides the goals, objectives, and approved programs that are used as the basis for budgetary development. In many cases, it formally approves the finalized budget, especially the cash budget and budgeted financial statements; these are critical when assessing financial condition, which is a primary responsibility of the board.

The CEO or administrator of the health care facility has overall responsibility for budgetary development. The budget is the administrator's tool in the overall program of management by exception, which enables the CEO to focus only on those areas where problems exist.

Controllers often serve as budget directors. Their primary function is facilitation: they are responsible for providing relevant data on costs and outputs and for providing budgetary forms that may be used in budget development. They are not responsible for either making or enforcing the budget.

Responsibility centers are the focal points of control. Managers of departments should be actively involved in developing budgets for their assigned areas of responsibility and are responsible for meeting the budgets developed for their areas.

Many large health care firms use a special budgetary committee to aid in budget develop-

ment and approval. Typically, this committee is composed of several department managers, headed by the controller. A committee structure such as this can help legitimize budgetary decisions that might appear arbitrary and capricious if made unilaterally by management.

Statistics Budget

Development of the statistics budget is the first step in budgeting. It provides the basis for subsequent development of the revenue and expense budgets. Together, these three budgets are sometimes referred to as the operating budget.

The objective of the statistics budget is to provide measures of workload or activity in each department or responsibility center for the next budget period. The following three issues are involved in this task:

1. output expectations,
2. responsibility for estimation, and
3. estimation methodology.

Output Expectation

Sales forecasts in many businesses reflect management's output expectations—how much of the business' product can be sold, given certain promotional efforts. There is some question about the extent to which health care firms can determine their volume of service, at least within the usual budgetary period. Although, in the long run, through the development or discontinuation of certain programs, volume may be changed, most health care firms implicitly assume while developing their statistics budget that they cannot affect their overall volume during the next budgetary period. Instead, they assume that they will provide services to meet their actual demand. This leads to a reliance on past-period service levels to forecast demand. Assuming that demand patterns in the budget period will be similar to prior periods can, however, be a costly mistake. First, foreseeable but uncontrollable forces may dramatically alter service patterns. For example, retirement of key medical staff with no replacement could drastically reduce admissions. Second, the health care facility may in fact control service levels in the short run and do so in a way that reduces costs. For example, a hospital may decide to develop clinical pathways in conjunction with its physicians, thus reducing total volume and total cost.

Responsibility for Estimation

The second issue regarding the statistics budget is the assignment of responsibility for developing projected output or workload indicators. Should department managers provide this information themselves, or should top management provide it to them? In some situations, department managers may tend to overstate demand. Overstatement of demand implies a greater need for resources within their own area and creates potential budgetary slack if anticipated volumes are not realized. The result of the information coming from top management may be the converse: understatement of demand may result in a lower total cost budget that might not provide adequate resources to meet actual output levels. Negotiation thus often becomes necessary when determining demand for budgetary purposes.

Estimation Methodology

The last area of statistics budget development concerns problems of estimation. In most health care facilities, department activity depends on a limited number of key indicators, such as patient days, outpatient visits, or covered lives.

Prior values for these indicators can be related to departmental volume through statistical analysis. The major problem becomes one of accurately forecasting values for the indicators.

The use of seasonal, weekly, and daily variations in volume poses an important estimation problem. Too often, yearly volume is assumed to be divided equally between the monthly periods throughout the year, even when that is clearly not the case. Recognition of seasonal, weekly, and daily patterns of variation in volume can in fact create significant opportunities for cost reduction, especially in labor staffing.

Finally, output at the departmental level is often multiple in nature. In fact, a department normally produces more than one type of output; for example, a laboratory may provide literally thousands of different tests. In such situations, a weighted unit of service is needed, such as the relative value units (RVUs) used in areas such as laboratory and radiology. Using weighted unit measures in the statistics budget is especially important when the mix of services is expected to change. Assume that a hospital is rapidly increasing its volume in outpatient clinics. This expansion in volume will increase activity in many other departments, including the pharmacy department. If, in such a situation, the filling of an outpatient prescription requires significantly more effort than the filling of an inpatient prescription, the use of an unweighted activity measure for prescriptions could provide misleading information for budgetary control purposes. Much less labor might be budgeted than is actually needed.

Expense Budget

With estimates of activity for individual departments developed in the statistics budget, department managers can proceed to develop expense budgets for their areas of responsibility. Expense budgeting is the area of budgeting "where the rubber meets the road." Management cost control efforts are finally reflected in hard numbers that the departments must live with—in most cases, for the budget period. Major categories of expense budgets at the departmental level include payroll, supplies, and other. In some situations, a budget for allocated costs from indirect departments also may be included, although departmental managers usually do not do this.

In our discussion of expense budgeting, we shall focus on the following four issues of budgeting that are of general interest:

1. length of the budget period,
2. flexible or forecast budgets,
3. standards for price and quantity, and
4. allocation of indirect costs.

Length of the Budget Period

Generally speaking, there are two alternative budget periods that may be used—fixed and rolling. Of the two, a fixed budget period is much more frequently used in the health care industry. A fixed budget covers some defined time from a given budget date, usually one year. This contrasts with a rolling budget, in which the budget is periodically extended on a frequent basis, usually a month or a three-month quarter. For example, in a rolling budget period with a monthly update, the entity always would have a budget that projected at least eleven more months. The same is not true in a fixed budget, in which, at fiscal year end, there may be only one week or one month remaining.

A rolling budget has many advantages, but it requires more time and effort and therefore more cost. Among its major advantages are the following:

• more realistic forecasts, which should improve management planning and control;
• equalization of the workload of budget development during the entire year; and

• improved familiarity and understanding of budgets by department managers.

Flexible or Forecast Budgets

The use of a flexible budget versus a forecast budget has been discussed heavily by health care financial people. Presently, few health care firms use a formal system of flexible budgeting. However, flexible budgeting is a more sophisticated method of budgeting than typical forecast budgeting and is being adopted by more and more health care firms as they become experienced in the budgetary process.

A flexible budget adjusts targeted levels of costs for changes in volume. For example, the budget for a nursing unit operating at 95-percent occupancy would be different from the budget for that same unit operating at an 80-percent occupancy. A forecast budget, in contrast, would make no formal differentiation in the allowed budget between these two levels.

The difference between a forecast and a flexible budget is illustrated by the historical data and projected use levels for the laboratory presented in Table 12–1. The forecast levels of volume in RVUs for 1999 are identical to the actual volumes of 1998, except that a 10-percent growth factor is assumed. The department manager using this statistics budget must develop a budget for hours worked in 1999. A common approach to this task is to assume that past work experience indicates future requirements. In this case, the average value for hours of work required per RVU in 1998 was .5061. A common method for developing a forecast budget is to multiply this value of .5061 by the estimated total workload for the budget period, which is expected to be 72,160, and spread the total product equally over each of the twelve months. This is the forecast budget depicted in Table 12-2.

A major difference between a flexible budget and a forecast budget is that a flexible budget must recognize and incorporate underlying cost behavioral patterns. In this laboratory example, hours worked might be written as a function of RVUs as follows:

Table 12-1 Laboratory Productivity Data

| | 1998 Actual | | 1999 |
	Hours Worked	RVUs	Expected RVUs
January	2,825	5,700	6,270
February	2,700	5,200	5,720
March	2,900	6,000	6,600
April	2,875	5,900	6,490
May	2,825	5,700	6,270
June	2,700	5,200	5,720
July	2,750	5,400	5,940
August	2,625	4,900	5,390
September	2,725	5,300	5,830
October	2,750	5,400	5,940
November	2,750	5,400	5,940
December	2,775	5,500	6,050
Total	33,200	65,600	72,160

Note: 1998 average hours/RVU = $\dfrac{33,200}{65,600}$ = .5061.

Hours worked = (1,400 hours per month) + (.25 × RVUs)

Application of this formula to the budgeted RVUs expected in 1999 yields the flexible budget presented in Table 12–2.

Two points should be made before concluding our discussion of flexible budgeting versus forecast budgeting. First, a flexible budget may be represented as a forecast budget for planning purposes. For example, in the laboratory problem of Table 12–2, the flexible budget would provide an estimated hours-worked requirement of 34,837 hours for 1999. However, in an actual control period evaluation, the flexible budget formula would be used. To illustrate, assume that the actual RVUs provided in January 1999 amounted to 6,500 instead of the forecasted 6,270. Budgeted hours in the flexible budget then would not total 2,967 but 3,025:

1,400 + (.25 × 6,500) = 3,025

This value would be compared with the actual hours worked, not the initially forecasted 2,967.

Second, dramatic differences in approved costs can result from the two methods. Recognizing the underlying cost behavioral patterns can change the estimated resource requirements approved in the budgetary process. In our laboratory example in Table 12–2, the forecast budget calls for 36,516 hours versus the flexible budget hours requirement of 34,837. The difference results from the method used to estimate hours worked. In a forecast budget method, the prior average hours per RVU relationship is used. In most situations, average hours or average cost should be greater than variable hours or variable cost. In departments with expanding volume, the estimated requirements for resources could be overstated. The converse may be true in departments with declining volume. In many cases, use of forecast budgeting methods is based on the incorporation of prior average cost relationships. This error is not made with flexible budgeting methods because their use depends on explicit incorporation of cost behavioral patterns that distinctly recognize variable and fixed costs.

Table 12-2 Alternative Hours-Worked Budget for Laboratory

	Forecast Budget*	Flexible Budget†
January	3,043	2,967
February	3,043	2,830
March	3,043	3,050
April	3,043	3,022
May	3,043	2,967
June	3,043	2,830
July	3,043	2,885
August	3,043	2,747
September	3,043	2,857
October	3,043	2,885
November	3,043	2,885
December	3,043	2,912
Total	36,516	34,837

*$(.5061 \times 72,160)/12 = 3,043.35$.

†January value $= 1,400 + (.25 \times 6,270)$.

A flexible budget makes sense when there are expenses that could vary with small changes in volume. Expense categories such as supplies are usually variable in nature. Labor costs may or may not be variable. The use of part-time labor, overtime, and outside pools all tend to make labor costs variable. In general, greater variability or uncertainty in volume forecasts should lead management to adopt more flexible staffing policies.

Standards for Price and Quantity

Earlier, three factors were identified that can create differences between budgeted and actual costs: volume, prices, and usage or efficiency. The use of flexible budgeting is an attempt to improve the recognition of deviations caused by changes in volume. The use of standards for prices and wage rates, coupled with standards for physical quantities, is an attempt to improve the recognition of deviations from budgets that result from prices and usage.

For example, assume that the flexible budget-hours requirement for the laboratory example is still hours worked $= 1,400 + (.25 \times \text{RVUs})$. As-

sume further that the budgeted wage rate is $15 per hour and the actual RVUs for January 1999 amounted to 6,500. Total payroll cost for hours worked (excluding vacations and sick pay) is assumed to be $49,600. If the actual hours worked amounted to 3,100, the variance analysis report presented in Table 12–3 would be applicable to the laboratory department.

The total unfavorable variance of $4,225 results from a $3,100 unfavorable price variance and a $1,125 unfavorable efficiency variance. Splitting the variance in this manner helps management quickly identify possible causes. For example, the $3,100 price variance may be due to a negotiated wage increase of $1 per hour. If this is the case, the department manager is clearly not responsible for the variance. If, however, the difference is due to an excessive use of overtime personnel or a more costly mix of labor, then the manager may be held responsible for the difference and should attempt to prevent the problem from occurring again. The unfavorable efficiency variance of $1,125 reflects excessive use of labor during the month in the amount of seventy-five hours. An explanation

Table 12–3 Standard Cost Variance Analysis for Labor Costs, Laboratory, January 1994

1. Price variance = (Actual hours worked) × (Actual wage rate)
   − (Actual hours worked) × (Budgeted wage rate)
   = (3,100 × $16.00) − (3,100 × $15.00)
   = $3,100 [Unfavorable]

2. Efficiency variance = (Actual hours worked) × (Budgeted wage rate)
   − (Budgeted hours worked) × (Budgeted wage rate)
   = (3,100 × $15.00) − (3,025 × $15.00)
   = $1,125 [Unfavorable]

3. Total variance = $3,100 + $1,125 = $4,225 [Unfavorable]

Note: Actual wage rate = $49,600/3,100 = $16.00.
Budgeted wage rate = $15.00.
Actual hours worked = 3,100.
Budgeted hours worked = (1,400) + (.25 × 6,500) = 3,025.

for this difference should be sought and steps taken to prevent its recurrence.

Standard costing techniques have been used in industry for many years as an integral part of management control. Although it is true that input and output relationships may not be as objective in the health care industry as they are in general industry, this does not imply that standard costing cannot be used. In fact, there are many areas of activity within a health care facility that have fairly precise input-output relationships—housekeeping, laundry and linen, laboratory, radiology, and many others. Standard costing can prove to be a valuable tool for cost control in the health care industry, if properly applied (this topic is explored in greater detail in Chapter 13).

Allocation of Indirect Costs

There probably has been more internal strife in organizations over the allocation of indirect costs than over any other single budgetary issue. A comment often heard is, "Why was I charged $3,000 for housekeeping services last month when my department didn't use anywhere near that level of service?"

A strong case can in fact be made for not allocating indirect costs in budget variance reports.

In most normal situations, the receiving department has little or no control over the costs of the servicing department. Allocation may thus raise questions that should not be raised. Although it is true that indirect costs need to be allocated for some decision-making purposes, such as pricing, they are generally not needed for evaluating individual responsibility center management.

However, an equally strong argument can be made for including indirect costs in the budgets of benefiting departments. They are legitimate costs of the total operation, and department managers should be aware of them. If department managers' decisions can influence costs in indirect areas, these managers should be held accountable for those costs. For example, maintenance, housekeeping, and other indirect costs can be influenced by the decisions of benefiting departments. Ideally, a charge for these indirect services should be established and levied against the using departments, based on their use. Labeling the cost of indirect areas as totally uncontrollable can stimulate excessive and unnecessary use of indirect services and thus have a negative impact on the total cost control program in an organization.

Revenue Budget

The revenue budget can be set effectively only after the expense budget and the statistics budget have been developed. Revenues must be set at levels that cover all associated expenses plus provide a return on invested capital. This is a fundamental rule of finance and is equally valid for both voluntary, not-for-profit firms and investor-owned firms. Moreover, some of the total revenue actually realized by a health care facility is directly determined by expenses because of the presence of cost-reimbursement formulas.

Rate Setting

In this discussion of the revenue budget, we shall focus on only one aspect of revenue budget development—pricing or rate setting. Specifically, we shall illustrate the rate-setting model discussed in Chapter 10 through an additional example.

Figure 12–5 illustrates the rate-setting model. Sources of information to define the variables of the model are identified. However, the following three parameters have no identified source:

1. desired profit,

2. proportion of charge-paying patients, and
3. proportion of charge-paying patient revenue not collected.

In most situations, separate figures for the percentage of write-offs on charge-paying patients and the percentage of charge-paying patients are not available on a departmental basis. Sometimes the best information available may be the percentage of bad-debt write-offs on total revenue for the institution as a whole. Using the example data for Department 1 in Table 12–4, a 1-percent write-off on 20 percent of the patients who paid charges in the department implies that 5 percent of the charge-paying patient revenue in that department is written off. The corresponding figure for department 2 is 50 percent. Using these data, and substituting the total or aggregate values for the percentage write-offs on charge-paying patients and the percentage of charge-paying patients, the following rates would be established:

Department 1 price =

$$\frac{\dfrac{\$10,000}{100} + \dfrac{\$500}{100 \times .4}}{1 - .3875} = \$183.67$$

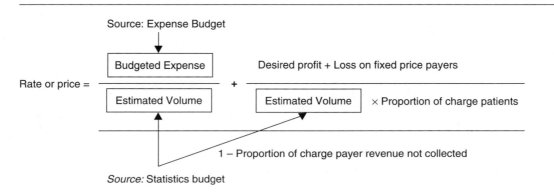

Source: Expense Budget

$$\text{Rate or price} = \frac{\text{Budgeted Expense}}{\text{Estimated Volume}} + \frac{\text{Desired profit} + \text{Loss on fixed price payers}}{\text{Estimated Volume} \times \text{Proportion of charge patients}}$$

1 – Proportion of charge payer revenue not collected

Source: Statistics budget

Note: The two source items indicate where values for budgeted expense and estimated volume may be found.

Figure 12–5 Rate Setting in the Revenue Budget

Table 12–4 Rate Setting Example Data

	Department 1	Department 2	Total
Less on fixed price payers	$ 0	$ 0	$ 0
Desired profit	$ 500	$ 500	$ 1,000
Budgeted expense	$10,000	$10,000	$20,000
Estimated volume	100	100	—
Percentage bad debt	1 percent	30 percent	15.5 percent
Percentage charge-paying patients	20 percent	60 percent	40 percent
Percentage bad debt on charge-paying patients	5 percent	50 percent	38.75 percent

Department 2 price =

$$\frac{\dfrac{\$10,000}{100} + \dfrac{\$500}{100 \times .4}}{1 - .3875} = \$183.67$$

Proper reflection of the departmental values, however, would produce the following rates:

Department 1 price =

$$\frac{\dfrac{\$10,000}{100} + \dfrac{\$500}{100 \times .2}}{1 - .05} = \$131.58$$

Department 2 price =

$$\frac{\dfrac{\$10,000}{100} + \dfrac{\$500}{100 \times .6}}{1 - .50} = \$216.67$$

In the former case, the use of aggregate or average values produces an inequitable pricing structure. The price for Department 1 was initially overstated, whereas the price for Department 2 was initially understated. If equity in rate setting is an objective, reliance on average values can prevent the development of an equitable rate structure along departmental lines. In many cases, the errors may be significant.

Desired Profit Levels

Determining a desired level of profit is not easy. In many cases, it is a subjective process, made to appear objective through the application of a quantitative profit requirement. For example, desired profit may be arbitrarily set at some percentage of budgeted expenses, such as 10 percent above expenses, or as a certain percentage of total investment. However, desired levels of profit can, in general, be stated as the difference between financial requirements and expenses as follows:

> Desired profit =
> Budgeted financial requirements –
> Budgeted expenses

Budgeted financial requirements are cash requirements that an entity must meet during the budget period. Four elements usually constitute total budgeted financial requirements:

1. budgeted expenses, excluding depreciation,
2. requirements for debt principal payment,
3. requirements for increases in working capital, and
4. requirements for capital expenditures not financed with debt.

Budgeted expenses at the departmental level should include both direct and indirect (or allocated) expenses. Depreciation charges are excluded because depreciation is a noncash requirement expense.

Debt principal payments include only the principal portion of debt service due. In some cases, additional reserve requirements may be established, which may require additional funding. Interest expense is already included in budgeted expenses and should not be included in debt principal payments.

Working capital requirements were discussed earlier. The maintenance of necessary levels of inventory, accounts receivable, and precautionary cash balances requires an investment. Changes in the total level of this investment must be funded from cash, additional indebtedness, or a combination of the two. Planned financing of increases in working capital is a legitimate financial requirement.

Capital expenditure requirements may be of two types. First, actual capital expenditures may be made for approved projects. Those projects not financed with indebtedness require a cash investment. Second, prudent fiscal management requires that funds be set aside and invested to meet reasonable requirements for future capital expenditures. This amount should be related to the replacement cost depreciation of existing fixed assets.

Any loss incurred on fixed-price payers, such as Medicare, must be added to the desired profit target. The amount of the loss would represent the projected difference between allocated costs or expenses and net revenue received from fixed-price payers. If revenues from fixed price payers exceed costs, the difference would be subtracted from the profit target. For example, if a firm received $5,000,000 in revenue from Medicare and incurred $4,800,000 in costs to provide care to Medicare patients, the difference of $200,000 would be subtracted from the desired profit target. The effect would be lower required rates or prices. (Chapter 10 provides more detail on price setting.)

A logical question is, "How is the desired profit requirement allocated to individual de-

partments?" Usually, it is just assigned on the basis of some percentage of budgeted expenses. If a nursing home budgets $5 million in expenses and determines that $500,000 profit is required, each department might set its rates to recover 10 percent above its expenses. However, the importance of cost reimbursement and bad debts at the departmental level also should be considered.

Discretionary Revenue Budget and Capital Budget

Discretionary revenue may be important, especially for institutions with large investment portfolios. A good management control system will have a budget for expected return on investments. Variations from the expected level then would be investigated. In some cases, changes in investment management may be necessary.

Capital budgeting can give many health care managers a major control tool. It can significantly affect the level of cost. This is especially true when not only the initial capital costs associated with given capital expenditures are considered but also the associated operating costs for salaries and supplies. (The capital budgeting process is examined in detail in Chapter 15.)

The Cash Budget and Budgeted Financial Statements

The cash budget is management's best indicator of the organization's expected short-run solvency. It translates all of the previous budgets into a statement of cash inflows and outflows. The cash budget is usually broken down by periods, such as months or quarters, within the total budget period. An example of a cash budget is shown in Table 12–5.

Departmental expense budgets, departmental revenue budgets, a discretionary revenue budget, and a capital budget that do not provide a sufficient cash flow can necessitate major revisions. If the organization cannot or will not finance the deficits, the budgets must be changed to main-

Table 12–5 Cash Budget, Budget Year 1999

| | 1st Quarter | | | | | |
	January	February	March	2nd Quarter	3rd Quarter	4th Quarter
Receipts from operations	$300,000	$310,000	$320,000	$1,000,000	$1,100,000	$1,100,000
Disbursements from operations	280,000	280,000	300,000	940,000	1,000,000	1,000,000
Cash available from operations	$20,000	$30,000	$20,000	$60,000	$100,000	$100,000
Other receipts						
Increase in mortgage payable				500,000		
Sale of fixed assets		20,000				
Unrestricted Income— endowment			40,000	40,000	40,000	40,000
Total other receipts	0	$20,000	$40,000	$540,000	$140,000	$140,000
Other disbursements						
Mortgage payments			150,000		150,000	
Fixed-asset purchase				480,000		
Funded depreciation			30,000	130,000	30,000	30,000
Total other disbursements	0	0	180,000	610,000	180,000	30,000
Net cash gain (loss)	$20,000	$50,000	$(120,000)	$(10,000)	$(40,000)	$110,000
Beginning cash balance	100,000	120,000	170,000	50,000	40,000	0
Cumulative cash	$120,000	$170,000	$50,000	$40,000	$0	$110,000
Desired level of cash	100,000	100,000	100,000	100,000	100,000	100,000
Cash above minimum needs (financing needs)	$20,000	$70,000	$(50,000)	$(60,000)	$(100,000)	$10,000

tain the solvency of the organization. A poor cash budget could cause an increase in rates, a reduction in expenses, a reduction in capital expenditures, or many other changes. These changes and revisions must be made until the cash budget reflects a position of short-run solvency.

The two major financial statements that are developed on a budgetary basis are the balance sheet and the statement of revenue and expense. These two statements are indicators of both short- and long-run solvency; however, they are more important in assessing long-run solvency. Changing projections in either statement might cause changes in any of the other budgets.

In short, the budgeted financial statements and the cash budget test the adequacy of the entire budgetary process. Budgets that result in an unfavorable financial position, as reflected by the budgeted financial statements and the cash budget, must be adjusted. Solvency is a goal that most organizations cannot sacrifice. Cash budgeting is explored in greater detail in Chapter 18.

ZERO-BASE BUDGETING

Zero-base budgeting is a term that has gained much publicity. It has been touted as management's most effective cost-containment tool. It also has been described as the biggest hoax of the century. The truth lies somewhere in the middle.

Zero-base budgeting, or zero-base review, as some prefer to call it, is a way of looking at existing programs. It is part of programming, but it focuses on existing programs instead of new programs. Zero-base budgeting assumes that no existing program is entitled to automatic approval. Many individuals have identified automatic approval with existing budgetary systems that are based on prior-year expenditure levels.

Zero-base budgeting looks at the entire budget and determines the efficacy of the entire expenditure. It thus requires a tremendous effort and investment of time. It cannot be done well on an annual basis. This is why many refer to it as zero-base review instead of zero-base budgeting. Some have suggested that a zero-base review of a given activity would be appropriate every five years.

Zero-base budgeting is a process of periodically reevaluating all programs and their associated levels of expenditures. Management decides the frequency of this reevaluation and may vary it from every year to every five years.

Although most decision makers agree with the concept of zero-base budgeting, in practice it poses the following two significant questions:

1. What evaluation methodology should be used in zero-base budgeting?
2. Who should be involved in the actual decision-making process?

In each case, the answers are important to the success or failure of the zero-base budget program. Yet, there still is not complete agreement among experts regarding the answers.

Nearly everyone would agree that cost-benefit analysis should be the evaluation methodology of zero-base budgeting. There are two important issues involved in the application of cost-benefit analysis to zero-base budgeting programs: (1) Are the services that are presently provided being delivered in an efficient manner? (2) Are these services being delivered in an effective manner in terms of the organization's goals and objectives? A procedure for quantitatively answering these two questions involves the following seven sequential steps:

1. Define the outputs or services provided by the program or departmental area.
2. Determine the costs of these services or outputs.
3. Identify options for reducing the cost through changes in outputs or services.
4. Identify options for producing the services and outputs more efficiently.
5. Determine the cost savings associated with options identified in Steps 3 and 4.
6. Assess the risks, both qualitative and quantitative, associated with the identified options of Steps 3 and 4.
7. Select and implement those options with an acceptable cost/risk relationship.

BENCHMARKING AT THE DEPARTMENTAL LEVEL

One of the critical aspects to management control at the departmental or responsibility center level is access to relevant productivity standards. How much labor should be used to produce a certain level of output? In general, there are three sources of productivity standards:

- Internally developed historical standards,
- Engineered standards, and
- Comparative group standards.

Internally developed standards based upon historical performance is the easiest and least costly method of productivity standard development. It is also the most commonly used method. For example, a hospital laundry and linen department may have a historical average of twenty hours of labor per 1,000 pounds of laundry. That historical average could be used to budget labor hours for the coming year. The biggest disadvantage of using this method is that historical averages don't provide information about relative efficiency. Is twenty hours of labor per 1,000 pounds of laundry an efficient level of productivity or not?

Engineered standards can be developed with internal staff, or they can be developed with the help of outside consultants. The key aspect to this method is an exhaustive study of the work setting and the definition of normative standards of productivity. For example, a consultant might determine that only fourteen hours of labor is required per 1,000 pounds of laundry. Significant opportunities for cost reduction may result because of this engineered standard. The management problem of achieving this standard still remains, however, and there is no guarantee that the projected savings can be realized soon, if ever. Management must act on the information that it was given if it is to realize savings. The

primary disadvantage of engineered standards is cost. The use of specialized internal staff or outside consultants can be costly.

Comparative group productivity standards are available in most health care industry sectors. Sometimes associations that represent health care firms collect data and distribute them to members, or private firms also may provide comparative group standards from survey data they have collected. Table 12–6 provides some hospital departmental standards from the Center for Healthcare Industry Performance Studies in Columbus, Ohio. The data indicate that the national average for productivity in hospital laundry departments was 12.02 hours per 1,000 pounds.

Comparative group data are usually less expensive to obtain than engineered standards, but there are several drawbacks. First, is the productivity standard comparable across all departments in the group? To be comparable, both the measure of cost and output must be defined in the same manner by all reporting members. For

Table 12–6 Productivity and Cost Standards for Selected Hospital Departments

Department	Output Unit	Paid Hours per Output Unit	Direct Cost per Output Unit
Nursing			
Combined ICU and CCU	Patient days	22.3	$453.71
Combined medical and surgical	Patient days	9.3	150.93
Labor and delivery	Deliveries	26.8	649.01
Psychiatric	Patient days	11.5	199.64
Professional Services			
Operating room	Hours	8.7	$440.45
Radiology-diagnostic	Weighted procedures	1.6	39.17
Laboratory	Billable procedures	.3	8.41
Physical therapy	Patient time units	.6	12.76
General Services			
Laundry and linen	1,000 pounds	12.0	$350.00
Housekeeping	1,000 square feet	68.2	710.00
Food services	Meal equivalents	0.3	5.11

Source: Center For Healthcare Industry Performance Studies, FACT Report, 1995.

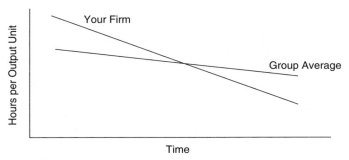

Figure 12–6 Closing the Performance Gap

example, is the number of pounds of laundry measured wet or dry? Does the measure of labor hours include vacation and sick time? Second, knowing there is a difference between a group average and your department's performance doesn't tell you why the difference exists. Our laundry may require twenty hours per 1,000 pounds, and the national average may be twelve hours, but how can we achieve that standard? Perhaps the equipment used is old and requires more labor costs. The difference does imply that something is wrong and that change is needed, but communication with other group members may be necessary to realize savings. Many of the comparative group reporting services provide mechanisms for interfirm communication to learn and adopt best practices. Ultimately, the objective is to achieve superior performance as Figure 12–6 illustrates.

SUMMARY

This chapter has focused on the process of management control that is used in organizations. Most management control processes involve the following four phases of activity: programming, budgeting, accounting, and analysis and reporting. Budgeting is an activity that many department managers view as the primary focus of management control because of its direct focus on resource allocation and emphasis on efficiency. Efficiency standards are primary inputs into the budgeting process and are often provided through comparative benchmarking data.

ASSIGNMENTS

1. Under what conditions is a flexible budget likely to be more effective than a forecast budget?
2. Can an organization be efficient but not effective? Discuss the circumstances in which this could be true.
3. The first step in the budgeting process is to develop the statistics budget. Why is this true?
4. Ann Walker, CPA, is the controller for your hospital. For a long time, Ms. Walker has been concerned about management control in the hospital, and she finally has developed a new departmental labor control system. It is based on the data in Table 12–7 for the obstetrics nursing unit.

   Using these data, Ms. Walker developed a two-factor variance model for labor costs in the obstetrics department. In Period 1, the variances in this model would be as follows:

   Labor rate variance = ($13.50 − $13.64) × 1,550 = $217.00 (Favorable)

   Labor usage variance = (1,550 − 4.33 × 350) × $13.64 = $470.58 (Unfavorable)

   A similar model for labor control has been adopted in all other departments. As the chief executive officer of the hospital, are you satisfied with this labor control system? What suggestions for revisions would you make?
5. Floyd Farley is the maintenance department head. His department is participating in a wage-incentive program in which he and his staff receive 20 percent of the department's income as supplemental income. Net income is defined as $25 multiplied by maintenance staff hours charged, less direct departmental expense. Do you see any problems with this system? If so, how might they be solved?
6. You have been asked to prepare a flexible budget for a forty-bed nursing unit. A schedule of staffing requirements by occupancy is presented in Table 12–8.

   Prepare a budget for management that shows expected personnel costs for this nursing unit by occupancy level.

Table 12–7 Budget Data for OB Example

Period	Patient Days	Hours Worked	Rate	Total Cost
1	350	1,550	$13.50	$ 20,925
2	400	1,700	13.80	23,460
3	300	1,400	13.20	18,480
4	375	1,625	13.80	22,425
5	450	1,850	13.80	25,530
Total	1,875	8,125		$110,820

Average rate = $13.64 = $110,820/8,125
Average hours/Patient day = 4.33 = 8,125/1,875

Table 12–8 Staffing Budget for Nursing Unit

	Below 60 Percent Occupancy	60 to 80 Percent Occupancy	80 to 100 Percent Occupancy
First shift			
Head nurse	1	1	1
Registered nurse	1	1	2
Licensed practical nurse	1	1	1
Aides	1	2	2
Second shift			
Registered nurse	2	2	2
Licensed practical nurse	1	1	1
Aides	2	3	3
Third shift			
Registered nurse	1	1	1
Licensed practical nurse	1	1	1
Aides	0	1	2

Daily personnel costs by job title and shift	
Head nurse	$175
Registered nurse—first shift	135
Second and third shifts	155
Licensed practical nurse—first shift	85
Second and third shifts	100
Aides—first shift	70
Second and third shifts	75

7. You must establish a pricing schedule for laboratory procedures. From a total hospital perspective, management has decided that the hospital must earn 5 percent above costs. The hospital has established that it loses 10 percent on each fixed-price payer (Medicare). That is, for every $100 of cost incurred to treat a fixed-price payer, the hospital receives only $90 in payment. You must build both the required profit and the expected loss on fixed-price payers into your rate structure. Payer mix for the laboratory is expected to be as presented in Table 12–9.

Medicare pays on a fixed price per diagnosis-related group for all inpatients. There is thus no separate payment for laboratory tests. Medicaid pays average costs for both inpatient and outpatient tests. Medicare also pays average costs for outpatient tests. Blue Cross pays 95 percent of charges for both inpatient and outpatient procedures. All other commercial insurance and health maintenance organization (HMO) patients pay 100 percent of charges. If budgeted expenses are $1,000,000 ($2.00 per RVU), what price must be set to meet management's profit expectations?

Table 12–9 Laboratory Pricing Data

	Budgeted RVUs		
	Inpatient	Outpatient	Total
Medicare	200,000	50,000	250,000
Medicaid	40,000	10,000	50,000
Blue Cross	80,000	20,000	100,000
Commercial insurance and HMOs	60,000	10,000	70,000
Bad debt and charity	15,000	15,000	30,000
Total RVUs	395,000	105,000	500,000

8. How would you calculate the amount of revenue to be realized as cash from patient sources in a fiscal period?
9. What is the major conceptual difference between zero-base budgeting and conventional budgeting?
10. In a hospital operation, what key variables are important when projecting volume at departmental levels?

SOLUTIONS AND ANSWERS

1. Two conditions are necessary for a flexible budget to be more useful than a forecast budget. First, there must be some indication that costs are variable, at least in part. Second, there must be some variability in activity levels, that is, volume is not expected to be constant in each period.

2. Efficiency relates to the costs per unit of output produced. Effectiveness relates to the attainment of organizational objectives given its outputs. It is possible for a firm to be efficient but not effective. For example, a hospital might provide inpatient care at an extremely low cost. However, this might not be effective if the provision of the inpatient' care is accomplished at rates that threaten the hospital's goal of financial solvency.

3. Figure 12–4 indicates that the statistics budget provides input for the development of the expense budget and the revenue budget. Projection of both expenses and revenues is a function of expected volume and variability of volume over the budget period. In cases when volume is expected to vary significantly, management may try to make more of their costs variable to maximize their ability to control costs, given volume changes. For example, more variable staffing may be used through the use of part-time employees, nursing pools, or overtime.

4. The primary weakness of Ms. Walker's model is its failure to incorporate fixed labor requirements. A flexible budgeting system should be put into effect instead. Using a high-low method, the following budget parameters for hours required can be estimated:

$$\text{Variable hours} = \frac{1{,}850 - 1{,}400}{450 - 300} = 3.0 \text{ hours per patient day}$$

$$\text{Fixed hours per period} = 1{,}850 - (3.0 \times 450) = 500 \text{ hours per period}$$

The deviation in hours worked per period is removed when the fixed labor requirement is recognized (Table 12–10).

5. Mr. Farley has an incentive to engage his staff in what might be needless maintenance. This could be controlled by setting limits on the absolute level of incentive payment that could be earned, for example, by basing the incentive payments on the difference between actual and budgeted costs or by establishing control systems for authorizing maintenance work.

6. The budget in Table 12–11 could be developed to show daily standard personnel costs by occupancy level for the nursing unit.

Table 12–10 Flexible Budget Comparison of Actual versus Budgeted Hours

Period	Actual Hours	Budgeted Hours (500 + 3.0 × PD)	Difference
1	1,550	1,550	0
2	1,700	1,700	0
3	1,400	1,400	0
4	1,625	1,625	0
5	1,850	1,850	0

Table 12–11 Nursing Unit budget

| | Occupancy | | |
	Below 60%	60% to 80%	80% to 100%
First shift			
Head nurse	$ 175	$ 175	$ 175
Registered nurse	135	135	270
Licensed practical nurse	85	85	85
Aides	70	140	140
Second shift			
Registered nurse	310	310	310
Licensed practical nurse	100	100	100
Aides	150	225	225
Third shift			
Registered nurse	155	155	155
Licensed practical nurse	100	100	100
Aides	0	75	150
Total Standard Personnel Costs	$1,280	$1,500	$1,710

7. Using the formula in Figure 12–5, the following rate structure can be established to meet management's profit expectations:

$$Price = \frac{\frac{\$1,000,000}{500,000} + \frac{(\$50,000 + \$40,000)}{500,000 \times .40}}{1 - .175} = \$2.9697$$

Desired profit = .05 × $1,000,000 = $50,000
Loss on fixed-price payers = .4 × $1,000,000 × .10 = $40,000

Proportion of charge payers = (100,000 + 70,000 + 30,000)/500,000 = .40

$$\text{Proportion of charge payer revenue not collected} = \frac{30,000 + .05 \times 100,000}{100,000 + 70,000 + 30,000} = .175$$

Budgeted Income

Medicare inpatient (.4 × $1,000,000 × .9)	$ 360,000
Medicare outpatient (.1 × $1,000,000)	100,000
Medicaid (.1 × $1,000,000)	100,000
Blue Cross (100,000 × $2.9697 × .95)	282,121
Commercial insurance and HMO (70,000 × $2.9697)	207,879
Bad debt and charity	0
Total revenue	$1,050,000
Less expenses	1,000,000
Budget profit	$ 50,000

8. Cash realized from patient sources could be expressed as follows:

   Cash flow = Net patient revenue + Beginning patient accounts receivable –
   Ending patient accounts receivable

9. Zero-base budgeting starts from a zero base. That is, all expenditures must be justified in the budgeting review. Conventional budgeting looks primarily at expenditures that are above prior levels.

10. The volume of actual cases treated (discharges or admissions) and outpatient activity are the key variables that affect departmental volumes. For example, laboratory tests are usually related to discharges and outpatient visits. Patient days are derived from discharges by assuming an average length of stay. Refinements in forecasting can be achieved by projecting case mix. Finally, more or fewer ancillary services per discharge may be required, depending on the type of case.

13

Cost Variance Analysis

Cost variance analysis is of great potential importance to the health care industry. Successful use of cost variance analysis requires a sound system of standard setting, or budgeting, and a related system of cost accounting. Perhaps the major factor impeding the widespread adoption of more effective cost variance analysis in the health care industry has been the lack of interaction between it and existing systems of cost accounting.

Cost accounting systems usually serve two basic informational needs. First, they supply data essential for product or service costing. Second, they provide information for managerial cost control activity. This second role is the major topic of this chapter.

COST CONTROL

The following conceptual model is used to discuss the major alternatives to cost control in organizations:

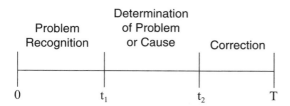

In general, there are three distinct time phases in an out-of-control situation:

1. recognition of problem (0 to t_1),
2. determination of problem or cause (t_1 to t_2), and
3. correction of problem (t_2 to T).

The unit of time used in the previous representation may be minutes, hours, days, weeks, or even months. The important point is that the longer the problem remains uncorrected (0 to T), the greater the cost to the organization.

The term "efficiency cost" is sometimes used to describe the total cost incurred by an organization as a result of an out-of-control situation. Efficiency cost may be represented as follows:

$$\text{Efficiency cost} = T \times R \times P$$

where:

T = total time units that the problem remains uncorrected
R = loss or cost per time unit
P = probability that the problem occurrence is correctable

The objective of management should be to minimize the efficiency cost in any given situation. While accomplishing this objective, two major alternatives are available to management: (1) the preventive approach and (2) the detection-correction (DC) approach.

In the preventive approach, management attempts to minimize the efficiency cost by minimizing the probability that a problem will occur (P). One of the major methods for reducing the value of P centers on staffing. Management attempts not only to hire the most competent individuals available but also to provide them with relevant training programs and materials to ensure consistently high levels of performance. The nature of the reward structure, both monetary and nonmonetary, also enters into this management strategy. The preventive approach is obviously used by most organizations, but the emphasis on it is usually greater in small organizations. In these organizations, the number of people supervised by one manager is usually smaller and the evaluation of individual performance is more direct.

The DC approach seeks to minimize efficiency cost by minimizing the time that a problem remains uncorrected (T). This method is directly related to the effectiveness of variance analysis. Effective variance analysis should result in a reduction of both the recognition of problem phase (0 to t_1) and the determination of cause phase (t_1 to t_2). The actual correction phase (t_2 to T) relies primarily on the effective motivation of management.

The development of cost variance analysis systems to reduce the recognition and determination phases usually involves the expenditure of funds. Prudent management dictates that the marginal expenditures of funds for system improvements be evaluated by their expected reductions in efficiency cost. For example, the frequency of reporting could be altered to reduce the problem recognition phase, or the number of cost areas reported could be increased to improve both recognition and determination times. However, these improvements are likely to result in increased cost and may not be justified. Areas of relatively small dollar expenditure or largely uncontrolled costs thus are not prime candidates for major system improvements.

INVESTIGATION OF VARIANCES

In the DC approach to cost control, cost variances are the clues that both signal that a potential problem exists and suggest a possible cause. These variances are usually an integral part of any management-by-exception plan of operations. A decision to investigate a given variance is not an automatic occurrence. It involves some financial commitment by the organization and thus should be weighed carefully against the expected benefits. Unfortunately, management rarely knows whether any given variance is due to a random or noncontrollable cause or to an underlying problem that is correctable or controllable.

Many organizations have developed rules to determine what variances will be investigated. Common examples of such rules are to investigate the following:

- all variances that exceed an absolute dollar size (for example, $500),
- all variances that exceed budgeted or standard values by some fixed percentage (for example, 10 percent),
- all variances that have been unfavorable for a defined number of periods (for example, three periods), and
- some combination of the previous rules.

Actual specification of criteria values in the previous rules is highly dependent on management judgment and experience. A variance of $1,000 may be considered normal in some circumstances and abnormal in others.

At some point, management may wish to determine whether the historical criteria values should be changed. In that case, some method of testing whether the historical values are acceptable or not acceptable must be developed. In general, there are two possible theories that may be used to develop this information: (1) classical statistical theory and (2) decision theory.

Classical Statistical Theory

One of the most commonly used means to determine which cost variances to investigate is the control chart. The control chart is often used to monitor a physical process by comparing output observations with predetermined tolerance limits. If actual observations fall between predetermined upper and lower control limits on the chart, the process is assumed to be in control.

Control charts can be established for determining when a cost variance should be investigated. The major assumption underlying the traditional development of control charts is that observed cost variances are distributed in accordance with a normal probability distribution. In a normal distribution, it can be anticipated that approximately 68.3 percent of the observations will fall within one standard deviation (σ) of the mean ($\bar{x}$), 95.5 percent will fall within two standard deviations ($\bar{x}\pm2\sigma$), and 99.7 percent will fall within three standard deviations ($\bar{x}\pm3\sigma$).

The control limits for any given variance will then be set at the following:

$$\bar{x} \pm K\sigma$$

If the costs of investigation are high relative to the benefits in a given situation, then K may be set to a high value (for example, 3.0). This will ensure that few investigations will be made and that some out-of-control situations may continue. Conversely, if benefits are high relative to the costs of investigation, then lower values of K may be selected that will ensure that more investigations will be performed and that some situations that are not out-of-control will be investigated.

To develop the control chart, the underlying distribution must be specified. An assumption that the distribution is normal means that the analyst must define both the mean ($\bar{x}$) and the standard deviation (σ). In most situations, this specification will result from an analysis of prior observations. To illustrate this process, assume that the pattern of labor variances in Table 13–1 occurred during the 13 biweekly pay periods:

The mean ($\bar{x}$) of these observations is calculated as follows:

$$\bar{x} = \frac{\Sigma x_i}{n} = \frac{0}{13} = 0$$

An estimate of the standard deviation (s) is calculated as follows:

$$s = \sqrt{\frac{\Sigma (x_i - \bar{x})^2}{n-1}} = 437.80$$

If the labor cost variances in this example are expected to follow a normal distribution in the future with $\bar{x} = 0$ and $\sigma = \$437.80$, control limits for investigation at the 95-percent level could be defined by multiplying the estimated standard deviation by 2. The following control chart would result:

$$\bar{x} + 2\sigma = 875.60$$
$$\bar{x} = 0$$
$$\bar{x} - 2\sigma = -875.60$$

Any observation falling within the control limits would not be investigated, whereas variances falling outside the established limits would be investigated.

Table 13–1 Labor Variances by Pay Period

Pay Period	Variances (xi)
1	800
2	400
3	−500
4	−100
5	200
6	−700
7	500
8	−300
9	−200
10	300
11	200
12	−200
13	−400
	0

The major deficiency in the classical statistical approach is that it does not relate the expected costs of investigation and benefits with the probability that the variance signals are out of control. The control chart can signal when a situation is likely to be out of control, but it cannot directly evaluate whether an investigation is warranted.

Decision Theory

Decision theory provides a framework for directly integrating the probability of the system being out of control and the costs and benefits of investigation into a definite decision rule. Central to this approach is the payoff table, which specifically considers costs and benefits. Table 13–2 provides an example of a payoff table, where

I = cost of investigation
C = cost of correcting an out-of-control situation
L = cost of letting an out-of-control situation continue (expected loss)

The payoff table is a conceptualization of the actual decision evaluation process. It can be applied to any cost variance situation. The objective is to minimize the actual cost for a given situation. To accomplish this, estimates of the probabilities for the two states, in control and out-of-control, are required.

Assume that P denotes the probability that the system is in control and that (1– P) represents the probability that the system is out of control. The

expected cost of the two courses of action can be defined as follows:

Expected cost of investigating
$= (P \times I) + (1 - P)(I + C)$
$= I + (1 - P)C$

Expected cost of not investigating
$= (P \times O) + (1 - P)L$
$= (1 - P)L$

By setting the two expected costs equal to each other, we can determine the value of P to which the decision-maker is indifferent. This break-even probability would be calculated as follows:

$$P^* = 1 - \frac{I}{L - C}$$

Evaluation of this formula provides a nice summarization of earlier comments concerning the costs and benefits of investigating variances. In situations of high investigation costs (I) and low net benefits (L – C), the critical value of P (P*) becomes low. This, of course, means that to justify an investigation, the probability that the system is actually in control (P) must be very low, or, alternatively, the probability that the system is actually out of control (1 – P) must be large.

To use the decision theory model just described, the analyst must have estimates of I, C, L, and P. In most situations, there is a reasonable expectation that I and C will be relatively constant. These costs are usually directly related to the labor involved in the analysis. L, however, usually varies, depending on the size of the cost

Table 13–2 Variance Investigation Payoff Table

Action	State	
	In Control	Out of Control
Investigate	I	I + C
Do not investigate	O	L

variance. In short, the loss depends on the proportion of the variance to be saved in future periods and the number of periods over which the loss is expected to occur if the situation is not corrected.

The value of P is, in many respects, the most difficult of the parameter values to specify. Either objective or subjective approaches may be used. An objective method may be used to develop an estimated probability distribution for the system. If the underlying distribution is assumed to be normal, estimating the mean and standard deviation from prior observations will enable the analyst to specify the distribution from this estimated distribution. The probability that any given system is under control (P) then can be defined.

Subjective estimates of P are possible on both a prior basis and an ex post facto basis. A subjective normalized distribution of variances can be built in advance as a basis for the estimate. The analyst might ask department managers between which two values they would expect 50 percent of actual observations to fall. If the budget cost for labor in a department is $4,000 per pay period, the department manager might specify that he or she expects actual observations to fall between $3,700 and $4,300 50 percent of the time. Using this information, a normalized distribution could be defined as presented in Figure 13–1.

Subjective estimates of P also may be made after an actual variance occurred and then related directly to the actual size of the cost variance. This assessment then can be related to a table of critical values of P necessary for an investigation decision of a given variance. This permits analysts to directly use sensitivity analysis in their decisions. For example, assume that I is $100 and that C is $200. Assume further that L is equal to two times the absolute size of the variance. Table 13–3 of critical values of P could then be defined.

This table is relatively straightforward. As the dollar size of the variance increases, the probability that the system is under control must increase to justify a "do not investigate" decision. For example, if a variance of $600 occurred, the analyst must believe that there is at least a 90-percent probability that the system is under control.

VARIANCE ANALYSIS CALCULATIONS

Variance analysis is simply an examination of the deviation of an actual observation from a standard. For the purposes of this chapter, the following two types of standards for comparative purposes are used: (1) prior-period values and (2) departmental values. In each case, the objective of cost-variance analysis is to explain why actual costs are different, either from budgeted values or from prior-period actual values. This objective is an important element in the cost-control process of the organization.

Prior-Period Comparisons

Relevant Factors

An evaluation of the difference between current levels of cost and prior costs should suggest to management which factors have contributed to the change. In general, the following three major factors influence costs: (1) input prices, (2) productivity of inputs, and (3) output levels.

Input prices usually may be expected to increase over time. It is important, however, from management's perspective, to evaluate what portion, if any, of that increase was controllable

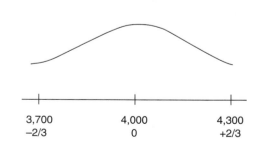

| 3,700 | 4,000 | 4,300 |
| -2/3 | 0 | +2/3 |

Figure 13–1 Normal Distribution of Labor Cost Utilization

Table 13–3 Relationship of P* to Variance Size

Critical Value of P (P*)	Size of Variance
0.50	$200
0.75	300
0.83	400
0.88	500
0.90	600

where:

P = input prices
I = physical quantities of inputs
X = services required per unit of output
Q = output level

In the previous cost equation, P represents the effect of input prices, I/X represents the effect of productivity, X/Q represents the effect of service intensity, and Q represents the influence of output. Changes in cost can result from changes in any one of these four terms.

Macroanalysis

There are many occasions when it is important to discover and communicate the causes for cost increases at the organizationwide level, whether that organization is a hospital, nursing home, or surgicenter. For example, your board may want to know why your total costs have increased 60 percent in the last three years. A useful framework can be developed to provide answers to questions such as this, provided that some critical pieces of information can be defined.

- There must be one measure of activity or output for the entire organization. This might be an adjusted discharge, patient day, visit, or other measure.
- It must be possible to define a measure of activity for each department within the organization and to define a cost per unit for that measure. It may not be necessary to define an output unit for indirect departments—those departments that do not directly provide a product or service to the patient—provided that the costs of the indirect departments have been allocated to the direct departments.

We will now develop a model and example for a hospital to illustrate the use of this macroanalysis. First, we will assume that our measure of activity is an adjusted discharge. The term adjusted simply reflects that outpatient ac-

or avoidable. Rapidly increasing prices for some commodities may signal opportunities for resource substitutions, for example, by switching to a less expensive mix of labor or substituting one supply item for another. Measuring productivity has, in fact, become increasingly important in the health care industry as a result of the emphasis on cost containment. One of the major difficulties in evaluating productivity, however, has been the changing nature of health care services. Comparison of productivity within a hospital for two periods requires that the services in each period be identical. For example, a comparison of full-time equivalents (FTEs) per patient day in 1998 with FTEs per patient day of care in 1995 is meaningless unless a patient day of care in 1998 is identical to a patient day of care in 1995. Finally, changes in output levels also influence the level of costs. This influence may occur in two ways. First, the absolute level of output provided may affect the quantity of resources necessary to produce the output level. Second, service intensity may affect resource requirements. Any increase in the number of services required per unit of output will directly affect costs. For example, a change in the number of laboratory procedures performed per patient day of care probably will affect the total cost per patient day of care.

This discussion can be summarized in the following cost function:

$$\text{Total cost} = P \times \frac{I}{X} \times \frac{X}{Q} \times Q$$

tivity has been recognized. This recognition may have occurred through a simple ratio of inpatient revenue to total patient revenue at the organizationwide level or at the individual departmental level.

The general cost per discharge (CPD) can be defined in the following equation:

$$CPD^t = C^t \times Q^t$$

where:

C^t = cost (direct and indirect) per unit of output in each department
Q^t = units of output in each department required per adjusted discharge

The following example is now presented to help clarify the previous concepts. The data in Table 13–4 represent cost and volume information for the year 1998. These data are compared with cost and volume data for 1996.

In this example, the CPD increased 31.6 percent from 1996 to 1998. Causes for the increase could be partitioned into the following two possible areas:

1. Intensity of service—More units of intermediate services are required per discharge, such as laboratory tests and days in intensive care unit.
2. Cost—Cost increases could have resulted from higher prices paid for inputs such as wage and salary changes in the nature of the service provided (such as a change in the proportion of routine chest radiographs to computed tomography scans) or a change in efficiency of production.

The following two indices capture the impact of each of these two areas.

$$\frac{CPD^t}{CPD^o} = \frac{C^t Q^t}{C^o Q^o} = HCI \times HII$$

The hospital cost index (HCI) is defined as the following:

$$HCI = \frac{C^t Q^o}{C^o Q^o}$$

The HCI measures the change in cost attributed to both price increases and productivity changes. The other index, the hospital intensity index (HII) is defined as the following:

$$HII = \frac{C^o Q^t}{C^o Q^o}$$

The HII measures the change in cost due to changes in service intensity.

Using this framework in our example data would yield the following values:

$$HCI = \frac{\begin{array}{l}(\$714.29 \times .4000) + \\ (\$308.12 \times 6.6000) + \\ (\$500.00 \times 1.5000) + \\ (\$85.71 \times 5.0000) + \\ (\$285.71 \times 2.0000)\end{array}}{\begin{array}{l}(\$562.50 \times .4000) + \\ (\$252.52 \times 6.6000) + \\ (\$472.22 \times 1.5000) + \\ (\$75.00 \times 5.000) + \\ (\$150.00 \times 2.0000)\end{array}} =$$

$$\frac{\$4,069}{\$3,275} = 1.242$$

$$HII = \frac{\begin{array}{l}(\$562.50 \times .4828) + \\ (\$252.52 \times 6.1552) + \\ (\$472.22 \times 1.7241) + \\ (\$75.00 \times 6.0345) + \\ (\$150.00 \times 2.4138)\end{array}}{\begin{array}{l}(\$562.50 \times .4000) + \\ (\$252.52 \times 6.6000) + \\ (\$472.22 \times 1.5000) + \\ (\$75.00 \times 5.0000) + \\ (\$150.00 \times 2.0000)\end{array}} =$$

$$\frac{\$3,455}{\$3,275} = 1.045$$

The previous calculations show that the increase in CPD from 1996 to 1998 could be broken down as follows:

Table 13–4 Summary of Cost per Discharge (1998 and 1996)

1998 Cost Summary
11,600 Discharges

Department	Volume	Cost (000s)	Cost/ Unit (C')	Units/ Discharge (Q')
Intensive care unit	5,600	$ 4,000	$714.29	.4828
Routine nursing	71,400	22,000	308.12	6.1552
Operating room	20,000	10,000	500.00	1.7241
Laboratory	70,000	6,000	85.71	6.0345
Radiology	28,000	8,000	285.71	2.4138
		$50,000		

CPD = $50,000,000/11,600 = $4,310.34

1996 Cost Summary
12,000 Discharges

Department	Volume	Cost (000s)	Cost/ Unit (C')	Units/ Discharge (Q')
Intensive care unit	4,800	$ 2,700	$562.50	.40000
Routine nursing	79,200	20,000	252.52	6.6000
Operating room	18,000	8,500	472.22	1.5000
Laboratory	60,000	4,500	75.00	5.0000
Radiology	24,000	3,600	150.00	2.0000
		$39,300		

CPD = $39,300,000/12,000 = $3,275.00

Percentage increase due to cost increases	24.2%
Percentage increase due to intensity	5.5
Joint cost and intensity	1.9
Total increase	31.6%

For those who wish to further break down the causes for the increase in CPD during the two-year period, some individual departmental analysis could be done. For example, in 1998, the average laboratory CPD was $517.22 ($85.71 × 6.0345), compared with $375.00 ($75.00 × 5.000) in 1996. This represents a 37.9-percent increase and could be broken down into cost and intensity factors also. The next section addresses the issue of departmental analysis of cost variances.

Departmental Analysis of Variance

The preceding indices are useful for analyzing cost changes at the total facility level. In such situations, a measure of output for the facility as a whole—such as patient days, admissions, discharges, visits, or enrollees—would be used. However, although this type of analysis may be useful, it is also often desirable to analyze the reasons for cost changes at the departmental level. In general, the primary reason for a cost change at the departmental level between two periods can be stated as a function of the following three factors:

1. changes in input prices,
2. changes in input productivity (efficiency), and
3. changes in departmental volume.

The following variances can be calculated to compute the effects of these three factors:

Price variance = (Present price – Old price) × Present quantity

Efficiency variance = (Present quantity – Expected quantity at old productivity) × Old price

Volume variance = (Present volume – Old volume) × Old cost per unit

These formulas may be applied to the laundry example found in Table 13–5. It is assumed that the laundry has only two inputs: soap and labor.

With these calculations, Table 13–6 summarizes the factors that created cost changes in the laundry department.

Table 13–6 indicates that increased volume was the largest source of the total change in cost. It is often useful to factor this volume variance into two areas:

Intensity = (Change in volume due to intensity difference) × Old cost per unit

Pure volume = (Change in volume due to change in overall service) × Old cost per unit

Here, the intensity variance represents the change in volume due to increased intensity of

---

Table 13–5 Cost Data for Laundry/Linen Department

	1996	1998
Pounds of laundry	140,000	180,000
Units of soap	1,400	1,800
Soap units per pound of laundry	.01	.01
Price per soap unit	$40.00	$50.00
Productive hours worked	19,600	27,000
Productive hours per pound of laundry	.14	.15
Wage rate per productive hour	5.25	6.00
Total cost	$158,900	$252,000
Cost per pound	$1.135	$1.40
Patient days	70,000	80,000

Price variances
   Soap = ($50.00 – $40.00) × 1,800 = $18,000 (Unfavorable)
   Labor = ($6.00 – $5.25) × 27,000 = $20,250 (Unfavorable)
Efficiency variances
   Soap = (1,800 – [.01 × 180,000]) × $40.00 = 0
   Labor = (27,000 – [.14 × 180,000]) × $5.25 = $9,450 (Unfavorable)
Volume variances
   Volume variance = (180,000 – 140,000) × $1.135 = 45,400 (Unfavorable)

Table 13–6 Variance Analysis Summary

Causes of Laundry Department
Cost Change—1996 to 1998

	Dollars	*% Change*
Increase in wages	$20,250	21.8
Increase in soap price	18,000	19.3
Decline in labor efficiency	9,450	10.1
Increase in volume	45,400	48.8
Total change in cost	$93,100	100.0

service. For example, in 1998, 2.25 pounds of laundry were provided per patient day (180,000/ 80,000). The corresponding value for 1996 was 2.00 pounds per patient day (140,000/70,000). The two volume variances would be the following:

Intensity variance = ([2.25 − 2.00] × 80,000) × $1.135 = $22,700

Pure volume = 2.00 × (80,000 − 70,000) × $1.135 = $22,700

The system of cost variance analysis described previously should be a useful framework in which to discuss factors causing changes in departmental costs. Aggregation of some resource categories probably will be both necessary and desirable. There would be little point in calculating price and efficiency variances for each of 100 or more supply items. Only major supply categories should be examined. The supply items that are aggregated together could not be broken down in terms of individual price and efficiency variances because there would be no common input quantity measure. For example, the addition of pencils, sheets of paper, and boxes of paper clips would not produce a comparable unit of measure. For these smaller areas of supply or material costs, a simple change in cost per unit of departmental output may be just as informative as detailed price and efficiency variances.

VARIANCE ANALYSIS IN BUDGETARY SETTINGS

A final area in which variance analysis can be applied is the operation of a formalized budgeting system. The presentation that follows assumes a budgeting system that is based on a flexible model. This means that the management must have identified those elements of cost that are presumed to be fixed and those that are presumed to be variable in the budgetary process. Although relatively few health care organizations use flexible budgeting models at the present time, a trend toward their adoption is clearly visible. In this context, the variance analysis models examined here may be applied to any budgetary situation, fixed or flexible.

The cost equation for any given department may be represented as follows:

$$Cost = F + (V \times Q)$$

where:

F = fixed costs
V = variable costs per unit of output
Q = output in units

The fixed and variable cost coefficients are the sum of many individual resource quantity and unit price products. These terms can be represented as follows:

$$F = I_f \times P_f$$
$$V = I_v \times P_v$$

where:

I_f = physical units of fixed resources
P_f = price per unit of fixed resources
I_v = physical units of variable resources per unit of output
P_v = price per unit of variable resources

In most budgeting situations, there are three levels of output or volume that are critical in cost variance analysis. The first is the actual level of volume produced in the budget-reporting period. This level of activity is critical because, if management has established a set of expectations concerning how costs should behave, given changes in volume from budgeted levels, an adjustment to budgeted cost can be made for a change in volume.

The second critical level is that of budgeted or expected volume. It is on this expected volume level that management establishes its commitments for resources, and therefore incurs cost. An unjustified faith in volume forecasts can lock management into a sizable fixed-cost position, especially regarding labor costs.

The third critical level is that of standard volume. Standard volume is equal to actual volume, unless there is some indication that not all of the output was necessary. For example, a utilization review committee may determine that a certain number of patient days were medically unnecessary or that some surgical procedures were not warranted. Alternatively, in some indirect departments, such as maintenance, it may be important to identify the difference between actual and standard, or necessary, output. The cost effect of these output decisions needs to be isolated, and control should be directed to the individual(s) responsible.

The expected level of costs to be incurred at each of the three levels of volume (actual, budgeted, and standard) may be expressed as follows:

$$FB^a = F + (V \times Q_a)$$
$$FB^b = F + (V \times Q_b)$$
$$FB^s = F + (V \times Q_s)$$

where:

FB^a = flexible budget at actual output level
FB^b = flexible budget at budgeted output level
FB^s = flexible budget at standard output level
Q^a = actual output
Q^b = budgeted output
Q^s = standard output

The major categories of variances now can be defined to explain the difference between actual cost (AC) and applied cost ($Q^s \times FB^b/Q^b$) (Table 13–7).

For control purposes, it is important to further break down the spending variance into individual resource categories, and also to isolate the change due to price and efficiency factors. This will not only better isolate control for budget deviations but also improve the problem definition and determination phase times discussed earlier in the detection-correction approach to cost control. The spending variances are broken down as follows:

$$\text{Efficiency} = (I^a - I^b)P^b$$
$$\text{Price} = (P^a - P^b)I^a$$

where:

I^a = actual physical units of resource
I^b = budgeted physical units of resource
P^a = actual price per unit of resource
P^b = budgeted price per unit of resource

With this background, we must now relate the structure we developed for standard costing in Chapter 11 to our analyses of budgetary variances. The following two sets of standards are involved: (1) standard cost profiles (SCPs) and

Table 13–7 Categories of Budgetary Variances

Variance Name	Definition	Cause
Spending	$(AC - FB^a)$	Price and efficiency
Utilization	$(Q^a - Q^s) \times (FB^b/Q^b)$	Excessive services
Volume	$(Q^b - Q^a) \times (F/Q^b)$	Difference from budgeted volume

(2) standard treatment protocols (STPs). SCPs are developed at the departmental level. They reflect the quantity of resources that should be used and the prices that should be paid for those resources to produce a specific departmental output unit, defined as a service unit (SU). Table 13–8 provides an SCP for a nursing unit, with the SU defined as a patient day.

Using Table 13–8, a standard variance analysis could be performed for any period. For example, the data in Table 13–9 reflect actual experience in the most recent month.

In this example, the nursing unit would have incurred actual expenditures of $49,650 during the month. It would have charged its standard cost times the number of patient days to treated patients:

Cost charged to patients = $48,540 = $80.90 × 600

The total variance to be accounted for would be the difference ($49,650 – $48,540), or $1,110, which is an unfavorable variance. The individual variances that constitute this total are shown in the following calculations:

1. Spending variances
   - Efficiency variances ($[I^a - I^b]P^b$)
     a. Head nurse = (180 – 189) × $15.00 = $135.00 (Favorable)
     b. RN = (1,800 – 1,830) × $12.00 = $360.00 (Favorable)
     c. LPN = (1,200 –1,200) × $8.00 = 0
     d. Aides = (2,400 – 2,430) × $5.00 = $150.00 (Favorable)
     e. Supplies = (1,300 – 1,200) × $2.20 = $220.00 (Unfavorable)

   - Price variances ($[P^a - P^b]I^a$)
     a. Head nurse = ($15.50 – $15.00) × 180 = $90.00 (Unfavorable)
     b. RN = ($12.50 – $12.00) × 1,800 = $900.00 (Unfavorable)
     c. LPN = ($8.10 – $8.00) × 1,200 = $120.00 (Unfavorable)
     d. Aides = ($4.80 – $5.00) × 2,400 = $480.00 (Favorable)
     e. Supplies = ($2.40 – $2.20) × 1,300 = $260.00 (Unfavorable)
2. Volume variance ($[Q^b - Q^a] [F/Q^b]$)
   - Volume variance = (630 – 600) × $21.50 = $645.00 (Unfavorable)

Price—Head nurse	$ 90.00	(Unfavorable)
Price—RN	900.00	(Unfavorable)
Price—LPN	120.00	(Unfavorable)
Price—Aides	480.00	(Favorable)
Price—Supplies	260.00	(Unfavorable)
Efficiency—Head nurse	135.00	(Favorable)
Efficiency—RN	360.00	(Favorable)
Efficiency—LPN	0.00	
Efficiency—Aides	150.00	(Favorable)
Efficiency—Supplies	220.00	(Unfavorable)
Volume	645.00	(Unfavorable)
Total	$1,110.00	(Unfavorable)

A few additional statements about the calculation of the efficiency variances may be necessary. The formula states that the difference between actual quantity (I^a) and budgeted quantity (I^b) is multiplied by budgeted price (P^b). The most difficult calculation is that for budgeted quantity. It represents the quantity of resource

Table 13–8 Standard Cost Profile for Nursing Unit

Standard Cost Profile
Nursing Unit Number 6
Patient Day = Service Unit
Expected Patient Days = 630

Resource	Quantity Variable	Quantity Fixed	Unit Cost	Variable Cost	Average Fixed Cost	Average Total Cost
Head nurse	0.00	.30	$15.00	$ 0.00	$ 4.50	$ 4.50
Registered Nurse (RN)	2.00	1.00	12.00	24.00	12.00	36.00
Licensed Practical Nurse (LPN)	2.00	0.00	8.00	16.00	0.00	16.00
Aides	3.00	1.00	5.00	15.00	5.00	20.00
Supplies	2.00	0.00	2.20	4.40	0.00	4.40
Total				$59.40	$21.50	$80.90

that should have been used at the actual level of output, or the sum of the budgeted fixed requirement plus the variable requirement at actual output (600 patient days). Table 13–10 shows the calculation of fixed and variable requirements for the individual resource categories.

The calculation for volume variance also may require some further explanation. This variance is simply the product of the difference between budgeted and actual volume $(Q^a - Q^b)$ and the average fixed cost budgeted (F/Q^b). The average fixed cost, as calculated in the SCP amounted to $21.50. You will notice that in our example volume variance is unfavorable because actual volume of patient days (600) was less than budgeted patient days (630). Because actual volume was less than that budgeted, the average fixed cost per unit will increase. The reverse situation would have existed if actual volume had exceeded budgeted volume. In that situation, the volume variance would have been favorable.

The third type of variance, utilization variance, results from a difference between actual volume and standard volume, or the quantity of volume actually needed. The measure of standard volume is generated from the STPs, which

Table 13–9 Actual Costs for Nursing Unit

Actual Month's Cost
Nursing Unit Number 6
Actual Patient Days = 600

Resource	Quantity Used	Unit Cost	Total Cost
Head nurse	180	$15.50	$2,790.00
RN	1,800	12.50	22,500.00
LPN	1,200	8.10	9,720.00
Aides	2,400	4.80	11,520.00
Supplies	1,300	2.40	3,120.00
Total			$ 49,650

Table 13–10 Calculation of Budgeted Resource Requirements

1 Resource Category	2 Average Fixed Requirement/ Unit	3 Budgeted Fixed Requirement (Col. 2 × 630)	4 Average Variable Requirement/ Unit	5 Budgeted Variable Requirement (Col. 4 × 600)	6 Total Requirement (Col. 3 + Col. 5)
Head nurse	.30	189	0.00	0	189
RN	1.00	630	2.00	1,200	1,830
LPN	0.00	0	2.00	1,200	1,200
Aides	1.00	630	3.00	1,800	2,430
Supplies	0.00	0	2.00	1,200	1,200

define how much output or how many SUs are required per treated patient type.

Let us generate a hypothetical set of data to apply to our nursing-unit example. Assume that the patients treated in Nursing Unit Number 6 are all in diagnosis-related group (DRG) 209 (major joint procedures) and are all associated with one physician, Dr. Mallard. Our STP for DRG 209 calls for a 14-day length of stay. A review of Dr. Mallard's patient records reveals that only 560 patient days of care should have been used (40 cases at 14 days per case). Dr. Mallard had twenty patients with lengths of stay greater than 14 days. These twenty patients accounted for an excess of 80 patient days. Dr. Mallard also had ten patients with shorter lengths of stay. These patients offset 40 days of the 80 day surplus. Thus, although 600 patient days of care were provided, only 560 should have been used. This creates an unfavorable utilization variance, calculated as the product of budgeted cost per unit and the difference between actual and standard volume. In our example of Nursing Unit Number 6, the utilization variance would be as follows:

Utilization variance = (600 − 560) ×
$80.90 = $3,236.00 (Unfavorable)

This variance is not charged to the nursing department. It is charged to the manager of patient treatment, in this case Dr. Mallard.

Figure 13–2 depicts the flow of costs and the variances associated with each account.

This delineation of variances represents a powerful analytical tool for analyzing cost variances from budgeted cost levels. The existence of a flexible budget model is not a prerequisite to its use. The only real prerequisite is that major resource cost categories be separated into price and utilization components. Because effective cost control appears to be predicated on a separate analysis of price and utilization decisions, this does not seem too difficult a task, considering the potential payoff. Finally, it should be noted that there is no requirement to formally include these variances into the budget-reporting models. They can be calculated on an ad hoc basis to investigate and explain large cost variances.

VARIANCE ANALYSIS IN MANAGED CARE SETTINGS

Variance analysis is an important analytical tool that has become useful to managed care firms that are seeking to monitor and control their costs. Because most managed care firms operate with relatively small margins, and because most of their cost is variable, changes in budgetary assumptions can have a sizable influence on costs and, therefore, profitability.

The following relationships will help us to formulate a variance analysis model that will

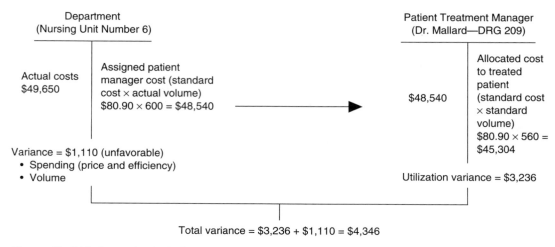

Figure 13–2 Variance Analysis Summary

separate cost variations into factors that are suggestive of cause and should lead to corrective actions more quickly.

- Total cost = Inpatient cost (IPC) + Outpatient cost (OPC)

Inpatient Cost (IPC)
- IPC = Admissions × Cost per admission
  - Admissions = Enrollees (E) × Admissions per member (APM)
  - Cost per admission = Cost per admission at case mix of 1.0 (CPA) × Admission case-mix index (ACMI)
- IPC = E × APM × CPA × ACMI

Outpatient Cost (OPC)
- OPC = Visits × Cost per visit
  - Visits = Enrollees (E) × Visits per member (VPM)
  - Cost per visit = Cost per visit at case mix of 1.0 (CPV) × Visit case-mix index (VCMI)
- OPC = E × VPM × CPV × VCMI

The previous formulas define the following primary cost drivers:

1. enrollment (E),
2. utilization (APM or VPM),
3. efficiency (CPA or CPV), and
4. patient mix (ACMI or VCMI).

Costs in a managed care setting can increase because of changes in any one of these four factors. An increase in enrollment most likely will lead to an increase in costs, but this increase in costs may be offset by an increase in revenues, and profits may actually improve. Increases in utilization most likely will lead to an increase in costs because more units of service, either more admissions or more visits, are being provided per member. An increase in costs per unit (CPA or CPV) would signal a decline in efficiency and lead to an increase in costs. If the managed care organization is not fully integrated and is not affected by increased production costs, this may not be a concern. If, however, the managed care firm owns the providers of care, then increases in their costs will adversely affect profitability of the consolidated firm. Finally, changes in patient mix, ACMI or VCMI, can adversely affect costs. Utilization of more costly procedures can have a negative effect on profits.

To illustrate the use of this framework, a case example is presented in Table 13–11.

Table 13–11 Managed Care Budget to Actual Comparison

	Budget	Actual
Enrollees (E)	10,000	11,000
Admissions Per Member (APM)	.075	.080
Admissions (E × APM)	750	880
Visits Per Member (VPM)	4.5	5.0
Visits (E × VPM)	45,000	55,000
Cost Per Admission (CPA)	$5,000	$5,200
Admission Case-Mix Index (ACMI)	1.0	1.02
Actual Cost Per Admission (CPA × ACMI)	$5,000	$5,304
Cost Per Visit (CPV)	$75	$80
Visit Case-Mix Index (VCMI)	1.10	1.15
Actual Cost Per Visit (CPV × VCMI)	$82.50	$92.00
Inpatient Costs	$3,750,000	$4,667,520
Outpatient Costs	$3,712,500	$5,060,000
Total Costs	$7,462,500	$9,727,520

The total variance to account for in the case presented inTable 13–11 is shown in Table 13–12.

The numbers indicate that costs were much higher than expected, but they do not relay the cause of the variance. The definition of individual variances can help explain causes for the total variance and suggest possible solutions. We know from the case in Table 13–11 that there were 880 actual inpatient admissions and that the actual cost per case was $5,304, which generated actual inpatient costs of $4,667,520. There were 750 budgeted inpatient admissions, and budgeted costs per case were $5,000, which generated an expected or budgeted cost of $3,750,000. Costs were higher than budgeted because we admitted more patients and the cost to treat them was higher than expected. Let's use the framework described previously to partition the total variance into areas that might suggest possible causes and solutions.

Volume-Related Variances

We know that we admitted 130 more patients than expected (880 – 750) and experienced 10,000 more outpatient visits than expected (55,000 – 45,000). This deviation in volume can result from two possible causes:

- changes in enrollees, and
- changes in utilization rates.

Table 13–12 Summary of Cost Variance

	Inpatient Costs	Outpatient Costs	Total Costs
Actual costs	$4,667,520	$5,060,000	$9,727,520
Less budgeted costs	3,750,000	3,712,500	7,462,500
Variance	$ 917,520	$1,347,500	$2,265,020

Table 13–13 Variance Definitions—Enrollment

Variance Formula	Calculation	Variance
Inpatient = $(E^a - E^b) \times APM^b \times$ CPA$^b \times$ ACMI^b	$(11,000 - 10,000) \times .075 \times \$5,000 \times 1.0$	\$375,000
Outpatient = $(E^a - E^b) \times$ VPM$^b \times$ CPV$^b \times$ VCMI^b	$(11,000 - 10,000) \times 4.5 \times \$75 \times 1.1$	\$371,250
Total Enrollment Variance		\$746,250

Enrollment Variances

Enrollment variances are simply the product of budgeted cost per unit times the change in enrollment times budgeted utilization. The formulas for these variances are presented in Table 13–13.

Utilization Variances

Utilization variances are simply the product of the change in volume due to the change in usage rates calculated at the actual number of enrollees times budgeted cost per unit (Table 13–14).

Note that the change in inpatient volume attributed to enrollment variance is 75 (1,000 × .075) and that the change in inpatient volume attributed to utilization variance is 55 (.005 × 11,000). Added together, the two variances total 130, which was the difference between budgeted and actual inpatient cases. In a similar manner, the outpatient volume difference of 10,000 can be factored into 4,500 attributed to enrollment variance and 5,500 attributed to utilization variance. Multiplying these variations in volume by the budgeted costs of $5,000 per case and $82.50

per visit yield the variances calculated previously.

Cost-Related Variances

The actual cost of treating an inpatient case was $5,304 compared to a budgeted cost per case of $5,000, a difference of $304 per case. The outpatient difference between actual and budgeted cost per visit was $9.50 ($92.00 – $82.50). These differences in costs contributed to the overall unfavorable variance, but, as before, there are two possible causes for this deviation in cost per unit:

- changes in the efficiency of production, and
- changes in the case mix of patients seen.

Efficiency Variance

Efficiency variances are a reflection of a change in the underlying cost of production, keeping case mix constant. The efficiency variance is the product of the difference between actual and budgeted costs for a constant case mix equal to one times the actual case mix of patients

Table 13–14 Variance Definitions—Utilization

Variance Formula	Calculation	Variance
Inpatient = $(APM^a - APM^b) \times E^a \times$ CPA$^b \times$ ACMI^b	$(.080 - .075) \times 11,000 \times \$5,000 \times 1.0$	\$275,000
Outpatient = $(VPM^a - VPM^b) \times$ E$^a \times$ CPV$^b \times$ VCMI^b	$(5.0 - 4.5) \times 11,000 \times \$75 \times 1.10$	\$453,750
Total Utilization Variance		\$728,750

Table 13–15 Variance Definitions—Efficiency

Variance Formula	Calculation	Variance
Inpatient = (CPA^a − CPA^b) × ACMI^a × E^a × APM^a	($5,200 − $5,000) × 1.02 × 11,000 × .080	$179,520
Outpatient = (CPV^a − CPV^b) × VCMI^a × E^a × VPM^a	($80 − $75) × 1.15 × 11,000 × 5.0	$316,250
Total Efficiency Variance		$495,770

seen times actual volume of patients (Table 13–15).

Case-Mix Variances

Case-mix variances reflect the change in cost per unit that has resulted not from a change in efficiency, but from a change in case mix of patients seen. This variance may not be controllable by the providers and may be a reflection of the nature of the insured population. Case-mix variances are the product of the change in case mix times the expected cost per unit at a case-mix standard value of 1.0 times the actual volume (Table 13–16).

The variation in cost per case was $304, of which $204 is attributed to efficiency variation and $100 is attributed to case-mix variation. The difference in cost per outpatient visit was $9.50, of which $5.75 is attributed to efficiency variation and $3.75 is attributed to case-mix variation. Multiplying these differences by the actual volumes of patients seen (880 cases and 55,000 visits) produces the variances reported previously.

It is now possible to summarize the variance analysis performed to date in a structure that may help management direct their attention to areas needing correction. This is done in Table 13–17.

Table 13–17 shows that the majority of the total variance can be attributed to enrollment variance and utilization variance. Of the two, enrollment variances accounted for approximately 32.9 percent of the total variation and is not likely to be a problem because increased enrollment most likely was offset by increased revenues. The utilization variances accounted for 32.2 percent of the total variation and could represent a serious problem that should be examined. Continuation of this trend could destroy the firm's profitability.

SUMMARY

In general, within the framework for cost control, the following two approaches are possible: (1) preventive and (2) detection-correction

Table 13–16 Variance Definitions—Case Mix

Variance Formula	Calculation	Variance
Inpatient = (ACMI^a − ACMI^b) × CPA^b × E^a × APM^a	(1.02 − 1.0) × $5,000 × 11,000 × .080	$88,000
Outpatient = (VCMI^a − VCMI^b) × CPV^b × E^a × VPM^a	(1.15 − 1.10) × $75 × 11,000 × 5.0	$206,250
Total Case-Mix Variance		$294,250

Table 13–17 Individual Variance Analysis Summary

Variance Cause	Inpatient Amount	Inpatient %	Outpatient Amount	Outpatient %	Amount	Total %
Enrollment	$375,000	40.8	$371,250	27.6	$746,250	32.9
Utilization	275,000	30.0	453,750	33.1	728,750	32.2
Efficiency	179,520	19.6	316,250	23.5	495,770	21.9
Case Mix	88,000	9.6	206,250	15.3	294,250	13.0
Total	$917,520	100.0	$1,347,500	100.0	$2,265,020	100.0

(DC). The DC approach is usually based on some system of variance analysis. From a decision-theory perspective, the investigation of a variance is based on the cost of investigation, the probability that a correctable problem exists, the potential loss if the problem is not corrected, and the costs of problem correction. It may not always be possible to develop truly objective measures for these values, but sensitivity analysis may offer a useful aid in such situations.

ASSIGNMENTS

1. Two general types of approaches to internal control are preventive and detection approaches. Preventive approaches stress the elimination of problems, whereas detection approaches stress the early recognition and correction of problems. What sorts of things could you do if you used a preventive approach to reduce costs?
2. What is a coefficient of variation, and how can that information be used in budgeting?
3. Which would you investigate first—a budget variance that is 1.0 standard deviation away from the expected value or one that is 1.5 standard deviations away from the value? Why?
4. When is the use of a flexible budget likely to be most effective?
5. Standard cost accounting systems often separate variance into price and efficiency components. Why?
6. Use of a multivariable flexible budget may reduce the time involved in investigating variances. Why might this be true?
7. Ned Zechman is the dietary manager of a large convalescent center. He is disturbed by variances, all highly unfavorable, in his food budget for the past three months. Ned has been reducing both the quantity and quality of delivered meals, but to date, there has been no reflection of this in his monthly budget variance report. A recent organizational change brought in Pat Schumaker, who is now responsible for all purchasing activity, including dietary. All purchased food costs are charged to dietary at the time of purchase. What do you think might explain Ned's problem, and how would you determine the cause?
8. Assume that the budgeted cost for a department is $10,000 per week and the standard deviation is $500. The decision to investigate a variance requires a comparison of expected benefits with expected costs. Suppose an unfavorable variance of $1,000 is observed. The normal distribution indicates the probability of observing this variance is .0228 if the system is in control. Furthermore, assume that the benefits would be 50 percent of the variance and that investigation costs are $200. Should this variance be investigated? Assume that the variance is still $1,000, but it is favorable. Should it still be investigated?
9. Departmental costs may be out of control if either the variance is outside specified limits or the number of successive observations, above or below expected costs, is excessive. The binomial distribution can be used as a basis for determining what is or is not excessive. If we assume that the probability of being either above or below budgeted costs is .50, then the probability of n successive observations of actual costs being greater than budgeted costs is $.50^n$. What is the probability of observing six successive periods in which actual costs are greater than budgeted costs?
10. You are evaluating the performance of the radiology department manager. The SU or output for this department is the number of procedures. A static budget was prepared at the beginning of the year. You are now examining that budget in relation to actual experience. The relevant data are included in Table 13–18.

   The department manager is pleased because he has a favorable $120,000 cost variance. Evaluate the effectiveness claims of the manager using the budgetary variance model described in this chapter.

Table 13–18 Radiology Department Data

	Actual	Original Budget	Variance	
Procedures	100,000	120,000	20,000	(Unfavorable)
Variable costs	$1,200,000	$1,320,000	$120,000	(Favorable)
Fixed costs	600,000	600,000	—	
Total costs	$1,800,000	$1,920,000	$120,000	(Favorable)

11. The data in Table 13–19 were assembled for a laundry department during the period from 1997 to 1998.

    Break down the total change in cost ($3,324) into the variance categories described in this chapter, that is, price, efficiency, intensity volume, and pure volume variances.

12. John Jones, CEO at Valley Hospital, is concerned by the rapid increase in cost per case during the last five years at his hospital. Five years ago, his average cost per case was $9,295; it is now $14,355. Using the data in Table 13–20, help John understand what factors have fueled the increase in costs during the last five years.

Table 13–19 Laundry Department Data

	1997	1998
Weighted patient days	24,140	24,539
Pounds of laundry	333,225	328,624
Pounds per day	13.80385	13.39191
Number of FTEs	3.0	3.0
FTEs per pound	.00000900292	.00000912897
Average salary	$7,260.67	$7,873.00
Salary cost per pound	$.065367	$.071872
Supply units	3,332	3,286
Supply units per pound	.01	.01
Cost per supply unit	$2.6946	$3.1848
Total cost	$30,761	$34,085
Cost per pound	$.092313	$.10372

Table 13–20 Valley Hospital DRG Costs

	Total Cost	Present Volume	Average Cost
DRG 106	$150,000	10	$15,000
DRG 107	200,000	20	10,000
DRG 103	95,000	1	95,000
	$445,000	31	$14,355

	Total Cost	Five Years Ago Volume	Average Cost
DRG 106	$114,750	9	$12,750
DRG 107	192,000	24	8,000
DRG 103	0	0	0
	$306,750	33	$9,295

13. You have just taken a position as a financial analyst with the American Health Plan, a partially integrated delivery system, contracting with major employers for health care services. The financial and utilization data in Table 13–21 were presented to you regarding the previous completed year.

Table 13–21 American Health Plan Budget

	Budget	Actual
Enrollees	10,000	11,000
Patient days Per 1,000 enrollees	600	550
Patient days	6,000	6,050
Visits per member	5.0	5.5
Visits	50,000	60,500
Cost per patient day	$1,000	$1,100
Cost per visit	$65	$62
Inpatient costs	$6,000,000	$6,655,000
Outpatient costs	$3,250,000	$3,751,000
Total costs	$9,250,000	$10,406,000
Per-member per-year costs	$925	$946

You have been asked to make some sense of this data and factor the total variance of $1,156,000 ($10,406,000 – $9,250,000) into some subaccounts that suggest possible causes. Please review these data and calculate variances for inpatient and outpatient into the following areas:

- enrollment variance,
- utilization variance, and
- efficiency variance (note that there is no case-mix intensity standard).

Even in situations when one person does have responsibility for both components, the separation is useful because it provides information for focused management correction.

SOLUTIONS AND ANSWERS

1. The following are some of the things you could do, using a preventive approach: improve employee training, increase inspection of material, improve equipment maintenance, and increase supervision.
2. The coefficient of variation is the ratio of the standard deviation to the mean. A large value implies great variability in the results. In a budgeting context, operations with large prior coefficients of variation typically require a more sophisticated budget model, such as a flexible budget, to account for deviations from average performance.
3. The budget variance that is 1.5 standard deviations from expected performance is more likely to be controllable and should be investigated first. However, adjustments for the relative differences in investigation costs and variance size should be considered.
4. A flexible budget is likely to be most effective when costs in a department are not fixed and are expected to vary with changes in output or other variables.
5. Standard cost accounting systems separate variances into price and efficiency components because, in many situations, one person does not have decision responsibility for both purchases and usage. Even in situations when one person does have responsibility for both components, the separation is useful because it provides information for focused management correction.
6. To the extent that a multivariable budget model reflects cost behavior more accurately, it may provide a better indication of when actual costs are out of control. This may reduce the number of times needless investigations or justification efforts are conducted.
7. Prices paid for food may have increased significantly either because of recent changes in food prices or because of ineptness or fraud on the part of Mr. Schumaker. An audit of purchasing costs should be initiated, especially if other departments in the center have similar problems.
8. The following calculations should be made as a basis for deciding whether an investigation should be conducted:

    Expected benefits = $.5 \times \$1{,}000 \times (1 - .0228)^* = \$488.60$
    Expected costs = \$200
    *(1 − .0228) = Probability that the variance is not a random occurrence

    Yes, the variance should be investigated, because the expected benefits are greater than the expected costs. Even if the variance is favorable, it should be investigated, because it may indicate that the budget is not accurate. A reduction of the budget may promote a future reduction in costs.
9. The probability of observing six successive periods in which actual costs are greater than budgeted costs is $.50^6 = .0156$.
10. In your evaluation, you can calculate spending and volume variances for the radiology department. The total variance would be calculated as

    Actual cost less assigned cost, or

    $\$1{,}800{,}000 - 100{,}000 \times (\$1{,}920{,}000 / 120{,}000) = \$200{,}000$ (Unfavorable)

    The radiology department has an unfavorable variance of \$200,000, as opposed to a favorable variance of \$120,000. The \$200,000 unfavorable variance can be broken into spending and volume variances:

Spending variance = Actual costs − Budgeted fixed costs − Budgeted variable cost
= $1,800,000 − $600,000 − ($11 × 100,000) = $100,000 (Unfavorable)

Volume variance = (Budgeted volume − Actual volume) × Budgeted average fixed cost
= (120,000 − 100,000) × ($600,000/120,000) = $100,000 (Unfavorable)

The department manager may not be responsible for the volume variance, but the unfavorable spending variance of $100,000 should be analyzed to see what caused it. More detail would permit further breakdowns by price and efficiency variances.

11. The causes of the change in cost and the resulting variances for the laundry department are presented in Table 13–22.

12. The primary cause for the increase in cost has been the initiation of a new DRG category that is expensive to produce. This case illustrates the importance of case mix and severity-adjusting cost data. Table 13–23 breaks the variances into price and cost and volume variances.

Table 13–22 Variances for Laundry Department

Labor price	1,837	(Unfavorable)	55.26%
Supply price	1,611	(Unfavorable)	48.47
Labor efficiency	301	(Unfavorable)	9.06
Pure volume	508	(Unfavorable)	15.28
Intensity volume	(933)	(Favorable)	(28.07)
Total	3,324		100.00%

Labor price = ($7,873.00 − $7,260.67) × 3.0 = $1,837 (Unfavorable)
Supply price = ($3.1848 − $2.6946) × 3,286 = $1,611 (Unfavorable)
Labor efficiency = (3.0 − .00000900292 × 328,624) × $7,260.67 = $301 (Unfavorable)
Pure volume = (13.80385 × [24,539 − 24,140]) × $.092313 = 508 (Unfavorable)
Intensity volume = ([13.80385 − 13.39191] × 24,539) × $.092313 = $933 (Favorable)

Table 13–23 Valley Hospital Variance Analysis

	Variance Analysis by DRG			
	Cost	Volume	New	Total
DRG 106	$22,500	$12,750	0	$35,250
DRG 107	40,000	(32,000)	0	8,000
DRG 103	0	0	95,000	95,000
	$62,500	(19,250)	$95,000	$138,250

13. Table 13–24 provides the variances in the required categories.
The calculations for the variances are the following:

Enrollment:
Inpatient = 1,000 × .600 × $1,000 = $600,000 (Unfavorable)
Outpatient = 1,000 × 5.0 × $65 = $325,000 (Unfavorable)

Utilization
Inpatient = (.550 − .600) × 11,000 × $1,000 = −$550,000 (Favorable)
Outpatient = (5.5 − 5.0) × 11,000 × $65 = $357,500 (Unfavorable)

Efficiency
Inpatient = ($1,100 − $1,000) × 6,050 = $605,000 (Unfavorable)
Outpatient = ($62 − $65) × 60,500 = − $181,500 (Favorable)

The data suggest that the vast majority of the variance was created by an increase in enrollment. Of the total $1,156,000 variance, $925,000 was the result of an increase in enrollment. This should not be a concern. There was, however, an increase in the price paid for inpatient care from $1,000 per day to $1,100 per day. It is not clear whether this is a result in the intensity of patients seen, or the use of more expensive hospitals. Inpatient utilization decreased significantly and created a favorable variance of $550,000. On the outpatient side, the situation was reversed. Outpatient utilization increased, resulting in an unfavorable variance of $357,500, whereas outpatient efficiency or prices paid actually declined, resulting in a favorable variance of $181,500.

Table 13–24 American Health Plan Variances

	Inpatient	Outpatient	Total
Enrollment	$600,000	$325,000	$925,000
Utilization	−550,000	357,500	−192,500
Efficiency	605,000	−181,500	423,500
Total	$655,000	$501,000	$1,156,000

14

Financial Mathematics

In this chapter, we examine the concepts and methods of discounting sums of money received at various points in time through the use of compound interest formulas and tables. This material is of special importance in the context of the next two chapters on capital budgeting (Chapter 15) and capital financing (Chapter 16). The present abbreviated discussion of financial mathematics is intended as a review for those who have had prior exposure; if this material is new to the reader, some background reading may be necessary.

The two major questions in the financial decision-making process of any business are the following: (1) Where shall we invest our funds? and (2) How shall we finance our investment needs? Investment decisions involve expending funds today while expecting to realize returns in the future. Financing decisions involve the receipt of funds today in return for a promise to make payments in the future. The evaluation of the relative attractiveness of alternative investment and financing opportunities is a major task of management. Differences in the timing of either receipts or payments can have a significant impact on the ultimate decision to invest or finance in a certain way. A payment that is made or received in the first year has a greater value than an identical payment made or received in the tenth year. The concept underlying this point is often referred to as the time value of money. A time value for money is simply the assignment of a cost or interest rate for money.

Money or funds can be thought of as a commodity, like any other commodity that can be bought or sold. The price for the commodity called money is often stated as an interest rate, for example, 10 percent per year. An interest rate of 10 percent per year implies exchange rates between money at different periods. When the interest rate is 10 percent, a dollar received one year from today is worth only .9091 of a dollar received today, and a dollar received ten years from today is worth only .3855 of a dollar today. Compound interest rate tables are merely values that provide relative weighting for money received or paid during different periods at specified prices or interest rates. With these relative weightings, money received or paid can be added or subtracted to produce some logical meaningful result. The major purpose of compound interest tables is to permit addition and subtraction of money paid or received during different periods. The resulting sums are usually expressed in dollars at one of the two following time points: (1) present value and (2) future value.

The compound interest tables we shall use in this chapter are categorized as either present value or future value tables. The present value tables provide the relative weights that should be used to restate money of future periods back to the present. Future value tables provide the relative weighting for restating money of one period to some designated future period.

SINGLE-SUM PROBLEMS

Future Value—Single Sum

There are many situations in which a business would be interested in the future value of a single sum. For example, a nursing home may want to invest $100,000 today in a fund to be used in two years for replacement. It would like to know what sum of money would be available two years from now.

This type of problem is easily solved, using the values presented in Table 14–1. The first step in solving the problem is to set up a time graph.

This involves the following four variables that make up any simple compound interest problem:

1. number of periods during which the compounding occurs (n),
2. present value of future sum (p),
3. future value of present sum (f), and
4. interest rate per period (i).

If you know the values of any three of these variables, you can solve for the fourth. The time graph is a simple device that helps you to conceptualize the problem and identify the known values to permit the problem to be solved. In the previous nursing-home investment example, a 10-percent interest rate per period would be reflected in Figure 14–1.

The value 0 on this time graph represents the present time, whereas the values 1 and 2 represent Year 1 and Year 2. In the nursing-home ex-

Table 14–1 Future Value of $1 Received in n Periods

Period	2%	4%	6%	8%	10%	12%	14%
1	1.0200	1.0400	1.0600	1.0800	1.1000	1.1200	1.1400
2	1.0404	1.0816	1.1236	1.1664	1.2100	1.2544	1.2996
3	1.0612	1.1249	1.1910	1.2597	1.3310	1.4049	1.4815
4	1.0824	1.1699	1.2625	1.3605	1.4641	1.5735	1.6890
5	1.1041	1.2167	1.3382	1.4693	1.6105	1.7623	1.9254
6	1.1262	1.2653	1.4185	1.5869	1.7716	1.9738	2.1950
7	1.1487	1.3159	1.5036	1.7138	1.9487	2.2107	2.5023
8	1.1717	1.3686	1.5938	1.8509	2.1436	2.4760	2.8526
9	1.1951	1.4233	1.6895	1.9990	2.3579	2.7731	3.2519
10	1.2190	1.4802	1.7908	2.1589	2.5937	3.1058	3.7072
11	1.2434	1.5395	1.8983	2.3316	2.8531	3.4785	4.2262
12	1.2682	1.6010	2.0122	2.5182	3.1384	3.8960	4.8179
13	1.2936	1.6651	2.1329	2.7196	3.4523	4.3635	5.4924
14	1.3195	1.7317	2.2609	2.9372	3.7975	4.8871	6.2613
15	1.3459	1.8009	2.3966	3.1722	4.1772	5.4736	7.1379
16	1.3728	1.8730	2.5404	3.4259	4.5950	6.1304	8.1372
17	1.4002	1.9479	2.6928	3.7000	5.0545	6.8660	9.2765
18	1.4282	2.0258	2.8543	3.9960	5.5599	7.6900	10.5752
19	1.4568	2.1068	3.0256	4.3157	6.1159	8.6128	12.0557
20	1.4859	2.1911	3.2071	4.6610	6.7275	9.6463	13.7435
30	1.8114	3.2434	5.7435	10.0627	17.4494	29.9599	50.9502
40	2.2080	4.8010	10.2857	21.7245	45.2593	93.0510	188.8835

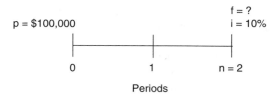

Figure 14–1

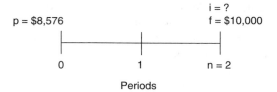

Figure 14–2

ample, we know three of the four variables and can, therefore, solve the problem through substitution in the following formula:

$$f = p \times f(i,n)$$

The factor f(i, n) is the future value of $1 invested today for n periods at i rate of interest per period. These values can be found in Table 14–1, using the previous generic formula. The following calculation then can be made to solve the problem:

$$f = \$100,00 \times f(10\%,2) \text{ or}$$

$$f = \$100,000 \times 1.210 \text{ or}$$

$$f = \$121,000$$

In some situations, it may be the interest rate that we wish to determine. Assume that we can invest $8,576 today in a discounted note that will pay us $10,000 two years from today. Figure 14–2 summarizes the problem.

The following calculation then can be made to solve the problem:

$$\$10,000 = \$8,576 \times f(i,2) \text{ or}$$
$$f(i,2) = 1.166$$

A check of the values in Table 14–1 indicates that the interest rate would be 8 percent (f[8%,2] = 1.166). If the previous value had not exactly matched a figure in the table, some interpolation would have been required.

A microcomputer or a calculator with a financial mathematics function also could be used to

solve the previous types of problems. It is still useful, however, to set up a time graph to conceptualize the problem before entering numbers into the calculator or computer.

Present Value—Single Sum

In some situations, it is the present value of a future sum that is of interest. This type of problem is similar to those we examined regarding the future value of a single sum. In fact, the same table of values could be used, except that now we would use division rather than multiplication.

The general equation used to solve present-value, single-sum problems is the following:

$$p = f \times p(i,n)$$

The factor p(i,n) represents the present value of $1 received in n periods at an interest rate of i. Values for p(i,n) can be found in Table 14–2.

Assume that your health maintenance organization (HMO) has a $100,000 debt service obligation due in two years. You are interested in learning how much money must be set aside today to meet the obligation if the expected yield on the investment is 12 percent. The relevant time graph is depicted in Figure 14–3.

The calculation to solve the problem would be the following:

$$p = f \times p(i,n) \text{ or}$$

$$p = \$100,000 \times p(12\%,2) \text{ or}$$

$$p = \$100,000 \times .797 \text{ or}$$

$$p = \$79,700$$

Table 14–2 Present Value of $1 Due in n Periods

Period	2%	4%	6%	8%	10%	12%	14%
1	0.9804	0.9615	0.9434	0.9259	0.9091	0.8929	0.8772
2	0.9612	0.9246	0.8900	0.8573	0.8264	0.7972	0.7695
3	0.9423	0.8890	0.8396	0.7938	0.7513	0.7118	0.6750
4	0.9238	0.8548	0.7921	0.7350	0.6830	0.6355	0.5921
5	0.9057	0.8219	0.7473	0.6806	0.6209 ⟩	0.5674	0.5194
6	0.8880	0.7903	0.7050	0.6302	0.5645	0.5066	0.4556
7	0.8706	0.7599	0.6651	0.5835	0.5132	0.4523	0.3996
8	0.8535	0.7307	0.6274	0.5403	0.4665	0.4039	0.3506
9	0.8368	0.7026	0.5919	0.5002	0.4241	0.3606	0.3075
10	0.8203	0.6756	0.5584	0.4632	0.3855	0.3220	0.2697
11	0.8043	0.6496	0.5268	0.4289	0.3505	0.2875	0.2366
12	0.7885	0.6246	0.4970	0.3971	0.3186	0.2567	0.2076
13	0.7730	0.6006	0.4688	0.3677	0.2897	0.2292	0.1821
14	0.7579	0.5775	0.4423	0.3405	0.2633	0.2046	0.1597
15	0.7430	0.5553	0.4173	0.3152	0.2394	0.1827	0.1401
16	0.7284	0.5339	0.3936	0.2919	0.2176	0.1631	0.1229
17	0.7142	0.5134	0.3714	0.2703	0.1978	0.1456	0.1078
18	0.7002	0.4936	0.3503	0.2502	0.1799	0.1300	0.0946
19	0.6864	0.4746	0.3305	0.2317	0.1635	0.1161	0.0829
20	0.6730	0.4564	0.3118	0.2145	0.1486	0.1037	0.0728
30	0.5521	0.3083	0.1741	0.0994	0.0573	0.0334	0.0196
40	0.4529	0.2083	0.0972	0.0460	0.0221	0.0107	0.0053

It is important to note that the values of Table 14–1 and Table 14–2 are reciprocals of each other. That is

$$f(i,n) = 1/p(i,n)$$

In effect, this means that only one of the two tables is necessary to solve either a present-value or future-value problem involving a single sum.

ANNUITY PROBLEMS

Future Value

In many business situations, there is more than one payment or receipt. In the case of multiple payments or receipts, when each payment or receipt is constant per time period, we have an annuity situation. Figure 14–4 depicts a time graph for an annuity.

In the graph in Figure 14–4, F represents the future value of the invested annuity deposits at the end of period n. (Note that F is used to denote future value for annuities, while f is used for single sums.) The values for R represent the periodic deposits that are constant for each period. It should be emphasized that the deposits are made at the end of each period. Such a system of deposits is often described as an ordinary annu-

Figure 14–3

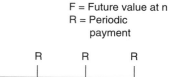

F = Future value at n
R = Periodic
    payment

Figure 14–4

ity. The values presented in Tables 14–3 and 14–4 assume an ordinary annuity situation in which deposits or receipts occur at the end of the period.

The basic equation for a future value annuity is

$$F = R \times F(i,n)$$

The factor F(i, n) represents the future value of $1 invested each period for n periods at i rate of interest. Values for F(i, n) can be found in Table 14–3. Again, if three of the four variables (F, R, i, and n) in the previous equation are known, the equation can be solved to determine the fourth. Thus, if we know F, i, and n, we can solve for R.

Assume that a hospital wants to know what the value of $50,000 worth of annual deposits in a trust fund for professional malpractice insurance will be in three years if the fund earns 8 percent per year. The time graph for this problem is depicted in Figure 14–5.

The calculation to solve the problem would be as follows:

$$F = R \times F(i,n) \text{ or}$$

$$F = \$50,000 \times F(8\%,3) \text{ or}$$

$$F = \$50,000 \times 3.2464 \text{ or}$$

$$F = \$162,320$$

Table 14–3 Future Value of $1 Received Each Period for n Periods

Period	2%	4%	6%	8%	10%	12%	14%
1	1.0000	1.0000	1.0000	1.0000	1.0000	1.0000	1.0000
2	2.0200	2.0400	2.0600	2.0800	2.1000	2.1200	2.1400
3	3.0604	3.1216	3.1836	3.2464	3.3100	3.3744	3.4396
4	4.1216	4.2465	4.3746	4.5061	4.6410	4.7793	4.9211
5	5.2040	5.4163	5.6371	5.8666	6.1051	6.3528	6.6101
6	6.3081	6.6330	6.9753	7.3359	7.7156	8.1152	8.5355
7	7.4343	7.8983	8.3938	8.9228	9.4872	10.0890	10.7305
8	8.5830	9.2142	9.8975	10.6366	11.4359	12.2997	13.2328
9	9.7546	10.5828	11.4913	12.4876	13.5795	14.7757	16.0853
10	10.9497	12.0061	13.1808	14.4866	15.9374	17.5487	19.3373
11	12.1687	13.4864	14.9716	16.6455	18.5312	20.6546	23.0445
12	13.4121	15.0258	16.8699	18.9771	21.3843	24.1331	27.2707
13	14.6803	16.6268	18.8821	21.4953	24.5227	28.0291	32.0887
14	15.9739	18.2919	21.0151	24.2149	27.9750	32.3926	37.5811
15	17.2934	20.0236	23.2760	27.1521	31.7725	37.2797	43.8424
16	18.6393	21.8245	25.6725	30.3243	35.9497	42.7533	50.9804
17	20.0121	23.6975	28.2129	33.7502	40.5447	48.8837	59.1176
18	21.4123	25.6454	30.9057	37.4502	45.5992	55.7497	68.3941
19	22.8406	27.6712	33.7600	41.4463	51.1591	63.4397	78.9692
20	24.2974	29.7781	36.7856	45.7620	57.2750	72.0524	91.0249
30	40.5681	56.0849	79.0582	113.2832	164.4940	241.3327	356.7868
40	60.4020	95.0255	154.7620	259.0565	442.5926	767.0914	1342.0251

Table 14–4 Present Value of $1 Received Each Period for n Periods

Period	2%	4%	6%	8%	10%	12%	14%
1	0.9804	0.9615	0.9434	0.9259	0.9091	0.8929	0.8772
2	1.9416	1.8861	1.8334	1.7833	1.7355	1.6901	1.6467
3	2.8839	2.7751	2.6730	2.5771	2.4869	2.4018	2.3216
4	3.8077	3.6299	3.4651	3.3121	3.1699	3.0373	2.9137
5	4.7135	4.4518	4.2124	3.9927	3.7908	3.6048	3.4331
6	5.6014	5.2421	4.9173	4.6229	4.3553	4.1114	3.8887
7	6.4720	6.0021	5.5824	5.2064	4.8684	4.5638	4.2883
8	7.3255	6.7327	6.2098	5.7466	5.3349	4.9676	4.6389
9	8.1622	7.4353	6.8017	6.2469	5.7590	5.3282	4.9464
10	8.9826	8.1109	7.3601	6.7101	6.1446	5.6502	5.2161
11	9.7868	8.7605	7.8869	7.1390	6.4951	5.9377	5.4527
12	10.5753	9.3851	8.3838	7.5361	6.8137	6.1944	5.6603
13	11.3484	9.9856	8.8527	7.9038	7.1034	6.4235	5.8424
14	12.1062	10.5631	9.2950	8.2442	7.3667	6.6282	6.0021
15	12.8493	11.1184	9.7122	8.5595	7.6061	6.8109	6.1422
16	13.5777	11.6523	10.1059	8.8514	7.8237	6.9740	6.2651
17	14.2919	12.1657	10.4773	9.1216	8.0216	7.1196	6.3729
18	14.9920	12.6593	10.8276	9.3719	8.2014	7.2497	6.4674
19	15.6785	13.1339	11.1581	9.6036	8.3649	7.3658	6.5504
20	16.3514	13.5903	11.4699	9.8181	8.5136	7.4694	6.6231
30	22.3965	17.2920	13.7648	11.2578	9.4269	8.0552	7.0027
40	27.3555	19.7928	15.0463	11.9246	9.7791	8.2438	7.1050

The values in Table 14–3 also could be determined through simple addition of the values for a single sum in Table 14–1. This can be seen easily by further examining our hospital example. Table 14–5 summarizes the relevant data.

Notice that the future value total in Table 14–5 is identical to that in the earlier annuity formula. Also note that the summation of the individual future value factors yields the value of the

annuity factor (3.2464). In general, a future value annuity factor can be expressed as follows:

$$F(i,n) = f(i,1) + f(i,2) +.... + f(i,n - 1) + 1.0$$

In many situations, a financial mathematics problem may be part annuity and part single sum. In such cases, the use of a time graph will help you spot this duality and solve the problem correctly. Assume that a hospital has a sinking fund payment requirement for the last ten years of a bond's life. At the end of that period, there must be $45 million available to retire the debt. The hospital has created a $5 million fund today, twenty years before debt retirement, to offset part of the future sinking fund requirement. If the investment yield is expected to be 10 percent per year, what annual deposit must be made to the sinking fund? Figure 14–6 summarizes the problem.

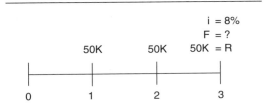

Figure 14–5

Table 14–5

Year	Future Value Factor (8%)	Future Value	Year Invested		
			1	2	3
1	1.1664	$ 58,320	$50,000		
2	1.0800	54,000		$50,000	
3	1.0000	50,000			$50,000
Total	3.2464	$162,320			

The first step is to determine the future value of the $5 million deposit, which is

f = $5,000,000 × f(10%,20) or

f = $5,000,000 × 6.7275 or

f = $33,637,500

This means that the amount of money that must be generated by the ten sinking fund deposits must equal $11,362,500 ($45,000,000 − $33,637,500). The following calculation provides the solution:

F − f = R × F(i,n) or

$11,362,500 = R × F(10%,10) or

$11,362,500 = R × 15.9374 or

R = $712,946

Present Value

While determining the present value of an annuity, the procedure is analogous to that used to determine the future value of an annuity, except that our attention is now on present value rather than future value. Figure 14–7 represents the typical present value annuity problem.

As noted earlier, this is an ordinary annuity situation because the payments are at the end of the period. The basic equation used to solve a present-value annuity problem is the following:

P = R × P(i,n)

The factor P(i,n) represents the present value of $1 received at the end of each period for n periods when i is the rate of interest. Values for P(i,n) are found in Table 14–4. (Note that P is used to denote an annuity problem, while p is used to denote a single sum problem.)

Assume that a hospital is considering buying an older hospital and consolidating its operations in another nearby facility. An actuary has estimated that pension payments of $100,000 per year for the next four years will be required to satisfy the obligation to vested employees. The hospital wants to know what the present value of this obligation is so that it can be sub-

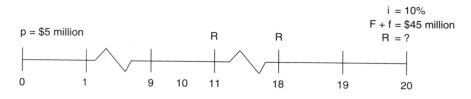

Figure 14–6

Figure 14–7

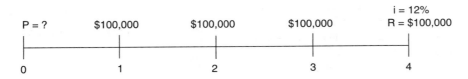

Figure 14–8

Table 14–6

Year	Present Value Factor (12%)	Present Value	Year of Payment			
			1	*2*	*3*	*4*
1	.893	$ 89,300	$100,000			
2	.797	79,700		$100,000		
3	.712	71,200			$100,000	
4	.636	63,600				$100,000
Total	3.038	$303,800				

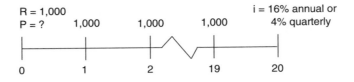

Figure 14–9

tracted from the negotiated purchase price. The obligation's discount rate is assumed to be 12 percent. The time graph for this problem is depicted in Figure 14–8.

The calculation to solve the problem is as follows:

$$P = \$100,000 \times P(12\%,4) \text{ or}$$

$$P = \$100,000 \times 3.037$$

$$P = \$303,700$$

Present-value annuity problems can be thought of as a series of individual single-sum problems. The present-value annuity factor $P(i,n)$ is the sum of the individual single-sum values of Table 14–2. The data in Table 14–6 summarize this calculation in our hospital example.

The small differences between the annuity values and the single-sum values in Table 14–6 are due to rounding errors.

The present-value annuity factor $[P(i,n)]$ can be expressed as follows:

$$P(i,n) = p(i,1) + p(i,2) +... + p(i,n) \,.$$

In most business situations, ordinary annuity problems do not arise. The classic exception to the ordinary annuity situation is a lease with front-end payments. Assume that a clinic wants to lease a computer for the next five years with quarterly payments of $1,000 due at the beginning of each quarter. If the clinic's discount rate is 16 percent per annum, what is the present value of the lease liability? The relevant time graph is presented in Figure 14–9.

The graph in Figure 14–9 indicates that the clinic has a nineteen-period ordinary annuity, with each period lasting three months. The effective interest rate for each quarter is 4 percent. The present value of the first payment is $1,000 because it occurs at the beginning of the first quarter. The following calculation provides the solution to the problem:

$$P = \$1,000 + \$1,000 \times P(4\%,19) \text{ or}$$

$$P = \$1,000 + \$1,000 \times 13.134 \text{ or}$$

$$P = \$14,134$$

SUMMARY

In the area of financial mathematics, compound interest rate tables provide us with values with which we can weight money flows that are received or paid during different periods. The relative weighting assigned to each period's money flow is a function of the price of money or the interest rate. The relative weightings permit us to add or subtract money flows from different periods and produce a meaningful measure. The value of money is usually expressed in terms of present value or value at some future specified date.

ASSIGNMENTS

1. Steven Hudson has agreed to settle a debt of $100,000 by paying $14,903 per year for ten years. What effective rate of interest is Steven paying under this agreement?

2. Findling Hospital is planning a major expansion project. The construction cost of the project is to be paid from the proceeds of serial notes. The notes are of equal amounts and include a provision for interest at an annual rate of 8 percent payable semiannually over the next 10 years. It is expected that receipts from the hospital will provide for the repayment of principal and interest on the notes. Allan Klein, controller of the hospital, has estimated that the cash flow available for repayment of principal and interest will be $450,000 per year. The construction project is expected to cost $3,420,000. Can the hospital meet the peak debt service with existing cash flows?

3. Jerry Scott has just accepted a position with a state agency that has a retirement pension plan calling for joint contributions by the employee and the employer. Jerry is now ten years from retirement age of sixty-five and expects to contribute $400 per year to the plan, which would make him eligible for payments of $1,000 per year for the remainder of his life, starting in ten years. Because this retirement plan is optional, Jerry is considering the alternative of investing annually an amount equal to his $400 per year contribution. If Jerry can assume that his investments would earn 8 percent annually, and that his life expectancy is eighty years, should he invest in his own plan or should he make contributions to his employer's fund?

4. Meany Hospital wishes to provide for the retirement of an obligation of $10,000,000 that becomes due July 1, 2005. The hospital plans to deposit $500,000 in a special fund each July 1 for eight years, starting July 1,1997. In addition, the hospital wishes to deposit on July 1, 1997, an amount that, with accumulated interest at 10 percent compounded annually, will bring the total value of the fund to the required $10,000,000 at the end of 2005. What dollar amount should the hospital deposit?

5. Jim Hubert, an investment banker with The Ohio Company, is arranging a financing package with Bill Andrews, president of Liebish Hospital. The financing package calls for $20 million in bonds to be repaid in twenty years. A decision must be made regarding the amount that must be deposited on an annual basis in a sinking fund. It is estimated that the sinking fund will earn interest at the rate of 8 percent compounded annually. What dollar amount must be set aside annually in the sinking fund to meet the $20 million payment in the twentieth year?

6. General Hospital is evaluating a zero-interest capital financing alternative. General would borrow $100,000,000 and receive $62,100,000 in cash. The $100,000,000 note would carry no interest payment but would be due at the end of the fifth year. The lender would require an annual sinking fund payment over the next five years to meet the maturity value of $100,000,000. If the fund is scheduled to earn interest at the rate of 6 percent annually, what amount must be deposited annually?

7. ABC Hospital is embarking on a major renovation program. The total cost of construction will be $50,000,000. Payments will be $10,000,000 at the end of Year 1, $30,000,000 at the end of Year 2, and $10,000,000 at the end of Year 3. ABC wants to set aside sufficient funds today to meet the expected construction draws. If the fund can be expected to earn 8 percent per annum, what amount should be set aside?

8. If you issue $100,000 of 10-percent bonds with interest payable semiannually over the next five years, what is the market value of the bonds if the required market rate of interest is 12 percent annually? Assume that no payment of principal is made until maturity.

9. You have agreed to buy an adjacent medical office building with quarterly payments of $100,000 for the next six years. Payments are due at the beginning of each quarter. If the cost of money to you is 16 percent per annum, would you pay $1,200,000 in cash today to the present owners?

10. You plan to invest $1 million per year for the next three years to meet future professional liability payments. If the fund earns interest at a rate of 10-percent per annum, how large will the balance be in five years? Assume that no payments for claims are made until then.

SOLUTIONS AND ANSWERS

1. The graph in Figure 14–10 and the following calculations show the effective rate of interest Steven is paying.

   $P = R \times P(i,n)$

   $\$100{,}000 = \$14{,}903 \times P(i,10)$

   $P(i,10) = 6.710$

   $i = 8\%$

2. In this hospital expansion project, it is necessary to recognize that debt service will be at the maximum or peak in the first year. This is the pattern that results with a serial note. Thus:

   Debt principal payment = \$3,420,000/20 = \$171,000 every six months

   Interest in first six months = .04 × \$3,420,000 = \$136,800

   Interest in second six months = .04 × (\$3,420,000 – \$171,000) = \$129,960

   Total first-year debt service = \$171,000 + \$136,800 + \$171,000 + \$129,960 = \$608,760

   Thus, Findling Hospital's project cannot be financed with the existing cash flow of \$450,000.

3. The graph in Figure 14–11 and the following calculations are relevant to Jerry's retirement fund decision.

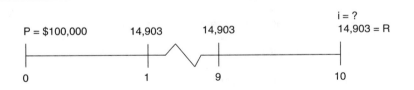

Figure 14–10

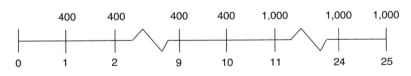

Figure 14–11

Calculation of the value of the state agency's payments at Year 10 is as follows:

P = $1,000 × P(8%,15)

P = $1,000 × 8.559

P = $8,559

Calculation of the value of Jerry's deposits at Year 10 is as follows:

F = $400 × F(8%,10)

F = $400 × 14.4866

F = $5,795

Thus, Jerry is better off with the state agency's retirement plan. His deposits of $400 would not provide a fund large enough to give him $1,000 a year for fifteen years.

4. The relevant calculations for Meany Hospital are as follows and depicted in Figure 14–12.

Calculation of the value of annual deposits at July 1, 2005 is as follows:

Future Value of Deposits = $500,000 × f(10%,8) + [$500,000 × F(10%,7)]f(10%,1)

F = $500,000 × 2.1436 + ($500,000 × 9.4872) × 1.10

F = $1,071,800 + $5,217,960 = $6,289,760

Calculation of the required deposit at July 1, 1997 is as follows:
Required amount at July 1, 2005 must equal $10,000,000 – $6,289,760, or $3,710,240.

p = $3,710,240 × p(10%,8) = required deposit at July 1, 1997

p = $3,710,240 × .467

p = $1,732,682 = deposit required at July 1, 1997

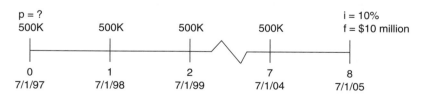

Figure 14–12

5. Figure 14–13 and the following calculations show the dollar amount that must be set aside annually in the sinking fund to meet the $20-million repayment in the twentieth year.

$F = R \times F(i,n)$

$\$20,000,000 = R \times F(8\%,20)$

$\$20,000,000 = R \times 45.7620$

$R = \$437,044$

6. Figure 14–14 and the following calculations show the amount that General Hospital will have to deposit in the sinking fund each year.

$F = R \times F(i,n)$

$\$100,000,000 = R \times F(6\%,5)$

$\$100,000,000 = R \times 5.6371$

$R = \$17,739,618$

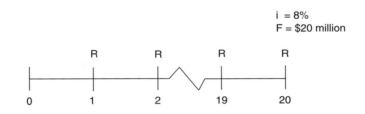

Figure 14–13

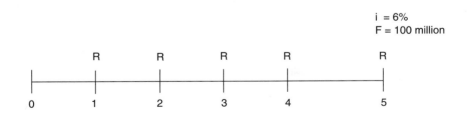

Figure 14–14

7. Figure 14–15 and the following calculations show the amount that ABC Hospital must set aside to meet expected construction draws.

p = $10,000,000 × p(8%,1) + $30,000,000 × p(8%,2) + $10,000,000 × p(8%,3)

p = $10,000,000 × .926 + $30,000,000 × .857 + $10,000,000 × .794

p = $42,910,000

8. The market value of the bonds may be calculated as follows (Figure 14–16):

Market Value = $5,000 × P(6%,10) + $100,000 × p(6%,10)

Market Value = $5,000 × 7.360 + $100,000 × .558

Market Value = $92,600

9. To determine whether you should pay $1,200,00 in cash today to the present owners, Figure 14–17 and the following calculations are relevant.

P = $100,000 + $100,000 × P(4%,23)

P = $100,000 + ($100,000 × 14.857)

P = $1,585,700

Yes, you should make the $1,200,000 cash payment to the present owners. The present value of an outright purchase price of $1,200,000 is less than the present value of the installment sale arrangement.

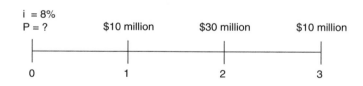

Figure 14–15

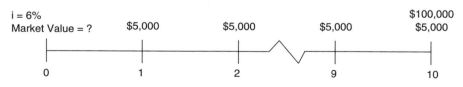

Figure 14–16

10. Figure 14–18 and the following calculations show the amount of the fund balance in five years.

Fund Value = $1,000,000 × F(10%,3) × f(10%,2)

Fund Value = $1,000,000 × 3.310 × 1.210

Fund Value = $4,005,100

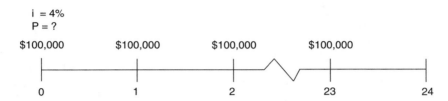

i = 4%
P = ?

$100,000 $100,000 $100,000 $100,000

0   1   2   23   24

Figure 14–17

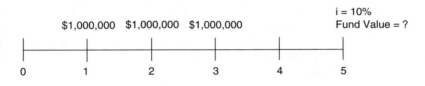

$1,000,000 $1,000,000 $1,000,000

i = 10%
Fund Value = ?

0   1   2   3   4   5

Figure 14–18

15

Capital Project Analysis

Capital project analysis occurs during the programming phase of the management control process. Whereas zero-base budgeting or zero-base review can be considered as the programming phase of management control concerned with old or existing programs, capital project analysis is the phase primarily concerned with new programs. Here, it is broadly defined to include the selection of investment projects.

Capital project analysis is an ongoing activity, but it is not usually summarized annually in the budget. The capital budget is the yearly estimate of resources that will be expended for new programs during the coming year. Capital budgeting may be considered as less comprehensive and shorter term than capital project analysis.

PARTICIPANTS IN THE ANALYTICAL PROCESS

The capital decision-making process in the health care industry is complex for several reasons. First, a health care firm, whether nonprofit or investor-owned, is likely to have more complex and less quantifiable objectives than firms in other industries. Provision of care to the indigent and community access to services as well as to quality standards are often critical objectives for health care firms in addition to profits. Second, the number of individuals involved in the

process, either directly or indirectly, is likely to be greater in the health care industry than in most other industries. Figure 15–1 illustrates the relationships of various parties involved in the capital decision-making process of a health care facility.

External Participants

Financing Sources

The option of obtaining funds externally for many new programs is an important variable in the capital decision-making process. A variety of individual organizations are involved in the credit-determination process, including investment bankers, bond-rating agencies, bankers, and feasibility consultants. Many of these entities and their roles are discussed in Chapter 16. At this juncture, it is important to recognize that, collectively, these entities may influence the amount of money that can be borrowed and the terms of the borrowing, and this can affect the nature and size of capital projects undertaken by a given health care facility.

Rate-Setting and Rate-Control Agencies

Government, both federal and state, often control or limit the rates that hospitals and other health care firms can charge for services. The

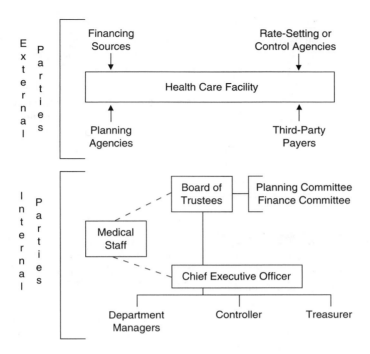

Figure 15-1 Capital Decision-Making Participants

influence exerted by rate-setting or rate-control organizations on capital decision making is indirect but still extremely important. Control of rates can limit both short-term and long-term profitability. This control can reduce a health care firm's ability to repay indebtedness and thus limit its access to the capital markets. More directly, rate-setting organizations can limit the amount of money available for financing capital projects by reducing the amount of profits that may be retained. One of the major effects of rate control is to significantly reduce the level of capital expenditures by health care firms.

Third-Party Payers

Like rate-setting and rate-control agencies, third-party payers can indirectly influence the capital decision-making process. Through their reimbursement provisions, third-party payers can affect both capital expenditure levels and

sources of financing. For example, many people believe that third-party cost reimbursement provides a strong incentive for increased capital spending: in most situations, such cost reimbursement provides for the reimbursement of depreciation and interest expense, which then may be used to repay financial requirements associated with any indebtedness. As a result, the risk associated with hospital-indebted indebtedness is reduced. In the past, third-party cost reimbursement favorably affected the availability of credit. Conversely, recent departures from cost reimbursement have had an adverse impact on credit availability.

Planning Agencies

In many states, state approval of capital expenditures is still required. Planning agencies review certificate-of-need applications and their recommendations are then passed on to the state authority responsible for final approval or disapproval. An unfavorable decision by the state can be appealed in court.

Internal Participants

Board of Trustees

Ultimately, the board of trustees is responsible for the capital expenditure and capital financing program of the health care firm. However, in most situations, the board delegates this authority to management and special board committees. The board's major function should be to clearly establish defined goals and objectives. The statement of goals and objectives is a prerequisite to the programming phase of management control, which includes capital expenditure analysis. Without a clear statement of goals and objectives, capital expenditure programs cannot be adequately defined and analyzed.

Another role of the governing board should be to approve a preliminary five-year capital expenditure program. This capital expenditure program should link back to the strategic financial plan discussed in Chapter 9. The list of capital expenditures should be generated by management and should reflect not just a "wish list" of capital expenditures that would be desirable to make, but should represent management's best guess concerning what future capital expenditures will be essential to meet and maintain the organization's mission.

Planning Committee

Many health care facility boards of trustees have established planning committees whose primary function is to define, analyze, and propose programs to help the organization attain its goals and objectives. These committees are specialized groups within the board of trustees that are directly involved in capital expenditure analysis.

Finance Committee

Some boards of trustees also have established finance committees that have authority in several key financial functional areas, including budgeting and capital financing. In the latter two areas, a finance committee may be involved with translating programs, perhaps identified by the planning committee, into financing requirements. These requirements may be operational or capital. The finance committee's major responsibility is to ensure adequate financing to meet program requirements. Many of the finance committee's budgetary functions are delegated to the controller; many of its capital financing functions are delegated to the treasurer.

Chief Executive Officer

The chief executive officer (CEO) is responsible on a day-to-day basis for implementing approved capital expenditure programs and developing related financing plans. The CEO must develop an organizational system that responds to the requests of department managers and medical staff for capital expenditures. Much of the authority vested in the chief executive officer's (CEO) position is delegated by the board of trustees. The administration also may seek board approval for its own programs.

Department Managers

Department managers make most of the internal requests for capital expenditure approval. In many health care facilities, formal systems for approving capital expenditures have been developed to receive, process, and answer departmental requests. The allocation of a limited capital budget to competing departmental areas is a difficult task for management. Careful definition of the criteria for capital decision making can help make this problem less political and more objective.

Medical Staff

Medical staff demands for capital expenditures are a problem unique to the health care industry. Medical staff members, in most situations, are not employees of the health care firm but rather use it to treat their private patients. Because of their ability to change a firm's utilization dramatically and thus affect financial solvency, administrators listen to, and frequently honor, medical staff members' wishes. Health care firms thus encounter strong pressure from individuals who have little financial interest in the organization and whose financial interest may, in fact, be contrary to that of the health care firm.

Controller

The controller facilitates approval of capital expenditures. The controller is usually responsible for developing capital expenditure request forms and for assisting department managers with preparing their capital expenditure proposals. The controller usually serves as an analyst, assisting the administrator with allocating the budget to competing departmental areas. In many small health care firms, the controller's function may be merged with that of the treasurer.

Treasurer

The treasurer is responsible for obtaining funds for both short- and long-term programs. The treasurer may work with the finance committee to negotiate for funds necessary to implement approved programs.

CLASSIFICATION OF CAPITAL EXPENDITURES

A capital expenditure is a commitment of resources that is expected to provide benefits during a reasonably long period—at least two or more years. Any system of management control must take into account the various types of capital expenditures. Different types of capital expenditures create different problems; they may require specific individuals to evaluate them or special methods of evaluation.

The more important classifications of capital expenditures are

- period during which the investment occurs,
- types of resources invested,
- dollar amounts of capital expenditures, and
- types of benefits received.

Period of Investment

Determining the amount of resources committed to a capital project depends heavily on the definition of the period. For example, how would you determine the capital expenditures needed by a project that had a low initial investment cost but will have a significant investment cost in future years? Should just the initial capital expenditure be considered, or should total expenditures over the life of the project be considered? If the latter is the answer, is it appropriate just to add the total expenditures together, or should expenditures made in later years be weighted to reflect their lower present value? If so, at what discount rate? These are not simple questions to answer, but they are important when evaluating capital projects.

A classic example of this type of problem in the health care industry is the initiation of programs that have been funded by grants. In many such situations, there appears to be little or no investment of capital, because the amounts are funded almost totally through the grant. The programs thus appear to be highly desirable. However, if there is a formal or informal commitment to continue the programs for a longer period, capital expenditures and additional operating funds for later periods may be required. In such cases, it is imperative that the grant-funded projects be classified separately and their long-run capital cost requirements be identified. The health care facility may very well not have a sufficient capital base to finance a program's continuation. Thus, granting agencies should assess the health care facility's financial capability to continue funded programs after the grant period expires.

Types of Resources Invested

When discussing capital expenditures, many people are apt to limit their attention just to the expenditure or resources invested in capital assets, that is, tangible fixed assets. This narrow focus has several shortcomings, however, and may result in ineffective capital expenditure decisions.

First, focusing on tangible fixed assets implies ownership; yet, many health care facilities lease a significant percentage of their fixed assets, especially in the major movable equipment area. If a lease is not construed to be a capital expenditure, it may escape the normal review and approval system. Lease payments should be considered as a capital expenditure. Furthermore, the contractual provisions of the lease should be considered when determining the total expenditure amount. Weight should be given to future payments or to the alternative purchase price of the asset.

Second, the capital costs of a capital expenditure are only one part of total cost; indeed, in the labor-intensive health care industry, capital costs may be just the "tip of the iceberg." All of the operating costs associated with beginning and continuing a capital project should be considered. Programs with low capital investment costs may not be considered as favorable when their operating costs are taken into account.

Lifecycle costing is a method for estimating the cost of a capital project that reflects total costs, both operating and capital, over the project's estimated useful life. The lifecycle cost of all contemplated programs should be considered; failure to do this can cause errors in the capital decision-making process, especially in the selection of alternative programs. Consider, for example, two alternative renal dialysis projects; both may have the same capacity, but one may have a significantly greater investment cost because it uses equipment requiring less monitoring and lower operating costs. Failure to consider the operating cost differences between these two projects may bias the decision in favor of the project with lower capital expenditures and result in higher expenses in the long run.

Amounts of Expenditures

Different systems of control and evaluation are required for different-sized projects. It would not be economical to spend $500 in administra-

tive time evaluating the purchase of a $100 calculator. Nor would it be wise to spend only $500 to evaluate a $25 million building program. Obviously, control over capital expenditures should be conditioned by the total amount involved; and, if appropriate, the amount should be based on the total lifecycle cost.

Control of capital expenditures in most organizations, including health care firms, typically follows one of three patterns:

1. approval required for all capital expenditures,
2. approval required for all capital expenditures above a pre-established limit, or
3. no approval required for individual capital expenditure projects below a total budgeted amount.

Retaining final approval of all capital expenditures allows management to exert maximum control over the resource-spending area. However, the cost of management time to develop and review expenditure proposals is high. In most organizations of any size, management review of all capital expenditure requests is not productive. However, some review is needed, so a limit must be established. For example, a given responsibility center or department need not submit any justification for individual capital expenditure projects requiring less than $500 in investment costs. In such cases, there is usually some formal or informal limitation on the total dollar size of the capital budget that will be available for small-dollar capital expenditures. This prevents responsibility-center managers from making excessive investments in capital expenditures that have no formalized reviewing system.

Another form of management control over capital expenditures is an absolute dollar limit; that is, any responsibility center manager may spend up to an authorized capital budget on any items in question. The real negotiation involves determining the size of the capital budget that will be available for individual departments. However, this system, although least costly in terms of review time, does not ensure that the capital expenditures actually made are necessarily in the best interests of the organization.

Types of Benefits

Depending on the types of benefits envisioned for a capital expenditure, different systems of management control and evaluation may be necessary. For example, investment in a medical-office building results in different benefits than investment in an alcoholic rehabilitation unit. Such differences make it inappropriate to rely exclusively on any one method of evaluating projects. It is important to note that traditional methods of evaluating capital budgeting may not be appropriate in the health care industry. Traditional methods evaluate only the financial aspects of a capital expenditure. However, projects in the health care industry may produce benefits that are much more important than a reduction in cost or an increase in profit.

The following are major categories of investment in which benefits may be differentially evaluated:

- operational continuance,
- financial, and
- other.

The first category of investment produces benefits that permit continued operations of the facility along present lines. Here, the governing board or management must usually answer the following two questions: (1) Are continued operations in the present form desirable? (In most cases, the answer is yes.) (2) Which alternative investment project can achieve continued operations in the most desirable way (for example, with lowest cost, patient safety, and so on)? A classic example of this type of investment is based on a licensure requirement for installation of a sprinkler system in a nursing home. Failure to make the investment may result in discontinuance of operations.

The second category of investment provides benefits that are largely financial, in terms of either reduced costs or increased profits to the organization. Many people may believe that these two are identical, that is, that reduced costs imply increased profits. However, as we will determine, this may not be true if cost reimbursement for either operating or capital costs is present. The important point to remember is that if the major benefits are financial, traditional capital budgeting methods may be more appropriate.

The third category of investments is a catch-all category. Investments here would range from projects that activate major new medical areas (such as outpatient or mental-health services) to projects that improve employee working conditions (such as employee gymnasiums). In this category, benefits may be more difficult to quantify and evaluate. Traditional capital-budgeting methods thus may be appropriate only in the selection of least costly ways to provide designated services.

THE CAPITAL PROJECT DECISION-MAKING PROCESS

Making decisions that will be the basis on which capital projects will be undertaken is not an easy task. In many respects, this may represent the most difficult and important management decision area. The allocation of limited resources to specific project areas will directly affect the efficiency and effectiveness and, ultimately, the continued viability of the organization.

For our purposes, we can divide the capital decision-making process into four interrelated activities or stages:

1. generation of project information,
2. evaluation of projects,
3. decisions about which projects to fund, and
4. project implementation and reporting.

Generation of Project Information

In this stage of the decision-making process, information is gathered that can be analyzed and evaluated later. This is an extremely important stage because inadequate or inaccurate information can lead to poor decision making. Specifically, there are six major categories of information that should be included in most capital expenditure proposals:

1. alternatives available,
2. resources available,
3. cost data,
4. benefit data,
5. prior performance, and
6. risk projection.

Alternatives Available

A major deficiency related to many capital expenditure decisions is the failure to consider possible alternatives. Too many times, capital expenditures are presented on a "take it or leave it" basis; yet, there usually are alternatives. For example, different manufacturers might be selected; different methods of financing could be used; or different boundaries in the scope of the project could be defined.

Resources Available

Capital expenditure decisions are not made in a vacuum. In most situations, there are constraints on the amount of available funding. This is the whole rationale behind capital expenditure decision making: scarce resources must be allocated among a virtually unlimited number of investment opportunities. There is little question that top-level management needs information concerning the availability of funding.

However, there is some question about its importance at the departmental level. On one hand, a budgetary constraint may temper requests for capital expenditures. On the other hand, it may encourage a department manager to submit only those projects that are in the department's best interests. These may, in fact, conflict with the broader goals and objectives of the organization as a whole.

Cost Data

It goes without saying that cost information is an important variable in the decision-making process. In all cases, the lifecycle costs of a project should be presented. Limiting cost information to capital costs can be counterproductive.

Benefit Data

We can divide benefit data into the following two categories: quantitative and nonquantitative. Some believe that many of the benefit data in the health care industry are nonquantitative. To a large extent, quantitative data are viewed as being synonymous with financial data. And because financial criteria are sometimes viewed as less important in the nonprofit health care industry, the assumption is that quantitative data are also less important. This is not true. Quantitative data can and should be used. Effective management control is predicated on the use of numbers that relate to the organization's stated goals and objectives. It may not be easy to develop quantitative estimates of benefits, but it is not impossible. For example, assume that a hospital in an urban area opens a clinic in a medically underserved area. One of the stated goals for the clinic is the reduction of unnecessary use of the hospital's emergency room for nonurgent care. A realistic and quantifiable benefit of this project should be a numerical reduction in the use of the hospital's emergency room for nonurgent care by individuals from the clinic area. However, no quantitative assessments are either projected or reported; the only quantitative statistics used are those of a financial nature. The management control process in this situation is less valuable than it should have been.

Prior Performance

Information on prior operating results of projects proposed by responsibility-center managers can be useful. A comparison of prior actual results with forecast results can give a decision maker some idea of the manager's reliability in forecasting. In too many cases, project planners are likely to overstate a project's benefits if the project interests them. Review of prior performance can help a manager evaluate the accuracy of the projections.

It is generally acknowledged that most people requesting capital expenditure approval for their projects will overstate benefits (revenues) and understate costs. This type of behavior is not necessarily intentional, but may reflect sincere faith and interest in the project. Individuals reviewing proposals must recognize this inherent bias and also recognize that not all people make the same magnitude of errors in forecasts.

Risk Projection

Nothing is certain in this world except death and taxes, especially when evaluating capital expenditure projects. It is important to ask "what-if" questions. For example, how would costs and benefits change if volume changed? Volume of service is a key variable in most capital expenditure forecasts, and its effects should be understood. In some situations, requiring projections for the highest, the lowest, and the most likely projections of volume can help answer the questions. The same types of calculations can be made for other key factors, such as prices of key inputs and technologic changes. This is an important area to understand because some capital expenditure projects are inherently more risky than others. Specifically, programs with extremely high proportions of fixed or sunk costs are much more sensitive to changes in volume than those with low percentages of fixed or sunk costs.

Evaluation of Projects

Although financial criteria are clearly not the only factors that should be evaluated while making capital expenditure decisions, there are few, if any, capital expenditure decisions that can omit financial considerations. Our focus is on the following two prime financial criteria: solvency and cost.

Solvency

A project that cannot show a positive rate of return in the long run should be questioned. If implemented, such a program will need to be subsidized by some other existing program area. For example, should a hospital subsidize an outpatient clinic? If so, to what extent? This is the kind of policy and financial question the governing board of the organization needs to determine. The fairness of some patients subsidizing other patients is one of the basic qualitative issues in capital project analysis. Operation of an insolvent program eventually can threaten the solvency of the entire organization. Thus, organizations that plan to subsidize insolvent programs must be in good financial condition, and assessment of financial condition can be done only after the organization's financial statements are examined.

Cost

Cost is the second important financial concern. An organization needs to select the projects that contribute most to the attainment of its objectives, given resource constraints. This type of analysis is often called cost-benefit analysis. Benefits differ from project to project. While evaluating alternative programs, decision makers must weight those benefits according to their own preferences and then compare them with cost.

There is a second dimension to the cost criterion. All projects that are eventually selected should cost the least to provide the service. This type of evaluation is sometimes called cost-effectiveness analysis. Least cost should be defined as the present value of both operating and capital costs (methods for determining this are discussed later in the chapter).

Decisions about Which Projects To Fund

At this juncture of the capital expenditure decision-making process, it is time to make the decisions. The decision makers possess lists of possible projects that may be funded. Each project should represent the lowest cost of providing the desired service or output. In addition, various benefit data on each project should be described. These data should be consistent with the criteria that the decision makers used in their capital expenditure decision making.

To illustrate this process, assume that the members of the governing board are deciding on how many, if any, of three proposed programs they will fund in the coming year. The three programs are a burn care unit, a hemodialysis unit, and a commercial laboratory. Assume further that the members have decided that there are only four criteria of importance to them:

1. solvency,
2. incremental management time required,
3. public image, and
4. medical staff approval.

Because none of the three projects clearly dominates, it is not clear which, if any, should be funded. Thus, the decision makers must weight the criteria according to their own preferences and determine the overall ranking of the three projects. For example, one manager might weight solvency and management time highly, relative to public image and the medical staff, and thus select the commercial laboratory project. Another manager might weight medical staff and public image more heavily and thus select the hemodialysis or burn-care-unit project.

In this example, the three projects can be ranked in terms of their relative standing on each of the four criteria in Table 15–1.

Project Implementation and Reporting

Most capital expenditure control systems are concerned primarily, if not exclusively, with analysis and evaluation prior to selection. However, a real concern should be focused on whether the projected benefits are actually being realized as forecast. Without this feedback on the actual results of prior investments, the capital expenditure control system's feedback loop is not complete.

The following are some of the specific advantages of establishing a capital expenditure review program:

- Capital expenditure review could highlight differences between planned versus actual performance that may permit corrective action. If actual performance is never evaluated, corrective action may not be taken. This could mean that the projected benefits might never be realized.
- Use of a review process may result in more accurate estimates. If people realize that they will be held responsible for their estimates, they may tend to be more careful with their projections. This will ensure greater accuracy in forecast results.

Table 15–1 Capital Project Ranking

	Project		
Criterion	Hemodialysis Unit	Burn-Care Unit	Commercial Laboratory
Solvency	2	3	1
Management time	2	3	1
Public image	2	1	3
Medical staff	1	2	3

- Forecasts by individuals with a continuous record of biased forecasts can be adjusted to reflect that bias. This should result in a better forecast of actual results.

JUSTIFICATION OF CAPITAL EXPENDITURES

In most health care organizations, there is a formalized process for approval of a capital expenditure. Usually, this approval process is initiated by a department or responsibility-center manager through the completion of a capital expenditure approval form. An example of a completed capital expenditure approval form is shown in Exhibit 15–1. Both the approval form and the approval process may vary across health care organizations, depending on the nature of the management control process in each case.

The approval form in Exhibit 15–1 is, in fact, more comprehensive than that used in most health care organizations. Thus, it provides a detailed summary of the following key aspects involved in capital expenditure approval:

- amount and type of expenditure,
- attainment of key decision criteria, and
- detailed financial analysis.

In most firms, small capital expenditures are usually not subjected to detailed analysis and do not require justification. For example, capital expenditures less than $2,000 are not reviewed according to the instructions in Exhibit 15–1. This does not mean that a department has an unlimited capital expenditures budget if it spends less than $2,000 per item; the department is most likely subject to some overall level for small capital expenditures. For example, a department such as physical therapy might have an $8,000 limit on small capital expenditure items. No justification for capital expenditure items less than $2,000 would be required if the aggregate limit of $8,000 is not violated.

Replacement items also are specially recognized. In the example in Exhibit 15–1, a replacement expenditure less than $20,000 is not subject to review. The rationale for this higher limit relates to the operational continuance of capital expenditures. Replacement expenditures are often viewed as essential to the continuation of existing operations. They are, therefore, not as closely evaluated as are expenditures for new pieces of equipment.

In any decision-making process, it is important to carefully define the criteria that will be used in the selection process. The example in Exhibit 15–1 has three categories of criteria:

1. need (management goals, hospital goals),
2. economic feasibility, and
3. acceptability (physicians, employees, community).

Most capital expenditure forms probably would request that data regarding economic or financial feasibility be included. Exhibit 15–1 provides data in other areas as well and also includes a means for scoring the project. For the specific project being appraised, a raw score of 16 and a priority score of 5 resulted. Different values could be obtained by changing the form's measures and their relative weightings.

The important point to recognize is that project selection usually involves the consideration of criteria other than financial criteria. Failure to collect data on the attainment of those additional criteria for specific projects often will lead to more subjectivity in the process. Without such relevant data, individuals may make inferences that are not legitimate.

A key aspect of the capital expenditure approval process is the financial or economic feasibility of the project. In most capital expenditure forms, there is some summary statistic that measures the project's overall financial performance. In general, such measures are usually categorized as either (1) discounted cash-flow methods (DCF) or (2) nondiscounted cash-flow methods. In the present discussion, we will not be concerned with nondiscounted cash-flow methods because they are usually regarded as less sophisticated than DCF methods.

Exhibit 15-1 Completed Capital Expenditure Approval Form

Appraisal Sheet for
Capital Expenditure Proposals

Department and no. ____Surgery #818____
Date of request for purchase ____1/7/98____
Summary description of item or package of items (attach original request for purchase)
IABP Model 10 with cardiac output computer and recorder (Intra Aortic Balloon Pump)
_____
_____

Total capital expenditure, including training, renovation, and purchase of equipment
(attach list) $19,500
Undepreciated value of equipment being replaced   0
  Total cost of implementation $19,500

Appraisal Instructions

Level I—Complete a Level I assessment for:
1. a new item having a total capital expenditure exceeding $2,000, or
2. a replacement item having a total capital expenditure exceeding $20,000, or
3. a proposed capital expenditure requiring an evaluation before a purchase
   (or lease) decision may be made.

Level II—Complete both a Level I and a Level II assessment for any proposed
capital expenditure that:

1. exceeds $100,000, or
2. initiates or modifies the scope or type of health services rendered in the community and
   may require a certificate of need, or
3. requires a more extensive evaluation than offered by a Level I review.

Appraisal Outcome	By (initials)	Date	Priority Status
Request denied	_____	_____	_____
Request accepted and pending	_____	_____	_____
Request approved	_____	_____	_____

Level I Review—Complete the following assessment for any proposed capital expenditure requiring either a Level I or Level II review.

A. Need
  1. Indicate whether the proposed capital expenditure contributes directly to the achievement
    of any of the following management goals (check those that apply)
      _____ Revenue
      _____ Hospital improvement study
      _____ Productivity
      ____X____ Quality assurance
      _____ Employee development
      _____ Management services consultant package
      _____ Other goal (specify)

Exhibit 15-1 continued

2. Indicate whether the proposed capital expenditure contributes directly to the achievement of any of the following hospital goals (check one or more goals)

      X   Patient care
              Medical and allied health education
      X   Community service
              Cost containment
              The leadership role
              Clinical research

3. Provide the following information on historical and projected utilization of items for the provision of patient care services. (See the finance department for assistance in completing this section.)

   a. For replacement items only:

   (1) Identify units of service, if any, provided through the utilization of existing equipment; the actual volume of services provided during the most recent year for which statistics are available; the current patient charge, if any, for these services; and the annual revenue realized.

   Unit of Service Historical Annual Volume Patient Charge Annual Review

Unit of Service	Historical Annual Volume	Patient Charge	Annual Revenue
1. _____	_____	_____	_____
2. _____	_____	_____	_____
3. _____	_____	_____	_____
4. _____	_____	_____	_____
Total	Units		$

   (2) Serial no. of item

   (3) Fixed asset tag no.

   b. For both new and replacement items:

   (1) Identify the units of service, if any, to be offered through acquisition of the proposed item and the estimated volume of services to be provided annually. If known, provide the proposed patient charge per unit of service.

Unit of Service	Estimated Annual Volume	Proposed Patient Charge
1. Ped open heart	161	$459.16 (Average)
2. _____	_____	_____
3. _____	_____	_____

   continues

Exhibit 15-1 continued

   (2) Identify any other services of which volume of utilization will be affected through acquisition of the proposed item.
   (3) Percentage of charge patients for department (from cost report) __93.1__
   (4) Estimated useful life of equipment: _____10_____ years.

4. Document the reasons justifying the acquisition of the proposed capital expenditure, particularly as they relate to the achievement of hospital, departmental, and management goals and objectives.
   <u>We presently borrow General Hospital's Balloon Pumps three or four times per month. This is a life-saving device. Without it, some patients cannot survive open-heart surgery.</u>

B. Economic feasibility
   1. Estimate any change in the annual operating costs associated with acquisition of this proposed capital expenditure. (See the finance department for assistance in completing this section.)

	Change in Annual Operating Cost
Personal	
Employee benefits @23%	
Physician cost	
Materials and supplies	
Maintenance contracts	
Insurance	
Other depreciation	$1,950
Total change in annual operating	$1,950

   Provide documentation in support of the previous estimates.

   2. Financial analysis (to be completed by finance):

Estimated Cost to Purchase
IAPB Model 10 with Cardiac Output Computer

Cash Expenditure	Cost Reimbursement @26%	Net Cash (Disbursed) Received	Present Value @6%
$(19,500)	$ 507	$(18,993)	$(17,918)
	507	507	451
	507	507	426
	507	507	402
	507	507	379
	507	507	357
	507	507	337
	507	507	318
	507	507	300
	507	507	283
$(19,500)	$5,070	$(14,430)	$(14,665)

Total present value (cost)	$(14,665)

Exhibit 15-1 continued

3. Space analysis:
   a. Change in the number of square feet of space required for item: <u>N/A</u>
   b. Is existing department space available for the item?

   (Circle one)   (Yes)   No
   If not, document plan for acquiring additional space.

C. Acceptability
   1. Physician impact of the capital expenditure decision:
      a) What is the scope of any physician attitude change? (check one)
         _____ 1 No change. (skip to Section C-2)
         ___X___ 2 One or two physicians will be affected.
         _____ 3 The majority of the physicians in a hospital service will be affected.

      b) What is the *intensity* of the effect on physician attitude? (check two answers—one for acceptance and one for nonacceptance)
         Not accepted:
         _____ 4 The physicians affected will move their practices to other hospitals.
         ___X___ 3 The physicians affected will tend to reduce their practices at the hospital.
         _____ 2 The physicians affected, at the very least, will be disgruntled and will tend to discuss in the community and with other physicians the lack of the expenditure or project.
         _____ 1 The physicians will be aware of the lack of support for the project and will be less likely to believe that the hospital is maintaining a proper level of patient care.
         _____ 0 No effect.

         Accepted:
         _____ 0 No effect.
         _____ 1 The physicians affected will be aware of the expenditure or project and will be satisfied that the hospital is maintaining a high level of patient care.
         ___X___ 2 The physicians affected will be very impressed and will tend to discuss the expenditure or project favorably in the community and with other physicians.
         _____ 3 The physicians affected will tend to increase their practices moderately in the hospital.
         _____ 4 The physicians affected will move their practices to the hospital.

   2. Employee impact of the capital expenditure decision:
      What is the effect on the attitude of hospital employees?
      (Check two answers—one for acceptance and one for nonacceptance.)
      Not accepted:
      _____ 4 Major and widespread negative impact on employee morale and attitude toward the hospital.
      _____ 3 Widespread disappointment with the hospital and some general negative effect on the hospital's image among employees.
      ___X___ 2 Negative reaction from a limited group of employees (one or two departments).
      _____ 0 No effect.

continues

Exhibit 15-1 continued

Accepted:

_____ 0 No effect.

_____ 1 Limited reaction from a few employees.

___X___ 2 Positive reaction from a limited group of employees (one or two departments).

_____ 3 Positive impact on nearly all employees.

_____ 4 Major and widespread impact with long-term effect on employee attitude toward the hospital.

3. Community impact of the capital expenditure decision:

What is the expected community impact?

(Check the answers below that best describe the expected community impact; check one for acceptance and one for nonacceptance.)

Not accepted:

_____ 4 Intense and widespread negative reaction in the community will affect hospital's image.

___X___ 3 A widespread negative effect on the hospital's general image and reputation will result.

_____ 1 The attitudes of relatively few people will be negatively affected.

_____ 0 No effect.

Accepted:

_____ 0 No effect.

_____ 1 Relatively few people will be positively affected.

_____ 2 Certain groups in the community will be favorably impressed.

___X___ 3 A widespread positive effect on the hospital's image and reputation will result.

_____ 4 Significant and widespread positive community reaction will contribute significantly to the hospital's general image and reputation.

APPRAISAL SCORE SHEET FOR
CAPITAL EXPENDITURE PROPOSALS

	Assigned Value	Raw Score	Priority Instruction	Priority Score
A. Need evaluation				
1. If proposal directly contributes to one or more management goals (I-A-2)	+1	+1		
2. If proposal directly contributes to one or more hospital goals (I-A-2)	+1	+1		

Exhibit 15-1 continued

	Assigned Value	Raw Score	Priority Instruction	Priority Score
(For Level II reviews only)				
3. Performance expectations (II-A-4)				
If negative or questionable	−1			
If positive	+1			
4. If certificate-of-need approval is necessary, but unlikely (II-A-5)	−3	___	Enter positive raw score as	___
Subtotal, need raw score		2	priority score.	2
B. Economic Evaluation				
1. If annual operating costs (including depreciation) are reduced (I-B-1-a)	+1			
2. Return on investment (I-B-2-a)				
If greater than 7.5%	+2			
If positive	0			
If negative	−2	−2		
3. If significant additional space is required (I-B-3)	−1			
(For Level II reviews only)				
4. If external financing is required (II-B-1)	−1	___	Enter positive raw score as	___
Subtotal, economic raw score		−2	priority score.	
C. Acceptability Evaluation				
1. Physician attitude				
a. Scope (enter score for response to question I-C-1-A)	1 to 3	1	If scope score is greater than 2, enter raw score in priority score column.	

continues

Exhibit 15-1 continued

	Assigned Value	Raw Score	Priority Instruction	Priority Score
b. Intensity (add responses to question I-C-1-b)	0 to 8	5	If raw score exceeds 4, the excess is priority score.	
2. Employee attitude (add responses to question I-C-3)	0 to 8	4	If raw score exceeds 4, the excess is priority score.	
3. Community attitude (add responses to question I-C-3)	0 to 8	6	If raw score exceeds 4, the excess is priority score.	2
Subtotal, acceptability raw score		16		3
Total raw score		16	Total priority score	5

Note: A capital expenditure proposal may be approved, disapproved, or deferred on the basis of an appraisal of the raw scores for need, economy, and acceptability, considered either independently or together. An approved capital expenditure proposal is ranked according to its priority score for future appropriation of capital expenditure funds.

DISCOUNTED CASH-FLOW METHODS

In this section, we examine three DCF methods that are relatively easy to understand and use:

1. net present value,
2. profitability index, and
3. equivalent annual cost.

Before examining these three methods, a word of caution is in order: In our view, the calculation of specific DCF measures is an important, but not a critical, phase of capital expenditure review. We strongly believe that the most important phase in the capital expenditure review process is the generation of quality project information. Specifically, the set of alternatives being considered must include the best ones; it does a firm little good to select the best five projects from a list of ten inferior ones. Beyond that, the validity of the forecasted data is critical; small changes in projected volumes, rates, or costs can have profound effects on cash flow. Determination of possible changes in both of these parameters is much more important than discussions about the appropriate discount rate or cost of capital.

Each of the previous three DCF methods is based on a time-value concept of money. Each is useful in evaluating a specific type of capital expenditure or capital financing alternative. Specifically, their areas of application are:

Method of Evaluation	Area of Application
Net present value	Capital financing alternative
Profitability index	Capital expenditures with financial benefits
Equivalent annual cost	Capital expenditures with nonfinancial benefits

Net Present Value

A net present value (NPV) analysis is a useful way to analyze alternative methods of capital financing. In most situations, the objective in such a situation is clear: the commodity being dealt with is money, and it is management's goal to minimize the cost of financing operations. (We will consider shortly how this goal may conflict with solvency when the effects of cost reimbursement are considered.)

NPV equals discounted cash inflows less discounted cash outflows. In a comparison of two alternative financing packages, the one with the highest NPV should be selected.

For example, assume that an asset can be financed with a four-year annual $1,000 lease payment or can be purchased outright for

$2,800. Assume further that the discount rate is 10 percent, which may reflect either the borrowing cost or the investment rate, depending on which alternative is relevant. (We will discuss the issue of an appropriate discount rate shortly.) The present value cost of the lease is $3,169. This amount is greater than the present value cost of the purchase, $2,800. With no consideration given to cost reimbursement, the purchase alternative is the lowest cost alternative method of financing.

However, for accuracy, the effects of cost reimbursement should be considered. Reimbursement of costs would mean that the facility would be entitled to reimbursement for depreciation if the asset was purchased, or the facility would be entitled to the rent payment if the asset was leased. (Some third-party cost payers limit reimbursement on leases to depreciation and interest if the lease is treated as an installment purchase.) Assuming that straight-line depreciation is used and that 20 percent of capital expenses are reimbursed by third-party cost payers, the present value of the reimbursed cash inflow (using the discount factors from Table 14–4) would be as presented in Table 15–2.

If the asset was purchased, the organization would pay $2,800 immediately. For each of the next four years, it would be reimbursed for the noncash expense item of depreciation in the amount of $700 per year ($2,800/4). However, because only 20 percent of the patients are capital cost payers, only $140 per year would be re-

Table 15–2 Present Value of Reimbursement

		Annual Reimbursement		Discount Factor		% of Cost Reimbursement	
Present value of reimbursed depreciation	=	$\frac{\$2,800}{4}$	×	3.170	×	.20	= $444
Present value of reimbursed lease payments	=	$1,000	×	3.170	×	.20	= $634

ceived (.20 × $700). If the asset was leased, the organization would be permitted reimbursement of the lease payment in the amount of $1,000 per year. However, because only 20 percent of the patients are capital cost payers, only $200 (.20 × $1,000) would be paid.

The NPV of the previous two financing methods for considering cost reimbursement would be as presented in Table 15–3.

In this example, it is clear that the best method of financing is outright purchase. By purchasing the asset, annual expenses will be $700 in depreciation, compared with $1,000 per year with the leasing plan. In addition, purchasing is also a plan that results in a lower NPV. Relative ratings regarding NPV could change quickly, however, given higher percentages of capital cost reimbursement. To see the impact of cost reimbursement on NPV, assume that 80 percent of capital costs will be reimbursed. When this change is reflected in the calculations in Table 15–2, leasing's NPV(–$633) is lower than purchasing's NPV (–$1,025).

Profitability Index

The profitability index method of capital project evaluation is of primary importance in cases when the benefits of the projects are mostly financial, for example, a capital project that saves costs or expands revenue with a primary purpose of increased profits. In these situations, there is usually a constraint on the availability of funding. Thus, those projects with the highest rate of return per dollar of capital invest-ment are the best candidates for selection. The profitability index attempts to compare rates of return. The numerator is the NPV of the project, and the denominator is the investment cost.

$$\text{Profitability index} = \frac{\text{NPV}}{\text{Investment cost}}$$

To illustrate the use of this measure, let us assume that a hospital is considering an investment in a laundry service shared with a group of neighboring hospitals. The initial investment cost is $100,000 for the purchase of new equipment and delivery trucks. Savings in operating costs are estimated to be $20,000 per year for the entire ten-year life of the project. If the discount rate is assumed to be 10 percent, the following calculations could be made, ignoring the effect of cost reimbursement and using the discount factors of Table 14–4.

Present value of operating savings =
$20,000 × 6.145 = $122,900

NPV = $122,900 – $100,000 = $22,900

$$\text{Profitability index} = \frac{\$22,900}{\$100,000} = .229$$

Values for profitability indices that are greater than zero imply that the project is earning at a rate greater than the discount rate. Given no funding constraints, all projects with profitability indices greater than zero should be funded. However, in most situations, funding constraints

Table 15–3 Net Present Value of Financing Alternatives

		Present Value of Reimbursement (Cash Inflows)		Present Value of Payments (Cash Outflows)		NPV
NPV of purchase	=	$444	–	$2,800	=	–$2,356
NPV of lease	=	$634	–	$3,170	=	–$2,536

do exist, and only a portion of those projects with profitability indices greater than zero are actually accepted.

The previous calculations give no consideration to the effects of cost reimbursement. If we assume that 80 percent of the facility's capital expenses are reimbursed and 20 percent of its operating expenses are reimbursed, then the following additional calculations must be made:

Present value of reimbursed depreciation =
$$\frac{\$100,000}{10} \times 6.145 \times .80 = \$49,160$$

Present value of lost reimbursement from operating savings =
$$\$20,000 \times 6.145 \times .20 = \$24,580$$

NPV = \$22,900 + \$49,160 - \$24,580
= \$47,480

$$\text{Profitability index} = \frac{\$47,480}{\$100,000} = .4748$$

The previous calculations require some clarification. We are adjusting the initially calculated NPV of \$22,900 to reflect the effects of cost reimbursement. Depreciation is the first item to be considered. Because 80 percent of the facility's patients are associated with capital cost reimbursement formulas, it can expect to receive 80 percent of the annual depreciation charge of \$10,000 (\$100,000/10) or \$8,000 per year as a reimbursement cash flow. The present value of this stream, \$49,160, is added to the initial net present value of \$22,900.

The second item to be considered is the operating savings. If the investment is undertaken, the facility can anticipate a yearly savings of \$20,000 for the next ten years. However, that savings will reduce its reimbursable costs by \$20,000 annually, which means that 20 percent of that amount, or \$4,000, will be lost annually in reimbursement. The present value of that loss for the ten years is \$24,580, which is subtracted from the initial NPV. The effect of cost reimbursement thus reduces increased costs associ-

ated with new programs, but it also reduces the cost savings associated with new programs.

The preceding example illustrates an important financial concept discussed in Chapter 2. Because some third-party payers still reimburse for actual capital costs, a strong financial incentive exists for investment in projects that reduce operating costs. In the previous example, the laundry facility's profitability index increased from .229 to .4748 when the effects of capital and operating cost reimbursement were considered.

Equivalent Annual Cost

Equivalent annual cost is of primary value when selecting capital projects for which alternatives exist. Usually, these are capital expenditure projects that are classified as operational continuance or other. (The profitability index measure just discussed is used for projects in which the benefits are primarily financial in nature.)

Equivalent annual cost is the expected average cost, considering both capital and operating cost, over the life of the project. It is calculated by dividing the sum of the present value of operating costs over the life of the project and the present value of the investment cost by the discount factor for an annualized stream of equal payments (as derived from Table 14–4):

Equivalent annual cost =

$$\frac{\text{Present value of operating cost} + \text{Present value of investment cost}}{\text{Present value of annuity}}$$

To illustrate use of this measure, assume that an extended care facility must invest in a sprinkler system to maintain its license. After investigation, two alternatives are identified. One sprinkler system would require a \$5,000 investment and an annual maintenance cost of \$500 during each year of its estimated ten-year life. An alternative sprinkler system can be purchased for \$10,000 and would require only \$200 in maintenance cost each year of its estimated twenty-year life. Ignoring cost reimbursement and assuming a discount factor of 10 percent, the following calculations can be made:

Equivalent annual cost of a $5,000 sprinkler system:

Present value of operating costs
= $500 × 6.145 = $3,073

Present value of investment = $5,000

Equivalent annual cost =
$$\frac{\$3,073 + \$5,000}{6.145} = \$1,314$$

Equivalent annual cost of a $10,000 sprinkler system:

Present value of operating costs
= $200 × 8.514 = $1,703

Present value of investment = $10,000

Equivalent annual cost =
$$\frac{\$1,703 + \$10,000}{8.541} = \$1,370$$

From this analysis, it can be determined that the $5,000 sprinkler system would produce the lowest equivalent annual cost, $1,314 per year, compared with the $1,370 equivalent annual cost of the $10,000 system.

Two points should be made regarding this analysis. First, the equivalent annual cost method permits comparison of two alternative projects with different lives. In this case, a project with a ten-year life was compared with a project with a twenty-year life. It is assumed that the technology will not change and that in ten years the relevant alternatives still will be the two systems being analyzed. However, in situations of estimated rapid technologic changes, some subjective weight should be given to projects of shorter duration. In the previous example, this is no problem, because the project with the shorter life also has the lowest equivalent annual cost.

Second, equivalent annual cost is not identical to the reported or accounting cost. The annual reported accounting cost for the two alternatives would be the annual depreciation expenses plus the maintenance cost. Thus

Accounting expense per year ($5,000 sprinkler system) =
$$\frac{\$5,000}{10} + \$500 = \$1,000$$

Accounting expense per year ($10,000 sprinkler system) =
$$\frac{\$10,000}{20} + \$200 = \$700$$

Reliance on such information that does not incorporate the time-value concept of money can produce misleading results, as it does in the previous example. The second alternative is not the lowest cost alternative when the cost of capital is included. In this case, the savings of $5,000 in investment cost between the two systems can be used either to generate additional investment income or to reduce outstanding indebtedness. It is assumed that the appropriate discount rate for each of these two alternatives would be 10 percent.

Once again, the effects of cost reimbursement should be considered. In our example, we assume that 50 percent of the extended care facility's capital costs will be reimbursed and 10 percent of its operating costs will be reimbursed. The following adjustments result:

Equivalent annual cost of a $5,000 sprinkler system:

Present value of reimbursed operating costs = $500 × 6.145 × .10 = $307.25

Present value of reimbursed depreciation =
$$\frac{\$5,000}{10} × 6.145 × .50 = \$1,536.25$$

Equivalent annual cost =
$$\$1,314 - \frac{(\$307.25 + \$1,536.25)}{6.145} = \$1,014$$

Equivalent annual cost of $10,000 sprinkler system:

Present value of reimbursed operating costs = $200 × 8.514 × .10 = $170.28

Present value of reimbursed depreciation =
$$\frac{\$10,000}{20} \times 8.514 \times .5 = \$2,128.50$$

Equivalent annual cost =
$$\$1,370 - \frac{(\$170.28 + \$2,128.50)}{8.514} = \$1,100$$

Again, some clarification of the calculations may be useful. To reflect the effect of cost reimbursement, the reimbursement of reported expenses for the two alternative sprinkler systems must be considered. The reported expense items for both sprinkler systems are depreciation and maintenance costs, which are referred to as operating costs. Depreciation for the $5,000 sprinkler system will be $500 per year ($5,000/10), and 50 percent of this amount ($250) will be paid for reimbursement each year. The present value of the reimbursed depreciation ($250 × 6.145) is $1,536.25. Using the same procedure, the present value of reimbursed depreciation for the $10,000 sprinkler system is $2,128.50 ($250 × 8.514). In a similar fashion, payment for reimbursement of the maintenance costs for the two sprinkler systems also will be made. For the $5,000 system, the annual $500 maintenance cost will yield $50 in new reimbursement (.10 × $500) per year. The present value of this reimbursement inflow is $307.25. Using the same calculations for the $10,000 sprinkler system yields a present value of $170.25. The present values of both reimbursed depreciation and maintenance costs are then annualized and subtracted from the initially calculated equivalent annual cost to derive new equivalent annual costs that reflect cost reimbursement effects.

In this case, cost reimbursement did not change the decision. The lower-cost sprinkler system, after consideration of the effects of re-imbursement, is still the best alternative. In fact, the relative difference has increased.

SELECTION OF THE DISCOUNT RATE

In the three DCF methods just discussed, to specify the discount rate we simply arbitrarily selected a number for each of our examples. In an actual case, however, the issue of how to select the appropriate discount rate requires careful attention.

Before discussing methods of determining the appropriate discount rate, it may be useful to evaluate the role of the discount rate in project selection. A natural question at this point is, would an alternative discount rate affect the list of capital projects selected? For example, if we used a discount rate of 10 percent and later learned that 12 percent should have been used, would our list of approved projects change? The answer is maybe. In some cases, alternative values for the discount rate would alter the relative ranking and therefore the desirability of particular projects.

Again, we believe that the definition of the discount rate is an important issue, but not a critical one—especially for health care organizations. This is true for several reasons. First, in the case of health care organizations, the financial criterion is not likely to be the only criterion. Other areas—such as need, quality of care, and teaching—also may be important. Second, a change in the relative ranking of projects is much more likely to result from an accurate forecast of cash flows than it is from an alternative discount rate. Efforts to improve forecasting would appear to be much more important than esoteric discussions about the relevancy of cost-of-capital alternatives.

In this context, we can examine three primary methods for defining a discount rate or the cost of capital for use in a DCF analysis:

1. cost of specific financing source,
2. yield achievable on other investments, and
3. weighted cost of capital.

The cost of a specific financing source is sometimes used as the discount rate. Usually, the identified financing source is debt. For example, if a firm can borrow money at 8 percent in the bond market, that rate would become its cost of capital or discount rate.

Another alternative is to use the yield rate possible on other investments. In many cases, this rate might be equal to the investment yield possible in the firm's security portfolio. For example, if the firm currently earned 10 percent on its security investments, then 10 percent would be its discount rate. This method, based on an opportunity cost concept, is relatively easy to understand.

The last alternative is to use the weighted cost of capital. This is the most widely discussed and used method of defining the discount rate. In its simplest form, it is calculated as follows:

Cost of capital = (% Debt × Cost of debt) + (% Equity × Cost of equity)

The advantage of this method is that it clearly represents the cost of capital to the firm. A major problem with its use, however, is the definition of the cost of equity capital. This is an especially difficult problem for nonprofit firms. How do you define the cost of equity capital? Detailed exploration of this issue and other aspects of discount rate selection are beyond the scope of the present discussion.

Readers who are interested in examining these topics in greater depth are referred to any good introductory finance textbook.

VALUATION

It is becoming an almost everyday occurrence to read about one health care entity buying or acquiring another related health care business. Hospitals buy other hospitals, nursing homes, physician practices, durable medical equipment firms, and other types of businesses. Nursing homes buy other nursing homes, home health firms, and other businesses. Although there are many tasks that need to be accomplished in any business acquisition, one of the most difficult and most important is valuation. Exactly what is the value of the business being acquired?

Valuation is really a subset of capital expenditure analysis. The business being acquired can be thought of as a capital expenditure that needs to be evaluated just as any other capital expenditure made in the organization. Nonfinancial criteria should be considered, and the contribution that the acquired business will make toward the acquiring firm's mission must be addressed.

Valuation of a business is not a scientific process that results in one objective measure of value. Different measures of value result for the following three reasons:

1. Different methods of valuation are used.
2. Different expectations regarding future performance of the acquired business are assumed.
3. Different values may be assigned by different prospective buyers.

Alternative Valuation Methods

In general, three major methods of valuation are often cited:

1. asset-based,
2. comparable sales, and
3. income/cash flow (DCF).

Asset-based approaches to valuation rely on the availability of objective measures for the assets being acquired. Usually, three alternative asset-based valuation approaches are identified. One approach is simply to take the tangible book value of the acquired firm's assets. Although this method is objective, there is great doubt about the relevance of the resulting value. For example, consider a computed tomography (CT) scanner that was acquired two years ago at a cost of $700,000 that now has a book value of $500,000, which reflects two years of depreciation. The $500,000 value is most likely not a good measure of this asset's value to an acquiring firm.

A second asset-based method would be to use the replacement cost of the assets. For example, assume that the CT scanner in the previous example now has a current replacement cost of $1,400,000. Recognizing two years' worth of depreciation would produce an adjusted replacement cost of $1,000,000.

Current replacement cost	$1,400,000
– Allowance for depreciation	400,000
Estimated replacement cost	$1,000,000

This estimate of value would be useful for a firm that anticipated using the CT scanner in the future. Replacement cost is often associated with "a going concern" basis of operation. A going concern basis simply means the business is expected to continue and will not be terminated. The acquired firm will continue to operate basically as it currently does and, therefore, the existing capital assets will be needed.

The third asset-based approach assumes that the assets are not really needed and will be sold. For example, the CT scanner referenced previously will be sold in a secondhand market for $600,000. This value is often associated with liquidation.

Comparable sales methods are widely used in real estate valuation. Real estate appraisers will look at properties similar to the one being valued that have sold in that location during a recent time interval. This method of valuation is not often used for health care businesses because there are not enough comparable sales to make the valuation meaningful. Common rules of thumb based on sales around the country are sometimes used. For example, nursing homes may sell in a range of $15,000 to $45,000 per bed depending on the payer mix and the present age of the facility. Other health care examples would include physician practice acquisition and health maintenance organizations (HMOs). Most physician practices are acquired for $100,000 to $200,000 per physician, whereas HMOs typically sell for $200 to $600 per member. Although these comparable sales values are useful, they usually are only a benchmark against which a calculated value is determined from an appraisal based on income or cash flow.

Table 15–4 includes information from a recent survey based on physician-practice acquisitions. Table 15–4 illustrates the wide ranges in value per physician.

The most common methods of valuing health care firms are usually based on some projections of income or cash flow. The three most common methods are

1. direct capitalization,
2. price earnings multiple, and
3. DCF.

In direct capitalization, a projected value for cash flow is determined. That number is then divided by some discount rate. The discount rate ideally represents the acquiring firm's cost of capital, but it is often adjusted up or down to reflect the riskiness of the business being acquired. For example, if a durable medical equipment (DME) firm was thought to have cash flow of $100,000 per year for the foreseeable future and the purchasing firm's cost of capital was 12 percent, the value of the DME firm would be the following:

$$\text{Value of DME firm} = \frac{\$100,000}{.12} = \$833,333$$

To reflect greater risk in the business, the discount rate could be increased to 20 percent. This increase would effectively reduce the value to $500,000. A preferable way to reflect risk rather than adjust the discount rate would be to conduct a sensitivity analysis on the forecast of cash flows. It is highly desirable to have at least the following three scenarios forecast: most likely, pessimistic, and optimistic.

A price earnings approach is similar to direct capitalization, except that it uses earnings rather than cash flow to discount, and multiplication rather than division is used. Assume that the pre-

Table 15–4 Physician Valuation by Specialty

Specialty	Median Value Per Physician	Range Per Physician
Family medicine	$112,000	$10,000 to $725,000
Internal medicine	$ 90,000	$ 8,000 to $383,000
OB/GYN	$163,000	$38,000 to $699,000
Pediatrics	$ 78,000	$13,000 to $184,000

Source: CHIPS, Physician Practice Acquisition Resource Book, 1996.

viously mentioned DME firm had earnings—not cash flow—of $125,000. If the purchasing firm applied a price/earnings ratio of 8 to the earnings, the value would be the following:

Value of DME firm = $125,000 × 8.0 = $1,000,000

A variation of the price earnings multiple is EBITDA (earnings before interest, taxes, depreciation, and amortization). Table 15–5 presents EBITDA multiples for major investor-owned health care firms as of May 1996.

The higher the EBITDA multiple, the greater the value assigned to the firm. In Table 15–5, Columbia/HCA had the highest EBITDA multiple, although all of the firms were fairly close. It is important to note that using an EBITDA multiple provides an estimate of the total value of the business. To value the equity portion, only the outstanding debt must be subtracted. Table 15–6 illustrates this concept for Phycor, a physician practice management company.

DCF methods are most commonly used in most health care firm valuations. The typical approach will estimate cash flows for each of the next five years. These cash flows are then discounted to reflect the present value of the firm. The last remaining requirement is to estimate what the value of the acquired firm will be at the end of Year 5, or whenever annual cash flows are no longer estimated. Generically, the value of a firm would be stated as follows:

Value = Present value of estimated future cash flows + Present value of residual value

To illustrate this method, assume that the DME firm described earlier is projected to generate $100,000 per year in annual cash flow for each of the next five years. Thereafter, the firm will continue to generate $100,000 of cash flow for as far as can be forecast into the future. If a discount rate of 12 percent is used, the value should be $833,333, the same value that resulted in direct capitalization (Table 15–7).

The residual value is derived by applying the direct capitalization method to the projected cash flows that are forecast to occur for every year past Year 5. The present value factors were taken from Table 14–2.

Applying the direct capitalization method to cash flows is not the only way to construct a residual value. In some cases, an estimate of the resale value of the firm might be used. Other methods might also be used in certain situations. The following point, however, is important: the residual value may be uncertain and, as a result, some alternative scenarios should be tested. One value should never be accepted. Alternative

Table 15–5 EBITDA Multiples

Firm	EBITDA
Columbia/HCA	7.5
OrNDA	7.2
Tenet	6.9
Quorum	7.3
Universal	6.1

Table 15–6 Phycor Valuation

	Year Ending 12/31/95
Net Income	$ 21,874,000
+ Interest	5,230,000
+ Income Taxes	13,923,000
+ Depreciation and Amortization	21,445,000
EBITDA	$ 62,472,000
× EBITDA multiple	22.2
	$1,386,878,400
Value	
–Debt	$ 125,274,000
Equity Value	$1,261,604,400

valuations under different assumptions should be sought.

Valuation Concepts

Before concluding our discussion of valuation, there are several concepts that are important to better understand valuation. Great emphasis has been placed on cash flow, but what exactly is cash flow for valuation purposes?

Cash flow is usually defined more broadly than net income plus depreciation for valuation purposes. Often, the term free cash flow is used. Free cash flow is defined as follows:

Net income + Depreciation + Interest
– Capital Expenditures – Working
capital expenditures

Most analysts think of depreciation plus net income as cash flow. Interest is added back in the previous concept of free cash flow to recognize that the business may be financed in a manner different from the way it is presently financed. If a business was purchased and the existing debt of that business was assumed by the purchaser, then interest should not be subtracted because the interest expense would be a cash expense assumed by the buyer. Capital ex-

penditures are subtracted to recognize that businesses need to renovate and replace their physical assets if they are to stay in business, and this, in fact, represents a reduction of available cash flow. In the same manner, expenditures for working capital also represent a drain on available funds, or free cash flow. A buildup in accounts receivable means that not all of the firm's net income is available.

It is also important to understand the term "goodwill." Goodwill is defined as the price or value paid for a business less the fair market value of the tangible assets acquired. For example, assume that a hospital paid $4,000,000 for a 100-bed nursing home. All of the tangible assets of the nursing home would be appraised at fair market value. A piece of land may have a recorded cost of $100,000 on the nursing home's books, but its current market value might be $800,000. The fair market value of the land would be $800,000. Alternatively, some equipment items might be reduced below their historical cost because they are no longer of value.

Goodwill is an intangible asset that will be amortized over future years. For example, assume that the fair market value of the acquired assets in the nursing home was $3,000,000. The amount of goodwill would be $1,000,000 ($4,000,000 – $3,000,000) and would be written

Table 15–7 Discounted Cash Flows of DME Company

Present Value of Cash Flows	Amount	Present Value Factor	Present Value
1st year	$100,000	.893	$89,300
2nd year	100,000	.797	79,700
3rd year	100,000	.712	71,200
4th year	100,000	.636	63,600
5th year	100,000	.567	56,700
Present value of residual value cash flows after Year 5	833,333	.567	472,500
Total value			$833,000

off as a cost of operation in the future. Goodwill plus fair market value will equal the price paid for the business.

SUMMARY

The capital decision-making process in the health care industry is complex, involving many independent decision-makers. In this chapter, we examined the process and focused on methods for evaluating capital projects. Although capital expenditure decisions in the health care industry are not usually decided exclusively on the basis of financial criteria, most health care decision makers regard financial factors as important elements in the process. In that context, the three DCF methods we have examined can serve as useful tools in capital project analysis for health care facilities.

ASSIGNMENTS

1. A health care firm's investment of $1,000 in a piece of equipment will reduce labor costs by $400 per year for the next five years. Eighty percent of all patients seen by the firm have a third-party payer arrangement that pays for capital costs on a retrospective basis. Ten percent of all patients reimburse for actual operating costs. What is the annual cash flow of the investment? Assume a five-year life and straight-line depreciation.

2. A hospital has just experienced a breakdown of one of its boilers. The boiler must be replaced quickly if the hospital is to continue operations. Should this investment be subjected to any analysis?

3. Few firms ever track the actual results achieved from a specific capital investment against projected results. What are the likely effects of such a management policy?

4. Santa Cruz Community Hospital is considering investing $90,000 in new laundry equipment to replace its present equipment, which is completely depreciated and outmoded. An alternative to this investment is a long-term contract with a local firm to perform the hospital's laundry service. It is expected that the hospital would save $20,000 per year in operating costs if the laundry service was performed internally. Both the expected life and the depreciable life of the projected equipment are six years. Salvage value of the present equipment is expected to be zero. Assuming that Santa Cruz Community Hospital can borrow or invest money at 8 percent, calculate the payback, the NPV, and the profitability index. Ignore any reimbursement effects.

5. Frances Gebauer, president of Lucas Valley Hospital System, is investigating the purchase of thirty-six television sets for rental purposes. The sets have an expected life of two years and cost $500 apiece. The possible rental income flows are presented in Table 15–8.

   If funds cost Lucas Valley 10 percent, calculate the expected NPV of this project.

6. Mr. Dobbs, administrator at Innovative Hospital, is considering opening a new health screening department in the hospital. However, he is concerned about the financial consequences of this action, because his board has indicated that because the current financial position of the hospital is not good, the project must pay for itself. Mr. Dobbs is thus especially interested in the establishment of a rate for the service and wishes to consult with you for your expert financial advice. He has prepared the cost and utilization data found in Table 15–9 for your review.

Table 15–8 Rental Revenues from TVs

Year 1		Year 2	
Rental Income	Conditional Probability	Rental Income	Conditional Probability
$12,000	.40	$4,000	.40
		7,000	.60
$15,000	.60	6,000	.30
		8,000	.70

Table 15–9 Projected Costs of Health Screening Unit

Year	Variable Cost	Fixed Costs*	Patients Screened
1	$ 96,000	$120,000	2,400
2	144,000	135,000	3,600
3	192,000	150,000	4,800
4	192,000	150,000	4,800
5	192,000	150,000	4,800

* Includes annual depreciation of $70,000.

Mr. Dobbs is aware of the rapid pace of technologic change and anticipates that the current equipment, costing $350,000, will need to be replaced at the end of Year 5 for $500,000. He is not concerned about price inflation for his other operating costs because he believes that the increased costs can be recovered by increased charges. However, he is concerned about establishing a current charge for the new service that will generate a fund of sufficient size to meet the Year 5 replacement cost. Mr. Dobbs believes that any invested funds will earn interest at a rate of 8 percent compounded annually. Assume that all payments and receipts are made at year end. What rate would you recommend charging for the new health screening service? Assume this rate to be effective for the entire five-year period.

7. Two hospitals are considering merging their laundry departments and constructing a new facility to take care of their future laundry requirements. Some relevant cost data are presented in Table 15–10.

The new laundry facility will cost approximately $40,000 to construct and will be located between the two hospitals in a leased building. Average life of the equipment is assumed to be eight years, which generates a $5,000 yearly depreciation charge. Lease payment is fixed at $3,000 per year for the next eight years. Financing for the project will be generated from available funds in each institution: $12,000 from hospital A and $28,000 from hospital B. Expenses will be shared using the same ratios (30 and 70 percent). Both hospitals use a discount factor of 10 percent on their cost-reduction investment projects. Given this information, do you think the merger would be beneficial to both hospitals? What other information would you like to have to help you evaluate this investment project?

Table 15–10 Laundry Merger Data

	Hospital A	Hospital B	Merged C
Variable cost/pound	.030	.032	.024
Pounds of laundry	300,000	700,000	1,000,000
Fixed costs/year			
Depreciation (lease)	$1,000	$5,000	$8,000
Maintenance	1,400	2,500	3,000
Administrative salaries	8,000	16,000	20,000
Transportation	0	0	3,000
Total fixed cost	$10,400	$23,500	$34,000

8. In the preceding laundry merger problem, assume that hospital B would expect to replace its present equipment with new equipment in two years at a cost of $64,000. The equipment would have an eight-year life. Ignoring cost-reimbursement considerations, does the merger make economic sense for hospital B under these conditions?
9. Scioto Valley Convalescent Center is considering buying a $25,000 computer to improve its medical-record and accounting functions. It is estimated that, with the computer, operating costs will be reduced by $7,000 per year. The computer has an estimated five-year life with an estimated $5,000 salvage value. What is this investment's profitability index if the discount rate is 8 percent? Ignore reimbursement considerations.
10. In problem 9, assume that capital costs are reimbursed 80 percent and there is no reimbursement based on operating costs. Further assume that Scioto Valley is a tax-paying entity with a marginal tax rate of 40 percent. What is the profitability index for this project now?
11. You have been asked to provide an estimate of the value for a nursing home that your client is interested in buying. Financial data and projections are presented in Table 15–11.

    Use an assumed discount rate of 10 percent to value the firm, and assume that the fifth-year cash flow will carry into the future. After you have completed your valuation, what additional information or steps would you suggest to the client?
12. As of June 21, 1996, United Healthcare sold at $48.75 per share with 175,215,000 outstanding shares. This creates a market value of United Healthcare shares of $8,541,731,000 ($48.75 × 175,215,000).

    Calculate the multiple of EBITDA that United Healthcare is trading, assuming the values in Table 15–12.

Table 15–11 Projected Nursing Home Cash Flows

	Year 1	Year 2	Year 3	Year 4	Year 5
Net income	$2,000	$2,200	$2,400	$2,700	$3,000
+ Depreciation	1,400	1,500	1,700	2,000	2,200
− Working capital	500	600	700	800	1,000
− Capital expenditures	4,000	4,000	5,000	300	300
Free cash flow	($1,100)	($900)	($1,600)	$3,600	$3,900

Table 15–12 United Healthcare Valuation Data

Net income	$285,964,000
Interest	771,000
Income taxes	170,205,000
Depreciation and amortization	94,458,000
EBITDA	$551,398,000
Debt	$ 38,970,000

SOLUTIONS AND ANSWERS

1. The cash flow of the equipment investment by the health care firm may be calculated as follows:

   Cash flow = Annual depreciation × Proportion of capital cost payers

   + (Annual operating savings × [1 – Proportion of operating cost payers])

   = $200 × .80 + ($400 × [1 – .10])

   = $160 + $360 = $520

2. The investment in a new boiler would benefit the hospital in the area of operational continuance. Failure to make the needed investment would mean discontinued service. In this case, less analysis is needed, but care still should be exercised when identifying alternatives. The lowest-cost alternative to meet the need should be selected.

3. If it does not compare actual with projected results, management may lose some of the benefits that were originally expected to be realized with its investment. If the control loop is not closed, management will not know, and therefore cannot correct for, deviations from forecasted results. It is also possible that some department managers will overstate benefits for their favorite capital projects and that such actions will not be perceived as having any adverse consequences, because no comparison of forecast with actual results was made.

4. The calculations in Table 15–13 show the payback, the NPV, and the profitability index for the laundry service investment.

5. The NPV of Lucas Valley's television purchase project is shown in the data in Table 15–14.

Table 15–13 Laundry Alternative Analysis

$$\text{Payback} = \frac{\text{Investment cost}}{\text{Annual cash flow}} = \frac{\$90,000}{\$20,000} = 4.5 \text{ years}$$

Net present value   = Present value of cash inflows – Investment cost
= $20,000 × P(8%,6) – $90,000
= $20,000 × 4.623 – $90,000 = $2,460

$$\text{Profitability index} = \frac{\text{Net present value}}{\text{Investment cost}} = \frac{\$2,460}{\$90,000} = .0273$$

Table 15–14 Expected NPV of TV Purchase

Item	Amount	Year	Probability	Expected Value	Present Value Factor	Expected Present Value
Rental income	$12,000	1	.40	$4,800	.909	$4,363.20
Rental income	15,000	1	.60	9,000	.909	8,181.00
Rental income	4,000	2	.16	640	.826	528.64
Rental income	7,000	2	.24	1,680	.826	1,387.68
Rental income	6,000	2	.18	1,080	.826	892.08
Rental income	8,000	2	.42	3,360	.826	2,775.36
TV cost	(18,000)	0	1.00	(18,000)	1.000	(18,000.00)
Expected NPV						$127.96

6. The first step in determining the rate that Mr. Dobbs should charge for the new health screening service is to calculate the present value of the cash flow requirements that need to be covered by the charge for the service (Table 15–15).

The second step is to define the rate that will generate the required present value as calculated in Table 15–15. If we define r as the required rate per screening, the following calculation can be made:

$1,255,929 = (2,400 × r × p[8%,1]) + (3,600 × r × p[8%,2])

+ (4,800 × r × p[8%,3]) +(4,800 × r × p[8%,4])

+ (4,800 × r × p[8%,5])

$1,255,929 = (2,400r [.926]) + (3,600r [.857]) + (4,800r [.794])

+ (4,800r [.735]) + (4,800r [.681])

Table 15–15 Present Value of Cash Operating Expenses

Item	Amount	Year	Present Value Factor (8%)	Present Value
Costs less depreciation	$146,000	1	.926	$135,196
Costs less depreciation	209,000	2	.857	179,113
Costs less depreciation	272,000	3	.794	215,968
Costs less depreciation	272,000	4	.735	199,920
Costs less depreciation	272,000	5	.681	185,232
Replacement	500,000	5	.681	340,500
				$1,255,929

$1,255,929 = 15,915.6r

$$r = \frac{\$1,255,929}{15,915.6}$$

r = $78.91

7. The relevant data and calculations in the laundry service merger between hospital A and hospital B are presented in Table 15–16.

   Thus, given present data, the merger would be beneficial to hospital A but not to hospital B. A key piece of additional data that is needed is the replacement cost of the existing equipment. If hospital B would need to acquire new equipment in the near future, the merger also might be favorable to it. The effects of cost reimbursement also should be considered.

Table 15–16 Discounted Cash Flow Analysis of Laundry Merger

	Hospital A	Hospital B
Cash outflow—unmerged		
Variable costs	$ 9,000	$22,400
Maintenance	1,400	2,500
Salaries	8,000	16,000
Total	$18,400	$40,900
Cash outflow—merged		
Variable costs	$ 7,200	$16,800
Lease	900	2,100
Maintenance	900	2,100
Salaries	6,000	14,000
Transportation	900	2,100
	$15,900	$37,100
Net savings	$ 2,500	$ 3,800

Hospital A:

Present value of savings = $2,500 × P(10%,8) = $2,500 × 5.335 = $13,337.50

$$\text{Profitability index} = \frac{\$1,337.50}{\$12,000.00} = .111$$

Hospital B:

Present value of savings = $3,800 × P(10%,8) = $3,800 × 5.335 = $20,273

$$\text{Profitability index} = \frac{-7,727}{28,000} = -.276$$

8. The laundry merger project in these new circumstances would require use of the equivalent annual cost method. The alternative of a merger (Figure 15–2) would have an eight-year life, whereas the alternative not including a merger (Figure 15–3) would have a ten-year cycle.

$$\text{Equivalent annual cost} = \frac{[\$37,100 \times P(10\%,8)] + \$28,000}{P(10\%,8)}$$

$$= \frac{(\$37,100 \times 5.335) + \$28,000}{5.335}$$

$$= \$42,348$$

The alternative of a merger is now more desirable for hospital B because it has a lower equivalent annual cost compared with the alternative that does not include a merger.

$$\text{Equivalent annual cost} = \frac{(\$40,900 \times P[10\%,10]) + (\$64,000 \times p[10\%,2])}{P(10\%,10)}$$

$$= \frac{(\$40,900 \times 6.145) + (\$64,000 \times .826)}{6.145} = \$49,503$$

| $28,000 | | $37,100 | | $37,100 | | $37,100 |

0   1   7   8

Figure 15–2 Cost of Merger—Hospital B

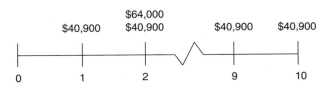

$64,000 / $40,900 / $40,900 / $40,900 / $40,900

0   1   2   9   10

Figure 15–3 Costs Unmerged—Hospital B

9. The profitability index for the computer investment by Scioto Valley Convalescent Center is calculated as follows:

Present value of cash inflows = ($7,000 × P[8%,5]) + ($5,000 × p[8%,5])

= ($7,000 × 3.993) + ($5,000 × .681)

= $31,356

Profitability index = $\dfrac{\$31{,}356 - \$25{,}000}{\$25{,}000}$ = .254

10. The calculation of the profitability index for the computer investment in these new circumstances is now the following:

Calculation of present value of cash inflows:

Operating savings	
$7,000 × (1 − .40) × 3.993 =	$16,770.60
Reimbursed depreciation	
$4,000 × .80 × (1 − .40) × 3.933 =	7,551.36
Depreciation tax shelter effect	
$4,000 × .40 × 3.933 =	6,292.80
Salvage value	
$5,000 × .681=	3,405.00
Total present value	$34,019.76

Profitability index = $\dfrac{\$34{,}019.76 - \$25{,}000}{\$25{,}000}$ = .361

11. Using the values from Table 14–2, the estimate of value in Table15–17 would result:

Table 15–17 Nursing Home Valuation

Present Value of Cash Flows	Amount	Present Value Factor	Present Value
Year 1	$(1,100)	.909	$(1,000)
Year 2	(900)	.826	(743)
Year 3	(1,600)	.751	(1,202)
Year 4	3,600	.683	2,459
Year 5	3,900	.621	2,422
Present value of residual value cash flows after Year 5	39,000	.621	24,220
Total value			$26,156

A sensitivity analysis should be performed, especially on cash flows in Year 5. Most of the total value is attributed to the residual value of the firm at the end of Year 5. Even small changes in this value will have a dramatic impact on the value.

12. (EBITDA $\times$ Multiple) $-$ Debt = Market value

($551,398,000 $\times$ Multiple) $-$ $38,970,000 = $8,541,731,000

$$\text{EBITDA Multiple} = \frac{\$8,580,701,000}{\$551,398,000} = 15.56$$

16

Capital Formation

In this chapter, we will examine the concepts and principles of capital formation in the health care industry. Few areas are more important to the financial well-being of a health care firm. A firm that cannot obtain the amounts of capital specified in its strategic financial plan will not be able to achieve its long-term objectives. Indeed, if the firm finds it difficult to acquire any amount of capital at a reasonable cost, its future survival may be questionable. Successful firms have the capability to provide capital financing when needed and at a cost that is reasonable.

Three key questions are relevant to our discussion of capital formation in the health care industry. First, how much capital is needed? Ideally, the firm should have defined its capital needs in its strategic financial plan. Capital needs should include working capital requirements and replacement reserves, as well as the funding needs for buildings and equipment.

Second, what sources of capital financing are available? At the time of this writing, the future availability of tax-exempt financing is unclear. Tax-exempt financing has been the largest source of capital for the hospital industry for the last twenty years. If it were eliminated, financing patterns would experience a major shift. The exact direction of this shift is unclear at this time, although it would seem that taxable sources of debt would have to be substituted for tax-exempt sources.

Third, how are the costs of capital financing provided for in third-party payment plans? This area is critical to the discussion of capital financing and selection of capital financing alternatives. At the time of this writing, Medicare and Medicaid provide for the payment of a portion of actual capital costs, such as interest expense. It is expected, however, that this situation will change and that cost reimbursement of capital costs will be replaced totally by prospective prices.

Table 16–1 presents a summary of investment and financing patterns in the hospital industry for the period of 1986 to 1995. In general, we can classify the sources of financing into the following two categories: (1) equity and (2) debt. In the hospital industry, approximately 50 percent of total assets are financed with equity and 50 percent are financed with debt. However, financing patterns may vary somewhat in different sectors of the health care industry. For example, many long-term care facilities have much higher proportions of debt. Debt financing in such facilities may run as high as 90 percent.

EQUITY FINANCING

In general, the following are the only ways in which a firm can generate new equity capital: (1) profit retention, (2) contributions, and (3) sale of equity interests. We already have stressed in past

Table 16-1 Percentage Balance Sheet for U.S. Hospitals, 1991–1995

	1991	*1992*	*1993*	*1994*	*1995*
Assets					
Cash and marketable securities	6.8%	6.2%	6.0%	5.7%	6.1%
Net accounts receivable	14.9%	15.4%	16.5%	17.1%	16.9%
Inventory	1.1%	1.1%	1.2%	1.2%	1.2%
Other current assets	1.9%	2.2%	2.2%	2.1%	2.3%
Total current assets	24.7%	24.9%	25.9%	26.1%	26.5%
Other investments	13.9%	13.8%	13.8%	14.1%	14.7%
Net fixed assets	50.0%	49.6%	49.3%	48.3%	47.5%
Other assets	11.4%	11.7%	11.0%	11.5%	11.4%
	100.0%	100.0%	100.0%	100.0%	100.0%
Liabilities and fund balance					
Current liabilities	12.3%	12.8%	13.2%	13.4%	13.7%
Long-term debt	36.6%	36.0%	35.6%	35.8%	35.1%
Other liabilities	2.2%	2.3%	2.2%	2.8%	3.0%
Fund balance	48.9%	48.9%	49.0%	48.0%	48.2%
	100.0%	100.0%	100.0%	100.0%	100.0%

Source: Center for Healthcare Industry Performance Studies.

chapters the importance of earning adequate levels of profit. Hence, our discussion at this point is focused primarily on contributions and sales of new equity. A contribution may be given to a firm for a variety of reasons. Normally, in tax-exempt health care firms, a contribution is given with no expectation of a future return. The donor may derive some immediate or deferred tax benefit, but there is no expectation of a financial return to be paid by the health care entity. In contrast, contributions are given to a taxable health care entity with the expectation of a future financial return. The contribution may be in the form of a stock purchase or a limited partnership unit. It is important to note that this form of contribution also may be available to tax-exempt entities through a corporate restructuring arrangement. We will discuss this point in more detail shortly.

Philanthropy is definitely not dead in our nation. In 1993, approximately 2 percent of our nation's gross national product, or $126.2 billion, was in the form of philanthropic gifts. Tables 16–2 and 16–3 provide data showing the sources and the distribution of giving for the period of 1988 to 1993. These data present an encouraging picture. Total giving increased during the five-year period of 1988 to 1993. Individuals were clearly the largest source of giving, representing more than 80 percent of total giving.

To be successful, a major philanthropic program should have the following key elements:

- A "case statement." This document should carefully and persuasively define why you need money.
- A designated development officer. This individual may not be a full-time employee, but duties and expectations should be precisely defined. Incentives for development

Table 16-2 Sources of Giving

	1988 Dollars (Billions) (Inflation Adj.)	%	1993 Dollars (Billions)	%
Individuals	$101.7	81.4%	$102.6	81.3%
Bequests	$8.4	6.7%	$8.5	6.7%
Foundations	$7.8	6.2%	$9.2	7.3%
Corporations	$7.1	5.7%	$5.9	4.7%
Total	$125.0	100.0%	$126.2	100.0%

officers should be related to expectations for giving.

- Trustee and medical staff involvement. People give to people, not to organizations.
- Prospect lists. You should know who in the community are prime prospects for giving.
- Programs for giving. This is critical. You should have a variety of methods and means to encourage giving. For example, you may have a number of deferred giving plans, such as unitrusts, annuity trusts, or pooled-income funds. Your development officer should be familiar with these methods.
- Goals. You need to define realistic targets for long-range planning.

There are many ways to encourage people to give to charitable, tax-exempt health care firms. Many large firms employ full-time development staff. These individuals can do much to increase charitable giving.

One of the most promising areas of philanthropic giving is in deferred gift arrangements. In a deferred giving plan, a taxpayer donor may get an immediate tax benefit in return for a gift to be given to the tax-exempt firm later. An interesting recent example of deferred giving is the case of a hospital in California that initiated a provocative new fund-raising effort, called the home value program (HVP). HVP is designed for senior citizens, aged seventy or older, who own mortgage-free homes. The homeowners sign a revocable agreement that, upon their

Table 16-3 Distribution of Giving

	1988 Dollars (Billions) (Inflation Adj.)	%	1993 Dollars (Billions)	%
Religion	$ 57.4	45.9%	$ 57.2	45.3%
Education	$ 13.0	10.4%	$ 15.1	12.0%
Health	$ 12.2	9.8%	$ 10.8	8.6%
Human services	$ 13.3	10.6%	$ 12.5	9.9%
Arts and culture	$ 8.6	6.9%	$ 9.6	7.6%
Other	$ 20.5	16.4%	$ 21.0	16.6%
Total	$125.0	100.0%	$126.2	100.0%

deaths, transfers the title to their homes to the hospital. In return, they receive a monthly payment that is based on a loan from the hospital. In concept, HVP is similar to the reverse annuity mortgages that are being used in some banking circles. An HVP program is also being used to finance long-term care for individual patients in nursing homes and home health agencies. It is especially useful for the elderly who have no means of supporting themselves other than the equity built up in their homes.

The following case illustrates the mechanics of HVP. Assume that Mrs. Jones, aged seventy, has a mortgage-free home with a market value of $100,000. The hospital, or its foundation, executes a loan of $50,000 at 12-percent interest that will pay Mrs. Jones $717 per month for ten years. Mrs. Jones signs a revocable agreement.

How does the hospital benefit? First, for a $50,000 loan, the hospital receives title to property that is valued at $100,000. Second, the hospital benefits from any appreciation on the property. In ten years, if the annual appreciation rate is 5 percent, Mrs. Jones' $100,000 home will be worth $163,000. Third, the hospital establishes a relationship with Mrs. Jones that may lead to other donations.

How does Mrs. Jones benefit? First, the monthly payment is considered tax-free income. Second, there is no risk to Mrs. Jones because the agreement is revocable and can be rescinded with payment of the loan plus a penalty. Third, HVP provides Mrs. Jones with a tangible way of supporting the hospital. The last factor is the key to the ultimate success of the program.

An HVP, or some adaptation of it, can provide a significant return to a hospital. However, some forethought is required. For one thing, working capital obviously is necessary. Payments to homeowners will precede any financial recovery through sale of the donated homes. Also, a significant amount of legal, accounting, and actuarial consulting is essential. Finally, such a program should not be perceived as a pure donation program. It is intended to be a method of investment diversification, albeit one with unusually high returns. Thus, a program such as an HVP can provide an excellent vehicle for long-term equity capital growth.

Both taxable and tax-exempt health care providers have shown great interest in the issuance of equity to investors. For taxable health care firms, this interest is not new; for most such firms, the issuance of equity has been a major source of financing over the years. Most taxable health care firms began with a small amount of venture capital. They were able to use that original funding to develop a successful track record of operations. Based on that record of success, an initial public offering (IPO) of stock was made. The resulting funds were then used to expand operations, part of which was fueled by leveraging funds acquired during the initial public offering.

The technique of expanding operations quickly through the issuance of equity and then leveraging that equity through the issuance of debt has been used extensively in the taxable sector. Table 16–4 illustrates the growth potential of a taxable entity.

Table 16–4 Capital Growth in Alternative Organizations

Organizational Type	Historical Net Income	Equity Issue (Stock)	Debt Addition	Possible Total Capital
Tax-exempt	$1.0	.0	$2.0	$3.0
Taxable	$.07	$14.0	$28.0	$42.7

These data indicate that a taxable entity could raise approximately fourteen times the amount of total capital that a tax-exempt entity could. Let us examine these data and their related assumptions more closely to clearly understand the underlying process behind capital formation. It is assumed that some business unit or firm has generated $1 million in before-tax income. If the firm was a taxable entity, it would be required to pay approximately 30 percent of this income as tax. However, the taxable firm could issue stock, limited partnership units, or some other type of equity security. Furthermore, it is assumed that a price-to-earnings multiple of 20 is in effect. This means that the taxable firm could raise $14 million in equity based on its net income of $700,000. Both the tax-exempt and the taxable firms could issue debt based on their equity positions. We have assumed that a leverage ratio of 2 to 1 exists; that is, the firms could borrow $2 for every $1 of equity. The taxable firm could issue $28 million in debt, whereas the tax-exempt firm would be limited to $2 million in debt. Total capital, both debt and equity, would be $3 million for the tax-exempt firm and $42.7 million for the taxable firm.

In the preceding example, some of the assumptions might be changed, but the relative growth potential would remain the same. In this situation, is there any way that a tax-exempt firm can take advantage of this growth potential? The answer is yes: a tax-exempt firm could change its status to taxable. This is not an easy thing to do, but it is not impossible. Several large health maintenance organizations (HMOs) started out as tax-exempt firms but changed their ownership status to maximize their growth potential.

An easier alternative method is to restructure the firm. Figure 16–1 presents a generic structure that is used by many tax-exempt health care firms to create an equity capital formation alternative. This structure involves the creation of taxable entities that can issue equity securities directly to investors. In the parent holding company model in Figure 16–1, there are several taxable entities that could issue equity to investors and help generate capital for the entire consolidated structure.

An actual case example may help to illustrate the potential for capital formation created by restructuring a tax-exempt health care firm. ABC hospital needed to replace its computed tomography (CT) scanner with a new one. The estimated cost of the new scanner was $1,160,000. The hospital did not wish to use any of its debt capacity in this project. The solution was to create a limited partnership and joint venture with its physicians. A new entity was created, called ABC Scanner, which was a limited partnership. The ABC Properties Company, which was a subsidiary of the hospital's parent holding company, was the general partner. A bank loan of $1,180,000 was obtained; the loan was guaranteed by the limited partners (thirty limited partners) and the general partner. The source and use-of-funds statement for the new structure is presented in Table 16–5.

Table 16–5 documents the capability of the new structure to enhance ABC hospital's capital position with little funding commitment from the hospital. The general partner, a member of the restructured health care entity, has contributed only $50,000 of cash and guaranteed $295,000 in loans. For this relatively modest level of commitment, total funding of $1,380,000 was made available.

LONG-TERM DEBT FINANCING

An examination of the specific sources of long-term debt financing in the health care industry can be a complex and confusing process. Part of the problem stems from the use of jargon by those involved. Unless one is familiar with this jargon, meaningful communication with financing people may be difficult. Before describing the alternatives for long-term debt financing in the health care industry, we should note five key characteristics of financing that greatly affect the relative desirability of alternative sources of financing. As we describe these char-

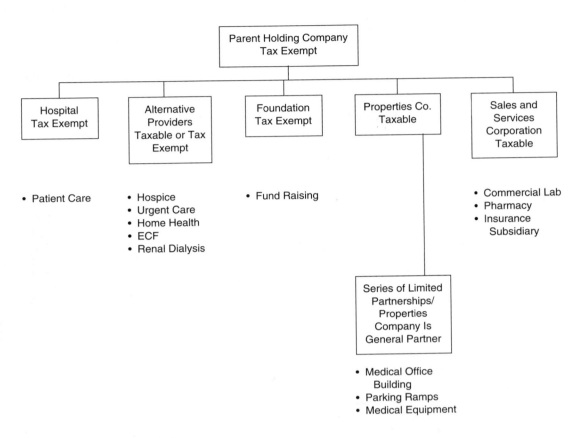

Note: ECF = extended care facility.

Figure 16–1 A Parent Holding Company

acteristics, we will introduce some new terminology that will facilitate later discussion.

The five key characteristics are

1. cost,
2. control,
3. risk,
4. availability, and
5. adequacy.

Cost

Interest rates are the most important characteristic that affects the cost of alternative debt fi-

nancing. The fixed return of a long-term debt instrument is often called the coupon rate. For example, a 9.8-percent revenue bond indicates that the issuer will pay the investor $98 annually for every $1,000 of principal. Sometimes the term "basis point" is used to describe differences in coupon rates. A basis point is 1/100 of 1 percent. For example, the difference between a coupon rate of 9.8 percent and 9.65 percent would be fifteen basis points.

Although interest is the primary measure of financing cost, it is not the only aspect of cost that should be considered. Issuance costs can be sizable in some types of financing. Issuance

Table 16–5 Source and Use of Funds for CT Scanner

Sources of		
bank loan		$1,180,000
Guaranteed by:		
General partner	$295,000	
Limited partners (@ $29,500)	885,000	
General partner's cash contribution		50,000
Limited partner's cash contribution (@ $5,000)		150,000
Total sources		$1,380,000
Uses of Funds		
Purchase and installation of CT scanner		$1,160,000
Leasehold (suite) improvements		95,000
Loan placement fee		35,400
Legal and other organizational expenses		15,000
Reserve for working capital		74,600
Total uses		$1,380,000

costs are simply those expenditures that are essential to consummate the financing. There is a great difference in the amount of issuance costs for publicly placed and privately placed issues. A privately placed issue is not sold to the general market but rather is purchased directly by only a few major buyers. In a publicly placed issue, there are a number of costs that must be incurred to legally sell the securities to the general public. Printing costs are associated with producing the official statements that will be sent to prospective clients. There are costs for attorneys and accountants who must certify various aspects of the issue, such as its financial feasibility and its tax-exempt status. Finally, there is the underwriter's spread that is charged by the investment banking firm that arranges the sale of the securities. The underwriter's spread represents the difference between the face value of the bonds and the price the underwriter or investment banker pays to purchase the bonds. When aggregated, issuance costs can sometimes amount to as much as 5 percent of the total issue. This means that an issuer must borrow $100 to get $95.

Another large cost of financing is reserve requirements. Some types of financing require the creation of fund balances in escrow accounts under the custody of the bond trustee. The bond trustee is designated by the issuer to represent the interests of the bondholders. The obligations of the trustee are defined in the Trust Indenture Act of 1939, which is administered by the Securities and Exchange Commission. There are two primary categories of reserve requirements. The first is the debt service reserve. This fund represents a cushion for the investors if the issuer gets into some type of fiscal crisis. It is usually set equal to one year's worth of principal and interest payments. The second category of reserve requirement is the depreciation reserve. This fund is sometimes set up to equal the cumulative difference between debt principal repayment and depreciation expense on the depreciable assets financed with debt. Usually, the amount of depreciation expense is greatest during the immediate years after a major construction program has been completed, when debt principal may be at its lowest level. Because depreciation may represent the primary source of debt principal payment, there is a need to accumulate these funds to ensure their availability in later years, when the amount of debt principal payment exceeds depreciation. Figure 16–2 presents a graphic display of this relationship.

Control

Ideally, when issuing debt financing, the issuer would like to have little or no interference by the investors in management. It is usually not possible to avoid such interference, however. The investors often will specify some conditions or restrictions that they would like included in the bond contract. Such conditions or restrictions are often known as covenants. These are explained in great detail in the indenture, which is the written contract between the investors and the issuing company.

One category of restrictive covenants concerns specific financial performance indicators. For example, most indentures define values for the firm's debt service coverage ratio and its current ratio. If actual values for these indicators are below the defined values, the bond trustee may take certain actions. The trustee may assume a position on the board of trustees, replace current management, or require the entire outstanding principal to be paid immediately.

Another category of covenants concerns future financing. A section in the indenture referred to as additional parity financing defines the conditions that must be satisfied before the firm can issue any additional debt. The most important condition is usually prior and projected debt service coverage.

There is a trend developing in the issuance of tax-exempt bonds to replace the projected debt service coverage provision with a stated level of debt to equity. For example, the initial bond placement may specify that new financing can be issued if long-term debt does not equal a multiple of 1.5 times present equity or net assets. This would permit large health care systems more flexibility when issuing future debt and is more closely akin to provisions that exist in the corporate taxable debt markets.

Risk

From the issuer's perspective, flexibility of repayment terms is highly desirable. An issuer

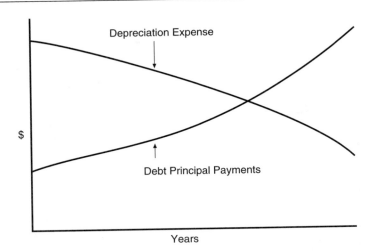

Figure 16–2 Depreciation Reserve Requirement: Relationship between Depreciation Expense and Debt Principal Payments

with flexible repayment terms can alter payments to meet the issuer's current cash flow. The investor, however, wants some guarantee that the principal will be repaid in accordance with some preestablished plan.

One of the most important indenture elements is the prepayment provision. This provision specifies the point in time at which the debt can be retired, and the penalty that will be imposed for an early retirement. For example, the indenture may prohibit the issuer from prepaying the debt for the first ten years of issue life. Thereafter, the debt may be repaid, but only if there is a call premium. The call premium is some percentage of the par or face value of the bonds. Thus, a call premium of 5 percent would mean that a $50 premium would be paid for each $1,000 of bonds. The issuer would like to have the option of retiring outstanding debt at any point with no call premium. However, investors do not usually permit this for debt that has a fixed interest rate.

Another aspect of risk relates to the debt principal amortization pattern. Most debt retirement plans can be categorized as level-debt service or level-debt principal. In a level-debt service plan, the amount of interest and principal that is repaid

each year remains fairly constant. This is the type of repayment that is usually associated with home mortgages. In the early years, the amount of interest is much greater than the debt principal. Over time, this pattern changes and the amount of principal repaid each year begins to exceed the interest payment. Figure 16–3 presents a graphic view of a level-debt service plan. Level-debt principal means that equal amount of debt principal is repaid each year. In this pattern of debt retirement, the total debt service payment decreases over time. Figure 16–4 shows this relationship.

Many financing plans approximate a level-debt service plan. This pattern of debt amortization extends the debt retirement life and may benefit the issuer. The benefit is predicated on three factors:

1. the ability of the issuer to earn a return greater than the interest rate on the debt,
2. the presence of reimbursement for capital costs, and
3. the availability of tax-exempt financing.

To illustrate the desirability of principal repayment delay, we will examine a simple case.

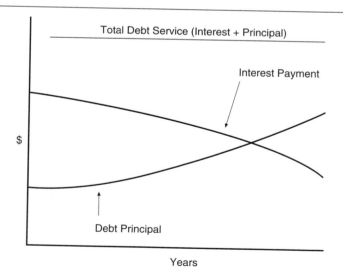

Figure 16–3 Level-Debt Service: Relationship between Interest Payment and Debt Principal

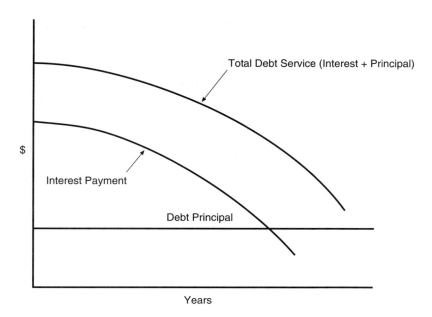

Figure 16–4 Level-Debt Principal: Relationship between Interest Payment and Total Debt Service

Let us assume that we have two alternative financing plans. One plan will permit us to borrow $10 million for five years with no payment of principal until the fifth year. We will be required to pay 10 percent per year as our interest payment for each of the five years. The second financing plan will permit us to borrow the same $10 million for five years; however, there will be an annual payment of principal equal to $2 million per year. The interest rate on this financing plan will be 8 percent per year, which is below the interest rate in the first plan. Let us further assume that 80 percent of our interest expense will be repaid by our third-party payers, who still pay us for the actual costs of capital incurred. Finally, let us assume that any differences in cash flow between the two plans could be invested at 10 percent. Table 16–6 provides a comparison of the net present values for these two financing plans. The values indicate that the higher-interest balloon payment plan is the lower cost source of financing. This is a direct

result of the large percentage (80 percent) of capital cost payment. An 80-percent capital cost payment means that the effective interest rate is $(1 - .80)$ times the interest rate. This means that the effective interest rate for the balloon repayment plan would be 2 percent, and the corresponding value for the equal principal plan would be 1.6 percent. The difference in interest rates has decreased from 2 percent to .4 of 1 percent. An investment yield of 10 percent means that we can make money from delaying principal payment. In short, our cost is less than our return. It is only natural to want to retain money as long as possible.

Availability

Once a health care firm decides that it needs debt financing, it usually wants to obtain the funds as quickly as possible. A delay can result in severe consequences and postpone the start of a construction program. This might increase the

Table 16–6 Cost of Alternative Debt Amortization Plans

Item	Amount before Reimbursement Effect	Amount after Reimbursement Effect	Years	Present Value Factor (10%)	Present Value
		Equal Principal Payment—8%			
Principal	$2,000,000	$ 2,000,000	1–5	3.791	$7,582,000
Interest	800,000	160,000	1	.909	145,440
Interest	640,000	128,000	2	.826	105,728
Interest	480,000	96,000	3	.751	72,096
Interest	320,000	64,000	4	.683	43,712
Interest	160,000	32,000	5	.621	19,872
Net present value cost					$7,968,848
		Balloon Principal—10%			
Interest	$ 1,000,000	$ 200,000	1–5	3.791	$ 758,200
Principal	10,000,000	10,000,000	5	.621	6,210,000
Net present value					$6,968,200

cost of the total program because of normal inflation in construction costs. A delay also could result in an unexpected increase in interest rates. Although privately placed issues usually can be arranged more quickly than publicly placed issues, there is usually a higher interest rate associated with privately placed issues. However, the difference in interest rates may more than offset the costs of delay.

Adequacy

A key requirement of any proposed plan of financing is that it cover all the associated costs. One of the key areas of adequacy is that of refinancing costs. In many situations, a new construction program that requires financing may not be possible unless existing financing can be retired or refinanced. Not all types of financing permit the issuer to include the costs of refinancing in the amount borrowed.

Funding during construction is another important area of financing. Some types of financing do not permit the issuer to borrow during the construction period. A loan will be issued only after the construction has been completed and the new assets are available for operations. In this situation, the issuer must arrange for a separate source of funding to finance the construction. Permanent financing then must be arranged upon completion of the construction program.

Interest incurred during construction can be sizable. For example, a $50 million construction program might incur $10 to $15 million in interest during the construction period. It is thus important to have a source of financing that also permits the issuer to borrow to cover interest costs.

Last, the percentage of financing available varies across financing plans. Some plans permit up to 100 percent of the cost, whereas others may limit the amount to 70 or 80 percent. Depending on the availability of other funds, these limitations may pose real problems in some situations.

ALTERNATIVE DEBT FINANCING SOURCES

Sources

Presently, the following four major alternative sources of long-term debt are available to health care facilities:

1. tax-exempt revenue bonds,
2. Federal Housing Administration (FHA)–insured mortgages,
3. public taxable bonds, and
4. conventional mortgage financing.

Table 16–7 compares these four sources of financing regarding the factors that affect capital financing desirability.

Tax-Exempt Revenue Bonds

Tax-exempt revenue bonds permit the interest earned on them to be exempt from federal income taxation. The primary security for such loans is usually a pledge of the revenues of the facility seeking the loan, plus a first mortgage on the facility's assets. If the tax revenue of a government entity is also pledged, the bonds are referred to as "general obligation bonds." Because of the income tax exemption, the interest rates on a tax-exempt bond are usually 1.5 to 2 percent lower than other sources of financing.

Most tax-exempt revenue bonds are issued by a state or local authority. The health care facility then enters into a lease arrangement with the authority. Title to the assets remains with the authority until the indebtedness is repaid.

Congress has issued legislation that has begun to limit both the total amount of tax-exempt revenue bonds that can be issued and the purpose for which the financing can be used. For example, a hospital can no longer issue tax-exempt revenue bonds to finance the construction of a medical office building.

FHA-Insured Mortgages

FHA-insured mortgages are sponsored by the Federal Housing Administration, but initial processing begins in the Department of Health and Human Services. Through the FHA program, the government provides mortgage insurance for both proprietary and nonproprietary hospitals. This guarantee reduces the risk of a loan to investors and thus lowers the interest rate that a hospital must pay. However, obtaining the appropriate approvals often can be a time-consuming process.

Public Taxable Bonds

Public taxable bonds are issued in much the same way as tax-exempt revenue bonds, except that there is no issuing authority and no interest income tax exemption. An investment banking firm usually underwrites the loan and markets the issue to individual investors. Interest rates are thus higher on this type of financing than they are on a tax-exempt issue.

Conventional Mortgage Financing

Conventional mortgage financing is usually privately placed with a bank, pension fund, savings and loan institution, life insurance company, or real estate investment trust. This source of financing can be arranged quickly, but, compared with other alternatives, does not provide as large a percentage of the total financing requirements for large projects. Thus, greater amounts of equity must be contributed.

Parties Involved

Figure 16–5 is a schematic representation of the parties involved and their relationships when issuing a public tax-exempt revenue bond. This schematic also could be used to illustrate the process of issuing a public taxable bond. The only change would be the deletion of the issuing

Table 16-7 Comparative Analysis: Long-Term Debt Alternatives for Hospitals

Program Characteristics	Conventional Mortgage	Taxable Bonds	Tax-Exempt Bonds	FHA-Insured Mortgage (GNMA Guarantee)
Security	First mortgage given to lender; pledge of gross revenues (substantially all hospital assets pledged)	First mortgage given to trustee bank for benefit of bondholder; pledge of gross revenue (substantially all assets pledged)	First mortgage given to trustee bank for benefit of bondholders; pledge of gross revenue (substantially all assets pledged)	First mortgage given to FHA-approved mortgagee for benefit of HUD; pledge of gross revenue (substantially all assets pledged)
Timing for alternative	1–6 months	4–8 months	3–6 months	6–12 months
Percentage financing available	Usually 70%–75% of eligible assets available to be pledged (as determined by appraisal)	Up to 100%, limited by available cash flow and available assets in some cases	Up to 100%, subject to available cash flow	
Construction financing	Normally required	Optional	Not required	Not required
Financing costs	Covers all costs of assets, excluding some movable equipment	Covers all costs	Covers all costs	Covers all costs, including startup costs
Term of financing	15–20 years	15–20 years (occasionally with balloon payment based on longer amortization)	30–35 years common	25 years subsequent to construction completion
Front-end fees	1%–2% commitment fee subject to amount financed; other fees $5–$25,000	1% underwriting (private placement) or 2%–4% underwriting (public offering); other expenses approximately 1/2 of 1% plus feasibility study	1% underwriting (private placement) or 2%–3.5% underwriting (public offering); other expenses approximate 1/2 of 1% plus feasibility study	1% placement fee, 0.8% filing fee, 0.5% insurance (FHA) fee, 0.25% GNMA fee
Continuing annual fee	1/8 of 1% servicing if multiple lenders	Trustee fees (nominal)	Trustee fees (nominal)	0.5% FHA insurance fee; 0.25% GNMA fee

Table 16-7 continued

Program Characteristics	Conventional Mortgage	Taxable Bonds	Tax-Exempt Bonds	FHA-Insured Mortgage (GNMA Guarantee)
Prepayment provisions	Normally 10 year, no prepayment; 5% penalty descending thereafter	Normally 5 year and prepayment; no penalty unless refinancing	10 year, no prepayment; 3% penalty descending thereafter	15% of loan may be prepaid each year; 3% penalty over 15%, declining by 1/8 of 1% each year
Required reserves	Usually none; depreciation reserve optional	None	Debt service reserve equal to 1 year's principal and interest (P & I); depreciation reserve equal to deficiency amount	Usually none
Restriction on leasing	Yes; subject to cash-flow levels by covenant	None	None	None
Additional parity financing	Yes; normally subject to lender approval	Yes; subject to approval of underwriter or to provisions of financing agreement; normally required coverage of 110%–150%	Yes; subject to meeting coverage requirement of 110%–150% on both historical and pro forma basis	Yes; only with FHA-compatible program
Payment	Monthly	Semiannually	Quarterly/semiannually	Monthly
Reporting	Lender(s) only	Lender(s) or bond trustee and underwriter as appropriate, and rating agencies	Bond trustee, under-writer, and rating agencies as appropriate	HUD and mortgagee

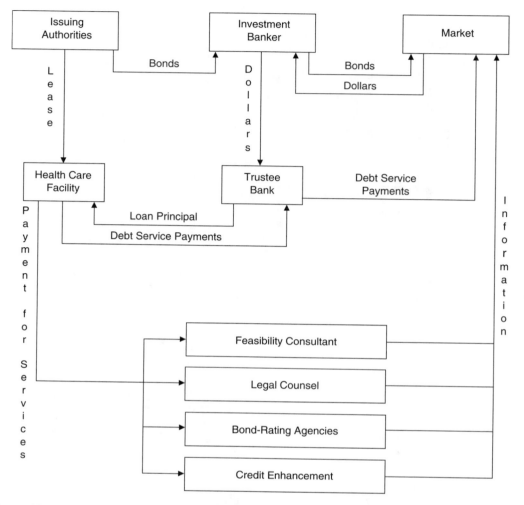

Figure 16–5 Parties Involved in a Public Tax-Exempt Revenue Bond Issue

authority and addition of a line showing the direct issuance of the bonds by the health care facility. The specific parties involved in financing a bond include the following:

- issuing authority,
- investment banker,
- health care facility,
- market,
- trustee bank,
- feasibility consultant,

- legal counsel, and
- bond-rating agency.

Issuing Authority

The issuing authority is involved only in tax-exempt financing. In most cases, the issuing authority is some state or local governmental authority, which may be specially created for the sole purpose of issuing revenue bonds. The issuing authority serves as a conduit between the health care facility and the investment banker. In a public taxable issue or in a situation in which tax-exempt revenue bonds are issued directly by the health care facility, the role of the issuing authority may be eliminated.

Investment Banker

In public or private issues, investment bankers have a dual role. First, they serve as advisors to the health care facility that is issuing the bonds. In many circumstances, they are the focal point for coordinating the services of the feasibility consultant, the legal counsel, and the bond-rating agencies. Their advice can be extremely important to obtaining timely funding under favorable conditions. Second, investment bankers serve as brokers between the market and the issuer of the bond. If investment bankers underwrite the issue, it means that they technically buy the entire issue and are at risk for the sale of the bonds to individual investors. If investment bankers place the issue on a best-efforts basis, they do not purchase the issue, and any unsold bonds become the property of the issuer.

Health Care Facility

The health care facility is the ultimate beneficiary of the bond issue. The health care facility is also responsible for repayment of the loan principal. The health care facility's financial condition and its ability to repay the indebtedness are thus the central concerns of the investor. To provide evidence of its financial condition and the risk of the investment to the market, the health care facility usually employs independent consultants who assess various aspects of the facility. Such consultants include the feasibility consultant, the legal counsel, and the bond-rating agencies.

Market

For any given bond issue, the market may consist of a large number of individual investors or it may consist of a small number of large institutional investors. In any case, the market purchases the bonds of the issuer with the expectation of some stated rate of return. The market also wants assurances that the bonds will be re-

paid on a timely basis and that there is not an unreasonable amount of risk.

Trustee Bank

A trustee bank serves as the market's agent once the bonds are sold. Typically, the trustee bank is a commercial bank—in some cases, the same bank at which the health care facility has its accounts. The trustee bank may receive the proceeds from the sale of the bond issue and deliver the monies directly to the hospital or to the contractor, as required. The trustee bank also receives the debt service payments from the health care facility and distributes these to the market or investors. It may retire outstanding bonds according to a prearranged schedule of retirement and hold additional reserve requirements deposited by the health care facility. Finally, the trustee bank ensures that the health care facility is adhering to the provisions of the bond contract or indenture, such as those concerning adequate debt service coverage and working capital positions.

Feasibility Consultant

The feasibility consultant is usually an independent, certified public accountant who may or may not be the health care facility's outside auditor. The feasibility consultant's primary function is to assess the financial feasibility of the project and the ability of the health care facility to meet the associated indebtedness. Financial projections are usually made for a five-year period. These projections provide a basis for the investor and the bond-rating agency to assess the risk of default.

Legal Counsel

Legal counsel is needed for several reasons. First, in a tax-exempt revenue bond issue, the market is concerned with the legality of the tax exemption. If the interest payments are not determined to be tax-exempt by the Internal Revenue Service, the investors will suffer a significant loss. Second, legal opinion is necessary to ensure that the security pledged by the health care facility, whether it be revenue or assets, is legal and enforceable.

Bond-Rating Agencies

Moody's and Standard & Poor's are the two primary bond-rating agencies, although other smaller ones exist. Their function is to assess the relative risk associated with a given bond issue. The two agencies have developed detailed coding systems to assess risk (Table 16–8). The resulting bond rating has important implications. First, there is a definite correlation between the interest rate that an issuer must pay and the bond rating associated with the issue. Generally speaking, the higher the bond rating, the lower the interest rate. Thus, a bond rated AAA by Standard & Poor's would be likely to have a much lower rate of interest than one rated BBB. Second, issues rated below BBB by Standard & Poor's or Baa by Moody's are not classified as investment grade. Many institutional investors are prohibited from investing in bonds that carry a rating lower than investment grade. Thus, the market for such issues is likely to be small.

Credit Enhancement

Credit enhancement is a term that has come into use in the health care financing field only recently. A credit enhancement device is simply a mechanism by which the risk of default can be shifted from the issuer to a third party. Thus, the FHA-insured mortgage program provides a form of credit enhancement.

Aside from the FHA program, two basic types of credit enhancement are commonly used. The first type is municipal bond insurance. Municipal bond insurance is a surety bond that ensures that the debt service will be repaid. When municipal bond insurance is used, the credit rating for the issue becomes the credit rating of the insurance firm that is writing the insurance. In most cases, this means that the bond rating would be AAA or Aaa. Table 16–9 presents a summary of the major firms that currently provide municipal bond insurance and gives some idea of the relative cost of such insurance.

The second form of credit enhancement is a letter of credit. A letter of credit, usually issued by a commercial bank, provides a formal assurance that a specified sum of money will be available during some defined period. Usually, the period matches the maturity of the debt, and the amount provided in the letter of credit corresponds to the amount of indebtedness. As with bond insurance, the credit rating of the bank would be substituted for the credit rating of the issuer. In most situations, this would mean an

Table 16–8 Bond Ratings

Classification	Moody's	Standard & Poor's
Investment grade	Aaa	AAA
	Aa	AA
	A1	A +
	A	A
	Baa1	BBB +
	Baa	BBB
Not investment grade	Ba	BB
	B	B
	Caa	CCC
	Ca	CC
	C	C

Table 16–9 Municipal Bond Insurers

Insurer	Types of Issues	Rating	Premiums	Principal and Interest Insured (Billions)	
				All Types	Health Care
AMBAC Indemnity (212-248-3307)	New-issue general obligation bonds (GOs), tax and revenue anticipation note	AAA Aaa	.33–.94%	$86.2	$12.9
MBIA (914-765-3893)	New-issue GOs, utility issues, commercial paper, hospital goods	AAA Aaa	.30–.90%	$157.7	$32.1
FGIC (212-607-3009)	New issues, GOs, revenue bonds, and unit investment trusts	AAA Aaa	NA	$92.6	NA
Capital Guarantee (415-995-8012)	New issues, GOs, and revenue bonds	AAA NR	.20–2.00%	$9.0	$.56
FSA (212-826-0100)	New issues, GOs, revenue bonds, and municipal utilities	AAA Aaa	NA	$21.6	$.67

Source: Prepared by James LeBuhn, Ziegler Securities, Chicago, Illinois.

automatic AAA or Aaa rating. The bank requires a fee for providing the letter of credit, and the issuer must determine whether the cost of the letter of credit exceeds any possible savings in reduced interest expense that would result from an improved bond rating.

NEW DEVELOPMENTS

The following four recent modifications in the traditional sources of long-term debt should be noted at this juncture:

1. variable rate financing,
2. pooled or shared financing,
3. zero-coupon and original issue discount bonds, and
4. interest rate swaps.

Variable Rate Financing

Recently in the health care sector, as well as in other industries, there has been a shift to the use of variable rate financing. In variable rate financing, the outstanding debt principal is fixed, but the interest rate on the principal is variable. This contrasts with the traditional situation in which the interest rate is fixed for the life of the bonds. Variable rate financing requires that the interest rate be adjusted periodically—in some cases, weekly—to a current market index.

A feature that is often associated with variable rate financing is the use of a tender option or put. A tender option or put permits investors to redeem their bonds at some predetermined interval—perhaps daily—at the face value. In reality, this type of financing is short-term, not long-term. As a result, the interest rate may be significantly below a comparable long-term rate at the initiation of the financing. Many firms—not just health care firms—have opted to use variable rate financing to achieve a lower cost of financing. Sometimes this strategy is referred to as "moving down the yield curve." Figure 16–6 shows a typical upward-sloping yield curve.

Pooled Financing

In the health care sector, there has been increasing interest in developing financing packages that encompass more than one entity. The major rationale for this interest lies in the relationship between size and cost of debt; larger organizations are better able to obtain debt capital and to realize lower costs of financing.

In general, there are three ways in which pooled or shared arrangements have been created in the health care sector. The first is through the use of master indenture financing by health care systems. In such cases, master indenture financing means that the debt is guaranteed by all the members who are a part of the master indenture. For example, a system of ten hospitals could finance through some master indenture arrangement in which all ten hospitals, or some subset of the ten hospitals, would be involved in the financing.

A second alternative is the use of pooled equipment financing programs. These programs are often sponsored by the state hospital association or some regional association. Individual hospitals are involved in the financing and can obtain funds from the pool. The interest rate is usually much lower because the risk is spread across several hospitals.

The third alternative is an arrangement similar to the previous, except that the sponsor is different. Here, the pooled approach is used either for equipment needs or, in some cases, for major building programs. The issuer and sponsor of the pool is not the state or regional association, however, but some voluntary association of health care entities. The Voluntary Hospitals of America have created such pooled financing for their members, and other associations are developing similar financing programs for their members.

Zero-Coupon and Original Issue Discount Bonds

Bonds that are issued at a great discount have a coupon rate of interest that is below the rate required by the market for that type of security. In a zero-coupon situation, there is no interest paid, thus the term zero coupon. Certain investors think advantages accompany purchasing zero-coupon bonds to meet their portfolio needs. There also may be advantages for the issuer. The major advantage for the issuer is the delay of interest payments. This can conserve needed cash flow and may match the cash needs of the issuer. There is also the possibility that the after-reimbursement cost of the debt will be below the in-

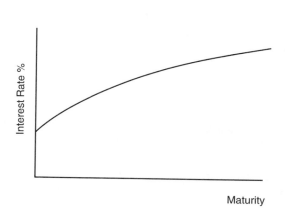

Figure 16–6 The Yield Curve

vestment yield. It is important to note that, in most zero-coupon situations, there is a periodic payment to a sinking fund. The sinking fund is an account under the control of the bond trustee, and the proceeds of the fund are used to retire the bonds at maturity.

The mechanics of a zero-coupon situation may be illustrated in the following case example. Assume that General Hospital issues $100,000,000 in zero-coupon, five-year bonds. General Hospital would receive $62,100,000 from the market if the current market rate of interest is 10 percent. Although no interest is paid, each year an amount is recorded for interest expense. This amount is an amortization of the difference between the face value of the bonds ($100,000,000) and the actual cash received ($62,100,000). Thus, during the five-year period, $37,900,000 will be recognized as interest expense. General also will be required to make semiannual payments of $7,586,793 to a sinking fund. This fund is assumed to earn interest at 12 percent annually or 6 percent semiannually. Assume also that equal amounts of the total discount will be recognized as interest expense each year. This would amount to $7,580,000 ($37,900,000/5). The calculation in Table 16–10 shows the net present value cost of this financing, assuming that 50 percent of capital costs are reimbursed and that the appropriate discount rate for the hospital is its investment yield of 12 percent.

The net present value cost of General Hospital's financing is $42,175,850, which is significantly less than the $62,100,000 that the hospital will receive. The sinking fund is not recognized as a capital expense item, which explains why the before and after reimbursement amounts are the same. The annual amortization of the discount, which is recognized by third-party payers as a reimbursable capital item, reduces the cost of the financing significantly. In some cases, this pattern of amortization may not be permitted by the payers. Instead, the payer may require a type of amortization called effective yield. This type of amortization requires that the same total amount of interest expense be recorded over the five years ($37,900,000), but the amounts in the earlier years would be less. This would reduce the present value of the benefit somewhat.

Interest Rate Swaps

Many hospitals and other health care providers have begun to use interest rate swaps. Interest rate swaps may enable firms to deal with the volatility in the financial markets and obtain lower-cost financing that better meets their needs. To understand an interest rate swap, three questions must be answered:

1. What is an interest rate swap?

Table 16–10 Net Present Value of Zero-Coupon Financing

Item	Amount before Reimbursement	Amount after Reimbursement	Years (Periods)	Present Value Factor (12%)	Present Value
Sinking fund	$7,586,793	$7,586,793	1–10*	7.360*	$55,838,800
Interest expense (amortization)	(7,580,000)	(3,790,000)	1–5	3.605	(13,662,950)
				Net present value cost	$42,175,850

*Ten semiannual payments; the present value factor is for ten periods at 6%.

2. Why are interest rate swaps beneficial? For every winner, won't there be a loser?
3. How can a swap arrangement be analyzed?

An interest rate swap is merely an exchange of interest rate payments between two firms, with a bank usually acting as a broker. For example, a firm that has issued fixed-rate debt may wish to make floating-rate payments. If a firm that makes floating-rate payments can be found that would like to substitute this type of payment with fixed-rate payments, a swap may be arranged. It is also possible to swap two different types of floating-rate debt. In a swap, only the coupon payments are exchanged, not the principal. Payments are also conditional. One party can break the deal at any time.

The basic nature of the swap is easy to understand. The aspect that is often puzzling is, how could both parties benefit from the swap? Many people believe that the only party that truly benefits is the broker.

The rationale for swaps is purely and simply a function of a supposed market imperfection. This means that one borrower has a better relative position in one maturity market than another. This difference is often ascribed to differential information and institutional restrictions that lead to differences in transaction costs. Because of these imperfections, the opportunity for financial arbitrage occurs.

To understand this concept more fully, let us assume that hospital A and hospital B encounter the interest rates in Table 16–11.

In the example in Table 16–11, hospital A has a better relative position in both markets, fixed

and floating. The differential, however, is much larger in the fixed-rate market [95 basis points (bps)] than in the floating-rate market (15 bps). The net differential is 80 (95 − 15). This difference implies that there is a swap opportunity present and that the total advantage is 80 bps. It is this 80 bps differential that will be split among hospital A, hospital B, and the broker.

Assume now that both hospitals issue $50 million of debt. Hospital A issues fixed-rate debt and hospital B issues floating-rate debt. A broker could put these two hospitals together, and the set of payments in Table 16–12 might result.

The data in Table 16–12 show that all parties have realized some financial advantage as a result of the swap.

Hospital A has reduced its floating rate to variable minus ten basis points from variable plus twenty-five basis points. This is a savings of thirty-five basis points from its initial position. Hospital B also has gained. It now has fixed-rate debt at 7.80 percent, which is thirty basis points under its projected rate of 8.10 percent. Of course, the broker has kept fifteen basis points for the time and effort required to bring the parties together.

This is the way in which a swap is supposed to work. Everyone has benefited. It is not always true, however, that every party will benefit, and each swap opportunity must be carefully analyzed to ensure that benefits will be realized.

EARLY RETIREMENT OF DEBT

In many cases, an issuer would like to retire an existing debt issue before its maturity. There are a variety of reasons for wanting to do this.

Table 16–11 Interest Rates for Two Hospitals

Type of Debt	Hospital A	Hospital B	Rate Differential
Fixed	7.15%	8.10%	95 bps
Floating	Variable + 25 bps*	Variable + 40 bps	15 bps

*bps = Basis point (1/100 of 1 percent).

Table 16–12 Interest Rate Swap Payments

Payments	Hospital A	Hospital B	Broker
To bondholders	715 bps	Variable + 40 bps	0
To broker	Variable + 15 bps	750 bps	Variable + 765 bps
From broker to A	740 bps	0	740 bps
From broker to B	0	Variable + 10 bps	Variable + 10 bps
Net payment	Variable − 10 bps	780 bps	15 bps
Advantage	35 bps	30 bps	15 bps

One important reason is that it permits the issuer to take advantage of a reduction in interest rates. An issue may have been marketed several years ago when interest rates were 10 percent, and rates may now have decreased to 7 percent. If the present lower interest rate could be substituted for the original rate, a major improvement in net income could result. Other reasons for wishing to retire an existing indebtedness might be that it would enable the issuer to avoid onerous covenants in the existing indenture or to take advantage of changes in bond ratings or changes in policy regarding tax-exempt financing. Whatever the reason, most health care issues, in fact, do not remain outstanding for their full life cycles; most are retired early.

The following are two common ways of retiring an issue early: (1) refinancing and (2) refunding. In a refinancing situation, the issuer buys back the outstanding bonds from the investors. This can be accomplished in either of two ways. In the first way, the issuer may have the option of an early call. If the outstanding bonds are callable, the issuer would notify the present bondholders that the bonds are being called and should be tendered for payment. The principal or face value would then be paid, along with any call premium plus accrued interest. A second way to effect a refinancing would be for the issuer to buy back the bonds in open-market transactions or to send a letter to existing bondholders, offering to buy the bonds at some stated dollar amount.

Early retirement of existing bonds also can be accomplished through refunding. In a refunding situation, the outstanding bonds are not acquired by the issuer, and the present bondholders continue to maintain their investment. Although the refunding does not actually retire the bonds, the bonds are not shown on the issuer's financial statements, and the covenants present in the indenture are now voided. The process of voiding existing indenture covenants and removing the bonds from the issuer's financial statements is called defeasance. In effect, defeasance in a refunding situation involves the deposit of a sum of money with the bond trustee, which is then used to buy specially designated securities of the federal government. With these securities, there is a guarantee that all future interest and principal payments can be met from the proceeds controlled by the bond trustee.

The following is a simple example to illustrate the refunding process: On January 1, 1998, $1 million of 15-percent, level-debt service bonds are issued. The bonds have a five-year life. The earliest call date is January 1, 2000. No call premium is involved. On January 1, 1999, interest rates have decreased to 7 percent, and management advance-refunds the January 1, 1998 issue. In this example, the original issue would have the debt service schedule included in Table 16–13.

To retire or advance-refund the issue on January 1, 1999, management must place on deposit with a trustee a sum of money that will guarantee

Table 16–13 Debt Service Schedule of January 1998 Issue

Date	Interest	Principal	Total Debt Service	Ending Debt Principal
Jan. 1, 1999	$150,000	$148,320	$298,320	$851,680
Jan. 1, 2000	127,750	170,570	298,320	681,110
Jan. 1, 2001	102,170	196,150	298,320	484,960
Jan. 1, 2002	72,740	225,580	298,320	259,380
Jan. 1, 2003	38,940	259,380	298,320	0

payment of the following amounts on January 1, 2000 (the earliest call date):

Interest due Jan. 1, 2000	$127,750
Debt principal due Jan. 1, 2000	170,570
Ending debt principal on Jan. 1, 2000	681,110
	$979,430

If management borrows all the funds necessary to meet the $979,430 payment on January 1, 2000, how much must it borrow on January 1, 1999? Ignoring placement fees and other debt issuance costs, the hospital would borrow $915,360. Why $915,360? It is assumed that the hospital will be able to invest the proceeds at 7 percent, the effective interest rate on January 1, 1999. In tax-exempt issues, an arbitrage restriction limits investment yields for all practical purposes to the interest rate of the refunding issue.

Is there any real savings in debt service costs? Yes; the new issue schedule in Table 16–14 shows annual savings of $28,080 ($298,320 – $270,240) for the next four years.

Thus far, the refinancing looks good. However, there is an accounting loss that must be recorded. At the end of the first year (January 1, 1999), the value for the old debt, $851,680, will be removed from the balance sheet. But the defeased debt will be replaced by $915,360 of new debt, and this will reduce income in that year by $63,680 ($915,360 – $851,680). This will be treated as an extraordinary loss during the period in which refunding takes place.

A "real-world" case may make the magnitude of these numbers more apparent. A hospital recently refunded $65 million of two-year-old debt with $79 million of new debt at a lower ef-

Table 16–14 Debt Service Schedule of January 1999 Issue

Date	Interest	Principal	Total Debt Service	Ending Debt	Savings in Debt Service
Jan. 1, 2000	$64,080	$206,160	$270,240	$709,200	$28,080
Jan. 1, 2001	49,640	220,600	270,240	488,600	28,080
Jan. 1, 2002	34,200	236,040	270,240	252,560	28,080
Jan. 1, 2003	17,680	252,560	270,240	0	28,080

fective interest rate. Estimated savings in debt service over the life of the issue were $22 million, but there was an accounting loss of approximately $13 million during the initial year. More important, this loss reduced the hospital's ratio of equity to assets from 26 percent to 16 percent. This is a sizable reduction that could have some impact on future credit availability. Many lenders establish target equity-to-debt ratios beyond which they will not lend funds at reasonable interest rates.

In sum, refunding to take advantage of reduced interest rates usually makes a lot of economic sense. But the presence of an accounting loss should be considered, especially when considering its potential impact on future credit availability.

SUMMARY

The major sources of capital financing available to health care firms may be categorized as (1) equity and (2) debt. Equity has become an important source of capital, even for traditional tax-exempt health care firms. Corporate restructuring can greatly facilitate the process of accessing equity capital. However, long-term debt probably will continue to represent the major source of capital for most health care firms. Evaluation of alternative sources of long-term debt requires more than a simple comparison of interest rates. The impact of other factors also should be carefully reviewed to determine the overall attractiveness of alternative financing packages.

ASSIGNMENTS

1. Explain the term defeasance. What does it mean?
2. Assuming a normal or typical yield curve (that is, upward sloping), discuss the advantages and disadvantages of borrowing money for a major construction program with three-year term financing.
3. When is a master trust indenture used, and what is its value?
4. Under what circumstances might your firm be interested in issuing zero-coupon bonds?
5. In an advance refunding of debt, accounting gains or losses usually occur. Under what conditions could there be an accounting gain?
6. United Hospital has received a leasing proposal from Leasing, Inc., for a Siemens cardiac catheterization unit. The terms are

   - five-year lease,
   - annual payments of $200,000 payable one year in advance,
   - payment of property tax estimated to be $23,000 annually, and
   - renewal at end of Year 5 at fair market value.

   Alternatively, United Hospital can buy the catheterization unit for $725,000. United Hospital must debt finance this equipment. It anticipates a bank loan with an initial down payment of $125,000 and a three-year term loan at 16 percent with equal principal payments. The residual value of the equipment at year 5 is estimated to be $225,000. The lease is treated as an operating lease. Depreciation is calculated on a straight-line basis. Assuming a discount rate of 14 percent, what financing option should United Hospital select? Assume that there is no reimbursement of capital costs.
7. Nutty Hospital wishes to advance-refund its existing 15-percent long-term debt. The present $30,000,000 is not callable until five years from today. The payout on the issue over the next five years is as presented in Table 16–15.

   At the end of the fifth year, the debt ($25,000,000 outstanding balance at that time) may be called with a 10-percent penalty. If present interest rates are 10 percent and the investment rate on the funds to be received from the new issue cannot exceed 10 percent, what amount must Nutty Hospital borrow today? Assume that underwriting fees and other issuance costs will be 5 percent of the issue and that all debt service on the old issue must be met from the proceeds of the refunding issue and related investment income.

Table 16–15 Nutty Hospital Debt Service Schedule

	Interest	Principal	Total
End of year 1	$4,500,000	$1,000,000	$5,500,000
End of year 2	4,350,000	1,000,000	5,350,000
End of year 3	4,200,000	1,000,000	5,200,000
End of year 4	4,050,000	1,000,000	5,050,000
End of year 5	3,900,000	1,000,000	4,900,000

8. You have the option of leasing an asset for $100,000 per year, with payments to be made at the end of each year of use. This lease cannot be cancelled. Alternatively, you may buy the asset for $248,700. For reimbursement purposes, the lease must be capitalized. If the asset is purchased, it will be debt-financed with $210,000 of three-year serial notes (that is, $70,000 of principal will be repaid each year). The effective interest rate on this loan will be 8 percent. Assume that the asset has an allowable useful life of three years with no estimated salvage value.

   • Determine the amount of expense that would be reported during each of the three years under the two financing plans.
   • Assuming that 80 percent of all reported capital expenses are reimbursed and that the discount rate is 6 percent, determine the present value of the asset in these two methods of financing.

9. Happy Valley is considering moving from its present location into a new 200-bed facility. The estimated construction cost for the new facility is $40 million. The hospital has no internal funds and is considering a twenty-year mortgage with interest scheduled to be 8 percent. The issue will be repaid over twenty years with equal annual principal payments of $2 million. Interest expense would decline each year by $160,000.

   The cost of the plant and fixed equipment would be 80 percent of the total cost or $32 million, and the movable equipment would be $8 million. The movable equipment would need to be replaced in ten years, and it is estimated that the replacement cost would be $17,271,200 (inflation is assumed to be 8 percent per year). The plant and fixed equipment would need to be replaced in thirty years at a cost of $322,006,400 (inflation again assumed to be 8 percent per year). All costs reflect only the investment required to provide inpatient services. A separate analysis will be done for outpatient services.

   Happy Valley anticipates that its operation will generate about 9,700 discharges per year. The hospital anticipates that its operating costs, excluding capital costs, will be $4,000 per discharge, or $38,800,000 in the first full year of operation.

   The payer mix at Happy Valley is expected to be 60 percent Medicare and Medicaid on the inpatient side. These payers will pay approximately $4,400 per discharge. This payment reflects both operating and capital cost payments. Approximately 10 percent of Happy Valley's operating and capital costs will be paid by payers who reimburse the hospital on a cost-related basis for both capital and operating costs. The remaining 30 percent of Happy Valley's business will be charge-based, but it is expected that discounts to commercial insurers and bad debt and charity write-offs will average 30 percent.

   Assuming that Happy Valley wishes to break even on a cash-flow basis during the first year of operation, what charge per discharge must be set? If the hospital wanted to include an element in its rate structure to reflect replacement cost of the building and movable equipment, what additional amount would that be? Assume that 50 percent of the movable equipment cost would be debt financed and 80 percent of the building and fixed equipment would be debt financed. Also assume that the hospital can earn 10 percent on any invested money, so use 10 percent as your discount rate.

10. Mayberry Hospital is considering a joint venture relationship with your physicians to acquire a full-body CT scanner. Projected revenues and expenses for the scanner are presented in Table 16–16.

Table 16–16 CT Scanner Financial Forecast

	Year 1	Year 2	Year 3	Year 4	Year 5
Revenues	$521,000	$531,000	$542,000	$533,000	$564,000
Less bad debts and discounts	52,100	53,100	54,200	53,300	56,400
Net revenues	468,900	477,900	487,800	479,700	507,600
Expenses					
Wages and employee benefits	60,000	63,000	66,150	69,459	72,930
Maintenance	55,000	57,750	60,638	63,669	66,853
Supplies	20,000	21,000	22,050	23,153	24,310
Rent	18,000	18,900	19,845	20,837	21,879
Administrative	10,000	10,500	11,025	11,576	12,155
Utilities	5,000	5,250	5,513	5,788	6,078
Insurance	5,000	5,250	5,513	5,788	6,078
Taxes	10,000	10,000	10,000	10,000	10,000
Depreciation	94,050	137,940	131,670	131,670	131,670
Interest	40,620	33,384	25,271	16,176	5,977
Total expenses	317,670	362,974	357,675	358,116	357,930
Net income before tax or interest	$151,230	$114,926	$130,125	$121,585	$149,670

The scanner is expected to cost $627,000 and have a useful life of five years. Two possible financing plans have been proposed. The first plan would be a limited partnership arrangement. There would be thirty-four shares; thirty-three would be sold to investors for $19,000 apiece. The thirty-fourth would be retained by the hospital for its development effort. In the second financing plan, a $380,000 level-debt service plan with a five-year maturity and interest at 10 percent would be arranged. The remainder of the funding would be generated through the sale of thirty-three limited partnership shares at $7,500 per share. Again, a thirty-fourth share would be issued to the hospital for its development efforts. Assuming that a 30-percent marginal tax rate will exist, project cash flow per partnership unit under each financing alternative for each of the five years.

SOLUTIONS AND ANSWERS

1. Defeasance means that upon final payment of all interest and principal, the rights of the bond trustee cease to exist; that is, they are defeased. The security covenants in an indenture also may be satisfied through the creation of a trust (escrow) in which sufficient monies are held to guarantee payment at some future date. Defeasance means that the issue defeased is no longer an obligation of the issuer and can be removed from the issuer's books.

2. The typical upward-sloping yield curve implies that a three-year interest rate probably will be much lower than a twenty- to twenty-five-year rate. Therefore, cost will be lower with a three-year construction loan. At the end of the third year, however, permanent financing must be sought; also, there is no guarantee that interest rates will not have increased during the period or that financing will be available at the end of the third year.

3. A master trust indenture usually pledges the assets and revenues of several firms in a combined financing package. It is often used by health care systems to gain better access to capital and lower interest rates.

4. Zero-coupon bonds are especially desirable if the issuer's effective interest rate on the bonds is well below the yield or discount rate of the issuer. In a zero-coupon bond issue, the postponement of interest payment maximizes the possibility for additional arbitrage, that is, for investing at a yield greater than the cost of funds.

5. Accounting gains usually take place when the advance-refunding issue has a higher rate of interest than the refunded issue. Accounting losses often occur when the reverse is true.

6. United Hospital's financing options for the cardiac catheterization unit are detailed in Table 16–17. From the data in Table 16–17, it can be seen that purchase of the catheterization unit would produce a lower net present value cost, compared with a lease.

Table 16–17 Lease/Purchase Analysis

Item	Amount before Reimbursement	Amount after Reimbursement	Years	Present Value Factor (14%)	Present Value
Lease					
Rent	$200,000	$200,000	0	1.000	$200,000
Rent	200,000	200,000	1–4	2.914	582,800
Property tax*	23,000	23,000	1–5	3.433	78,959
				Net present value cost of lease	$861,759

Item	Amount before Reimbursement	Amount after Reimbursement	Years	Present Value Factor (14%)	Present Value
Purchase					
Downpayment	$125,000	$125,000	0	1.000	$125,000
Principal	200,000	200,000	1–3	2.322	464,400
Interest	96,000	96,000	1	.877	84,192
Interest	64,000	64,000	2	.769	49,216
Interest	32,000	32,000	3	.675	21,600
Salvage	(225,000)	(225,000)	5	.519	(116,775)
				Net present value of purchase	$627,633

* Property tax would be passed on to the lessee or hospital. There is no property tax on the purchase because the hospital is a tax-exempt firm.

7. Nutty Hospital's present borrowing needs are detailed in Table 16–18.
8. The data in Exhibit 16–1 show the comparative expense and present values for leasing versus debt financing the asset during the three-year period.

Table 16–18 Nutty Hospital Refunding Requirements

Item	Amount Required	Years	Present Value Factor (10%)	Present Value
Debt service—year 1	$ 5,500,000	1	.909	$ 4,999,500
Debt service—year 2	5,350,000	2	.826	4,419,100
Debt service—year 3	5,200,000	3	.751	3,905,200
Debt service—year 4	5,050,000	4	.683	3,449,150
Debt service—year 5	4,900,000	5	.621	3,042,900
Principal at year 5	25,000,000	5	.621	15,525,500
Call premium	2,500,000	5	.621	1,552,500
			Net present value	$36,893,850

$$\text{Amount borrowed} = \frac{\$36,893,850}{.95} = \$38,835,631$$

Exhibit 16–1 Expenses for Leasing versus Purchase

- Expenses for Lease

  $248,700 = \$100,000 \times P\ (i,3)$

  $P\ (i,3) = 2.487$

  Interest Rate $(i) = 10\%$

- Interest expense per year

Year	Beginning Principal	Interest (at 10%)	Reduction in Principal	Total
1	$248,700	$24,870	$ 75,130	$100,000
2	173,570	17,357	82,643	100,000
3	90,927	9,073*	90,927	100,000
		$51,300	$248,700	$300,000

*Last year's interest is derived by subtracting the principal payment of $90.927 from the total payment of $100,000.

Exhibit 16–1 continued

- Depreciation expense per year: $248,700/3 = $82,900

- Expenses for debt financing

    Interest expense per year

Year	Interest
1	.08 × 210,000 = $16,800
2	.08 × 140,000 = 11,200
3	.08 × 70,000 = 5,600

    Depreciation expense per year: $82,900

- Comparison of expenses

	Lease Alternative			Debt Alternative		
Year	Interest	Depreciation	Total	Interest	Depreciation	Total
1	$24,870	$ 82,900	$107,770	$16,800	$ 82,900	$ 99,700
2	17,357	82,900	100,257	11,200	82,900	94,100
3	9,073	82,900	91,973	5,600	82,900	88,500
Totals	$51,300	$248,700	$300,000	$33,600	$248,700	$282,300

- Comparison of cash flows—present value basis

Item	Amount before Reimbursement	Amount after Reimbursement	Years	Present Value Factor (6%)	Present Value
Lease financing					
Rentals	$100,000	$100,000	1–3	2.673	$267,300
Depreciation	(82,900)	(66,320)	1–3	2.673	(177,273)
Interest*	(24,870)	(19,896)	1	.943	(18,762)
Interest*	(17,357)	(13,886)	2	.890	(12,358)
Interest*	(9,073)	(7,258)	3	.840	(6,097)
		Net present value cost of lease			$ 52,810

continues

Exhibit 16–1 continued

Item	Amount before Reimbursement	Amount after Reimbursement	Years	Present Value Factor (6%)	Present Value
Debt financing					
Down payment	$38,700	38,700	0	1.000	$ 38,700
Principal payment	70,000	70,000	1–3	2.673	187,110
Depreciation	(82,900)	(66,320)	1–3	2.673	(177,273)
Interest	16,800	3,360	1	.943	3,168
Interest	11,200	2,240	2	.890	1,993
Interest	5,600	1,120	3	.840	941
Net present value cost of debt					$54,639

*Interest is shown as a reduction of cost because the lease payment reflects the interest paid to the lessor. The interest deduction recognizes third-party payments for interest expense.

9. Exhibit 16–2 reflects the required charge that Happy Valley must set to break even on a cash-flow basis and the additional charge required to cover the funded depreciation requirement necessary for eventual replacement.

Exhibit 16–2 Happy Valley Rate Structure

Cash expenditures	
Principal payment	$ 2,000,000
Interest payment	3,200,000
Operating costs	38,800,000
Total cash cost	$44,000,000
Reimbursement	
Medicare and Medicaid ($4,400 × 5,820)	$25,608,000
Reimbursed interest (.10 × $3,200,000)	320,000
Reimbursed operating costs (.10 × 38,800,000)	3,880,000
Reimbursed equipment depreciation (.1 × $8,000,000/10)	80,000
Reimbursed building depreciation (.1 × $32,000,000/30)	106,667
Total payments	$29,994,667

Exhibit 16–2 continued

Required charge to cover cash expenditures	
Cash expenditures remaining after reimbursement	$14,005,333
Number of charge-paying discharges	2,910
Required charge without discount ($14,005,333/2,910)	$4,812.83
Required charge with discount ($4,812.83/.7)	$6,875.47
Required additional amounts for funded	
depreciation to meet replacement needs	
Annual deposit for movable equipment	$541,838
[.5 × $17,271,200/F(10%,10 years)]	
Annual deposit for building	391,506
[.2 × $322,006,400/F(10%,30 years)]	
Total Deposit Required	$933,344
Number of charge-paying discharges	2,910
Required charge without discount ($933,344/2,910)	$320.74
Required charge with discount ($320.74/.7)	$458.20

10. The data in Table 16–19 show the projected cash flow per partnership unit under the two financing alternatives.

Table 16–19 CT Scanner Cash Flow per Share

	Years				
	1	*2*	*3*	*4*	*5*
Alternative 1—no debt					
Income before tax					
and interest	$151,230	$114,926	$130,125	$121,585	$149,670
Less income tax	45,369	34,478	39,038	36,476	44,901
Income after tax	$105,861	$ 80,448	$ 91,087	$ 85,109	$104,769
Add depreciation	94,050	137,940	131,670	131,670	131,670
Cash flow	$199,911	$218,388	$222,757	$216,779	$236,439
Cash flow per share (34 shares)	$ 5,880	$ 6,423	$ 6,552	$ 6,376	$ 6,954
Percentage return	30.9%	33.8%	34.5%	33.6%	36.6%

continues

Table 16–19 continued

	Years				
	1	2	3	4	5
Alternative #2—debt financing					
Income before tax and interest	$151,230	$114,926	$130,125	$121,585	$149,670
Less interest	38,000	31,776	24,930	17,400	9,116
Taxable income	113,230	83,150	105,195	104,185	140,554
Less income tax	33,969	24,945	31,559	31,256	42,166
Income after tax	79,261	58,205	73,636	72,929	98,388
Add depreciation	94,050	137,940	131,670	131,670	131,670
Less principal	62,237	68,461	75,307	82,837	91,158
Cash flow	$111,074	$127,684	$129,999	$121,762	$138,900
Cash flow per share (34 shares)	$ 3,267	$ 3,755	$ 3,824	$ 3,581	$ 4,085
Percentage return	43.6%	50.1%	51.0%	47.8%	54.5%

17

Working Capital and Cash Management

Few topics in finance are more important than cash and investment management. Cash is the lifeblood of a business operation. A firm that controls its access to cash and the generation of cash usually will survive and thrive. A firm that ignores or manages its cash position poorly may fail. Experience has shown that more firms fail because of a lack of ready cash than for any other reason—even firms with sound profitability. It is important, therefore, to recognize and appreciate that profit and cash management are not the same thing.

It would seem logical to expect that great volumes of literature would be devoted to such an important topic as cash and investment management. Unfortunately, this is not the case. Although a major portion of a financial manager's time is devoted to working capital problems, relatively little space is devoted to them in most financial management textbooks. A typical text often contains only several chapters that deal with working capital management and perhaps a single chapter that discusses cash management.

Cash management is probably more important in the health care industry than in many other industries, but often it is less understood. Health care financial executives frequently advance through the accounting route. Finance texts provide little coverage on cash management, and accounting texts provide almost no

coverage. Many health care financial executives traditionally think of cash management in terms of receivables control. They often believe that better cash management will result if accounts receivable can be reduced or the collection cycle shortened. Although accounts receivable management in health care organizations is clearly important, limiting attention to this one area is myopic. Good cash management should focus not only on the acceleration of receivables, but also on the complete cash conversion cycle. Reduction of the cash conversion cycle, along with the related investment of surplus funds, should be a critical objective of financial managers.

Many hospitals and health care firms often are willing to allow their banks to handle most of their cash-management decisions. Although this strategy is acceptable in some situations, it may produce a result that is less than optimal. Risks are sometimes unnecessarily increased or yields on investments are sacrificed. Real or perceived conflicts of interest also exist if the bank is represented on the health care firm's governing board.

Why is cash and investment management important to health care executives? Hospitals have large sums of investable funds compared with firms of similar size in other industries. For example, in 1995, the average hospital maintained a $25.4 million investment, or 28.4 percent of its total assets, in short-term cash, marketable securities, or other investments. Hospitals and other health care firms are also more likely to have greater investment management needs than other industries for several reasons:

- Many health care firms are voluntary, not-for-profit firms and must set aside funds for replacement of plants and equipment. Investor-owned firms can rely on the issuance of new stockholders' equity to finance some of their replacement needs.
- Health care firms are increasingly beginning to self-insure all or a portion of their professional liability risk. This requires that sizable investment pools be available to meet estimated actuarial needs.
- Many health care firms receive gifts and endowments. Although these sums may not be large for individual firms, they can provide additional sources of investment.
- Many health care firms also have sizable funding requirements for defined-benefit pension plans and debt service requirements associated with the issuance of bonds. These funds are usually held by a trustee.

With greater investments, one should expect to find greater levels of investment income. For the average hospital in 1995, approximately 40 percent of total net income was derived from nonoperating revenue sources. Much of this nonoperating revenue is clearly related to investment income.

CASH AND INVESTMENT MANAGEMENT STRUCTURE

Effective cash management is often related to the cash conversion cycle, as depicted in Figure 17–1. In its simplest form, the cash conversion cycle represents the time that it takes a firm to go from an outlay of cash to purchase the needed factors of production, such as labor and supplies, to the actual collection of cash for the produced product or service, such as a completed treatment for a given patient. Usually, the objectives in cash management are to minimize the collection period and to maximize the payment period. Trade-offs often exist; for example, accelerating collection of receivables may result in lost sales, and delaying payments to vendors could result in increased prices.

The primary tool used in cash planning is the cash budget. (Cash budgeting is discussed more fully in Chapter 18.) Cash balances are affected by changes in working capital over time. Working capital may be defined as the difference between current assets and current liabilities. The following items are usually included in these two categories:

1. current assets
   - cash and investments
   - accounts receivable
   - inventories
   - other current assets
2. current liabilities
   - accounts payable
   - accrued salaries and wages
   - accrued expenses
   - notes payable
   - current position of long-term debt

The cash budget focuses on four major activities that affect working capital:

1. purchasing of resources,
2. production/sale of service,
3. billing, and
4. collection.

These activities represent intervals in the cash conversion cycle. The purchasing of resources relates to the acquisition of supplies and labor, such as the level of inventory necessary to maintain realistic production schedules and the staff required to ensure adequate provision of services. Production and sale are virtually the same in the health care industry; there is no inventory of products or services. However, there is a delay between the production of service and final

Figure 17–1 Cash Conversion Cycle

delivery. A patient may be in the hospital for ten to fifteen days or in a skilled nursing facility for two months, which could be regarded as the final point of sale. Billing represents the interval between the release or discharge of a patient and the generation of a bill. Collection represents the interval between the generation of a bill and the actual collection of the cash from the patient or the patient's third-party payer.

Estimating these four intervals is critical to cash budgeting and, therefore, cash planning. For example, the average collection period will dramatically influence the need for cash assets. During periods when sales are expected to increase, a long collection period will require the hospital to finance a larger amount of working capital in the form of increased receivables. The hospital must pay for its factors of production (that is, supplies and labor) at the beginning of the cycle and wait to receive payment from its customers at the end of the cycle.

The previous example also illustrates why a focus on a static measure of liquidity, such as a current ratio, sometimes can be deceiving. A rapid buildup in sales results in a large increase in accounts receivable, which increases the current ratio. Liquidity position, however, might not be improved in this case. The speed with which these receivables can be turned into cash is also an extremely important measure of liquidity.

The major purpose of a cash budget, an example of which is shown in Table 17–1, is to prepare an accurate estimate of future cash flows. With this estimate, the firm can arrange for short-term financing from a bank through a line of credit if it projects a period of cash deficiency, or it can invest surplus funds. Because yields are usually higher on longer-term investments, an investment for a six-month term is likely to result in greater income than an investment broken down into two three-month cycles. The cash budget, then, is the key document in terms of providing information regarding short-term investment and short-term financing decisions. A key factor in these projections is the desired level of cash balances that the firm would like to maintain. Firms that set low cash requirement levels are assuming more risks. The entire cash-management process can be broken down into five sequential steps.

1. Understand and manage the cash conversion cycle. In most situations, the objective is to minimize the required investment in working capital, when working capital is defined as current assets less current liabilities.
2. Develop a sound cash budget that accurately projects cash inflows and cash outflows during the planning horizon.
3. Establish the firm's minimum required cash balance. This level should be set in a manner consistent with the firm's overall risk assumption posture.
4. Arrange for working capital loans during those periods when the cash budget indicates that short-term financing will be needed.
5. Invest cash surpluses in a way that will maximize the expected yield to the firm, subject to a prudent assumption of risk.

Table 17–1 Sample Cash Budget

	First Quarter			Second Quarter	Third Quarter	Fourth Quarter
	January	February	March			
Recipients from operations	$300,000	$310,000	$320,000	$1,000,000	$1,100,000	$1,100,000
Less disbursements from operations	280,000	280,000	300,000	940,000	1,000,000	1,000,000
Cash available from operations	$20,000	$30,000	$20,000	$60,000	$100,000	$100,000
Other receipts						
Increase in mortgage payable				500,000		
Sale of fixed assets		20,000				
Unrestricted income—endowment			40,000	40,000	40,000	40,000
Total other receipts	0	$20,000	$40,000	$540,000	$40,000	$40,000
Other disbursements						
Mortgage payments			150,000		150,000	
Fixed-asset purchase				480,000		
Funded depreciation			30,000	130,000	30,000	30,000
Total other disbursements	0	0	180,000	610,000	180,000	30,000
Net cash gain (loss)	$20,000	$50,000	$(120,000)	$(10,000)	$(40,000)	$110,000
Beginning cash balance	100,000	120,000	170,000	50,000	40,000	0
Cumulative cash	$120,000	$170,000	$50,000	$40,000	$0	$110,000
Desired level of cash	100,000	100,000	100,000	100,000	100,000	100,000
Cash above minimum needs (financing needs)	$20,000	$70,000	$(50,000)	$(60,000)	$(100,000)	$10,000

MANAGEMENT OF WORKING CAPITAL

The management of working capital items is related to short-term bank financing and investment of cash surpluses, which are discussed in subsequent sections of this chapter. The balance sheet for ABC Medical Center in Table 17–2 presents a useful way to examine the relevant items of working capital management. As examples, the following two categories are discussed: (1) receivables and (2) accounts payable and accrued salaries and wages.

Receivables

Industry experience suggests that receivables constitute the most critical, but not exclusive, area of importance in cash management. In general, accounts receivable usually represent about 60 to 70 percent of a hospital's total investment in current assets. ABC Medical Center has $8,778,677 of receivables, or 51.6 percent of its total current assets, in 1999. This value is below the range cited previously, largely because ABC Medical Center has a relatively low value for days in accounts receivable (50.3 days). This situation, of course, is favorable and is an objective of most financial managers. In general, the following three objectives are usually associated with accounts receivable management:

1. Minimize lost charges.
2. Minimize write-offs for uncollectable accounts.
3. Minimize the accounts receivable collection cycle.

All three objectives are important, but our attention will be directed at the third—minimizing the collection cycle. Figure 17–2 provides a schematic that predicts intervals involved in the entire accounts receivable cycle. The following intervals usually exist in the hospital inpatient accounts receivable collection cycle:

- admission to discharge,
- discharge to bill completion,
- bill completion to receipt by payer,
- receipt by payer to mailing of payment,
- mailing of payment to receipt by hospital, and
- receipt by hospital to deposit in bank.

Figure 17–2 also provides the estimated time that could be involved in each interval, but these numbers vary widely among hospitals and payer categories within hospitals. They are intended only to show the relative importance of each interval in the overall accounts receivable collection cycle. The total number of days represented in Figure 17–2 is sixty-four, which is reasonably close to the national average of sixty-two days during 1995.

Admission to Discharge (Five Days)

Shortening this interval is not the critical objective from an accounts receivable perspective. This does not imply, however, that a reduction in length of stay is not an objective, because clearly it is. With fixed prices per case, reduced length of stay is particularly desirable from a cost management viewpoint.

In terms of managing the accounts receivable cycle, the real solution appears to be what occurs during this interval to expedite later collection. The following specific suggestions are provided:

- Determine whether interim billings are possible for patients with a long length of stay. Some third-party payers permit interim billings if the length of stay exceeds a specified interval. Often, this is twenty-one days. Although there may be relatively few patients in this category, it is important to recognize that the absolute value of accounts receivable represented by these patients can be large.
- Use advance deposits for nonemergent admissions. If insurance coverage can be verified, estimates of the total deductible and copayment amounts can be made. They can be requested from the patient before or dur-

Table 17–2 ABC Medical Center, Consolidated Balance Sheets, June 30, 1999 and 1998

	Assets	
	1999	*1998*
Current assets		
Cash	$1,216,980	$ 362,422
Investments	4,042,407	4,597,806
Patient accounts receivable (1999, $7,356,120; 1998, $6,253,629), less allowance for uncollectables	5,892,339	5,143,471
Other receivables		
Medicare	2,672,612	2,113,655
Miscellaneous	213,726	164,631
Inventories	1,302,598	1,174,295
Prepaid expenses	1,021,972	249,455
Current portion of deferred receivables from Medicare	454,404	502,904
Assets held by trustee	180,000	247,181
Total current assets	$16,997,038	$14,555,820
Other assets		
Investments	$ 10,642,621	$10,983,125
Accounts receivable—affiliated companies	4,510,105	2,036,436
Notes receivable—affiliated company	700,000	700,000
Assets held by trustee		
Temporary cash account	—	59,643
Construction fund	2,717,846	4,018,948
Sinking fund	6,751,942	6,112,530
Interest receivable	118,142	94,231
Self-insurance funds	10,942,749	7,875,602
Unamortized debt issuance expenses	934,535	954,078
Investment in ABC Insurance, Ltd.	209,655	—
Deferred receivables for Medicare	2,620,162	3,074,567
Prepaid pension cost	840,449	—
Unamortized past service cost	1,784,160	—
Total other assets	$42,772,366	$35,909,160
Property, plant, and equipment		
Land	$ 1,654,394	$ 1,649,912
Buildings	36,505,277	34,504,398
Improvements to land and leaseholds	1,272,205	1,263,959
Fixed equipment	8,812,615	8,713,615
Movable equipment	20,290,037	15,461,276
Capitalized leases	2,998,295	3,293,693
Total property, plant, and equipment	$71,532,823	$64,886,853
Less allowance for depreciation	27,763,195	22,037,503
	$43,769,628	$42,849,350
Construction and other work in progress	4,396,463	3,869,866
Total property, plant, and equipment	$48,166,091	$46,719,216
Total assets	$107,935,495	$97,184,196

Table 17–2 continued

| | Liabilities fund balances | |
	1999	1998
Current liabilities		
Accounts payable trade	$ 2,297,672	$ 2,531,257
Accrued salaries and wages	1,366,777	1,035,496
Accrued liability for compensated absences	1,232,586	1,119,800
Accrued Medicare liability	317,302	1,881,895
Accrued indigent care assessment	1,170,001	1,061,742
Other accrued liabilities	611,230	444,916
Current portion of long-term debt	1,528,910	1,442,420
Total current liabilities	$ 8,524,478	$ 9,517,526
Other liabilities		
Accounts payable—affiliated companies	$ 1,993,815	—
Self-insurance liabilities	8,904,000	$ 7,048,000
	$10,897,815	$ 7,048,000
Long-term debt, less current maturities		
Series B bonds, less unamortized discount		
(1991, $1,144,348; 1986, $1,186,425)	$ 45,745,652	$46,063,575
Notes payable	3,902,113	1,888,504
Capital leases payable	127,535	595,407
	$ 49,775,300	$48,547,486
Net assets	$ 38,737,952	$32,071,204
	$107,935,545	$97,184,216

ing admission. In situations when this is not possible, a financing plan should be developed jointly between the hospital and the patient. Many patients appreciate being told beforehand what their insurance will pay and what their individual liability is likely to be.

• Obtain required insurance and eligibility information before admission for non-emergent patients. For emergency admissions, obtain the same data during the hospital stay. This will permit the preparation of a bill during, or shortly after, discharge.

Discharge to Bill Completion (Fifteen Days)

Ideally, this interval should be reduced as much as possible. Although this may be an ob-

jective, there are clearly some cost/benefit trade-offs to be evaluated. For example, speeding up the processing of bills is desirable only if the cost involved does not exceed the benefits of more rapid bill preparation. Basic suggestions include the following:

• Implement more timely billing and remove "bottlenecks." Usually, bills are not prepared during discharge so that late charges can be posted. If certain ancillary departments experience constant delays, corrective steps should be taken to improve posting. A holding period longer than two to three days is probably not reasonable.
• Develop educational programs to show the effects of physicians delaying completing medical charts. Often, an incomplete medi-

Figure 17–2 Accounts Receivable Collection Cycle in Days

cal chart is the reason for delay in billing. Physicians must be informed of the effect these delays have on the hospital. Some hospitals have suspended admitting privileges of physicians who are constantly delinquent. Although this strategy may not be useful in many hospitals, it is worth considering in some situations.

Bill Completion to Receipt by Payer (Four Days)

The estimated four-day length of this interval is directly related to mail time. Several steps may be useful in shortening this interval including the following:

- Deliver bills to the post office as soon as they are prepared for mailing. Bills may be stacked in nice, neat piles and left on a desk for one or more days before being mailed.
- Consider electronic invoicing for large payers when this alternative is available. This decreases mail time to zero, and it may reduce the account receivable cycle for these payers by as much as four days.
- Try to settle all outpatient accounts at the point of discharge or departure. Each outpatient should be presented with a bill at the point of departure, and payment should be requested at this time.
- Submit a bill for any deductible and copayment amounts for hospital inpatients at the point of discharge. Settlement should take place at this point if the patient has been advised previously of the total amount due.

Receipt by Payer to Mailing of Payment (Thirty-Five Days)

This interval varies greatly by type of payer. Some self-pay patients may have outstanding accounts for more than a year. Insurance companies may take an inordinate amount of time to settle bills because of disputes over coverage or reasonableness. Steps to be considered include the following:

- Selling some accounts receivable. Until recently, hospitals could not legally sell Medicare accounts, but this is no longer true. More and more hospitals are considering selling accounts receivable because the rates of interest charged for these loans are relatively low. On a taxable basis, the interest rate will be slightly below prime for these asset-backed transactions.
- Using discounts for prompt payment. Many businesses have long provided discounts as financial incentives for early payment. This strategy may be used for self-pay portions of hospital bills and also for insurance payers. Sufficiently large discounts also can greatly reduce collection costs and write-offs. How large an inducement should be offered? This decision, of course, is firm-specific, but a 5-percent reduction for payment during discharge does not seem excessive.
- Creating a system to respond quickly to third-party requests for additional data. Third-party payers often delay payment until requested information has been received and reviewed. At a minimum, a log should

be maintained that shows dates of requests and responses.

- Claiming all bad debts on the Medicare deductible and copayment portion of hospital bills. Medicare is liable for payment of bad debts experienced in these areas. It is important, however, to document reasonable collection efforts on the part of the hospital before Medicare liability for payment can be ensured.
- Making frequent follow-up telephone calls to detect problems or concerns with bills. In many situations, self-pay hospital bills are not paid because there is a disagreement over the amount of the bill. This type of dispute can be avoided by a nonthreatening hospital employee promptly contacting the patient and inquiring about the patient's health and the amount of the bill. Sometimes this may be better handled by an independent party. When this approach has been used, reductions in bad debt write-offs have been large.

Payment Mailed to Receipt by Hospital (Four Days)

Mail time is the cause for this four-day interval. These delays cannot be prevented for most small, personal accounts. In the case of a government or large insurance payer, a courier service can be used. Checks are picked up as they become available. For large, out-of-town payers, a special courier arrangement can be used or direct deposits to an area bank can be initiated. Relatively large sums of money must be involved for these strategies to be cost effective. In addition, direct wire transfer of funds between payer and health care provider is also an alternative that makes great sense if available.

Receipt by Hospital to Deposit in Bank (One or More Days)

Perhaps the only effective way this interval can be shortened is through the use of a lockbox arrangement in which payments go directly to a post office box that is cleared at least once a day by bank employees. Bank employees deposit all payments, usually photocopy the checks, and send the copies—along with any enclosures—to the hospital for proper crediting. There is usually a cost for this service. The hospital must determine whether improvement in the cash flow, plus potential reduction in clerical costs are worth the fee charged.

Accounts Payable and Accrued Salaries and Wages

Accounts payable and accrued salaries and wages represent spontaneous sources of financing. This means that these amounts are not usually negotiated but vary directly with the level of operations. Table 17–2 shows that ABC Medical Center had $2,297,672 in accounts payable trade and $1,366,777 in accrued salaries and wages in 1999. In addition, $1,993,815 of accounts payable from affiliated companies also existed. These amounts are not small and represent a sizable proportion of ABC's total financing.

Managing accounts payable and accrued salaries is similar to the management of accounts receivable, except in a reverse direction. Instead of acceleration, most financial managers would like to slow payment to these accounts. A number of approaches, as discussed in the literature, attempt to do this. Several relevant approaches for a free-standing hospital are as follows:

- Delay payment of an account payable until the actual due date. Many hospitals often process invoices upon receipt and initiate payment even when the invoices are not due for several weeks or months. For example, many invoices for subscriptions to journals are sent out three to five months before their due dates. There is no reason to pay these invoices until they are actually due.
- Stretch accounts payable. This technique has been described frequently in the literature and is familiar to most individuals. Stretching accounts payable simply means

delaying payment until some point after the due date. Although this technique is often used, the ethics of the method are clearly debatable. In addition, delays may cause a hospital's credit rating to deteriorate. Vendors eventually will be unwilling to grant credit, or they may alter payment terms.

- Change the frequency of payroll. Although not a popular decision with employees, lengthening the payroll period can provide a significant amount of additional financing that is virtually free. For example, ABC Medical Center has an estimated weekly payroll of approximately $1,150,000. If ABC changes its payroll period from a weekly to a biweekly basis, it can create an additional source of financing equal to one week's payroll, or $1,150,000. Investing that money at 8 percent provides $92,000 in annual investment income. Fewer payroll periods may also reduce bookkeeping costs.
- Use banks in distant cities to pay vendors and employees. This method may delay check clearing and create a day or two of "float." Float is defined as the difference between the bank balance and the checkbook balance. It also may be a questionable practice, depending on applicable state laws.
- Schedule deposits to checking accounts to match expected disbursements on a daily basis. A daily cash report can be prepared for each account, using information obtained daily by calling to the bank or accessing the account electronically. The report can thus reconcile data on beginning cash balances and disbursements expected to be made that day. Separate accounts for payroll are often maintained to recognize the predictability of check clearing. For example, payroll checks issued on a Friday may have a highly predictable pattern of check clearing. Knowledge of this distribution enables the treasurer to minimize the amount of funds needed in the account on any given day to meet actual disbursements

and thus maximize the amount of invested funds.

SHORT-TERM BANK FINANCING

Many health care firms may experience a short-term need for funds during their operating cycles. The need for funds may have resulted from a predictable seasonality in the receipt and disbursement of cash or it may represent an unexpected business event, such as a strike. Commercial banks are the predominant sources of short-term loans, but other sources are also available. Several common arrangements used by health care firms to arrange for short-term loans include those discussed below.

Single-Payment Loan

The single-payment loan is the simplest credit arrangement and is usually given for a specific purpose, such as the purchase of inventory. The note can be either on a discount or an add-on basis. In the discount arrangement, the interest is computed and deducted from the face value of the note. The actual proceeds of the loan, then, would be in an amount less than the face of the note. In an add-on note, the interest is added to the final payment of the loan. In this arrangement, the borrower receives the full value of the loan when the loan is originated.

Line of Credit

A line of credit is an agreement that permits a firm to borrow up to a specified limit during a defined loan period. For example, a commercial bank may grant a $2 million line of credit to a hospital during a specific year. In that year, the hospital could borrow up to $2 million from the bank with presumably little or no additional paper work required. Lines of credit are either committed or uncommitted. In an uncommitted line, there is no formal or binding agreement on the part of the bank to loan money. If conditions change, the bank could decide not to loan any funds at all. In a committed line of credit, there is a written agreement that conveys the terms and conditions of the line of credit. The bank is legally required to lend money under the line as long as the terms and conditions have been met by the borrower. To cover the costs and risks incurred by the commercial bank in a committed line of credit, the bank charges a commitment fee. The fee is usually based on either the total credit line or the unused portion of the line.

Revolving Credit Agreements

A revolving credit is similar to a line of credit except that it is usually for a period longer than one year. Revolving credit agreements may be in effect for two to three years. Most revolving credit agreements are renegotiated before maturity. If the renegotiation occurs more than one year before maturity, a revolving credit agreement loan may be stated as a long-term debt and never appear as a current liability on a firm's balance sheet. Terms of revolving credit agreements are similar to those of lines of credit. Interest rates are usually variable and based on the prime rate or other money-market rates.

Term Loans

Term loans are made for a specific period, usually ranging between two and seven years. The loans usually require periodic installment payments of the principal. This type of loan is frequently used to finance a tangible asset that will produce income in future periods, such as a computed tomography scanner. The asset acquired with the loan proceeds may be pledged as collateral for the loan.

Letters of Credit

Some hospitals use letters of credit as a method of bond insurance. A letter of credit is simply a letter from a bank stating that a loan will be made if certain conditions are met. In

hospital bond financing, a letter of credit from a bank guarantees payment of the loan if the hospital defaults.

INVESTMENT OF CASH SURPLUSES

The term surplus is confusing, even among financial executives. For the purpose of this discussion, cash surplus is defined as money exceeding a minimum balance that the firm prefers to maintain to meet immediate operating expenses and minor contingencies, plus any compensating balance required at its banks.

The balance sheet for ABC Medical Center shown in Table 17–2 lists a cash balance of $1,216,980 plus $4,042,407 in short-term investments as of June 30, 1999. These are the funds that are most often referred to as surplus cash when discussing short-term investment strategy. It is important to note that ABC Medical Center has significant investments in other areas. Most hospitals follow this procedure. For example, ABC Medical Center, as of June 30, 1999, has $10,642,621 in an investments account under the "other assets" section of the balance sheet. These funds probably are designated for the eventual replacement of the hospital plant. In addition, sizable balances of funds are maintained with a trustee. For example, there is $2,717,846 in the construction fund account, $6,751,942 in the sinking fund account, $118,142 in the interest receivable account, and $10,942,749 in the self-insurance fund account. Most hospitals and health care firms maintain similar fund balances. It is critical for management to make investments that will meet the objectives of each specific fund and maximize the potential yield to the firm.

Often, a portion of a firm's investment funds is restricted to money-market investments. The term money market refers to the market for short-term securities, including U.S. Treasury bills, negotiable certificates of deposit, bankers' acceptances, commercial paper, and repurchase agreements. Maturities for money-market investments can range from one day to one year.

Funds invested in money-market securities usually serve two roles. They represent (1) a liquidity reserve that can be used if the firm experiences a need for these funds and (2) a temporary investment of surplus funds that can result in the earning of a return.

If the funds are invested for periods longer than one year (for example, the investment of a replacement reserve fund), higher yields often result. These longer-term maturity investments may not be referred to as money-market securities.

When evaluating alternative investment strategies, there are usually five basic criteria that should be reviewed:

1. price stability,
2. safety of principal,
3. marketability,
4. maturity, and
5. yield.

Price Stability

The importance of price stability, especially for money-market investments, cannot be overemphasized. If a firm has a sudden need for cash, most major money-market investments can be sold without any serious capital losses. Generally, U.S. Treasury bills are the most credit-worthy money-market investments, followed closely by other U.S. Treasury obligations and federal agency issues. Investment in securities with long-term maturities are subject to risk if interest rates increase. This explains why money-market investments are usually restricted to maturities of less than one year.

Safety of Principal

Financial managers expect that the principal of their investment is generally not at risk. Treasury and federal agency obligations have little risk of principal loss through default. Bank securities (such as negotiable certificates of deposit and bankers' acceptances) and corporate obliga-

tions (such as commercial paper) are different matters. There may be a loss of principal through default, and care should be exercised when choosing these instruments. Information on banks is available in *Polk's World Bank Directory* and *Moody's Bank and Finance Manual*. There is no reason why a firm should not review the creditworthiness of its banks as carefully as banks review the financial position of loan applicants. It should be noted, however, that erosion of principal can occur through increases in money-market interest rates, and these increases subsequently will have an impact on fixed-rate securities.

Marketability

Marketability varies among money-market instruments. The term refers to the ability to sell a security quickly and with little price concession before maturity. In general, an active secondary trading market must exist to ensure the presence of marketability. Most major money-market instruments do have active secondary markets, especially obligations of the U.S. Treasury. Some commercial paper, especially that of industrial firms, may be difficult to redeem before maturity.

Maturity

There is a clear relationship between the yield of a security and its maturity that can be summarized in a yield curve. Table 17–3 shows a set of values for treasury bills on June 20, 1996. Some firms use a strategy of investment described as "riding the yield curve." This strategy relies on the existence of an upward-sloping yield curve. Investments are made in longer-term securities that are sold before maturity.

Yield

Yield is a measure of the investment's return and is an important consideration. Yield is usually affected by maturity, expected default risk

Table 17-3 Yield to Maturity for Treasury Bills, June 20,1996

Days to Maturity	Annualized Yield (%)
16	4.61
30	4.77
44	4.96
58	4.99
72	5.08
86	5.10
100	5.11
114	5.14
128	5.15
142	5.18

of principal, marketability, and price stability. In addition, taxability is often an issue. A tax-exempt health care firm has no incentive to invest in securities that are exempt from federal income taxes.

SUMMARY

Working capital management involves decisions that have an impact on operating cash flows of the firm. Ideally, the objective of most working capital management systems is to accelerate the collection of cash from customers and to slow down the payment to suppliers and employees. Investment management is important in many health care firms because of the relative size of their investment portfolios. Hospitals, for example, generate about 40 percent of their total net income from nonoperating sources, largely investment income. With so much at stake, health care firms need to improve performance in the cash and investment management area.

ASSIGNMENTS

1. Data from Table 17–2 indicate that $8,778,677 of accounts receivable were present at the end of 1999. If this value represented fifty days of average net patient revenue, and the hospital believed that this value could be reduced to forty days, what dollar amount of new cash flow would be generated? If these funds were invested at 8.5 percent, how much additional investment income would result per year?

2. Alpha Home Health Inc. has received an invoice for medical supplies for $5,000 with terms of a 2-percent discount if paid within ten days. The invoice is due on the thirtieth day. What is the annual effective cost of interest on this invoice? If the 2-percent discount still could be taken even though the invoice was not paid until the twentieth day, what would the effective interest rate be?

3. Pauly Hospital has been thinking about changing its payroll period from biweekly to monthly. Pauly currently has 600 employees with an annual payroll of $18,000,000. If Pauly could earn 9.5 percent on invested funds, what amount of new investment income could be generated on an annual basis? If the cost of writing a payroll check is $1.50, what additional amount could be saved on an annual basis from switching to a monthly payroll period?

4. Your firm has negotiated a $1,000,000 line of credit with your local bank. The terms of the line of credit call for an interest rate of 2 percent above prime on any borrowing plus 0.5 percent on any unused balance. If the line is not used during the year, what cost will your firm incur?

5. ABC Medical Center (Table 17–2) expects its revenues to increase by 10 percent next year. If the firm can increase its current liabilities by 12 percent through payment extensions and limit its increase in current assets, excluding cash and investments, to 8 percent, what additional cash will be required to finance working capital?

SOLUTIONS AND ANSWERS

1. The amount of new cash flow would be $1,755,735:

   [($8,778,677)/50] × [50 – 40]

   The amount of additional investment income per year would be $149,238 (.085 × $1,755,735).
2. The 2-percent discount would be realized for making payment twenty days before required. The annual interest cost would be approximately 36 percent:

   2% × [360 days/20days] = 36%

   The new effective rate would be 18 percent if payment was delayed until the twentieth day.
3. There are two ways to estimate the annual savings. The easiest method would be to multiply the difference in average wages payable by 9.5 percent:

$$\left[\frac{(18,000,000 / 12)}{2} - \frac{(18,000,000 / 26)}{2} \right] \times .095 = \$38,365$$

Alternatively, the difference in average payable amount per day can be calculated and multiplied times the average daily interest rate (.095/360), which is shown in Table 17–4.

Table 17–4 Investment Income from Longer Payroll Cycle

Day	Average Payable Balance		Incremental Amount Invested	Investment Income
	Monthly	Biweekly		
1	$49,315	$49,315	$0	$0.00
2	98,630	98,630	0	0.00
3	147,945	147,945	0	0.00
4	197,260	197,260	0	0.00
5	246,575	246,575	0	0.00
6	295,890	295,890	0	0.00
7	345,205	345,205	0	0.00
8	394,521	394,521	0	0.00
9	443,836	443,836	0	0.00
10	493,151	493,151	0	0.00
11	542,466	542,466	0	0.00
12	591,781	591,781	0	0.00
13	641,096	641,096	0	0.00
14	690,411	690,411	0	0.00
15	739,726	49,315	690,411	182.19
16	789,041	98,630	690,411	182.19
17	838,356	147,945	690,411	182.19
18	887,671	197,260	690,411	182.19

continues

Table 17–4 continued

Day	Average Payable Balance Monthly	Average Payable Balance Biweekly	Incremental Amount Invested	Investment Income
19	936,986	246,575	690,411	182.19
20	986,301	295,890	690,411	182.19
21	1,035,616	345,205	690,411	182.19
22	1,084,932	394,521	690,411	182.19
23	1,232,877	443,836	690,411	182.19
24	1,183,562	493,151	690,411	182.19
25	1,232,877	542,466	690,411	182.19
26	1,282,192	591,781	690,411	182.19
27	1,331,507	641,096	690,411	182.19
28	1,380,822	690,411	690,411	182.19
29	1,430,137	49,315	1,380,822	364.38
30	1,479,452	98,630	1,380,822	364.38
Monthly Total				$3,279.42

Assuming that the pattern presented in Table 17–4 holds, the annual return would be $39,353 ($12 \times$ \$3,279.42). The savings from reduced checks would be $12,600 = [600(26–12) \times$ \$1.50].
4. The firm must pay 0.5 percent on the entire $1,000,000, or $5,000 (.005 × $1,000,000).
5. The schedule presented in Table 17–5 shows the increase in net working capital.

Table 17–5 Net Increase in Working Capital

Present current assets	$16,997,038
– Cash	1,216,980
– Investments	4,042,407
Noncash current assets	$11,737,651
8% Increase	.08
Increase in noncash current assets	$939,012
Present current liabilities	$8,524,478
× 12% increase	.12
Increase in current liabilities	$1,022.937
Net increase in working capital	($83,925)

18

Developing the Cash Budget

Chapter 17 stressed the importance of developing a sound cash budget that accurately projects cash inflows and cash outflows in the cash-management process. Cash budgets embody the key source of information that permits management to determine the firm's short-term needs for cash. When a cash budget is modified to include the effects of alternative outcomes, financial executives can better assess the issue of liquidity risk and make decisions that will reduce the probability of a liquidity crisis. One of the following three courses of action can be taken:

1. Increase the level of cash and investment reserves.
2. Restructure the maturity of existing debt.
3. Arrange a line of credit with a bank.

DETERMINING REQUIRED CASH AND INVESTMENT RESERVES

Historically, the finance literature has identified the following three major types of reasons for holding cash balances:

1. transactional,
2. precautionary, and
3. speculative.

The transactional motive relates to the need to maintain cash balances to allow routine expenditures for such things as payroll, supplies, and capital investment. The precautionary motive is related to the concept of risk. Most firms do not know what their actual disbursements and receipts will be during any interval. To avoid this risk, many firms add some "cushion" to their cash balances so that they can meet unexpected contingencies. The speculative motive represents management's desire to have access to cash to take advantage of special investment opportunities that promise unusually high returns.

In the health care sector, which comprises many voluntary firms, there is another major need for holding cash and investment reserves—replacing fixed assets. Voluntary health care providers are not in a position to raise new equity from the stock market; therefore, they must set aside cash to meet normal replacement needs. Failure to set aside adequate levels of replacement reserves ultimately will result in excessive levels of debt financing, closure, or both.

Firms differ regarding their needs for cash to meet transactions and their precautionary motives. Firms that have greater instability in cash flows need to carry more liquid assets to reduce the risk of cash insolvency. Access to short-term lines of credit also may be important when determining required cash position. Although these factors and others may affect the level of cash carried to meet transactional and precautionary motives, there are some reasonable and generally accepted norms. For example, the average length of days' cash on hand for both the hospital industry and the Standard & Poor's 400 industrials generally is from fifteen to twenty-five days. (See Chapter 7 for a further discussion of this indicator.) For most health care providers, a sum of twenty days' cash on hand seems like a reasonable target.

Some funds also should be set aside to meet future replacement needs. As a general rule of thumb, most voluntary health care firms should try to have the following amount of cash available for replacement needs:

(100% – Desired debt policy %) × Replacement cost need

The firm's desired debt policy represents the expected overall percentage of future capital needs that will be financed with debt. This represents the target for all capital expenditures, not just major renovation projects. For many voluntary health care firms, this percentage appears to be about 50 percent. Health care firms may finance major renovation projects with 80- to 90-percent debt, but then they will use 80- to 90-percent equity on smaller routine replacement projects, such as capital equipment. The replacement cost need is equal to the amount of accumulated depreciation that would currently exist if the fixed assets were stated in current replacement cost dollars rather than historical acquisition dollars. Table 18–1 illustrates this concept.

The replacement cost need in Table 18–1 would be $14,000,000. The firm has a plant base that would require $42,000,000 to replace in today's market, but it already has used up one-third of that plant base because one-third of the historical cost has depreciated to date. If the firm's board had established a debt policy of 50 percent, the firm would need $7,000,000 worth of investments to meet this debt target. A firm with a target debt policy of 50 percent would require a replacement viability ratio of 0.5. (See Chapter 7 for a discussion of this indicator.)

Table 18–2 illustrates how a firm might calculate its desired cash and investment position. In the example in Table 18–2, there is a surplus of short-term cash because the firm has 30.5 days' cash on hand when its required target is only 20.0. The firm, however, is deficient in the area of replacement reserves because its replacement viability ratio is only 0.34 and the target ratio is 0.50. Overall, the firm has a total cash deficiency of $2,836,000.

There are several other areas in which a firm must maintain cash and liquid asset investments that result from legal or regulatory requirements. For example, health-care firms that self-insure their professional liability are usually required to maintain stipulated levels of funds with a trustee, usually a bank. In a similar manner, funding for pension or retirement programs also requires cash and investment balances to be set aside. Finally, most long-term lenders require borrowers to maintain reserves of cash and investments to meet several stipulated purposes, such as debt service reserve.

Table 18-1 Estimating Replacement Cost Need

	Acquisition Cost	Replacement Cost
Gross property, plant, and equipment	$24,000,000	$42,000,000
Less accumulated depreciation	8,000,000	14,000,000
Net property, plant, and equipment	$16,000,000	$28,000,000

Table 18-2 Calculation of Required Cash and Investment Position

	Short-Term Cash	Replacement Reserves	Total
Present balance	$4,200,000	$ 9,100,000	$13,300,000
Present ratio*	30.5	.34	
Desired target ratio	20.0	.50	
Multiplier			
(Desired/present)	20.0/30.5	.50/.34	
Required position	$2,754,000	$13,382,000	$16,136,000
Surplus (deficiency)	$1,446,000	($ 4,282,000)	($2,836,000)

*Days' cash on hand ratio is the short-term ratio used, and replacement viability ratio is the replacement reserve ratio used.

SOURCES AND USES OF CASH

In its most basic form, a cash budget is a statement that projects how the firm's cash balance position will change between two points in time. Changes to cash position are categorized as either sources of cash flow (sometimes called receipts) or uses of cash flow (sometimes called disbursements). Sources of cash include

- collection of accounts receivable,
- cash sales,
- investment income,
- sale of assets,
- financings, and
- capital contributions.

Uses of cash include

- payments to employees,
- payments to suppliers,
- payments to lenders for interest and principal,
- purchase of fixed assets, and
- investments.

It is important to note that the definition of income and the definition of cash flows are not the same. This means that the amount reported for revenues in any given period most likely will not equal the actual amount of cash realized. The only exception would be a case in which all revenues were produced by cash sales. In most health care settings, there is a lag between the recording of revenue and the collection of the resulting account receivable. In the same manner, expenses reported for wages and salaries and supplies may not actually equal the amount of cash expended within the period. As the period expands, for example, from a month to a year, the differences between revenues and expenses and receipts and disbursements begin to narrow. If one expanded the period from one year to twenty years, the difference between cash flows and income would be minimal. Unfortunately, most financial managers are interested in cash flows over much shorter periods. Many firms have cash budgets defined on at least a monthly basis, and some have biweekly or weekly cash budgets.

When cash flows are extremely volatile but reasonably forecastable, cash budgets for shorter terms are desirable. If cash flows are reasonably stable, a cash budget defined on a quarterly basis may be appropriate. Although most firms develop cash budgets on a monthly basis, it is common for these budgets to be revised periodically because original budget assumptions often prove to be inaccurate.

The primary factor affecting the validity of the cash budget is the accuracy of the forecasts for individual cash-flow categories. The greater the degree of possible variation between actual and forecasted cash flow, the higher the liquidity need of the firm. Firms that cannot predict cash flow with much certainty should increase their cash balances or negotiate lines of credit to escape the possibility of severe cash insolvency problems.

PREPARING THE CASH BUDGET

The most important area in cash budgeting is the revenue forecast. The revenue for health care providers will be a function of the following two factors: (1) volumes by product line and (2) expected prices by payer category.

Most firms use a variety of methods to estimate volumes of services during the cash budget period. As discussed in Chapter 12 and shown in Figure 18–1, the revenue budget is critically related to the statistics budget. In general, the following two major categories of methods are used to develop estimates of volumes: (1) subjective forecasts and (2) statistical forecasts.

In reality, most forecasts probably combine elements of both subjective and statistical methods. Subjective forecasts are often referred to as "seat of the pants" methods and other less flattering names. Subjective forecasts do, however, have a place in the estimation of product line volumes. The critical factors in the reliability of a subjective forecast are the wisdom and understanding of the forecaster. In cases when future volumes are likely to deviate from historical patterns, subjective forecasts may be the most reliable method of forecasting. Surveying medical staff members regarding their expected utilization during the next year is a form of subjective forecasting, but one that may be extremely reliable.

Statistical forecasts run the gamut from major econometric studies to simple time series techniques. Whatever the method, an underlying assumption surrounds a statistical forecast that states the future can be predicted based on some mathematical model extrapolated from the past. If the relationships or models on which the forecasts are based have changed, future forecasts can be misleading.

In some cases, predicting prices for the firm's products and services may be almost as difficult as projecting volumes. Health care firms are price takers in most situations. This means that they rely on someone else to establish prices for their services. Medicare and Medicaid are two organizations that set prices and exert tremendous influence on a major portion of the total revenue budget. One would think that these payers would establish prices far enough in advance so that forecasting prices would be a simple matter. Unfortunately, sometimes interim prices

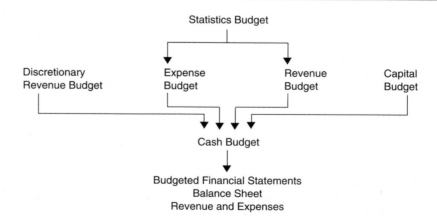

Figure 18–1 Integration of the Budgetary Process

stay interim for longer than expected, and promised increases never materialize. Although the differences between expected and actual prices may be relatively small, the volume of the Medicare and Medicaid book of business is so large that small changes in prices have a major impact on net cash flows. Most health care providers operate with relatively small margins—somewhere between 1 and 5 percent. When Medicare and Medicaid account for 50 percent or more of a firm's total business, a small forecast error of 1 or 2 percent in the final prices to be paid by Medicare and Medicaid can have a disastrous impact on final operating margins.

Health care firms also increasingly are being asked to discount more and more of their business to other major groups such as health maintenance organizations (HMOs), preferred provider organizations, commercial insurers, and self-insured employers. This makes projecting actual realized net prices more and more difficult.

Projecting revenues does not equate to projecting cash flows. Collections will lag the actual booking of revenues for some period. One common way to develop forecasts of patient receipts is through the use of "decay curves." These curves relate future collections to past billings. Figure 18–2 depicts a decay curve with the following pattern of collections:

1. The first 15 percent of any month's revenue is collected in the first month.

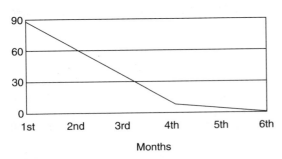

Figure 18–2 Decay Curve Analysis: Percentage Uncollected by Month after Billing

2. The next 30 percent of any month's revenue is collected in the second month.
3. The next 25 percent of any month's revenue is collected in the third month.
4. The next 20 percent of any month's revenue is collected in the fourth month.
5. The next 5 percent of any month's revenue is collected in the fifth month.
6. The remaining 5 percent of any month's revenue is written off and not collected.

Table 18–3 presents a cash receipts summary for the first six months of the year. The collection pattern reflected in the decay curve of Figure 18–2 can be seen in Table 18–3. For example, of the $2,000,000 of January revenue, 15 percent ($300,000) is collected in January, 30 percent ($600,000) is collected in February, 25 percent ($500,000) is collected in March, 20 percent ($400,000) is collected in April, 5 percent ($100,000) is collected in May, and the remaining 5 percent ($100,000) is written off and not collected. The revenues in the following months reflect the same collection pattern. Although cash receipts and revenues are most often correlated, it is not always true that the months producing the highest revenue will be the months with the highest cash collection. For many health care firms, the highest cash collection month is often one to two months after the highest revenue month.

Changes in collection patterns of major third-party payers can have a significant effect on cash flows and should be reflected immediately in revised cash budgets. For example, if Medicaid decides to delay the payment of patient bills by sixty days to conserve cash, the cash budget must be revised to reflect this new payment pattern. Increasing values for deductibles and copayments under many health care insurance plans also may delay collection patterns and increase eventual write-offs because the self-pay portion of the total health care bill may not be paid by the patient.

Additional cash receipts may come from sources other than revenue collection. Investment income and sale of assets are identified as

Table 18–3 Cash Receipts Summary (in Thousands)

	January	February	March	April	May	June
Beginning accounts						
receivable revenue	$3,600	$1,600	$1,000	$500	$100	
January sales	2,000	300	600	500	400	100	0
February sales	2,100	0	315	630	525	420	105
March sales	2,000	0	0	300	600	500	400
April sales	1,900	0	0	0	285	570	475
May sales	1,800	0	0	0	0	270	540
June sales	1,800	0	0	0	0	0	270
Subtotal		$1,900	$1,915	$1,930	$1,910	$1,860	$1,790
Other cash receipts						
Investment income		20	20	50	20	20	50
Sale of assets		0	0	25	0	0	0
Subtotal		$ 20	$ 20	$ 75	$ 20	$ 20	$ 50
Estimated cash						
receipts		$1,920	$1,935	$2,005	$1,930	$1,880	$1,840

the only other sources in Table 18–3, but other sources also may exist. Contributions, sale of stock, and the issuance of new debt are also possibilities.

After forecasting cash receipts, a schedule of expected cash disbursements is necessary before the cash budget is complete. The two largest categories in most health care firms are labor and supplies. Labor costs or payroll most often represent about 60 percent or more of a health care firm's total expenses. The expense budget will identify expected labor or payroll expenses by month, but payroll expenses do not translate into cash disbursements. Most health care firms meet the majority of their payroll obligations on a biweekly basis, which necessitates some accruals. For example, labor expense in January might be $1,200,000, but actual payroll might be $1,731,000 because there were three biweekly payroll periods. (There are twenty-six biweekly payroll periods in a year. Every month will have at least two payroll periods, but two months will have three.) Conversely, in other months during which only two biweekly pay periods were present, actual payroll disbursements might be less than labor expense.

Payroll expense also must be adjusted for withholding and other deductions. For example, the January payroll of $1,731,000 might be broken down as presented in Table 18–4.

In Table 18–4, the figure for net payroll—$1,190,000—does not include additional payroll taxes, such as workers' compensation, unemployment, and the employer's share of social security. Other fringe benefits such as pension and

Table 18–4 Payroll Disbursements

Total payroll	$1,731,000
Less:	
Income taxes	330,000
Social Security	126,000
Other deductions	85,000
Net payroll disbursed to	$1,190,000
employees	

Table 18–5 Cash Disbursements Summary (in Thousands)

	January	February	March	April	May	June
Salary and wages	$1,190	$900	$980	$880	$850	$840
Fringe benefits	155	130	135	125	115	110
Purchases	315	385	405	390	385	385
Other disbursements	185	205	225	190	210	250
Capital expenditures	25	15	100	350	45	60
Debt service	0	0	300	0	0	300
Estimated disbursement	$1,870	$1,635	$2,145	$1,935	$1,605	$1,945

health insurance also are not included.

As with payroll, the expense budget will include a value for supplies expense, but that value will not equal the actual disbursement for supplies. Table 18–5 presents a schedule of expected cash disbursements.

The only remaining task is to combine the cash receipts summary and the cash disbursements summary to create the cash budget. Before doing so, a desired level of cash balances must be defined. For this example, it will be assumed that a short-term cash balance of $1,350,000 is required to meet the firm's transactional and precautionary motives. If the firm cannot maintain this balance, it must make a decision whether it will transfer funds from its replacement reserves or whether it will borrow short-term through a line-of-credit arrangement.

Table 18–6 combines the cash receipt and cash disbursement summaries to produce the cash budget. The cash budget shows that the firm will experience negative cash flows in some months. However, in this initial six-month forecast, no month will show a balance less than the required cash balance of $1,350,000. If the forecast proves to be accurate, the firm will not need to arrange any short-term financing, nor will it need to transfer any replacement reserves. In fact, it could transfer some of the short-term cash balances that are more than the required minimal balance of $1,350,000 to replacement reserves. The firm could transfer all of the $50,000 in cash flow that occurs in January to replacement reserves, but only $160,000 of the $300,000 net cash flow in February could be transferred to replacement reserves. Because the months of March and April have negative cash flows, some of the February surplus ($300,000) will be needed to meet the deficits in March and April.

Table 18–6 Cash Budget Summary (in Thousands)

	January	February	March	April	May	June
Beginning cash balance	$1,350	$1,400	$1,700	$1,560	$1,555	$1,830
Add receipts	1,920	1,935	2,005	1,930	1,880	1,840
Less disbursements	1,870	1,635	2,145	1,935	1,605	1,945
Cash flow	50	300	(140)	(5)	275	(105)
Ending cash balance	$1,400	$1,700	$1,560	$1,555	$1,830	$1,725

By examining the pattern of expected cash flows, the treasurer of the firm can better decide the duration and maturity of possible investments. Usually, longer-term securities will yield higher returns. Therefore, if the funds are not expected to be needed for six months, the firm would be better off to invest in a six-month treasury bill than a thirty-day treasury bill.

SUMMARY

Cash budgets are critical pieces of information that financial executives in all health care firms need to prepare and monitor closely. The forecast of cash flows should help management determine whether additional financing will be needed, in what amounts, and for what duration. The information also will permit the short-term investment of surplus funds so that yields on those investments might be improved.

Cash budgets are forecasts, and there is no guarantee that the results forecast will be achieved. It is important for management to test the sensitivity of the forecasts regarding alternative scenarios, such as slowdowns in collections or declines in revenues.

ASSIGNMENTS

1. Morgan Village is a voluntary, nonprofit, continuing care retirement center. Presently it has $1,200,000 set aside for replacement and renovation. If its replacement viability ratio is presently .35 and it would like a target replacement viability ratio of .75, how much additional funding must it set aside for replacement purposes?

2. Huntley Hospital must maintain $3.3 million in a debt service reserve fund maintained by the bond trustee. The board members would like to count this balance when determining the amount of cash that they should carry for meeting normal transaction needs. Is this reasonable?

3. Dean Nursing Home has a payer mix of approximately 60 percent Medicaid and 40 percent private pay. The state Medicaid program recently has experienced major funding problems, and the frequency of payment for Medicaid beneficiaries is unclear for the next year. How might this information affect Dean's cash management?

4. Prepare a cash budget for Aztec Home Health Agency for the months of May, June, and July. The firm wishes to maintain a $200,000 minimum cash balance during the period, and it presently has a $220,000 balance as of April 30. Revenues are presented in the following:

January	$ 500,000
February	500,000
March	600,000
April	600,000
May	700,000
June	800,000
July	1,000,000
August	1,000,000

The firm collects 30 percent of its revenue in the month billing occurred, 30 percent in the next month, and 25 percent in the following month. The firm fails to collect 15 percent of its revenue because of either bad debt or contractual allowances. Expense budget relationships are presented in the following:

Payroll = $50,000 per month plus .50 × Revenues
Supplies = .10 × Revenues
Rent = $50,000 per month
Debt service = $150,000 in July
Capital expenditures = $75,000 in June

Eighty percent of payroll expense is paid in the month this expense was incurred, and 20 percent is paid in the following month. Supplies expense is paid in the following month. All other items are paid in the month reported. Determine during which months Aztec will be able to invest surplus funds and during which months it might need to borrow.

SOLUTIONS AND ANSWERS

1. The total amount of required replacement reserves should be $(.75/.35) \times \$1,200,000$, or $2,571,428. Morgan Village must therefore set aside $1,371,428 in additional reserves.
2. No. The debt service reserve fund is not under the control of Huntley Hospital management and could not be used to meet normal transactional needs for cash such as payroll and purchases.
3. Because cash flows are likely to be more volatile next year, Dean should consider enhancing its liquidity position. This might be accomplished by increasing the amount of short-term cash reserves or negotiating a line of credit.
4. Surplus funds will be available during May and June, but a loan will need to be obtained during July, as the cash budget in Table 18–7 shows.

Table 18–7 Cash Budget for Aztec Home Health Agency

	May	June	July
Receipts			
March revenue	$150,000	$ 0	$ 0
April revenue	180,000	150,000	0
May revenue	210,000	210,000	175,000
June revenue	0	240,000	240,000
July revenue	0	0	300,000
Total receipts	$540,000	$600,000	$715,000
Disbursements			
Payroll			
April	$ 70,000	$ 0	$ 0
May	320,000	80,000	0
June	0	360,000	90,000
July	0	0	440,000
Total payroll disbursed	$390,000	$440,000	$530,000
Supplies	$ 60,000	$ 70,000	$ 80,000
Rent	50,000	50,000	50,000
Debt service	0	0	150,000
Capital expenditures	0	75,000	0
Total disbursements	$500,000	$635,000	$810,000
Net cash flow	$ 40,000	($35,000)	($95,000)
Beginning balance	$220,000	$260,000	$225,000
Ending cash	260,000	225,000	130,000
Less required minimum	200,000	200,000	200,000
Net investment (borrowing)	$ 60,000	$ 25,000	($70,000)

Index